OLD AND MIDDLE ENGLISH LANGUAGE STUDIES

AMSTERDAM STUDIES IN THE THEORY AND HISTORY OF LINGUISTIC SCIENCE

General Editor
E.F. KONRAD KOERNER
(University of Ottawa)

Series V

LIBRARY & INFORMATION SOURCES IN LINGUISTICS

Advisory Editorial Board

Mohammed H. Bakalla (Riyadh); Jivco Boyadjiev (Sofia)
Frank Di Trolio (Gainesville, Fla.); Leszek M. Karpinski (Vancouver, B.C.)
Salvatore C. Sgroi (Catania); Joseph L. Subbiondo (Santa Clara, Calif.)
Matsuji Tajima (Fukuoka, Japan)

Volume 13

Matsuji Tajima (comp.)

*Old and Middle English Language Studies
A Classified Bibliography 1923-1985*

OLD AND MIDDLE ENGLISH LANGUAGE STUDIES
A CLASSIFIED BIBLIOGRAPHY 1923-1985

Compiled by

MATSUJI TAJIMA
Kyushu University
Fukuoka, Japan

JOHN BENJAMINS PUBLISHING COMPANY
Amsterdam/Philadelphia

1988

Library of Congress Cataloging-in-Publication Data

Tajima, Matsuji, 1942-
   Old and Middle English language studies : a classified bibliography, 1923-1985 / compiled by Matsuji Tajima.
       p.   cm. -- (Amsterdam studies in the theory and history of linguistic science. Series V, Library & information sources in linguistics, ISSN 0165-7267; v. 13)
Includes index.
1. English language -- Old English, ca. 450-1100 -- Bibliography. 2. English language -- Middle English, 1100-1500 -- Bibliography. I. Title. II. Series.
Z2015.A1T3   1988
[PE123]
016.429 -- dc 19   88-10429
                                                                            CIP
ISBN 90 272 3732 8 (alk. paper)

© Copyright 1988 - John Benjamins B.V.
No part of this book may be reproduced in any form, by print, photoprint, microfilm, or any other means, without written permission from the publisher.

For
Professor Tamotsu Matsunami, D. Litt.
with respect and gratitude

CONTENTS

Preface	xi
Abbreviations	xv

I. Bibliographies — 1
   A. General — 1
   B. Individual — 6
   C. Annual — 9

II. Dictionaries, Concordances, and Glossaries — 13
   A. Historical — 13
   B. Old English — 15
   C. Middle English — 19

III. Histories of the English Language — 25

IV. Grammars — 39
   A. Historical — 39
   B. Old English — 41
   C. Middle English — 48

V. General and Miscellaneous — 53
   A. General — 53
   B. Old English — 56
   C. Middle English — 59

VI. Language of Individual Authors or Works — 67
   A. Old English — 67
   B. Middle English — 68

VII.	**Orthography and Punctuation**	77
	A. General	77
	B. Old English	78
	C. Middle English	81
VIII.	**Phonology and Phonetics**	85
	A. General	85
	B. Old English	90
	C. Middle English	107
IX.	**Morphology**	119
	A. General	119
	B. Old English	121
	C. Middle English	128
X.	**Syntax**	133
	A. General	133
	B. Old English	150
	C. Middle English	176
XI.	**Lexicology, Lexicography, and Word-Formation**	199
	A. General	199
	B. Old English	208
	C. Middle English	266
XII.	**Onomastics**	313
	A. General	313
	B. Old English	315
	C. Middle English	330
XIII.	**Dialectology**	337
	A. General	337
	B. Old English	337
	C. Middle English	339
XIV.	**Stylistics**	347
	A. General	347

B. Old English	348
C. Middle English	351

Index of Names   357

PREFACE

Exactly sixty years have passed since A.G. Kennedy's monumental *Bibliography of Writings on the English Language* appeared in 1927, in which he surveyed the whole field of English philology from the beginning of printing to the end of 1922. Whereas bibliographical interests in Modern English have been served quite well by G. Scheurweghs and E. Vorlat's five-volume *Analytical Bibliography of Writings on Modern English Morphology and Syntax* (Louvain, 1963-1979), no recent bibliography has systematically surveyed the Old and Middle English scholarship that has accumulated since 1922. The need for an updated bibliography of Old and Middle English language studies that is as comprehensive and detailed as Kennedy's has, therefore, become a desideratum.

With the aim of at least partially filling this bibliographical lacuna, the present work lists books, monographs, dissertations, articles, notes, and reviews on Old and Middle English *language*, published since Kennedy's cut-off date. Although designed to be a comprehensive listing of appropriate publications from 1923 through 1985, this bibliography does, in fact, include a number of items published as recently as the summer of 1987. In compiling this bibliography, I have consulted not only all available bibliographies and serial publications, but also bibliographies and footnotes appended to all books and articles I could lay my hands on. The vast majority of the items listed here have actually been examined by me or others on my behalf. Nevertheless, I have also included, rather than ignored, some items which I have not been able to inspect. In such cases, however, I have made every possible effort to verify them.

This bibliography makes no claim to being complete. Important contributions may have escaped my scrutiny; however, certain omissions were the result of careful deliberation. It has not been my intention to include purely theoretical studies with only marginal references to Old or Middle English. All publications in Slavic languages, in which I have no competence, and most of the Japanese publications, which are virtually unavailable outside Japan, have also been intentionally excluded. (Those interested in the latter are referred to Yoshio Terasawa's listing — no. 21 in the present bibliography — of Japanese publications on Medieval English language and literature up to June 1982.) Because of their brevity, reviews in *The Year's Work in English Studies* have also been omitted.

Each entry provides full bibliographical details. A special effort has been made to spell out the first and the middle, in addition to the last, names of authors as this information often facilitates their location in card catalogues. Wherever titles do not clearly indicate their content or scope, notes have been appended in square brackets. Some entries include cross-references to related items, or additional information on reprintings or other publication matters. Reviews have been listed under the entry for the work reviewed, because they often contain relevant information.

Most scholarship defies simple classification, since any given work may deal with several subjects. This bibliography divides the items listed into fourteen, fairly broad categories, according to their main subject-matter. Most of these categories are subdivided into three sections: General (covering both Old and Middle English), Old English (to about 1100), and Middle English (about 1100-1500). Within each section, works are listed alphabetically by authors and their publications are arranged chronologically, by date of publication. Items authored collectively are entered only after the first author's individual works; however, the index provides references to all co-authors as well. The heading 'Language of Individual Authors or Works' deals with scholarship on the language in general of individual authors or works. The heading 'Stylistics' includes only those studies which may be correctly classified as *linguistic* stylistics. Since this bibliography only purports to cover scholarship of a purely linguistic nature, studies relating to paleography, versification, literary stylistics, variation, and oral-formulaic theory have been excluded. (For the last field, J.M. Foley's exhaustive bibliography — no. 30 in the present bibliography — may be consulted.)

This bibliography is the result of over ten years' research. Searching, assembling, verifying, and editing the materials were all undertaken single-handedly. Despite my various efforts to obtain research grants in my own country, I have had no financial assistance and no paid staff at my disposal. This fact largely explains why it has taken me too long a time to complete this work. Under such conditions, this book would have been an impossible undertaking had I not greatly benefited from the assistance and goodwill of

PREFACE   xiii

a number of institutions and individuals. The bulk of this work was conducted at the University of Ottawa Library during regular studies at the university in the years 1977-79 and a subsequent sojourn in the Canadian capital in the summer of 1983. At various times, I have also researched at the libraries of the University of British Columbia, Simon Fraser University, and Carleton University in Canada; Princeton University in the U.S.A.; and Tohoku Gakuin University, Seinan Gakuin University, and my own university, Kyushu University, in Japan. To all those libraries, from whose excellent resources, facilities, and staff I have so immensely benefited, and, above all, to the staff of the inter-library loan section of the University of Ottawa Library, who were particularly helpful in obtaining a number of obscure materials on my behalf, I extend my deepest appreciation. As for help from individual scholars and friends, I would first like to thank my long-time friend Prof. E.F.K. Koerner of the University of Ottawa without whose constant help and encouragement, expert advice on editorial matters, and many valuable suggestions I could hardly have carried through with this project. For having provided me with bibliographical information, offprints, and notices of articles and books, I am very grateful to the following: Prof. Norman Blake, University of Sheffield; Prof. François Chevillet, Université de Grenoble III; Prof. Michael Cummings, York University (Canada); Prof. Norman Davis, University of Oxford; Dr. David Denison, University of Manchester; Prof. Klaus Dietz, Freie Universität Berlin; Prof. Jacek Fisiak, Adam Mickiewicz University, Poznań; Dr. Risto Hiltuonen, University of Helsinki; Dr. Erik S. Kooper, University of Utrecht; Prof. Robert E. Lewis, University of Michigan; Prof. Akio Oizumi, Doshisha University (Japan); Prof. Thomas F, Shannon, University of California, Berkeley; and Prof. Bertil Sundby, University of Bergen (Norway). In particular, I feel deeply indebted to Prof. Eiichi Suzuki of Tohoku Gakuin University who made it possible for me to make use of his university library and also graciously and patiently responded to my frequent queries on specific items. I also wish to thank Prof. David Staines, mentor and friend, at the University of Ottawa; my old Canadian friend Mr. John R. Anscomb; and my colleagues at Kyushu University, especially Professors Yukito Nakano, Keiichi Onizuka, Tetsuo Yoshida, Kazuto Ono, and Atsuo Kurumisawa, for their unfailing support and encouragement throughout this and other projects. My warm thanks are further due to Prof. Sukeaki Matsuda of Oita University who most generously gave of his time and energy in preparing the preliminary version of the Index of Names and also in reading the proofs, and to Mr. Kenji Matsuse of Kumamoto University and Mr. Kazuyuki Urata and Miss Yoko Iyeiri, both of Kyushu University, who helped me with the typing and/or proofreading.

Matsuji Tajima

Kyushu University
Fukuoka, Japan
10 October 1987

ABBREVIATIONS

Abbreviations are listed below under three headings: 1. periodicals and serials; 2. collections: festschriften and miscellaneous; and 3. others. Publications not listed herein are cited by full title in the main text.

1. Periodicals and Serials

AA	Anglistische Arbeitshefte. Tübingen.
AAA	*Arbeiten aus Anglistik und Amerikanistik.* Graz 1 (1976)-.
AASF	Annales Academiae Scientiarum Fennicae. Helsinki.
ABAG	*Amsterdamer Beiträge zur älteren Germanistik.* Amsterdam 1 (1972)-.
AEB	*Analytical and Enumerative Bibliography.* Northern Illinois Univ., DeKalb, IL 1 (1977)-.
AF	Anglistische Forschungen. Heidelberg.
AION-SG	*Annali Istituto Universitario Orientale di Napoli, Sezione Germanica.* Napoli 1 (1958)-.
AION-SL	*Annali Istituto Universitario Orientale di Napoli, Sezione Linguistica.* Napoli 1 (1958)-.
AJP	*American Journal of Philology.* Baltimore 1 (1880)-.
ALH	*Acta Linguistica (Hafniensia).* Copenhagen 1 (1939)-.
ALLCB	*Association for Literary and Linguistic Computing Bulletin.* Cambridge 1 (1973)-.
ALPS	Alabama Linguistic and Philological Series. University, AL.
AN&Q	*American Notes and Queries.* Lexington, KY 1 (1962)-.
ANF	*Arkiv för Nordisk Filologi.* Christina (Oslo) 1(1883)-4(1888); Lund 5 (1889)-.
Anglia	*Anglia. Zeitschrift für englische Philologie.* Halle 1 (1878)-68 (1944); Tübingen 69 (1950)-.
Anglia B	*Beiblatt zur Anglia.* Halle 1 (1890/91)-55 (1944).
AnM	*Annuale Mediaevale.* Duquesne Univ., Pittsburgh, PA 1 (1960)-.
APS	*Acta Philologica Scandinavica.* Copenhagen 1 (1926)-.
ARBA	*American Reference Books Annual.* Littleton, CO 1 (1970)-.
Archiv	*Archiv für das Studium der neueren Sprachen und Literatur-*

	en. Braunschweig 1 (1846)-.
ArchL	Archivum Linguisticum: A Review of Comparative Philology and General Linguistics. Glasgow 1 (1949)-17 (1965); Menston, Yorkshire n.s. 1 (1970)-.
AS	American Speech. New York, currently University, AL 1 (1925/26)-.
ASE	Anglo-Saxon England. Cambridge 1 (1972)-.
ASSAH	Anglo-Saxon Studies in Archaeology and History. Oxford 1 (1980)-.
AUBud-L	Annales Universitatis Scientiarum Budapestensis de Rolando Eötvös nominatae. Sectio Linguistica. Budapest.
AUL	Acta Universitatis Lundensis.
AUMLA	AUMLA: Journal of the Australasian Universities Language and Literature Association. [Formerly Journal of Australian Universities Modern Language Association.] [Place of publication varies] 1 (1933)-.
AUT	Annales Universitatis Turkuensis.
BEP	Beiträge zur englischen Philologie. Bochum-Langendreer.
BFS	Bulletin de la Faculté des Lettres de Strasbourg. Strasbourg.
BGDSL (H)	Beiträge zur Geschichte der deutschen Sprache und Literatur. Halle/Saale 1 (1874)-.
BGDSL (T)	Beiträge zur Geschichte der deutschen Sprache und Literatur. Tübingen 77 (1955)-.
BN	Beiträge zur Namenforschung. Heidelberg 1 (1949)-16 (1965); N.F. 1 (1966)-.
BPG	Bibliothèque de Philologie Germanique. Paris.
BPTJ	Biuletyn Polskiego Towarzystwa Językoznawczego/Bulletin de la Société polonaise de Linguistique. Wrocław & Crakow 1 (1927)-.
BRP	Beiträge zur romanischen Philologie. Berlin 1 (1961)-.
BSE	Brno Studies in English. Prague, later on Brno 1 (1959)-.
BSEP	Bonner Studien zur englischen Philologie. Bonn.
BSL	Bulletin de la Société de Linguistique de Paris. Paris 1 (1869)-.
CCC	College Composition and Communication. Urbana, IL 1 (1950)-.
CCM	Cahiers de Civilisation Médiévale. Poitiers 1 (1958)-.
CE	College English. Urbana, IL 1 (1939/40)-.
ChauN	The Chaucer Newsletter: A Publication of the New Chaucer Society. Knoxville, TN 1 (1982)-.
ChauR	The Chaucer Review. University Park, PA 1 (1966)-.
Choice	Choice (Association of College and Research Library). Middletown, CT 1 (1964)-.
CHum	Computers and the Humanities. Flushing, NY 1 (1966)-.
CJL	Canadian Journal of Linguistics/Revue Canadienne de Linguistique. Toronto 1 (1954)-.

ABBREVIATIONS

CL	Comparative Literature. Eugene, OR 1 (1949)-.
ČMF	Časopis pro Moderní filologii. Prague 1 (1911)-. [Continued as PP.]
Comments on Etymology.	Rolla, Missouri 11 (1982) & 12 (1983).
CP	Classical Philology. Chicago 1(1906)-.
CSL	Cambridge Studies in English.
DA	Dissertation Abstracts/Dissertation Abstracts International. Ann Arbor, MI 1(1938)-.
Diachronica	Diachronica: International Journal for Historical Linguistics. Hildesheim-Zürich-New York 1 (1984)-.
Dictionaries	Dictionaries: Journal of the Dictionary Society of North America. Terre Haute, IN 1 (1979)-.
DL	Deutsche Literaturzeitung. Leipzig 1 (1930)-.
DLZ	Deutsche Literaturzeitung für Kritik der internationalen Wissenschaft. Berlin & Leipzig 1 (1880)-.
DQR	DQR: the Dutch Quarterly Review of Anglo-American Letters. Amsterdam 1 (1971)-.
DUJ	The Durham University Journal. Durham 1 (1876)-.
EA	Études Anglaises. Paris 1 (1937)-.
E&S	Essays and Studies by Members of the English Association. Oxford 1 (1910)-32 (1946). Superseded by Essays and Studies for the English Association. Oxford n.s. 1 (1948)-.
E&S, UCPE	Essays and Studies, Univ. of California Publications in English.
EASG	English and American Studies in German: Summaries of Theses and Monographs. Supplements to Anglia. Tübingen 1 (1969)-.
EBSK	Erlanger Beiträge zur Sprach- und Kunstwissenschaft. Nürnberg.
EETS	Early English Text Society.
EGerm	Études Germaniques. Paris 1 (1946)-.
EGS	English and Germanic Studies. Birmingham 1 (1947)-7 (1960/61). [Continued as EPS.]
EHR	English Historical Review. London 1 (1886)-.
EIC	Essays in Criticism. Oxford 1 (1951)-.
EJ	English Journal. E. Lansing, MI 1 (1912)-28 (1939). [College edition, superseded by CE.]
ELH	ELH. [Formerly Journal of English Literary History.] Baltimore, MD 1 (1934)-.
ELN	English Language Notes. Boulder, CO 1 (1963)-.
EM	English Miscellany. Roma, Italy 1 (1950)-.
English	English. [The Journal of The English Association.] Oxford 1 (1935)-.
EPS	English Philological Studies. Cambridge 8 (1961)-11 (1968). [Continuation of EGS.]

Erasmus	*Erasmus: Speculum Scientiarum. International Bulletin of Contemporary Scholarship/Bulletin international de la science contemporaine.* Wiesbaden.
ES	*English Studies.* Amsterdam 1 (1919)-.
ESA	*English Studies in Africa.* Johannesburg 1 (1958)-.
ESC	*English Studies in Canada.* Fredericton, New Brunswick 1 (1975)-.
EStn	*English Studien.* Leipzig 1 (1877)-76 (1944).
EurH	Europäische Hochschulschriften/Publications Universitaires Européennes/European Univ. Studies. Frankfurt a. M./Bern.
Expl	*The Explicator.* Washington, DC 1 (1942/43)-.
FL	*Foundations of Language.* Dordrecht 1 (1965)-13 (1975). [Continued as *SLang.*]
FLH	*Folia Linguistica Historica.* The Hague 1 (1980)-.
FMLS	*Forum for Modern Language Studies.* Univ. of St. Andrews 1 (1965)-.
FoL	*Folia Linguistica. Acta Societatis Linguisticae Europaeae.* The Hague 1 (1967)-.
GB	Germanische Bibliothek. Heidelberg.
GBEP	Grazer Beiträge zur englischen Philologie. Graz.
GHÅ	*Göteborgs Högskolas Årsskrift.* Göteborg 1 (1895)-60 (1954). [Superseded by *GUÅ*.]
GL	*General Linguistics.* Lexington, KY, later on University Park, PA 1 (1955)-.
Glossa	*Glossa: An International Journal of Linguistics.* Burnaby, British Columbia, Canada 1 (1967)-.
GothSE	Gothenburg Studies in English. Göteborg & Stockholm.
GR	*The Germanic Review.* New York 1 (1926)-.
GRLH	Garland Reference Library of the Humanities. New York.
GRM	*Germanisch-Romanische Monatsschrift.* Heidelberg 1 (1909)-31 (1943); N.F. 1 (1950/51)-.
GSU-ZF	*Godišnik na Sofijskija Universitet, Fakultet po zapadni filologii.* Sofija.
GUÅ	*Göteborgs Universitets Årsskrift.* Stockholm & Göteborg 61 (1955)-. [Supersedes *GHÅ*.]
HAR	*The Humanities Association Review.* [Formerly *Humanities Association Bulletin.*] Queens Univ., Kingston, Ontario 1 (1954)-.
Hist. Today	*History Today.* London.
HSE	*Hungarian Studies in English.* Debrecen 1 (1963)-.
IALR	*International Anthropological and Linguistic Review.* Miami, FL 1 (1953)-.
IF	*Indogermanische Forschungen.* Strassburg, later on Berlin 1 (1892)-.
In Geardagum	*In Geardagum: Essays on Old and Middle English Language and Literature.* The Society for New Language, Denver 1 (1974)-.

InLi	*Incontri Linguistici.* Trieste, later on Firenze 1 (1974)-.
IRAL	*IRAL: International Review of Applied Linguistics in Language Teaching/Internationale Zeitschrift für angewandte Linguistik in der Spracherziehung.* Heidelberg 1 (1963)-.
JAF	*Journal of American Folklore.* Washington, DC 1(1888)-.
JanL	*Janua Linguarum.* The Hague.
JČ	*Jazykovedný Časopis.* Bratislava 1 (1951)-.
JEGP	*The Journal of English and Germanic Philology.* Bloomington, IN, later on Urbana, IL 1 (1897)-.
JEngL	*Journal of English Linguistics.* Bellingham, WA 1 (1967) - 16 (1983); Whitewater, WI 17 (1984)-19:1(1986); Athens, GA 19:2(1986)-.
JEPNS	*Journal of the English Place-Name Society.* Cambridge 1 (1924)-15 (1942); Nottingham 1 (1969)-.
JIES	*The Journal of Indo-European Studies.* Washington, DC 1(1973)-.
JL	*Journal of Linguistics.* Edinburgh, later on London 1 (1965)-.
JNT	*Journal of Narrative Technique.* Eastern Michigan Univ., Ypsilanti 1 (1971)-.
JSA	*Journal of the Society of Archivists.* London 1 (1955)-.
Kalbotyra	*Kalbotyra. Lietuvos TSR Aukstuju mokyklu mokslo darbai.* Vilnius 1 (1945)-.
KBAA	*Kieler Beiträge zur Anglistik und Amerikanistik.* Neumünster.
KN	*Kwartalnik Neofilologiczny.* Warsaw 1 (1954)-.
Kratylos	*Kratylos. Kritisches Berichts- und Rezensionsorgan für indogermanische und allgemeine Sprachwissenschaft.* Wiesbaden 1 (1956)-.
LA	*Linguistische Arbeiten.* Tübingen.
Lang&S	*Language and Style.* Carbondale, IL 1 (1968)-9 (1976); Flushing, NY 10 (1977)-.
LangQ	*USF Language Quarterly.* Tampa, FL 1 (1962)-.
LangS	*Language Sciences.* Bloomington, IN 1 (1968)-48(1977).
Language	*Language: Journal of the Linguistic Society of America.* Baltimore, MD 1 (1925)-.
LanM	*Les Langues Modernes.* Paris 1 (1903)-.
LB	*Leuvense Bijdragen. Tijdschrift voor Germaanse filologie.* Leuven 1 (1896)-.
LeSt	*Lingua e Stile.* Bologna 1 (1966)-.
LGRP	*Literaturblatt für germanische und romanische Philologie.* Heilbronn & Leipzig 1 (1880)-66 (1944).
Library	*Library: Transactions of the Bibliographical Society.* London 1 (1892)-.
LingA	*Linguistic Analysis.* Seattle, WA 1 (1975)-.
LingB	*Linguistische Berichte.* Braunschweig, later on Wiesbaden 1 (1969)-.

LingI	*Linguistic Inquiry.* Cambridge, MA 1 (1970)-.
Lingua	*Lingua. International Review of General Linguistics.* Amsterdam 1 (1947/48)-.
Linguistics	*Linguistics. An International Review.* The Hague 1 (1963)-.
Linguistique	*La Linguistique. Revue de la Société internationale de linguistique fonctionnelle.* Paris 1 (1965)-.
LISL	Library and Information Series in Linguistics. Amsterdam.
LM	Language Monographs published by the Linguistic Society of America. Philadelphia.
Litera	*Litera: Studies in Language and Literature.* Istanbul, Turkey 1 (1954)-.
Litteris	*Litteris. An International Critical Review of the Humanities.* Lund 1 (1924)-7 (1930).
LMS	*London Medieval Studies.* London 1 (1937)-.
Lore&L	*Lore and Language.* Sheffield 1 (1969)-.
LOS	*Literary Onomastic Studies.* Brockport, NY 1 (1974)-.
LPosn	*Lingua Posnaniensis.* Poznań 1 (1949)-.
LSE	*Leeds Studies in English and Kindred Languages* (Old Series); *Leeds Studies in English* (New Series). Leeds 1 (1932)-8 (1952); n.s. 1 (1967)-.
LT	*Levende Talen.* Groningen 1 (1914)-.
LUÅ	Lunds Universitets Årsskrift.
LundSE	Lund Studies in English.
MAE	*Medium Ævum.* Oxford 1 (1932)-.
M&H	*Medievalia et Humanistica.* North Texas State Univ., Denton, TX 1(1943)-9(1955); n.s. 1 (1970)-.
MASO	*Meijerbergs arkiv för svensk ordforskning.* Göteborg 1 (1937)-.
MESN	*Mediaeval English Studies Newsletter.* Tokyo 1 (1979)-.
METh	*Medieval English Theatre.* Lancaster 1 (1979)-.
MGS	*Michigan Germanic Studies.* Ann Arbor, MI 1 (1975)-.
MichA	*Michigan Academician.* Ann Arbor, MI 1 (1969)-.
MLing	*Modèles Linguistiques.* Lille 1 (1979)-.
MLJ	*The Modern Language Journal.* [Place of publication varies] 1 (1916/17)-.
MLN	*Modern Language Notes.* Baltimore 1 (1886)-.
MLQ	*Modern Language Quarterly.* Seattle 1 (1940)-.
MLR	*The Modern Language Review.* Cambridge 1 (1905/06)-.
MP	*Modern Philology.* Chicago 1 (1903/04)-.
MS	*Mediaeval Studies.* Toronto 1 (1939)-.
MSAAF	Meddelanden från Stiftelsens för Åbo Akademi Forskningsinstitut. Åbo [Turku].
MScan	*Mediaeval Scandinavia.* Odense, Denmark 1 (1968)-.
MSE	*Massachusetts Studies in English.* Amherst, MA 1 (1958)-.
MSL	Mémoires de la Société de Linguistique de Paris. Paris 1 (1868)-23 (1935).

ABBREVIATIONS

MSNH	Mémoires de la Société Néophilologique de Helsinki. Helsinki 1 (1893)-.
MSpr	Moderna Språk. Malmö, later on Stockholm 1 (1907)-.
MSS	Münchener Studien zur Sprachwissenschaft. München 1 (1956)-.
Museum	Museum: Maandblad voor Philologie en Geschiedenis. Groningen; Leiden; etc. 1 (1893)-.
MWPL	Montreal Working Papers in Linguistics. Montreal
Names	Names: Journal of the American Name Society. Youngstown, OH, later on Potsdam, NY 1 (1953)-.
N&Q	Notes and Queries. Oxford 1 (1849/50)-198 (1953); n.s. 1 (1954)-.
NBEP	Neue Beiträge zur englischen Philologie. Münster.
Neophil	Neophilologus. [Subtitle varies.] Groningen 1 (1916)-.
NHLS	North-Holland Linguistic Series. Amsterdam.
Nku	Naamkunde. Leuven 1 (1969)-.
NM	Neuphilologische Mitteilungen. Helsinki 1 (1899)-.
NMon	Neuphilologische Monatsschrift.
NMS	Nottingham Mediaeval Studies. Univ. of Nottingham 1 (1957)-.
NoB	Namn och Bygd. Tidskrift för nordisk ortnamnsforskning. Uppsala 1 (1913)-.
Nomina	Nomina: A Newsletter of Name Studies related to Great Britain and Ireland. Univ. of Hull 1 (1977)-.
Northern History	Northern History: A Review of the History of England. Leeds 1 (1966)-.
NOWELE	NOWELE: North-Western European Language Evolution. Odense 1 (1983)-.
NS	Die neueren Sprachen. Marburg 1 (1893/94)-51 (1943); N.F. Frankfurt am Main 1 (1951)-.
NSE	Norwegian Studies in English. Oslo.
NSM	Nuovi studi medievali. Bologna 1 (1923/24)-3 (1927).
NTF	Nordisk Tidsskrift for Filologi. Series 4. Copenhagen 1 (1911)-.
NTS/NJL	Norsk Tidsskrift for Sprogvidenskap/Norwegian Journal of Linguistics. Oslo 1 (1928)-.
NYRB	New York Review of Books. New York 1 (1963)-.
NYTB	New York Times Book Review. New York 1 (1896)-.
NZ	Neuphilologische Zeitschrift. Berlin & Hannover 1 (1949)-4 (1952).
OEN	Old English Newsletter. Columbus, OH, later on Binghamton, NY 1 (1967)-.
Onoma	Onoma: Bibliographical and Information Bulletin. Louvain 1 (1950)-.
Orbis	Orbis: Bulletin international de documentation linguistique. Louvain 1 (1952)-.

OSE	Oslo Studies in English. [Superseded by NSE.]
Paideia	*Paideia. Rivista letteraria di informazione bibliografica.* Brescia, Italy 1 (1946)-.
Parergon	*Parergon: Bulletin of the Australian and New Zealand Association for Medieval and Renaissance Studies.* Canberra 1 (1968)-32 (1982); n.s. 1 (1983)-.
PBA	*Proceedings of the British Academy.* London 1 (1903)-.
PELL	*Papers on English Language and Literature.* Carbondale, IL. [Continued as *PLL*.]
PIL	*Papers in Linguistics.* Edmonton, Alberta & Champaign, IL 1 (1969)-.
PLL	*Papers on Language and Literature.* Edwardsville, IL 1 (1965)-. [Continuation of *PELL*.]
PMASAL	*Papers of the Michigan Academy of Science, Arts, and Letters.*
PMLA	*Publications of the Modern Language Association of America.* Baltimore, then Mensha, WI and later on New York 1 (1884)-.
Poetica	*Poetica: International Journal of Linguistic-Literary Studies.* Tokyo 1 (1974)-.
PP	*Philologica Pragensia.* Praha 1 (1958)-11 (1968).
PQ	*Philological Quarterly.* Iowa City 1 (1922)-.
PSE	*Pragu Studies in English.* Praha 1 (1924)-.
Q&F	Quellen und Forschungen zur Sprach- und Kulturgeschichte der germanischen Völker. Strassbourg & Berlin.
QJS	*Quarterly Journal of Speech.* [Place of publication varies] 1 (1915)-.
QQ	*Queen's Quarterly.* Kingston, Ontario 1 (1893/94)-.
RBPH	*Revue Belge de Philologie et d'Histoire.* Brussels 1 (1922)-.
RCEL	*Revista Canaria de Estudios Ingleses.* Tenerife, Spain 1 (1978)-.
RES	*The Review of English Studies.* Oxford 1 (1925)-25 (1949); n.s. 1 (1950)-.
RESL	*Revista Española de Lingüística.* Madrid 1 (1971)-.
RG	*Revue Germanique.* Paris 1 (1905)-30 (1939).
RLB	*Recueil linguistique de Bratislava.* Bratislava 1 (1948)-.
RLM	*Rivista di Letterature Moderne.* Asti, Italy 1 (1946)-.
RLV	*Revue des Langues Vivantes.* Brussels 1 (1932)-.
RMRLL	*Rocky Mountain Review of Language and Literature.* [Place of publication varies] 1 (1967)-.
RP	*Romance Philology.* Berkeley & Los Angeles 1 (1947/48)-.
RUO	*Revue de l'Université d'Ottawa.* Ottawa, Ontario 1 (1931)-. [Continued as the *University of Ottawa Quarterly.*]
SAA	Schweizer anglistische Arbeiten. (Swiss Studies in English.)
SAB	*South Atlantic Bulletin.* Athens, GA-Chapel Hill, NC-Knoxville, TN 1 (1935)-.

SAC	Studies in the Age of Chaucer. Knoxville, TN 1 (1979)-.
Saga-Book	Saga-Book of the Viking Society for Northern Research. London 1 (1892)-; Text Series 1 (1953)-.
SAP	Studia Anglica Posnaniensia. Poznań 1 (1968)-.
SAU	Studia Anglistica Upsaliensia. Uppsala.
SB	Studies in Bibliography. Charlottesville, VA 1 (1948)-.
Schede Medievali	Schede Medievali. Palermo, Italy 1 (1981)-.
ScoS	Scottish Studies. Edinburgh 1 (1957)-.
Scripta Minora	Scripta Minora Regiae Societatis Humaniorum Litterarum Lundensis.
SEA	Studies in English and American. R. Eötvös Univ., Budapest.
SEL	Studies in English Literature. Tokyo 1 (1919)-
Semiotica	Semiotica: Journal of the International Association for Semiotic Studies. The Hague, later on Amsterdam 1 (1969)-.
SEP	Studien zur englischen Philologie. Halle/Saale.
SFFBU	Sborník prací Filosofické Fakulty Brněnské University. Brno 1 (1923)-.
SFQ	Southern Folklore Quarterly. Univ. of Florida, Gainesville, FL 1 (1937)-.
SGerm	Studi Germanici. Florence 1 (1935)-; nuova serie, Rome 1 (1963)-.
SGG	Studia Germanica Gandensia. Ghent, Belgium 1 (1959)-.
SIL	Studies in Linguistics, Buffalo, NY 1 (1942)-18 (1964/66); Dallas, TX 19 (1967)-21 (1969/70); Dekalb, IL 22 (1971/72)-25 (1975).
SKGGD	Sammlung kurzer Grammatiken germanischer Dialekte. Tübingen.
SL	Studia Linguistica. Lund 1 (1947)-.
SLang	Studies in Language. Amsterdam 1 (1977)-. [Continuation of FL.]
SMC	Studies in Medieval Culture. Western Michigan Univ., Kalamazoo, MI 1 (1971)-.
SMed	Studi Medievali. 3a serie. Spoleto, Italy 1 (1904)-.
SML	Statistical Methods in Linguistics. Stockholm 1 (1961)-.
SMSpr	Studier i Modern Sprakvetenskap/Stockholm Studies in Modern Philology. Stockholm 1 (1898)-19 (1956); n.s. 1 (1960)-.
SN	Studia Neophilologica. Uppsala 1 (1928)-.
SNF	Studier i nordisk filologi. Helsingfors 1 (1910)-.
SOPL	Stanford Occasional Papers in Linguistics. Stanford 1 (1971)-.
SP	Studies in Philology. Chapel Hill, NC 1 (1928)-.
Speculum	Speculum: A Journal of Mediaeval Studies. Cambridge, MA 1 (1926)-.
Sprache	Die Sprache. Zeitschrift für Sprachwissenschaft. Wien 1 (1949)-.

Sprachw	*Sprachwissenschaft*. Heidelberg 1 (1976)-.
SRAZ	*Studia Romanica et Anglica Zagrabiensia*. Zagreb 1 (1956)-.
SRL	*The Saturday Review of Literature*. New York 1 (1924/25)-.
SSE	Stockholm Studies in English.
SSF-CHL	Societas Scientiarum Fennica: Commentationes Humanarum Litterarum.
StHum	*Studies in the Humanities*. Indiana, PA 1 (1969)-.
Style	*Style*. Univ. of Arkansas, Fayetteville, AK 1 (1967)-.
TBL	Tübinger Beiträge zur Linguistik.
TCLP	*Travaux du Cercle Linguistique de Prague*. Prague 1 (1929)-8 (1939).
TLP	*Travaux Linguistiques de Prague*. Prague 1 (1964)-.
TLSM	Trends in Linguistics: Studies and Monographs. Berlin.
TLS	*The Times Literary Supplement*. London 1 (1902)-.
TNTL	*Tijdschrift voor Nederlandse Taal- en Letterkunde*. Leiden 1 (1888)-.
TOES	Toronto Old English Series.
TPS	*Transactions of the Philological Society*. Oxford 1854-.
TRHS	*Transactions of the Royal Historical Society*. London 1 (1918)-.
TSE	*Tulane Studies in English*. New Orleans, LA 1 (1949)-.
TSLL	*Texas Studies in Literature and Language*. Austin, TX 1 (1959/60)-.
TYDS	*Transactions of the Yorkshire Dialect Society*. Leeds 1 (1897)-.
UCPE	University of California Publications in English.
UCPL	University of California Publications in Linguistics.
UCTSE	*University of Cape Town Studies in English*. Cape Town 1 (1970)-.
UppsalaE&S	English Institute in the University of Uppsala: Essays and Studies in English Language and Literature.
USFLQ	University of South Florida Language Quarterly. Tampa, FL 1 (1962)-.
USE	*Unisa English Studies*. Univ. of South Africa, Pretoria 1 (1968)-.
Us Wurk	*Us Wurk. Tydskrift foar Frisistyk*. Groningen 1 (1952)-.
UTQ	*University of Toronto Quarterly*. Toronto 1 (1931/32)-.
UUÅ	Uppsala Universitets Årsskrift.
UWPE	University of Washington Publications in English.
UWPLL	University of Washington Publications in Language and Literature.
UWSLL	University of Wisconsin Studies in Language and Literature.
Viator	*Viator: Medieval and Renaissance Studies*. Los Angles 1 (1970)-.
WBEP	Wiener Beiträge zur englischen Philologie.

Word	*Word: Journal of the Linguistic Circle of New York/Journal of the International Linguistic Association.* New York 1 (1945)-.
WSt	*Word Study.* Springfield, MA 1 (1925/26)-38 (1962/63).
WZHU	*Wissenschaftliche Zeitschrift der Humboldt-Universität, Berlin. Gesellschafts- und sprachwissenschaftliche Reihe.* Berlin 1 (1951)-.
WZUR	*Wissenschaftliche Zeitschrift der Wilhelm-Pieck-Universität Rostock. Gesellschafts- und sprachwissenschaftliche Reihe.* Rostock 1 (1951)-.
YES	*The Yearbook of English Studies.* Cambridge 1 (1971)-.
YPL	*York Papers in Linguistics.* York.
YR	*The Yale Review: A National Quarterly.* New Haven, CT n.s. 1 (1911/12)-.
YSE	*Yale Studies in English.*
YWES	*The Year's Work in English Studies.* London 1921-.
ZAA	*Zeitschrift für Anglistik und Amerikanistik.* Leipzig 1 (1953)-.
ZDA	*Zeitschrift für deutsches Altertum und deutsche Literatur.* Berlin, later on Wiesbaden 1 (1841)-.
ZDL	*Zeitschrift für Dialektologie und Linguistik.* Wiesbaden 37 (1970)-. [Supersedes and continues *ZMaF*.]
ZDP	*Zeitschrift für deutsche Philologie.* Halle, later on Berlin 1 (1869)-.
ZFEU	*Zeitschrift für französischen und englischen Unterricht.* Berlin 1 (1902)-33 (1934). [Continued as *ZNU*.]
ZMaF	*Zeitschrift für Mundartforschung.* Halle 11 (1935)-19 (1944); Wiesbaden 20 (1945)-36 (1969). [Superseded by *ZDL*.]
ZNU	*Zeitschrift für neusprachlichen Unterricht.* Berlin 34 (1935)-42 (1943). [Continuation of *ZFEU*.]
ZNUL	*Zeszyty naukowe Uniwersytetu Łódzkiego.* Seria I. Łódź 1 (1955)-.
ZON	*Zeitschrift für (Orts)namenforschung.* München & Berlin 1 (1925)-.
ZPhon	*Zeitschrift für Phonetik, Sprachwissenschaft und Kommunikationsforschung.* [Formerly *Zeitschrift für Phonetik und Allgemeine Sprachwissenschaft*.] Berlin 1 (1947)-.
ZRP	*Zeitschrift für romanische Philologie.* Halle, later on Tübingen 1 (1876)-.
ZVS	*Zeitschrift für vergleichende Sprachforschung auf dem Gebiete der indogermanischen Sprachen.* Berlin 1 (1852)-.

2. Collections: Festschriften and Miscellaneous

Anglistentag 1981 = *Anglistentag 1981: Vorträge*, ed. Jörg Hasler. (= Trierer Studien zur Literatur, 7.) Frankfurt am Main: Peter Lang, 1983.

Barley & Hanson = *Christianity in Britain, 300-700*, ed. M.W. Barley and R.P.C. Hanson. Leicester: Leicester Univ. Press, 1968.

Behre Papers = Frank Behre, *Papers on English Vocabulary and Syntax, Edited on the Occasion of his Sixty-fifth Birthday*, ed. Alvar Ellegård and Yngve Olsson. (= Gothenburg Studies in English, 10.) Göteborg: Elanders Boktryckeri Aktiebolag; Stockholm: Almqvist & Wiksell.

Bennett Festschrift = *Medieval Studies for J.A.W. Bennett*, ed. P.L. Heyworth. (= Aetatis Suae, 70.) Oxford: Clarendon Press, 1981.

Brodeur Festschrift = *Studies in Old English Literature in Honor of Arthur G[ilchrist] Brodeur*, ed. Stanley B. Greenfield. Eugene, OR: Univ. of Oregon Press, 1963.

Blake & Jones = *English Historical Linguistics: Studies in Development*, ed. N.F. Blake and Charles Jones. (= Centre for English Cultural Tradition and Language Conference Papers Series, 3.) Sheffield: The Centre for English Cultural Tradition and Language, Univ. of Sheffield, 1984.

Buyssens Festschrift = *Linguistique contemporaine: Hommage à Eric Buyssens*, ed. Jean Dierickx and Yvan Lebrun. Brussels: Éditions de l'Institute de Sociologie de l'Université Libre, 1970.

Cameron Studies = *Problems of Old English Lexicography: Studies in Memory of Angus Cameron*, ed. Alfred Bammesberger. (= Eichstätter Beiträge, 15: Absteilung Sprach und Literatur.) Regensburg: Friedrich Pustet, 1985.

Chadwick Festschrift = *The Early Cultures of North-West Europe (H.M. Chadwick Memorial Studies)*, ed. Cyril Fox and Bruce Dickins. Cambridge: Cambridge Univ. Press, 1950.

Christophersen Festschrift = *Studies in English Language and Early Literature in Honour of Paul Christophersen*, ed. P.M. Tilling. (= Occasional Papers in Linguistics and Language Teaching, 8.) Coleraine, N. Ireland: New Univ. of Ulster.

Computers and OE Concordances = *Computers and Old English Concordances*, ed. Angus Cameron, Roberta Frank, and John Leyerle. Toronto: Univ. of Toronto Press (in association with the Centre for Medieval Studies, Univ. of Toronto), 1970.

Coseriu Festschrift = *Logos Semantikos: Studia Linguistica in honorem Eugenio Coseriu 1921-81*, ed. Horst Geckeler, et al. Berlin & New York: de Gruyter; Madrid: Gredos, 1981.

Crépin LSSME/10 = *Linguistic and Stylistic Studies in Medieval English*, Vol. 10, ed. André Crépin. (= Publications de l'Association des Médiévistes de l'Enseignement Superieur, 10.) Paris: L'Association des Médiévistes Anglicistes, 1984.

Current Research 1980 = *Current Research in Dutch Universities on Old English, Middle English, and Historical Linguistics* (Second Philological Symposium 1980), ed. Johan Kerling. Utrecht: Engels Instituut, Univ. of Utrecht, 1981.

Current Research 1983 = *Current Research in Dutch and Belgian Universities on Old English, Middle English and Historical Linguistics* (Fifth Philological Symposium 1983), ed. Erik (S.) Kooper. Utrecht: Engels Instituut, Univ. of Utrecht, 1984.

Current Research 1984 = *Current Research in Dutch and Belgian Universities on Old English, Middle English and Historical Linguistics* (Sixth Philological Symposium 1984), ed. Frans Diekstra. Utrecht: Engels Instituut, Univ. of Utrecht, 1985.
Current Topics in EHL = *Current Topics in English Historical Linguistics*, ed. Michael Davenport, et al. (= Odense University Studies in English, 4.) Odense: Odense Univ. Press, 1983. [= Proceedings of the Second International Conference on English Historical Linguistics Held at Odense University 13-15 April, 1981.]
Dating Beowulf = *The Dating of Beowulf*, ed. Colin Chase. (= Toronto Old English Series, 6.) Toronto: Univ. of Toronto Press (in association with the Centre for Medieval Studies, Univ. of Toronto), 1981.
Davis Festschrift = *Middle English Studies Presented to Norman Davis in Honour of his Seventieth Birthday*, ed. Douglas Gray and E.G. Stanley. Oxford: Clarendon Press, 1983.
Deutschbein Festschrift = *Englische Kultur in sprachwissenschaftlicher Deutung: Max Deutschbein zum 60. Geburtstag*, ed. W. Schmidt. Leipzig: Quelle und Meyer, 1936.
Dickins Festschrift = *The Anglo-Saxons: Studies in Some Aspects of Their History and Culture Presented to Bruce Dickins*, ed. P. Clemoes. London: Bowes & Bowes, 1959.
Dobson Festschrift = *Five Hundred Years of Words and Sounds for Eric John Dobson*, ed. E.G. Stanley and Douglas Gray. Cambridge: D.S. Brewer; Totowa, NJ: Biblio, 1983.
DOE Plan = *A Plan for the Dictionary of Old English*, ed. Roberta Frank and Angus Cameron. Toronto: Univ. of Toronto Press (in association with the Centre for Medieval Studies, Univ. of Toronto), 1973.
Edinburgh Studies = *Edinburgh Studies in English and Scots*, ed. A.J. Aitken, Angus McIntosh, and Herman Palsson. London: Longman, 1971.
Einarsson Festschrift = *Nordica et Anglica: Studies in Honour of Stefán Einarsson*, ed. Allan H. Orrick. (= Janua Linguarum, Series Maior, 22.) The Hague & Paris: Mouton, 1968.
Ekwall Festschrift = *A Philological Miscellany Presented to Eilert Ekwall*. Parts I-II. Uppsala: A.-B. Lundequistska, 1942. [= *Studia Neophilologica* 14 & 15.]
Ekwall Papers = Eilert Ekwall, *Selected Papers*. (= Lund Studies in English, 33.) Lund: Gleerup; Copenhagen: Ejnar Munksgaard, 1963.
Enkvist Festschrift = *Style and Text: Studies Presented to Nils Erik Enkvist*, ed. Håkan Ringbom, et al. Stockholm: Skriptor; Åbo: Åbo Akademi Forskningsinstitut, 1975.
Erlangen Proceedings = *The Study of the Personal Names of the British Isles: Proceedings of a Working Conference at Erlangen 21-24 September 1975*, ed. Herbert Voitle. Erlangen: Institut für Anglistik und Amerikanistik, Universität Erlangen-Nürnberg, 1976.
Essays Sound Pattern = *Essays on the Sound Pattern of English*, ed. Didier L. Goyvaerts and Geoffrey K. Pullum. Ghent: Story-Scientia, 1975.
Fifteenth-Century Studies = *Fifteenth-Century Studies: Recent Essays*, ed. Robert F. Yeager. Hamden, CT: Archon, 1984.
Flasdieck Festschrift = *Britannica: Festschrift für Hermann M. Flasdieck*, ed. Wolfgang Iser and Hans Schabram. Heidelberg: Carl Winter, 1960.
Förster Festschrift = *Britannica: Max Förster zum sechzigsten Geburtstage*. Leipzig: Tauchnitz, 1929.

Fries Festschrift = *Studies in Language and Linguistics in Honor of Charles C. Fries*, ed. Albert Henry Marckwardt. Ann Arbor, MI: The English Language Institute, Univ. of Michigan, 1964.
Funke Aufsätze = Otto Funke, *Gesammelte Aufsätze zur Anglistik und Sprachtheorie.* (= Schweizer anglistische Arbeiten, 56.) Bern: Francke, 1965.
Garmonsway Festschrift = *Medieval Literature and Civilization: Studies in Memory of G.N. Garmonsway*, ed. Derek A. Pearsall and Ronald A. Waldron. London: The Athlone Press, Univ. of London, 1969.
Gerritsen Festschrift = *Historical & Editorial Studies in Medieval & Early Modern English for Johan Gerritsen*, ed. Mary-Jo Arn and Hanneke Wirtjes with Hans Jansen. Groningen: Wolters-Noordhoff, 1985.
Greenfield Festschrift = *Modes of Interpretation in Old English Literature: Essays in Honour of Stanley B. Greenfield*, ed. Phyllis R. Brown, Georgia R. Crampton, and Fred C. Robinson. Toronto-Buffalo-London: Univ. of Toronto Press, 1986.
Grimshaw Papers = *Papers in the History and Structure of English*, ed. Jane B. Grimshaw. (= Univ. of Massachusetts Occasional Papers in Linguistics, 1.) Amherst, MA: Dept. of English, Univ. of Massachusetts, 1975.
Haugen Festschrift = *Studies for Einar Haugen, Presented by Friends and Colleagues*, Evelyn S. Firchow, et al. (= Janua Linguarum, Series Maior, 59.) The Hague: Mouton, 1972.
Historical Morphology = *Historical Morphology*, ed. Jacek Fisiak. (= Trends in Linguistics: Studies and Monographs, 17.) The Hague-Paris-New York: Mouton, 1980.
Historical Phonology = *Recent Developments in Historical Phonology*, ed. Jacek Fisiak. (= Trends in Linguistics: Studies and Monographs, 4.) The Hague-Paris-New York: Mouton, 1978.
Historical Semantics = *Historical Semantics · Historical Word-Formation*, ed. Jacek Fisiak. (= Trends in Linguistics: Studies and Monographs, 29.) Berlin-New York-Amsterdam: Mouton, 1985.
Historical Syntax = *Historical Syntax*, ed. Jacek Fisiak. (= Trends in Linguistics: Studies and Monographs, 23.) Berlin-New York-Amsterdam: Mouton, 1984.
Jespersen Festschrift = *A Grammatical Miscellany Offered to Otto Jespersen on his Seventieth Birthday*, ed. Niels Bøgholm, et al. Copenhagen: Levin & Munksgaard; London: George Allen & Unwin, 1930.
Joly & Fraser Studies = *Studies in English Grammar*, ed. André Joly and Thomas K.H. Fraser. (= Centre Interdisciplinaire de Recherche en Linguistique, 2.) Lille: Univ. de Lille III, 1975.
Klaeber Festschrift = *Studies in English Philology: A Miscellany in Honor of Frederick Klaeber*, ed. Kemp Malone and Martin Brown Ruud. Minneapolis: Univ. of Minnesota press, 1929.
Koziol Festschrift = *Festschrift Prof. Dr. Herbert Koziol zum siebzigsten Geburtstag*, ed. Gero Bauer, Franz K. Stanzel and Franz Zaic. (= Wiener Beiträge zur englischen Philologie, 75.) Wien & Stuttgart: Wilhelm Braumüller, 1973.
Kurath Festschrift = *Lexicography and Dialect Geography: Festgabe für Hans Kurath*, ed. Harald Scholler and John Reidy. (= Zeitschrift für Dialektologie und Linguistik, Beiheft, N.F. 9.) Wiesbaden: Franz Steiner, 1973.

LACUS/6 = *The Sixth LACUS Forum 1979*, ed. William C. McCormack and Herbert J. Izzo. Columbia, SC: Hornbeam Press, 1980.
LACUS/7 = *The Seventh LACUS Forum 1980*, ed. James E. Copeland and Philip W. Davis. Columbia, SC: Hornbeam Press, 1981.
LACUS/11 = *The Eleventh LACUS Forum 1984*, ed. Robert A. Hall. Columbia, SC: Hornbeam Press, 1985.
Lane Festschrift = *Studies in Historical Linguistics in Honor of George Sherman Lane*, ed. Walter W. Arndt, et al. (= Univ. of North Carolina Studies in the Germanic Languages and Literatures, 58.) Chapel Hill, NC: Univ. of North Carolina Press, 1967.
Lass EHL = *Approaches to English Historical Linguistics: An Anthology*, ed. Roger Lass. New York & London: Holt, Rinehart & Winston, 1969.
LEXeter '83 = *LEXeter '83: Papers from the International Conference on Lexicography at Exeter, 9-12 September 1983*, ed. Reinhard R.K. Hartmann. (= Lexicographia, Series Maior, 1.) Tübingen: Max Niemeyer, 1984.
Linguistique et Philologie = *Linguistique et Philologie (Applications aux Textes Médiévaux): Actes du Colloqus des 29 et 30 avril 1977, Université de Picardie*, ed. Danielle Buschinger. Paris: Champion, 1977.
Lombard Festschrift = *Mélanges de Philologie offerts à Alf Lombard à l'occasion de son soixante-cinquième anniversaire par ses collègues et ses amis*. (= Études Romanes de Lund, 18.) Lund: CWK Gleerup, 1969.
Luick Festschrift = *Neusprachliche Studien: Festgabe für Karl Luick zu seinem 60. Geburtstage*, ed. Friedrich Wild. (= *Die neueren Sprachen* 33, Beiheft 6.) Marburg: Elwert, 1925.
Magoun Festschrift = *Franciplegius: Medieval and Linguistic Studies in Honor of Francis Peabody Magoun, Jr.*, ed. Jess B. Bessinger, Jr. and Robert P. Creed. New York: New York Univ. Press, 1965.
Malone Festschrift = *Philologica: The Malone Anniversary Studies*, ed. Thomas A[ustin] Kirby and Henry B[osley] Woolf. Baltimore: The Johns Hopkins Press, 1949.
Marchand Festschrift = *Wortbildung, Syntax und Morphologie: Festschrift zum 60. Geburtstag von Hans Marchand am 1. Oktober 1967*, ed. Herbert E. Brekle and Leonhard Lipka. (= Janua Linguarum, Series Maior, 36.) The Hague & Paris: Mouton, 1968.
Maxwell Festschrift = *Iceland and the Mediaeval World: Studies in Honour of Ian Maxwell*, ed. Gabriel Turville-Petre and John Stanley Martin. Melbourne: Melbourne Univ. Press, 1974.
McIntosh Festschrift (A) = *Language Form and Linguistic Variation: Papers Dedicated to Angus McIntosh*, ed. John Anderson. (= Current Issues in Linguistic Theory, 15.) Amsterdam: John Benjamins, 1982.
McIntosh Festschrift (E) = *So Meny People Longages and Tonges: Philological Essays in Scots and Mediaeval English Presented to Angus McIntosh*, ed. Michael Benskin and M[ichael] L[ouis] Samuels. Edinburgh: Michael Benskin & M.L. Samuels, 1981.
Meritt Festschrift = *Philological Essays: Studies in Old and Middle English Language and Literature in Honour of Herbert Dean Meritt*, ed. James L. Rosier. The Hague: Mouton, 1970.

Michigan Essays and Studies = *Essays and Studies in English and Comparative Literature, by Members of the English Department of the University of Michigan*. (= Univ. of Michigan Publications, Language and Literature, 13.) Ann Arbor, MI: Univ. of Michigan Press, 1935.

Mossé Festschrift = *Mélanges de Linguistique et de Philologie: Fernand Mossé in Memoriam*. Paris: Marcel Didier, 1959.

MSC Aachen 1983 = *Medieval Studies Conference: Aachen; Language and Literature*, ed. Wolf-Dietrich Bald and Horst Weinstock. (= Bamberger Beiträge zur Englischen Sprachwissenschaft, 15.) Frankfurt am Main-Bern-New York-Nancy: Peter Lang, 1984.

Mustanoja Festschrift = *Studies Presented to Tauno F. Mustanoja on the Occasion of his Sixtieth Birthday*. Helsinki: Société Néophilologique, 1972. [= *Neuphilologische Mitteilungen* 73, nos. 1 & 2.]

Papajewski Festschrift = *Studien zur englischen und amerikanischen Sprache und Literatur: Festschrift für Helmut Papajewski*, ed. P.G. Buchloh, et al. (= Kieler Beiträge zur Anglistik und Amerikanistik, 10.) Neumünster: Wachholtz, 1974.

Penzl Festschrift = *Linguistic Method: Essays in Honor of Herbert Penzl*, ed. Irmengard Rauch and Gerald F. Carr. (= Janua Linguarum, Series Maior, 79.) The Hague-Paris-New York: Mouton, 1979.

Philologie und Sprachwissenschaft = *Philologie und Sprachwissenschaft: Akten der 10. Osterreichischen Linguisten-Tagung Innsbruck, 23.-26. Oktober 1982*, ed. Wolfgang Meid and Hans Schmeja. (= Innsbrucker Beiträge zur Sprachwissenschaft, 43.) Innsbruck: Institut für Sprachwissenschaft der Universität Innsbruck, 1983.

PCLS = *Papers from the -th Regional Meeting of the Chicago Linguistic Society*. Chicago.

PICEHL/4 = *Papers from the 4th International Conference on English Historical Linguistics, Amsterdam, 10-13 April, 1985*, ed. Roger Eaton, et al. (= Current Issues in Linguistic Theory, 41.) Amsterdam: John Benjamins, 1985 [1986].

PICHL/1 & 2 = *Proceedings of the First (Second) International Conference on Historical Linguistics*. (= North-Holland Linguistics Series, 12 & 31.) Amsterdam & Oxford: North Holland, 1974 & 1976.

PICHL/3, 4, 5, 6 = *Papers of the Third* (etc.) *International Conference on Historical Linguistics*. (= Current Issues in Linguistic Theory, 13, 14, 21, 34.) Amsterdam: John Benjamins, 1982, 1980 [sic], 1982, 1985.

PICL = *Proceeding of the -th International Congress of Linguists*. [Date and place of publication varies.]

Pinsker Festschrift = *Festgabe für Hans Pinsker zum 70. Geburtstag*, ed. Richild Acobian. Wien: V[erband der] W[issenschaftlichen] G[esellschaften] Ö[sterreichs], 1979.

PMALC/1971 = *From Soundstream to Discourse: Papers from the 1971 Mid-American Linguistics Conference*, ed. Daniel G. Hays and Donald M. Lance. Columbus, MO: Univ. of Missouri, 1972.

Pope Festschrift = *Old English Studies in Honour of John C. Pope*, ed. Robert B. Burlin and Edward B. Irving, Jr. Toronto: Univ. of Toronto Press, 1974.

Quirk Essays = Randolph Quirk, *Essays on the English Language — Medieval and Modern*. London: Longmans, 1968.

Reports on Text Linguistics = *Reports on Text Linguistics: Approaches to Word Order*, ed. Nils Erik Enkvist and Viljo Kohonen. (= Meddelanden från Stiftelsens för Åbo Akademi Forskningsinstitut, 8.) Åbo [Turku]: Åbo Akademi Forskningsinstitut, 1976.
Robbins Festschrift = *Chaucer and Middle English Studies in Honour of Rossell Hope Robbins*, ed. Beryl Rowland. London: George Allen & Unwin; Kent, OH: Kent State Univ. Press, 1974.
Rynell Festschrift = *Studies in English Philology, Linguistics and Literature Presented to Alarik Rynell 7 March 1978*, ed. Mats Rydén and Lennart A. Björk. (= Stockholm Studies in English, 46.) Stockholm: Almqvist & Wiksell, 1978.
Sawyer Med.Settlement = *Medieval Settlement: Continuity and Change*, ed. P.H. Sawyer. London: Arnold; New York: Crane, Russak, 1976.
Schibsbye Festschrift = *Essays Presented to Knud Schibsbye* (on his 75th birthday 29 November 1979), ed. Michael Chestnut, et al. (= Publications of the Department of English, Univ. of Copenhagen, 8.) Copenhagen: Akademisk Forlag, 1979.
Schlauch Festschrift = *Studies in Language and Literature in Honour of Margaret Schlauch*, ed. Mieczysław Brahmer, et al. Warzawa: Państowe Wydawnictwo Naukowe; New York: Russell & Russell, 1965.
Schneider Festschrift = *Festschrift für Karl Schneider zum 70. Geburtstag am 18. April 1982*, ed. Ernst S. Dick and Kurt R. Jankowsky. Amsterdam: John Benjamins, 1982.
Scott & Erickson = *Readings for the History of the English Language*, ed. Charles T. Scott and Jon L. Erickson. Boston: Allyn & Bacon, 1968.
Sievers Festschrift = *Germanica: Eduard Sievers zum 75. Geburtstage 25. November 1925*. Halle: Max Niemeyer, 1925.
Smith Festschrift = *Early English and Norse Studies: Presented to Albert Hugh Smith in Honour of his Sixtieth Birthday*, ed. Arthur Brown and Peter G. Foote. London: Methuen, 1963.
Sofia English Studies = *English Studies: Articles on English and American Literature and the English Language*. Sofija: Sofijski Univ. "Kliment Ochridski", 1980.
South Saxons = *The South Saxons*, ed. Peter Brandon. London: Phillimore, 1978.
Steenbergen Festschrift = *Een Spyeghel voor G. Jo Steenbergen, huldealbum aangeboden bij zijn emeritaat*, ed. Fr. Daems and L. Goossens. Leuven & Amersfoort: Acco, 1983.
Studies in Lexicography = *Studies in Lexicography*, ed. Robert W. Burchfield. Oxford: Clarendon Press, 1987.
Syntactic Variation I = *Papers from the Scandinavian Symposium on Syntactic Variation, Stockholm, May 18-19, 1979*, ed. Sven Jacobson. (= Stockholm Studies in English, 52.) Stockholm: Almqvist & Wiksell International, 1980.
Syntactic Variation II = *Papers from the Second Scandinavian Symposium on Syntactic Variation, Stockholm May 15-16, 1982*, ed. Sven Jacobson. (= Stockholm Studies in English, 57.) Stockholm: Almqvist & Wiksell International, 1983.
Syntactic Variation III = *Papers from the Third Scandinavian Symposium on Syntactic Variation, Stockholm, May 11-12, 1985*, ed. Sven Jacobson. (= Stockholm Studies in English, 65.) Stockholm: Almqvist & Wiksell International, 1986.
The Vikings = *The Vikings: Proceedings of the Symposium of the Faculty of Arts of*

Uppsala University, June 6-9, 1977, ed. Thorsten Andersson and Karl Inge Sandred. (= Symposia Universitatis Upsaliensis annum quingentesimum celebrantis, 8.) Uppsala: Uppsala Univ. Press; Stockholm: Almqvist & Wiksell International, 1978.

Tolkien Festschrift = *English and Medieval Studies: Presented to J.R.R. Tolkien on the Occasion of his 70th Birthday*, ed. Norman Davis and Charles L. Wrenn. London: George Allen & Unwin, 1962.

Trnka Papers = Bohumil Trnka, *Selected Papers in Structural Linguistics: Contributions to English and General Linguistics written in the years 1928-1978*, ed. Vilém Fried. (= Janua Linguarum, Series Maior, 88.) Berlin-New York-Amsterdam: Mouton, 1982.

Untersuchungen zur Flur = *Untersuchungen zur eisenzeitlichen und fruhmittelalterlichen Flur in Mitteleuropa und ihrer Nutzung: Bericht über die Kolloquien der Kommission für die Altertumskunde Mitel- und Nordeuropas in den Jahren 1975 und 1976, I-II*, ed. Heinrich Beck, et al. (= Abhandlungen der Akademi der Wissenschaften in Göttingen, Philologisch-historische Klasse, 3:115 & 116.) Göttingen: Vandenhoeck & Ruprecht, 1979.

Utley Festschrift = *Medieval Literature and Folklore Studies: Essays in Honor of Francis Lee Utley*, ed. Jerome Mandel and Bruce A. Rosenberg. New Brunswick, NJ: Rutgers Univ. Press, 1970.

von Feilitzen Festschrift = *Otium et Negotium: Studies in Onomatology and Library Science Presented to Olog von Feilitzen*, ed. Folke Sandgren. (= Acta Bibliotheca Regiae Stockholmiensis, 16.) Stockholm: Kungliga Biblioteket, 1973. [Also separate ed., Stockholm: P.A. Norstedt & Söner.]

Whitelock Festschrift = *England before the Conquest: Studies in Primary Sources Presented to Dorothy Whitelock*, ed. Peter Clemoes and Kathleen Hughes. Cambridge: Cambridge Univ. Press, 1971.

Wild Festschrift = *Anglistische Studien: Festschrift zum 70. Geburtstag von Prof. Dr. Friedrich Wild*, ed. Karl Brunner, Herbert Koziol and Siegfried Korninger. (= Wiener Beiträge zur englischen Philologie, 66.) Wien & Stuttgart: Braumüller, 1958.

Willard Festschrift = *Studies in Language, Literature, and Culture of the Middle Ages and Later: Studies in Honor of Rudolph Willard*, ed. E. Bagby Atwood and Archbald A. Hill. Austin, TX: Univ. of Texas at Austin, 1969.

Winchester Studies = *Winchester in the Early Middle Ages: An Edition and Discussion of the Winston Domesday*, ed. Martin Biddle. (= Winchester Studies, 1.) Oxford: Clarendon Press, 1976.

Wrenn Word and Symbol = Charles Leslie Wrenn, *Word and Symbol: Studies in English Language*. (English Language Series.) London: Longmans, Green & Co, 1967.

Zandvoort Festschrift = *English Studies Presented to R.W. Zandvoort on the Occasion of his Seventieth Birthday*. Amsterdam: Swets & Zeitlinger, 1964. [= A Supplement to *English Studies* 45.]

3. Others

Abstr.	abstract
AN	Anglo-Norman
Anon.	Anonymous
AS	Anglo-Saxon
Aufl.	Auflage
c.	circa
cf.	compare
chap.	chapter
comp(s).	compiler(s), compiled by
CT	Geoffrey Chaucer, *The Canterbury Tales*
Dept.	Department
diss.	(doctoral) dissertation
DOST	*A Dictionary of the Older Scottish Tongue*
ed(s).	edition(s), editor(s), edited by
enl.	enlarged
et al.	and others
ff.	(and the) following
IE	Indo-European
ME	Middle English
MED	*Middle English Dictionary*
ModE	Modern English
MS(S)	manuscript(s)
N.F.	Neue Folge
no(s).	number(s)
n.s.	new series
OE	Old English
OED	*The Oxford English Dictionary*
OF	Old French
ON	Old Norse
o.s.	original series
p(p).	page(s)
pt.	part
pub(s).	publication(s), published
rev.	revision, revised
repr.	reprint(ed)
ser.	series
transl.	translation, translated
Univ.	University/Universität/Universitaire
vol(s).	volume(s)

N.B. In the place of publication, the US state name is identified by its zip-code symbol, as in MA for Massachusetts.

I. BIBLIOGRAPHIES

A. General

(i) Comprehensive

1. Allen, Harold Byron, comp. 1966. *Linguistics and English Linguistics.* (Goldentree Bibliographies.) New York: Appleton-Century-Crofts, xi + 108 pp. [A selective bibliography of publications since 1922, the cut-off date of Kennedy [no. 11].]

   Review: Helmut Gneuss in *Anglia* 88.103-04 (1970).

2. ———, comp. 1977. *Linguistics and English Linguistics.* 2nd ed. Arlington Heights, IL: AHM Publishing Corp., xvi + 175 pp.

   Review: Pablo Domínguez in *RCEI* 5.141-43 (1982).

3. Bateson, Frederick Wilse, ed. 1940. *The Cambridge Bibliography of English Literature. I: 600-1660.* Cambridge: Cambridge Univ. Press, xl + 912 pp.

4. Beale, Walter H. 1976. *Old and Middle English Poetry to 1500: A Guide to Information Sources.* Detroit: Gale Research, xxvi + 454 pp. [Contains 'OE Language' (pp. 53-55) and 'ME Language' (pp. 205-07).]

5. Crosby, Everett Uberto, C. Julian Bishko, and Robert L. Kellogg. 1983. *Medieval Studies: A Bibliographical Guide.* (= GRLH, 427.) New York: Garland, xxv + 1131 pp. [Contains 'English Language and Literature' (pp. 791-97).]

6. Fisiak, Jacek, ed. 1977. *Bibliografia anglistyk polskiej 1945-1975. Językoznawstwo-literaturoznawstwo* [Bibliography of Writings on English Language and Literature in Poland, 1945-75]. Warsaw: Państwowe Wydawnictwo Naukowe, 205 pp.

7. ———, ed. 1983. *A Bibliography of Writings for the History of the English Language.* (= Uniwersytet im. Adama Mickiewicza w Poznaniu, Seria Filologia Angielska, 20.) Poznań: Wydawnictwo Naukowe Uniwersytetu im. Adama Mickiewicza w Poznaniu, 166 pp.

Reviews: E.G. S[tanley] in *N&Q* n.s. 31.437 (1984); Ruta Nagucka in *JEngL* 17.116-18 (1984); Hans Heinrich Hock in *World Englishes* (Oxford & New York) 4.290-91 (1985).

8. Funke, Otto. 1950. *Englische Sprachkunde: Ein Überblick ab 1935*. (= Wissenschaftliche Forschungsberichte, Geisteswissenschaftliche Reihe, 10.) Bern: A. Francke, 163 pp.

    Reviews: H.M. Flasdieck in *Anglia* 69.450 (1950); N. Davis in *ArchL* 3. 212-13 (1951); A.A. Prins in *Museum* 56.144 (1951); S.B. Liljegren in *SN* 24.225 (1951/52); R. Derolez in *RBPH* 30.253-55 (1952); N.E. Eliason in *MLN* 67.352-53 (1952); F. Mossé in *EA* 5.175 (1952); V. Pisani in *Paideia* (Brescia, Italy) 7.139-40 (1952); Randolph Quirk in *MLR* 47.59-60 (1952); E.V.K. Dobbie in *Word* 9.86-87 (1953); H.C. Matthes in *Archiv* 189.60 (1953); M.L. Samuels in *RES* n.s. 4.88-89 (1953); R.W. Zandvoort in *ES* 35.231-32 (1954); Ernst Leisi in *GRM* 38.90-92 (1957).

9. Greenfield, Stanley Brian and Fred Colson Robinson. 1980. *A Bibliography of Publications on Old English Literature to the End of 1972*. Toronto & Buffalo: Univ. of Toronto Press; Manchester: Manchester Univ. Press, xxii + 437 pp. [Using the collections of E.E. Ericson. Linguistic studies which deal with specific OE texts are included, but not more general works on language.]

    Reviews: Anon. in *British Book News*, August 1981, p. 462; Eugene P. Sheehy in *College & Research Libraries* (Chicago) 42.351 (1981); E.G. Stanley ("The Scholarly Recovery of the Significance of Anglo-Saxon Records in Prose and Verse: a New Bibliography") in *ASE* 9.223-62 (1980 [1981]); Carl T. Berkhout in *Speculum* 57.897-99 (1982); Alan Bliss in *N&Q* n.s. 29.353-54 (1982); J.D. Burnley in *Lore&L* 3:6.134 (1982); Donald K. Fry in *AEB* 6.183-86 (1982) and *ELN* 20.11-20 (1982); Valmai Fenster in *American Reference Books Annual* 13.664-65 (1982); Helmut Gneuss in *Anglia* 100.487-93 (1982); M.L. Samuels in *Library Review* (Glasgow) 31.298-99 (1982); Roberta Frank in *UTQ* 52.302-03 (1983); M.R. Godden in *MAE* 52.311-12 (1983); Patrizia Lendinara in *Schede Medievali* 5.491-92 (1983); Bruce Mitchell in *RES* n.s. 34.320-21 (1983); Matti Rissanen in *NM* 84.271-73 (1983); Rolf H. Bremmer, Jr. in *ES* 65.38 (1984); J.E. Cross in *MLR* 79.412-14 (1984).

10. Heusinkveld, Arthur H. and Edwin J. Bashe. 1931. *A Bibliographical Guide to Old English: A Selective Bibliography of the Language, Literature, and History of the Anglo-Saxons*. (= Univ. of Iowa Humanistic Studies, 4:5.) Iowa City: Univ. of Iowa Press, 153 pp. [Repr., Folcroft, PA: Folcroft Library Editions, 1971. For linguistic studies, see pp. 32-35.]

    Reviews: A. B[randl] in *Archiv* 161.145 (1932); F. Klaeber in *Anglia B* 43.200-02 (1932); F.P. Magoun, Jr. in *Speculum* 7.286-89 (1932); K. M[alone] in *MLN* 49.352 (1934); J. Hoops in *EStn* 69.432 (1934/35).

11. Kennedy, Arthur Garfield. 1927. *A Bibliography of Writings on the English Language from the Beginning of Printing to the End of 1922.* Cambridge, MA: Harvard Univ. Press; New Haven, CT: Yale Univ. Press; London: Milford, xvii + 517 pp. [Repr., New York & London: Hafner, 1961, 1967.]
    Reviews: Anon. in *TLS*, June 16, 1927, p. 428; George P. Krapp in *SRL*, Dec. 3, 1927, 4.376; Hermann M. Flasdieck in *Anglia B* 39.166-74 (1928); George T. Flom in *JEGP* 27.437-40 (1928); Louise Pound in *AS* 3.239-40 (1927/28); James F. Royster in *MP* 25.495-97 (1928); R.B. Mck[errow] in *RES* 5.120-21 (1929); Arvid Gabrielson in *SN* 2.117-68 (1929); R.M. Wilson in *MLR* 58.150 (1963).

12. ———— and Donald B. Sands. 1972. *A Concise Bibliography for Students of English.* 5th ed. Revised by William E. Colburn. Stanford, CA: Stanford Univ. Press, xvi + 300 pp. [1st ed. by A.G. Kennedy, 1940; Rev. eds. by A.G. Kennedy, 1945 and 1954, vii + 162 pp.; 4th ed. rev. by D.B. Sands, 1960.]

13. Kohl, Norbert. 1970. *Bibliographie für das Stadium der Anglistik.* Band I: *Sprachwissenschaft. Mit einem allgemeinen bibliographischen und lexikalischen Teil.* (= Schwerpunkte Anglistik, 2.) Bad Homburg v.d.H.: Athenäum, 270 pp.

14. Markey, Thomas Lloyd, Robert Lange Kyes, and Paul T. Roberge, with the assistance of Barbara E. Hagerman. 1977. *Germanic and Its Dialects: A Grammar of Proto-Germanic. III: Bibliography and Indices.* Amsterdam: John Benjamins, xlviii + 504 pp. [Contains quite a number of OE and ME studies.]

15. Matthews, William, comp. 1968. *Old and Middle English Literature.* (Golden Bibliographies in Language and Literature.) New York: Appleton-Century-Crofts, xvi + 112 pp. ['OE Language' (pp. 8-9) and 'ME Language' (pp. 38-39).]

16. Müller-Schwefe, Gerhard. 1962. *Einführung in das Studien der englischen Philologie mit Bibliographie.* Tübingen: Max Niemeyer, xii + 186 pp.

17. Oizumi, Akio. 1966. *A Classified Bibliography of Writings on English Philology and Medieval English Literature.* Tokyo: Nan'un-do, xiii + 108 pp.

18. ————. 1968. *A Classified Bibliography of Writings on English Philology and Medieval English literature.* Rev. and enl. ed. Tokyo: Nan'un-do, xvi + 182 pp. ['Addenda and Corrigenda' to the 1st ed. (pp. 93-96) and 'First Supplement' (pp. 96-165).]

19. Robinson, Fred Colson. 1970. *Old English Literature: A Selective Bibliography.* (= TMB, 2.) Toronto: Univ. of Toronto Press, xvi + 64 pp.

Reviews: D.A.H. Evans in *SN* 42.485-86 (1970); R. D[erolez] in *ES* 52.192 (1971); P. Lendinara in *AION-SG* 14.600 (1971); P. Grenzel in *ZAA* 20.305-06 (1972); H. Gneuss in *Anglia* 92.439-41 (1974).

20. Severs, Jonathan Burke and Albert E. Hartung, gen. eds. 1967-. *A Manual of the Writings in Middle English, 1050-1500*. 7 vols. (to date). New Haven, CN: The Connecticut Academy of Arts and Sciences. (Order from: Hamden, CN: Archon Books/The Shoe String Press.) ["Based upon *A Manual of the Writings in Middle English 1050-1400* by John Edwin Wells, New Haven, 1916, and Supplements 1-9, 1919-1951".]

    Contents to date are as follows:
    Vol. 1: I. *Romances*, 1967, 338 pp. Vol. 2: II. *The Pearl Poet*; III. *Wyclyf and His Followers*; IV. *Translations and Paraphrases of the Bible, and Commentaries*; V. *Saints' Legends*; VI. *Instructions for Religious*, 1968, 10 + 339-668 pp. Vol 3: VII. *Dialogues, Debates, and Catechisms*; VIII. *Thomas Hoccleve*; IX. *Malory and Caxton*, 1972, 10 + 669-960 pp. Vol. 4: X. *Middle Scots Writers*; XI. *The Chaucerian Apocrypha*, 1973, 10 + 961-1313 pp. Vol. 5: XII. *Dramatic Pieces*; XIII. *Poems Dealing with Contemporary Conditions*, 1975, 10 + 1315-1742 pp. Vol.6: XIV. *Carols*; XV. *Ballads*; XVI. *John Lydgate*, 1980, 10 + 1743-2194 pp. Vol. 7: XVII. *John Gower*; XVIII. *Piers Plowman*; XIX. *Travel and Geographical Writings*; XX. *Works of Religious and Philosophical Instruction*, 1986, x + 2195-2595 pp.

    Reviews: Vol. 2 by Anne Hudson in *MAE* 43.199-201 (1974); Vol. 3 by Derek Pearsall in *MAE* 43.87-90 (1974); Vol. 5 by Raymond St-Jacques in *HAR* 29.106-08 (1978); Vol. 6 by Richard L. Hoffman in *Literary Research Newsletter*. (Manhattan College, Bronx, NY) 7.30-34 (1982).

21. Terasawa, Yoshio, gen. ed. 1983. *A Bibliography of Publications on Medieval English Language and Literature in Japan*. Tokyo: Centre for Mediaeval English Studies, Univ. of Tokyo, ix + 259 pp. [In Japanese.]

22. ———, gen. ed. 1986. *A Bibliography of Publications on Medieval English Language and Literature in Japan from April 1983 to March 1985*. (= *MESN*, Special Issue, 1.) Tokyo: Centre for Mediaeval English Studies, Univ. of Tokyo, [i +] 34 pp. [Lists only the works voluntarily reported to the Centre.]

23. Watson, George, ed. 1957. *The Cambridge Bibliography of English Literature. Vol. V: Supplement: A.D. 600-1900*. Cambridge: Cambridge Univ. Press, xiv + 710 pp. [Covers scholarship to 1955.]

24. ———, ed. 1958. *The Concise Cambridge Bibliography of English Literature, 600-1950*. Cambridge: Cambridge Univ. Press, xi + 271 pp. [2nd ed. 1965.]

25. ———, ed. 1974. *The New Cambridge Bibliography of English Literature, I:*

600-1600. Cambridge: Cambridge Univ. Press, xxxii + 1253 pp. [The cut-off point is the end of 1972. See esp. cols. 53-186.]

Reviews: Peter Davison in *Library* (London) 30.146-49 (1975); Goerges and Élizabeth Bourcier in *EA* 29.203-05 (1976); John Mulryan in *Cithara* (St Bonaventure, NY) 15.132-34 (1976); W.H. Toppen in *DQR* 7.143-46 (1977); Fred C. Robinson in *Anglia* 97.511-17 (1979); Johan Gerritsen in *ES* 61.466-67 (1980).

(ii) Specialized

26. Bailey, Richard Weld and Dolores M. Burton, S.N.D. 1968. *English Stylistics: A Bibliography*. Cambridge, MA & London: The M.I.T. Press, xxii + 198 pp.

    Reviews: Donald McClusky in *GL* 9.132-34 (1969); Samuel R. Levin in *MLJ* 54.41 (1970); Henry Kučera in *FL* 7.455-56 (1971).

27. Becker, Russell. 1978. "Materials for English Historical Linguistics: An Annotated Bibliography of Concordances". *JEngL* 12.1-11. [Includes the concordances of *Beowulf*, Chaucer, *Pearl*-Poet, and Malory.]

28. Bennett, James R. 1968. "English Prose Style from Alfred to More: A Bibliography". *MS* 30.248-59. [Annotated.]

29. Cameron, Angus (Fraser), Allison Kingsmill, and Ashley Crandell Amos. 1983. *Old English Word Studies: A Preliminary Author and Word Index*. (= TOES, 8.) Toronto: Univ. of Toronto Press (in association with the Centre for Medieval Studies, Univ. of Toronto), xvi + 192 pp. + 5 microfiches.

    Reviews: Patrizia Lendinara in *Schede Medievali* 5.476-77 (1983); Rolf H. Bremmer, Jr. in *ES* 66.380 (1985); Susan Cooper in *MAE* 54.290-91 (1985); Constance B. Hieatt in *ESC* 11.231-32 (1985); Theodore H. Leinbaugh in *Speculum* 60.214-15 (1985); Ilkka Mönkkönen in *NM* 86.599-601 (1986); Karl Toth in *Anglia* 104.178-82 (1986).

30. Foley, John Miles. 1985. *Oral-Formulaic Theory and Research: An Introduction and Annotated Bibliography*. (= Garland Folklore Bibliographies, 6.) New York: Garland, xvi + 718 pp.

31. Guimier, Claude. 1981. *Prepositions: An Analytical Bibliography*. (= Library and Information Sources in Linguistics, 8.) Amsterdam: John Benjamins, vii + 244 pp.

32. Juilland, Alphonse G. 1953. "A Bibliography of Diachronic Phonemics". *Word* 9.198-208. [Of 174 items listed, only 11 are concerned with English.]

33. Mitchell, Bruce and Allison Kingsmill. 1980. "Prepositions, Adverbs, Prepositional Adverbs, Postpositions, Separable Prefixes, or Inseparable Prefixes, in Old English?: A Supplementary Bibliography". *NM* 81.313-17. [Cf. Mitchell [no. 1542].]

34. Patch, Howard Rollin and Robert J. Menner. 1923. "A Bibliography of Middle English Dialects". *SP* 20.479-95.

35. Roberts, Richard Julian. 1958/59 [1961]. *Bibliography of Writings on English Place- and Personal Names*. Louvain: International Centre of Onomastics, 82 pp. [= *Onoma: Bibliographical and Information Bulletin*, 8:3.]

36. Seymour, Richard K. 1968. *A Bibliography of Word Formation in the Germanic Languages*. Durham, NC: Duke Univ. Press, xv + 158 pp.

    Reviews: Bengt Pamp in *ANF* 84.263-64 (1970); Klaus R. Grinda in *Anglia* 89.241-43 (1971).

37. Smith, Elsdon Coles, comp. 1952. *Personal Names: An Annotated Bibliography*. New York: New York Public Library, 226 pp. [New ed., Detroit, MI: Gale, 1965.]

    Review: Edward J. Alfonsin in *Names* 14.127 (1966).

38. Stein, Gabriele. 1973. *English Word-Formation over two Centuries*. In Honour of Hans Marchand on the Occasion of his Sixty-Fifth Birthday, 1 October 1972. (= TBL, 34.) Tübingen: TBL-Verlag, 356 pp.

    Reviews: R. D[erolez] in *ES* 55.595-96 (1974); Herbert E. Brekle in *JL* 11.357-59 (1975); Klaus Hansen in *ZAA* 23.76-79 (1975).

39. Terasawa, Yoshio, gen. ed. 1980. "Publications on Middle English Dialectology by Professors A. McIntosh and M.L. Samuels, and their Associates". *MESN* 3.3-7.

B. Individual

40. Andrew, Malcolm. 1979. *The 'Gawain'-Poet: An Annotated Bibliography, 1839-1977*. (= GRLH, 129.) New York & London: Garland, xxviii + 256 pp.

    Review: Rossell Hope Robbins in *AEB* 4.241-52 (1980).

41. Baird, Lorrayne Y. 1977. *A Bibliography of Chaucer, 1964-73*. Boston: G.K. Hall, xxiv + 287 pp. [Continues Crawford [no. 46]. For linguistic studies, see pp. 62-65.]

    Review: Dieter Mehl in *Archiv* 216.168-69 (1979).

42. Baugh, Albert Croll, comp. 1968. *Chaucer.* (Goldentree Bibliographies in Language and Literature.) New York: Appleton-Century-Crofts, xv + 128 pp.

43. ———, comp. 1977. *Chaucer.* 2nd ed. (Goldentree Bibliographies in Language and Literature.) Arlington Heights, IL: AHM Publishing Corp., xiv + 160 pp. [For linguistics studies, see pp. 30-33.]

44. Blake, Norman Francis. 1985. *William Caxton: A Bibliographical Guide.* (= GRLH, 524.) New York & London: Garland, x + 227 pp. [Includes the section 'Language and Style' (pp. 99-107).]

    Review: A.S.G. Edwards in *ES* 68.95-98 (1987).

45. Blanch, Robert J. 1983. *Sir Gawain and the Green Knight: A Reference Guide.* Troy, NY: Whitson, 298 pp. [All items are placed in chronological order from 1824 to 1978.]

    Reviews: Tadahiro Ikegami in *SAC* 7.166-67 (1985); G.C. Britton in *N&Q* n.s. 33.212-13 (1986).

46. Crawford, William R. 1967. *Bibliography of Chaucer 1954-63.* (= UWPLL, 17.) Seattle & Lodnon: Univ. of Washington Press, xliv + 144 pp. [Continues Griffith [no. 51].]

    Reviews: Beryl Rowland in *AN&Q* 6.45-46 (1967); E.G. Stanley in *N&Q* n.s. 15.42 (1968); Paul Bacquet in *EA* 21.300 (1968); Anon. in *TLS*, 22 Feb. 1968, p. 184; R.S. Rainbow, Jr. in *MP* 66.273-74 (1969); Rossell Hope Robbins in *Archiv* 205.65-66 (1969); P.M. Vermeer in *ES* 52.164-65 (1971).

47. Colaianne, A.J. 1978. *Piers Plowman: An Annotated Bibliography of Editions and Criticism, 1550-1977.* (= GRLH, 121.) New York & London: Garland, xi + 195 pp. [Originally Univ. of Cincinnati diss. For linguistic studies, see Chap. IV (pp. 151-64).]

    Reviews: P.M. Kean in *RES* n.s. 30.457-58 (1979); Barbara Raw in *N&Q* n.s. 26.566-67 (1979).

48. Fisher, John Hurt. 1977. "Bibliography [of Chaucer]". *The Complete Poetry and Prose of Geoffrey Chaucer*, 973-1032. New York: Holt, Rinehart and Winston. [This bibliography "includes all books and articles from 1964 through 1974" (p. 975).]

49. Fry, Donald K. 1969. *Beowulf and the Fight at Finnsburh: A Bibliography.* Charlottesville, VA: The Univ. Press of Virginia, for the Bibliographical Society of the Univ. of Virginia, xx + 222 pp. ["Every work published before July 1967 which deals with *Beowulf* or *Finnsburh* in any useful or significant way is, regardless of quality, is included" (p. xii).]

Reviews: Anon. in *Virginia Quarterly Review* (Charlottesville), Summer 1970, p. xcviii; Hugh Keenan in *Library Journal* (New York), 1 May, 1970; Stephen Manning in *Papers of the Bibliographical Society of America* (Austin, TX) 64.363-64 (1970); L. Whitbread in *ES* 53.249-50 (1970); Donald C. Baker in *ELN* 10.127-28 (1972).

50. Griffith, Dudley David. 1926. *A Bibliography of Chaucer, 1908-1924*. (= UWPLL, 4:1.) Seattle: Univ. of Washington Press, 148 pp. [Incorporated in Griffith [no. 51].]

Reviews: John Koch in *EStn* 61.440-41 (1927); Martin B. Ruud in *MLN* 42.343-44 (1927); W.F. Schirmer in *NS* 36.24-25 (1928).

51. ———. 1955. *Bibliography of Chaucer 1908-1953*. (= UWPLL, 13.) Seattle: Univ. of Washington Press, xviii + 398 pp.

Reviews: Anon. in *TLS*, Sept. 2, 1955, p. 514; Rolf Berndt in *ZAA* 4.494-96 (1956); H.M. Flasdieck in *Anglia* 74.252-53 (1956); Joseph G. Fucilla in *JEGP* 55.501-02 (1956); F. Mossé in *EA* 9.42 (1956); Howard R. Patch in *MLN* 72.210-12 (1957); J.A.W. Bennett in *RES* n.s. 8.180-81 (1957); Ursula Brown in *MAE* 27.39-43.

52. Huang Do, Merdeka Thien-Ly. 1980. "*Sir Gawain and the Green Knight*: An Annotated Bibliography, 1973-1978". *Comitatus* (Univ. of California, Los Angeles) 11.66-110.

53. Leyerle, John and Anne Quick. 1986. *Chaucer: A Bibliographical Introduction*. (= TMB, 10.) Toronto: Univ. of Toronto Press (in association with the Centre for Medieval Studies, Univ. of Toronto), xx + 321 pp. [Based on the material up to the end of 1979. For linguistic studies, see the section 'Language and Versification' (pp. 17-26).]

54. Life, Page West. 1980. *Sir Thomas Malory and the 'Morte Darthur': A Survey of Scholarship and Annotated Bibliography*. Charlottesville: The Univ. Press of Virginia, xiii + 297 pp. [Originally Univ. of North Carolina at Chapel Hill diss. 1979; Abstr. in *DA* 40.4587A (1980). Includes 41 linguistic studies, 7 of which are pre-1923 publications.]

Reviews: Peter Brown in *Library* (London) 36.248-49 (1981); Barry Gaines in *South Atlantic Review* (Knoxville, TN) 46:2.109-12 (1981).

55. Martin, Willard E., Jr. 1935. *A Chaucer Bibliography 1925-1933*. (Duke Univ. Publications.) Durham, NC: Duke Univ. Press, xii + 97 pp.

56. Pickford, Cedric E. and Rex Last (with the assistance of Christine R. Barker), eds. 1981-83. *The Arthurian Bibliography*. I: *Author Listing*; II: *Subject Index*. (= Arthurian Studies, 3 & 6.) Cambridge: D.S. Brewer; Woodridge,

Suffolk: Boydel & Brewer, xxxiv + 820 pp.; (xx +) 117 pp. [Claims to be a complete bibliography in two volumes of Arthurian literature to 1978.]

57. Short, Douglas D. 1980. *'Beowulf' Scholarship: An Annotated Bibliography.* (= GRLH, 193.) New York & London: Garland, xvi + 353 pp. [Part I covers the period 1705-1949, and Part II the period 1950-1978.]

58. Yeager, Robert F. 1981. *John Gower Materials: A Bibliography through 1979.* (= GRLH, 266.) New York & London: Garland, xi + 155 pp. [Contains the sections 'Bibliographies, Lexicons, Concordances' (pp. 29-31) and 'Language Studies' (pp. 39-47).]
    Review: Pamela Gradon in *N&Q* n.s. 29.357-58 (1982).

C. Annual

59. *Abstracts of English Studies.* Boulder, CO: National Council of Teachers of English, 1958-1980; Calgary, Alberta: Dept. of English, Univ. of Calgary, 1981-.

60. *American Speech: A Quarterly of Linguistic Usage.* New York: Columbia Univ., 1925/26-.
    "Bibliography: General and Historical Studies" 1 (1925/26)-43 (1968). [Suspended 1968.]

61. *Anglo-Saxon England.* Cambridge: Cambridge Univ. Press, 1972-.
    "Bibliography for ..." [Annual bibliography dating from 1971.]

62. *Annual Bibliography of English Language and Literature for ...* Cambridge: The Modern Humanities Research Association, 1921-. [Begins with listings from 1920. Also includes book reviews.]

63. *Bibliographie Linguistique de l'Année ... et complément des années précédentes/ Linguistic Bibliography for the Year ... and supplement for previous years.* Published by the Permanent International Committee of Linguists under the auspices of the International Council of Philosophy and Humanistic Studies. Utrecht & Antwerp: Spectrum, 1949-1975; Dordrecht-Boston-Lancaster: Martinus Nijhoff, 1976-. [Vol. 1 (1949) covers the period 1939-1947.]

64. *Bibliographie Linguistischer Literatur: Bibliographie zur allgemeinen Linguistik und zur anglistischen, germanistischen und romanistischen Linguistik*, ed. Elke Suchan and Paul Georg Meyer. Frankfurt am Main: Vittorio Klostermann, 1976-. [Vol. 1 (1976) contains entries for 1971-1975.]

65. *Chaucer Review.* University Park, PA: Pennsylvania State Univ., 1967-. "Chaucer Research" 1966-.

66. *Dissertation Abstracts (International)* [formerly *Microfilm Abstracts*]. Ann Arbor, MI: University Microfilms, 1952-.

67. *English and American Studies in German: Summaries of Theses and Monographs.* A Supplement to *Anglia.* Ed. Werner Habicht (vols. 1968-82)/Horst Weinstock (vols. 1982-). Tübingen: Max Niemeyer, 1969-.

68. *International Guide to Medieval Studies: A Quarterly Index to Periodical Literature.* Darien, CN: American Bibliographic Service, 1961-.

69. *International Medieval Bibliography.* Leeds: Univ. of Leeds, 1967-.

70. *Journal of the English Place-Name Society.* Univ. of Nottingham, 1969-. "Bibliography" 1967-. [Coverage is on an annual basis for the second year back; thus 1969 covers 1967. Lists personal name studies as well.]

71. *MLA International Bibliography of Books and Articles on the Modern Languages and Literatures.* New York: Modern Language Association of America, 1970-. [Supersedes no. 74.]

72. *Neuphilologische Mitteilungen.* Bulletin de la Société Néophilologique/Bulletin of the Modern Language Society. Helsinki: Modern Language Society of Helsinki, 1899-.
"Old English Research in Progress" 1964 [Vol. 66 (1965)]-.
"Middle English Research in Progress" 1963 [Vol. 65 (1964)]-.
"Chaucer Research in Progress" 1969 [Vol. 70 (1969)]-.

73. *Old English Newsletter.* Published by the Old English Group of the Modern Language Association of America, 1967-68; published by the Old English Group of the Modern Language Association of America and the Center for Medieval and Renaissance Studies, Ohio State University, 1969-76; published for the Old English Division of the Modern Language Association of America by the Center for Medieval and Early Renaissance Studies, State Univ. of New York-Binghamton, 1977-.
"Old English Bibliography" 1964-. [Publishes in alternate issues an annual bibliography and the "Year's Work in Old English Studies".]

74. *Publications of the Modern Language Association [PMLA].* New York: Modern Language Association of America, 1884-.
"Annual Bibliography", published as the June issue of *PMLA*, 1922-1969. [International coverage since 1956. Superseded by *MLA International Bibliography* [no. 71].]

75. *Quarterly Check-list of Medievalia: An International Index of Current Books, Monographs, Brochures and Separates.* Darien, CN: American Bibliographic Service, 1958-.

76. *Studies in the Age of Chaucer.* Norman, OK: The New Chaucer Society [Univ. of Oklahoma], 1979-.
"An Annotated Chaucer Bibliography" 1975-. [Vol. 1 (1979) covers items for 1975 and 1976, and Vol. 2 (1980) for 1977 and 1978. Beginning with Vol. 3 (1981), coverage is on an annual basis for the second year back.]

77. *The Year's Work in English Studies.* London: The English Association, 1921-. [The series begins with listings from 1919. Selective, but amply annotated. The current publisher for the Association is John Murray, London, and Humanities Press, Atlantic Highlands, NJ.]

II. DICTIONARIES, CONCORDANCES, AND GLOSSARIES

A. Historical

78. Burchfield, Robert William, ed. 1972-86. *A Supplement to the Oxford English Dictionary.* 4 vols. Oxford: Clarendon Press. Vol. I: A-G, 1972, xxiii + 1331 pp.; Vol. II: H-N, 1976, xvii + 1282 pp.; Vol. III: O-Scz, 1982, xvii + 1579 pp.; Vol. IV: Se-Z, 1986, xxiii + 1409 + 45 (Bibliography) pp.

   Reviews: Vol. I: Donald C. Baker in *ELN* 11.156-57 (1973); Johannes Hedberg in *MSpr* 67.255-60 (1973); Fred C. Robinson in *Yale Review* (New Haven, CT) 62.450-56 (1972); J.S. Ryan in *AUMLA* 39.167-69 (1973); Lawrence S. Thompson in *American Book Collector* (New York) 23:5.9-10 (1973); J.D.A. Widdowson in *Lore&L* 1:9.218-21 (1973); Simeon Potter in *RES* n.s. 24.461-64 (1973); M.M. Mathews in *MP* 72.218-21 (1974); Barbara M.H. Strang in *N&Q* n.s. 21.2-13 (1974); Donald B. Sands in *CE* 37.710-18 (1976).— Vol. II: Kingsley Amis in *Observer*, 21 May, 1976, p. 31; Anthony Burgess in *TLS* 19 Nov. 1976, p. 1443; Johannes Hedberg in *MSpr* 70.367-69 (1976); Fred C. Robinson in *Yale Review* 67.94-99 (1977); Donald C. Baker in *ELN* 15.157-59 (1977); J.D.A. Widdowson in *Lore&L* 2:9.112-13 (1978); (together with Vol. I) Hans Heinrich in *ES* 60.648-60 (1979). — Vol. III: Pablo Domínguez in *RCEI* 5.144-46 (1982); Roy Harris in *TLS* 3 Sept. 1982, pp. 935-36; D.A.N. Jones in *Listener* 16 Sept. 1982, p. 27; Martin Lehnert in *ZAA* 31.163-65 (1983); Gabriele Stein in *Anglia* 101.468-75 (1983); Basil Cottle in *RES* n.s. 35.517-18 (1984); Johannes Hedberg in *MSpr* 78.347-49 (1984); Knud Sørensen in *ES* 65.86-90 (1984) and 68.293-96 (1987).

79. Finkenstaedt, Thomas, Ernst Leisi, and Dieter Wolff. 1970. *A Chronological English Dictionary, Listing 80,000 Words in Order of Their Earliest Known Occurrence.* Heidelberg: Carl Winter, xvi + 1395 pp.

   Reviews: René Derolez in *ES* 53.144-52 (1972); Klaus Hansen in *ZAA* 20.74-76 (1972); Hans Karlgren in *SML* 8.102-06 (1972); Wilhelm Kesselring in *ZRP* 88.196-201 (1972) and *NS* 72.673-75 (1973); W. Martin in *ITL* (Louvain) 15.80-83 (1972); Susie I. Tucker in *YES* 2.226-27 (1972); J. Dierickx in *RBPH* 52.264-66 (1974); Josef Vachek in *IRAL* 12.367-68 (1974); Hans Käsmann in *Archiv* 212.356-59 (1975).

80. Murray, James Augustus Henry, Henry Bradley, William Alexander Craigie, and Charles Talbut Onions, eds. 1933. *The Oxford English Dictionary, Being A Corrected Re-issue with an Introduction, Supplement, and Bibliography of A New English Dictionary on Historical Principles* founded mainly on the materials collected by the Philological Society. 13 vols. Oxford: Clarendon Press. Vol. I: A-B, xxxvi + 1240 pp.; Vol. II: C, 1308 pp.; Vol. III: D-E, 740 + 488 pp.; Vol. IV: F-G, 628 + 532 pp.; Vol. V: H-K, 516 + 758 pp.; Vol. VI: L-M, 528 + 820 pp.; Vol. VII: N-Poy, 277 + 1216 pp.; Vol. VIII: Poy-Ry, 1217-1676 + 936 pp.; Vol. IX: S-Soldo, 800 + 386 pp.; Vol. X: Sole-Sz, 387-1211 + 396 pp.; Vol. XI: T-U, 404 + 565 + 493 pp.; Vol. XII: V-Z, 332 + 334 + 400 + 105 pp.; Supplement and Bibliography, viii + 542 + 336 + 91 pp. [For the new *Supplement*, see Burchfield [no. 78].]

Reviews and notes: too numerous to enumerate.

81. Onions, Charles Talbut. 1933. *The Shorter Oxford English Dictionary*. Prepared by William Little, Henry Watson Fowler, and Jessie Coulson. Revised and edited by C.T. Onions. 2 vols. Oxford: Clarendon Press. Vol. I: A-M, xxi + 1306 pp; Vol. II: N-Z, 1307-2475 pp. [2nd ed. 1936; 3rd ed. with corrections and revised addenda, 1944, xxii + 1306; [iv +] 1307-2515 pp. — 3rd ed. completely reset with etymologies revised by George Washington Salisbury Friedrichsen and with revised addenda. 2 vols. 1973. Vol. I: A-Markworthy, xxix + 1280 pp.; Vol. II: Marl-Z and Addenda, xi + 1281-2672 pp.]

Reviews: Anon. in *N&Q* 164.251-52 (1933); L.L. Schücking in *Anglia B* 44.266-69 (1933); A. Brandl in *DLZ* 54.833-38 (1933); F. Mossé and R.W. Zandvoort in *ES* 15.119-23 (1933); H.C. Wyld in *RES* 10.85-93 (1934).

82. Shipley, Joseph T. 1955. *Dictionary of Early English*. With a Foreword by Mark van Doren. New York: Philosophical Library, xiii + 753 pp. [A dictionary of words and senses no longer in use; the period covered is from the 8th to the 19th century, but little is included that is earlier than the 15th century.]

Reviews: Basil Cottle in *JEGP* 55.499-501 (1956); S.M. Kuhn in *Language* 32.769-74 (1956); Martin Lehnert in *ZAA* 4.491-94 (1956); T.M. Pearce in *Western Folklore* (Los Angeles) 15.294-95 (1956); Anon. in *TLS*, Mar. 22, 1957, P. 178; A. Culioli in *EA* 10.139-40 (1957); E.V.K. Dobbie in *AS* 32.54-55 (1957).

83. Zupko, Ronald Edward. 1968. *A Dictionary of English Weights and Measures from Anglo-Saxon Times to the Nineteenth Century*. Madison: Univ. of Wisconsin Press, xvi + 224 pp.

84. ———. 1985. *A Dictionary of Weights and Measures for the British Iles: The Middle Ages to the Twentieth Century*. (= Memoirs, 168.) Philadelphia: American Philosophical Society, xxxviii + 520 pp.

Review: Lorraine Attreed in *Speculum* 62.522 (1987).

B. Old English

85. Bammesberger, Alfred. 1979. *Beiträge zu einem etymologischen Wörterbuch des Altenglischen: Berichtigungen und Nachträge zum Altenglischen etymologischen Wörterbuch von Ferdinand Holthausen.* (= AF, 139.) Heidelberg: Carl Winter, viii + 156 pp. [For Holthausen's *Altenglisches etymologisches Wörterbuch*, see no. 98.]

    Reviews: Ernst A. Ebbinghaus in *GL* 20.224-26 (1980); E.G. Stanley in *N&Q* n.s. 29.150-53 (1982); Karl Toth in *Anglia* 104.174-78 (1986).

86. Barney, Stephen A., with the assistance of Ellen Wertheimer and David Stevens. 1977. *Word-Hoard: An Introduction to Old English Vocabulary.* New Haven, CT & London: Yale Univ. Press, xvi + 108 pp. [2nd ed. 1985, xv + 79 pp.]

    Reviews: Anon. in *Choice* 14.366 (1977); Peter J. Lucas in *N&Q* n.s. 24.385-86 (1977); Anon. in *British Studies Monitor* (Bowdoin College, Brunswick, ME) 8:3.78 (1978); André Crépin in *EA* 31.374 (1978); Geoffrey Cubbin in *MAE* 47.324-25 (1978); Thomas D. Hill in *Speculum* 53.786 (1978); M. Görlach in *Anglia* 96.465-67 (1978); Robert A. Peters in *MLJ* 62.217 (1978); Alan Ward in *RES* n.s. 29.329-30 (1978); Patrizia Lendinara in *AION-SG* 22.416-17 (1979). — 2nd ed.: Alan Ward in *RES* n.s. 38.125 (1987).

87. Bergman, Madeleine M. 1982 [1985]. "Supplement to a *Concordance to the Anglo-Saxon Poetic Records*". *Mediaevalia* 8.9-52. [Cf. Bessinger [no. 90].]

88. Bessinger, Jess Balsor, Jr. 1960. *A Short Dictionary of Anglo-Saxon Poetry in a Normalized Early West-Saxon Orthography.* Toronto: Univ. of Toronto Press, xvii + 87 pp. [Based primarily on the text of *The Anglo-Saxon Poetic Records* (New York: Columbia Univ. Press, 1931-53) and claims to be a gloss to the crucial 40 per cent of the poetic vocabulary. 4th rev. printing, 1967.]

    Reviews: Anon. in *TLS* 17 April 1961, p. 222; R. MacGregor Dawson in *Dalhousie Review* (Halifax, Nova Scotia) 41.418 (1961); James L. Rosier in *JEGP* 60.560-63 (1961); L.K. Shook in *UTQ* 30.419-20 (1961); C.L. Wrenn in *MAE* 30.206-07 (1961); A. Campbell in *RES* n.s. 13.436-37 (1962); K. Grinda in *Archiv* 199.417-18 (1962/63).

89. ———, ed. 1969. *A Concordance to Beowulf.* Programmed by Philip H. Smith, Jr. (The Cornell Concordances.) Ithaca, NY: Cornell Univ. Press, xxxiv + 373 pp. [A computer-assisted concordance, based on *The Anglo-Saxon Poetic Records*, Vol. IV (1953).]

    Reviews: L.D. Benson in *Speculum* 45.273-75 (1970); Alistair Campbell in *N&Q* n.s. 17.116-17 (1970); C.J.E. Ball in *MAE* 39.366-68 (1970); W.F. Bolton in *RES* n.s. 21.189-90 (1970); J.L. Rosier in *JEGP* 69.161-63 (1970); E.G. Stanley in *MLR* 65.863-65 (1970); Gerhard Graband in *Archiv* 208.123-26 (1971/72); Martin Lehnert in *ZAA* 19.73-75 (1971); L. Whitbread in *ES* 52.444-46 (1971); Dieter Wolff in *Anglia* 89.508-13 (1971); Paul M. Clogan in *CHum* 6.233-34 (1972).

90. ———, ed. 1978. *A Concordance to 'The Anglo-Saxon Poetic Records'*. Programmed by Philip H. Smith, Jr. With an Index of Compounds compiled by Michael W. Twomey. (The Cornell Concordances.) Ithaca, NY & London: Cornell Univ. Press, xl + 1510 pp. [The copy-text for the *Concordance* is that of the individual poems edited in six volumes as *The Anglo-Saxon Poetic Records: A Collective Edition*, ed. George Philip Krapp and Elliot Van Kirk Dobbie (New York: Columbia Univ. Press, 1931-1953), plus a single late poem in OE edited as "Instructions for Christians" by James L. Rosier in *Anglia* 82.4-22 (1964), with addenda in *Anglia* 84.74 (1966).]

Reviews: Anon. in *Choice* 15.1191 (1978); Thomas Elwood Hart in *CHum* 13.229-35 (1979); Bruce Mitchell in *N&Q* n.s. 26.347-49 (1979); E.G. Stanley in *RES* n.s. 30.328-31 (1979); Joseph B. Trahern, Jr. in *JEGP* 78.242-44 (1979); Deborah Jane Brewer in *ARBA* 10.606 (1979).

91. Borden, Arthur R., Jr. 1982. *A Comprehensive Old English Dictionary*. Washington, DC: Univ. Press of America, vi + 1606 pp.

Review: Robert J. Reddick in *Allegorica* (Univ. of Texas at Arlington) 6:1.192 (1981 [1982]).

92. Braasch, Theodor. 1933. *Vollständiges Wörterbuch zur sog. Caedmonschen Genesis*. (= AF, 76.) Heidelberg: Carl Winter, vii + 157 pp. [A complete glossary of the OE *Genesis* (*A* and *B*).]

Reviews: A. B[randl] in *Archiv* 164.129-30 (1933); R. Girvan in *MLR* 28.497 (1933); F. Klaeber in *EStn* 68.431-32 (1934); J. Daniels in *Museum* 41.145-46 (1934); F. Holthausen in *Anglia B* 45.227-28 (1934); A. Szogs in *LGRP* 55.99-100 (1934).

93. Campbell, Alistair. 1972. *Enlarged Addenda and Corrigenda to the Supplement by T. Northcote Toller to 'An Anglo-Saxon Dictionary', Based on the Manuscript Collections of Jeseph Bosworth*. Oxford: Clarendon Press, viii + 68 pp. [Issued separately or as part of the *Supplement*. Cf. Joseph Bosworth and Thomas Northcote Toller, *An Anglo-Saxon Dictionary Based on the Manuscript Collections of the late Joseph Bosworth*, edited and enlarged by Thomas N. Toller, Oxford: Clarendon Press, 1898, xii + 1302 pp; Thomas N. Toller, *An Anglo-Saxon Dictionary Based on the Manuscript Collections of Joseph Bosworth: Supplement*, Oxford: Clarendon Press, 1921, viii + 768 pp.]

Reviews: M.L. Samuels in RES n.s. 25.111 (1974); R.I. Page in MAE 44.65-68 (1975).

94. Dobyns, Mabel Falberg. 1973. *Wulfstan's Vocabulary: A Glossary of the 'Homilies' with Commentary*. Univ. of Illinois at Urbana-Champaign diss., 138 pp. [Abstr. in *DA* 34.7701-02A (1974).]

95. Gneuss, Helmut. 1962/63. "Ergänzungen zu den altenglischen Wörterbüchen". *Archiv* 199.17-24. [Addenda and errata for the Bosworth-Toller and Clark Hall dictionaries.]

96. Hall, John Richard Clark. 1931. *A Concise Anglo-Saxon Dictionary*. 3rd ed., rev. and enlarged. Cambridge: Cambridge Univ. Press, xv + 437 pp. [1st ed. 1894, xvi + 369 pp.; 2nd ed. 1916, xiv + 372 pp.]

    Reviews: F. Klaeber in *Anglia B* 43.197-200 (1932); F.P. Magoun, Jr. in *Speculum* 7.286-89 (1932); A.H. Smith in *Yearbook of the Viking Society* 23/24. 11-12 (1931/32); A.E.H. Swaen in *Neophil* 17.300-02 (1932); F. Holthausen in *EStn* 69.392-93 (1934/35).

97. ———. 1960. *A Concise Anglo-Saxon Dictionary*. 4th ed., with a Supplement by Herbert Dean Meritt. Cambridge: Cambridge Univ. Press, xv + 432 + 20 pp. [Repr. as "Medieval Academy Reprints for Teaching, 14", Toronto: Univ. of Toronto Press, 1984.]

    Reviews: R.W. Zandvoort in *ES* 42.269 (1961); E.G. Stanley in *N&Q* n.s. 9.155-56 (1962); L.A. Muinzer in *JEGP* 62.786-87 (1963); Hans Schabram in *Anglia* 84.83-88 (1966).

98. Holthausen, Ferdinand. 1934 [1932-34]. *Altenglisches etymologisches Wörterbuch*. (= GB, 4:7.) Heidelberg: Carl Winter, xxviii + 428 pp. [2nd ed., with revised bibliography by H.C. Matthes, 1963, xxxvi + 428 pp.]

    Reviews: R. Girvan in *MLR* 28.375-76; 496-97 (1933) and 29.180 (1934); F.P. Magoun, Jr. in *Speculum* 8.94-96 (1933); F. Mossé in *ES* 15.60-65 (1933) and 16.196-201 (1934); J. Raith in *Anglia B* 44.36-39 (1933) and 45.33-34 (1934); A.E.H. Swaen in *Neophil* 18.303-04 (1933) and 19.298-99 (1934); A. Meillet in *BSL* 34.127 (1933) and 35.121 (1934); Karl Jost in *IF* 52.80-81 (1934); C.L. W[renn] in *RES* 10.242-44 (1934); F. Fiedler in *ZNU* 34.121-22 (1935); J. Weisweiler in *LGRP* 56.233-40 (1935); W. Wokatsch in *Archiv* 168.103-05 (1935).

99. ———. 1941-42. "Zum altenglischen Wortschatz. I-II". *Anglia B* 52.40-41; 53.35-37. [Additions and corrections to Holthausen [no. 98].]

100. Jember, Gregory K., John C. Carrell, Robert P. Lundquist, Barbara M. Olds, and Raymond P. Tripp, Jr. 1975. *A Modern English-Old English Dictionary*. Denver, CO: Society for New Language Study, 23 pp.

101. ———, John C. Carrell, Robert P. Lundquist, Barbara M. Olds, and Raymond P. Tripp, Jr. eds. 1975. *English-Old English, Old English-English Dictionary*. Boulder, CO: Westview Press, xxxiii + 178 pp.

    Reviews: Anon. in *Choice* 13.348 (1976); Bruce Mitchell in *RES* n.s. 28.248 (1977); J. Verdonck in *ES* 58.575-76 (1977).

102. ——— and Fritz Kemmler. 1981. *A Basic Vocabulary of Old English Prose/ Grundwortschatz altenglische Prosa*. Tübingen: Max Niemeyer, xvi + 48 pp.

    Reviews: Cinzia Marino in *Schede Medievali* 3.468-69 (1982); Alfred Bammesberger in *IF* 89.371-73 (1984); Bernhard Diensberg in *Archiv* 221.355-56 (1984).

103. Lehnert, Martin. 1956. *Poetry and Prose of the Anglo-Saxons: Dictionary*. Berlin: Deutscher Verlag der Wissenschaften, 247 pp. [An etymological glossary to Lehnert's *Poetry and Prose of the Anglo-Saxons*, Vol. I: *Texts, Introduction, Bibliography*, 1955, xv + 173 pp.]

    Reviews: T.F. Mustanoja in *NM* 57.269-70 (1956); H.B. Woolf in *Language* 32.766-69 (1956); H. Marcus in *Archiv* 193.207 (1956/57); W.C. Greet in *JEGP* 57.332 (1958); P. Mertens-Fonck in *RBPH* 56.522-25 (1958); R. Quirk in *MLR* 53.300 (1958); R. Derolez in *ES* 41.31-33 (1960).

104. Madden, John F. and Francis Peabody Magoun, Jr. 1954. *A Grouped Frequency Word-List of Anglo-Saxon Poetry*. Cambridge, MA: Harvard Univ. Press, xi + 52 pp. [Repr. with corrections 1957, 1960, 1964. Also repr. in 1966 as "Harvard Old English Series, 2".]

    Reviews: Allan H. Orrick in *MLN* 70.438 (1955); E.G. Stanley in *N&Q* n.s. 14.402 (1967).

105. Marckwardt, Albert Henry, ed. 1952. *Laurence Nowell's Vocabularium Saxonicum*. (= Univ. of Michigan Pubs. in Language and Literature, 25.) Ann Arbor, MI: Univ. of Michigan Press, ix + 198 pp. [An edition of the earliest OE dictionary, compiled about 1565 and never before published.]

    Reviews: H.M. Flasdieck in *Anglia* 61.476-78 (1953); J.A.W. Bennett in *RES* n.s. 5.398-99 (1954); E.V.K. Dobbie in *JEGP* 53.451-53 (1954); S.B. Liljegren in *SN* 26.180-82 (1953/54); F.P. Magoun, Jr. in *Speculum* 29.144-45 (1954); R. Quirk in *MLR* 49.61-62 (1954); B.J. Timmer in *ES* 35.263-64 (1954); H.B. Woolf in *MLN* 69.288-89 (1954).

106. Mertens-Fonck, Paule. 1960. *A Glossary of the 'Vespasian Psalter and Hymns' (Brit. Mus. Ms. Cotton Vespasian A 1) with a Latin-Mercian Index. Part I: The Verb.* (= Bibliothèque de la Faculté de Philosophie et Lettres de l'Univ. de Liege, 154.) Paris: Société d'édition "Les Belles Lettres", 387 + 19 pp.

Reviews: A. Campbell in *MAE* 30.107-08 (1961); James L. Rosier in *JEGP* 60.563-66 (1961); E.G. Stanley in *MLR* 57.142-43 (1962); C.L. Wrenn in *RES* n.s. 13.325 (1962); Sherman M. Kuhn in *Speculum* 38.383-88 (1963); William G. Stryker in *NM* 64.405-10 (1963); R. Vleeskruyer in *ES* 44.134-35 (1963); Klaus R. Grinda in *Anglia* 82.502-05 (1964).

107. Oda, Takuji, ed. 1982. *A Concordance to the Riddles of the Exeter Book.* Tokyo: Gaku Shobo, viii + 294 pp.

Reviews: E.G. Stanley in *N&Q* n.s. 30.1 (1983); André Crépin in *EA* 37.183-84 (1984).

108. Smith, Andrea B. 1985. *The Anonymous Parts of the Old English Hexateuch: A Latin-Old English/Old English-Latin Glossary.* Cambridge: D.S. Brewer, xvii + 471 pp. [Originally Cambridge diss.]

Review: E.G. Stanley in *N&Q* n.s. 34.248-49 (1987).

109. Venezky, Richard Lawrence and Antonette diPaolo Healey, comps. 1980. *A Microfiche Concordance to Old English.* (= Pubs. of the Dictionary of Old English, 1.) Toronto: Centre for Medieval Studies, Univ. of Toronto, xviii + 201 pp.; 418 microfiches (= 126, 876 pp.). [Also available from E.J. Brill, Leiden.]

Reviews: Donald K. Fry in *ELN* 20.11-20 (1982); Fred C. Robinson in *Speculum* 57.133-35 (1982); E.G. Stanley in *N&Q* n.s. 29.385-86 (1982).

110. ———— and Sharon Butler, comps. 1984. *A Microfiche Concordance to Old English: The High-Frequency Words.* (= Pubs. of the Dictionary of Old English, 2.) Toronto: Pontifical Institute of Mediaeval Studies; Leiden: E.J. Brill, 24 pp.; xviii + 201 pp.; 253 microfiches.

C. Middle English

111. Ackerman, Robert W. 1952. *An Index of the Arthurian Names in Middle English.* (= Stanford Univ. Pubs. in Language and Literature, 10.) Stanford, CA: Stanford Univ. Press, xxvi + 250 pp.

Reviews: J.A.W. Bennett in *MLR* 49.221-22 (1954); Jean Frappier in *RP* 7.372-74 (1953/54); Auvo Kurvinen in *NM* 55.223-25 (1954); Roger S. Loomis in *Speculum* 29.244-46 (1954); Kemp Malone in *Names* 2.64 (1954); Robert H. Wilson in *JEGP* 53.100-04 (1954).

112. Bense, Johan Frederik. 1926-39. *A Dictionary of the Low-Dutch Element in the English Vocabulary*. The Hague: Martinus Nijhoff; London: Oxford Univ. Press/Humphrey Milford, xxxii + 663 pp. [Issued in five parts. Aims to record all the words that have, or may have, passed into the English language from Low-Dutch, i.e. the continental Low German dialects (Flemish, Dutch and Low German) since the 13th century. For the author's diss. on "Anglo-Dutch Relations", see no. 311.]

    Reviews: O.K. Schram in *MLR* 32.123-26 (1937); F. Holthausen in *Anglia B* 51.122-23 (1940); C.B. van Haeringen in *ES* 22.141-47 (1940); Henning Larsen in *PQ* 20.95-96 (1941); G.V. Smithers in *RES* 17.494-99 (1941).

113. Berger, Sidney Elliot. 1971. *A Concordance to Layamon's 'Brut'*. Part I: *A-F*. Iowa diss., 511 pp. [Abstr. in *DA* 32.2631A (1971).]

114. Bitterling, Klaus. 1970. *Der Wortschatz von Barbours 'Bruce'*. Berlin: Dissertationsdruckstelle, 566 pp. [Freie Univ. Berlin diss.]

    Reviews: Janet M. Templeton in *SN* 43.579-80 (1971); Martin Lehnert in *ZAA* 21.201 (1973); Karl Reichl in *Archiv* 210.180 (1973).

115. Bowman, Walter Parker and Robert Hamilton Ball. 1961. *Theatre Language: A Dictionary of Terms in English of the Drama and Stage from Medieval to Modern Times*. New York: Theatre Arts Books, xii + 428 pp.

    Reviews: Louis Bonnerot in *EA* 14.356-57 (1961); Herbert L. Carson in *QJS* 47.439-40 (1961).

116. Buehler, Philip Grether. 1968. *A Glossary to the Middle English 'Genesis and Exodus'*. Pennsylvania diss., 434 pp. [Abstr. in *DA* 30.1157A (1969).]

117 Carter, Henry Holland. 1961. *A Dictionary of Middle English Musical Terms*. Ed. George B. Gerhard, et al. (= Indiana Univ. Humanities Ser., 45.) Bloomington: Indiana Univ. Press, xv + 655 pp. [Cf. Gerhard [no. 3033].]

    Reviews: C.L. Bunting in *SIL* 16.64 (1962); John Reidy in *Language* 38.85-92 (1962); Richard L. Greene in *MAE* 32.80-82 (1963); Helmut Gneuss in *Anglia* 82.229-31 (1964); John Stevens in *RES* n.s. 15.62-64 (1964).

118. Chapman, Coolidge Otis. 1951. *An Index of Names in 'Pearl', 'Purity', 'Patience', and 'Gawain'*. (= Cornell Studies in English, 38.) Ithaca, NY: Cornell Univ. Press; London: Oxford Univ. Press, ix + 66 pp.

    Reviews: R.W. Ackerman in *JEGP* 50.538-39 (1951); Henry Savage in *Speculum* 27.364-66 (1952); Thomas A. Kirby in *MLN* 68.582 (1953); A[ngus] Macdonald in *RES* n.s. 4.276-78 (1953).

119. Conroy, Kenneth Clement. 1964. *A Glossary of John Trevisa's Translation of the*

'De Regimine Principum' of Aegidius Romanus. Univ. of Washington diss., 291 pp. [Abstr. in DA 25.7241 (1965).]

120. Craigie, William Alexander, Adam Jack Aitken, and James A.C. Stevenson. 1931-. *A Dictionary of the Older Scottish Tongue from the Twelfth to the End of the Seventeenth*, founded on the collections of Sir William A. Craigie. 5 vols. (to date). Chicago: Univ. of Chicago Press, 1931- ; London: Oxford Univ. Press, 1931-68/Univ. of Chicago Press, 1969- ; Aberdeen: Aberdeen Univ. Press, 1983-.
Vol. I: A-Cythariste, 1931-37, xi + 799 + 37 (Additions and Corrections) pp.; Vol. II: D-Gyte, 1938-51, 764 pp.; Vol. III: H-Lyv(e)tennandry, 1952-64, 1012 + xxxii pp.; Vol. IV: M-Nyxttocum, 1967-72, 618 + xii pp.; Vol. V: O-Pn, 1975-83, 620 pp. [Editors: W.A. Craigie, 1925-55; A.J. Aitken, 1955-; J.A.C. Stevenson, 1973-.]

Reviews: Anon. in *N&Q* 162.288 (1932), 163.216 (1932), 166.198 (1934), 168.88 (1935), 169.196-97 (1935), 172.52-53 (1937), 173.107-08 (1937), 175.376-77 (1938) 179.161-62 (1940), 190.220 (1946), 192.439-40 (1947), 194.417-18 (1949), 197.284-85 (1952), 198.500 (1953), n.s. 11.2-3 (1964); Anon. in *TLS*, Mar.10, 1932, p. 171, June 1, 1946, p. 260, Mar. 7, 1952, p. 173; A. Mawer in *RES* 8.320-21 (1932), 9.95-97 (1933), 10.349-50 (1934), 12.480-90 (1936), 13.245-46 (1937), 14.496 (1938), 17.372-73 (1941); B. Dickins in *MLR* 28.243-44 (1933); P.W. Long in *JEGP* 32.235-38 (1933); A. Macdonald in *RES* n.s. 2.402-04 (1951) and *N&Q* n.s. 6.294 (1959); John Braidwood in *MLR* 51.455 (1956), 59.86-87 (1964); Kurt Wittig in *Anglia* 78.462-67 (1960) and *Erasmus* 17.597-603 (1965); Hans Heinrich Meier in *ES* 43.444-48 (1962); A. Fenton in *ScoS* 10.198-205 (1966); E.G. Stanley in *N&Q* n.s. 12.162-63 (1965), 15.282-83 (1968), 20.442 (1974).

121. Davis, Norman, Douglas Gray, Patricia Ingham, and Anna Wallace-Hadrill. 1979. *A Chaucer Glossary*. Oxford: Clarendon Press, xx + 185 pp. [Based primarily on Skeat's six-volume edition (Oxford, 1894; 2nd ed. 1900).]

Reviews: T.A. Shippey in *TLS*, Nov. 30, 1979, p. 73; Basil Cottle in *RES* n.s. 31.445-46 (1980); J.J. Anderson in *Critical Quarterly* (Manchester) 23:2.82 (1981); W. Bruce Finnie in *SAC* 3.134-37 (1981); M. Gretsch in *Anglia* 99.500-02 (1981); Stephen A. Barney in *MLR* 77.920-21 (1982).

122. De Weever, Jacqueline Elinor. 1971. *A Dictionary of Classical, Mythological and Sideral* [sic] *Names in the Works of Geoffrey Chaucer*. Pennsylvania diss., 246 pp. [Abstr. in DA 32.4559A (1972).]

123. Dillon, Bert. 1974. *A Chaucer Dictionary: Proper Names and Allusions, Excluding Place-Names*. Boston: G.K. Hall; London: Prior, xix + 266 pp. [Originally Duke Univ. diss. 1972; Abstr. in DA 33.5118-19A (1973).]

Review: Jill Mann in *MAE* 47.159-61 (1978).

124. Fisher, John Lionel. 1968. *A Medieval Farming Glossary of Latin and English Words, taken mainly from Essex Records*. London: National Council of Social Service, for the Standing Conference for Local History, xii + 41 pp.

125. Gburek, Hubert. 1977. *Der Wortschatz des Robert Mannyng of Brunne in 'Handlyng Synne'*. Bamberg: M. Schadel, 730 pp. [Erlangen diss.]

    Reviews: M. Görlach in *Archiv* 215.398-99 (1978); E.G. Stanley in *N&Q* n.s. 25.99-100 (1978); Hans Käsmann in *Anglia* 97.496-98 (1979); Stephen Sullivan in *MAE* 49.139-40 (1980); Martin Lehnert in *ZAA* 29.70-74 (1981).

126. Kato, Tomomi. 1974. *A Concordance to the Works of Sir Thomas Malory*. Tokyo: Univ. of Tokyo Press, ix + 1659 pp.

    Reviews: Anon. in *Library Journal* (New York) 99.2954 (1974); Robert W. Ackerman in *CHum* 9.44-45 (1975); Yuji Nakao in *SEL* English No. 1975, 121-31 (1975).

127. Kinneavy, Gerald Byron. 1986. *Concordance to the York Plays*. (= GRLH, 626.) New York & London: Garland, xxxviii + 936 pp.

128. Kottler, Barnet and Alan M. Markman. 1966. *A Concordance to Five Middle English Poems: Cleanness, St. Erkenwald, Sir Gawain and the Green Knight, Patience, Pearl*. Pittsburg, PA: Univ. of Pittsburg Press, xxxiii + 761 pp.

    Reviews: Larry D. Benson in *Speculum* 42.382-84 (1967); J.B. Bessinger, Jr. in *CHum* 2.53-56 (1968); Norman Davis in *MAE* 37.324-28 (1968).

129. Kurath, Hans, Sherman McAllister Kuhn, and Robert Enzer Lewis, eds. 1952-. *Middle English Dictionary*. Ann Arbor, MI: Univ. of Michigan Press.
    Plan and Bibliography: Plan and Methods — Hans Kurath; Bibliography — Margaret S. Ogden, Charles E. Palmer, and Richard L. McKelvey, 1954, xii + 105 pp.; Plan and Bibliography, Supplement I: Plan and Methods — Robert E. Lewis; Bibliography — Mary Jane Williams, 1984, v + 35 + 1 ("Errata in the 1954 Bibliography") pp.; A-B, 1956-58, [iii +] 1245 pp.; C-D, 1959-62, [ii +] 1371 pp.; E-F, 1952-55, [ii +] 952 pp.; G-H, 1963-67, [ii +] 1053 pp.; I-L, 1968-73, 1318 pp.; M-N, 1975-79, [ii+] 1141 pp.; O-P, 1980-83, [ii +] 1408 pp.; Q-R, 1984-86, [ii +] 893 pp.; S.1-2, 1986, [ii +] 256 pp. [Editors: Hans Kurath, A-F; Sherman M. Kuhn, G-P; Robert E. Lewis, Q-. The last fascicle published as of the summer of 1987 was S.2 [savāciõun — sē] (1986). For the present and future of the *MED* project, see Lewis [no. 3139].]

    Reviews: too numerous to enumerate; they have frequently appeared in *Anglia*, *EA*, *ES*, *JEGP*, *Language*, *MAE*, *MLN*, *MLR*, *NM*, *RES*, *Speculum*, *Word*, *ZAA*, and many other important journals.

DICTIONARIES, CONCORDANCES, AND GLOSSARIES 23

130. Magoun, Francis Peabody, Jr. 1961. *A Chaucer Gazetteer*. Chicago: Univ. of Chicago Press; Stockholm: Almqvist & Wiksell, 173 pp. [A dictionary of geographical names occurring in Chaucer's works; combines three separate articles originally published in *MAE*: "Chaucer's Ancient and Biblical World", *MAE* 15.107-36 (1953); "Chaucer's Great Britain", *MAE* 16.131-56 (1954); "Chaucer's Mediaeval World outside of Great Britain", *MAE* 17.117-42 (1955).]

    Reviews: J. Hedberg in *MSpr* 55.277-80 (1961); T.F. Mustanoja in *NM* 62.233-34 (1961); R.T. Davies in *N&Q* n.s. 9.159-60 (1962); Thomas Finkenstaedt in *Anglia* 79.480 (1962).

131. Mindt, Dieter. 1971. *Der Wortschatz der 'Lambeth Homilies': Das Adjektiv*. (= Braunschweiger Anglistische Arbeiten, 2.) Braunschweig: Inst. für Anglistik und Amerikanistik, Technische Univ. Carolo-Wilhelmina zu Braunschweig, 88 pp.

132. Ohlander, Urban. 1972. *A Middle English Metrical Paraphrase of the Old Testament, V. Glossary*. (= GothSE, 24.) Göteborg (distr.: Almqvist & Wiksell, Stockholm), 113 pp. [A glossary to H. Kalen, ed., *A Middle English Metrical Paraphrase of the Old Testament, I* (Göteborg: Elanders Boktr., 1921) and U. Ohlander, ed., *A Middle English Metrical Paraphrase of the Old Testament, II-IV* (= GothSE, 5, 11, and 16) (Göteborg: Elanders Boktr., 1955, 1961, and 1963).]

133. Pfleiderer, Jean Diane and Michael J. Preston. 1981. *A Complete Concordance to 'The Chester Mystery Plays'*. (= GRLH, 249.) New York & London: Garland, xxii + 513 pp.

134. Preston, Michael J. 1975. *A Concordance to the Middle English Shorter Poems, I-II*. (= Compendia. Computer-Generated Aids to Literary and Linguistic Research, 6.) Leeds: W.S. Maney and Son, xviii + 2455 pp. [Part I: A-M; Part II: N-Z.]

    Reviews: W.R.J. Barron in *ALLCB* 5.102-04 (1977); H. Gneuss in *Anglia* 95.220-24 (1977); R.T. Davies in *MLR* 73.595-96 (1978); Nils Erik Enkvist in *SN* 50.325-26 (1978); Douglas Gray in *MAE* 48.306-08 (1979).

135. —— and Jean Diane Pfleiderer. 1982. *A KWIC Concordance to the Plays of the Wakefield Master*. (= GRLH, 248.) New York: Garland, xxi + 427 pp.

136. Roach, Bruce Vincent. 1972. *A Concordance to Layamon's 'Brut' Lines 1-8020 with Introductory Essay Descriptive and Illustrative of the Structure and Uses of the Concordance for Literary Scholars*. Washington Univ. diss., 2425 pp. [Abstr. in *DA* 33.4361A (1973).]

137. Robinson, Mairi, ed. 1985. *The Concise Scots Dictionary*. Aberdeen: Aberdeen Univ. Press, xli + 815 pp. [One-volume dictionary of the Scots language from the 12th century to the present, based on two major works, the *Scottish National Dictionary* for the modern period from 1700 to the present, and the *Dictionary of the Older Scottish Tongue* [see no. 120] for the centuries up to 1700.]

138. Ross, Thomas W. 1972. *Chaucer's Bawdy*. New York: Dutton; Toronto & Vancouver: Clarke, Irwin and Co., x + 246 pp. [A glossary of bawdy and indecorous words in Chaucer.]

   Review: Paul E. Beichner in *Notre Dame English Journal* (Univ. of Notre Dame, IN) 8.52-54 (1972).

139. Scott, A.F. 1974. *Who's Who in Chaucer*. With a Foreword by Nevil Coghill. London: Elm Tree Books; New York: Taplinger, xii + 145 pp. [A glossary of characters in Chaucer.]

140. Tatlock, John Strong Perry and Arthur Garfield Kennedy. 1927. *A Concordance to the Complete Works of Geoffrey Chaucer and to the Romaunt of the Rose*. Washington, DC: The Carnegie Institution of Washington, xiii + 1110 pp. [Repr., Gloucester, MA: Peter Smith, 1963. Based on the Globe edition of Chaucer, *The Works of Geoffrey Chaucer*, ed. Alfred W. Pollard, et al. (London: Macmillan, 1898). See also Tatlock's "The Chaucer Concordance", *MLN* 38.504-06 (1923).]

   Reviews: Anon. in *TLS*, Nov. 10, 1927, p. 816; A. Brandl in *Archiv* 153.264-66 (1928); W. Fischer in *Anglia B* 39.259-62 (1928); J. Hoops in *EStn* 63.86-89 (1928); Robert J. Menner in *MLN* 43.332-36 (1928); Clark S. Northup in *JEGP* 27.238-40 (1928); James F. Royster in *SP* 25.62-69 (1928).

141. Whiting, Bartlett Jere, with the collaboration of Helen Wescott Whiting. 1968. *Proverbs, Sentences, and Proverbial Phrases from English Writings Mainly before 1500*. Cambridge, MA: Harvard Univ. Press; Toronto: Saunders; London: Oxford Univ. Press, li + 733 pp. [A compilation of ME proverbs.]

   Reviews: Anon. in *TLS*, July 24, 1969, p. 794; A.C. Baugh in *JEGP* 68.688-89 (1969); Albert C. Friend in *Speculum* 44.674-76 (1969); P.W. Rogers in *QQ* 76.361-62 (1969); Helmut Gneuss in *Anglia* 88.529-31 (1970); E.G. Stanley in *N&Q* n.s. 17.187-88 (1970); A.G. Rigg in *RES* n.s. 22.326-33 (1971); Norman Davis in *MAE* 41.164-68 (1972).

III. HISTORIES OF THE ENGLISH LANGUAGE

142. Aiken, Janet Rankin. 1930. *English Present and Past*. With an Introduction by George Philip Krapp. New York: Ronald Press, xii + 287 pp.

143. Alexander, Henry. 1940. *The Story of Our Language*. Toronto: Nelson, x + 242 pp. [Paperback repr., Garden City, NY: Doubleday; London: W.H. Allen, 1962.]

    Reviews: G.H.C. in *QQ* 48.193-94 (1941); Helge Kökeritz in *AS* 17.54-56 (1942) and *SN* 15.377-79 (1942/43).

144. Armour, J.S. 1935. *The Genesis and Growth of English: An Outline of Philology for Students*. New York: Oxford Univ. Press. xii + 189 pp. [Originally published in 1934 under the title *Genesis and Growth of English: A Philological Sketch for Indian Students*. Bombay: Oxford Univ. Press.]

    Review: C.M. Lotspeich in *JEGP* 36.263 (1937).

145. Bambas, Rudolph C. 1980. *The English Language: Its Origin and History*. Norman, OK: Univ. of Oklahoma Press, xiv + 241 pp.

    Reviews: Catherine von Schon in *Library Journal* (New York) 105.2328 (1980); Arleta Adamska-Sałaciak in *SAP* 16.291-95 (1983); Daniel Brink in *RMRLL* 37.102-03 (1983).

146. Barber, Charles Laurence. 1964. *The Story of Language*. London: Pan Books, 286 pp. [Rev. ed. 1972, viii + 294 pp.]

    Review: Vladímira Chourová in *ČMF* 51.184-85 (1969).

147. ———. 1965. *The Flux of Language*. London: Allen and Unwin, 288 pp. [A hard-cover reprint of the preceding item.]

    Reviews: Anon. in *TLS*, July 29, 1965, p. 660; P. Mertens-Fonck in *RLV* 33.437 (1967); Simeon Potter in *MLR* 62.105-06 (1967).

148. Barnett, Lincoln. 1964. *The Treasure of Our Tongue: The Story of English from Its Obscure Beginnings to Its Present Eminence as the Most Widely Spoken Language on Earth*. New York: Knopf, viii + 304 pp. [Also published in 1970 as *History of the English Language*. London: Sphere, 253 pp.]

Reviews: Anon. in *Modern Age* (Chicago) 9.200-02 (1965); Richard T. Baker in *Columbia Journalism Review* 4.36-38 (1965); Nathaniel Benchley in *Book Week/World*, Jan. 10, 1965, p. 19; Robert Root in *Journalism Quarterly* 42.128-29 (1965); Anon. in *TLS*, Nov. 24, 1966, p. 1102; James Macris in *AS* 41.284-86 (1966); Raven I. McDavid, Jr. in *South Atlantic Quarterly* (Durham, NC) 65.143-45 (1966).

149. Baugh, Albert Croll. 1935. *A History of the English Language*. New York: Appleton-Century Company, xiii + 509 pp. [First published in England in 1951, London: Routledge & Kegan Paul.]

   Reviews: R.G. Kent in *Language* 12.72-75 (1936); B.C. Williams in *AS* 11.85-87 (1936); R.W. Zandvoort in *ES* 19.90-94 (1937); E. Ekwall in *SN* 10.189-92 (1938).

150. ———. 1957. *A History of the English Language*. 2nd ed. (revised). New York: Appleton-Century-Crofts, xviii + 506 pp. [Also, London: Routledge & Kegan Paul, 1959.]

   Reviews: Morton W. Bloomfield in *JEGP* 57.796 (1958); Lee S. Hultzén in *QJS* 44.198 (1958).

151. ——— and Thomas Cable. 1978. *A History of the English Language*. 3rd ed. Englewood Cliffs, NJ: Prentice-Hall; London: Routledge & Kegan Paul, xvi + 438 pp.

   Reviews: Robert A. Peters in *JEngL* 13.94-95 (1979); Joseph B. Trahern, Jr. in *JEGP* 78.242 (1979).

152. Berndt, Rolf. 1982. *A History of the English Language*. Leipzig: VEB Verlag Enzyklopädie, 240 pp. [Includes Michael Benskin's 'On the present state of Middle English dialectology' (pp. 207-08) as Appendix. 2nd (unchanged) ed. 1984.]

   Reviews: Grzegorz Kleparski in *KN* 31.97-100 (1984); Josef Vachek in *PP* 27.47-49 (1984); Herbert Penzl in *JEngL* 18.71-74 (1985); Gillis Kristensson in *ES* 67.378-79 (1986).

153. Bloomfield, Morton Wilfred and Leonard Newmark. 1963. *A Linguistic Introduction to the History of English*. New York: Knopf. xviii + 375 + xx pp. [Repr. with corrections in 1979.]

   Reviews: G.L. Brook in *MLR* 59.440-41 (1964); Jacek Fisiak in *International Journal of American Linguistics* (Chicago) 30.305-09 (1964); Thomas Gardner in *Anglia* 82.346-51 (1964); Paul Goodman in *NYRB*, May 14, 1964, pp. 15-18; James Sledd in *Language* 40.465-83 (1964); E.C. Garcia in *Word* 20.101-05 (1964); Alfred Bammesberger in *NS* N.F. 14.495-96 (1965); Guy Bourquin in *Linguistics* 12.70-72 (1965); Norman Davis in *MAE* 34.171-73 (1965); J. Randolph Fisher in *College Language Association Journal* (Baltimore) 8.302-03 (1965); Raven I. McDavid, Jr. in *CE* 26.324-25 (1965); J.A. van Ek in *ES* 46.353-55 (1965); Veronika Kniezsa in *ALH* 16.197-98 (1966).

154. Bøgholm, Niels. 1939. *English Speech from an Historical Point of View*. Copenhagen: Nyt Nordisk Forlag; London: Allen and Unwin. 389 pp.

    Reviews: Anon. in *TLS*, Dec. 23, 1939, p. 747; Louis Hjelmslev in *ALH* 2.131 (1941).

155. Bolton, Whitney French. 1967. *A Short History of Literary English*. London: Edward Arnold, x + 86 pp. [2nd ed. 1972.]

    Reviews: André Crépin in *EA* 21.186 (1968); Susie I. Tucker in *MLR* 63.668 (1968); Gero Bauer in *Anglia* 87.418-21 (1969).

156. ———. 1982. *A Living Language: The History and Structure of English*. New York: Random House, x + 461 pp.

    Reviews: John Algeo in *Word* 34.235-40 (1983); Joseph L. Subbiondo in *Diachronica* 1.261-65 (1984); Seth Lerer in *MP* 81.330-33 (1984); B.D.H. Miller in *RES* n.s. 37.67-68 (1986).

157. Bourcier, Georges. 1978. *Histoire de la langue anglaise: Du Moyen Âge à nos jours*. (Collection Études. Section Anglais.) Paris: Bordas, 304 pp.

    Reviews: Cecily Clark in *EA* 32.212-14 (1979); André Crépin in *BSL* 75:2.157-58 (1980).

158. ———. 1981. *An Introduction to the History of the English Language*. English Adaptation by Cecily Clark. Cheltenham: Stanley Thornes, viii + 230 pp.

    Reviews: Sheila M. Embleton in *CJL* 27.183-84 (1982); François Chevillet in *EA* 37.176-77 (1984); Alwin Fill in *Anglia* 102.145-47 (1984); B.D.H. Miller in *RES* n.s. 35.216-17 (1984); E.G. S[tanley] in *N&Q* n.s. 31.437-38 (1984); Barbara M.H. Strang in *MLR* 79.410-12 (1984).

159. Bradley, Henry. 1968. *The Making of English*. Revised by Simeon Potter. London: Macmillan, ix + 203 pp. [1st ed. 1904. Revision and chapters 7 & 8 are by Potter. American ed., New York: Walker, 1967.]

160. Brook, George Leslie. 1958. *A History of the English Language*. (The Language Library.) London: André Deutsch, 224 pp.

    Reviews: Bergen Evans in *Saturday Review* (New York), July 19, 1958, p. 33; Anon. in *TLS*, April 17, 1959, p. 227; N.E. Eliason in *MLR* 54.453-54 (1959); Bertil Sundby in *MSpr* 53.62-65 (1959); R.W. Zandvoort in *ES* 41.221-22 (1960); Martin Lehnert in *ZAA* 9.190-91 (1961).

161. Brunner, Karl. 1950-51. *Die englische Sprache: Ihre geschichtliche Entwicklung.* (= SKGGD, B 6.) 2 vols. Halle/Saale: Max Niemeyer. Vol. I: *Allgemeines, Lautgeschichte,* 1950, xix + 351 pp.; Vol. II: *Die Flexionsformen, ihre Verwendung,* 1951, vi + 424 pp.

Reviews: W. Schmidt-Hidding in *Die Lebenden Fremdsprachen* 2.379-82 (1950) and *NS* N.F. 2.278-80 (1953); H.C. Matthes in *Archiv* 188.142-43 (1951) and 189.57 (1952/53); F. Mezger in *Anglia* 70.118-20 (1951) and 73.87-92 (1955); G. Scheurweghs in *LB* 41. Bijblad 99-100 (1951); R. Derolez in *RBPH* 30.896-99 (1952); A.A. Hill in *JEGP* 51.90-91 (1952); J.J. Campbell in *JEGP* 51.401-02 (1952); G. Kirchner in *NZ* 4.210-13 (1952); S. Potter in *RES* n.s. 3.404-06 (1952) and 4.194-95 (1953); A.A. Prins in *Neophil* 36.119-22 (1952); R. Quirk in *MLR* 47.381-82 (1952) and 48.452-54 (1953); J. Raith in *DLZ* 73.720-22 (1952); A. Sommerfelt in *NTS* 16.454-56 (1952) and 17.568-70 (1954); T.F. Mustanoja in *NM* 54.369-71 (1953); H. Penzl in *Language* 29.96-98 (1953); F.Th. Visser in *ES* 34.24-29 and 73-79 (1953); R.W. Zandvoort in *Museum* 58.168-73 (1953); F. Mossé in *EA* 7.313-14 (1954); A.J.Th. Eisenring in *Erasmus* 9.138-41 (1956).

162. ———. 1960-62. *Die englische Sprache: Ihre geschichtliche Entwicklung.* (= SKGGD, B 6.) 2., überarbeitete Aufl. 2 vols. Tübingen: Max Niemeyer. Vol. I: *Allgemeines, Lautgeschichte,* 1960, xxii + 416 pp.; Vol. II: *Die Flexionsformen und ihre Verwendung,* 1962, xii + 454 pp. [The softcover 1984 reprint of this 2nd rev. ed. has 16-page 'Nachträge und Erganzungen' by Klaus Faiss.]

Reviews: T.F. Mustanoja in *NM* 61.344-45 (1960); B. Carstensen in *NS* N.F. 11.56 (1961) and 12.435-36 (1963); H. Penzl in *Language* 37.147-50 (1961) and 39.521-23 (1963); H. Schabram in *Anglia* 79.53-58 (1961) and 82.220-27 (1964); E.G. Stanley in *MLR* 57.140-41 (1962) and 58.620-21 (1963); S. Standop in *Archiv* 199.121-23 (1962/63) and 201.129 (1964/65); R. Berndt (review-article) in *ZAA* 16.156-76 (1968).

163. Bryant, Margaret M. 1948. *Modern English and Its Heritage.* New York & London: Macmillan, xii + 407 pp.

Reviews: L.S. Hultzén in *QJS* 35.257-58 (1949); Sanford B. Meech in *AS* 24.206-08 (1949); M. Schlauch in *New Republic* (Washington, DC), June 27, 1949, p. 18; A.L. Davis in *CE* 11.228-29 (1949/50); O. Arngart in *MSpr* 46.112 (1952); S.B. Liljegren in *SN* 26.171 (1953/54).

164. ———. 1962. *Modern English and Its Heritage.* 2nd rev. ed. New York & London: Macmillan, xvi + 492 pp.

Review: Bernard J. Weiss in *QJS* 48.441-42 (1962).

165. Burchfield, Robert William. 1985. *The English Language.* Oxford: Oxford Univ. Press, xiii + 194 pp.

Reviews: Johannes Hedberg in *MSpr* 79.71-73 (1985); Hans Käsmann in *Anglia* 103.411-18 (1985); M.L. Samuels in *N&Q* n.s. 33.197-98 (1986); Basil Cottle in *RES* n.s. 37.400-01 (1986); Jean Pauchard in *EA* 39.194 (1986); W. Nelson Francis in *Language* 62.712-13 (1986) N.F. Blake in *Lore&L* 5:1.102 (1986).

166. Cannon, Garland. 1972. *A History of the English Language.* New York: Harcourt Brace Jovanovich, xi + 242 pp.

    Review: S.F.D. Hughes in *CCC* 24.59-61 (1973).

167. Claiborne, Robert. 1983. *Our Marvelous Native Tongue: The Life and Times of the English Language.* New York: Times Books, xi + 339 pp.

168. Clark, John Williams. 1957. *Early English: A Study of Old and Middle English.* (The Language Library.) London: André Deutsch: Fair Lawn, NJ: Essential Books, 176 pp. [Also, New York: Norton, 1964.]

    Reviews: Morton W. Bloomfield in *AS* 33.198-99 (1958); R.M. Wilson in *English* 12.18-19 (1958); Rolf Berndt in *ZAA* 7.305-07 (1959); Stanley B. Greenfield in *MLN* 74.59-60 (1959); F.E. Harmer in *MLR* 54.139-40 (1959); Albert H. Marckwardt in *Language* 41.143-46 (1965).

169. ———. 1967. *Early English: A Study of Old and Middle English.* Rev. ed. (The Language Library.) London: André Deutsch, 174 pp.

    Reviews: F.G.A.M. Aarts in *LT* 1968, p. 577; Josef Vachek in *Linguistics* 50.105-07 (1969).

170. Cook, Albert B., III. 1969. *Introduction to the English Language: Structure and History.* New York: Ronald Press, x + 354 pp.

    Review: E.A. Ebbinghaus in *GL* 10.181-82 (1970).

171. Crépin, André. 1967. *Histoire de la Langue Anglaise.* (= Collection QUE SAIS-JE? 1265.) Paris: Presses Universitaires de France, 128 pp.

    Reviews: L. Heilmann in *LeSt* 2.403 (1967); Klaus Hansen in *ZAA* 16.295-97 (1968); A.R. Tellier in *BSL* 65.113-14 (1970); Jaroslav Macháček in *Linguistics* 82.126-28 (1972); Herbert Koziol in *Archiv* 209.394-96 (1972/73).

172. ———. 1978. *Problèmes de grammaire historique: de l'indo-européen au vieil-anglais.* Paris: Presses Universitaires de France, 150 pp.

    Reviews: Juliette De Caluwé-Dor in *EA* 33.338-40 (1980); S. Kalifa in *BSL* 75:2.155-57 (1981).

173. ———. 1978. *Grammaire historique de l'anglais: du XIIe siècle à nos jours.* Paris: Presses Universitaires de France, 127 pp.

Reviews: Juliette De Caluwé-Dor in *EA* 33.338-40 (1980); S. Kalifa in *BSL* 75:2.155-57 (1981).

174. Delcourt, Joseph. 1944. *Initiation à l'étude historique de l'anglais*. (= Bibliothèque de philologie germanique, 4.) Paris: Aubier, 224 pp.

    Reviews: Tauno F. Salminen in *NM* 45.185-88 (1944); R.W. Zandvoort in *ES* 26.96 (1944); A.A. Prins in *Neophil* 30.94 (1945); W. Horn in *Archiv* 185.147-48 (1948).

175. Donahue, Delia. 1979. *Outline of the Growth and Development of English Language*. (= Bibl. di Cultura, 159.) Roma: Bulzoni, 111 pp.

176. Faiss, Klaus. 1977. *Aspekte der englischen Sprachgeschichte*. (= TBL, 71.) Tübingen: Gunter Narr, x + 426 pp.

    Review: Hans Jürgen Diller in *IF* 82.365-68 (1977).

177. Fernandez, Francisco. 1982. *Historia de la Lengua Inglesa*. Madrid: Editorial Gredos, 738 pp.

    Review: J[osé] S.G. S[oliño] in *RCEI* 5.155 (1982).

178. Fosty, Angeline. 1974. *External History of English*. Montreal: McGill Univ., Dept. of English, 55 pp.

179. Görlach, Manfred. 1974. *Einführung in die englische Sprachgeschichte*. (= Uni-Taschenbücher, 383.) Heidelberg: Quelle & Meyer, 228 pp. [2nd ed. 1983, 231 pp.]

    Reviews: Manfred Scheler in *Archiv* 212.361-62 (1975); Wolfgang Blumbach in *Anglia* 97.483-88 (1979); J.M. Kirk in *Lore&L* 3:1.79-81 (1979); Gabriella Del Lungo Camiciotti in *StG* 45/46.544-45 (1978)

180. Hook, J.N. 1975. *History of the English Language*. New York: The Ronald Press, viii + 372 pp.

181. Huchon, René. 1923. *Histoire de la Langue Anglaise*. Tome I: *Des Origines à la conquête normand (450-1066)*. Paris: Armand Colin, xii + 327 pp.

    Reviews: Otto Jespersen in *MLR* 19.348-50 (1924); A. Mawer in *Litteris* 2.63-65 (1925); L. Grootaers in *Humanitas* 2.63-64 (1927); W. van der Gaaf in *ES* 9.85-89 (1927).

182. ————. 1930. *Histoire de la Langue Anglais*. Tome II: *De la Conquête normande à l'Introduction de l'Imprimerie (1066-1475)*. Paris: Armand Colin, vii + 392 pp.

Reviews: F. Klaeber in *Anglia B* 41.258-61 (1930); W. van der Gaaf *ES* 12.184-87 (1930); Karl Brunner in *NS* 39.66-67 (1931); J. Mansion in *RBPH* 10.232-35 (1931); S.B. Liljegren in *LGRP* 57.169-71 (1936).

183. Iarovici, Edith. 1970. *A History of the English Language*. Bucarest: Editura Didactică şi Pedagogică, 312 pp. [2nd ed. 1973.]

184. Jespersen, Otto. 1923. *Growth and Structure of the English Language*. 4th ed. rev. Oxford: Blackwell; New York: Appleton; Leipzig: Teubner, iv + 255 pp. [1st ed. 1905, Leipzig: Teubner, iv + 260 pp.; 8th ed. 1935, iv + 239 pp.; 9th ed. 1938, iv + 244 pp.; 10th ed., with a five-page foreword by Randolph Quirk, 1982, vii + 244 pp.]

    Reviews: 4th ed.: Max F. Mann in *Anglia B* 34.366-67 (1923); Fritz Karpf in *NS* 32.441-43 (1924). — 8th ed.: A. Långfors in *NM* 35.139-40 (1934); W. Fischer in *Anglia B* 46.182-83 (1935); E. Zellmer in *ZNU* 35.280 (1936); A.E.H. Swaen in *Neophil* 21.169-71 (1936); R.W. Zandvoort in *ES* 19.90-94 (1937). — 9th ed.: F. Mossé in *BSL* 120.127-28 (1939); S.B. Liljegren in *SN* 12.264-65 (1939/40).

185. Jungandreas, Wolfgang. 1949. *Geschichte der deutschen und der englischen Sprache*. Teil III: *Geschichte der englischen Sprache*. Göttingen: Vandenhoeck und Ruprecht, 270 pp.

    Reviews: W.F. Leopold in *JEGP* 49.574-77 (1950); W.E. Collinson in *MLR* 46.123-25 (1951); L. Grootaers in *LB* 41.16-17 (1951)

186. Kisbye, Torben. 1975. *A Short History of the English Language*. Aarhus, Denmark: Aarhus Univ. (Dept. of English), 151 pp. [2nd rev. ed., Aarhus: Akademisk Boghandel, 1977.]

187. Koziol, Herbert. 1967. *Grundzüge der Geschichte der englischen Sprache*. (= Grundzüge, 9.) Darmstadt: Wissenschaftliche Buchgesellschaft, 242 pp.

    Reviews: Klaus Hansen in *ZAA* 16.402-05 (1968); Z[andvoort] in *ES* 49.88 (1968); Gerhard Nickel in *Archiv* 207.461-64 (1970/71); Horst Weinstock in *Anglia* 90.163-65 (1972)

188. Krapp, George Philip. 1969. *Modern English: Its Growth and Present Use*. Revised by Albert H. Marckwardt. New York: Scribner's, xvi + 316 pp. [1st ed. 1909.]

    Review: John Algeo in *JEngL* 5.122-25 (1971).

189. Lanzisera, Francesco. 1948. *History of the English Language with a Short Historical Grammar*. Bari & Napoli: Adriatica Editrice. 222 pp.

190. Leith, Dick. 1983. *A Social History of English*. London-Boston-Melbourne-Henry: Routledge & Kegan Paul, ix + 224 pp.

Reviews: Mª. Teresa Gilbert in RCEI 8.172-73 (1984); Manfred Markus in AAA 9.212-16 (1984).

191. Lindelöf, Uno. 1928. *Grundzüge der Geschichte der englischen Sprache*. 2nd enl. and corrected ed. Leipzig: Teubner, vi + 160 pp. [1st ed. 1912, vi + 141 pp.]

    Reviews: Friedrich Wild in DLZ 50.220-22 (1929); F. Karpf in NS 37:2.168-69 (1929); H.M. Flasdieck in Anglia B 41.72-73 (1930).

192. Marckwardt, Albert Henry. 1942. *Introduction to the English Language*. New York: Oxford Univ. Press, xviii + 347 pp.

    Reviews: Henry Alexander in AS 17.259-61 (1942); Norman E. Eliason in MLQ 3.476 (1942); James R. Hulbert in MP 40.213 (1942); Henry Lee Smith, Jr. in Language 18.250-52 (1942); C.K. Thomas in QJS 28.362-63 (1942); Rudolph Willard in CE 4.147-48 (1942/43); Henry B. Woolf in MLN 58.326-27 (1943).

193. McLaughlin, John C. 1970. *Aspects of the History of English*. New York & London: Holt, Rinehart & Winston, xv + 375 pp.

    Reviews: Angus Cameron in CJL 16.55-57 (1970); John Algeo in JEngL 5.122-29 (1971) and CE 33.936-40 (1972); Charles Carlton in GL 11.119-23 (1971); J.A. Johnson in Language 47.703-08 (1971); Harold Kane in CCC 22.74-77 (1971); C.J.E. Ball in JL 8.340-42 (1972); D.L. Goyvaerts in Linguistics 159.97-111 (1975).

194. McKnight, George Harley, with the assistance of Bert Emsley. 1928. *Modern English in the Making*. New York: Appleton, xii + 590 pp. [Repr. as *The Evolution of the English Language: from Chaucer to the twentieth century*. New York: Dover Publications, 1968.]

    Reviews: George Philip Krapp in SRL, Nov. 17, 1928, 5.374; Anon. in TLS, Feb. 21, 1929, p. 130; R.S. Forsythe in Quarterly Journal (Univ. of North Dakota) 19.327-29 (1929); J.R. H[ulbert] in MP 27.243 (1929); A.G. K[ennedy] in AS 4.317-18 (1929); C.M. Lotspeich in JEGP 29.139-40 (1930). — Review of the 1968 repr.: Dora Maček in Linguistics 137.111-15 (1974).

195. Measham, D.C. 1965. *English Now and Then*. Cambridge & New York: Cambridge Univ. Press, viii + 137 pp.

196. Mossé, Fernand. 1947. *Esquisse d'une Histoire de la Langue Anglaise*. (= Collection 'Les Langues du Monde', 2.) Lyon: Imprimerie Artistique en Couleur, xv + 268 pp. [2nd ed. 1958, xiii + 204 pp.]

    Reviews: R.M. Lumiansky in JEGP 47.291-92 (1948); Randolph Quirk in MLR 43.521-22 (1948); J. Vendryes in BSL 44.116-19 (1948); E.V.K. Dobbie in *AS* 24.58-59 (1949); S. Einarsson in *MLN* 64.193-94 (1949); F.Th. Visser in *ES* 30.45-48 (1949); G. Scheurweghs in *LB* 38. Bijblad 15-16 (1948); V. Pisani in *Paideia* 3.178-80 (1948); S.B. Liljegren in *SN* 21.78-79 (1948/49); B. Trnka in *Lingua* 2.90 (1949); K. Brunner in *Erasmus* 3.469-70 (1950); A. Macdonald in *RES* n.s. 1.92 (1950); T.F. Mustanoja in *NM* 51.45-46 (1950); G. Kirchner in *NZ* 4.279-82 (1952).

197. Myers, L.M. 1966. *The Roots of Modern English*. Boston: Little, Brown, x + 323 pp. [2nd ed. rev. by Richard L. Hoffman, 1979.]

   Reviews: Donald C. Freeman in *CE* 28.543-46 (1967); Donald W. Lee in *CCC* 19.43-44 (1968).

198. Nist, John. 1966. *A Structural History of English*. New York: St. Martin's Press, xvii + 426 pp.

   Reviews: Elizabeth Bowman in *JEngL* 1.67-73 (1967); Donald C. Freeman in *CE* 28.543-46 (1967) and *Linguistics* 45.101-14 (1968); Jan McCarthy in *Southern Speech Communication Journal* (Knoxville, TN) 32.249 (1967); Alicja Wegner in *SAP* 3.169-71 (1970).

199. Pei, Mario. 1952. *The Story of English*. Philadelphia: Lippincott, 381 pp. [British ed., London: George Allen & Unwin, 1953.]

   Reviews: Joseph Wood Krutch in *New York Herald Tribune Book Review*, Nov. 16, 1952, p. 4; H. Reynolds in *NYTB*, Nov. 16, 1952. p. 20; Anon. in *TLS*, Aug. 21, 1953, p. 538; Norman E. Eliason in *AS* 28.198-99 (1953); Raven I. McDavid, Jr. in *SIL* 11.1-2 (1953); Edwin Muir in *Observer*, July 5, 1953, p. 9; L.S. Hultzén in *QJS* 39.105-06 (1953); Anon. in *ELT* 8.105-07 (1953/54).

200. ———. 1967. *The Story of the English Language*. Revised ed. Philadelphia & New York: Lippincott, viii + 430 pp. [British ed., London: George Allen & Unwin, 1968.]

   Reviews: J. Donald Adams in *NYTB*, Aug. 27, 1967, p. 8; J.M. Lalley in *Modern Age* (Chicago) 12.182-88 (1968); Donald C. Freeman in *Massachusetts Review* (Amherst) 10.198-200 (1969); Joe E. Pierce in *Linguistics* 64.99-103 (1970).

201. Peters, Robert Anthony. 1968. *A Linguistic History of English*. Boston: Houghton Mifflin, xvi + 352 pp.

   Reviews: Allan A. Metcalf in *California English Journal* (Upland) 1970, 62-64; Thomas Gardner in *Anglia* 89.480-82 (1971); V.J. Plotkin in *Linguistics* 84.85-89 (1972).

202. Pezzini, Domenico. 1981. *Storia della lingua inglese. I: Dalle origine al Quattrocento.* (= Pubbl. del Centro di linguistica dell'Univ. cattolica. Trattati e manuali, 3.) Brescia: La scuola, 217 pp.

203. Potter, Simeon. 1950. *Our Language* (= Pelican Books, A 227.) Harmondsworth: Penguin Books, 202 pp.

    Reviews: H.E. Collins in *AS* 26.279-80 (1951); R.W. Zandvoort in *ES* 32.183-86 (1951); Randolph Quirk in *MLR* 47.98-99 (1952).

204. Pyles, Thomas. 1964. *The Origins and Development of the English Language.* New York: Harcourt, Brace and World, xi + 388 pp.

    Reviews: C.L. Wrenn in *RES* n.s. 16.449-50 (1965); Broder Carstensen in *NS* N.F. 15.343-44 (1966); Jacek Fisiak in *Linguistics* 21.120-26 (1966); Rupert E. Palmer, Jr. in *Language* 42.122-34 (1966); Charles Barber in *MLR* 62.505-06 (1967); Thomas Gardner in *Anglia* 86.365-68 (1968).

205. ———. 1971. *The Origins and Development of the English Language.* 2nd ed. New York: Harcourt Brace Jovanovich, xi + 413 pp.

    Review: Johannes Hedberg in *MSpr* 65.256-61 (1971).

206. ——— and John Algeo. 1982. *The Origins and Development of the English Language.* 3rd ed. New York: Harcourt Brace Jovanovich, xi + 383 pp.

207. Robertson, Stuart. 1934. *The Development of Modern English.* New York: Prentice-Hall, 568 pp. [Revised and enlarged ed. 1938, xi + 571 pp.]

    Reviews: H.M. Ayres in *AS* 10.65-66 (1935); M.B. Ruud in *EJ* 24.856-57 (1935); Anon. in *TLS*, July 11, 1936, p. 581; E. Weekly in *Observer*, May 24, 1936; R. Huchon in *MLR* 32.462-64 (1937).

208. ———. 1954. *The Development of Modern English.* 2nd ed., revised by Frederic G[omes] Cassidy. Englewood Cliffs, NJ: Prentice-Hall, ix + 469 pp.

    Reviews: C.M. Wise in *QJS* 40.341-43 (1954); E.G. Stanley in *EGS* 6.120-21 (1957).

209. Schibsbye, Knud. 1972-77. *Origin and Development of the English Language.* 3 vols. Copenhagen: Nordisk Sprog- og Kulturforlag. Vol. I: *Phonology*, 1972, ix + 121 pp; Vol. II: *Morphology and Syntax: Verbs, with an Excursus on Semantic Change*, 1974, 158 pp.; Vol. III: *Morphology and Syntax: Substantives, Adjectives, Adverbs, Numerals, Pronouns*, 1977, 226 pp.

    Reviews: Torben Kisbye in *SN* 45.437-39 (1973); Herbert Koziol in *ES* 60.89-91 (1979).

210. Schlauch, Margaret. 1952. *Outline of the English Language 1400 to the Present.* Warszawa: Państowe Wydawnictwo Naukowe, 137 pp.

211. ———. 1959. *The English Language in Modern Times (since 1400).* Warszawa: Państowe Wydawnictwo Naukowe; Oxford: Clarendon Press, xiv + 316 pp. [2nd ed. 1964.]

 Reviews: Simeon Potter in *N&Q* n.s. 7.313-14 (1961); R.M. Wilson in *MLR* 56.568-69 (1961); Josef Vachek in *SFFBU* 10 (A9).214-06 (1961); R.W. Zandvoort in *ES* 42.173-75 (1961); Thomas Finkenstaedt in *Anglia* 80.427-29 (1962); T. Grzebieniowski in *KN* 9.312-16 (1962); G. Kirchner in *ZAA* 10.299-304 (1962); E.J. Dobson in *RES* n.s. 14.316-19 (1963).

212. Schmidt, Gertrude. 1978. *A History of the English Language.* Timişoara, Romania: Timişoara Univ. Press, 206 pp.

213. Scott, H.F., W.L. Carr, and G.T. Wilkinson. 1935. *Language and Its Growth: An Introduction to the History of Language.* Chicago: Scott, Foresman, vii + 389 pp. [Chapter XI gives an account of the history of English.]

 Review: Lyman Spicer Judson in *QJS* 21.595-96 (1935).

214. Shipley, Joseph Twadell. 1977. *In Praise of English: The Growth & Use of Language.* New York: Times Books, ix + 310 pp.

 Review: Doris Grumbach in *NYTB*, Jan. 29, 1978, p. 16.

215. Smith, Logan Pearsall. 1952. *The English Language.* 2nd ed., with an Epilogue by R.W. Chapman. (= The Home Univ. Library of Modern Knowledge, 45.) London: Oxford Univ. Press, v + 178 pp. [1st ed. 1912; 3rd ed. published in 1966 as Oxford Paperbacks, Univ. Series, 7; 138 pp.]

216. Sparke, William. 1966. *Story of the English Language.* Illustrated with drawings by Wayne Gallup. London & New York: Abelard-Schuman, 190 pp.

217. Stevick, Robert D. 1968. *English and Its History: The Evolution of a Language.* Boston: Allyn and Bacon, 339 pp.

 Review: Sidney E. Bellamy in *JEngL* 4.95-96 (1970).

218. Strang, Barbara M.H. 1970. *A History of English.* London: Methuen, xxiv + 453 pp. [Also as paperback in: Univ. Paperback, 514. London: Methuen, 1974.]

 Reviews: Joseph A. DeVito in *QJS* 57.126 (1971); Roger Fowler in *Lang&S* 4.316-18 (1971); R.M. Wilson in *English* 20.22-23 (1971); Avril Bruten in *RES* n.s. 23.62-63 (1972); Veronika Kniezsa in *ALH* 22.240-42 (1972); John C. McLaughlin in *JL* 8.301-06 (1972); K.C. Phillipps in *ES* 53.184-88 (1972)

Rupert E. Palmer, Jr. in *Language* 48.941-47 (1972); Alarik Rynell in *SN* 44.180-88 (1972); P.M. Vermeer in *DQR* 2.134-37 (1972); Broder Carstensen in *NS* 72.568-69 (1973); T.G. Duncan (review-article) in *FMLS* 10.79-92 (1974); Jerzy Wełna in *SAP* 5.204-09 (1974); Derek A. Britton in *Studies* (Dublin) 64.97-99 (1975); Horst Weinstock in *NM* 76.342-48 (1975); Lilo Moessner in *Linguistics* 176.89-93 (1976); Helmut Gneuss in *Archiv* 214.123-25 (1977); Rolf Berndt in *ZAA* 27.167-69 (1979).

219. Tellier, André R. 1962. *Histoire de la langue anglaise.* (= Collection Almand Colin. Section langages et littératures, 363.) Paris: A. Colin, 224 pp.

Reviews: L. Geschiere in *Het Franse Boek* (Amsterdam) 33.91-92 (1963); E. Buyssens in *RBPH* 42.1143 (1964); Barbara Lewandowska in *KN* 13.346-48 (1966).

220. Vachek, Josef. 1969-72. *A Brief Survey of the Historical Development of English.* 2 vols. Bratislava: Univerzita Komenského; Leiden: State Univ. Vol. I: *Old English*, 1969, 80 pp.; Vol. II: *Middle English and Early Modern English*, 1972, 85 pp.

221. ———. 1977. *Standard English in Historical Perspective.* Košice: Univ. P.J. Šafárika, 146 pp.

222. Vallins, George Henry. 1966. *The Pattern of English.* Rev. ed. (The Language Library.) London: André Deutsch, 188 pp. [1st ed. 1956.]

Review: J. Mitchell Morse in *Journal of General Education* (University Park, PA) 18.223-24 (1966).

223. Weber, Georg. 1934. *Der Bau der englischen Sprache.* (= Palaestra, 192.) Leipzig: Mayer und Müller, iv + 135 pp.

Reviews: R.S. in *NS* 42.425-26 (1934); F. Fiedler in *ZNU* 34.123 (1935); O. Jespersen in *LGRP* 56.161-63 (1935).

224. Weekly, Ernest. 1928. *The English Language.* (= Benn's Sixpenny Library, 35.) London: Ernest Benn, 80 pp.

225. ———. 1952. *The English Language.* Rev. ed., with a Chapter on the History of American English by John Williams Clark. (The Language Library.) London: André Deutsch, 138 pp.

Review: F. Mossé in *EA* 7.107 (1954).

226. Williams, Joseph M. 1975. *Origins of the English Language: A Social and Linguistic History.* New York: The Free Press; London: Collier Macmillan, ix + 422 pp.

Reviews: Jeffrey F. Huntsman in *Language Sciences* (Bloomington) 48.27-29 (1977); Barbara M.H. Strang in *JL* 13.107-11 (1977); J.D. Burnley in *Lore&L* 2:8.46 (1978).

227. Wood, Frederick T. 1969. *An Outline History of the English Language.* 2nd ed. London: Macmillan, x + 305 pp. [1st ed. 1941.]

228. Wrenn, Charles Leslie. 1949. *The English Language.* (= Home Study Books, 8.) London: Methuen, vi + 236 pp. [Repr., with minor revisions, 1952.]

    Reviews: G. Kirchner in *NZ* 3.440-42 (1951); R.W. Zandvoort in *ES* 32.183-86 (1951); O. Arngart in *MSpr* 46.112-14 (1952); M. Lehnert in *ZAA* 1.210-13 (1952).

229. Wyld, Henry Cecil. 1927. *A Short History of English.* With a bibliography of recent books on the subject, and lists of texts and editions. 3rd ed., rev. and enl. London: John Murray, viii + 294 pp. [1st ed. 1914; 2nd ed. 1921.]

    Reviews: C.B. in *MLR* 23.387-88 (1928); Rudolph Willard in *MLN* 43.496-97 (1928); Walther Preusler in *Anglia B* 40.142-44 (1929); R.E. Zachrisson in *SN* 2.219-22 (1930); E. Kruisinga in *ES* 12.231-32 (1930)

230. ———. 1936. *A History of Modern Colloquial English.* 3rd ed., with additions. Oxford: Blackwell; New York: Peter Smith, xviii + 433 pp. [1st ed. 1920.]

    Reviews: Anon. in *AS* 12.217 (1937); H.M. Flasdieck in *Anglia B* 48.257-64 (1937); K. Malone in *Language* 13.325 (1937); C.K. Thomas in *QJS* 23.489-90 (1937); C.L. W[renn] in *Oxford Magazine*, Nov. 11, 1937, 56.166-68 (1937); E. Ekwall in *ES* 21.225 (1939).

IV. GRAMMARS

A. Historical

231. Catalini Fennel, Claire. 1976. *Lezioni di antico e medio inglese per il corso di filologia germanica.* (= Linguistica generale e storia, 7.) Bologna: Patron, 63 pp. [2nd ed. 1978, 81 pp.]

232. Ekwall, Eilert. 1956. *Historische neuenglische Laut- und Formenlehre.* Dritte, durchgesehene Auflage. (= Sammlung Göschen, 735.) Berlin: de Gruyter, 150 pp. [1st ed. 1914; 2nd ed. 1922; 4th = last ed. 1965.]

    Reviews: K. Brunner in *Anglia* 74.474 (1956); M. Martorelli in *Archivio Glottologico Italiano* (Rome) 41.188-89 (1956); G. Storms in *LT* 1957, 284 (1957); K. Schneider in *Archiv* 194.331 (1957/58).

233. ———. 1975. *A History of Modern English Sounds and Morphology.* Transl. and ed. by Alan Ward. Oxford: Basil Blackwell; Totowa, NJ: Roman & Littlefield, xvi + 133 pp. [Transl. of the 4th ed. of Ekwall [no. 232].]

234. Jespersen, Otto [Jens Otto Harry]. 1909-49. *A Modern English Grammar on Historical Principles.* 7 Vols. Heidelberg: Carl Winter; Copenhagen: Ejnar Munksgaard; London: George Allen & Unwin.

    Part I: Sounds and Spelling. Heidelberg, 1909; Copenhagen & London, 1949, xi + 485 pp.

    Part II: Syntax. First Volume. Heidelberg, 1913; Copenhagen & London, 1949, xxviii + 512 pp.

    Part III: Syntax. Second Volume. Heidelberg, 1927; Copenhagen & London, 1949, x + 415 pp. *Reviews*: Anon. in *TLS*, Nov. 10, 1927, p. 815; E. Kruisinga in *ES* 9.196-202 (1927); E.S. Sonnenschein in *Saturday Review*, Jan. 21, 3769, 68 (1928); A.G. K[ennedy] in *AS* 3.334-39 (1927/28); G.O. Curme in *Language* 4.135-48 (1928); W.E. Collinson in *Litteris* 6.33-38 (1929); W. Franz in *EStn* 63.402-05 (1929); W. Preusler in *ZFEU* 28.234-35 (1929); M. Redin in *SN* 2.75-77 (1929); M.B. Ruud in *JEGP* 28.532-39 (1929).

    Part IV: Syntax. Third Volume. Time and Tense. Heidelberg, 1931; Copenhagen & London, 1949, xxxii + 400 pp. *Reviews*: F. Delatte in *RBPH* 10.648-49

(1931); G.O. Curme in *JEGP* 31.586-90 (1932); W. Franz in *EStn* 57.249-52 (1932); E. Ekwall in *Anglia B* 44.129-32 (1933); F. Fiedler in *ZFEU* 32.46-47 (1933); F. Wild in *DL* 6.419-22 (1935).

Part V: Syntax. Fourth Volume. Copenhagen, 1940; London, 1946, xvi + 528 pp. *Reviews*: W. Preusler in *Anglia B* 52.99-105 (1941); R.W. Zandvoort in *ES* 23.44-51 and 80-82 (1941); C.A. Bodelsen in *ALH* 2.117-22 (1941); H. Koziol in *EStn* 75.74-78 (1942/43); A.A. Prins in *Museum* 49.156 (1942) and 51.86-89 & 107-09 (1944); F. Mossé in *BSL* 42:2.143-46 (1942-45).

Part VI: Morphology. Written with the Assistance of Paul Christophersen, Niels Haislund and Knud Schibsbye. Copenhagen, 1942; London, 1946, xii + 570 pp. *Reviews*: C.A. Bodelsen in *ALH* 2.259-61 (1942); W. Preusler in *Anglia B* 54.13-15 (1943); H. Koziol in *EStn* 76.121-24 (1944); R.W. Zandvoort in *ES* 26.145-53 (1944/45); K. Malone in *MLN* 64.553-55 (1949); F. Wild in *DLZ* 66/68.76-79 (1947); (Parts V & VI) S. Potter in *MLR* 42.367-70 (1947).

Part VII: Syntax. Completed and Published by Niels Haislund. Copenhagen, 1949; London, 1949, xiii + 683 pp. *Reviews*: C.A. Bodelsen in *ES* 30.281-87 (1949); E. Dieth in *Erasmus* 6.348-49 (1953). See also R.W. Zandvoort ("A Critique of Jespersen's *Modern English Grammar*") in *EA* 5.2-10 (1952).

235. ———. 1927. *Appendix to A Modern English Grammar. Part II: Syntax*. Heidelberg: Carl Winter, 28 pp.

Review: E. Kruisinga in *ES* 9.162-63 (1927).

236. Luick, Karl. 1964 [1914-40]. *Historische Grammatik der englischen Sprache*. Mit dem nach den hinterlassenen Aufzeichnungen ausgearbeiteten zweiten Kapitel herausgegeben von Friedrich Wild und Herbert Koziol. 2 vols. Stuttgart: Tauchnitz; Oxford: Basil Blackwell, xiv + 548; xiv + 549-1257 pp. [Photographic repr. of the first ed., issued in parts, 1914-40: Erster Band: Einleitung, Lautgeschichte. 1. Abteilung, 1914-21, xiv + 548 pp.; 2. Abteilung, 1929-40, xiv + 549-1257 pp. — First pub. by Tauchnitz, Leipzig.]

Reviews: W.F. Bryan in *JEGP* 29.606-11 (1930); E. Ekwall in *Anglia B* 42.193-97 (1931); E. Fischer in *LGRP* 52.352-56 (1931); F. Fiedler in *ZFEU* 30.637-41 (1931); F. Holthausen in *Anglia B* 51.265-67 (1940); E.G. Stanley in *MLR* 62.304 (1967).

237. Mincoff, Marco K. [Minkov, Marko K.] 1955. *English Historical Grammar*. Sofija: Nauka i izkustvo, 448 pp. [2nd ed. 1967; 3rd ed. 1972, 396 pp.]

238. Moore, Samuel. 1925. *Historical Outlines of English Phonology and Morphology (Middle English and Modern English)*. Ann Arbor, MI: George Wahr, viii + 153 pp. [Based on Moore's *Historical Outlines of English Phonology and Middle English Grammar* (Ann Arbor: George Wahr, 1919).]

Reviews: H. Flasdieck in *Anglia B* 36.263-64 (1925); E.G. Ingram in *RES* 2.240-41 (1926); Martin B. Ruud in *JEGP* 25.269-73 (1926); Karl Brunner in *Archiv* 154.257-59 (1928).

239. ———. 1951. *Historical Outlines of English Sounds and Inflections*. Rev. by Albert Henry Marckwardt. Ann Arbor, MI: George Wahr, vii + 179 pp. [A complete rev. of Moore [no. 238].]

Reviews: Elliot V.K. Dobbie in *AS* 28.122 (1953); K. Malone in *MLN* 68.143 (1953).

240. Pinsker, Hans Ernst. 1959. *Historische englische Grammatik: Elemente der Laut- und Formenlehre*. München: Max Hueber, xii + 200 pp.

Reviews: B. Carstensen in *NS* N.F. 9.196-97 (1960); E. Standop in *Archiv* 197.210-11 (1960/61); Hans Schabram in *GRM* 42.231-33 (1961); K. Hansen in *ZAA* 9.191-94 (1961); J. Nosek in *Sprache* 8.123-24 (1962).

241. ———. 1963. *Historische englische Grammatik: Elemente der Laut-, Formen- und Wortbildungslehre*. 2., verbesserte und erweiterte Aufl. München: Max Hueber, xvi + 281 pp. [4th ed. 1974.]

Reviews: E.G. Stanley in *MLR* 59.621-22 (1964); Klaus Hansen in *ZAA* 13.301-04 (1965); Torben Kisbye in *Archiv* 202.127-29 (1965); Ewald Standop in *IF* 70.110-11 (1965); Hans Schabram in *Anglia* 84.196-99 (1966).

242. Wełna, Jerzy. 1978. *A Diachronic Grammar of English. Part One: Phonology*. Warszawa: Państowe Wydawnictwo Naukowe, 280 pp.

Review: Donka Minkova in *FLH* 2.151-56 (1981).

243. Wright, Joseph and Elizabeth Mary Wright. 1924. *An Elementary Historical New English Grammar*. London: Oxford Univ. Press, xii + 224 pp.

Reviews: E. Kruisinga in *ES* 7.121-23 (1925); F. Wild in *EStn* 60.214-16 (1925); K. Brunner in *Archiv* 149.285-86 (1926); J.H.G. Grattan in *MLR* 21.446-47 (1926); M.B. Ruud in *JEGP* 25.120-25 (1926); E. Ekwall in *Anglia B* 36.257-60 (1925).

B. Old English

244. Alston, Robin Casfrae. 1961. *An Introduction to Old English*. Evanston, IL & Elmsford, NY: Row, Peterson; Toronto: The Copp Clarke, xii + 167 pp.

Reviews: C. Dean in *QQ* 69.650-51 (1962/63); A. Renoir in *CE* 24.158 (1962/63); G.G. Počepcov in *ZAA* 12.67-70 (1964).

245. ———. 1967. *An Introduction to Old English.* Leeds: Leeds Univ. Press, 59 pp.

246. Anderson, Marjorie and Blanche Colton Williams. 1935. *Old English Handbook.* Boston: Houghton Mifflin, vii + 503 pp. [Contains 'Grammar' (pp. 3-131).]

   Review: Anon. in *TLS* 12 Sept. 1935, p. 567.

247. Blakely, Leslie. 1964. *Teach Yourself Old English.* London: English Universities Press, xiii + 193 pp.

   Review: Barbara Lewandowska in *KN* 12.324-26 (1965).

248. Bright, James Wilson. 1935. *An Anglo-Saxon Reader.* Rev. and enl. by James Root Hulbert. New York: Holt, cxxxii + 395 pp. [Contains 'An Outline of Anglo-Saxon Grammar' (pp. ix-lxxxvi) slightly expanded by Hulbert. 1st ed. 1891. 2nd ed. of Hulbert's rev., 1961. For 3rd ed., see Cassidy & Ringler [no. 253].]

249. Brook, George Leslie. 1955. *An Introduction to Old English.* Manchester: Manchester Univ. Press, xi + 138 pp. [2nd ed. 1962.]

   Reviews: Kenneth R. Brooks in *ArchL* 8.158-59 (1956) and *MLR* 51.622 (1956); H.M. Flasdieck in *Anglia* 74.249-50 (1956); T.F. Mustanoja in *NM* 57.269-70 (1956); M.L. Samuels in *RES* n.s. 7.188 (1956); G. Storms in *Neophil* 40.154-55 (1956); Paul Bacquet in *Bulletin de la Faculté des Lettres de Strasbourg* (Strasbourg) 35.449-50 (1956/57); A. Culioli in *EA* 10.139 (1957); J.L.N. O'Loughlin in *MAE* 26.120-21 (1957); L.A. Muinzer in *JEGP* 56.122-23 (1957); O. Funke in *ES* 41.259-61 (1960).

250. Brunner, Karl. 1942. *Altenglische Grammatik, nach der angelsächsischen Grammatik von Eduard Sievers.* (= SKGGD, A 3.) Halle/Saale: Max Niemeyer, x + 450 pp. [2nd rev. ed. 1951, x + 468 pp.; 3rd rev. ed., Tübingen: Max Niemeyer, 1965, x + 436 pp.]

   Reviews: F. Mossé in *BSL* 42.136-38 (1942-45); E. Kruisinga in *Taal en Leven* (Den Haag) 6.142-44 (1942/43); F. Klaeber in *Archiv* 182.131-35 (1943); S.B. Liljegren in *SN* 15.367-70 (1942/43); A.A. Prins in *Museum* 50.102 (1943). — 2nd ed.: F.Mossé in *EA* 5.239-40 (1952); B.J. Timmer in *MLR* 47.421 (1952); H.C. Matthes in *Archiv* 189.56 (1952/53).

251. Campbell, Alistair. 1959. *Old English Grammar.* Oxford: Clarendon Press, xvi + 423 pp. [Concentrates on OE phonology and inflections.]

   Reviews: K. Brunner in *Anglia* 77.346-49 (1959); E. Standop in *Archiv* 196.340 (1959/60); C.E. Bazell in *MAE* 29.27-30 (1960); G.L. Brook in *RES* n.s. 11.193-94 (1960); Daniel Cook in *MLN* 75.344-47 (1960); Norman E. Eliason in *Speculum* 35.435-38 (1960); Pierre Janelle in *Le Moyen Age* (Brussels) 66.378-79 (1960); A.R. Tellier in *EA* 13.48 (1960); R. Vleeskruyer in *MLR* 55.94-95 (1960); A. Reszkiewicz in *KN* 8.93-98 (1961); R. Derolez in *RBPH* 41.990-92 (1963); O. Funke in *ES* 44.205-09 (1963).

252. Casieri, Sabino. 1973. *Grammatica dell'Inglese Antico*. Milan: Cisalpino-Goliardica, vii + 167 pp.

253. Cassidy, Frederic Gomes and Richard N. Ringler, eds. 1971. *Bright's Old English Grammar and Reader*. 3rd ed. New York & London: Holt, Rinehart and Winston, xiv + 494 pp. [A thorough rev. and updating of Bright [no. 248]. 2nd corrected printing, 1974. For the "Grammar", see pp. 1-101.]

    Reviews: David L. Shores in *AS* 46.148-52 (1971 [1974]); J.L. Mitchell in *NM* 78.328-38 (1977).

254. Diamond, Robert E. 1970. *Old English Grammar and Reader*. Detroit: Wayne Univ. Press, 304 pp.

    Reviews: Marjory Rigby in *MLR* 66.654-55 (1971); C.E. Bazell in *Linguistics* 143.102-03 (1975); J.L. Mitchell in *NM* 78.328-38 (1977).

255. Dürmüller, Urs and Hans Utz. 1977. *Altenglisch: eine Einführung*. (= AA, 12.) Tübingen: Max Niemeyer, viii + 116 pp.

    Reviews: T. Fraser in *EA* 32.226 (1979); Claus-Dieter Wetzel in *IF* 84.364-72 (1979); Anna Maria Luiselli Fadda in *SMed* 20.443-44 (1979); Franz Wenisch in *Anglia* 99.162-67 (1981).

256. Flom, George T. 1930. *Introductory Old English Grammar and Reader*. Boston: D.C. Heath and Co., xiv + 413 pp. [2nd ed. 1930, xiv + 423 pp.]

    Reviews: Anon. in *Oxford Magazine* 49.147-48 (1930/31); H.M. Flasdieck in *Anglia B* 44.7-8 (1933); E.E. Ericson in *Anglia B* 48.35-36 (1937); S. Einarsson in *MLN* 46.482-83 (1931); F. M[ossé] in *RG* 23.148-49 (1932).

257. Girvan, Ritchie. 1931. *Angelsaksisch Handboek*. (= Oudgermaansche Handboeken, 4.) Haarlem: H.D. Tjeenk Willink & Zoon, xvi + 409 pp.

    Reviews: F. Holthausen in *Anglia B* 43.327-29 (1932); C.L. W[renn] in *MAE* 1.141-45 (1932); A.G. Kennedy in *JEGP* 32.229-31 (1933); A. van Loey in *RBPH* 13.261-62 (1934); A.E.H. Swaen in *EStn* 70.262-64 (1935).

258. Hieatt, Constance B. 1968. *Essentials of Old English: Readings with Keyed Grammar and Vocabulary*. New York: Crowell, xiv + 90 pp.

259. Hill, Joyce, A.R. Taylor, and R.L. Thomson. 1977. *Beginning Old English:*

Materials for a One-Year Course. (Leeds Studies in English.) Leeds: Univ. of Leeds School of English, vii + 130 pp.

260. Kieckers, Ernst. 1935. *Altenglische Grammatik.* (Huebers kurz Grammatiken.) München and Leipzig: Max Hueber, xx + 199 pp.

    Reviews: A B[randl] in *Archiv* 167.300 (1935); P.N.U. Harting in *Museum* 42.295-97 (1935); W. Preusler in *Anglia B* 46.170-78 (1935); R.W. Zandvoort in *ES* 17.222-24 (1935).

261. Kispert, Robert J. 1971. *Old English: An Introduction.* New York: Holt, Rinehart & Winston, x + 275 pp.

    Reviews: Joseph B. Trahern, Jr. in *GL* 13.123-28 (1973); J.L. Mitchell in *NM* 78.328-38 (1978).

262. Lehnert, Martin. 1939. *Altenglisches Elementarbuch. Einführung, Grammatik, Texte mit Übersetzung und Wörterbuch.* (= Sammlung Göschen, 1125.) Berlin: de Gruyter, 118 pp.

    Reviews: K. Brunner in *Anglia B* 50.292-94 (1939); G.T. Flom in *JEGP* 38.472 (1939); G. Linke in *EStn* 75.215-16 (1942).

263. ———. 1950. *Altenglisches Elementarbuch. Einführung, Grammatik, Texte mit Übersetzung und Wörterbuch.* 2. verbesserte und vermehrte Aufl. (= Sammlung Göschen, 1125.) Berlin: de Gruyter, 176 pp. [3rd ed. 1955, 178 pp.; 4th ed. 1959; 5th ed. 1962; 6th ed. 1965; 7th ed. 1969, 179 pp.; 8th ed. 1973; 9th ed. 1978 (= Sammlung Göschen, 2210).]

    Reviews: H.M. Flasdieck in *Anglia* 69.291 (1950); H. Marcus in *NZ* 2.496 (1950); E. Stürzl in *Sprache* 2.246-47 (1952). — 3rd ed.: F. Mossé in *EA* 8.337 (1955); Wolfgang Schmidt-Hidding in *NS* N.F. 4.286-87 (1955); K.R. Brooks in *MLR* 51.622-23 (1956); Hermann M. Flasdieck in *Anglia* 74.250 (1956); M.L. Samuels in *RES* n.s. 7.188-89 (1956); Friedrich Schubel in *ZAA* 4.114-15 (1956); L.A. Muinzer in *JEGP* 56.121-22 (1957). — 4th ed.: S.B. Liljegren in *ZAA* 7.413 (1959); G. Storms in *LT* 1959, 685; N.E. Eliason in *Language* 36.165-66 (1960). — 5th ed.: S.B. Liljegren in *LB* 51. Bijblad 105 (1962). — 6th ed.: Hans Schabram in *Anglia* 83.483-88 (1965); L. Heilmann in *LeSt* 1.123 (1966); Ján Šimko in *ZAA* 14.389-91 (1966); A.R. Tellier in *BSL* 62:2.71-72 (1968). — 9th ed.: Paul T. Roberge in *ZDL* 49.372-73 (1978); Josef Vachek *ZAA* 28.66 (1980); Ludmila Urbanová in *BSE* 14.169-70 (1981).

264. Marckwardt, Albert Henry and James L. Rosier. 1972. *Old English: Language and Literature.* New York: Norton, xviii + 394 pp.

    Reviews: T.F. Hoad in *N&Q* n.s. 21.63-66 (1974); Patrizia Lendinara in *AION-SG* 17.253-54 (1974); Mechthild Gretsch in *Anglia* 94.492-96 (1976).

265. Mazzuoli Porru, Giulia. 1977. *Manuale di inglese antico*. (= Orientamenti linguistica, 1.) Pisa: Giardini, 303 pp.

    Reviews: Franco Ivan Nucciarelli in *AION-SG* 21.369-76 (1978); M.G. Arcamone in *SMed* 20.468-79 (1979).

266. Mitchell, Bruce. 1965. *A Guide to Old English*. Oxford: Basil Blackwell, xvi + 160 pp.

    Reviews: R.I. Page in *MAE* 35.175-76 (1966); J.E. Cross in *RES* n.s. 18. 57-58 (1967); A.M.L. Knuth in *Neophil* 51.421-23 (1967); L. Seiffert in *EPS* 10.62-64 (1967).

267. ———. 1968. *A Guide to Old English*. 2nd ed. Oxford: Basil Blackwell, xvi + 169 pp. [With corrections, additions, and two new appendices.]

    Review: T.P. Dobson in *AUMLA* 31.92-94 (1969).

268. ——— and Fred Colson Robinson. 1982. *A Guide to Old English*. Revised with Texts and Glossary [3rd ed.]. Oxford: Basil Blackwell, xiv + 271 pp. [4th rev. ed. 1986, xvi + 354 pp.]

    Reviews: Fran Colman in *FLH* 4.325-30 (1983); Malcolm Godden in *TLS* 8 July 1983, p. 736; Katherine O'Brien O'Keeffe in *CEA Critic* (Centenary College of Louisiana, Shreveport) 45:3/4.48-49 (1983); Carmela Rizzo in *Schede Medievali* 5.505 (1983); Rolf H. Bremmer, Jr. in *ES* 65.366 (1984); Daniel G. Calder in *Speculum* 59.416-19 (1984); M.A.L. Locherbie-Cameron in *MAE* 53.111-12 (1984); Hans Peters in *Anglia* 102.147-49 (1984); Matti Rissanen in *NM* 85.523-24 (1984); Jane Roberts in *N&Q* n.s. 31.253-54 (1984); E.G. Stanley in *RES* n.s. 36.141 (1985).

269. Moore, Samuel and Thomas A. Knott. 1940. *The Elements of Old English: Elementary Grammar, Reference Grammar, and Reading Selections*. 8th ed. Ann Arbor, MI: George Wahr, viii + 339 pp. [1st ed. 1930. This 8th ed. adds about ninety pages (pp. 199-284) of reading selections, arranged in order of difficulty. 9th ed. 1942. 10th ed. rev. by James R. Hulbert, 1955.]

270. Mossé, Fernand. 1945. *Manuel de l'Anglais du Moyen Âge des Origines au XIVe Siècle. I. Vieil-anglais*. 2 vols. (= BPG, 8.) Paris: Aubier. Vol. I: Grammaire et textes, 345 pp.; Vol. II: Notes et glossaire, 203 pp. [2nd ed. 1950.]

    Reviews: S. Einarsson in *MLN* 61.559-62 (1946); J. Vendryes in *BSL* 43.81-85 (1946); E. Buyssens in *RBPH* 25.685-87 (1946/47); B. Trnka in *ČMF* 30.272-73 (1946/47); Henning Larsen in *JEGP* 46.434-35 (1947); A. Macdonald in *MLR* 42.493-94 (1947); R.W. Zandvoort in *ES* 28.15-19 (1947); E.V.K. Dobbie in *Language* 24.241-44 (1948).

271. Pilch, Herbert. 1970. *Altenglische Grammatik*. (= Commentationes Societatis Linguisticae Europaea, 1:1.) München: Max Hueber, 267 pp. [Designed as a companion to Pilch's *Altenglischer Lehrgang: Begleitband zur Altenglischen Grammatik*, 1970, 82 pp.]

Reviews: R. Zimmermann in *Kratylos* 15.191-97 (1970); C.R. Barrett in *AUMLA* 36.221-24 (1971); Klaus Hansen in *ZAA* 19.413-16 (1971): Herbert Koziol in *Archiv* 209.139-42 (1972); Jiří Nosek in *PP* 15.40-42 (1972); Wolfgang Viereck in *JEngL* 6.71-73 (1972); M. Perrelet-Bridges and P.B. Taylor in *Linguistics* 102.118-22 (1973); Lars-G. Hallander in *SN* 50.135-41 (1978); E. Kolb in *Anglia* 96.459-65 (1978).

272. ———. 1970. "Altenglisch". *Kurzer Grundriss der germanischen Philologie bis 1500, I: Sprachgeschichte*, ed. Ludwig Erich Schmitt, 144-89. Berlin: de Gruyter. [An abridged version of Pilch [no. 271].]

273. Prokosch, Eduard. 1939. *A Comparative Germanic Grammar*. (William Dwight Whitney Linguistic Ser.) Philadelphia: Linguistic Society of America, 353 pp.

274. Quirk, Randolph and Charles Leslie Wrenn. 1955. *An Old English Grammar*. (Methuen's Old English Library.) London: Methuen, x + 166 pp. [2nd ed. 1957.]

Reviews: Anon. in *TLS* 23 Sept. 1955, p. 563; K.R. Brooks in *ArchL* 8.158-62 (1956); Karl Brunner in *MLR* 51.419-20 (1956); S. Chatman in *Language* 32.535-40 (1956); H.M. Flasdieck in *Anglia* 74.459 (1956); Celia Sisam in *MAE* 25.52-53 (1956); P. Bacquet in *BFS* 35.447-48 (1956/57); John Braidwood in *RES* n.s. 8.43-45 (1957); A. Culioli in *EA* 10.140-41 (1957); S. Einarsson in *MLN* 72.204-06 (1957); A. Rynell in *MSpr* 51.145-49 (1957); Alfred Reszkiewicz in *KN* 4.324-26 (1957); S.M. Kuhn in *JEGP* 57.114-17 (1958); Ralph W.V. Elliott in *DUJ* 20.131-32 (1959); O. Funke in *ES* 41.259-61 (1960).

275. Raw, Barbara C. 1967. *A Programmed Course in Old English*. (= Keele Univ. Lib. Occasional Pub., 5.) Keele, Staffordshire: Keele Univ. Lib., iii + 152 (mimeographed) pp.

276. Reszkiewicz, Alfred. 1964. *Old English Essentials*. Warszawa & Łódź: Państwowe Wydawnictwo Naukowe, 72 (mimeographed) pp. [An English version, slightly enlarged, of the author's *Elementy Gramatyki Historycznej Języka Angielskiego, I. Język Staroangielski*. Cracow: PWN, 1951, 52pp.]

Review: Aleksander Szwedek in *KN* 12.206-08 (1965).

277. ———. 1971. *Synchronic Essentials of Old English: West-Saxon*. Warszawa:

Państwowe Wydawnictwo Naukowe, 121 pp. [An expansion of Reszkiewicz [no. 276].]

Review: Angus Cameron in Anglia 92.412-13 (1974).

278. ———. 1973. *A Diachronic Grammar of Old English. Part I: Phonology and Inflections.* Warszawa: Państwowe Wydawnictwo Naukowe, 175 pp.

279. Ross, Alan Strode Campbell. 1948. *The Essentials of Anglo-Saxon Grammar.* Cambridge: W. Heffer & Sons, 19 pp.

Reviews: Anon. in *TLS* 1 Jan. 1949, p. 15; C.G. Cecioni in *RLM* 2.392-93 (1952).

280. Rot, Sándor. 1982. *Old English.* Budapest: Tankönyvkiadó, 628 pp.

Reviews: Martin Lehnert in *ZAA* 31.52-53 (1983); Josef Vachek in *PP* 27.101-02 (1984).

281. Setzler, Edwin Boinest, Edwin Lake Setzler, and Hubert Holland Setzler. 1938. *The Jefferson Anglo-Saxon Grammar and Reader.* New York: Macmillan, xiv + 198 pp.

Reviews: E.V.K. Dobbie in *AS* 13.208-10 (1938); W.F. Bryan in *MLN* 54.157-58 (1939).

282. Sievers, Eduard. 1941. *Abriss der altenglischen (angelsächsischen) Grammatik.* 10. Aufl. neu bearbeitet von Karl Brunner. (= SKGGD, C 2.) Halle/Saale: Max Niemeyer, viii + 78 pp. [1st ed. 1895; 11th ed. 1948; 12th ed. 1950, viii + 90 pp.; 15th ed. 1959 (Tübingen: Max Niemeyer); 16th ed. 1963.]

Reviews: W. Fischer in *Anglia B* 52.97 (1941); A.A. Prins in *Museum* 49.71 (1942); W. Horn in *Archiv* 185.152 (1948). — 11th ed.: H. Marcus in *DLZ* 70.495 (1949); A.A. Prins in *Museum* 54.43 (1949); B.J. Timmer in *ES* 32.78-79 (1951); F. Rau in *Anglia* 71.230-32 (1953).

283. ———. 1975. *Compendio di grammatica antico inglese*, 16th ed. rev. by Karl Brunner. Transl. by M. Augusta Coppola. Messina: Peloritana, x + 132 pp.

Review: Patrizia Lendinara in *AION-SG* 19.216-19 (1976).

284. Sweet, Henry, 1953. *Anglo-Saxon Primer.* 9th ed., rev. throughout by Norman Davis. Oxford: Clarendon Press, vii + 129 pp. [1st ed. 1882; 8th ed. 1905.]

Reviews: Anon. in *DUJ* 14.121 (1953); H.M. Flasdieck in *Anglia* 71.461 (1953); F.P. Magoun, Jr. in *Speculum* 28.876-77 (1953); F. Mossé in *EA* 7.314 (1954); R. Quirk in *MLR* 49.111-12 (1954); M.L. Samuels in *RES* n.s. 5.274 (1954).

285. Weimann, Klaus. 1982. *Einführung ins Altenglische.* (= Uni-Taschenbücher, 1210.) Heidelberg: Quelle und Meyer, 248 pp.

286. Wright, Joseph and Elizabeth Mary Wright. 1923. *An Elementary Old English Grammar.* Oxford: Clarendon Press, viii + 192 pp.

   Reviews: Anon. in *N&Q* 144.500 (1923); H.M. Flasdieck in *Anglia B* 34.263-64 (1923); B. Borowski in *EStn* 60.206-13 (1925); Kemp Malone in *JEGP* 24.286-91 (1925); George T. Flom in *JEGP* 26.276-77 (1927).

C. Middle English

287. Bähr, Dieter. 1975. *Einführung ins Mittelenglische.* (= Uni-Taschenbücher, 361.) München: Wilhelm Fink, 191 pp.

   Review: M. Görlach in *Anglia* 95.477-81 (1977).

288. Berndt, Rolf. 1960. *Einführung in das Studium des Mittelenglischen unter Zugrundlegung des Prologs der 'Canterbury Tales'.* Halle/Saale: Max Niemeyer, xviii + 398 pp. [Part I (pp. 1-224) deals with ME phonology; nothing on morphology or syntax.]

   Reviews: A. Reszkiewicz in *KN* 8.335-40 (1961); M. Schlauch in *ZAA* 9.296-99 (1961); B. Trnka in *ČMF* 43.109-10 (1961); Pamela Gradon in *Anglia* 81.462-64 (1963); Samuel R. Levin in *JEGP* 62.791-94 (1963); Simeon Potter in *MLR* 58.455-56 (1963); E.G. Stanley in *Archiv* 201.62-64 (1964).

289. Brunner, Karl. 1938. *Abriss der mittelenglischen Grammatik.* (= SKGGD, C 6.) Halle/Saale: Max Niemeyer, 90 pp. [2nd ed. 1948, viii + 114 pp.; 3rd ed. 1953 (Tübingen: Max Niemeyer); 4th ed. 1959; 5th ed. 1962.]

   Reviews: G.L. Brook in *MAE* 8.235-37 (1939); S.R.T.O. D'Ardenne in *ES* 21.272-75 (1939); Rolf Kaiser in *Archiv* 176.84-85 (1939); E.L. Deuschle in *Museum* 47.140 (1940) and *Neophil* 25.232 (1940); Will Héraucourt in *EStn* 74.214-15 (1940); W. Fischer in *Anglia B* 52.98-99 (1941).— 2nd ed.: A.A. Prins in *Museum* 55.83 (1950); T.F. Mustanoja in *NM* 52.72 (1951). — 3rd ed.: R. Vleeskruyer in *Museum* 55.47-49 (1955).— 4th ed.: Klaus Hansen in *ZAA* 8.85-88 (1960); Hans Marcus in *Archiv* 196.339-40 (1960.)

290. ———. 1963. *An Outline of Middle English Grammar.* Transl. by Grahame K.W. Johnston. Oxford: Basil Blackwell; Cambridge, MA: Harvard Univ. Press, viii + 111 pp. [Transl. of Brunner [no. 289], 5th ed., 1962.]

   Reviews: Pamela Gradon in *Anglia* 81.464 (1963); A.D. Miller in *N&Q* n.s. 11.193-94 (1964); E.G. Stanley in *MLR* 59.254 (1964).

291. Cecioni, Cesare G. 1974. *Grammatica del medio-inglese*. (= Collana di filologia germanici, 6.) Milan: Mursia, viii + 152 pp.

   Review: Gabriella Del Lungo Camiciotti in *SGerm* 12.445-49 (1974).

292. Dürmüller, Urs and Hans Utz. 1974. *Mittelenglisch: eine Einführung*. (= AA, 6.) Tübingen: Max Niemeyer, 100 pp.

   Reviews: X. Dekeyser in *LB* 65.108-09 (1976); M. Görlach in *Anglia* 94.459-62 (1976).

293. Fisiak, Jacek. 1964. *Outlines of Middle English. Part I: Graphics, Phonology and Morphology*. Łódź: Uniwersytet Łódzki, 207 pp.

   Reviews: Ruta Sikora in *KN* 12.208-10 (1965); J. Boswinkel in *ES* 48.68-69 (1967).

294. ———. 1968. *A Short Grammar of Middle English. Part I: Graphemics, Phonemics and Morphemics*. Warszwa: Państwowe Wydawnictwo Naukowe; London: Oxford Univ. Press, 139 pp. [5th ed. 1980.]

   Reviews: Alfred Reszkiewicz in *KN* 16.207-10 (1969); L.W. Collier in *MAE* 41.177-78 (1972); Robert D. Stevick in *Speculum* 47.119-22 (1972); Horst Weinstock in *Anglia* 90.367-69 (1972); R.M. Wilson in *MLR* 67.163 (1972).

295. Jones, Charles. 1972. *An Introduction to Middle English*. New York & London: Holt, Rinehart and Winston, xi + 228 pp. [A transformational treatment.]

   Reviews: Eugene J. Crook in *JEGP* 71.439-41 (1972); Johan Kerling in *ES* 55.557-58 (1974); Gero Bauer in *FL* 13.135-39 (1975); Ann Squires in *MAE* 45.121-24 (1976).

296. Jordan, Richard. 1925. *Handbuch der Mittelenglischen Grammatik. I. Teil: Lautlehre*. (= GB, 1:13.) Heidelberg: Carl Winter, xvi + 273 pp.

   Reviews: Cyril Brett in *MLR* 21.78 (1926); Eilert Ekwall in *Litteris* 3.153-58 (1926); F. Klaeber in *EStn* 60.317-22 (1926); K. Luick in *Anglia B* 37.193-98 (1926); Kemp Malone in *MLN* 41.400-01 (1926); J. Mansion in *Bulletin Bibliographique et Pédagogique du Musée Belge* 30.39-42 (1926); Robert J. Menner in *JEGP* 25.415-18 (1926); G. Binz in *LGRP* 48.357-60 (1927); F. Wild in *NS* 35.57-59 (1927).

297. ———. 1934. *Handbuch der mittelenglischen Grammatik. Teil I: Lautlehre*. (= GB, 1:13.) 2., durchgesehene Aufl., bearbeitet von Heinrich Christoph Matthes. Heidelberg: Carl Winter, xiv + 294 pp.

   Reviews: E. Eckhardt in *EStn* 69.240-42 (1934/35); A. B[randl] in *Archiv* 166.137-38 (1935); F. Fiedler in *ZNU* 34.122 (1935); G. Weber in *LGRP*

56.163 (1935); O. Boerner in *NS* 44.485 (1936); C.L. W[renn] in *RES* 12.374-75 (1936); C.T. O[nions] in *MAE* 7.159-61 (1938).

298. ———. 1968. *Handbuch der mittelenglischen Grammatik. Lautlehre.* (= GB, 1:13.) 3. Aufl. Nachdruck der von H.Ch. Matthes bearbeiteten 2. Aufl., mit einem bibliographischen Nachtrag von Klaus Dietz. Heidelberg: Carl Winter, xii + 308 pp. + 1 map.

299. ———. 1974. *Handbook of Middle English Grammar: Phonology.* (=JanL, Ser. Practica, 218.) Transl. and rev. [with considerable expansion] by Eugene Joseph Crook. The Hague: Mouton, xxxiv + 331 pp. [Originally Univ. of Illinois at Urbana-Champaign diss., 1970; Abstr. in *DA* 32.3976A (1971). This transl. is based on Jordan [no. 298].]

Reviews: Margaret 'Espinasse in *YES* 7.183-84 (1977); Jerzy Wełna in *SAP* 9.226-30 (1977); Gillis Kristensson in *ES* 59.156-57 (1978); Mechthild Gretsch in *Anglia* 98.122-25 (1980).

300. Mossé, Fernand. 1949. *Manuel de l'anglais du Moyen-Age des origines au XIVème siècle. II. Moyen-anglais.* 2 vols. (= BPG, 12.) Paris: Aubier. Vol. I: Grammaire et textes, 380 pp.; Vol. II: Notes et glossaire, 192 pp.

Reviews: V. Pisani in *Paideia* (Genoa) 4.333-34 (1949); S. Einarsson in *MLN* 65.123-27 (1950); A. Macdonald in *MLR* 45.276-77 (1950); G. Scheurweghs in *LB* 40.Bijblad 26-27 (1950); E. Buyssens in *RBPH* 29.880 (1951); A. Basil Cottle in *RES* n.s. 2.65-67 (1951); J.R. Hulbert in *MP* 48.58 (1950/51); T.F. Mustanoja in *NM* 52.70-71 (1951); A.A. Prins in *ES* 32.119-20 (1951); J. Vendryes in *BSL* 47.181-82 (1951).

301. ———. 1952. *A Manual of Middle English.* Transl. by James Albert Walker. Baltimore: The Johns Hopkins Press, xxvi + 495 pp. [Transl. of Mossé [no. 300].]

Reviews: Anon. in *TLS*, Sept. 11, 1953, p. 576; H.M. Flasdieck in *Anglia* 71.462 (1953); A. Macdonald in *EA* 6.148-49 (1953); H. Marcus in *Archiv* 190.134 (1953/54); T.F. Mustanoja in *NM* 54.89 (1953); Randolph Quirk in *MLR* 48.496-97 (1953); Norman E. Eliason in *MLN* 69.135-38 (1954); R.M. Wilson in *RES* n.s. 5.107 (1954); Martin Lehnert in *ZAA* 6.62-64 (1958).

302. ———. 1969. *Handbuch des Mittelenglischen.* Übersetzt von Herbert Pilch und Ursula Siewert. München: Hueber, 565 pp. [Transl. of Mossé [no. 300].]

Review: Klaus Hansen in *ZAA* 18.324-25 (1970).

303. ———. 1973. *Mittelenglische Kurzgrammatik: Lautlehre, Formenlehre, Syntax.* Übersetzt von Herbert Pilch und Ursula Siewert. (= Hueber-Hochschulreihe, 11.) München: Hueber, 154 pp. [Transl. of extracts of Mossé [no. 300]. 2nd. ed. 1977.]

Review: Martin Lehnert in *ZAA* 24.182-83 (1976).

304. Moessner, Lilo and Ursula Schaefer. 1974. *Proseminar Mittelenglisch: Lehrbuch mit Texten, Grammatik und Übungen*. Darmstadt: Thesen, 147 pp.

    Review: M. Görlach in *Anglia* 94.456-59 (1976).

305. Rosenborough, Margaret M. 1938. *An Outline of Middle English Grammar*. New York: Macmillan, x + 112 pp. [Repr., Westport, CT: Greenwood Press, 1970.]

306. Wardale, Edith Elizabeth. 1937. *An Introduction to Middle English*. London: Kegan Paul, x + 130 pp. [Repr., New York: AMS, 1977.]

    Reviews: R.M. Wilson in *MLR* 33.317 (1938); Albert C. Baugh in *EStn* 74.91-94 (1940).

307. Weinstock, Horst. 1968. *Mittelenglisches Elementarbuch: Einführung, Grammatik, Texte mit Übersetzung und Wörterbuch*. (= Sammlung Göschen, 1226/1226a/1226b.) Berlin: de Gruyter, 239 pp.

    Reviews: Klaus Hansen in *ZAA* 17.276-79 (1969); F.C. de Vries in *MAE* 39.78-80 (1970); Klaus Dietz in *IF* 77.126-37 (1972); Gero Bauer in *Archiv* 209.142-46 (1972/73); Margret Popp in *Anglia* 93.458-67 (1975).

308. Wright, Joseph and Elizabeth Mary Wright. 1923. *An Elementary Middle English Grammar*. London: Oxford Univ. Press, xii + 214 pp. [2nd ed. 1928, xiv + 226 pp.]

    Reviews: Eilert Ekwall in *Anglia B* 35.226-28 (1924); F. Holthausen in *LGRP* 45.302-05 (1924); E. Kruisinga in *ES* 6.162-63 (1924); J.M. Toll in *Archiv* 149.108-09 (1925); F. Wild in *EStn* 59.96-99 (1925).— 2nd ed.: G.B.H. in *RES* 5.246-47 (1929); F. Holthausen in *LGRP* 50.346-48 (1929); F. Wild in *EStn* 63.401-02 (1928/29).

V. GENERAL AND MISCELLANEOUS

A. General

309. Anderson, James Maxwell. 1973. *Structural Aspects of Language Change.* (= Longman Linguistics Library, 13.) London: Longman, xiii + 250 pp.

    Review: T.F. Hoad in *N&Q* n.s. 22.76-77 (1975).

310. Bammesberger, Alfred. 1984. *English Etymology.* (= Sprachwissenschaftliche Studienbücher: Erste Abteilung [unnumbered].) Heidelberg: Carl Winter, 163 pp. [Despite the title, the book is an outline of historical phonology and word-formation.]

    Reviews: M.L. Samuels in *N&Q* n.s. 33.198-99 (1986); Roger W. Wescott in *Language* 62.713 (1986).

311. Bense, Johan Frederik. 1924. *The Anglo-Dutch Relations from the Earliest Times to the Death of William III.* Being an Historical Introduction to a Dictionary of the Low-Dutch Element in the English Vocabulary. The Hague: Martinus Nijhoff, xv + 206 pp. [Amsterdam diss. Also published in 1925 by Oxford Univ. Press/Humphrey Milford, London, xx + 293 pp. For the *Dictionary*, see Bense [no. 112].]

312. Berndt, Rolf. 1968. "Erwiderungen und Ergänzungen: Bemerkungen zur geschichtlichen Entwicklung der englischen Sprache". *ZAA* 16.156-76. [Apropos of Brunner [no. 162].]

313. Blake, Norman Francis. 1976. "The English Language in Medieval Literature". *SN* 48.59-75.

314. ———. 1977. *The English Language in Medieval Literature.* (Everyman's Univ. Library.) London-Melbourne-Toronto: J.M. Dent; Totowa, NJ: Rowman & Littlefield, 190 pp. [Repr., London: Methuen, 1979.]

    Reviews: Anon. in *Choice* 14.1642 (1978); Alan Bliss in *N&Q* n.s. 25.353-56 (1978); C. Clark in *MAE* 47.367-69 (1978); Earl F. Guy in *Ariel* (Calgary) 9:2.99-101 (1978); Henry Hargreaves in *RES* n.s. 29.330-31 (1978); K.C. Phillipps in *TLS* 20 Jan. 1978, p. 68; Robert D. Stevick in *Speculum* 53.788-90 (1978); N. Williams in *Lore&L* 2:9.138 (1978); G. Kristensson in *ES* 60.321-23

(1979); Ian Baird in *Cahiers Élisabéthains* (Montpellier) 17.107-08 (1980); Martin Lehnert in *ZAA* 29.70-74 (1981); G.S. Ivy in *DUJ* n.s. 43.135-36 (1981/ 82); B. Goedhals in *UES* 20:2.30 (1982); Domenico Pezzini in *SMed* 25.239-44 (1984).

315. Burgschmidt, Ernst and Dieter Götz. 1973. *Historische Linguistik: Englisch.* (= AA, 2.) Tübingen: Max Niemeyer, viii + 104 pp. [Uses examples from the history of English.]

   Reviews: Wolfgang Blumbach in *Kratylos* 18.96-98 (1973); X. Dekeyser in *LB* 63.355-57 (1974); Manfred Görlach in *Anglia* 92.408-12 (1974); Klaus Hansen in *ZAA* 23.264-65 (1975).

316. Cameron, Angus Fraser. 1974. "Middle English in Old English Manuscripts". *Robbins Festschrift*, 218-29. [An examination of annotations recorded from the 13th to the 16th century.]

317. Dietz, Klaus. 1984. "Soziolinguistik und englische Sprachgeschichte". *Berliner Wissenschaftliche Gesellschaft Jahrbuch 1983*, 55-60. Berlin: Duncker & Humblot.

318. Ekwall, Eilert. 1930. "How Long did the Scandinavian Language Survive in England". *Jespersen Festschrift*, 17-30. [Repr. in *Ekwall Papers*, 54-67.]

319. Geipel, John. 1971. *The Viking Legacy: The Scandinavian Influence on the English and Gaelic Languages*. Newton Abbot, Devon: David & Charles, 225 pp.

   Reviews: R.M. Wilson in *English* 108.97 (1971); Gilliam Fellows Jensen in *Danske Studier* (Copenhagen) 67.126-29 (1972).

320. Hogan, J.J. 1934. *An Outline of English Philology, Chiefly for Irish Students*. Dublin & Cork: Educational Co. of Ireland, vii + 179 pp. [Partly historical and partly descriptive.]

321. Holthausen, Ferdinand. 1933. "Der Name des Buchstaben *y*". *Anglia B* 64.255-56.

322. Kretzschmar, William A., Jr. 1985. "English in the Middle Ages: the Struggle for Acceptability". *The English Language Today*, ed. Sidney Greenbaum, 20-29. Oxford: Pergamon Press.

323. Kruisinga, Etsko. 1925. "A Guide to English Studies: The Study of Old and Middle English". *ES* 7.129-36.

324. Kurath, Hans. 1969. "Some Aspects of the History of the English Language".

Linguistics Today, ed. Archibald A. Hill, 71-78. New York & London: Basic Books.

325. Kurban, Nabeel. 1978. *The Evolution of the Written Standard for Late West Saxon, from the Ninth to the Twelfth Centuries*. Indiana diss., 470 pp. [Abstr. in *DA* 39.6734A (1979). Discusses phonology and inflection.]

326. Magoun, Francis Peabody, Jr. 1937. "Colloquial Old and Middle English". *Harvard Studies and Notes in Philology and Literature* 19.167-73.

327. Milroy, James. 1984. "The History of English in the British Isles". *Language in the British Isles*, ed. Peter Trudgill, 5-31. Cambridge & New York: Cambridge Univ. Press.

328. Monteser, Frederick. 1966. "Internal Literary Evidence of Linguistic Maturation of the English Language". *Linguistics* 23.69-80.

329. Partridge, Astley Cooper. 1982. *A Companion to Old and Middle English Studies*. London: André Deutsch; Totowa, NJ: Barnes & Noble, xi + 462 pp. [Attempts 'a synthesis of cultural, political and language elements'.]

   Reviews: Bernard O'Donoghue in *TLS* 26 Nov. 1982, p. 1314; Kevin Crossley-Holland in *Times Educational Supplement* 13 May 1983, p. 50; S.G. Kossick in *UES* 21:1.25 (1983); Richard Abels in *Classical Bulletin* (Univ. of Saint Louis) 60.105 (1984); Carl T. Berkhout in *Speculum* 60.448-49 (1985).

330. Poussa, Patricia. 1982. "The Evolution of Early Standard English: The Creolization Hypothesis". *SAP* 14.69-85. [Concerning the fundamental changes which took place between standard literary OE and Chancery Standard English.]

331. Samuels, Michael Louis. 1965. "The Role of Functional Selection in the History of English". *TPS* 1965, 15-40.

332. ———. 1972. *Linguistic Evolution with Special Reference to English*. (= CSL, 5.) Cambridge: Cambridge Univ. Press, 203 pp.

   Reviews: A.J. Bliss in *N&Q* n.s. 21.182-86 (1974); D.A. Britton in *MAE* 44.95-98 (1974); Gero Bauer in *Anglia* 93.446-50 (1975); Henry M. Hoenigswald in *Language* 51.457-61 (1975); Josef Vachek in *Lingua* 37.81-86 (1975); Veronika Kniezsa in *Acta Linguistica* (Budapest) 26.256-59 (1976).

333. Šimko, Ján. 1963. "The Origin and Development of the Modern English Literary Language". *PP* 6.71-85. [A survey of the development of English from a language predominantly synthetic (as in Old English) to one basically analytical.]

B. Old English

334. Amos, Ashley Crandell. 1980. *Linguistic Means of Determining the Dates of Old English Literary Texts*. (= Medieval Academy Books, 90.) Cambridge, MA: Medieval Academy of America, xiii + 210 pp. [Originally Yale diss. 1976, submitted under her maiden name Ashley Crandell. Concerned with the validity of tests ('metrical and phonological', 'syntactical and grammatical', 'lexical' and 'stylistic') rather than with dating particular texts.]

   Reviews: Matti Rissanen in *Speculum* 57.112-14 (1982); Petra Herzog in *Sprache* 28.106 (1982); Hiroshi Ogawa in *Poetica* 14.99-109 (1983); Celia Sisam in *MAE* 52.138-39 (1983); Claus-Dieter Wetzel in *Anglia* 101.487-96 (1983); Gilda Cilluffo in *Schede Medievali* 4.171-73 (1983); Hans Sauer in *IF* 89.369-71 (1984); M.R. Godden in *RES* n.s. 35.346-47 (1984); Jane Roberts in *YES* 15.268-69 (1985); Thomas Cable in *JEGP* 85.93-95 (1986).

335. Arngart, Olof. 1947/48. "Some Aspects of the Relation between the English and the Danish Element in the Danelaw". *SN* 20.73-87. [Based largely on the consideration of personal names and place-names.]

336. Bahnick, Karen R. 1973. *The Determination of Stages in the Historical Development of the Germanic Languages by Morphological Criteria: An Evaluation*. (= JanL, Ser. Practica, 139.) The Hague & Paris: Mouton, 215 pp.

   Reviews: Anon. in *Sprache* 21.104 (1975); Christopher Wells in *RES* n.s. 26.192-94 (1975).

337. Bately, Janet Margaret. 1970. "King Alfred and the Old English Translation of *Orosius*". *Anglia* 88.433-60. [Considers the authorship of the OE *Orosius* on the basis of its syntax and vocabulary.]

338. ———. 1985. "Linguistic Evidence as a Guide to the Authorship of Old English Verse: a Reappraisal, with Special Reference to *Beowulf*". *Learning and Literature in Anglo-Saxon England: Studies Presented to Peter Clemoes on the Occasion of his Sixty-Fifth Birthday*, ed. Michael Lapidge and Helmut Gneuss, 409-31. Cambridge: Cambridge Univ. Press.

339. Bessinger, Jess Balsor, Jr. 1969. "Computers and Old English: A Conference Report". *CHum* 3.267-68.

340. Bibire, Paul and Alan Strode Campbell Ross. 1981. "The Differences between Lindisfarne and Rushworth Two". *N&Q* n.s. 28.98-116. [On various linguistic differences between the two glosses.]

341. Blockley, Mary Eva. 1984. *Linguistic and Stylistic Differences between Old English Verse and Old English Prose*. Yale diss., 426 pp. [Abstr. in *DA* 46.1283A (1985). Deals with lexical and syntactical features.]

342. Bodden, Mary Catherine. 1987. "Anglo-Saxon Self-Consciousness in Language". *ES* 68.24-39. [Concerns the Anglo-Saxons' technique of translation.]

343. Bremmer, Rolf H., Jr. 1982. "Old English–Old Frisian: the Relationship Reviewed". *Philologia Frisica Anno 1981* (=Utjefte Fryske Akademy, 618), 79-90. Ljouwert: Fryske Akademy.

344. Brook, George Leslie. 1959. "The Relation between the Textual and the Linguistic Study of Old English". *Dickins Festschrift*, 280-91.

345. Cerasano, S.P. 1980. "The Computer in the Meadhall: Standardizing Anglo-Saxon". *ALLCB* 8.111-24. [Intended to facilitate textual and dialectal comparisons.]

346. Cross, Samuel H. 1931. "Notes on King Alfred's North: *Osti, Este*". *Speculum* 6.296-99. [Apropos of Malone [no. 357].]

347. Derolez, René. 1958. "Norm and Practice in Late Old English". *Proceedings of the Eighth International Congress of Linguists*, ed. E. Silvertsen, 415-17. Oslo: Oslo Univ. Press. [On scribal practice.]

348. ———. 1974. "Cross-Channel Language Ties". *ASE* 3.1-14. [On OE dialectal differences.]

349. Eble, Connie C. 1978. "Aelfric and Bilingualism in Anglo-Saxon England". *The Fourth LACUS Forum 1977*, ed. Michael Paradis, 423-31. Columbia, SC: Hornbeam.

350. Faraci, Mary. 1982. "Phenomenology: Good News for Old English Studies". *Lang&S* 15.219-24. [Discusses the debate between the interpretation of *swa* (*The Wanderer* 43) defended by Stanley Greenfield (in *The Interpretation of Old English Poems* [London & Boston: Routledge & Kegan Paul, 1972]) and the one defended by Mitchell [no. 359].]

351. Gneuss, Helmut. 1972. "The Origin of Standard Old English and Æthelwold's School at Winchester". *ASE* 1.63-83.

352. Hansen, Bente Hyldegaard. 1984. "The Historical Implications of the Scandinavian Linguistic Element in English: a Theoretical Evaluation". *NOWELE* 4.53-95.

353. Hofmann, Dietrich. 1955. *Nordisch-englische Lehnbeziehungen der Wikingerzeit*. (= Bibliotheca Arnamagnæana, 14.) Copenhagen: Ejnar Munksgaard, 296 pp. [On the mutual influences of English and Norse prior to 1066.]

354. Kruisinga, Etsko. 1926. "How to Study Old English Syntax". *ES* 8.44-49.

355. Langenfelt, Gösta. 1931/32. "Notes on the Anglo-Saxon Pioneers". *EStn* 66.161-244; 471 (addenda). [I. The Earliest Homesteads on the Continent; II. Native Traditions; III. Anglo-Saxon Runes; IV. Colonists in Britain; V. Communications with the North; VI: The *Widsiþ* folk-names, and finally on some problems in *Beowulf.*]

356. Loyn, H.R. 1980. "The Norman Conquest of the English Language". *Hist. Today* 30.35-39.

357. Malone, Kemp. 1930. "King Alfred's North: A Study in Medieval Geography". *Speculum* 5.139-67. [Cf. Cross [no. 346].]

358. Marino, Matthew. 1979. "Linguistics, Literary Criticism, and Old English". *Mediaevalia* 5.1-14.

359. Mitchell, Bruce. 1975. "Linguistic Facts and the Interpretation of Old English Poetry". *ASE* 4.11-28. [With special reference to *swa* in *The Wanderer* 43 and the pluperfects of *The Wife's Lament* 11 & 15.]

360. Mitchell, John Lawrence and Kellen C. Thornton. 1981. "Computer-Aided Analysis of Old English Manuscripts". *Computing in the Humanities*, ed. Peter C. Patton and Renee A. Holoien, 105-12. Lexington, MA: Lexington Books. [Concerns lexical variants in MSS.]

361. Murphy, Michael. 1968. "Methods in the Study of Old English in the Sixteenth and Seventeenth Centuries". *MS* 30.345-50.

362. Nielsen, Hans Frede. 1975. "Morphological and Phonological Parallels between Old Norse and Old English". *ANF* 90.1-18.

363. ———. 1981. *Old English and the Continental Germanic Languages: a Survey of Morphological and Phonological Interrelations.* (= Innsbrucker Beiträge zur Sprachwissenschaft, 33.) Innsbruck: Institut für Sprachwissenschaft, Univ. Innsbruck, 311 pp. [2nd rev. ed. 1985.]

   Reviews: Rolf H. Bremmer, Jr. in *ES* 63.565-66 (1982); Thomas L. Markey in *Kratylos* 27.133-38 (1982 [1983]).

364. ———. 1986. "On the Origins of Emigrant Languages with Special Reference to the Dialectal Position of Old English Within Germanic". *JEngL* 19.94-105.

365. Page, Raymond Ian. 1959. "Language and Dating in OE Inscriptions". *Anglia* 77.385-406. [Points out the incompleteness of our present knowledge of the OE stone inscriptions, and the inadequacy of linguistic conclusions drawn from them.]

366. ———. 1971. "How Long Did the Scandinavian Language Survive in England? The Epigraphical Evidence". *Whitelock Festschrift*, 165-81.

367. Pilch, Herbert. 1967. "Altenglisch in synchronischer Sicht". *IF* 72.110-15. [Suggests approaches to the synchronic analysis of OE, independently of Indo-European.]

368. Pinsker, Hans (unter Mitarbeit von Udo Fries and Peter Bierbaumer). 1976. *Altenglisches Studienbuch*. (= Studienreihe Englische, 10.) Düsseldorf: A. Bagel; Bern & München: Francke, 247 pp.

    Reviews: Manfred Görlach in *Archiv* 215.156-59 (1978); Raymond Hickey in *Archiv* 221.357-60 (1984).

369. Prudent, R. 1929. *Gotisch-Angelsächsisch*. Darmstadt: Hofmann, 94 pp.

370. Rositzke, Harry August. 1935. *The Speech of Kent before the Norman Conquest*. Harvard diss. (no pagination available). [Abstr. in *Harvard Univ. Summaries of Theses* 1935, 281-82.]

371. Wrenn, Charles Leslie. 1933. "'Standard' Old English". *TPS* 1933, 65-88. [Repr. in *Wrenn Word and Symbol*, 57-77.]

C. Middle English

372. Benson, Robert G. 1980. *Medieval Body Language: A Study of the Use of Gesture in Chaucer's Poetry*. (= Anglistica, 21.) Copenhagen: Rosenkilde and Bagger, 170 pp. [Originally Univ. of North Carolina at Chapel Hill diss., 1974.]

    Reviews: Edmund Reiss in *South Atlantic Review* (Knoxville, TN) 46:1.100-01 (1981); R.T. Davis in *N&Q* n.s. 29.157-58 (1982); Werner Habicht in *Anglia* 100.500-01 (1982); Helen S. Houghton in *MAE* 51.261-62 (1982); Alasdair A. MacDonald in *ES* 63.474-75 (1982); Barry Windeatt in *SAC* 4.144-46 (1982).

373. Berndt, Rolf. 1965. "The Linguistic Situation in England from the Norman Conquest to the Loss of Normandy (1066-1204)". *PP* 8.145-63. [Repr. in *Lass EHL*, 369-71.]

374. ———. 1972. "The Period of the Final Decline of French in Medieval England (Fourteenth and Early Fifteenth Centuries)". *ZAA* 20.341-69.

375. ———. 1976. "French and English in Thirteenth-Century England: An Investigation into the Linguistic Situation after the Loss of the Duchy of Normandy and Other Continental Dominions". *Aspekte der anglistischen Forschungen*

in der DDR: Martin Lehnert zum 65. Geburtstag, 129-50. Berlin: Akademie-Verlag.

376. Blake, Norman Francis. 1970. "The Fifteenth Century Reconsidered". *NM* 71.146-57. [Considers the linguistic character of the 15th century under two heads: the rapid pace of change and the development of a standard.]

377. ———. 1981. *Non-Standard Language in English Literature.* (The Language Library.) London: André Deutsch; Boulder, CO: Westview Press, 217 pp. [A historical survey of the way in which non-standard language has been used in English literature from Chaucer to the present day.]

    Review: William Nelson Francis in *Language* 59.924-25 (1983).

378. Bolton, Whitney French. 1986. "Middle English in the Law Reports and Records of 11-13 Richard II". *ELN* 24.1-8.

379. Bornstein, Diane. 1977. "French Influence on Fifteenth-Century English Porse as Exemplified by the Translation of Christine de Pisan's *Livre du corps de policie*". *MS* 39.369-86. [Discusses vocabulary, syntax, and style.]

380. Bromwich, John. 1966. "Bilingualism in Fourteenth-Century England and Twentieth-Century South Africa". *ESA* 9.184-91.

381. Bühler, Curt Ferdinand. 1960. *William Caxton and His Critics: A Critical Reappraisal of Caxton's Contributions to the Enrichment of the English Language.* Syracuse, NY: Syracuse Univ. Press, viii + 30 pp. [With Caxton's Prologue to *Eneydos* in facsimile, and rendered into Present-day English.]

382. Cable, Thomas. 1984. "The Rise of Written Standard English". *The Emergence of National Languages,* ed. Aldo Scaglione (= Speculum Artium, 11), 75-94. Ravenna: Longo.

383. Clark, Cecily. 1976. "People and Languages in Post-Conquest Canterbury". *Journal of Medieval History* (Amsterdam) 2.1-33.

384. Cottle, Basil. 1969. *The Triumph of English 1350-1400.* London: Blandford; New York: Barnes and Noble, 318 pp. [Some general observations on the period.]

385. Covella, Francis D. 1976. "Grammatical Evidence of Multiple Authorship in *Piers Plowman*". *Lang&S* 9.3-16. [A comparison of the grammatical characteristics of the second half-lines of the A-, B-, and C-texts.]

386. Davis, Norman. 1974. "Chaucer and Fourteenth-Century English". *Geoffrey Chaucer* (Writers and their Background), ed. Derek Brewer, 53-84. London: G. Bell & Sons; Athens, OH: Ohio Univ. Press.

387. ———. 1977. "Chaucer and the English Language". *Geoffrey Chaucer: Conferenze organizzate dall'Accademia Nazionale dei Lincei in collaborazione con la British Academy. Accademia Nazionale dei Lincei, Anno CCCLXXIV — 1977, Quaderno No. 234. Problemi Attuali di Scienza e di Cultura* (Roma), 23-34.

388. ———. 1985. "Notes on Grammar and Spelling in the Fifteenth Century". *The Oxford Book of Late Medieval Verse and Prose*, ed. Douglas Gray, 493-508. Oxford: Clarendon Press.

389. Derolez, René. 1958. "Periodisering en Continuïteit, of: 'When Did Middle English Begin?' (K. Malone)". *Album Edgard Blancquaert: De gehuldigde aangeboden ter gelegenheid van zijn emeritaat door kollega's, vakgenoten en oud-leerlingen*, 77-84. Tongeren: George Michiels. [Cf. Malone [no. 412].]

390. ———. 1981. "Authorship and Statistics: The Case of the *Pearl*-Poet and the *Gawain*-Poet". *Christophersen Festschrift*, 41-51. [Apropos of Kjellmer [no. 407].]

391. Dickins, Bruce and Richard Middlewood Wilson. 1951. "Characteristics of Early Middle English". *Early Middle English Texts*, ed. Bruce Dickins and R.M. Wilson, 136-50. London: Bowes and Bowes; New York: Norton.

392. Domingue, Nicole Z. 1977. "Middle English: Another Creole?". *Journal of Creole Studies* (Kepellen, Belgium) 1.89-100.

393. Dürmüller, Urs. 1984. "Sociolinguistics and the Study of Medieval English". *Crépin LSSME*/10, 5-22. [Based on Chaucer's *Pardoner's Tale*.]

394. Fisher, John Hurt. 1977. "Chancery and the Emergence of Standard Written English in the Fifteenth Century". *Speculum* 52.870-99.

395. ———. 1979. "Chancery Standard and Modern Written English". *JSA* 6.136-44.

396. ———. 1984. "Caxton and Chancery English". *Fifteenth-Century Studies*, 161-85.

397. Fisiak, Jacek. 1977. "Sociolinguistics and Middle English: Some Socially Motivated Changes in the History of English". *KN* 24.247-59. [Concentrates on two sociolinguistic phenomena in ME: 1. multilingualism as a source of numerous changes in the period; 2. changes in the system of address — the use of the second person pronoun.]

398. Flasdieck, Hermann Martin. 1923. "Studien zur me. Grammatik, I-V". *Anglia B* 34.20-32; 116-28; 314-19. [I & II: "Gab es eine mkent. Diphtongierung $g\bar{o}$- > guo-, $b\bar{o}$- > buo-, $h\bar{e}$- > hie-, $cl\bar{e}$- > $clie$-?"; III: "Zur Assibilierungsfrage"; IV: "Über me. *agān* und Verwandtes"; V: "Gab es einen mundartlichen Lautwandel -$\bar{o}d$ > -$\bar{u}d$ im Me?".]

399. ———. 1923. "Der sprachgeschichtliche Wert der mittelenglischen Überlieferung". *GRM* 11.361-72.

400. Hart, Paxton. 1982. "Chaucer's Regard for English". *Interpretations: Studies in Language and Literature* (Memphis State Univ., TN) 14.1-10. [Argues that there is no evidence that Chaucer himself is embarrassed to use English as his medium of composition.]

401. Hinckley, Henry B. 1935. "The Riddle of the *Ormulum*". *PQ* 14.193-216. [Concerned to date the work on linguistic and paleographic criteria.]

402. Horner, Patrick J. 1977. "The Use and Knowledge of Spoken French in Early Fifteenth-Century England". *N&Q* n.s. 24.488.

403. Hudson, Anne. 1966. "Tradition and Innovation in Some Middle English Manuscripts". *RES* n.s. 17.359-72. [A linguistic analysis of variants in the MSS of Robert of Gloucester's *Chronicle*.]

404. Hughes, Susan Eileen Streett. 1978. *English in the Letter-Books and Plea and Memoranda Rolls of the Corporation of London, 1377-1422, in Comparison with Contemporaneous Chancery English: Their Possible Roles in the Evolution of Chancery Standard and Modern English.* Tennessee diss., 221 pp. [Abstr. in *DA* 39.6739-40A (1979).]

405. ———. 1980. "Guildhall and Chancery English, 1377-1422". *Guildhall Studies in London History* 4.53-62.

406. Hulbert, James Root. 1946. "A Thirteenth-Century English Literary Standard". *JEGP* 45.411-14. [Discusses the conclusions reached by Tolkien [no. 435].]

407. Kjellmer, Göran. 1975. *Did the "Pearl Poet" Write 'Peral'?* (= GothSE, 30.) Göteborg: Acta Universitatis Gothoburgensis, 105 pp. [Aims to establish the authorship of the Cotton Nero poems and *St. Erkenwald* according to seven linguistic categories.]

Reviews: Jan Svartvik in *MSpr* 70.63-64 (1976); Rima Handley in *N&Q* n.s. 23.480 (1976); P.M. Kean in *YES* 7.198-99 (1977); Gillis Kristensson in *SL* 34.79-80 (1980).

408. Kuhn, Sherman McAllister. 1974. "The Language of Some Fifteenth-Century Chaucerians: A Study of Manuscript Variants in the *Canterbury Tales*". *SMC* 4.472-82. [Shows different types of vocabulary and as many different textual problems as possible.]

409. Langenfelt, Gösta. 1933. *Select Studies in Colloquial English of the Late Middle Ages.* Lund: Håkan Ohlsson, xxv + 129 pp. [A collection of essays on colloquial English in ME and early ModE.]

Reviews: M. Day in *RES* 10.489-91 (1934); H. Koziol in *EStn* 69.243-47 (1934/ 35); W. van der Gaaf in *ES* 17.96-100 (1935).

410. Machan, Tim William. 1984. *Chaucer as Philologist: The 'Boece'*. Univ. of Wisconsin-Madison diss., 254 pp. [Abstr. in *DA* 45.1393A (1984).]

411. ———. 1985. *Techniques of Translation: Chaucer's 'Boece'*. Norman, OK: Pilgrim Books, xii + 163 pp. [Aims to investigate the 'mechanics of Chaucer's translation technique', discussing his lexicon and syntax.]

    Review: N.R. Havely in *N&Q* n.s. 34.252-53 (1987).

412. Malone, Kemp. 1930. "When Did Middle English Begin?". *Curme Volume of Linguistic Studies*, ed. James T. Hatfield, et al. (= LM, 7), 110-17. Philadelphia: Linguistic Society of America. [Examines the levelling of inflectional endings in the four main OE poetic codices. Cf. Derolez [no. 389].]

413. Markus, Manfred. 1983. "Metasprachliche Elemente im Spätmittelenglischen und Frühneuenglischen". *Philologie und Sprachwissenschaft*, 159-74.

414. McColly, William and Dennis Weier. 1983. "Literary Attribution and Likelihood-Ratio Tests: The Case of the Middle English *Pearl*-Poems". *CHum* 17.65-75.

415. Oakden, James Parker. 1930. *Alliterative Poetry in Middle English: Dialectal and Metrical Survey*. (= Pubs. of the Univ. of Manchester, 205: English Ser., 18.) Manchester: Manchester Univ. Press, xii + 273 pp. [Repr., together with no. 416, in one volume, Hamden, CT: Archon Books, 1968.]

    Reviews: Anon. in *TLS*, Sept. 17, 1931, p. 703; A. Brandl in *Archiv* 159.293-96 (1931); K. Brunner in *Anglia B* 42.334-41 (1931); J.R. Hulbert in *MP* 28.485-86 (1931); W. van der Gaaf in *ES* 13.142-45 (1931); E.E. Ericson in *SP* 29.123-29 (1932); K. Luick in *LGRP* 53.233-38 (1932); A.H. Smith in *MLR* 27.72-75 (1932); F. Wild in *EStn* 66.406-11 (1932); C.T. Onions in *RES* 9.89-94 (1933); C.L. W[renn] in *Oxford Magazine*, Jan. 26, 1933, p. 350.

416. ———, with the assistance from Elizabeth R. Innes. 1935. *Alliterative Poetry in Middle English: A Survey of the Traditions*. (= Pubs. of the Univ. of Manchester, 236: English Ser., 22.) Manchester: Manchester Univ. Press, x + 403 pp. [Treats of its vocabulary, phraseology, and style, and gives some account of the Early ME alliterative poetry and prose; also, of the poems of the alliterative revival.]

    Reviews: Anon. in *TLS*, Jan. 25, 1936, p. 67; K. Brunner in *Anglia B* 47.231-34 (1936); J.R. Hulbert in *MP* 34.198-200 (1936); R. Kaiser in *Archiv* 170.113-16 (1936); E.C. Knowlton in *JEGP* 36.120-23 (1937); H.L. Savage in *MLN* 52.430-33 (1937); G.V. Smithers in *RES* 13.217-25 (1937).

417. Orr, John. 1948. *The Impact of French upon English*. (The Taylorian Lecture, 1948.) Oxford: Clarendon Press, 28 pp. [Deals more particularly with the influence of French on ME syntax.]

   Reviews: George Kane in *MLR* 44.95 (1949); A. McIntosh in *French Studies* (Oxford) 3.90-91 (1949); J. Jud in *Vox Romanica* (Bern) 11.353 (1950).

418. Price, Hereward T. 1947. *Foreign Influences on Middle English*. (= Univ. of Michigan Contributions in Modern Philology, 10.) Ann Arbor, MI: Univ. of Michigan Press, 45 pp. [Studies the remarkable parallellism between the use of prepositions and adverbs in ME on the one hand and OF, ON, and Medieval Latin on the other.]

   Reviews: A.W. Reed in *MLR* 43.248 (1948); Gardiner Stillwell in *JEGP* 47.190-91 (1948); A. Macdonald in *RES* 25.89 (1949).

419. Richardson, Malcolm, II. 1978. *The Influence of Henry V on the Development of Chancery English*. Univ. of Tennessee diss., 252 pp. [Abstr. in *DA* 39.3604A (1978). The reign of Henry V: 1413-22.]

420. ———. 1980. "Henry V, the English Chancery, and Chancery English". *Speculum* 55.726-50. [Cf. Fisher [no. 394].]

421. Richter, Michael. 1979. *Sprache und Gesellschaft im Mittelalter: Untersuchungen zur mündlichen Kommunikation in England von der Mitte des 11. bis zum Beginn des 14. Jahrhunderts*. (= Monographien zur Geschichte des Mittelalters, 18.) Stuttgart: Hiersemann, viii + 235 pp.

   Reviews: Ian Short in *Speculum* 56.650-52 (1981); A.J. Holden in *CCM* 25.157-60 (1982); H. Käsmann in *Anglia* 100.455-59 (1982); H. Goebl in *ZRP* 99.184-87 (1983); M. Görlach in *Language Problems and Language Planning* (Austin, TX.) 7:1.99-101 (1983).

422. ———. 1985. "Towards a Methodology of Historical Sociolinguistics". *FLH* 4.41-61. [An investigation of the languages spoken in England in the second half of the 12th century.]

423. Riehle, Wolfgang. 1977. "The Problem of Walter Hilton's Possible Authorship of *The Cloud of Unknowing* and its Related Tracts". *NM* 78.31-45. [An investigation of the vocabulary and style of both Hilton and the *Cloud*.]

424. Rothwell, William. 1983. "Language and Government in Medieval England". *Zeitschrift für französische Sprache und Literatur* (Wiesbaden) 93. 258-70.

425. Salmon, Vivian. 1975. "The Representation of Colloquial Speech in *The Canterbury Tales*". *Enkvist Festschrift*, 263-77.

426. Sandved, Arthur Olav. 1981. "The Rise of Standard English". *Papers from the First Nordic Conference for English Studies, Oslo, 17-19 September, 1980*, ed. Stig Johansson and Bjørn Tysdahl, 398-404. Oslo: Institute of English Studies, Univ. of Oslo, vii + 447 pp.

427. ———. 1981. "Prolegomena to a Renewed Study of the Rise of Standard English". *McIntosh Festschrift* (E), 31-42.

428. Shores, David Lee. 1970. "The Peterborough Chronicle: Continuity and Change in the English Language". *SAB* 35:4.19-29.

429. Smith, Jeremy John. 1983. "Linguistic Features of Some Fifteenth-Century Middle English Manuscripts". *Manuscripts and Readers in Fifteenth-Century England: The Literary Implications of Manuscript Study*, ed. Derek Pearsall, 104-12. Cambridge: D.S. Brewer; Totowa, NJ: Biblio. [Based on Chaucer's *Canterbury Tales* and Gower's *Confessio Amantis*.]

430. Smithers, Geoffrey Victor. 1966. "Early Middle English". *Early Middle English Verse and Prose* (with a glossary by Norman Davis), ed. Jack Arthur Walter Bennett and G.V. Smithers, xviii-lviii. Oxford: Clarendon Press.

431. Soliño, José S. Gómez. 1985. "William Caxton y la estandarización de la lengua inglesa en el siglo XV". *RCEI* 10.95-118. [On Caxton's role in the standardization of the English language.]

432. ———. 1985. "La génesis del inglés estándar moderno: historia y estado actual de la cuestión". *RCEI* 11.81-106.

433. Suggett, Helen. 1946. "The Use of French in England in the Later Middle Ages". *TRHS*, 4th ser., 28.61-83. [The Alexander Prize Essay, read 16 June 1945.]

434. Taylor, John. 1956. "Notes on the Rise of Written English in the Late Middle Ages". *Proceedings of the Leeds Philosophical and Literary Society*, Literary and Historical Section 8:2.128-36.

435. Tolkien, John Ronald Reuel. 1929. "*Ancrene Wisse* and *Hali Meiðhad*". *E&S* 14.104-26. [Points out the close relationship in language as well as spelling, almost amounting to identity, between the Corpus MS of the *Ancrene Riwle* and the Bodley MS of the *Katherine Group*. Cf. Hulbert [no. 406].]

436. ———. 1934. "Chaucer as a Philologist: *The Reeve's Tale*". *TPS* 1934, 1-70. [Cf. Blake [no. 3745].]

437. Vachek, Josef. 1972. "Middle and Modern English". *Current Trends in Linguis-*

tics IX: Linguistics in Western Europe, ed. Thomas A. Sebeok, 1407-60. The Hague: Mouton.

438. Von Lindheim, Bogislav. 1937. "Sprachliche Studien zu Texten des MS. Cotton Galba E IX". *Anglia* 61.65-71. [Determines by means of spellings certain features of the pronunciation of the *scribe* of the versions of *Ywain and Gawain* and *The Seven Sages of Rome* in this MS.]

439. Whitehall, Harold. 1939. "A Most Ancient Petition (Pro. Sc. 8, 192/95, 80)". *PQ* 18.306-10. [Calls attention to the importance of the whole body of Ancient Petitions in the Public Record Office as sources of linguistic information.]

440. Wilson, Richard Middlewood. 1943. "English and French in England 1100-1300". *History* n.s. 28.37-60.

441. Woodbine, G.E. 1943. "The Language of English Law". *Speculum* 18.395-436. [On the French and English languages in England in the Middle Ages.]

442. Wyld, Henry Cecil. 1940. "Aspects of Style and Idiom in Fifteenth-Century English". *E&S* 26.30-44. [Discusses vocabulary, various features of style (such as the synonym habit and word-order), double negatives, group possessives, and various idiomatic phrases and usages.]

443. Zachrisson, R.E. 1925. "Det engelska rikssprakets uppkomst och utveckling". *NTF* n.s. 1.396-408. [A survey of the origin and development of Standard English.]

VI. LANGUAGE OF INDIVIDUAL AUTHORS OR WORKS

A. Old English

444. Anderson, George Kumler. 1941. "Notes on the Language of Ælfric's English *Pastoral Letters* in Corpus Christi College 190 and Bodleian Junius 121". *JEGP* 40.5-13.

445. Ball, Christopher J.E. 1970. "The Language of the Vespasian Psalter Gloss: Two Caveats". *RES* n.s. 21.462-65. [Apropos of Alistair Campbell's account of the language of the gloss in *The Vespasian Psalter* (with a contribution on the gloss by Alistair Campbell), ed. David H. Wright. Copenhagen: Rosenkilde and Bagger, 1967.]

446. Britton, Geoffrey C. and Alan Strode Campbell Ross. 1960. "Aldrediana X: Manifesta". *Anglia* 78.129-68. [Aldred's *Lindisfarne* gloss: orthography, phonology, and morphology.]

447. Bromwich, John. 1950. "Who Was the Translator of the Prose Portion of the Paris Psalter?". *Chadwick Festschrift*, 289-303. [Examines the language.]

448. Cameron, Angus, Ashley Crandell Amos, and Gregory Waite, with the assistance of Sharon Butler and Antonette diPaolo Healey. 1981. "A Reconsideration of the Language of *Beowulf*". *Dating Beowulf*, 33-75.

449. Closs, Olwen Eleanor Elizabeth. 1964. *A Grammar of Alfred's 'Orosius'*. Univ. of California, Berkeley, diss., 268 pp. [Abstr. in *DA* 25.1899-1900 (1964) and *Linguistics* 14.110-12 (1965).]

450. Gneuss, Helmut. 1968. *Hymnar und Hymnen im englischen Mittelalter: Studien zur Überlieferung, Glossierung und Übersetzung lateinischer Hymnen in England. Mit einer Textausgabe der lateinisch-altenglischen Expositio hymnorum.* (= Buchreihe der *Anglia*, 12.) Tübingen: Niemeyer, xiv + 447 pp. [München Habilitationsschrift. Contains a chapter on 'The Language of the OE Hymn Glosses' (pp. 157-93).]

Reviews: Friedrich Stephan in *Mittellateinisches Jahrbuch* (Stuttgart) 5.283-84 (1968); Fred C. Robinson in *BGDSL*(T) 91.397-400 (1969); E.G. Stanley in

Archiv 206.136-38 (1969/70); A. Brounts in *Scriptorium* 24.465-66 (1970); S. Rossi in *SMed* 12.540-41 (1971); Celia Sisam in *Anglia* 89.523-26 (1971); R.H. Robbins in *Speculum* 47.759-61 (1972).

451. Horgan, Dorothy M. 1981. "The Lexical and Syntactic Variants Shared by Two of the Later Manuscripts of King Alfred's Translation of Gregory's *Cura Pastoralis*". *ASE* 9.213-21.

452. Jost, Karl. 1950. *Wulfstanstudien*. (= SAA, 23.) Bern: Francke, 271 pp. [Discusses Wulfstan's stylistic peculiarities in vocabulary and syntax.]

    Reviews: Angus McIntosh in *ES* 32.163-68 (1951); Claes Schaar in *SL* 5.50-52 (1951); B.J. Timmer in *MLR* 47.568-69 (1952); Dorothy Bethurum in *MLN* 68.125-29 (1953).

453. Negro, Pier Giorgio. 1980. "Nota sulla *Durham Admonition*". *Rendiconti dell'Istituto Lombardo di Scienze e Lettere, Classe di lettere e scienze morali e storiche* (Milano) 114.181-96. [Linguistic analysis.]

454. Sprockel, Cornelis. 1965. *The Language of the Parker Chronicle. I: Phonology and Accidence*. The Hague: Martinus Nijhoff, xxviii + 274 pp. [Amsterdam diss.]

    Reviews: H.J. de Vriend in *LT* 1965, 715-17 (1965); Joyce Bazire in *JEGP* 65.575-78 (1966); A. Campbell in *Anglia* 84.199-200 (1966); C.L. Wrenn in *RES* n.s. 17.423-25 (1966); G. Storms in *Neophil* 51.423-25 (1967); R.M. Wilson in *MLR* 62.305-06 (1967); Martin Lehnert in *ZAA* 16.293-94 (1968); Paule Mertens-Fonck in *ES* 51.442-44 (1970).

455. ———. 1973. *The Language of the Parker Chronicle. II: Word-Formation and Syntax*. The Hague: Martinus Nijhoff, xiv + 284 pp.

    Reviews: Bruce Mitchell in *RES* n.s. 25.452-54 (1974); Martin Lehnert in *ZAA* 23.164-66 (1975); Roberto Gusmani in *SGerm* 44.221 (1978).

456. Varnas, Lazaros Anastasios. 1965. *The Language of the Parker Chronicle*. Pennsylvania diss., 151 pp. [Abstr. in *DA* 26.3322 (1965). Deals with the phonology and morphology of the chronicle.]

B. Middle English

457. Bennett, Jacob. 1960. *A Linguistic Study of 'The Castle of Perseverance'*. Boston diss., 189 pp. [Abstr. in *DA* 21.872 (1960/61). Discusses phonological, morphological, and lexical features.]

458. ———. 1973. "The Language and the Home of the *Ludus Coventriae*". *Orbis* 22.43-63. [Analyses the phonological and morphological characteristics of the work and considers certain orthographic idiosyncracies as well.]

459. Blake, Norman Francis. 1965. "English Versions of *Reynard the Fox* in the Fifteenth and Sixteenth Centuries". *SP* 62.63-77. [Reviews the text and language of the early versions of the work.]

460. ———. 1966. "Caxton's Language". *NM* 67.122-32. [Explores Caxton's personal vocabulary.]

461. ———. 1969. *Caxton and His World*. (The Language Library.) London: André Deutsch, 256 pp. [Chapter 9 ('Caxton and the English Language', pp. 171-93) investigates Caxton's syntax, vocabulary and orthography.]

Reviews: Anon. in *Papers of the Bibliographical Society of America* (Univ. of Texas, Austin) 64.261 (1970).

462. Bøgholm, Niels. 1944. *The Layamon Texts: A Linguistic Investigation*. (= Travaux du Cercle Linguistique de Copenhague, 3.) Copenhagen: Einar Munksgaard, 85 pp. [Analyses and records the linguistic difference between MSS A and B under the heads of Vocabulary, Scandinavian Loan-words, Sounds and Orthography, and Grammar.]

Reviews: H. Penzl in *JEGP* 45.451-54 (1946); A.A. Prins in *Museum* 52.258 (1947); F. Mossé in *BSL* 44.122 (1947/48); R.W. Ackerman in *AJP* 69.460-62 (1948); E. Buyssens in *RBPH* 27.1112 (1949); H.C. Matthes in *Anglia* 71.480 (1953).

463. Brunner, Karl. 1940. "Die Sprache der Handschrift Junius 24". *Anglia B* 51.207-13. [On the 12th-century MS which contains the legend of *St. Chad*.]

464. Burchfield, Robert William. 1956. "The Language and Orthography of the *Ormulum* MS". *TPS* 1956, 56-87.

465. Burnley, (John) David. 1983. *A Guide to Chaucer's Language*. London: Macmillan, xvi + 264 pp. [Covers 'Chaucer's Grammar', 'Time and Tense', 'Negation', 'Textual Coherence'; 'Linguistic Diversity', 'Chaucer's Vocabulary', 'Register and Propriety', 'Levels of Style', and 'The Architecture of Chaucer's Language'.]

Reviews: Jeffrey Coffey in *PIL* 18.479-84 (1985); André Crépin in *EA* 38.110 (1985); Norman Davis in *RES* n.s. 36.554-55 (1985); M.L. Samuels in *SAC* 7.172-75 (1985); R.A. Waldron in *ES* 66.465-66 (1985); Manfred Markus in *Anglia* 104.489-93 (1986); Derek Pearsall in *MLR* 82.440-41 (1987); G.C. Britton in *N&Q* n.s. 34.257-58 (1987).

466. Cawley, Arthur Clare. 1938. *A Study of the Language of the Various Texts of Trevisa's Translation of Higden's 'Polychronicon'*. Univ. College London M.A. diss., 260 pp. [For a portion of this diss., see Cawley [no. 571].]

   Review: H.H. Meier in *ES* 34.291-92 (1953).

467. Colledge, Edmund and Cyril Smetana. 1972. "Capgrave's *Life of St. Norbert*: Diction, Dialect and Spelling". *MS* 34.422-34.

468. Collins, Janet Duthie. 1972. *The Paston Letters: A New Approach to Diachrnoic Linguistic Change*. Saint Louis Univ. diss., 102 pp. [Abstr. in *DA* 34.5942A (1974). Mainly concerned with syntactic and phonological features.]

469. Craigie, William Alexander. 1939 [1940]. "The Language of the *Kingis Quair*". *E&S* 25.22-38.

470. Davis, Norman. 1949. "The Text of Margaret Paston's Letters". *MAE* 18.12-28. [Contains linguistic notes on phonology and spelling.]

471. ———. 1955. *The Language of the Pastons*. (Sir Israel Gollancz Memorial Lecture 1954.) London: Oxford Univ. Press, 26 pp. [Repr. from *PBA* 40.119-44 (1954).]

   Reviews: Simeon Potter in *MAE* 25.125-26 (1956); R.M. Wilson in *MLR* 51.306 (1956).

472. ———. 1952. "A Paston Hand". *RES* n.s. 3.209-21. [On a number of features of spelling and language of some of the letters standing in the name of Margaret Paston.]

473. ———. 1953. "The Letters of William Paston". *Neophil* 37.36-41. [Contains a discussion of the characteristic features of the language of the letters, such as spellings, sounds, forms, and syntax.]

474. ———. 1969. "Two Unprinted Dialogues in Late Middle English, and Their Language". *RLV* 35.461-72. [Observations mainly on the language of the texts.]

475. ———. 1969. "The Epistolary Usages of William Worcester". *Garmonsway Festschrift*, 249-74. [A detailed survey of opening and closing formulas, personal characteristics, syntactical, morphological, and orthographical forms.]

476. ———. 1981. "Language in Letters from Sir John Fastolf's Household". *Bennett Festschrift*, 329-46. [Chiefly on their spelling habits.]

477. ———. 1983. "The Language of Two Brothers in the Fifteenth Century". *Dob-*

son *Festschrift*, 23-28. [Chiefly concerned with the spelling of two men of the Paston family.]

478. Ekwall, Eilert. 1949. "An Early London Text". *SMSpr* 17.39-46. [Examines the language of *The Prisoner's Prayer*, a 13th century poem.]

479. Elliott, Ralph Warren Victor. 1974. *Chaucer's English*. (The Language Library.) London: André Deutsch, 447 pp.

    Reviews: Cecily Clark in *MAE* 45.336-38 (1976); Akio Oizumi in *Poetica* 5.74-81 (1976); K.C. Phillipps in *ES* 57.258-60 (1976).

480. Francovich Onesti, Nicoletta. 1983. *La lingua delle ultime sezioni della Cronaca di Peterborough*. Firenze: All'Insegna del Giglio (Univ. degli Studi di Firenze, Istituto di lingue e lett. germ., sl. e ugrofinniche), 192 pp.

    Review: Cinzia Leone in *Schede Medievali* 6/7.229-30 (1984).

481. Fries, Udo. 1985. *Einführung in die Sprache Chaucers: Phonologie, Metrik und Morphologie*. (= AA, 20.) Tübingen: Max Niemeyer, xii + 111 pp.

    Reviews: J.D. Burnley in *Speculum* 62.187-89 (1987); Lilo Moessner in *Anglia* 105.204-06 (1987); G. Bourcier in *EA* 40.196-97 (1987); E.G. Stanley in *MAE* 56.153 (1987).

482. Görlach, Manfred. 1978. "Chaucer's English: What Remains to Be Done". *AAA* 4.61-79. [Argues that virtually all aspects of Chaucer's English need further work.]

483. Irvine, Annie Sowell. 1929. *Studies in the Language of John Wycliffe*. Univ. of Texas diss., 734 pp.

484. Jack, George Barr. 1979. "Archaizing in the Nero Version of *Ancrene Wisse*". *NM* 80.325-26. [Provides further evidence to support Ladd [no. 490].]

485. Kellog, Allen B. 1944. *The Language of the Alliterative 'Siege of Jerusalem'*. Chicago diss., 64 pp.

486. Kerkhof, Jelle. 1966. *Studies in the Language of Geoffrey Chaucer*. (= Leidse Germanistische en Anglistische Reeks van de Rijksuniversiteit te Leiden, 5.) Leiden: Universitaire Pers Leiden, viii + 251 pp. [Leiden diss.]

    Reviews: Norman Davis in *RES* n.s. 19.187-90 (1968); N.F. Blake in *Neophil* 53.336-37 (1969); H.H. Meier in *LT* 1969, 617-18 (1969); K.C. Phillipps in *ES* 51.153-57 (1970).

487. ———. 1982. *Studies in the Language of Geoffrey Chaucer*. Second, Rev. and

Enl. ed. (= Leidse Germanistische en Anglistische Reeks van de Rijksuniversiteit te Leiden, 5.) Leiden: E.J. Brill/Leiden Univ. Press, xii + 503 pp.

Reviews: F.N.M. Diekstra in ES 65.564-67 (1984); Manfred Görlach in AAA 10.279-80 (1985).

488. Kjerrström, Bengt. 1946. *Studies in the Language of the London Chronicles: Vocabulary, Phonology, Notes on Accidence*. Uppsala: Almqvist & Wiksell, 327 pp. [Uppsala diss. Mainly concerned with the text usually referred to as *Gregory's Chronicle* (c1475).]

489. Kuhn, Sherman McAllister. 1968. "The Preface to a Fifteenth-Century Concordance". *Speculum* 43.258-73. [Prints 'The preface to a fifteenth-century concordance' to the Wycliffite New Testament in B.M. MS Royal 17.B. and discusses its language (dialect and vocabulary).]

490. Ladd, Charles Anthony. 1961. "A Note on the Language of the *Ancrene Riwle*". *N&Q* n.s. 8.288-90. [Observes that archaic forms in the Nero MS are in fact innovations by the scribe. See also Jack [no. 484].]

491. Lee, Berta Grattan. 1974. *Linguistic Evidence for the Priority of the French Text of the 'Ancrene Wisse'*. Based on the Corpus Christi College Cambridge 402 and the British Museum Cotton Vitellius F VII Versions of the Ancrene Wisse. (= JanL, Ser. Practica, 242.) The Hague: Mouton, 90 pp. [Originally Nevada diss. 1970; Abstr. in *DA* 31.3509A (1971). Examines vocabulary, proper names, negation, morphology, and word order.]

Review: H. Peter Schwake in *ZRP* 91.664-66 (1975).

492. Lindberg, Conrad. 1984. "The Language of the Wyclif Bible". *MSC Aachen 1983*, 103-10. [A study of the vocabulary.]

493. Logan, H.M. 1973. *The Dialect of the 'Life of Saint Katherine': A Linguistic Study of the Phonology and Inflections*. (= JanL, Ser. Practica, 130.) The Hague: Mouton, 259 pp. [A rev. version of his Pennsylvania diss. 1966.]

Reviews: H.L.C. Tristram in *Linguistics* 201.78-83 (1978); Bernhard Diensberg in *Anglia* 98.125-30 (1980).

494. Magoun, Francis Peabody, Jr. 1937. "Kleine Beiträge zur *Sir Gawain*". *Anglia* 61.129-35. [Some notes on the punctuation, orthography, and vocabulary of the poem.]

495. Masui, Michio. 1964. *The Structure of Chaucer's Rime Words: An Exploration into the Poetic Language of Chaucer*. Tokyo: Kenkyusha, xxii + 371 pp. [Mainly concerned with 'The Syntactic Structure of Chaucer's Rime Words'.]

Reviews: Guy Bourquin in *EA* 18.301-02 (1965); Tauno F. Mustanoja in *NM* 66.262-63 (1965); Margaret Schlauch in *KN* 12.102-03 (1965); E.G. Stanley in *N&Q* n.s. 12.389-90 (1965); Thomas A. Kirby in *ES* 51.450-51 (1970).

496. McIntosh, Angus. 1965. "Some Linguistic Reflections of a Wycliffite". *Magoun Festschrift*, 290-93. [In BM MS Royal 17.B.i (15th century).]

497. ———. 1976. "The Language of the Extant Versions of *Havelok the Dane*". *MAE* 45.36-49.

498. Mitchell, John Lawrence. 1974. "The Language of the *Peterborough Chronicle*". *Computers in the Humanities*, ed. J.L. Mitchell, 132-45. Minneapolis: Univ. of Minnesota Press.

499. Mohr, Eugene Vincent. 1964. *Morphology and Syntax of AB, a Dialect of Early Middle English*. Univ. of California, Berkeley, diss., 184 pp. [Abstr. in *DA* 25.4136 (1965) and *Linguistics* 18.94-95 (1965).]

500. Munderloh, Heinrich. 1935. *Die Sprache der Lincoln Diocese Documents (1450-1544): Ein Beitrag zur Dialektkunde von Lincolnshire*. Oldenburg: Littmann, vi + 69 pp. [Münster diss.]

501. Nakashima, Kunio, 1981. *Studies in the Language of Sir Thomas Malory*. Tokyo: Nan'un-do, xi + 411 pp. [Devoted to the syntax of Malory's *Morte Darthur*.]

Review: N.F. Blake in *ES* 63.558 (1982).

502. Peters, Robert Anthony. 1980. *Chaucer's Language*. (= *JEngL*, Occasional Monographs, 1.) Bellingham, WA: *Journal of English Linguistics*, Western Washington Univ., vii + 125 pp.

Review: Walter S. Phelan in *SAC* 4.178-81 (1982).

503. Pheifer, Joseph D., ed. 1974. *Old English Glosses in the Épinar-Erfurt Glossary*. Oxford: Clarendon Press, xci + 166 pp. [The Introduction contains extensive discussion on language and orthography.]

Reviews: J.B. Wynn in *RES* n.s. 26.458-60 (1975); André Crépin in *EA* 29.79 (1976); Günter Kotzor in *BGDSL*(T) 98.306-12 (1976); Herbert D. Meritt in *MAE* 45.109-12 (1976); Alan K. Brown in *Speculum* 52.1031-37 (1977); E.G. Stanley in *Archiv* 214.131-34 (1977); J. Griffhorn in *Anglia* 96.204-212 (1978); R.I. Page in *SN* 51.161-63 (1979); H. Schabram in *IF* 85.373-78 (1980).

504. Rainbow, Raymond Scott, Jr. 1960. *A Linguistic Study of 'Wynnere and Wastoure' and 'The Parlement of the Three Ages'*. Chicago diss., 118 pp.

505. Raiter, Gladys Wilhelmina. 1935. *The Phonology and Morphology of the Auchinleck 'Sir Tristrem'*. Northwestern diss. (no pagination available).

[Abstr. in *Summaries of Doctoral Dissertations, Northwestern Univ.*, 3.5-7 (1935).]

506. Relihan, Mary Patricia. 1977. *The Language of the English Stonor Letters, 1420-1483*. Univ. of Tennessee diss., 312 pp. [Abstr. in *DA* 38.5438-39A (1978). Explores the emergence of a standard written language in the 15th century.]

507. Rønberg, Gert. 1985. "The Two Manuscripts of *The Wars of Alexander*: A Linguistic Comparison". *Neophil* 69.604-10. [Points out notable differences in orthography and morphology between MS Ashmole 44 and MS Trinity College Dublin 213.]

508. Sandved, Arthur Olav. 1959. "A Note on the Language of Caxton's Malory and that of the Winchester MS". *ES* 40.113-14. [A morphological study.]

509. ———. 1968. *Studies in the Language of Caxton's Malory and that of the Winchester Manuscript.* (= Norwegian Studies in English, 15.) Oslo: Norwegian Universities Press; New York: Humanities Press, 449 pp. [Concentrates on the morphology of the verb.]

Reviews: Basil Cottle in *JEGP* 68.289-90 (1969); N.F. Blake in *MAE* 38.216-18 (1969); Pamela Gradon in *RES* n.s. 20.485-87 (1969); Roland Hagenbüchle in *Erasmus* 20.332-34 (1969); J.F. Vanderheyden in *Orbis* 18.272 (1969); Michael J. Wright in *SN* 41.475-76 (1969); E.G. Williams in *ArchL* n.s. 1.104-06 (1970); Bertil Sundby in *NTS* 24.326-29 (1971); Peter H. Salus in *ES* 52.264-65 (1971); Ján Šimko in *YES* 1.219-22 (1971); Broder Carstensen in *Anglia* 90.228-30 (1972); J.R. Simon in *EA* 25.56-59 (1972); Klaus Faiss in *Linguistics* 64.103-07 (1970).

510. ———. 1985. *Introduction to Chaucerian English.* (= Chaucer Studies, 11.) Cambridge: D.S. Brewer; Dover, NH: Boydell and Brewer, [x +] 107 pp. [A brief description of Chaucer's phonology and morphology.]

Reviews: N.F. Blake in *SAC* 8.241-45 (1986); Norman Davis in *RES* n.s. 37.551-52 (1986); Roger Lass in *NM* 87.599-602 (1986); J.D. Burnley in *Speculum* 62.187-89 (1987); Udo Fries in *Anglia* 105.207-09 (1987).

511. Spearing, Anthony Colin. 1965. "Chaucer's Language". *An Introduction to Chaucer*, ed. Maurice Hussey, A.C. Spearing and James Winny, 89-114. Cambridge: Cambridge Univ. Press.

512. Stanley, Eric Gerald. 1969. "Laȝamon's Antiquarian Sentiments". *MAE* 38.23-37. [On the language (spelling, vocabulary, and syntax) of Laȝamon's *Brut*.]

513. Stevens, Martin. 1956. *The Language of the Towneley Plays: A Comparative Analysis of the Identical York and Towneley Plays, the 'Caesar Augustus', the*

'*Talents' and the Stanzas of the Wakefield Master*. Michigan State Univ. diss., 283 pp. [Abstr. in *DA* 16.1446-47.]

514. ———. 1959. "The Composition of the Towneley *Talents* Play: A Linguistic Examination". *JEGP* 58.423-33.

515. Taglicht, J. 1966. "Notes on the Language of *Ywain and Gawain*". *Studies in English Language and Literature*, ed. Alive Shalvi and A.A. Mendilow (= Scripta Hierosolymitana, 17), 301-09. Jerusalem: Hebrew Univ. [Contains 'The indication of vowel length in the spelling', and 'Initial *h-* in the MS'.]

516. Trusler, Margaret. 1936. "The Language of the Wakefield Playwright". *SP* 33.15-39. [A lexical, phonological and morphological study of his rime-words.]

517. Von Lindheim, Bogislav. 1937. *Studien zur Sprache des Manuscriptes Cotton Galba E IX*. (= WBEP, 59.) Wien & Leipzig: Braumüller, xiii + 131 pp. [A study of the language of the scribes of *Ywain and Gawain, The Seven Sages of Rome*, and *The Pricke of Conscience* in the MS.]

Reviews: Kurt Wittig in *Anglia B* 49.306-09 (1938); K. Brunner in *EStn* 73.253 (1939).

518. Weber-Liel, Bruno. 1939. *Die Sprache Winchesters im Spatmittelalter*. (= Forschungen zur engl. Philologie, 8.) Jena: Frommann, vii + 128 pp.

519. Wiencke, Helmut. 1930. *Die Sprache Caxtons*. (= Kölner Anglistische Arbeiten, 11.) Leipzig: Tauchnitz, 226 pp. [Köln diss. A detailed account of the phonology and morphology of Caxton's language, based on *The Recuyell of the Historyes of Troye, The History of Jason, The Fables of Aesop*, and *Eneydos*.]

520. Zettersten, Arne. 1965. *Studies in the Dialect and Vocabulary of the 'Ancrene Riwle'*. (= LundSE, 34.) Lund: C.W.K. Gleerup; Copenhagen: Ejnar Munksgaard, 331 pp. [Lund diss. The main portion comprises a complete examination of the phonology of vowels in words of Germanic origin.]

Reviews: Cecily Clark in *Neophil* 50.477-79 (1966); Ulf Jacobsson in *SN* 38.181-94 (1966); Basil Cottle in *JEGP* 66.116-18 (1967); Marilyn Powell Felperin in *Speculum* 42.415-18 (1967); Pamela Gradon in *RES* n.s. 18.183-84 (1967); R.M. Wilson in *MAE* 36.81-83 (1967) and *MLR* 63.161 (1968); Sven Bäckman in *ES* 49.453-62 (1968); Klaus Faiss in *Linguistics* 50.107-12 (1969).

VII. ORTHOGRAPHY AND PUNCTUATION

A. General

521. Adams, G.B. 1972. "Ash, Thorn, Eth, Wen, Yogh — A Brief History of our Lost Letters". *Irish Booklore* (Belfast) 2.103-11.

522. Bourcier, Georges. 1978. *L'orthographe de l'anglais: Histoire et situation actuelle*. (Le Monde Anglophone.) Paris: Presses Universitaires de France, 253 pp.

    Reviews: A.C. Gimson in *EA* 32.216-17 (1979); Paule Mertens-Fonck in *SN* 58.271-72 (1986).

523. Buck, Carl Darling. 1923. "The Letter *Y*". *The Manly Anniversary Studies in Language and Literature*, 340-50. Chicago: Univ. of Chicago Press. [On the history of the letter *y*.]

524. Clemoes, Peter. 1952. *Liturgical Influence on Punctuation in Late Old English and Early Middle English Manuscripts*. (= Univ. of Cambridge, Dept. of Anglo-Saxon, Occasional Papers, 1.) Cambridge: Dept. of Anglo-Saxon, Univ. of Cambridge, 22 pp.

    Reviews: H. Silvestre in *Scriptorium* (Brussels) 1954, p. 151; C.G. Harlow in *RES* n.s. 8.177-78 (1957).

525. Conner, Jack Edward. 1953. *A History of Double Vowels in English Spelling*. Stanford diss., 345 pp. [Abstr. in *Stanford Univ. Abstracts of Diss.*, 1952, pp. 211-13.]

526. Grosse, Eginhard. 1937. *Die neuenglische 'ea'-Schreibung: Ein Beitrag zur Geschichte der englischen Orthographie*. (= Palaestra, 208.) Leipzig: Mayer und Müller, viii + 271 pp. [Contains the history of the spelling *-ea* in OE and ME.]

    Review: G. Linke in *Archiv* 173.85-87 (1938).

527. Lindelöf, Uno, 1923. *Engelska Språkets Ortografi i Historisk Belysning*. (= Finska Vetenskaps-Societeten: Minnesteckningar och Föredrag, 2:1.) Helsingfors: Söderström, 18 pp.

528. Scragg, Donald George. 1974. *A History of English Spelling*. (= Mount Follick Ser., 3.) Manchester: Manchester Univ. Press; New York: Barnes & Noble, x + 130 pp.

Reviews: A.J. Bliss in *N&Q* n.s. 22.508-11 (1975); N.E. Osselton in *ES* 57.252-53 (1976); Vivian Salmon in *MLR* 71.879-81 (1976); Josef Hladký in *SAP* 12.198-99 (1980).

529. Sheard, John Albert. 1954. *Spelling*. (The Language Library.) London: André Deutsch, 200 pp.

530. Venezky, Richard Lawrence. 1965. *A Study of English Spelling-to-Sound Correspondences on Historical Principles*. Stanford diss., 239 pp. [Astr. in *DA* 26.3942 (1966).]

531. Vallins, George Henry. 1954. *Spelling*. With a Chapter on American Spelling by John Williams Clark. (The Language Library.) London: André Deutsch, 198 pp.

Reviews: Anon. in *TLS*, July 9, 1954, p. 438; Anon. in *Listener* 52.330 (1954); James Reeves in *Observer*, July 18, 1954, p. 9; Gerhard Graband in *ZAA* 3.486-87 (1955); F. Mossé in *EA* 8.250 (1955); F. Wölcken in *Archiv* 192.204-05 (1956).

532. ———. 1965. *Spelling*. With a Chapter on American Spelling by John Williams Clark. 2nd ed., rev. by D.G. Scragg. (The Language Library.) London: André Deutsch, 208 pp.

533. Wokatsch, Werner. 1932. *Unhistorisches 'ea' in angelsächsischen und frühmittelenglischen Handschriften*. Leipzig: Mayer und Müller, 58 pp. [Berlin diss.]

Reviews: F. Klaeber in *Archiv* 162.243-45 (1932); F. Holthausen in *Anglia B* 44.325 (1933).

534. Wrenn, Charles Leslie. 1943. "The Value of Spelling as Evidence". *TPS* 1943, 14-39. [Notes relating to all periods of English.]

B. Old English

535. Antonsen, Elmer H. 1967. "On the Origin of Old English Digraph Spellings". *SIL* 19.5-17.

536. Blake, Norman Francis. 1961. "A Note on *hw* in Old English". *N&Q* n.s. 8.165-66. [On scribal practice of recording the digraph *hw* as *h* or *w* in OE poetic MSS.]

537. Brunner, Alice. 1947/48. "A Note on the Distribution of the Variant Forms of the Lindisfarne Gospels". *EGS* 1.32-52.

538. Elliott, Ralph Warren Victor. 1955. "The Runes in *The Husband's Message*". *JEGP* 54.1-8.

539. ———. 1959. *Runes: An Introduction*. Manchester: Manchester Univ. Press; New York: Philosophical Library, xvi + 124 pp.
Reviews: S. Einarsson in *MLN* 75.703-04 (1960); A.S.C. Ross in *N&Q* n.s. 7.116 (1960); K. Schneider in *Anglia* 78.357-62 (1960); A.R. Taylor in *MLR* 55.617-18 (1960); E.A. Stephenson in *CE* 22.201 (1960/61); J.M. Bately in *MAE* 30.38-42 (1961); R.L.M. Delorez in *ES* 44.209-11 (1963).

540. ———. 1959. "Two Neglected English Runic Inscriptions: Gildon and Overchurch". *Mossé Festschrift*, 140-47.

541. Emerson, Oliver Farrar. 1926. "The Punctuation of *Beowulf* and Literary Interpretation". *MP* 23.393-405.

542. Fisher, John Hurt. 1951. "The Ancestry of the English Alphabet". *Archaeology* (The Archaeological Institute of America) 4.232-42. [Mainly on OE spelling.]

543. Guinn, Lawrence E. 1959. *English Runes and Runic Writing: The Development of the Runes and their Employment*. Pennsylvania diss., 391 pp. [Abstr. in *DA* 23.1365 (1962).]

544. Harlow, Christopher Geoffrey. 1959. "Punctuation in Some Manuscripts of Ælfric". *RES* n.s. 10.1-19.

545. Horgan, Dorothy M. 1980. "Old English Orthography: A Short Contribution". *ES* 61.385-89. [Based on Alfred's *Pastoral Care*.]

546. Kline, Edward A. 1968. "A Computer-Assisted Graphemic Analysis of *Beowulf*: Purpose and Procedure". *CHum* 2.211-13.

547. Linke, G. 1938. "Zur Präposition *betweoh* und zum Zahlwort *tuwa* im ags. Beda". *Archiv* 173.71-72. [On the forms of the words.]

548. Lutz, Angelika. 1984. "Spellings of the *Waldend* Group — Again". *ASE* 13.51-64. [Cf. Stanley [no. 561].]

549. ———. 1985. "Die Worttrennung am Zeilende in altenglischen Handschriften: Phonologische Betrachtungen zu Claus-Dieter Wetzels gleichnamigen Buch". *IF* 90.227-38.

550. ———. 1986. "The Syllabic Basis of Word Division in Old English Manuscripts". *ES* 67.193-210.

551. McCracken, Robert Ewing. 1971. *Punctuation, Capitalization, and Paragraphing in the Vercelli Poems Based on the Manuscript*. Michigan diss., 315 pp. [Abstr. in *DA* 32.6384A (1972).]

552. McGovern, D.S. 1983. "Unnoticed Punctuation in the Exeter Book". *MAE* 52.90-99.

553. Meling, Kjell. 1979. "The Cross as a Principle in the Formation of Certain Old English Runes". *NM* 80.36-38.

554. Mitchell, Bruce. 1980. "The Dangers of Disguise: Old English Texts in Modern Punctuation". *RES* n.s. 31.385-413.

555. Page, Raymond Ian. 1962. "The Use of Double Runes in Old English Inscriptions". *JEGP* 61.897-907.

556. ———. 1973. *An Introduction to English Runes*. London: Methuen; New York: Harper & Row, 253 pp.

   Reviews: Joan Turville-Petre in *MAE* 43.267-68 (1974); Klaus Düwel in *N&Q* n.s. 23.78-79 (1976); Karl Schneider in *Anglia* 94.117-24 (1976); Elmer H. Antonsen in *JEGP* 76.56-57 (1977).

557. Ross, Alan Strode Campbell. 1943. "Prolegomena to an Edition of the Old English Gloss to the Lindisfarne Gospels". *JEGP* 42.309-21. [Deals exhaustively with the contracted forms of the gloss.]

558. ———. 1959. "Aldrediana XI: The U-Orthographies". *SGG* 1.115-19.

559. Schneider, Karl. 1968. "Six OE Runic Inscriptions Reconsidered". *Einarsson Festschrift*, 37-52.

560. Squires, Ann. 1973. "Some Curious Abbreviations in the Durham Ritual". *N&Q* n.s. 20.403-09.

561. Stanley, Eric Gerald. 1969. "Spellings of the *Waldend* Group". *Willard Festschrift*, 38-69. [See Lutz [no. 548].]

562. Wetzel, Claus-Dieter. 1981. *Die Worttrennung am Zeilenende in altenglischen Handschriften*. (= EurH, 14; Angelsächsische Sprache und Literatur, 96.) Frankfurt am Main & Bern: Peter D. Lang, xxxiii + 495 pp. + 6 microfiches. [Göttingen diss.]

Reviews: Alfred Bammesberger in *Anglia* 101.500-01 (1983); Patrizia Lendinara in *Schede Medievali* 5.529-30 (1983); Celia Sisam in *MAE* 52.313 (1983); Carl T. Berkhout in *Speculum* 60.465-66 (1985).

563. Willard, Rudolph. 1950. "The Punctuation and Capitalization of Ælfric's Homily for the First Sunday in Lent". *The University of Texas Studies in English* 29.1-32.

C. Middle English

564. Aitken, Adam Jack. 1971. "Variation and Variety in Written Middle Scots". *Edinburgh Studies*, 177-209. [Discusses some problems of distribution of certain types of variant spelling in Middle Scots.]

565. Arakelian, Paul G. 1975. "Punctuation in a Late Middle English Manuscript". *NM* 76.614-24. [The MS is entitled *Pageant of the Birth, Life and Death of Richard Beauchamp Earl of Warwick K.G. 1389-1439*.]

566. Bateson, Frederick Wilse. 1975. "Could Chaucer Spell?". *EIC* 25.2-24. [See also Schmidt & Bateson [no. 599].]

567. Benskin, Michael. 1982. "The Letters <þ> and <y> in Later Middle English and Some Related Problems". *JSA* 7.13-30.

568. Bliss, Alan J. 1957. "The Spelling of *Sir Launfal*". *Anglia* 75.275-89.

569. Bolognesi, Giancarlo. 1981. "Notes about the History of English". *Coseriu Festschrift*, 5.277-82.

570. Brook, George Leslie. 1972. "A Piece of Evidence for the Study of Middle English Spelling". *Mustanoja Festschrift* = *NM* 73.25-28.

571. Cawley, Arthur Clare. 1937. "Punctuation in the Early Versions of Trevisa". *LMS* 1.116-33. [Portion of Lawley [no. 466].]

572. Cusack, Bridget. 1971. "*Not wreton with penne and ynke*: Problems of Selection Facing the First English Printer". *Edinburgh Studies*, 29-54. [Discusses matters of typography in relation to orthography.]

573. Davis, Norman. 1951/52. "A Scribal Problem in the Paston Letters". *EGS* 4.31-64. [Studies various details of spelling.]

574. ———. 1959. "Scribal Variation in Late Fifteenth-Century English". *Mossé Festschrift*, 95-103.

575. Erdmann, Peter H. 1973. [1974]. "On the Graphemic Representation of ME /g/ in Modern English". *SAP* 5.45-56.

576. Farish, John. 1957. "Some Spellings and Rhymes in the Scots *Sege of Troy*". *ES* 38.200-06.

577. Francis, Winthrop Nelson. 1962. "Graphemic Analysis of Late Middle English Manuscripts". *Speculum* 37.32-47.

578. Golson, Eva O. 1942. *The Spelling System of the Glasgow MS of 'The Canterbury Tales'*. Chicago diss., iii + 95 pp.

579. Gradon, Pamela. 1983. "Punctuation in a Middle English Sermon". *Dobson Festschrift*, 39-48. [The sermon examined is John Wyclif's "Sermon for Vigil of the Assumption".]

580. Gumbert, J.P. and P.M. Vermeer. 1971. "An Unusual *yogh* in the Bestiary Manuscript — A Paleographical Note". *MAE* 40.56-57.

581. Hamer, Richard. 1983. "Spellings of the Fifteenth-Century Scribe Richardus Franciscus". *Dobson Festschrift*, 63-73.

582. Heyworth, Peter Lorriman. 1972. "The -us Abbreviation in Middle English Manuscripts". *Scriptorium* (Paris) 26:1.63-64.

583. ———. 1981. "The Punctuation of Middle English Texts". *Bennett Festschrift*, 139-57. [The texts analysed are *Troilus and Criseyde, The Canterbury Tales* (The Clerk's Tale), and Thomas Usk's *The Testament of Love*.]

584. Jack, George Barr. 1976. "*Oþer* in the 'AB Language'". *Anglia* 94.431-35.

585. Killough, George Boyd. 1978. *The Virgule in the Poetry of the 'Canterbury Tales'*. Ohio Univ. diss., 305 pp. [Abstr. in *DA* 39.5496A (1979).]

586. ———. 1982. "Punctuation and Caesura in Chaucer". *SAC* 4.87-107.

587. Kim, Suksan. 1971. "Diacritical Functions of the Letter ȝ in Middle English". *JEngL* 5.94-100.

588. Kline, Edward A. 1967. *A Graphemic Analysis of 'The Owl and the Nightingale' from British Museum Manuscript Cotton Caligula A. ix*. St. Louis Univ. diss., 206 pp. [Abstr. in *DA* 28.3168A (1968).]

589. Kristensson, Gillis. 1981. "Another Piece of Evidence for the Study of Middle English Spelling". *NM* 82.159-61. [A comparison between two duplicated passages in the Lay Subsidy Rolls for Lindsey (Lincolnshire) in 1327.]

590. Lucas, Peter J. 1971. "Sense-Units and the Use of Punctuation-Markers in John Capgrave's *Chronicle*". *ArchL* n.s. 2.1-24.

591. ———. 1973. "Consistency and Correctness in the Orthographic Usage of John Capgrave's *Chronicle*". *SN* 45.323-55.

592. ———. 1981. "Computer Assistance in the Editorial Expansion of Contractions in a Middle English Text". *ALLCB* 9:3.9-10. [The text used is John Capgarve's *Chronicle*.]

593. McIntosh, Angus. 1956. "The Analysis of Written Middle English". *TPS* 1956, 26-55. [Discusses some of the problems of 'graphemic analysis'. Repr. in *Lass EHL*, pp. 35-57.]

594. ———. 1974. "Towards an Inventory of Middle English Scribes". *NM* 75.602-24.

595. ———. 1975. "Scribal Profiles from Middle English Texts". *NM* 76.218-35. [Repr. in *Linguistics at the Crossroads*, ed. Adam Makkai, et al., pp. 262-75. Lake Bluff, IL: Jupiter Press; Padua: Liviana Editrice, 1977.]

596. Rønberg, Gert. 1983. "Two North-West Midland Manuscripts Revisited". *Neophil* 67.463-67. [An orthographical examination of the two MSS of *the Destruction of Troy*.]

597. Samuels, Michael Louis, 1983. "Chaucer's Spelling". *Davis Festschrift*, 17-37.

598. Sands, Donald B. 1970. "Orthographic Changes in Middle English Verse: Hazards and Virtues". *NM* 71.461-67.

599. Schmidt, Aubrey Vincent Carlyle and Frederick Wilse Bateson. 1975. "Could Chaucer Spell?". *EIC* 25.391-93. [Refers to Bateson [no. 566].]

600. Seymour, Michael C. 1968. "A Fifteenth-Century East Anglian Scribe". *MAE* 37.166-73.

601. Stevick, Robert David. 1965. "Plus Juncture and the Spelling of the *Ormulum*". *JEGP* 64.84-89.

602. Thomson, S. Harrison. 1938. "Wyclif or Wyclyf". *EHR* 53.675-78. [Argues for the spelling "Wyclyf".]

603. Turville-Petre, J.E. 1947. "Studies on the *Ormulum* MS". *JEGP* 46.1-27. [Includes a survey of *eo* and *e* spellings (pp. 6-13).]

604. Umpfenbach, H. 1935. *Die 'oa'-Schreibung im Englischen: Ein Beitrag zur Ge-*

schichte der englischen Orthographie. (= Palaestra, 201.) Leipzig: Mayer und Müller, vii + 116 pp. [Covers the whole ground from ME times.]

Review: H. Marcus in Archiv 169.292-94 (1936).

605. Von Appel, M. Frelin. 1936. "Zur Schreibung der interdentalen Spirans im Mittelenglischen". EStn 71.14-26.

606. Weiss, H. 1937. Die 'ie(ee)'-Schreibung im Englischen und ihre Geschichte: Ein Beitrag zur Geschichte der englischen Orthographie. Bottrop: Postberg, 188 pp. [Berlin diss. A study of the ModE spellings ie and ee for ME close ē.]

607. Whitehall, Harold. 1930. "A Note on a North-West Midland Spelling". PQ 9.1-6.

608. ———. 1935. "Some Fifteenth-Century Spellings from the Nottingham Records". Michigan Essays and Studies, 61-71.

609. Wilson, Edward. 1974. "The Earliest 'Tis = 'It Is'". N&Q n.s. 21.127-28. [Refers to the form found in a manuscript in 1372 by John of Grimestone.]

VIII. PHONOLOGY AND PHONETICS

A. General

610. Aiken, Janet Rankin. 1929. *Why English Sounds Change*. New York: Ronald Press, vii + 146 pp. [Columbia diss.]

    Reviews: Dorores Benardete in *AS* 5.308-10 (1929/30); Josef Vachek in *ES* 18.234-36 (1936).

611. Alexander, James D. 1985. "*R*-Metathesis in English: A Diachronic Account". *JEngL* 18.33-40.

612. Anderson, John Mathieson. 1980. "On the Internal Structure of Phonological Segments: Evidence from English and its History". *FLH* 1.185-212.

613. —— and Charles Jones. 1977. *Phonological Structure and the History of English*. (= NHLS, 33.) Amsterdam: North-Holland, viii + 189 pp.

    Reviews: A.R. Tellier in *BSL* 73.308-12 (1978); F. Villa in *Studi Italiani di Linguistica Teorica ed Applica* (Padova) 7.292-97 (1978).

614. Antonsen, Elmer Harold. 1961. "Germanic Umlaut Anew". *Language* 37.215-30. [With particular emphasis on Old Icelandic and OE.]

615. Başkan, Özcan. 1959. "Some Notes on Sound Changes in Connection with the English Vowels Descending from the Proto-Germanic /a/-phoneme". *Litera* 6.25-30.

616. Bennett, William H. 1955. "The Southern English Development of Germanic Initial [f s þ]". *Language* 31.367-71.

617. Boisson, Claude. 1982. "Remarques sur la chronologie interne du grand changement vocalique en anglais". *Apports français à la linguistique anglaise* (= Univ. de Saint-Etienne, Travaux 35.), 9-30. Saint-Etienne: Centre Interdisciplinaire d'Etude et de Recherche sur l'Expression Contemporaine.

618. Brook, George Leslie. 1935. *Notes on Some English Sound-Changes*. Leeds: School of English Language, Univ. of Leeds, 32 pp.

619. ———. 1957. *English Sound-Changes*. Manchester: Manchester Univ. Press, 32 pp. [A revised version of the above [no. 618].]

620. Coates, Richard. 1982. "Phonology and the Lexicon: A Case Study of Early English Forms in *-gg-*". *IF* 87.195-222.

621. Cooley, Marianne. 1972. *Velars in English: A Diachronic Generative Analysis*. Univ. of Texas at Austin diss., 152 pp. [Abstr. in *DA* 33.3616A (1973).]

622. Dekeyser, Xavier. 1978. "Some Considerations on Voicing with Special Reference to Spirants in English and Dutch: A Diachronic-Contrastive Approach". *Historical Phonology*, 99-121.

623. Durand, M. 1959. "La Palatalisation en anglais". *Mossé Festschrift*, 113-21. [On various types of palatalization at different periods of English.]

624. Eckhardt, Eduard. 1938. "Die konsonantische Dissimilation im Englischen". *Anglia* 62.81-99. [Covers all periods of English.]

625. Eliason, Norman Ellsworth and Roland Clark Davis. 1939. *The Effects of Stress upon Quantity in Dissyllables: An Experimental and Historical Study*. (= Indiana Univ. Pubs., Science Ser., 8.) Bloomington: Indiana Univ., 56 pp.

626. Erdmann, Peter H. 1972. *Tiefenphonologische Lautgeschichte der englischen Vokale*. (= Athenäum-Skripten Linguistik, 4.) Frankfurt am Main: Athenäum, 279 pp.

627. Fetting, Hans Frederick. 1970. *A Study in Phylogenetic Change: Old English /d/ to Modern English /ð/ Reexamined*. Michigan State Univ. diss., 132 pp. [Abstr. in *DA* 31.6032A (1971).]

628. Fisiak, Jacek. 1968. "Prevocalic Consonant Clusters in the History of English". *SAP* 1.3-14.

629. Flasdieck, Hermann Martin. 1958. "Die Entstehung des engl. Phonems [ʃ], zugleich ein Beitrag zur Geschichte der Quantität". *Anglia* 76.339-410.

630. Gburek, Hubert. 1985. "The Vowel /a:/ in English". *PICHL*/6, 139-48.

631. Gonzo, Susan Thiede. 1978. *English Historical Phonology: Some Issues in the Theory of Phonological Change*. Univ. of Wisconsin-Madison diss., 211 pp. [Abstr. in *DA* 39.4918-19A (1979).]

632. Greene, Christopher L. 1979 [1980]. "The Gospel of the Blessed Bramble". *SAP* 11.41-47. [On vowel quantity in OE and ME.]

633. Harris, David Payne. 1954. *The Phonemic Patterning of the Initial and Final Consonant Clusters of English from Late Old English to the Present: A Structural Approach to their Historical Development.* Michigan diss., 268 pp. [Abstr. in *DA* 14.1083-84 (1954).]

634. Jones, Charles. 1976. "Some Constraints on Medial Consonant Clusters". *Language* 52.121-30.

635. Kisbye, Torben. 1969. *An Historical Survey of English Vowel Changes (the vowels of accented syllables).* Aarhus: Akademisk Boghandel, 26 pp. [Survey in diagrammatical form of developments from Germanic through ModE.]

636. Kniezsa, Veronika. 1984. "On the Phonology of Compounded Words from Late Old English to Early Middle English". *Blake & Jones*, 44-55.

637. Kristensson, Gillis. 1976. "A Note on Palatalization of Germanic *k* in English". *SN* 48.321-24.

638. Lass, Roger. 1976. *English Phonology and Phonological Theory: Synchronic and Diachronic Studies.* (= CSL, 17.) Cambridge: Cambridge Univ. Press, xii + 241 pp.

   Reviews: L. Bauer in *ES* 58.570-72 (1977); R. Hogg in *JL* 13.340-45 (1977); W.F. Koopman in *Neophil* 63.148-59 (esp. 153-59) (1979).

639. ———. 1983. "Velar /r/ and the History of English". *Current Topics in EHL*, 67-94.

640. Lauttamus, Timo. 1981. "A Note on the Development of Old English [x] to Middle English [f]". *NM* 82.1-4.

641. Malone, Kemp. 1959. "Diphthong and Glide". *Mossé Festschrift*, 256-66. [A historical study of Germanic and English diphthongal patterns.]

642. Malsch, Derry Lawrence. 1971. *Redundancy Rules and Phonological Change in the History of English.* Wisconsin diss., 162 pp. [Abstr. in *DA* 32.5766A (1972).]

643. ———. 1976. "Syllable, Mora, and Length in the Development of English". *PICHL*/2, 83-93.

644. McCue, George S. 1958. *A Graphic History of English Stressed Vowels.* Denver, CO: Alan Swallow, 32 pp.

   Review: Herbert Pilch in *IF* 65.112 (1960).

645. Milroy, James. 1983. "On the Sociolinguistic History of /h/-Dropping in English". *Current Topics in EHL*, 37-53.

646. O'Neil, Wayne. 1973. "Some Remarks on Old and Middle English Stress". *Halle Festschrift*, 158-65.

647. Phillips, Betty Steedley, 1983. "Lexical Diffusion and Function Words". *Linguistics* 21.487-99.

648. ———. 1983. "Constraints on Syllables and Quantitative Changes in Early English". *Linguistics* 21.879-95.

649. Plotkin, V.Y. 1972. *The Dynamics of the English Phonological System*. (= JanL, Ser. Practica, 155.) The Hague: Mouton, 98 pp. [Transl. of *Dinamika anglijskoj fonologičeskoj sistemy*, Novosibirsk, 1967.]

    Review: G. Knowles in *Lingua* 38.79-84 (1976).

650. Prins, Anton Adriaan. 1966. *A Synopsis of the History of English Tonic Vowels*. Leiden: Univ. Pers Leiden, ii + 28 pp.

    Reviews: J. Van Roey in *LB* 56.99 (1967); Erwin Mayer in *Anglia* 85.421-23 (1967); E.J. Dobson in *SN* 41.213-17 (1969).

651. ———. 1972. *A History of English Phonemes: From Indo-European to Present-day English*. Leiden: Univ. Pers Leiden, 265 pp. [2nd ed. 1974, 268 pp.]

    Reviews: H.H. Meier in *DQR* 3.92-94 (1973); A.R. Tellier in *BSL* 68.256 (1973); Richard M. Hogg in *Neophil* 58.136-38 (1974); Ulf Magnusson in *SL* 28.115-31 (1974); John Nist in *RBPH* 52.253-56 (1974); Frank-G. Berghaus in *Anglia* 93.166-72 (1975); Wolfgang Blumbach in *IF* 80.171-76 (1975); Leiv Egil Breivik in *ES* 56.273-76 (1975); Klaus Dietz in *Archiv* 213.163-68 (1976); Jerzy Wełna in *KN* 23.359-64 (1976).

652. Ross, Alan Strode Campbell. 1939/40. "Old Norse Diphthongs in English". *APS* 14.1-10.

653. Scott, Charles T. 1986. "English Front Round Vowels: A Synchronic and Diachronic Interpretation". *SAP* 18.3-14.

654. Somerset, R.D.-N. 1928. *Some Important Points in Historical English Grammar*. Oxford: Basil Blackwell, 39 pp. [Concerned with phonology.]

    Review: E.G. Ingram in *RES* 5.245-46 (1929).

655. Stemmler, Theo. 1965. *Die Entwicklung der englischen Haupttonvokale: Eine Übersicht in Tabellenform*. Göttingen: Vandenhoeck & Ruprecht, 8 pp. + 11 tables.

Review: Erwin Mayer in *Anglia* 84.410 (1966).

656. Stene, Aasta. 1954. *Hiatus in English: Problems of Catenation and Juncture*. (= Anglistica, 3.) Copenhagen: Rosenkilde og Bagger, 102 pp. [Includes a historical section describing the development of the various linking devices and of the gradual drift, from OE to the present, toward less hiatus.]

   Reviews: Norman E. Eliason in *MLN* 70.458-59 (1955); Herbert Koziol in *Anglia* 73.257-58 (1955); A. Culioli in *EA* 9.147 (1956) and *BSL* 52.149-50 (1956); P.A. Erades in *Lingua* 9.110-12 (1960).

657. Stockwell, Robert P. 1962. "On the Utility of an Overall Pattern in Historical English Phonology". *PICL*/9, 663-71. [Also repr. in *Lass EHL*, 88-96 and *Scott & Erickson*, 206-13.]

658. ———. 1969. "Mirrors in the History of English Pronunciation". *Willard Festschrift*, 20-37.

659. Vachek, Josef. 1933. "Prof. Karl Luick and Problems of Historical Phonology". *ČMF* 19.273-92.

660. ———. 1957. "On the Interplay of Quantitative and Qualitative Aspects in Phonemic Development: A Contribution to the History of Some English Consonant Phonemes". *ZAA* 5.5-28.

661. ———. 1959. "Notes on the Quantitative Correlation of Vowels in the Phonemic Development of English". *Mossé Festschrift*, 444-56.

662. ———. 1964. "On Peripheral Phonemes in Modern English". *BSE* 4.7-109. [Chapters II-VIII deal with the historical development of various phonemes from OE.]

663. ———. 1974. "Some Remarks on the Historical Development of English seen from the Functionalist Perspective". *PICHL*/1, 1.315-37.

664. Van Kemenade, Ans. 1981. "The Role of the Feature [Grave] in Old and Middle English Phonology". *Current Research 1980*, 1-16.

665. Van Langenhove, George Charles. 1923. "Cockney *H* in Old and Middle English". *LB* 15.1-50

666. ———. 1925. *On the Origin of the Gerund in English (Phonology)*. (= Recueil de travaux publiés par la Faculté de Philosophie et Lettres de l'Université de Gand, 56.) Gand: van Rysselberghe & Rombaut; Paris: Edouard Champion, xxviii + 132 pp.

Reviews: Anon. in N&Q 149.287-88 (1925); A. Carnoy in LB 17. Bijblad 97-98 (1925); C.B. in MLR 21.345 (1926); A. Western in Anglia B 37.25-27 (1926); E. Pons in RBPH 5.1042-43 (1926); W.F. Bryan in MLN 43.478-81 (1928); Morgan Callaway, Jr. in PQ 7.203-04 (1928); Kemp Malone in JEGP 27.398-400 (1928); M.S. Serjeantson in ES 14.235-36 (1932).

B. Old English

667. Anderson, John Mathieson. 1970 [1971]. "'Ablaut' in the Synchronic Phonology of the Old English Strong Verb". IF 75.166-97.

668. ———. 1977. "Noch einmal ae. *samcucu*". YPL 7.67-75. [Written in English (despite the title) on brace notation in OE phonology.]

669. ———. 1985 [1987]. "The Status of Voiced Fricatives in Old English". FLH 6:2.215-43.

670. Ångström, Margareta. 1937. *Studies in Old English Manuscripts, with Special Reference to the Delabialisation of ȳ (ŭ + i) to ī*. Uppsala: Almqvist and Wiksell, 176 pp. + 5 plates.

Review: H. Kökeritz in SN 10.83-93 (1937/38).

671. Antonsen, Elmer Harold. 1961. *The Investigation of 'I'-Mutation in the Germanic Languages*. Illinois diss., 537 pp. [Abstr. in DA 21.3774 (1961).]

672. Armalytė, O. 1979. "Smoothing in the West Mercian Dialect of Old English". Kalbotyra 30:3.7-13.

673. Armborst, David. 1976/77. "Evidence for Phonetic Weakening in Inflectional Syllables in *Beowulf*". LSE n.s. 9.1-18.

674. ———. 1977. "The Germanic Diphthongs *ai and au in Old Frisian and Old English and the Origin of the Old English (West Saxon) Digraph IE". SAP 9.55-69.

675. Awedyk, Wiesław. 1970. "Some Remarks on the Phonology of Old English". SAP 3.69-74.

676. ———. 1975. *The Syllable Theory and Old English Phonology*. Wrocław, Poland: Zakład im. Ossolińskich, 84 pp. [Originally Poznań diss. entitled *The Structure of Old English Syllable*, 1968.]

677. ———. 1975. *Palatal Umlaut versus Velar Umlaut and Breaking: A Comparative*

Study of the Palatalization and Velarization of Vowels in Germanic Languages. Poznań: Adam Mickiewicz Univ., 71 pp. [Habilitationsschrift.]

678. Ball, Cecil R. 1955. *A Phonemic Analysis of Early West Saxon*. Johns Hopkins diss., 930 pp.

679. Ball, Christopher J.E. 1962. "Mercian 'Second Fronting'". *ArchL* 14.130-45.

680. ———— and Patrick Stiles. 1983. "The Derivation of Old English *Geolu* 'Yellow', and the Relative Chronology of Smoothing and Back-Mutation". *Anglia* 101.5-28.

681. Barber, Charles Clyde. 1933. *Die vorgeschichtliche Betonung der germanischen Substantiva und Adjectiva*. Heidelberg: Carl Winter, xi + 232 pp.

   Reviews: J. Raith in *Anglia B* 44.361-63 (1933); F. Holthausen in *EStn* 69.237-40 (1934).

682. Barquist, Claudia Russell. 1985. *Phonological Patterning in 'Beowulf'*. Catholic Univ. of America diss., 234 pp. [Abstr. in *DA* 46.1263A (1985).]

683. Barrack, Charles Michael. 1970. "Old English Back Umlaut: A Case of Progressive Environmental Simplification". *Proceedings: Pacific Northwest Conference on Foreign Languages. Twenty-First Annual Meeting, April 3-4, 1970*, ed. Ralph W. Baldner, 187-89. Victoria, British Columbia: Univ. of Victoria.

684. ————. 1975. *A Diachronic Phonology from Proto-Germanic to Old English Stressing West-Saxon Conditions*. (= JanL, Ser. Practica, 144.) The Hague: Mouton, 136 pp. [Originally Univ. of Washington diss. 1969; Abstr. in *DA* 30.4961A (1970).]

   Reviews: P. Beade in *Lingua* 41.194-95 (1977); Gerald F. Carr in *German Quarterly* (Lancaster, PA) 51.189-90 (1978); Klaus Dietz in *Kratylos* 26.164-67 (1981).

685. ————. 1981. "Natural Generative Phonology and Old English Breaking". *Sprache und Literatur: Festschrift für Arval L. Streadbeck zum 65. Geburtstag*, ed. Gerhard P. Knapp, et al. (= Utah Studies in Literature and Linguistics, 20.), 9-13. Bern: Lang.

686. Bauer, Gerd. 1956. "The Problem of Short Diphthongs in Old English". *Anglia* 74.427-37.

687. Bauer, Gero. 1973. "Die altenglische Palataldiphthongierung". *Koziol Festschrift*, 7-21.

688. ———. 1979. "Zum Problem der Rekonstruktion von 'Lautwerten' im älteren Englisch". *Pinsker Festschrift*, 16-32.

689. Bazell, Charles Ernest. 1956. "Old English Diphthongs". *Litera* 3.115-20.

690. Bennett, Hobart. 1969. "Manifestations of *i*-Umlaut in Old English". *Linguistics* 50.5-26.

691. Bennett, William H. 1946. "The Cause of the West Germanic Consonant Lengthening". *Language* 22.14-18.

692. Bliss, Alan J. 1949/50. "The OE Long Diphthongs *ēo* and *ēa*". *EGS* 3.82-87.

693. Blumbach, Wolfgang. 1974. *Studien zur Spirantisierung und Entspirantisierung altenglischer Konsonanten. I: Labiale und Tektale.* Hauptband: Text, xiv + 355 pp.; Zusatzband: Anmerkungen, 93 pp. Göttingen: Philosophische Fakultät der Georg-August-Universität. [Göttingen diss.; Abstr. in *AESG* 1974.24-26 (1975) and *DA* 37.3148C (1977).]

    Reviews: Herbert Schendl in *IF* 81.406-11 (1976); J. Verdonck in *ES* 59.469-71 (1978).

694. Borowski, Bruno. 1924. *Lautdubletten im Altenglischen.* (= Sächsische Forschungsinstitute in Leipzig, Forschungsinstitut für neuere Philologie, 3.3.) Halle: Niemeyer, vii + 84 pp.

    Review: M. Flasdieck in *LGRP* 46.295-97 (1925).

695. Brink, Daniel. 1983. "Old English Dialects and the Ingvaeonic Hypothesis". *The Southwest Journal of Linguistics* (El Paso, TX) 6.185-95.

696. Britton, Geoffrey C. 1961. "Aldrediana IV: The *ę*- and *i*- Diphthongs". *EGS* 7.1-19.

697. ———. 1970. "Aldrediana XII: *æ~e*". *EPS* 12.1-34.

698. Brosnahan, Leonard Francis. 1953. *Some Old English Sound Changes: An Analysis in the Light of Modern Phonetics.* Cambridge: Heffer, xii + 141 pp. [Leiden diss.]

    Reviews: G. Graband in *ZPhon* 8.418-21 (1954/55); R. Derolez in *RBPH* 33.382-84 (1955); Barbara M.H. Carr in *RES* n.s. 6.74-76 (1955); Karl Brunner in *ES* 37.17-18 (1956); H.M. Flasdieck in *Anglia* 74.459-61 (1956); Sherman M. Kuhn in *JEGP* 55.491-93 (1956).

699. Brunner, Karl. 1953. "The Old English Vowel Phonemes". *ES* 34.247-51.

700. ———. 1955. "Die altenglische Ebnung". *BGDSL* (T) 77.67-70.

701. Cercignani, Fausto. 1983. "The Development of */k/ and */sk/ in Old English". *JEGP* 82.313-23.

702. Chatman, Seymour. 1958. "The *a/æ* Opposition in Old English". *Word* 14.224-36.

703. Coates, Richard. 1984. "On an Early Date for Old English *i*-Mutation". Crépin *LSSME*/10, 25-38.

704. Colman, Fran. 1983. "Old English /a/ ⁓ /æ/ or [a]~[æ]?". *FLH* 4.265-85.

705. ———. 1983. "'Vocalisation' as Nucleation". *SL* 37.30-48. [Deals with what evidence the digraph *ie* may offer about the nature and operation of the so-called 'vocalisation' in OE.]

706. ———. 1984. "Anglo-Saxon Pennies and Old English Phonology". *FLH* 5.91-143. [Discusses name-spellings as evidence for OE phonology.]

707. ———. 1985. "Old English *ie*: Quid Est?". *Lingua* 67.1-23.

708. ——— and John Anderson. 1983. "Front Umlaut: A Celebration of 2nd Fronting, *i*-Umlaut, Life, Food and Sex". *Current Topics in EHL*, 165-90. [Vowel fronting in *Vespasian Psalter*.]

709. Dal, Ingerid. 1947. "Name und Sache: zur Benennung "*u*-Umlaut" im Altenglisch". *NTS* 14.313-14.

710. Danchev, Andrei. 1975 [1976]. "On the Phonemic and Phonetic Values of the Short *ea* and *eo* Digraphs in Old English". *GSU-ZF* 70:1.33-88.

711. ———. 1980. "On Vowel Quantity in Old English". *Sofia English Studies*, 62-78.

712. Daunt, Marjorie. 1939. "Old English Sound Changes Reconsidered in Relation to Scribal Tradition and Practice". *TPS* 1939, 108-37.

713. ———. 1952 [1953]. "Some Notes on Old English Phonology: A Reply to Mr. M. Samuels' Paper". *TPS* 1952, 48-52. [Cf. Samuels [no. 842].]

714. Davidsen-Nielsen, Niels. 1984. "Old English Short Vowels before Nasals". *Blake & Jones*, 12-23.

715. ——— and Henning Ørum. 1978. "The Feature 'Gravity' in Old English and Danish Phonology". *ALH* 16.201-13.

716. Dietz, Klaus. 1970. "Zur Vokalquantität ae. Wörter des Typus *W(e)alh — W(e)alas*". *Anglia* 88.1-25.

717. Dimler, G. Richard. 1974. "Notes on the Phonetic Status of the Initial Consonant Cluster /sk/ in Old English Alliterative Verse". *SIL* 24.21-29.

718. Dresher, Bezalel Elan. 1980. "The Mercian Second Fronting: A Case of Rule Loss in Old English". *LingI* 11.47-73.

719. ———. 1984. "Second Fronting in the Old English Dialect of the Omont Leaf". *Cahiers Linguistiques d'Ottawa* (Univ. of Ottawa) 12.39-48.

720. ———. 1985. *Old English and the Theory of Phonology*. New York: Garland, xi + 272 pp. [Originally Univ. of Massachusetts (Amherst) diss., 1978; Abstr. in *DA* 39.261A (1978).]

721. Eckhardt, Eduard. 1939. "Die vokalische Dissimilation im Altenglischen". *EStn* 73.161-79.

722. Ekwall, Eilert. 1923. "On the Old English Fracture of *a* before *l* Followed by a Consonant". *ES* 5.57-63. [Criticism of Mary S. Serjeantson's "The Dialectal Distribution of Certain Phonological Features in Middle English", *ES* 4 (1922) 93-109, 191-98, and 223-33.]

723. ———. 1963. "A Problem of Old Mercian Phonology in the Light of West Midland Place-Names". *NoB* 51.16-48.

724. Eliason, Norman Ellsworth. 1948. "Old English Vowel Lengthening and Vowel Shortening before Consonant Groups". *SP* 45.1-20. [Portion of Johns Hopkins diss.]

725. Faulkner, Dewey Randolph. 1968. *The Phonology of British Museum Manuscript Royal 7.C.xii, Folios 25^v-45^v and 91-218*. Univ. of North Carolina at Chapel Hill diss., 311 pp. [Abstr. in *DA* 29.2258A (1969). The MS (dated 911) is the oldest known one of any Ælfric's Works.]

726. Fisiak, Jacek. 1967. "The Old English <wr-> and <wl->". *Linguistics* 32.12-14.

727. Flasdieck, Hermann Martin. 1930. "Miszellen zur ae. Grammatik: I. Zur relativen Chronologie des Velarumlauts im Westmittelland". *Anglia B* 41.283-88. [The material is taken from *Vespasian Psalter*.]

728. ———. 1950. "The Phonetic Aspect of Old Germanic Alliteration". *Anglia* 69.266-94. [Concerns the history of Germanic, and especially of OE sounds.]

729. Flom, George T. 1937. "Breaking in Old Norse and Old English with Special Reference to the Relations between Them". *Language* 13.123-36.

730. Förster, Max. 1935. "Zur *i*-Epenthese im Altenglischen". *Anglia* 59.287-98.

731. Fourquet, Jean. 1959. "Le système des éléments vocaliques longs en vieil-anglais. Considérations 'structurales'". *Mossé Festschrift*, 148-60.

732. Giffhorn, Jürgen. 1974. *Phonologische Untersuchungen zu den altenglischen Kurzdiphthongen*. München: Wilhelm Fink, 326 pp. [Bonn diss.]

   Reviews: Elmar Seebold in *Kratylos* 19.126-30 (1974); Manfred Scheler in *Anglia* 95.162-64 (1977); Roberto Gusmani in *SGerm* 44.220-21 (1978); Angelika Lutz in *Archiv* 219.184-87 (1982); Peter Bierbaumer in *JEngL* 11.51-57 (1977).

733. Göhler, Theodor. 1933. *Lautlehre der ae. Hexameron-Homilie des Abtes Ælfric*. Weida i. Thüringen: Thomas, 183 pp. [München diss.]

   Reviews: A. B[randl] in *Archiv* 164.130 (1933); G.T. F[lom] in *JEGP* 33.599 (1934); H. Koziol in *LGRP* 55.168-69 (1934); A.A. Prins in *Neophil* 19.231 (1934); Arthur Szogs in *Anglia B* 45.228-29 (1934); C.L. W[renn] in *RES* 11.374 (1935).

734. Goossens, Louis. 1969. "A Chronology for the Falling Together of Late Old English *hr* and *r*". *ES* 50.74-79.

735. ———. 1985. "Framing the Linguistic Actions Scene in Old and Present-day English: *cweþan, secgan, sp(r)ecan* and Present-day English *speak, talk, say* and *tell* compared". *PICHL*/6, 149-70.

736. Gradon, Pamela. 1962. "Studies in Late West-Saxon Labialization and Delabialization". *Tolkien Festschrift*, 63-76.

737. Grant, Clyde M. 1968. "A Note on the First Consonant Shift: Some Old English and Latin Cognates". *TAIUS* (Texas A & I Univ.) 1.61-64.

738. Grundt, Alice Wyland. 1980. "Diphthongs in Old English". *American Indian and Indo-European Studies: Papers in Honor of Madison S. Beeler*, ed. Kathryn Klar, et al. (= TLSM, 16.), 327-36. The Hague-Paris-New York: Mouton.

739. Hald, Kristian. 1978. "*A*-Mutation in Scandinavian Words in England". *The Vikings*, 99-106.

740. Hallqvist, Henning. 1948. *Studies in Old English Fractured 'ea'*. (= LundSE, 14.) Lund: Gleerup, 168 pp.

Reviews: K. Malone in *MLN* 64.561-62 (1949); Robert J. Menner in *Speculum* 24.579-80 (1949); F. Mossé in *BSL* 45.170 (1949); R. Quirk in *MLR* 44.256-58 (1949); R. Derolez in *RBPH* 28.583-85 (1950); E.V.K. Dobbie in *Word* 6.245-47 (1950); S.M. Kuhn in *Language* 26.319-23 (1950); A.A. Prins in *Museum* 55.31-33 (1950); M. Lehnert in *Anglia* 70.106-08 (1951).

741. Hamer, Richard F.S. 1967. *Old English Sound Changes for Beginners*. Oxford: Blackwell, 35 pp.

    Review: M.L. Samuels in *MAE* 37.245 (1968).

742. Harl, W. 1936. "Die überkurzen Vokale in den historischen indo-germanischen Sprachen". *ZVS* 63.1-28. [Discussion of OE epenthesis and breaking, pp. 23-26.]

743. Heald, Ann Ridgely Barber. 1965. *Some Graphic Evidence for Vowel Length in Three Old English Manuscripts*. Univ. of Texas diss., 201 pp. [Abstr. in *DA* 26.2199 (1965).]

744. Hickey, Raymond. 1984. "Remarks on Assimilation in Old English". *FLH* 5.279-303.

745. ———. 1985. "Velar Segments in Old Irish and Old English". *PICHL*/6, 267-79.

746. Hockett, Charles Francis. 1959. "The Stressed Syllabics of Old English". *Language* 35.575-97.

747. Hogg, Richard M. 1971. "Gemination, Breaking, and Reordering in the Synchronic Phonology of Old English". *Lingua* 28.48-69.

748. ———. 1974. "Further Remarks on Breaking and Gemination". *ArchL* n.s. 5.47-52.

749. ———. 1975. "The Place of Analogy". *Neophil* 59.109-13. [Concerns the occurrence of *sloh/slog* forms as singular partners of *slogon* by Verner's Law.]

750. ———. 1976. "The Status of Rule Reordering". *JL* 12.103-23. [The examples are taken from OE and Germanic.]

751. ———. 1977. "The Chronology and Status of Second Fronting". *ArchL* n.s. 8.70-81. [Examines the changes of *a>æ* and *æ>e* in the Mercian dialect of OE.]

752. ———. 1977. "Old English *r*-Metathesis and Generative Phonology". *JL* 13.165-75.

753. ———. 1979. "Old English Palatalization". *TPS* 1979, 89-113.

754. ———. 1980. "Æ1". *YPL* 8.49-54.

755. ———. 1982. "Was There Ever an /ɔ/-Phoneme in Old English?". *NM* 83.225-29.

756. ———. 1982. "Two Geminate Consonants in Old English?". *McIntosh Festschrift* (A), 187-202. [Discusses [ff] and [gg].]

757. Hollifield, Henry. 1985. "On the Phonological Development of Monosyllables in West Germanic and the Germanic Words for 'Who' and 'So'". *IF* 90.196-206.

758. Holthausen, Ferdinand. 1933. "Zu ae. ī für ē". *Anglia B* 44.26-27; 191-92.

759. Howell, Robert Busby. *Contribution to a Theory of Consonantal Influence in Germanic: Gothic Breaking and Old English Breaking and Velar Umlaut.* Cornell diss., 179 pp. [Abstr. in *DA* 44.2750-51A (1984).]

760. Hubmayer, Karl. 1983. "Phonetische Aspekte der Dehnung altenglischer Kurzvokale vor 'homorganer' Doppelkonsonanz". *Philologie und Sprachwissenschaft*, 93-105.

761. Ivanova, I.P. 1965. "'Overlapping' of /ĭ/, /ў/ in Old English". *PP* 8.220-23.

762. Jones, Charles. 1978. "Rounding and Fronting in Old English Phonology". *Lingua* 46.157-68.

763. ———. 1980. "Rounding and Fronting in Old English Phonology: A Dependency Approach". *FLH* 1.125-37.

764. Karstien, Carl. 1926/27. "Ags. *nāmon — ȝeāfon*". *EStn* 61.1-8.

765. Keyser, Samuel Jay. 1975. "Metathesis and Old English Phonology". *LingI* 6.377-411. [Also in *Grimshaw Papers*, 125-63.]

766. ——— and Wayne O'Neil. 1983. "Exceptions to High Vowel Deletion in the Vespasian Psalter and Their Explanation". *Current Topics in EHL*, 137-64.

767. Kim, Suksan. 1967. *A Phonemic Interpretation of the Vocalic Graphemes of Old English 'Pastoral Care' (MS Hatton 20)*. Michigan diss., 146 pp. [Abstr. in *DA* 28.2666-67A (1968).]

768. ———. 1971. "The Vowel Shift in Unstressed Syllables of Old English". *Language Research* (Seoul) 7.1-10.

769. ———. 1973. "Long Consonants in Old English". *Linguistics* 102.83-90.

770. ———. 1977. *A History of the Vowels of Early (West Saxon) Old English. The Old English 'Pastoral Care': the Manuscript and the Vowels*. Seoul: Pan Korea Book Corp., 272 pp.

   Review: Herbert Penzl in *Language* 55.253-54 (1979).

771. ———. 1984. "Old English <ie> and Its Phonetic Identification". *Blake & Jones*, 24-43.

772. Kiparsky, Paul and Wayne O'Neil. 1976. "The Phonology of Old English Inflections". *LingI* 7.527-57. [Cf. Keyser [no. 765].]

773. Kisbye, Torben. 1982. "A Chronology of Old English Vowel Changes". *OEN* 15:2.20-25.

774. Kniczsa, Veronika. 1975. "On the Phonology of Old English Prefixes: Based on the Material of the Peterborough Chronicle". *SEA* 2.349-70.

775. ———. 1976. "The Development of the Old English Short Vowel System: Based on the Material of the Peterborough Chronicle". *AUBud-L* 7.159-69.

776. ———. 1977. "The Development of the Old English Consonant System: Based on the Material of the Peterborough Chronicle". *SEA* 3.97-128.

777. ———. 1977. "The Development of the Old English Long Vowel System and Diphthongs as Reflected in the Material of the Peterborough Chronicle". *AUBud-L* 8.55-64.

778. Koopman, W.F. 1976. "Mercian Second Fronting and Ordering Theories". *Neophil* 60.280-96.

779. Koziol, Herbert. 1951. "Zur Alliteration im AE.". *Anglia* 70.43-45. [Notes to Flasdieck [no. 728].]

780. Kristensson, Gillis. 1983. "Old English 'Second Fronting' Revisited". *NOWELE* 1.61-76.

781. Krupatkin, Yakob B. 1963. "Germanic *ai, au* in Old English". *PP* 6.130-34.

782. ———. 1964. "Old English Breaking (A Step to a Phonemic Approach)". *PP* 7.62-64.

783. ———. 1965. "A Synchronic Problem Diachronically Solved (The Pre-English Nasalized Vowels)". *PP* 8.251-55.

784. Kuhn, Sherman McAllister. 1945. "*E* and *Æ* in Farman's Mercian Glosses". *PMLA* 60.631-69.

785. ———. 1961. "On the Syllabic Phonemes of Old English". *Language* 37.522-38. [Repr. in *Scott & Erickson*, 146-64.]

786. ———. 1970. "On the Consonantal Phonemes of Old English". *Meritt Festschrift*, 16-49.

787. ——— and Randolph Quirk. 1953. "Some Recent Interpretations of Old English Digraph Spellings". *Language* 29.143-56. [Repr. in *Quirk Essays*, 38-54.]

788. ——— and Randolph Quirk. 1955. "The Old English Digraphs: A Reply". *Language* 31.390-401. [A rejoinder to Stockwell & Barritt [no. 863]. Repr. in *Quirk Essays*, 55-69.]

789. Lass, Roger. 1970. "Palatals and Umlaut in Old English." *ALH* 13.75-98.

790. ———. 1971. "Boundaries as Obstruents: Old English Voicing Assimilation and Universal Strength Hierarchies". *JL* 7.15-30.

791. ———. 1977. "On the Phonetic Specification of Old English /r/". *SAP* 9.3-16.

792. ——— and John Mathieson Anderson. 1975. *Old English Phonology*. (= CSL, 14.) Cambridge: Cambridge Univ. Press, xv + 326 pp.

Reviews: Richard M. Hogg in *YPL* 6.187-93 (1976); Ruth P.M. Lehmann in *JEGP* 75.579-88 (1976); Josef Vachek in *PP* 19.196-98 (1976); John Algeo in *GL* 18.236-42 (1978); P. Beade in *LB* 67.183-89 (1978); B.E. Dresher in *Language* 54.432-46 (1978); Betty S. Phillips in *AS* 53.75-78 (1978); W.F. Koopman in *Neophil* 63.148-59 (esp. 148-53) (1979); Alan Ward in *MAE* 48.272-73 (1979); H. Weinstock in *ES* 60.313-18 (1979).

793. Lehmann, Winfred Philipp. 1959. "Metrical Evidence for Old English Suprasegmentals". *TSLL* 1.66-72.

794. ———. 1968. "Post-Consonantal *l m n r* and Metrical Practice in *Beowulf*". *Einarsson Festschrift*, 148-67.

795. Lester, Mark Pro. 1964. *The Phonological Implications of Graphic Variation in Ælfric's 'Catholic Homilies'*. Univ. of California, Berkeley, diss., 250 pp. [Abstr. in *DA* 25.5919-20 (1965) and *Linguistics* 20.108-10 (1966).]

796. Linke, G. 1938. "Zum Velarumlaut in der starken Verbalflexion der Hs. T des ags. Beda". *Archiv* 173.210-12.

797. ———. 1939. "Quantität und Quantitätsbezeichnungen im ags. Beda". *Archiv für vergleichende Phonetik* (Berlin) 3.40-42. [A study of the accent marks and the doubling of long vowels in MSS T and B of the Alfredian Bede.]

798. Lockwood, William Burley. 1952/53 [1954]. "Welsh *Ystwryian* and *I*-Epenthesis in Old English; and Related Problems". *EGS* 5.90-98.

799. Maling, Joan M. 1971. "Sentence Stress in Old English". *LingI* 2.379-99.

800. Malone, Kemp. 1932. "On the OE. Sound-shift $\bar{e} > \bar{\imath}$". *Anglia B* 43.284-87.

801. ———. 1933. "The OE. Sound-shift $\bar{e} > \bar{\imath}$ Once More". *Anglia B* 44.190-91; 193.

802. Malsch, Derry L. 1972. "Lexical Redundancy and Historical Alternation of Tenseness in English Vowels". *Glossa* 6.74-82. [On the so-called 10th-century lengthening.]

803. McCalla, Kim. 1984. "The Evolution of the Consonant System of Germanic into Old English". *FLH* 5.145-69.

804. McLaughlin, John C. 1979. "The i-Umlaut of the Old English West Saxon Diphthongs (Again)". *JL* 15.289-94. [Apropos of Lass & Anderson [no. 792].]

805. McMillan, John Terry. 1979. *A Computer Assisted Study of Vowel Length in Old English*. Univ. of Mississippi diss., 140 pp. [Abstr. in *DA* 40.4007A (1980). The main corpus is the language of *Beowulf*.]

806. Neuman, Erik. 1929. "Det nordiska *i*-omljudet". *APS* 4.193-246. [Contains remarks bearing on *i*-umlaut in OE.]

807. Newfield, Madeleine. 1981 [1983]. "The Disintegration of Germanic Verbal Ablaut in Old English". *Orbis* 30.114-34.

808. Ney, James W. 1968. "Old English Vowel Digraph Spellings". *Linguistics* 45.36-49.

809. Nielsen, Hans F. 1983 [1984]. "Germanic *ai* in Old Frisian, Old English and Old Norse". *IF* 88.156-64.

810. ———. 1984. "A Note on the Origin of Old English Breaking and Back Mutation". *ABAG* 22.73-81.

811. Nist, John Albert. 1958. "Phonemics and Distinctive Features of *Beowulf*". *SIL* 13.25-33.

812. O'Neil, Wayne A. 1970. "Explaining Vowel Gradation in Old English". *GL* 10.149-63.

813. ———. 1970. "Breaking in the Environment *-ll*: A Problem in the History of Old English". *PICL*/10, 733-38.

814. Pak, Tae-Yong. 1969. *Runic Evidence of Laminoalveolar Affrication in Old English*. Bowling Green State Univ. diss., 180 pp. [Abstr. in *DA* 30.4969A (1970).]

815. ———. 1969. "Phonology of Laminoalveolar Affrication in Old English According to Runic Evidence". *NEMLA Newsletter: A Publication of the Northeast Modern Language Association* (Brockport, NY) 1:3.8-20.

816. ———. 1972. "Position and Affrication in Northumbrian Old English". *Linguistics* 82.52-62. [Also printed in *Neophil* 57.74-82 (1973). Refutes Watson [no. 887].]

817. Peeters, Christian. 1971. "e_1 in Gothic, Old English, and Old High German: A Phonological Study". *Linguistics* 72.26-30.

818. Penzl, Herbert. 1944. "A Phonemic Change in Early Old English". *Language* 20.84-87. [A phonemic interpretation of medial and final *f* and *b* in the oldest OE texts.]

819. ———. 1947. "The Phonemic Split of Germanic *k* in Old English". *Language* 23.34-42.

820. ———. 1958. "Zur Vorgeschichte von westsächsisch *ae* und zur Methode des Rekonstruierens". *Wild Festschrift*, 158-69.

821. Peters, Robert Anthony. 1967. "Phonic and Phonemic Long Consonants in Old English". *SIL* 19.1-4.

822. Phillips, Betty Steedley. 1978. *A Natural Generative Phonology of Old English Based on King Alfred's Translation of Gregory's 'Pastoral Care'*. Univ. of Georgia diss., 274 pp. [Abstr. in *DA* 39.4219A (1979).]

823. ———. 1980. "Old English *an~on*: A New Appraisal". *JEngL* 14.20-23.

824. ———. 1980. "Two Approaches to a Phonological Problem". *Word* 31.275-85. [Concerns the *a~æ* alternation in OE.]

825. ———. 1981. "The Phonetic Basis of a Late Old English Sound Change". *Phonologica 1980: Akten der 4. Internationalen Phonologie-Tagung, Wien, 29. Juni — 2. Juli 1980*, ed. Wolfgang U. Dressler, et al. (= IBS, 36.), 337-41. Innsbruck: Inst. für Sprachwissenschaft der Univ. Innsbruck.

826. Pilch, Herbert. 1968 [1970]. "Altenglische historische Lautlehre als phonologisches Problem". *Linguistic Studies Presented to André Martinet on the Occasion of His Sixtieth Birthday, Part II: Indo-European Linguistics*, ed. Alphonse Juilland, 350-70. New York: Linguistic Circle of New York. [Also pub. as *Word* 24.350-70.]

827. ———. 1969 [1971]. "The Phonemic Interpretation of Old English Spelling Evidence". *ALH* 12.29-43.

828. Pyles, Thomas. 1943. "The Pronunciation of Latin Learned Loan Words and Foreign Words in Old English". *PMLA* 58.891-910.

829. Reszkiewicz, Alfred. 1953. "The Phonemic Interpretation of Old English Digraphs". *BPTJ* 12.179-87.

Review: F. Mossé in *BSL* 50:2.137 (1954).

830. ———. 1971. "The Elimination of the Front Rounded and Back Unrounded Short Vowel Phonemes from Medieval English: A Reinterpretation". *KN* 18.279-95.

831. ———. 1972. "On the Rise of Old English Secondary Non-Front Short Vowel Phonemes". *SAP* 4.23-33.

832. Richards, Michael D. 1972. "Ablaut Alternations in Resonant Stems of Old English Strong Verbs". *Glossa* 6.83-88.

833. Ritter, Otto. 1925. "Zum Vokalismus von ae. *tien*, *tēn*, zehn". *EStn* 59.155-57.

834. Robb, K.A. 1968. "Some Changes in Kentish OE Phonology". *Lingua* 20.177-86.

835. Ross, Alan Strode Campbell. 1951. "Old English *æ~a*". *ES* 32.49-56; 116.

836. ———. 1951. *Tables for Old English Sound Changes*. Cambridge: W. Heffer and Sons, 10 pp. + 5 tables.

Reviews: J.T.P. in *MAE* 20.104 (1951); R.M. Smith in *JEGP* 51.294 (1952).

837. ———. 1960. "A Hitherto Unnoticed Anglo-Saxon Sound-Change". *Flasdieck Festschrift*, 215-20. [= Aldrediana VIII.]

838. ———. 1968. "Aldrediana XV: On the Vowel of Nominal Composition". *NM* 69.361-74.

839. ———. 1974. "Anglo-Saxon 'e' to 'i' before 'u'". *N&Q* n.s. 21.123.

840. Rousse, Jean. 1968. "Les consonnes du vieil-anglais: Essai de classement phonétique et phonologique". *Caliban* (Paris) 5:1.3-14.

841. Rydland, Kurt. 1977. "Old Northumbrian *æw*-Spellings for Original /ēo/ + /w/: Scribal Error or Vowel Change? Some Evidence from Modern Northern Dialects". *ES* 58.289-95.

842. Samuels, Michael Louis. 1952. "The Study of Old English Phonology". *TPS* 1952, 15-47. [Comments on theories put forward by Daunt [no. 712]; Daunt's reply [no. 713].]

843. Scargill, Matthew Henry. 1951. *Notes on the Development of the Principal Sounds of Indo-European through Proto-Germanic and West Germanic into Old English*. Toronto: Univ. of Toronto Press; London: Oxford Univ. Press, 44 pp.

   Review: R.M. Smith in *JEGP* 51.294 (1952).

844. Schendl, Herbert. 1979. "Zur Chronologie des Wandels /xs/ zu /ks/ im Altenglischen". *Pinsker Festschrift*, 157-74.

845. Schmierer, Richard Joseph. 1977. *Theoretical Implications of Gothic and Old English Phonology*. Univ. of Massachusetts diss., 233 pp. [Abstr. in *DA* 38.4795-96A (1978).]

846. Schubel, Friedrich. 1941/42. "Die Aussprache des auslautenden ae. *sc*". *SN* 14.255-76.

847. Schultz, Manfred. 1977. *Untersuchungen zum anlautenden Velaren /g/ im Altenglischen*. Göttingen diss., xxxii + 218 pp. [Abstr. in *DA* 39.4681C (1979) and *EASG* 1978, 21-22 (1979).]

848. Scott, Forrest S. 1954. *Diagrams Illustrating Some West Saxon Sound-Changes*. Manchester: Manchester Univ. Press, 16 pp.

849. Scragg, Donald George. 1970. "Initial *h* in Old English". *Anglia* 88.165-96.

850. Serjeantson, Mary Sydney. 1923. "A Note on the Study of O.E. Dialects". *ES* 5.208-09. [Reply to Ekwall [no. 722].]

851. Sihler, Andrew L. 1977. "Morphologically Conditioned Sound Change and OE Past Participles in *-en*". *GL* 17.76-91.

852. Simon, J.-R. 1975. "Sur quelques problèmes de phonologie vieil-anglaise". *Tradition et innovation, Littérature et paralittérature: Actes du Congrès de Nancy (1972)*, 33-52. Paris: Didier.

853. Slettengren, Emrik. 1943. "On the Development of OE initial *sc*". *SMSpr* 15.45-50.

854. Speedie, David C. 1971. "A Note on Old English Diphthongization of Back Vowels after Initial *i*". *ArchL* n.s. 2.147-50. [Apropos of A. Campbell [no. 251], §§170-89.]

855. Stanley, Eric Gerald. 1952/53. "The Chronology of *r*-Metathesis in Old English". *EGS* 5.103-15.

856. Staun, Jørgen. 1983. "The Old English Obstruent System and Its History: A Dependency Account". *SL* 37.9-29.

857. ———. 1983. "Retraction of Old English [æ æ] and Bifurcation of Danish [ɑ] and the Articulatory Gesture in Dependency Phonology". *Lingua* 59.355-73.

858. Steponavičius, A. 1971. "The English Vowel System in the Period of the Oldest Written Records (VIII-Xcc.)". *Kalbotyra* 22:3.19-30.

859. ———. 1973. "The Development of Old English Diphthongs". *Kalbotyra* 24:3.57-73.

860. Stiles, Patrick. 1983. "The Attestation of Early Old English *wudu* 'wood': a Note on the Evidence for the Date of Combinative Back-Mutation". *NM* 84.415-18.

861. Stockwell, Robert P. 1958. "The Phonology of Old English: A Structural Sketch". *SIL* 13.13-24. [Repr. in *Scott & Erickson*, 136-45.]

862. ——— and Carlyle Westbrook Barritt. 1951. *Some Old English Graphemic-Phonemic Correspondences — æ, ea, and a.* (= *SIL*, Occasional Papers, 4.) Washington, DC: Georgetown Univ., 39 pp. [Repr., New York: Johnson Reprint, 1963, 1970.]

863. ——— and Carlyle Westbrook Barritt. 1955. "The Old English Short Digraphs: Some Considerations". *Language* 31.372-89. [A reply to Kuhn & Quirk [no. 787]. Cf. also Kuhn & Quirk [no. 788].]

864. ——— and Carlyle Westbrook Barritt. 1961. "Scribal Practice: Some Assumptions". *Language* 37.75-82. [On vowel phonemes of OE, apropos of Hockett [no. 746]. Repr. in *Lass EHL*, 133-41.]

865. ———— and Rudolph Willard. 1959. "Further Notes on Old English Phonology". *SIL* 14.10-13. [Cf. Stockwell [no. 861].]

866. Storms, Godfrid. 1956. "The Weakening of O.E. Unstressed *i* to *e* and the Date of Cynewulf". *ES* 37.104-10.

867. Strøjer, Lisbeth. 1984. "Aspects of West Saxon Breaking". *Blake & Jones*, 1-11.

868. Suzuki, Seiichi. 1982. "Phonetic Values of Old English Vocalic Digraphs". *Linguistics* 20.323-38.

869. ————. 1984. "A New Interpretation of the Development of Pre-OE *$\bar{e}a$Co $\left\{{i \atop j}\right\}$ in Non-West Saxon". *FLH* 5.257-77.

870. Syrochvatova, V.P. 1981. "The Development of the Palatal Fricative [γ'] in Old English". *Kalbotyra* 32:3.140-43.

871. Takahashi, Sakutaro. 1973. *The State of 'i'-Umlaut in Early West Saxon*. Northwestern Univ. diss., 188 pp. [Abstr. in *DA* 34.4237A (1974).]

872. Terrebonne, Robert Alexis. 1970. *A Generative Phonology of the Mercian Old English Verb*. Louisiana State Univ. and Agricultural and Mechanical College diss., 235 pp. [Abstr. in *DA* 31.4751A (1971).]

873. Toon, Thomas Edward. 1975. *Variation in the Vowel Systems of Early Mercian Old English*. Michigan diss., 155 pp. [Abstr. in *DA* 36.4458A (1976).]

874. ————. 1976. "The Variationist Analysis of Early Old English Manuscript Data". *PICHL*/2, 71-81. [A study of the process of Early OE sound change.]

875. ————. 1977. "The Actuation and Implementation of an Old English Sound Change". *The Third LACUS Forum 1976*, ed. Robert J. Di Pietro and Edward L. Blansitt, Jr., 614-22. Columbia, SC: Hornbeam Press.

876. ————. 1978. "Dialect Mixture and Language Change: Some Old English Data". *PICL*/12, 623-26.

877. ————. 1983. *The Politics of Early Old English Sound Change*. (Quantitative Analyses of Linguistic Structure Series.) New York: Academic Press, xv + 229 pp. [The period covered is A.D. 700-850.]

Review: Richard M. Hogg in *JL* 21.245-50 (1985).

878. Touster, Eva K. 1954. "Phonological Aspects of the Metre of *Beowulf*". *Essays in Honor of Walter Clyde Curry* (= Vanderbilt Studies in the Humanities, 2), 27-38. Nashville, TN: Vanderbilt Univ. Press.

879. Trnka, Bohumil. 1948. "From Germanic to English: A Chapter from the Historical English Phonology". *RLB* 1.139-49. [Repr. in *Trnka Papers*, 245-52.]

880. ———. 1975. "The Old English Vowel System and the Problem of Monophonemes". *Studii și Cercetări Lingvistice* (Bucharest) 26.429-31. [Repr. in *Trnka Papers*, 281-84.]

881. Vachek, Josef. 1971. "On One Point of Old English Phonology". *PSE* 14.133-42. [A critical note on Pilch [no. 826].]

882. Van der Rhee, Florus. 1977. "Palatalisierung, Mouillierung und Assibilierung von urgerm. /k/ im Altenglischen und Alfriesischen". *Us Wurk* 26.33-44.

883. Van Essen, A.J. 1967. "Some Remarks on Old English Phonology". *Linguistics* 32.83-86.

884. Van Langenhove, George Charles. 1930. "The Assibilation of Palatal Stops in Old English". *Jespersen Festschrift*, 69-75.

885. Watson, John Wilbur, Jr. 1941. *A Phonemic Study of the Northumbrian Dialect of Old English*. Univ. of Virginia diss., 617 pp. [Abstr. in *Univ. of Virginia Abstracts of Diss. 1942*, 19-22.]

886. ———. 1946. "Northumbrian Old English *ēo* and *ēa*". *Language* 22.19-26.

887. ———. 1947. "Non-initial *k* in the North of England". *Language* 23.43-49. [Mainly concerned with Northumbrian OE. Cf. Pak's criticism [no. 816].]

888. ———. 1951. "Smoothing and Palatalumlaut in Northumbrian". *English Studies in Honor of James Southall Wilson* (= Univ. of Virginia Studies, 4), ed. Fredson Bowers, 167-74. Charlottesville, VA: Univ. of Virginia.

889. Weber, Goerg. 1927. *Suffixvocal nach kurzer Tonsilbe vor r, n, m im Angelsächsischen*. (= Palaestra, 156.) Leipzig: Mayer und Müller, xiv + 142 pp. [Berlin diss.]

Reviews: A.J. W[yatt] in *RES* 4.496 (1928); Hermann Flasdieck in *Anglia B* 40.257-61 (1929).

890. Whitesell, James Edwin. 1935. *Accented Vowels in the Northumbrian Dialect of Old English*. Harvard diss. [Abstr. in *Harvard Univ. Summaries of Theses* 1935, 286-89.]

891. Wilson, Baxter D. 1952. *A Comparative Study of the Initial Consonant Clusters of Old English and Certain Cognate Languages*. Univ. of Virginia diss., 199 pp. [Abstr. in *Univ. of Virginia Abstracts of Diss. 1952*, 14-17.]

892. Woolfson, Arnold P. 1967. *A Graphemic, Diaphonemic, and Morphophonic Interpretation of the Early and Late Old English Dialects*. State Univ. of New York at Buffalo diss., 344 pp. [Abstr. in *DA* 28.453B (1967).]

893. Yoder, Emily K. 1977. "Germanic and Old English *b* and *p* as Developed from Proto-Indo-European: a Historical Reconstruction through Diachronic Phonological Frequency Analysis". *USFLQ* 16:1/2.21-26.

894. Zabulienė, L. 1979. "Back Mutation in Old English" *Kalbotyra* 30:3.79-86.

895. ———. 1981. "On Front Mutation in the System of Old English Diphthongs <ru>". *Kalbotyra* 32:3.134-39.

C. Middle English

896. Adamska-Sałaciak, Arleta. 1984 [1985]. "Some Notes on the Origin of Middle English /a/". *SAP* 17.51-62.

897. Aitken, Adam Jack. 1977. "How to Pronounce Older Scots". *Bards and Makars: Scottish Language and Literature, Medieval and Renaissance*, ed. Adam J. Aitken, et al., 1-21. Glasgow: Glasgow Univ. Press.

898. Arend, Zygeryd Marjan. 1931. "Linking in *Cursor Mundi*. A Phonological Investigation". *TPS* 1925-30, 200-59. [A rev. version of Poznań diss. 1926.]

899. Baader, Theodor. 1939. "'The Great Vowel Shift'. Einige Bemerkungen zur Chronologie der sog. 'mittelenglischen' Lautveränderungen". *Tijdschrift voor Taal en Letteren* (Tilburg) 27.293-303.

900. Bachmann, Walter. 1927. *Lautlehre des älteren Teiles der Chronik von Peterborough*. Weida: Thomas and Hubert, 143 pp. [Leipzig diss.]

901. Bailey, Charles-James N. 1970. "The English Great Vowel Shift Past and Present". *PIL* 3.173-78.

902. Bazire, Joyce. 1952. "ME $\bar{e}$ and $\bar{\varepsilon}$ in the Rhymes of *Sir Gawain and the Green Knight*". *JEGP* 51.234-35.

903. ———. 1957. "An Examination of Rhymes Containing Middle English $\bar{\varepsilon}$". *SN* 29.111-22.

904. Beade, Pedro. 1975. "Vowel Length in Middle English: Continuity and Change". *LB* 64.313-20.

905. Bliss, Alan J. 1948/49. "Three Middle English Studies". *EGS* 2.40-54. [1. The chronology of some sound-changes; 2. The diphthong *qu*; 3. Two notes on *The Bestiary*.]

906. ———. 1952-53. "Vowel-quantity in Middle English Borrowings from Anglo-Norman". *ArchL* 4.121-47; 5.22-47. [Repr. in *Lass EHL*, 164-207.]

907. Bond, George. 1937. *Umlaut in Middle English: A Report of a Theory Interpreting the English Vowel Shift as the Result of Umlaut in the Middle English Period*. South Methodist Univ. diss. [Abstr. in *South Methodist Univ. Abstracts of Theses* (Dallas, TX), No.5, pp. 25-26 (1938).]

908. Bonebrake, Veronica. 1980. *Historical Labial-Velar Changes in Germanic: A Study of the Counter-Directional Sound Changes in English and Netherlandic*. (= Umeå Studies in the Humanities, 29.) Umeå, Sweden: Acts Universitatis Umensis, ix + 220 pp. [Umeå diss.]

909. Bradley, Ruth J. 1943. "The Use of Cockney Dialect by Chaucer". *QJS* 29.74-76. [Shows that Chaucer did not sound initial [h].]

910. Carter, Richard. 1975. "Some Theoretical Implications of the Great Vowel Shift". *Essays Sound Pattern*, 369-76.

911. Coates, Richard. 1981. "More on Variation Between Initial 'c' and 'g' in English". *N&Q* n.s. 28.398-99. [Using largely the medieval orthography of relevant place-names as the data. Cf. A.S.C. Ross's "The Variation of Initial [k] and [g] in English" in *N&Q* n.s. 25 (1978).339-43, which is concerned with ModE.]

912. Conner, Jack E. 1963. "Old French Dissyllables and the Great Vowel Shift". *ES* 44.341-49.

913. Davies, Constance. 1934. *English Pronunciation from the Fifteenth Century to the Eighteenth: A Handbook to the Study of Historical Grammar*. London: Dent, xiv + 167 pp. [Illustrative documents.]

  Reviews: Anon. in *TLS*, May 23, 1935, p. 330; C.G. in *AS* 10.222 (1935); C.L. W[renn] in *RES* 12.372-74 (1936); G. Weber in *Anglia B* 50.136 (1939).

914. Diensberg, Bernhard. 1982. "Romanische Lehnwörter des Mittelenglischen als angebliche Zeugen für eine Diphthongierung von vulgärlat. *u* (≙ nfranz. *ü*) im Altfranzösischen". *Sprachw* 7.75-81.

915. ———. 1984 [1985]. "Historical Phonology and Markedness". *SAP* 17.39-50. [Mainly on ME diphthongs.]

916. ———. 1985. *Untersuchungen zur phonologischen Rezeption romanischen Lehnguts in Mittel- und Frühneuenglischen: Die Lehnwörter mit mittelenglisch* oi/ui *und ihre phonologische Rezeption.* (= TBL, 268.) Tübingen: Gunter Narr, xvii + 257 pp.

917. Dietz, Klaus. 1968. *Die Rezeption des vorkonsonantischen 'l' in romanischen Lehnwörtern des Mittelenglischen und seine Reflexe im neuenglischen Standard.* 2 vols. München: Fink, xxiv + 317; viii + 318-519 pp.

   Reviews: Horst Weinstock in *SN* 41.460-63 (1969); Margaret Popp in *Anglia* 88.523-29 (1970); Bertil Sundby in *IF* 75.337-41 (1970); Udo Fries in *Archiv* 207.121-23 (1970/71); Lothar Wolf in *ZRP* 88.539-40 (1972).

918. ———. 1974. "Zur Phonologie der mittelenglischen Tektalspiranten: die südmittelenglischen Reflexe von ae. *ē(o)g/h*". *Papajewski Festschrift*, 11-36.

919. ———. 1981. "Mittelenglisch *oi* in heimischen Ortsnamen und Personennamen: I.: Der Typus *Croydon*; II.: Das Namenelement *Boi(e)* und die Etymologie von *boy*". *BN* 16.269-340; 361-405.

920. ———. 1981. "Me. *oi* heimischer Provenienz". *Weltsprache Englisch in Forschung und Lehre: Festschrift für Kurt Wächtler*, ed. Peter Kunsmann and Ortwin Kuhn, 81-109. Berlin: Schmidt.

921. Dobson, Eric John. 1962 [1963]. "Middle English Lengthening in Open Syllables". *TPS* 1962, 124-48.

922. Eckhardt, Eduard. 1942. "Der Übergang zur germanischen Betonung bei den Wörtern französischer Herkunft im Mittelenglischen" *EStn* 75.9-66.

923. Ek, Karl-Gustav. 1972. *The Development of OE 'ȳ' and 'ēo' in South-Eastern Middle English* (= LundSE, 42.) Lund: Gleerup, 133 pp. [Lund diss.]

924. ———. 1975. *The Development of OE ĕ (i-Mutated ă) before Nasals and OE ǣ in South-Eastern Middle English.* (= AUL, 1:22.) Lund: LiberLäromedel/ Gleerup, 64 pp.

   Reviews: Andreas Fischer in *ES* 59.369 (1978); Charles M. Barrack in *ZDL* 49.374-75 (1982).

925. Ekselius, Paul. 1940. *A Study on the Development of the Old English Combinations* aht/oht *in Middle English.* Uppsala: Appelberg, xvi + 156 pp. [Uppsala diss.]

   Review: S.B. Liljegren in *Anglia B* 51.267-72 (1940).

926. Ekwall, Eilert. 1940. "Development of Middle English *ū*". *AS* 15.306-10.

927. Erdmann, Peter H. 1972. "The English Great Vowel Shift and Generative Phonology". *Lingua* 29.243-73.

928. Erickson, Karen. 1971. "Northern Middle English *qu-* and Scandinavian *hw-*: A Study" *MSE* 3.46-53.

929. Fausbøll, Else. 1979. "Some Examples of the Vacillation between [þ]/[ð] and [d] in Middle English". *Schibsbye Festschrift*, 32-50.

930. Fetting, Hans Frederick. 1972. "Some Nonphonetic Aspects of a Fifteenth Century Sound Change". *PMALC*/1971, 12-19. [Also printed in *Papers from the Michigan Linguistic Society Meeting, October 9, 1971*, ed. David Lawton, 7-24. Mt. Pleasant, MI: Dept. of English, Central Michigan Univ., 1972.]

931. Fischer, Erna. 1927. *Der Lautbestand des südmittelenglischen Oktavian, verglichen mit seinen Entsprechungen im Lybeaus Desconus und im Launfal.* (= AF, 63.) Heidelberg: Carl Winter, viii + 216 pp.

   Reviews: R. Willard in *MLN* 43.567 (1928); E. von Erhardt-Siebold in *JEGP* 28.547-49 (1929); F. Wild in *LGRP* 50.183 (1929); M.S. Serjeantson in *RES* 5.455-57 (1929); W. van der Gaaf in *ES* 11.27-31 (1929); E. Ekwall in *Anglia B* 41.14 (1930).

932. ———. 1929. "Ae. *ēa* im Südostmittelenglischen und die Heimat des südlichen *Octavian*". *EStn* 64.1-19.

933. Fisiak, Jacek. 1982. "Middle English *-ong* > *-ung* Revisited". *SAP* 14.17-27.

934. ———. 1984 [1985]. "The Voicing of Initial Fricatives in Middle English". *SAP* 17.3-16 (+ 7 maps).

935. Flasdieck, Hermann Martin. 1923. "Die Sprachliche Einheitlichkeit des Orrmulums". *Anglia* 47.289-331.

936. ———. 1924. "Ein südostmittelenglischer Lautwandel". *EStn* 58.1-23.

937. ———. 1925. "Studien zur Mittelenglischen Grammatik. O.E. *o + w* in Spätmittelenglischen". *Anglia B* 36.240-49.

938. ———. 1930. "Zur Datierung des ae. Wandels i̯ǫ>ę̄ǫ im westlichen Mittelland". *Anglia B* 41.37-39.

939. Friederici, Hans. 1937. *Der Lautstand Londons um 1400.* (= Forschungen zur englischen Philologie, 6.) Jena: Frommann, ix + 95 pp. [Jena diss.]

Reviews: H. Koziol in *EStn* 73.63-65 (1938); G. Weber in *Anglia B* 50.136-37 (1939).

940. Giffhorn, B. 1976. *Der Mittelenglische Typus 'waishen': Untersuchungen zu den englischen Dialekten*. Bonn diss., 393 pp. [Abstr. in *DA* 40.1492C (1979/ 80).]

941. Giffhorn, Jürgen. 1979. *Studien am "Survey of English Dialects": Wörter des Typus "know" und "grow" mit den Reflexen der me. Phoneme /au/ und /u/*. München: Wilhelm Fink, 151 pp. [Uses the material of the *Survey of English Dialects*, ed. Harold Orton, et al. (Leeds: E.J. Arnold, 1962-71).]

    Reviews: Josef Vachek in *PP* 24.56-57 (1981); Gillis Kristensson in *ES* 63.371-73 (1982); David Jost in *Speculum* 57.883-84 (1982).]

942. Hill, Archibald Anderson, 1940. "Early Loss of [r] before Dentals". *PMLA* 55.308-59.

943. Holthausen, Ferdinand. 1941. "Zur englischen Lautgeschichte". *Anglia B* 52.134-35. [1. Me. *b>w*; 2. zum ne. Lautwandel *sj>š*.]

944. Horn, Wilhelm and Martin Lehnert. 1954. *Laut und Leben: Englische Lautgeschichte der neuren Zeit (1400-1950)*. 2 vols. Berlin: Deutscher Verlag der Wissenschaften, xii + 736; viii + 737-1414 pp. [Begun by Horn and completed by Lehnert after Horn's death.]

    Reviews: H. Penzl in *MLJ* 39.433-34 (1955); H. Koziol in *ZPhon* 9.277-82 (1956); E.G. Stanley in *MLR* 51.88-90 (1956); B. Trnka in *ČMF* 38.56-58 (1956); F. Wild in *DLZ* 77.185-92 (1956); Karl Schneider in *Archiv* 193.200-03 (1956/57); Karl Brunner in *Anglia* 75.350-57 (1957); A.A. Prins in *Museum* 63.169-74 (1958); Helge Kökeritz in *ES* 41.325-31 (1960).

945. Hubmayer, Karl. 1982. "Silbenstruktur und Lautwandel: phonetisch-phonologische Aspekte der Dehnung mittelenglischer Kurzvokale in offener Silbe". *Klagenfurter Beiträge zur Sprachwissenschaft* (Klagenfurt) 8.157-74.

946. Ikegami, Masa T. 1984. *Rhyme and Pronunciation: Some Studies of English Rhymes from Kyng Alisaunder to Skelton*. (= Hogaku-Kenkyu, Keio Univ., Extra Ser., 5.) Tokyo: Hogaku-Kenkyu-Kai, Keio Univ., xv + 402 pp.

    Reviews: E.G. Stanley in *N&Q* n.s. 33.532-33 (1986); Alan Ward in *MAE* 56.116-17 (1987).

947. Jespersen, Otto. 1937. "Voicing of Spirants in English". *ES* 19.69-71. [Criticizes Trnka [no. 1019] concerning the changes of ME spirants.]

948. Kelly, Francis Marion, Jr. 1957. *The Origin of the Use of 'I' as a Sign of Length in Middle Scots*. Columbia diss., 189 pp. [Abstr. in *DA* 17.1548-49 (1957).]

949. Kihlbom, Asta. 1926. *A Contribution to the Study of Fifteenth Century English, I.* (= UUÅ 1926. Filosofi, Språkvetenskap och Historiska Vetenskaper, 7.) Uppsala: A.-B. Lundequistska Bokhandeln, xxxii + 203 pp. [Uppsala diss. Examines the development of ME vowel-sounds.]

Reviews: H.M. Flasdieck in *Anglia B* 39.128-31 (1928); J.M. Steadman, Jr. in *MLN* 43.338-40 (1928); E. Fischer in *Archiv* 161.112-13 (1932); W. van der Gaaf in *ES* 16.63-65 (1934).

950. King, Robert D. and Marianne Cooley. 1975. "An Ordering Problem in Early Middle English". *Glossa* 9.3-12.

951. Kivimaa, Kirsti and Leena Lehto. 1970. *The Great Vowel Shift — A Combinatory Change?* (= Pubs. of the Institute of Phonetics, Univ. of Helsinki, 23.) Helsinki: Institute of Phonetics, Univ. of Helsinki, iii + 41 pp.

Reviews: Klaus Hansen in *ZAA* 19.304-05 (1971); Klaus Dietz in *Anglia* 90.168-71 (1972); Horst Weinstock in *SN* 44.444-48 (1972); F. Cercignani in *ES* 54.168-69 (1973).

952. Kniezsa, Veronika. 1981. "On the Origin of <ei, ey> Spellings in Middle English". *On the Development of English*, ed. S. Rot, 88-100. Budapest: L. Eötvös Univ.

953. ———. 1983. "The Problem of the Merger of Middle English /aː/ and /ai/ in Northern English". *Current Topics in EHL*, 95-102.

954. ———. 1983. "<ai> and <e> in Medieval Northern English Manuscripts". *FLH* 4.45-53.

955. Kökeritz, Helge. 1954. *A Guide to Chaucer's Pronunciation*. Stockholm: Almqvist & Wiksell; New Haven, CT: Whitlock, 32 pp. [Repr., New York: Holt, Rinehart and Winston, 1961, 1962. Also repr. as "Medieval Academy Reprints for Teaching, 3", Toronto-Buffalo-London: Univ. of Toronto Press in association with the Medieval Academy of America, 1978.]

Reviews: [R.W.] Z[andvoort] in *ES* 35.285 (1954); T.F. Mustanoja in *NM* 56.73 (1955); T. Pyles in *MLN* 71.297-99 (1956); D.W. Robertson, Jr. in *QJS* 42.326-27 (1956).

956. ———. 1959. "English *i* for Old French *ü*". *Mossé Festschrift*, 218-24.

957. Kohler, K.J. 1967. "Aspects of Middle Scots Phonemics and Graphemics: The Phonological Implications of the Sign <i>". *TPS* 1967, 32-61.

958. Koziol, Herbert. 1937. "Der Abfall des nachtonigen -*e* im Mittelenglischen". *Anglia B* 48.307-09.

959. Kristensson, Gillis. 1977. "A Case of the Role of Functional Load". *Anglia* 95.450-53. [Discusses the ME development of OE /ø(:)/ and /y(:)/ in the West Midlands and the South-West of England.]

960. ———. 1978. "A Note on OE /e:ow/ and OFr /y/ in Middle English". *SN* 50.25-27.

961. ———. 1979. "On the Evidence for Phonemic Change". *NM* 80.304-07. [Demonstrates the value of 'inverted spellings' as evidence for phonemic *mergers* in ME.]

962. ———. 1985. "OE ěo in the West Midlands in Late Middle English". *Gerritsen Festschrift*, 97-112.

963. Kurath, Hans. 1956. "The Loss of Long Consonants and the Rise of Voiced Fricatives in Middle English". *Language* 32.435-45.

964. Kuryłowicz, Jerzy. 1965. "A Remark on the Great Vowel Shift". *Word* 21.183-87.

965. Lass, Roger. 1985 [1987]. "Minkova *noch einmal*: MEOSL and the Resolved Foot". *FLH* 6:2.245-65. [Apropos of Minkova [no. 982]. MEOSL = Middle English Open Syllable Lengthening.]

966. Liberman, A.S. 1965. "Some Notes on the History of Middle English /e/ and /o/ in Open Syllables". *ZAA* 13.21-24.

967. ———. 1966. "On the History of Middle English *ā* and *a*". *NM* 67.66-71.

968. Lieber, Rochelle. 1979. "On Middle English Lengthening in Open Syllables". *LingA* 5.1-27.

969. Liedholm, A. 1941. *A Phonological Study of the Middle English Romance 'Arthour and Merlin' (MS Auchinleck)*. Uppsala: Almqvist & Wiksell, xxiii + 192 pp. [Uppsala diss.]

   Review: S.B. Liljegren in *Anglia B* 53.13 (1942).

970. Mackenzie, Barbara A. 1926/27. "A Special Dialectal Development of O.E. *ēa* in Middle English". *EStn* 61.386-92.

971. ———. 1927. "Unfractured Forms in Thirteenth-Century Essex Place-Names". *RES* 3.453-55.

972. Magnusson, Ulf. 1971. *Studies in the Phonology of the 'Ayenbite of Inwyt'*. (= Lund Theses in English, 1.) Lund: Dept. of English, Lund Univ., vii + 268 pp. [Lund diss.]

973. Mahling, Carl. 1928. *Über Tonvokal + ht im Frühmittelenglischen*. Leipzig: Mayer und Müller, 200 pp. [Berlin diss.]

   Reviews: A. Eichler in *Anglia B* 40.263-64 (1929); W. van der Gaaf in *ES* 11.124 (1929); F. Wild in *EStn* 65.77-79 (1930).

974. Malone, Kemp. 1925/26. "Studies in English Phonology, II: *AI*". *MP* 23.483-90. [Mainly concerned with Chaucerian phonology. For the first of the series, see K. Malone, "Studies in English Phonology, I: *au*", *MP* 20 (1922), 189-200.]

975. ———. 1956. "Chaucer's Double Consonants and the Final *e*". *MS* 18.204-07.

976. Malsch, Derry L. and Roseanne Fulcher. 1975. "Tensing and Syllabication in Middle English". *Language* 51.303-14.

977. Matthes, Heinrich Christoph. 1931. "Das Orrmulum und die Frage der intonationsgerechten Orthographie". *Anglia* 55.400-11.

978. Matthews, William. 1937. "The Vulgar Speech of London in the XV-XVII Centuries". *N&Q* 172.2-5; 21-24; 40-42; 56-60; 77-79; 92-96; 112-15; 130-33; 149-51; 167-70; 186-88; 204-06; 218-21; 241-42. [An analysis of the pronunciation.]

979. McJimsey, Ruth Buchanan. 1942. *Chaucer's Irregular -e: A Demonstration among Monosyllabic Nouns of the Exceptions to Grammatical and Metrical Harmony*. New York: King's Crown Press, x + 248 pp.

   Reviews: S. Potter in *MLR* 38.138-39 (1943); Dorothy Everett in *RES* 20.234-36 (1944); A. Marckwardt in *Language* 20.257-60 (1944).

980. McLaughlin, John C. 1963. *A Graphemic-Phonemic Study of a Middle English Manuscript*. The Hague: Mouton, 162 pp. [Originally Indiana Univ. diss. 1961; Abstr. in *DA* 22.1617-18 (1961). The manuscript investigated is MS Cotton Nero A.x. which contains *Sir Gawain and the Green Knight, Pearl, Purity,* and *Patience*.]

   Reviews: Angus McIntosh in *ArchL* 16.78-80 (1964); R. Sikora in *KN* 11.299-300 (1964); H.E. Brekle in *Linguistics* 11.82-90 (1965); E.V.K. Dobbie in *Language* 41.151-54 (1965); M.C. Seymour in *Lingua* 16.433-35 (1966); H.H. Meier in *LT* 246.237-38 (1968); Jane Crawford in *ES* 50.Anglo-American Suppl. lxxix-lxxxii (1969).

981. Minkova, Donka. 1980. "Unstressed Final -*e* in the Ormulum". *Sofia English Studies*, 162-80.

982. ———. 1982. "The Environment for Open Syllable Lengthening in Middle English". *FLH* 3.29-58.

983. ———. 1983. "Middle English Final -*e* from a Phonemic Point of View". *Current Topics in EHL*, 191-209. [Also printed in *Edinburgh Univ. Dept. of Linguistics Work in Progress* 15.27-44 (1982).]

984. ———. 1984. "On the Hierarchy of Factors Causing Schwa Loss in Middle English". *NM* 85.445-53.

985. ———. 1984. "Early Middle English Metric Elision and Schwa Deletion". *Blake & Jones*, 56-66.

986. ———. 1985. "Of Rhyme and Reason: Some Foot-Governed Quantity Changes in English". *PICEHL*/4, 163-78. [Chiefly concerned with ME.]

987. Nakao, Toshio. 1978. *The Prosodic Phonology of Late Middle English*. Tokyo: Shinozaki Shorin, v + 206 pp.

988. ———. 1984. "On Late Middle English Word Stress". *Blake & Jones*, 87-100.

989. Nieuwint, P.J.G.M. 1981. "What Happened to Middle English /(u)(x)/?". *Neophil* 65.440-67.

990. Ogura, Mieko. 1980. "The Development of ME $\bar{e}$: A Case of Lexical Diffusion". *SEL* English No. 1980, 39-57.

991. Phillips, Betty Steedley. 1983. "Middle English Diphthongization, Phonetic Analogy, and Lexical Diffusion". *Word* 34.11-23.

992. Plotkin, V.Y. 1965. "Phonological Statistics and Diachronic Phonology". *PP* 8.283-85. [The examples are from Late ME.]

993. Poussa, Patricia. 1985. "A Note on the Voicing of Initial Fricatives in Middle English". *PICEHL*/4, 235-52.

994. Prins, Anton Adriaan. 1940. *The Great Vowel Shift*. Groningen: Noordhoff, 19 pp.

Review: E. Kruisinga in *Taal en Leven* (Den Haag) 5.46-47 (1941/42).

995. ———. 1942. "The Great Vowel Shift Reconsidered". *ES* 24.161-68.

996. ———. 1942. "A Few Early Examples of the Great Vowel Shift". *Neophil* 27.134-37.

997. ———. 1971. "The Great Vowel Shift: A Refutation". *Neophil* 55.317-27. [Argues against Trnka [no. 1021] and Vachek [no. 661].]

998. Rau, Reinhold. 1956. *Die schriftsprachliche Entwicklung der mittelenglischen e-Laute in Verbindung mit r im Neuenglischen.* Heidelberg diss., xiii + 439 pp.

999. Reaney, Percy Hide. 1925. "On Certain Phonological Features of the Dialect of London in the Twelfth Century". *EStn* 59.321-45.

1000. ———. 1928. "Unfractured Forms in Thirteenth-Century Essex Place-Names". *RES* 4.331-34. [Cf. Mackenzie [no. 971].]

1001. Romaine, Suzanne. 1984. "The Sociolinguistic History of T/D Deletion". *FLH* 5.221-55. [Examines the so-called t/d deletion found operative in the history of English in texts dating from at least the beginning of the ME period.]

1002. Sandahl, B. 1964. "On Old Norse *jó, jú* in English". *SN* 36.266-76. [In ME.]

1003. Schmidt, Ursula. 1963. *Die Rezeption des a-nasals romanischer Lehnwörter in Mittelenglischen und seine Weiterentwicklung in Standard u. Dialekten.* Heidelberg diss., xliii + 313 pp.

Reviews: A.J. Bliss in *MAE* 34.173-74 (1965); Bertil Sundby in *SN* 37.415-18 (1965); A.A. Prins in *ES* 51.451-52 (1970).

1004. Serjeantson, Mary Sydney. 1927. "The Development of Old English *ēa, ēah* in Middle English". *JEGP* 26.198-225 and 350-400.

1005. ———. 1931. "Middle English *-ong> -ung*". *RES* 7.450-52.

1006. Sheldon, Esther K. 1937. "The Vulgar Speech of London in the XV-XVII Centuries". *N&Q* 173.409-10. [Apropos of Matthews [no. 978].]

1007. Smithers, Geoffrey Victor. 1983. "The Scansion of *Havelok* and the Use of ME *-en* and *-e* in *Havelok* and by Chaucer". *Davis Festschrift*, 195-234.

1008. Stern, Gustaf. 1941. *Old English æ in the Earlier Text of Layamon.* (= *GHÅ*, 47.) Göteborg: Wettergren & Kerber, 31 pp.

Reviews: S.R.T.O. d'Ardenne in *ES* 24.179-81 (1942); Erik Tengstrand in *SN* 15.380-85 (1942/43).

1009. Stockwell, Robert P. 1952. *Chaucerian Graphemics and Phonemics: A Study in Historical Methodology.* Univ. of Virginia diss., iii + 211 pp. [Abstr. in *Univ. of Virginia Abstracts of Diss.* 1952, 11-13.]

1010. ———. 1961. "The Middle English 'Long Close' and 'Long Open' Mid Vowels". *TSLL* 2.529-38. [Repr. in *Lass EHL*, 154-63.]

1011. ———. 1972. "Problems in the Interpretation of the Great Vowel Shift". *Studies in Linguistics in Honor of George L. Trager* (= JanL, Ser. Maior, 52), ed. M. Estelle Smith, 344-62. The Hague: Mouton.

1012. ———. 1978. "Perseverance in the English Vowel Shift". *Historical Phonology*, 337-48.

1013. ———. 1985. "Assessment of Alternative Explanations of the Middle English Phenomenon of High Vowel Lowering when Lengthened in the Open Syllable". *PICEHL*/4, 303-18.

1014. Storms, Godfrid. 1960. "A Note on Chaucer's Pronunciation of French *u*". *ES* 41.305-08.

1015. Sundby, Bertil. 1956. "Middle English Overlapping of *V* and *W* and Its Phonemic Significance". *Anglia* 74.438-44.

1016. Taylor, A.B. 1924. "On the History of Old English $\bar{ea}$, $\bar{eo}$ in Middle English". *MLR* 19.1-10.

1017. Thomason, S.G. and T.S. Kaufman. 1976. "Contact-Induced Change: Loanwords and the Borrowing Language's Pre-Borrowing Phonology". *PICHL*/2, 167-79. [Discusses the impact of Anglo-Norman on ME.]

1018. Tillman, Nathaniel Patrick. 1941. *Lydgate's Rimes as Evidence of his Pronunciation*. Wisconsin diss., 617 pp. [Abstr. in *Summaries of Doctoral Diss., Univ. of Wisconsin* 6.293-95 (1942).]

1019. Trnka, Bohumil. 1936. "On the Phonological Development of Spirants in English". *Proceedings of the Second International Congress of Phonetic Sciences* (Cambridge), 60-64. [On the voicing of [f, θ, s] in late ME.]

1020. ———. 1938. "The Phonemic Development of Spirants in English". *ES* 20.26-31. [A rejoinder to Jespersen's criticism [no. 947] of Trnka [no. 1019].]

1021. ———. 1959. "A Phonemic Aspect of the Great Vowel-Shift". *Mossé Festschrift*, 440-43. [Repr. in *Trnka Papers*, 258-62.]

1022. Vachek, Josef. 1954. "Notes on the Phonological Development of the NE Pronoun *She*". *SFFBU* 3 (A2).67-80.

1023. ———. 1965. "The English Great Vowel Shift Again". *PSE* 11.3-13.

1024. Van der Gaaf, Willem. 1933. "The Evolution of Nasal *a* in Anglo-Norman and in English". [In ME.]

1025. Viel, Michel. 1975. "Vowel Alternations in English and the Great Vowel Shift". *Joly & Fraser*, 31-58.

1026. Weinstock, Horst. 1984. "Aspects of the Great Vowel Shift". *MSC Aachen 1983*, 155-68.

1027. Wilson, Richard Middlewood. 1935. "$æ^1$ and $æ^2$ in Middle English". *Proceedings of the Leeds Philosophical and Literary Society: Literary and Historical Section*, 3.342-46.

1028. Western, August. 1930. "Aphesis, Syncope and Apocope in Middle and Early Modern English". *Jespersen Festschrift*, 133-43.

1029. Wittig, Kurt. 1951. "Über die mittelenglische Dehnung in offener Silbe und die Entwicklung der $ēr$-Laute im Frühneuenglischen". *Anglia* 70.47-69.

1030. Wolfe, Patricia M. 1970. "Some Theoretical Questions on the Historical English Vowel Shift". *PIL* 3.221-35.

1031. ———. 1972. *Linguistic Change and the Great Vowel Shift in English*. Berkeley & Los Angeles: Univ. of California Press, x + 198 pp. [Originally Univ. of California, Los Angeles, diss. 1969; Abstr. in *DA* 30.4973A (1970).]

   Reviews: Anon. in *TLS*, 3 August, 1973, p. 909; Törbjörn Söderholm and Nils Erik Enkvist in *SN* 46.551-54 (1974); L.W. Collier in *JL* 11.371-72 (1975); Marianne Cooley in *Language* 51.478-80 (1975); Robin Smith in *ES* 56.176-78 (1975); Robert St. Clair in *PQ* 54.540-41 (1975); Alan Ward in *RES* n.s. 26.250-51 (1975).

1032. ———. 1975. "On the Validity of the Chomsky-Halle Analysis of the Historical English Vowel Shift". *Essays Sound Pattern*, 355-67.

IX. MORPHOLOGY

A. General

1033. Bammesberger, Alfred. 1984. *A Sketch of Diachronic English Morphology.* (= Eichstätter Materialen, 7: Sprach und Literatur.) Regensburg: Friedrich Pustet, 94 pp.

   Reviews: Martin Peters in *Sprache* 30.163-64 (1984); C. Robin Barrett in *Diachronica* 2.239-44 (1985); Alan Bliss in *N&Q* n.s. 32.508-09 (1985); R.L. Thomson in *GL* 25.133-40 (1985); Sheila M. Embleton in *Language* 62.212-13 (1986); Gero Bauer in *ZVS* 98.313-14 (1985).

1034. Bazell, Charles Ernest. 1962. "Six Questions of Old and Middle English Morphology". *Tolkien Festschrift*, 51-62. [1. OE nom.-acc. plural *suna*; 2. West-Saxon preterite indicative *funde*; 3. Consonantal alteration in the declension of OE *spræc*; 4. The preterite type *brāk*; 5. Northern *thire* 'these'; 6. West-Midland dat. plural *-es*.]

1035. Cooke, William G. 1987. "Notes on the Development of the English Pronouns". *ELN* 24:3.1-6.

1036. Gericke, Bernhard and Walter Greul. 1934. *Das Personalpronomen der 3. Person in spätangelsächsischen und frühmittelenglischen Texten. Ein Beitrag zur altenglischen Dialektgeographie.* (= Palaestra, 193.) Leipzig: Mayer und Müller, vii + 144 pp. [Contains two separate monographs: Gericke [no. 1082] and Greul [no. 1150].]

   Reviews: A. B[randl] in *Archiv* 166.293-94 (1935); H. Marcus in *Archiv* 167.138-39 (1935); M.S. Serjeantson in *ES* 20.42-44 (1938).

1037. Heller, Louis G. and James Macris. 1969 [1975]. "Typological Recycling and the Anomaly/Ungrammaticality Dichotomy: The Evolution of the English Verbal Endings". *AS* 44.106-17.

1038. Heltveit, Trygve. 1952. "Notes on the Development of the Personal Pronouns in English". *NTS* 16.377-86.

1039. ———. 1953. *Studies in English Demonstrative Pronouns: A Contribution to the History of English Morphology.* Oslo: Akademisk Forlag, 138 pp. [Oslo diss. Repr., Oslo: Universitetsforlaget, 1967.]

   Reviews: A. Culioli in *EA* 8.251-52 (1955) and *BSL* 52.145-47 (1956); E.V.K. Dobbie in *Word* 11.334-35 (1955); G. Shepherd in *MLR* 50.238-39 (1955); Alan Ward in *RES* n.s. 6.403-04 (1955); K. Schneider in *Archiv* 192.313-14 (1955/56); Karl Brunner in *Anglia* 74.258-60 (1956); Gerhard Graband in *ZAA* 4.373-75 (1956); G. Scheurweghs in *LB* 45.Bijblad 14-15 (1956); Eric Buyssens in *RBPH* 37.454-55 (1959); Walther Preusler in *IF* 64.326-27 (1959); B.D.H. Miller in *N&Q* n.s. 15.239-40 (1968).

1040. Janda, Richard D. 1980. "On the Decline of Declensional Systems: The Overall Loss of OE Nominal Case Inflections and the ME Reanalysis of *-es* as *his*". *PICHL*/4, 243-52.

1041. Kastovsky, Dieter. 1972. "Probleme der historischen Morphologie aus generativer Sicht: das englische konsonantische Präteritum und 2. Partizip". *Linguistik 1971. Referate des 6. Linguistischen Kolloquiums, 11.-14. August 1971 in Kopenhagen*, ed. Karl Hyldgaard-Jensen, 252-65. Frankfurt am Main: Athenäum.

1042. Keller, Wolfgang. 1925. "Skandinavischer Einfluss in der englischen Flexion". *Probleme der englischen Sprache und Kultur. Festschrift für Johannes Hoops zum 60. Geburtstag* (= Germanische Bibliothek, 2:20), ed. W. Keller, 80-87. Heidelberg: Carl Winter.

1043. Marckwardt, Albert Henry. 1935. "Origin and Extension of the Voiceless Preterite and the Past Participle Inflections of the English Irregular Weak Verb Conjugation". *Michigan Essays and Studies*, 151-328.

1044. Mezger, Fritz. 1937. "Zur Ineinanderbildung der verschiedenen Wurzeln und Formen im Präsens Indic. des Verbum Substantivum im Westgermanischen". *Archiv* 171.145-49.

1045. O'Neil, Wayne. 1982. "Simplifying the Grammar of English". *McIntosh Festschrift* (A), 285-306. [Discusses the simplification of case-realization and the sharpened distinction between derivational and inflectional morphemes in the grammar of English.]

1046. Peinovich, Michael Peter. 1972. *A Re-examination of Morphological Change in Old and Middle English Nouns*. Univ. of Wisconsin-Madison diss., 161 pp. [Abstr. in *DA* 33.6895A (1973).]

1047. ———. 1979. *Old English Noun Morphology: A Diachronic Study.* (= NHLS,

41.) Amsterdam: North-Holland, xii + 243 pp. [Despite the title, the period covered is 1050-1300.]

Reviews: Betty S. Phillips in *Word* 32.225-30 (1981); T.F. Hoad in *N&Q* n.s. 29.64-65.

1048. Peters, Robert Anthony. 1985. "Historical Development of Noun Plural *-(e)s*". *JEngL* 18.25-32.

1049. Reed, David Wooderson. 1950. *The History of Inflectional 'n' in English Verbs before 1500*. (= UCPE, 7:4.157-328.) Berkeley & Los Angeles: Univ. of California Press, x + 172 pp. [Originally Michigan diss. 1949.]

Reviews: K.R. Brooks in *MLR* 47.99-100 (1952); A.A. Hill in *Language* 27.594-97 (1951); James A. Walker in *AS* 27.36-39 (1952).

1050. Rooth, Erik. 1941/42. "Zur Geschichte der englischen Partizip-Präsens-Form auf *-ing*". *Ekwall Festschrift* = *SN* 14.71-85. [Discusses how and why OE *-ende* became *-ing*.]

1051. Scott, James Robert. 1975. *Morphology in Historical Change*. Univ. of Texas at Austin diss., 156 pp. [Abstr. in *DA* 36.2783-84A (1975). Partly concerned with OE and ME.]

1052. Wolff, Dieter. 1975. *Grundzüge der diachronischen Morphologie des Englischen*. (= AA, 7.) Tübingen: Max Niemeyer, x + 102 pp.

Reviews: Manfred Görlach in *IF* 84.411-15 (1976); Barbara M.H. Strang in *YES* 8.309-11 (1978); Hans Sauer in *Anglia* 100.459-63 (1982).

B. Old English

1053. Bammesberger, Alfred. 1969. "Die kurzsilbigen femininen *i*-Stämme im Altenglischen". *Sprache* 15.46-52.

1054. ———. 1975. "Die Flexion der altenglischen Abstrakta auf *-(ð)u*". *ZVS* 89.283-90.

1055. ———. 1982. "Der Optativ bei athematischen Verbalstämmen im Altenglischen". *Anglia* 100.413-18.

1056. ———. 1985. "Die Endung für Nom. Akk. Pl. bei altenglischen *u*-Stämmen". *Anglia* 103.365-70.

1057. Bazell, Charles Ernest. 1940. "Case-Forms in *-i* in the Oldest English Texts". *MLN* 55.136-39.

1058. ———. 1959. "Some Problems of Old English Morphology". *Mossé Festschrift*, 27-31. [1. The distribution of forms in the 2nd weak conjugation; 2. Northumbrian *-s* in the present indicative; 3. Nom.-acc. plural *-as*.]

1059. ———. 1960 [1961]. "A Question of Syncretism and Analogy". *TPS* 1960, 1-12. [The examples are mainly drawn from OE.]

1060. ———. 1968. "Notes on Old English Metre and Morphology". *Marchand Festschrift*, 17-19. [Contains the section 'Locative singulars in *-um*'.]

1061. Berndt, Rolf. 1956. *Form und Funktion des Verbums in nördlichen Spätaltenglischen*. Halle/Saale: Max Niemeyer, 311 pp. [Originally Humboldt Univ. Berlin diss., entitled *Die Flexion des Verbums im Nordhumbrischen und Mercischen im späten 10. Jahrhundert. Eine Untersuchung der sprachlichen Formen und ihrer syntaktischen Beziehungsbedeutungen*; Abstr. in *WZHU* 4.141-48 (1954/55). Concerned with *Lindisfarne* and *Rushworth Gospels* and *Durham Ritual*.]

Reviews: Ewald Standop in *Archiv* 194.329-30 (1957/58); Tauno F. Mustanoja in *NM* 59.221-24 (1958); M.L. Samuels in *ArchL* 10.139-43 (1958); A.S.C. Ross in *EPS* 8.45-47 (1963).

1062. ———. 1958. "Zum s/ð-Problem in der nordhumbrischen Verbalflexion". *ZAA* 6.46-50.

1063. Blakeley, Leslie. 1947/48. "Accusative-Dative Syncretism in the Lindisfarne Gospels". *EGS* 1.6-31.

1064. ———. 1949/50. "The Lindisfarne s/ð Problem". *SN* 22.15-47. [On the origin of the *s*-forms of the English verb.]

1065. Bloomfield, Leonard. 1930. "Old English Plural Subjunctive in *-e*". *JEGP* 29.100-13.

1066. Cowgill, Warren (Crawford). 1965. "The Old English Present Indicative Ending *-e*". *Symbolae Linguisticae in Honorem Georgii Kuryłowicz*, 44-50. Wrocław-Warszawa-Kraków: Polska Akademia Nauk.

1067. Dahl, Ivar. 1938. *Substantival Inflexion in Early Old English: Vocalic Stems*. (= LundSE, 7.) Lund: Gleerup, xvi + 206 pp.

Reviews: O. Arngart in *SN* 12.152-55 (1939/40); A.G. van Hamel in *Museum* 47.171 (1940); F. Mossé in *BSL* 125.138-39 (1942/45).

1068. Eble, Connie Clare. 1970. *Noun Inflection in Royal 7 C. XII, Ælfric's First Series of Catholic Homilies*. Univ. of North Carolina diss., 96 pp. [Abstr. in *DA* 32.946A (1971).]

1069. Eliason, Norman Ellsworth. 1967. "The Origin of Irregular -*t* in Weak Preterits like *sent* and *felt*". *Lane Festschrift*, 210-20.

1070. Erdmann, Peter H. 1974. "Die Ableitung der altenglischen Substantivparadigmen". *Linguistics* 130.5-53.

1071. Flasdieck, Hermann Martin. 1934. "Die zweite Person des Singulars im ae. Verbalsystem". *Anglia* 58.113-21.

1072. ———. 1935. "Untersuchungen über die germanischen schwachen Verben III. Klasse (unter besonderer Berücksichtigung des Altenglischen)". *Anglia* 59.1-192. [Also separately, Halle: Max Niemeyer, 192 pp. Cf. Ross [no. 1124].]

1073. ———. 1936. "Die reduplizierenden Verben des Germanischen (unter besonderer Berücksichtigung des Altenglischen)". *Anglia* 60.241-65.

1074. ———. 1936-38. "Das altgermanische Verbum Substantivum unter besonderer Berücksichtigung des Altenglischen". *EStn* 71.321-49; 72.158-60.

1075. ———. 1937. "Das Verbum *wollen* im Altgermanischen (unter besonderer Berücksichtigung des Altenglischen)". *Anglia* 61.1-42.

1076. ———. 1937. "Ae. *dōn* and *ʒān*". *Anglia* 61.43-64. [On OE forms of the verbs.]

1077. Förster, Max. 1941. "Die spätae. deiktische Pronominalform *pæʒe* und ne. *they*". *Anglia B* 52.274-80.

1078. ———. 1942. "Nochmals ae. *pæʒe*". *Anglia B* 53.86-87.

1079. Fourquet, Jean. 1941/42. "Anglo-Saxon *ēode*, *dyde*, et la théorie du prétérit faible". *Ekwall Festschrift* = *SN* 14.420-26.

1080. Fullerton, G. Lee. 1977. *Historical Germanic Verb Morphology*. (= Studia Linguistica Germanica, 13.) Berlin & New York: Walter de Gruyter, 123 pp.

    Reviews: Paul T. Roberge in *MGS* 4:1.101-14 (1978); Thomas W. Juntune in *CJL* 23.154-58 (1978).

1081. Fullmer, Daniel Henry. 1969. *Generative Inflectional Morphology and Phonology of Mercian Old English*. Michigan diss., 372 pp. [Abstr. in *DA* 30.3927A (1970).]

1082. Gericke, Bernhard. 1933. *Die Flexion des Personalpronomens der dritten Person im Spätangelsächsischen*. Berlin diss., 90 pp. [See Gericke and Greul [no. 1036].]

1083. Gough, John Vaughan. 1973. "Old English *cuman* and *niman*". *ES* 54.521-25.

1084. Hedberg, Johannes. 1945. *The Syncope of the Old English Present Endings: A Dialect Criterion*. (= LundSE, 12.) Lund: Gleerup; London: Williams and Norgate; Copenhagen: Ejnar Munksgaard, 310 pp. [Lund diss. A survey of the 2nd and 3rd sg. pres. ind. of the OE strong verbs, and of the weak verbs of Class I.]

Reviews: R.J. Menner in *JEGP* 47.415-18 (1948); Norman Davis in *RES* 25.160-61 (1949); K. Malone in *MLN* 64.559 (1949); Simeon Potter in *MLR* 44.95-97 (1949); F. Mossé in *BSL* 44.119-20 (1947/48); Edgar C. Polomé in *RBPH* 26.613-16 (1948); M.T. Löfvenberg in *SN* 22.225-29 (1949/50); H.C. Matthes in *Archiv* 187.129-30 (1950).

1085. Heidemann, Gerhard. 1924. "Die Flexion des Verbums substantivum im Angelsächsischen". *Archiv* 147.30-46.

1086. Herold, Curtis Paul. 1968. *The Morphology of King Alfred's Translation of the 'Orosius'*. (= JanL, Ser. Practica, 62.) The Hague: Mouton, 80 pp. [Originally Indiana diss. 1961: Abstr. in *DA* 22.3196 (1962).]

Reviews: Robert Howren in *Language* 45.374-78 (1969); Janet M. Bately in *Anglia* 89.516-23 (1971); E.M. Liggins in *MAE* 40.266-68 (1971).

1087. Hogg, Richard M. 1980. "Analogy as a Source of Morphological Complexity". *FLH* 1.277-84. [Based on OE.]

1088. Holthausen, Ferdinand. 1925/26. "Die Endung der I. Sgl. Ind. Präs. im Altenglischen". *EStn* 60.119.

1089. Howren, Robert. 1967. "The Generation of Old English Weak Verbs". *Language* 43.674-85.

1090. Keller, Wolfgang. 1925. "Keltisches im englischen Verbum". *Anglica: Untersuchung zur englischen Philologie, Alois Brandl zum 70. Geburtstage überreicht* (= Palaestra, 147), 55-66. Leipzig: Mayer und Müller. [See especially pp. 56-60 (i.e. I. Altenglisch *bið* = Kymrisch *byð*).]

1091. Keyser, Samuel Jay and Wayne O'Neil. 1985. "The Simplification of the Old English Strong Nominal Paradigms". *PICEHL*/4, 85-107.

1092. Lehmann, Winfred Philipp. 1954. "Old English and Old Norse Secondary Preterits in *-r-*". *Language* 30.202-10.

1093. Levin, Samuel R. 1964. "A Reclassification of the Old English Strong Verbs". *Language* 40.156-61.

1094. Linke, G. 1938/39. "*Standeþ* und *stent* und dergleichen in ags. sicher fixierten Hss". *EStn* 73.321-30. [On umlaut and syncope in the OE verb inflection.]

1095. Löfvenberg, Mattias Teodor. 1949. *On the Syncope of the Old English Present Endings.* (= Essays and Studies on English Language and Literature, 1.) Uppsala: Lundequist; Copenhagen: Munksgaard; Cambridge, MA: Harvard Univ. Press, 52 pp. [= *SN* 21.231-76. Cf. Hedberg [no. 1084].]

   Reviews: Randolph Quirk in *MLR* 45.276 (1950); A.A. Hill in *SIL* 9.97-98 (1951); G. S[cheurweghs] in *LB* 41.33-34 (1951).

1096. Lotspeich, C.M. 1933. "Germanic Strong Verbs of Class VII". *JEGP* 32.281-92.

1097. Malone, Kemp. 1936. "The Inflexion of OE. *gar* 'spear'". *Anglia B* 47.219-20.

1098. Marckwardt, Albert Henry. 1949. "Verb Inflections in Late Old English". *Malone Festschrift*, 79-88.

1099. Mertens-Fonck, Paule. 1984. "The Place of the *Vespasian Psalter* in the History of English". *Crépin LSSME*/10, 39-46. [Also printed in *SAP* 17.17-28 (1985). Discusses: (1) the 1st sg. pres. ind. *-e* and (2) confusion of Classes I and II of weak verbs.]

1100. ———. 1984. "The Old English 1st Sg. Pres. Ind. in *-e* Reconsidered". *Current Research 1983*, 29-38.

1101. Motherwell, George McCormick. 1959. *Old English Morphemic Structures: A Grammatical Restatement.* Indiana Univ. diss., 157 pp. [Abstr. in *DA* 20.1359-60 (1959).]

1102. Parker, Frank. 1975. "Inflectional Endings on Old English Past Participles". *Linguistics* 162.5-14.

1103. Peeters, Christian. 1970. "A Formal Description of the Use of Some Verbal Endings in Old English". *Buyssens Festschrift*, 151-59.

1104. Penhallurick, John M. 1978. "Change in a Grammatical System: The Case of West Saxon 1st sg. pres. *-e*". *ALH* 16.121-46.

1105. Peters, Robert Anthony. 1965. "Case-Number Morphs of Old English Nouns". *Linguistics* 14.41-51.

1106. ———. 1967. "Morphemic Classification of Old English Adverb Subsets". *CJL* 13.20-23.

1107. Prewitt, Terry. 1979. "Contextual and Pattern Variation of Old English Auxiliary Verbs: Implications for Documentation of Language Change Processes". *Papers of the 1978 Mid-American Linguistics Conference at Oklahoma*, ed. Ralph E. Cooley, et al., 134-43. Norman, OK: Dept. of Communication, Univ. of Oklahoma.

1108. Prokosch, Eduard. 1927. "The Old English Weak Preterites without Medial Vowel". *PMLA* 17.331-38.

1109. Quirk, Randolph. 1950. "On the Problem of Morphological Suture in Old English". *MLR* 45.1-5. [Slightly rev. and repr. as "On the problem of inflexional juncture in Old English" in *Quirk Essays* (pp. 30-37).]

1110. Ross, Alan Strode Campbell. 1933. "The 1st Sg. Pres. Ind. *-e* in Old English". *NM* 34.232-39.

1111. ———. 1934. "The Origin of the *S*-Endings of the Present Indicative in English". *JEGP* 33.68-73. [Concerned with OE. Cf. Erik Holmqvist, *On the History of the English Present Inflections, Particularly '-th' and '-s'*. Heidelberg: Carl Winter, 1922.]

1112. ———. 1934. "The Plural Present Indicative in English and Low German". *NM* 35.169-70. [Concerned with OE.]

1113. ———. 1935. "The Nom. Acc. SG. Fem. and the Nom. Acc. Pl. of the Anglo-Frisian *hi*-Pronoun". *LSE* 4.14-23.

1114. ———. 1937. *Studies in the Accidence of the Lindisfarne Gospels*. (= Leeds School of English Language, Texts and Monographs, 2.) Leeds: School of English, Univ. of Leeds, 179 pp.

Reviews: G. Linke in *Archiv* 174.112-13 (1938); F. M[ossé] in *RG* 29.62 (1938); S. Potter in *MLR* 33.574-75 (1938); Josef Raith in *Anglia B* 49.132-34 (1938); Ingerid Dal in *ES* 21.75-78 (1939).

1115. ———. 1967. "*This* in the Lindisfarne Gospels and the Durham Ritual". *N&Q* n.s. 14.284-88. [= Adrediana XVI. Analyzes Aldred's forms of *this*.]

1116. ———. 1968. "Aldrediana XX: Notes on the Preterite-Present Verbs". *EPS* 11.44-50.

1117. ———. 1968. "On Some Forms of the Anomalous and Contracted Verbs in the Anglo-Saxon Glosses to the Lindisfarne Gospels and the Durham Ritual". *TPS* 1968, 67-105. [= Aldrediana XIX.]

1118. ———. 1968. "*You* in the North". *N&Q* n.s. 15.323-24. [Derives the Northern pronoun *you* not from West Saxon OE *ēow*, but from Northumbrian OE *īuh*.]

1119. ———. 1970. "Aldrediana XXI: The Correspondent of West Saxon *Wunian*". *NM* 71.529-33.

1120. ———. 1971. "Two Vestigial Distinctions in the Late Northumbrian Dialect of Anglo-Saxon". *ArchL* n.s. 2.117-27.

1121. ———. 1971. "Aldrediana XXIII: Notes on the Accidence of the Durham Ritual". *LSE* n.s. 5.53-67.

1122. ———. 1976. "Notes on the Accidence of Rushworth^1". *NM* 77.492-509.

1123. ———. 1977. "Notes on the Accidence of Rushworth^2". *NM* 78.300-08.

1124. ———. 1981. "Aldredian Comments on Two Articles by the Late Professor Flasdieck". *Anglia* 99.390-93. [A list of corrections and amendments to H.M. Flasdieck's work [nos. 1072 & 1075].]

1125. Seebold, Elmar. 1966. "Die ae. schwundstufigen Präsentien (Aoristpräsentien) der *ei*-Reihe". *Anglia* 84.1-26.

1126. ———. 1967. "Die ae. starken Partizipia Praeteriti mit Umlaut". *Anglia* 85.251-69.

1127. Seelig, Fritz. 1930. *Die Komparation der Adjektiva und Adverbien im Altenglischen*. (= AF, 70.) Heidelberg: Carl Winter, xi + 79 pp.

Reviews: A.H. Smith in *MLR* 27.98-99 (1932); H.C. Matthes in *EStn* 66.402-04 (1931/32); E. Fischer in *Anglia B* 44.8-10 (1933); A. Rohr in *LGRP* 54.236-37 (1933); W. van der Gaaf in *ES* 18.75-76 (1936).

1128. Shields, Kenneth, Jr. 1984. "OE *sind(on)*: Its Germanic and Indo-European Origins". *AMAG* 22.1-9.

1129. Singh, Prem and Swadesh K. Premsingh. 1976. "The Old English 6th Class Verb". *Papers in Linguistic Analysis* (Delhi Univ.) 1.51-54.

1130. Stark, Detlef. 1982. *The Old English Weak Verbs: A Diachronic and Synchronic Analysis*. (= LA, 112.) Tübingen: Max Niemeyer, viii + 148 pp. [Originally Univ. of Wisconsin-Madison diss. 1979; Abstr. in *DA* 40.3275A (1979).]

Reviews: Carmela Rizzo in *Schede Medievali* 5.520 (1983); Georges Bourcier in *EA* 37.183 (1984); Lilo Moessner in *Anglia* 102.150-53 (1984); Uwe Carls in *ZAA* 33.171 (1985); Richard Hamer in *MAE* 54.345-46 (1985).

1131. Stewart, A.H. 1975. "A Note on Case Conflation in the Old English Nominal Declension". *PIL* 8.165-76.

1132. Watson, George. 1936. "Dialect Survivals of Anglo-Saxon Inflections". *JEGP* 35.44-60.

1133. Weyhe, Hans. 1925. "Zur altenglischen Flexion". *Sievers Festschrift*, 313-22.

1134. Yerkes, David. 1982. "The Differences of Inflection between the Two Versions of the Old English Translation of Gregory's *Dialogues*". *NM* 83.260-65.

C. Middle English

1135. Andrew, Samuel Ogden. 1929. "The Preterite in North-Western Dialects". *RES* 5.431-36.

1136. Awedyk, Wiesław. 1974. "Middle English *shē*". *SAP* 6.125-27.

1137. Britton, G.C. 1959. "N-Plurals in the Nouns of *Havelok the Dane*". *NM* 60.175-79.

1138. Burnley, David. 1982. "Inflexion in Chaucer's Adjectives". *NM* 83.169-77.

1139. Christensen, Inger G. 1971. "Kasusendelserne og deres funktion i sent old-engelsk og tidligt middelengelsk belyst ud fra *The Peterborough Chronicle* (Laud MS) og *Twelfth Century Homilies* (MS Bodley 343)". *Extracta: Resumeer af Specialeopgaver fra det Filosofiske Fakultet ved Københavns Universitet* 3.51-54.

1140. De Caluwé-Dor, Juliette. 1980. "L'intégration morphologique des verbes d'origine scandinave dans le *Katherine Group*". *Linguistics in Belgium/Linguistiek in België/Linguistique en Belgique* (Brussels: Didier) 3.40-53.

1141. Diensberg, Bernhard. 1975. *Morphologische Untersuchungen zur 'Ancrene Riwle': Die Verbalflexion nach den MSS Corpus Christi College Cambridge 402, B.M. Cotton Cleopatra C.VI, B.M. Cotton Nero A.XIV*. Bonn: Rheinische Friedrich-Wilhelms-Universität, xxvii + 786 pp. [Bonn diss.; Abstr. in *EASG* 1974 (1975), 27-28.]

Reviews: George Jack in *ES* 57.384 (1976); A. Bammesberger in *Kratylos* 22.191-92 (1977); K. Bitterling in *Anglia* 96.470-71 (1978); E.G. Stanley in *N&Q* n.s. 25.290 (1978).

1142. Dieth, Eugen. 1955. "*Hips*: A Geographical Contribution to the 'she' Puzzle". *ES* 36.209-17. [Concerns the origin of the pronoun *she*.]

1143. Fisiak, Jacek. 1965. *The Morphemic Structure of Chaucer's English*. (= ALPS, 10.) University, AL: Univ. of Alabama Press, 125 pp.

 Reviews: Norman Davis in *RES* n.s. 18.303-05 (1967); Elizabeth Closs Traugott in *Language* 43.966-69 (1967); J. Boswinkel in *ES* 49.244-45 (1968); Ruta Nagucka in *LPosn* (Poznań) 14.153-55 (1969).

1144. Forsström, Gösta. 1948. *The Verb 'To Be' in Middle English: A Survey of the Forms*. (= LundSE, 15.) Lund: Gleerup; Copenhagen: Munksgaard; London: Williams and Norgate, 237 pp. [Lund diss.]

 Reviews: A. Rynell in *SN* 21.305-10 (1948/49); K. Malone in *MLN* 64.562 (1949); R. Quirk in *MLR* 44.438 (1949); E.V.K. Dobbie in *Word* 6.244-45 (1950); Mary McDonald Long in *Speculum* 25.130-31 (1950); David W. Reed in *Language* 26.162-67 (1950); B. Trnka in *ČMF* 33.84-85 (1951); H.C. Matthes in *Archiv* 189.59 (1953) and *Anglia* 71.237-42 (1952/53).

1145. Francovich Onesti, Nicoletta. 1980/81. "Sulle forme dell'articolo determinativo nelle ultime sezioni della *Cronaca di Peterborough*". *InLi* 6.7-20.

1146. Füller, L. 1937. *Das Verbum in der Ancren Riwle*. Jena: Nevenhahn, 38 pp. [Jena diss. 1938.]

1147. Garcia, Erica C. 1970. "Inflection as a Derivational Device: The M.E. Midlands Plural Endings". *NM* 71.614-21.

1148. Gburek, Hubert. 1981. "Was *Are* Possible for the 2nd Sg. Pres. of Middle English 'To Be'?". *N&Q* n.s. 28.194-96. [Cf. Forsström [no. 1144].]

1149. Gleissner, Reinhard. 1979. "Middle English *-ind->-ing-*? And Bavarian *-ind-> -ing-*: A Note". *Bavarica Anglica, I: A Cross-Cultural Miscellany Presented to Tom Fletcher* (= Forum Anglisticum, 8), ed. Otto Hietsch, 53-60. Frankfurt am Main: Peter Lang.

1150. Greul, W. 1934. *Das Personalpronomen der 3. Person Pluralis im Frühmittelenglischen*. Berlin diss., 54 pp. [See Gericke and Greul [no. 1036].]

1151. Ingargiola, Nina. 1972. *Analogy in the Inflectional Endings of the Noun Forms of the 'Saint Katherine Group'*. City Univ. of New York diss., 271 pp. [Abstr. in *DA* 32.6405A (1972).]

1152. Iwasaki, Haruo. 1979 [1981]. "A Survey of the Noun Declensions in Laʒamon's *Brut*". *Poetica* 12.77-81.

1153. Jack, George Barr. 1977. "*Luste* in *Ancrene Wisse*". *NM* 78.24-26. [Argues that *luste<lusten* can be used as an indicative as well as subjunctive.]

1154. Kobayashi, Eichi. 1964. *The Verb Forms of the 'South English Legendary'*. (= JanL, Ser. Practica, 15.) The Hague: Mouton, 87 pp. [Originally Michigan diss. 1961; Abstr. in *DA* 23.230-31 (1962).]

   Reviews: M.C. Seymour in *Lingua* 16.437-38 (1966); Kenneth R. Brooks in *ES* 51.448-49 (1970).

1155. Lawson, Dorothy Day. 1956. *The Strong Verb in Gower's 'Confessio Amantis'*. New York: New York Univ., 18 pp. [An abridgement of New York Univ. diss. 1953, 345 pp.]

1156. Lehnert, Martin. 1953. *Sprachform und Sprachfunktion im 'Orrmulum' (um 1200): Die Deklination*. (= *ZAA*, Beiheft 1.) Berlin: Deutscher Verlag der Wissenschaften, xi + 199 pp. [Also in *WZHU* 2.1-58 (1952/53).]

   Reviews: S.B. Liljegren in *SN* 25.194 (1952/53); W. Schmidt-Hidding in *NS* 4.285-86 (1955); T.F. Mustanoja in *NM* 57.82-84 (1956).

1157. Long, Mary McDonald. 1944. *The English Strong Verb from Chaucer to Caxton*. Menasha, WI: George Banta, xvi + 314 pp. [New York Univ. diss. 1943.]

   Reviews: Herbert D. Meritt in *MLQ* 6.495-96 (1945); E.J. Bashe in *PQ* 24.94 (1945); F.P. Magoun, Jr. in *Speculum* 20.250-51 (1945); Simeon Potter in *MLR* 40.134-35 (1945); F. Mossé in *BLS* 127.85 (1946); Hereward T. Price in *JEGP* 45.108 (1946).

1158. Markey, Thomas L. 1972. "West Germanic *he/er—hiu/siu* and English 'she'". *JEGP* 71.390-405. [On the rise of *she*.]

1159. Mezger, Fritz. 1933. "Middle English *run*". *PMLA* 48.1036-40.

1160. Moore, Samuel. 1927. "Loss of Final *n* in Inflectional Syllables of Middle English". *Language* 3.232-59.

1161. ———. 1928. "Earliest Morphological Changes in Middle English". *Language* 4.238-66.

1162. Öfverberg, William. 1924. *The Inflections of the East Midland Dialects in Early Middle English. (Substantives, Adjectives, Numerals and Pronouns.)* Lund: Gleerup, xii + 179 pp. [Lund diss.]

1163. Palmatier, Robert A. 1972. "Metrical *-e* in the *Ormulum*". *JEngL* 6.35-45. [Concerns the leveling of nominal inflections in early ME.]

1164. Rettger, James Frederick. 1934. *The Development of Ablaut in the Strong Verbs of the East Midland Dialects of Middle English*. (= Supplement to *Language*: Language Dissertations, 18.) Philadelphia: Univ. of Pennsylvania Press, for the Linguistic Society of America, 186 pp. [Yale diss.]

    Reviews: A. B[randl] in *Archiv* 167.300-01 (1935); K. Jost in *IF* 54.308-09 (1936); M.S. Serjeantson in *ES* 20.42-44 (1938).

1165. Ruud, Martin B. 1926. "*She* Once More". *RES* 2.201-04. [A sequel to the author's "A Conjecture concerning the Origin of Modern English *she*", *MLN* 35.222-25 (1920).]

1166. Senff, H. 1937. *Die Nominalflexion im 'Ayenbite of Inwyt'*. (= Forschungen zur englischen Philologie, 7.) Jena: Walter Biedermann Formmann; Leipzig: Noske, iv + 101 pp.

1167. Smith, Albert Hugh. 1925. "Some Place-Names and the Etymology of *She*". *RES* 1.437-40.

1168. Stanley, Julia P. and Susan W. Robbins. 1978. "Going through the Changes: The Pronoun *She* in Middle English". *PIL* 11.71-88.

1169. Stevick, Robert David. 1964. "The Morphemic Evolution of Middle English *She*". *ES* 45.381-88.

1170. Stobie, Margaret M.R. 1940. "The Influence of Morphology on Middle English Alliterative Poetry". *JEGP* 39.319-36. [Attributes the changes in the character of alliterative verse in considerable measure to the loss of inflectional endings and changes in vowel quantity in ME.]

1171. Topliff, Delores E. 1970. "Analysis of Singular Weak Adjective Inflection in Chaucer's Works". *JEngL* 4.78-89.

1172. Valentine, Grace Evelyn Whysner. 1971. *A Study of the Noun and Pronoun Inflections of the N-Town Plays*. Univ. of Missouri-Columbia diss., 138 pp. [Abstr. in *DA* 32.5215A (1972).]

1173. Ziegler, Julian. 1952. "Eighteen Personal Pronouns of the Fifteenth Century". *MLN* 67.542-43. [Notes various pronominal forms not recorded in *OED*.]

X. SYNTAX

A. General

1174. Ahlgren, Arthur. 1946. *On the Use of the Definite Article with 'Nouns of Possession' in English.* (= SSE, 2.) Uppsala: Appelberg, xv + 221 pp. [Stockholm diss. Covers the whole period from the earliest times up to the present.]

   Reviews: Norman E. Eliason in *MLR* 45.362-63 (1950); Norman Davis in *ArchL* 3.78 (1951); R. Fricker in *Anglia* 70.324-27 (1951) and *ES* 33.83-85 (1952).

1175. Allen, Cynthia Louise. 1977. *Topics in Diachronic English Syntax.* Univ. of Massachusetts diss., 431 pp. [Abstr. in *DA* 38.4781A (1978). Discusses the history of certain syntactic constructions (e.g. relative clauses, questions, etc.) from OE to late ME.]

1176. Anderson, John Mathieson. "The Natural History of Dative Sentences". *Blake & Jones*, 241-78.

1177. Appleby, Mary Jane. 1967. *The Infinitive: Form and Syntax from Old English to Modern English.* Wisconsin diss., 338 pp. [Abstr. in *DA* 28.3164-65A (1968).]

1178. Armentrout, Ruth Evans. 1978. *The Development of Subordinating Conjunctions in English.* Pennsylvania State Univ. diss., 310 pp. [Abstr. in *DA* 39.846A (1978). Based on some 30 OE and 40 ME prose texts.]

1179. Arngart, Olof. 1979. "Adverbial Phrases with *Thing*". *NM* 80.46-47. [Discusses OE and ME examples.]

1180. ———. 1981. "The Word *Thing* in Adverbial Phrases". *NM* 82.368-69. [Deals with some additional OE examples (and the adverbial phrase *sure thing* of American origin).]

1181. Baron, Dennis E. 1974. *Case Grammar and Diachronic English Syntax.* (= JanL, Ser. Practica, 223.) The Hague: Mouton, 132 pp. [Originally Michigan diss. 1971; Abstr. in *DA* 32.6401A (1972). Treats the genitive object.]

Reviews: Manfred Görlach in *IF* 81.415-18 (1976); Lilo Moessner in *Linguistics* 178.65-70 (1976); D.A. Cruse in *SLang* 2.131-47 (1978); Christian Peeters in *RBPH* 59.736-37 (1981).

1182. Baron, Naomi S. 1971. "A Reanalysis of English Grammatical Gender". *Lingua* 27.113-40. [Also printed in *SOPL* 1.54-88 (1971).]

1183. ———. 1972. "Language Acquisition's Role in Diachrony: The Evolution of English Periphrastic Causatives". *SOPL* 2.47-63.

1184. Behre, Frank. 1961. "'It Cannot Be; It Is Impossible': A Study in Diachronic Grammar". *Behre Papers*, 128-58. [Traces the earlier use of the idiom and its predecessors in OE and ME.]

1185. Bennett, Paul A. 1980. "English Passives: A Study in Syntactic Change and Relational Grammar". *Lingua* 51.101-14.

1186. Bergener, Carl. 1928. *A Contribution to the Study of the Conversion of Adjectives into Nouns in English*. Lund: Gleerup, xvi + 222 pp. [Uppsala diss. The period covered is from the earliest times to the present-day.]

Reviews: A.G. Kennedy in *AS* 5.247-49 (1930); E. Kruisinga in *ES* 12.234-35 (1930).

1187. Berman, Arlene. 1970. "The Relative Clause Construction in Old and Middle English". *Mathematical Linguistics & Automatic Translation*, Report No. NSF-26, ed. Susumu Kuno, 1-43. Cambridge, MA: The Computation Laboratory of Harvard Univ.

1188. Biese, Yrjö Moses. 1941. *Origin and Development of Conversions in English*. (= AASF B 45:2.) Helsinki: Kirjallisuuden, vi + 495 pp. + 33 diagrams [497-522].

Reviews: W. Horn in *Archiv* 185.145-46 (1948); F. Mossé in *BSL* 46.152 (1950).

1189. Bock, Hellmut. 1931. "Studien zum präpositionalen Infinitiv und Akkusativ mit dem *To*-Infinitiv". *Anglia* 55.114-249.

1190. Breivik, Leiv Egil. 1977. "A Note on the Genesis of Existential *There*". *ES* 58.334-48. [Argues that existential *there* existed alongside locative *there* in both Old and Middle English.]

1191. ———. 1983. *Existential 'There': A Synchronic and Diachronic Study*. (= Studia Anglistica Norvegica, 2.) Bergen: Dept. of English, Univ. of Bergen, xiv + 458 pp. [Originally Univ. of Tromsø diss. 1981.]

Reviews: Roderick A. Jacobs in *Language* 60.663-64 (1984); Jürgen Esser in *Anglia* 103.421-24 (1985); Bent Jacobsen (review article) in *ES* 67.250-62 (1986).

1192. ———. 1986. "Variation in Existential Sentences in a Synchronic-Diachronic Perspective". *Syntactic Variation* III, 171-80.

1193. Brinton, Laurel Jean Teresa. 1981. *The Historical Development of Aspectual Periphrases in English*. Univ. of California, Berkeley, diss., 296 pp. [Abstr. in *DA* 42.5105-06A (1982).]

1194. Bungenstab, Edith. 1933. *Der Genitiv beim Verbum und sein Ersatz im Laufe der englischen Sprachgeschichte*. Breslau: Eschenhagen, xii + 62 pp. [Breslau diss.]

1195. Butler, Milton Chadwick. 1980. *Grammatically Motivated Subjects in Early English*. (= Texas Ling. Forum, 16.) Austin, TX: Dept. of Linguistics, Univ. of Texas, x + 321 pp. [Univ. of Texas at Austin diss. 1980; Abstr. in *DA* 41.3084A (1981).]

1196. Callaway, Morgan, Jr. 1929. "Concerning the Origin of the Gerund in English". *Klaeber Festschrift*, 32-49. [Also separately printed, Minneapolis: Univ. of Minnesota, 1929, 18 pp.]

Review: F. Karpf in *Anglia B* 41.290-91 (1930).

1197. Carlson, Anita M. 1978. "A Diachronic Treatment of English Quantifiers". *Lingua* 46.295-328. [Also printed in *Montreal Working Papers in Linguistics* 7.41-72 (1976).]

1198. Closs, Elizabeth. 1965. "Diachronic Syntax and Generative Grammar". *Language* 41.402-15. [Based on the history of the verbal auxiliary in English.]

1199. Culioli, Antoine. 1960. *Contribution à l'étude du subjonctif et de la coordination en moyen-anglais*. Paris diss., ii + 495 pp.

1200. Curme, George Oliver. 1929. "The Forms and Functions of the Subjunctive in the Classical and Modern Languages". *MP* 26.387-99.

1201. Dahl, Torsten. 1936. *Form and Function: Studies in Old and Middle English Syntax*. (= Acta Jutlandica, Aarsskrift for Aarhus Universitet, 8:1.) Aarhus: Universitetsforlaget; Copenhagen: C.A. Reitzel, 258 pp.

Review: Karl Jost in *Anglia B* 48.353-55 (1937).

1202. Dal, Ingerid. 1952. "Zur Entstehung des englischen Participium Praesentis auf -*ing*". *NTS* 16.5-116.

Review: Rudolf Keller in *ES* 37.75-78 (1956).

1203. De Garcia, Erica Charola. 1964. *History of the English Tense System*. Columbia diss., 379 pp. [Abstr. in *DA* 26.2197-98 (1965).]

1204. Dekeyser, Xavier. 1975. "On the Diachronic Expansion of BE + PrP". *LB* 64.151-66.

1205. ———. 1980. "The Diachrony of the Gender Systems in English and Dutch". *Historical Morphology*, 97-111.

1206. Dekker, Arie. 1938. "The Pseudo-Pronoun *So*". *Neophil* 23.134-45. [From the OE period on.]

1207. De la Cruz, Juan M. 1969. *Origins and Development of the Phrasal Verb to the End of the Middle English Period*. Queen's Univ., Belfast, diss. [No further information available.]

1208. ———. 1972. "The Origins of the Germanic Phrasal Verb". *IF* 77.73-96.

1209. ———. 1972. "A Syntactical Complex of Isoglosses in the North-Western End of Europe (English, North Germanic and Celtic)". *IF* 77.171-80.

1210. ———. 1973. "Notas para el Estudio del Desarrollo Angloescandinavo de los Verbos Preposicionales: los Datos del Inglés Antiguo y Medio". *RESL* 3.369-413.

1211. ———. 1976. "Context-Sensitivity in Old and Middle English". *SAP* 8.3-43. [Concerns word-order.]

1212. Denison, David. 1981. *Aspects of the History of English Group-Verbs: With Particular Attention to the Syntax of the 'Ormulum'*. Oxford diss., viii + 329 pp. [A diachronic study of a range of texts from Alfredian prose to the *Paston Letters*, with some later examples, and a synchronic study of the *Ormulum*.]

1213. Diekstra, F.N.M. 1984. "Ambiguous *that*-Clauses in Old and Middle English". *ES* 65.97-110.

1214. Diensberg, Bernhard. 1983. "Zur Genese und Entwicklung des neuenglischen Phrasal Verbs". *FLH* 4.247-64.

1215. Dolan, T.P. 1977. "On Claims for Syntactical Modernity in Early English Prose". *MP* 74.305-10. [Criticizes West [no. 1348].]

1216. Einenkel, Eugen. 1923. "Neues aus dem Gebiete der historischen Syntax". *Anglia* 47.274-86.

1217. Ellegård, Alvar. 1953. *The Auxiliary 'Do': The Establishment and Regulation of its Use in English.* (= GothSE, 2.) Stockholm: Almqvist & Wiksell, 320 pp. [Göteborg diss.]

Reviews: G. Gougenheim in *Le Français Moderne* (Paris) 22.222 (1954); M.L. Samuels in *ArchL* 6.143-45 (1954); E.V.K. Dobbie in *Word* 11.330-33 (1955); Hermann Heuer in *Archiv* 192.70-71 (1955/56); H.B. Woolf in *MLN* 70.543-44 (1955); B. Danielsson in *MSpr* 50.470-77 (1956); Herbert Koziol in *ES* 38.75-78 (1957).

1218. Elmer, Willy. 1981. *Diachronic Grammar: The History of Old and Middle English Subjectless Constructions.* (= LA, 97.) Tübingen: Max Niemeyer, xi + 177 pp.

Reviews: E. Burgschmidt in *Kratylos* 27.138-41 (1982); Lilo Moessner in *AAA* 8.102-05 (1983); Jerzy Wełna in *LB* 72.189-92 (1983); Hans Bennis in *ES* 65.276-77 (1984); Georges Bourcier in *EA* 37.85 (1984); Patrizia Lendinara in *Schede Medievali* 6/7.224-25 (1984); David W. Lightfoot in *Diachronica* 1.267-71 (1984).

1219. Erdmann, Peter. 1980. "On the History of Subject Contact-Clauses in English". *FLH* 1.139-70.

1220. Finkenstaedt, Thomas. 1963. *'You' und 'Thou': Studien zur Anrede im Englischen (Mit einem Exkurs über die Anrede im Deutschen).* (= Q&F, N.F. 10.) Berlin: de Gruyter, xi + 301 pp. [Gives a comprehensive account of the uses of the second person pronouns from OE to the present day.]

Reviews: M. Schentke in *ZAA* 11.303-04 (1963); J. Boswinkel in *LT* 1964, 128-29 (1964); Gerhard Graband in *Anglia* 82.120-23 (1964); T. Kisbye in *JEGP* 63.328-30 (1964); H. Marchand in *IF* 69.88-92 (1964); B.D.H. Miller in *RES* n.s. 15.410-11 (1964); S. Potter in *MLR* 59.88 (1964); L.W. Collier in *ES* 46.256-58 (1965); Ewald Standop in *Archiv* 201.449-52 (1964/65); G. Scheurweghs in *LB* 44.Bijblad 132-33 (1965); Hans Utz in *Kratylos* 13.75-77 (1968).

1221. Foster, Robert. 1975. "The Use of *þa* in Old and Middle English Narratives". *NM* 76.404-14.

1222. Fries, Charles Carpenter. 1940. "On the Development of the Structural Use of Word-Order in Modern English". *Language* 16.199-208.

1223. Funke, Otto. 1949. "On the Use of the Attributive Adjective in OE Prose and Early ME". *ES* 30.151-56. [Repr. in *Funke Aufsätze*, 22-28.]

1224. Gehse, Heinrich. 1938. *Die Kontaminationen in der englischen Syntax.* (= Sprache und Kultur der germanischen und romanischen Völker, A. Anglistische Reihe, 27.) Breslau: Priebatsch, xii + 116 pp. [Berlin diss.]

Reviews: G.T. Flom in JEGP 38.472 (1939); F. Mossé in EA 3.144 (1939); B. von Lindheim in Anglia B 50.164-68 (1939).

1225. Goedsche, C. Rudolf. 1932. "The Terminate Aspect of the Expanded Form: Its Development and Its Relation to the Gerund". *JEGP* 31.469-77.

1226. Goossens, Louis. 1982. "On the Development of the Modals and of the Epistemic Function in English". *PICHL*/5, 74-84.

1227. Grad, Anton. 1955. "A Contribution to the Problem of Word-Order in Old and Middle English". *Slavistična Revija* (Ljubljana) 8: *Linguistica* 1:1.11-27.

1228. Harder, Bernhard D. 1969. "Syntactic Changes of the Verbal Auxiliary from Old English to Middle English: A Transformational Approach". *PIL* 1.391-98.

1229. Harsh, Wayne. 1968. *The Subjunctive in English.* (= ALPS. 15.) University, AL: Univ. of Alabama Press, 174 pp. [Originally Univ. of California, Berkeley, diss. 1963; Abstr. in *DA* 24.3740 (1964) and *Linguistics* 9.109-10 (1964). Deals with the decline of the inflected subjunctive in English and the development of substitute constructions.]

1230. Hausmann, Robert B. 1974. "The Origin and Development of Modern English Periphrastic *do*". *PICHL*/1, 1.159-89.

1231. Hayes, Rosemary. 1971. *A Diachronic Study of the Relative Clause in English.* Univ. of Iowa diss., 133 pp. [Abstr. in *DA* 32.5212A (1972).]

1232. Helgander, John. 1971. *The Relative Clause in English and Other Germanic Languages: A Historical and Analytical Survey.* Göteborg: Dept. of English, Univ. of Gothenburg, vii + 307 pp. [Göteborg diss.]

1233. Hiltunen, Risto. 1982. "The Inseparable Verbal Prefixes in Old and Early Middle English: A Case of Language Change". *NM* 83. Supplement 23-37. [The Supplement = *Papers on English Philology read at the Symposium arranged by the Modern Language Society at Tvärminne on 26-28 November, 1981.*]

1234. ———. 1983. *The Decline of the Prefixes and the Beginnings of the Phrasal Verb: the Evidence from Some Old and Early Middle English Texts.* (= Turun Yliopiston Julkaisuja/Annales Universitatis Turkuensis, B 160.) Turku: Turun Yliopisto, 251 pp. [Originally Oxford diss. 1982.]

Review: E.G. S[tanley] in *N&Q* n.s. 31.1 (1984).

1235. ———. 1983. "Syntactic Variation in the Early History of the English Phrasal Verb". *Syntactic Variation* II, 95-108. [Covers OE and early ME (up to c1250).]

1236. Hladký, Josef. 1969. "A Note on the Quantitative Evaluation of the Verb in English". *BSE* 8.95-98.

1237. Hoffmann, G. 1934. *Die Entwicklung des umschriebenen Perfektums im Altenglischen und Frümittelenglischen.* Ohlau: Eschenhagen, 57 pp. [Part of Breslau diss.]

1238. Hols, Edith Jones. 1970. *Grammatical Roles of Three Sets of Prepositions in 'Beowulf' and 'King Horn'.* Univ. of Iowa diss., 196 pp. [Abstr. in *DA* 31.4748A (1971).]

1239. Horn, Wilhelm. 1928. "Untersuchungen zur historischen englischen Syntax. 1. Die syntaktische Verwendung von *though*". *Archiv* 154.213-23.

1240. Irwin, Betty J. 1967. *The Development of the '-ing' Ending of the Verbal Noun and the Present Participle from c.700 to c.1400.* Wisconsin diss., 210 pp. [Abstr. in *DA* 28.653-54A (1967).]

1241. Jack, George Barr. 1978. "*Rome's Destruction* and the History of English". *JL* 14.311-12. [Refuting Lightfoot [no. 1272], argues that phrases such as *Rome's destruction* were current in OE and early ME and that (in Lightfoot's words) 'the rule of NP Preposing' was part of the grammar of English long before the late ME period.]

1242. Jacobson, Sven. 1981. *Preverbal Adverbs and Auxiliaries: A Study of Word Order Change.* (= SSE, 55.) Stockholm: Almqvist & Wiksell, 100 pp. [A descriptive study of preverb/auxiliary word order up to the modern period, mainly in OE and ME.]

   Reviews: L.E. Breivik in *Lingua* 63.205-11 (1984); Suzette Haden Elgin in *Language* 60.457-58 (1984); Rüdiger Zimmermann in *Anglia* 103.125-27 (1985).

1243. Jambeck, Thomas J. 1973. "The Syntax of Petition in *Beowulf* and *Sir Gawain and the Green Knight*". *Style* 7.21-29.

1244. Johannesson, Nils-Lennart. 1985. "*Oh gracyous god my herte it burstes* — On the Historical Development of Unmarked and Marked Topics in English". *LACUS*/11, 432-46.

1245. Johansson, Karl Albert Stig. 1968. *Studies in the History and Development of the English Language.* Indiana Univ. diss., 161 pp. [Abstr. in *DA* 29.1525-26A (1968). Studies the origin and development of the auxiliary *do* and the rise of the prop-word *one*.]

1246. Joly, André. 1967. *Negation and the Comparative Particle in English.* (= Cahiers de psychomécanique du langage, 9.) Québec: Presses de l'Université Laval, 44 pp. [Suggests that the conjunction *than* originally contained a negative particle.]

Reviews: H.A.W. Kühlwein in *IRAL: International Review of Applied Linguistics in Language Learning* (Heidelberg) 6.291-94 (1968); Pieter A.M. Seuren in *Neophil* 52.337-38 (1968).

1247. ———. 1982. "*But*, signe de l'exception et de la restriction dans l'histoire de l'anglais". *MLing* 4.151-75.

1248. Karlberg, Göran. 1954. *The English Interrogative Pronouns: A Study of Their Syntactic History*. (= GothSE, 3.) Stockholm: Almqvist & Wiksell, 353 pp. [Göteborg diss.]

Reviews: W. Barritt in *Language* 31.301-03 (1955); Karl Brunner in *Anglia* 73.376-78 (1955); P.A. Erades in *ES* 36.172-76 (1955); U. Ohlander in *SN* 27.172-75 (1955); S. Potter in *MSpr* 49.316-18 (1955); N.E. Eliason in *MLN* 71.208-09 (1956); R. Quirk in *RES* n.s. 7.299-300 (1956); G. Shepherd in *MLR* 51.305-06 (1956).

1249. Keel, William D. 1980. "Passives and Grammatical Subject in Old/Middle English". *Papers from the 1979 Mid-American Linguistics Conference*, ed. Robert S. Haller, 376-83. Lincoln, NB: Area Studies Committee in Linguistics, Univ. of Nebraska-Lincoln.

1250. Kiffer, Theodore Edwin. 1965. *A Diachronic and Synchronic Analysis and Description of English Phrasal Verbs*. Pennsylvania State Univ. diss., 152 pp. [Abstr. in *DA* 26.4632-33 (1966). From *Beowulf* to the works of Milton.]

1251. Kihlbom, Asta. 1938. "Concerning the Present Subjunctive in Conditional Clauses". *SN* 11.257-66.

1252. Kirch, Max S. 1959. "Scandinavian Influence on English Syntax". *PMLA* 74.503-10. [A historical consideration of (1) relative clauses, (2) the omission of the conjunction *that*, (3) the particular use of *shall* and *will* in ME, and (4) the genitive before nouns.]

1253. Kisbye, Torben. 1963. *An Historical Survey of English Syntax. Part I: The Non-Finite Parts of the Verb*. Aarhus: Dept. of English, Aarhus Univ., 131 pp. [Intended for class-teaching at Aarhus Univ.]

1254. ———. 1964. *An Historical Survey of English Syntax. Part II: Pronouns, Adjectives and Adverbs (Sections E-M)*. Aarhus: Akademisk Boghandel, 177 pp. [Intended for class-teaching at Aarhus Univ.]

1255. ———. 1965. *An Historical Survey of English Syntax. Part III: Articles, Numer-*

als, Gender and Case, the Finite Forms of the Verb. Aarhus: Dept. of English, Aarhus Univ., 170 pp. [Intended for class-teaching at Aarhus Univ.]

1256. ———. 1971. *An Historical Outline of English Syntax. Part I.* Aarhus: Akademisk Boghandel, v + 207 pp. [A thoroughly revised version of Kisbye [nos. 1253-1255].]

1257. ———. 1972. *An Historical Outline of English Syntax. Part II.* Aarhus: Akademisk Boghandel, vii + 185 pp. [A thoroughly revised version of Kisbye [nos. 1253-1255].]

1258. Knispel, Eva. 1932. *Der altenglische Instrumental bei Verben und Adjektiven und sein Ersatz im Verlaufe der englischen Sprachgeschichte.* Breslau: Eschenhagen, x + 82 pp. [Breslau diss.]

1259. Kohonen, Viljo. 1974. "On the Problem of Sample Length in the Study of Major Word Order Patterns in Old English and Early Middle English Narrative Prose". *Reports on Text Linguistics: Four Papers on Text, Style and Syntax* (= MSAAF, 1), ed. Nils Erik Enkvist, 94-117. Åbo [Turku]: Åbo Akademi Forskningsinstitut.

1260. ———. 1978. *On the Development of English Word Order in Religious Prose around 1000 and 1200 A.D.: A Quantitative Study of Word Order in Context.* (= MSAAF, 38.) Åbo [Turku]: Åbo Akademi Forskningsinstitut, 242 pp. [Turku diss.; Abstr. in *DA* 41.4564C (1981). The material is from Ælfric's First Series of *Catholic Homilies, Vices and Virtues,* and *Sawles Warde.*]

Review: Sven Jacobson in *SL* 34.220-23 (1980).

1261. ———. 1979. "Observations on Syntactic Characteristics of Binominals in Late Old English and Early Middle English Prose". *NM* 80.143-63.

1262. König, Ekkehard. 1985. "On the History of Concessive Connectives in English: Diachronic and Synchronic Evidence". *Lingua* 66.1-19.

1263. Koopman, Willem F. 1985. "Verb and Particle Combinations in Old and Middle English". *PICEHL*/4, 109-21.

1264. Koziol, Herbert. 1936/37. "Zum Gebrauch der englischen Tempora". *EStn* 71.383-92. [Miscellaneous notes on the history of tenses in English.]

1265. Kruisinga, Etsko. 1927. "Contributions to English Syntax. XVII: On the History of Conversion in English". *ES* 9.103-08.

1266. Krzyszpień, Jersy. 1984 [1985]. "On the Impersonal-to-Personal Transition in English". *SAP* 17.63-69.

1267. LaBrum, Rebecca Wheelock. 1982. *Conditions on Double Negation in the History of English with Comparison to Similar Developments in German*. Stanford diss., 326 pp. [Abstr. in *DA* 43.157-58A (1982).]

1268. Lassaut, J. and Xavier Dekeyser. 1977. "Aspects of Sentence Embedding in Old and Middle English". *LB* 66.327-43.

1269. Lebow, Daniel B. 1954. *An Historical Study of Syntax: The Evolution of English from Inflectional to Prepositional Constructions*. New York Univ. diss., 660 pp. [Abstr. in *DA* 15.1235 (1955).]

1270. Lehnert, Martin. 1957. "The Interrelation between Form and Function in the Development of the English Language". *ZAA* 5.43-56.

1271. Lightfoot, David. 1974. "The Diachronic Analysis of English Modals". *PICHL/* 1, 1.219-49.

1272. ———. 1977. "Syntactic Change and the Autonomy Thesis". *JL* 13.191-216. [Refuted by Jack [no. 1241].]

1273. ———. 1979. *Principles of Diachronic Syntax*. (= CSL, 23.) Cambridge: Cambridge Univ. Press, x + 429 pp. [Using data almost wholly from the history of English.]

1274. Lindkvist, Karl-Gunnar. 1978. *'AT' versus 'ON', 'IN', 'BY': On the Early History of Spatial 'AT' and Certain Primary Ideas Distinguishing 'AT' from 'ON', 'IN', 'BY'*. (= SSE, 49.) Stockholm: Almqvist & Wiksell International, 90 pp. [An investigation of the use of the preposition *at* in a local sense in OE, ME, and ModE.]

Reviews: Bruce Mitchell in *RES* n.s. 30.244 (1979); Zdenka Strnadová in *PP* 23.46-47 (1980); J. Lachlan Mackenzie in *Anglia* 99.182-85 (1981).

1275. ———. 1978. "Some Notes on *At* as a Preposition of Place in English". *Rynell Festschrift*, 102-07.

1276. Macháček, Jaroslav. 1969. "Historical Aspects of the Accusative with Infinitive and the Content Clause in English". *BSE* 8.123-32.

1277. Magers, Mildred Kirtland. 1944. *The Development of the Grammatical Use of Word-Order for Relationships Expressed by the Accusative with Special Reference to the Development in Subordinate Clauses*. Michigan diss., 82 pp.

1278. Manabe, Kazumi. 1979. *Syntax and Style in Early English: Finite and Non-Finite Clauses c.900 — 1600*. Tokyo: Kaibunsha, 184 pp.

Review: Kikuo Yamakawa in *SEL* English No. 1981, 102-11.

1279. Mann, Gerd. 1950. "Die Entstehung des finalen Infinitivs im Englischen". *Archiv* 187.10-24.

1280. Marchand, Hans. 1938. "Remarks about English Negative Sentences". *ES* 20.198-204. [Discusses the history of the use of the negative sentence from OE to ModE.]

1281. ———. 1951. "The Syntactical Change from Inflectional to Word Order System and Some Effects of This Change on the Relation 'Verb/Object' in English: A Diachronic-Synchronic Interpretation". *Anglia* 70.70-89.

Review: Waltraut Reinhardt in *ZAA* 2.51-55 (1954).

1282. Marckwardt, Albert Henry. 1970. "*Much* and *Many*: The Historical Development of a Modern English Distributional Pattern". *Meritt Festschrift*, 50-54.

1283. Matsunami, Tamotsu. 1961. "A Historical Consideration of the Disjunctive Formula: *It Is I That Am To Blame*". *SEL* English No. 1961, 1-15.

1284. McCawley, Noriko A. 1976. "From OE/ME 'Impersonal' to 'Personal' Constructions: What Is a 'Subject-less' S?". *Papers from the Parasession on Diachronic Syntax, April 22, 1976*, ed. Sanford B. Steever, et al., 192-204. Chicago: Chicago Linguistic Society.

1285. Meritt, Herbert Dean. 1938. *The Construction ἀπὸ κοινοῦ in the Germanic Languages*. (= Stanford Univ. Pubs. in Language and Literature, 6:2.) Stanford: Stanford Univ. Press, 114 pp. [Originally Princeton diss. 1931; repr., New York: AMS Press, 1967. A collection and analysis of examples of the *apo koinou* construction from Old and Middle Germanic languages.]

Review: Frederick Klaeber in *Anglia B* 50.257-61 (1939)

1286. Mitchell, John Lawrence. 1971. *A Study in Diachronic Syntax: The Auxiliary from Old English to Modern English*. Univ. of Iowa diss., 194 pp. [Abstr. in *DA* 32.1497-98A (1971).]

1287. Moessner, Lilo. 1985. "Some English Relative Constructions". *Linguistique* 20:1.57-79. [From OE through ModE.]

1288. Mossé, Fernand. 1925. "Le renouvellement de l'aspect en germanique". *Mélanges linguistiques offerts a M.J. Vendryès* (= Collection Linguistique publiée par la Societé de Linguistique de Paris, 17), 287-99. Paris: Champion.

1289. ———. 1938. *Histoire de la forme périphrastique* 'être + participe présent' *en Germanique*. 2 vols. (= Collection linguistique publiée par la Societé de Linguistique de Paris, 42 & 43.) Paris: Klincksieck. Partie I: Introduction, Ancien germanique, Vieil-anglais, vi + 126 pp. Partie II: Moyen-anglais et Anglais moderne, xi + 301 pp. [Paris diss.]

Reviews: C.A. Bodelsen in *ES* 20.205-09 (1938); H. Koziol in *Anglia B* 50.261-66 (1939); René Huchon in *EA* 3.253-56 (1939); E. Pons in *Les Langues Modernes* (Paris) 38:3.278-81 (1939); A. Macdonald in *MLR* 35.226-27 (1940).

1290. Mustanoja, Tauno Frans. 1973. "*Almighty* in Early English: A Study in Positional Syntax". *Koziol Festschrift*, 204-12.

1291. Mutt, Oleg. 1968. "The Use of Substantives as Premodifiers in Early English". *NM* 69.578-96.

1292. Nagucka, Ruta. 1981. "A Reflexive Function of the Personal Pronoun in Old and Middle English". *BPTJ* 38.33-46.

1293. ———. 1983. "On Transitivity and Intransitivity of the Same (?) Verb in English". *SAP* 16.25-43. [The material is taken from all periods of English.]

1294. ———. 1984. "Explorations into Syntactic Obsoleteness: English *a-X-ing* and *X-ing*". *Historical Syntax*, 363-81.

1295. Nehls, Dietrich. 1974. *Synchron-diachrone Untersuchungen zur Expanded Form im Englischen: eine strukturral-funktionale Analyse*. (= Linguistische Reihe, 19.) München: Max Hueber, 193 pp.

Reviews: Hans Finger in *IRAL* 13.241-42 (1975); M. Görlach in *Archiv* 213.383-85 (1976); Gero Bauer in *Anglia* 95.173-77 (1977); R. Kupetz in *ZAA* 26.378-79 (1978); L. Dušková in *PP* 22.213-14 (1979).

1296. Nevanlinna, Saara. 1974. "Background and History of the Parenthetic *As Who Say/Saith* in Old and Middle English Literature". *NM* 75.568-601.

1297. Ohlander, Urban. 1943/44. "Omission of the Object in English". *SN* 16.105-27. [From OE to Shakespeare.]

1298. Pasicki, Adam. 1983. "*While*-Clauses in Old and Early Middle English". *FLH* 4.287-303.

1299. Peltola, Niilo. 1969. "Contributions to the Study of Intensives, I-II". *NM* 70.33-53. [I. On the genetic background of intensifying adverbial adjectives. II. *Boiling hot* and cognate expressions.]

1300. Potter, Simeon. 1966. "Limits of Functional Shift". *Schlauch Festschrift*, 307-12. [Traces the history of grammatical conversion in English and lists the possible functional shifts in current English.]

1301. ———. 1969. "Attributes and Attributive Adjectives". *BSE* 8.161-66. [Gives examples of the order of adjectives from various periods of English.]

1302. Preusler, Walther. 1942. "Keltischer Einfluss im Englischen". *Anglia* 66.121-28.

1303. ———. 1956. "Keltischer Einfluss im Englischen". *RLV* 22.322-50.

1304. Recktenwald, Robert Peter. 1975. *The English Progressive: Semantics and History*. Brown diss., 221 pp. [Abstr. in *DA* 37.269A (1976).]

1305. Rissanen, Matti. 1967. *The Uses of 'One' in Old and Early Middle English*. (= MSNH, 31.) Helsinki: Société Néophilologique, xxx + 325 pp.

   Reviews: R.C. Alston in *MAE* 37.245-46 (1968); M.L. Samuels in *N&Q* n.s. 15.395-96 (1968); T.F. Mustanoja in *NM* 70.165-67 (1969); J.R. Simon in *EA* 22.302-03 (1969); Torben Kisbye in *SN* 42.250-53 (1970); G. Bauer in *ES* 52.543-45 (1971); Simeon Potter in *YES* 1.203-04 (1971); Broder Carstensen in *Anglia* 89.492-94 (1971); Hans Heinrich Meier in *Archiv* 209.147-49 (1972/73).

1306. ———. 1969. "The Uses of *One* in Old and Early Middle English". *NM* 70.165.

1307. ———. 1972. "The Use of *One* and the Indefinite Article with Plural Nouns in English". *Mustanoja Festschrift* = *NM* 73.340-52.

1308. Romaine, Suzanne. 1983. "Syntactic Change as Category Change by Re-Analysis and Diffusion: Some Evidence from the History of English". *Curent Topics in EHL*, 9-27.

1309. Rot, Sandor. 1984. "Inherent Variability and Linguistic Interference of Anglo-Old Scandinavian and Anglo-Norman French Language Contacts in the Formation of Grammatical Innovations in Late Old English and Middle English.". *Blake & Jones*, 67-86.

1310. Rydén, Mats. 1979. *An Introduction to the Historical Study of English Syntax*. (= SSE, 51.) Stockholm: Almqvist & Wiksell, 58 pp.

   Reviews: Matti Rissanen in *NM* 81.446-47 (1980); Knud Sørensen in *ES* 62.488 (1981); Bengt Löfstedt in *Language* 57.499-500 (1981); X. Dekeyser in *LB* 71.231-32 (1982).

1311. ———. 1980. "Syntactic Variation in a Historical Perspective". *Syntactic Variation* I, 37-45. [Chiefly concerned with the study of historical English syntax.]

1312. Sabatini, Raymond N. 1979. "The Disappearance of the Impersonal Construction in English". *South Central Bulletin* (Univ. of Houston, TX) 39.151-53.

1313. Scheffer, Johannes. 1975. *The Progressive in English*. (= NHLS, 15.) Amsterdam & Oxford: North-Holland: New York: Elsevier, xvii + 397 pp. [Contains a detailed history of the English progressive (pp. 131-273).]

   Reviews: M. Görlach in *Archiv* 213.385-86 (1976); Robert I Binnick in *Lingua* 42.248-49 (1977); J.D. Burnley in *Lore&L* 2:7.43-44 (1977); G. Storms in *DQR* 7.157-60 (1977); Eugene A. Nida in *Linguistics* 204.89-90 (1978).

1314. Schmidt, Deborah Ann. 1980. *A History of Inversion in English*. The Ohio State Univ. diss., 315 pp. [Abstr. in *DA* 41.3089-90A (1981).]

1315. Small, George William. 1924. *The Comparison of Inequality: The Semantics and Syntax of the Comparative Particle in English*. Baltimore: The Johns Hopkins Univ., ix + 173 pp. [Johns Hopkins diss. 1923.]

   Reviews: Albert Morey Sturtevant in *MLN* 40.492-501 (1925); C.B. in *MLR* 21.345-46 (1926); A. Bosker in *ES* 8.81-83 (1926); Morgan Callaway, Jr. in *AJP* 47.198-99 (1926); J.H.G. Grattan in *RES* 2.241-42 (1926); E.H. Sturtevant in *Language* 2.197 (1926); Jacob Zeitlin in *JEGP* 26.136 (1927).

1316. Smith, Evan Shreeve. 1982. *Relative 'That' and 'As': A Study in Category Change*. Indiana Univ. diss., 199 pp. [Abstr. in *DA* 43.2985-86A (1983). Relatively little on OE.]

1317. Sørensen, Knud. 1957. "Latin Influence on English Syntax: A Survey with a Bibliography". *Travaux du Cercle Linguistique de Copenhague* 11 (= Acta Congressus Madvigiani, 5).131-55.

1318. ———. 1983. "The Growth of Cataphoric Personal and Possessive Pronouns in English". *Current Topics in EHL*, 225-38.

1319. Spamer, James B. 1979. "The Development of the Definite Article in English: A Case Study of Syntactic Change". *Glossa* 13.241-50.

1320. Stewart, Ann Harleman. 1976. "The Development of the Verb-Phrase Complement with Verbs of Physical Perception in English: Historical Linguistics as a Source of Deep Structures". *JEngL* 10.34-53.

1321. Stockwell, Robert P. 1984. "On the History of the Verb-Second Rule in English". *Historical Syntax*, 573-92.

1322. Storms, Godfrid. 1961. *The Origin and the Functions of the Definite Article in English*. Amsterdam: Meulenhoff, ii + 27 pp. [Inaugural address, Univ. of Nijmegen.]

SYNTAX 147

Review: R.W. Zandvoort in ES 42.190 (1961).

1323. Süsskand, Peter. 1935. *Geschichte des unbestimmten Artikels im Alt- und Frühmittelenglischen.* (= SEP, 85.) Halle: Max Niemeyer, x + 187 pp.

Reviews: E. Eckhardt in *DL* 6.1912-14 (1935); G.L. Brook in *MAE* 5.136-39 (1936); G.T. Flom in *JEGP* 35.602-05 (1936); W. Preusler in *Anglia B* 47.171-74 (1936); H. Heuer in *LGRP* 59.22-23 (1939).

1324. Suter, Kurt. 1955. *Das Pronomen beim Imperativ im Alt- und Mittelenglischen.* Aarau: H.R. Sauerländer, 167 pp. [Zürich diss.]

Reviews: Ewald Standop in *Anglia* 74.461-62 (1956); Hans Marcus in *Archiv* 194.238 (1957/58); E. Bagby Atwood in *Language* 33.244-46 (1957); A.A. Prins in *ES* 39.132-33 (1958).

1325. Tellier, André. 1962. *Les verbes perfecto-présents et les auxiliaires de mode en anglais ancien (VIIIe S. — XVIe S.).* (Études linguistiques, 1.) Paris: Klincksieck, 359 pp.

Reviews: Ewald Standop in *Anglia* 82.351-55 (1964); S.R.T.O. d'Ardenne in *EA* 18.171-72 (1965); J. Fourquet in *BSL* 60:2.121-23 (1965).

1326. Terasawa. Jun. 1985. "The Historical Development of the Causative Use of the Verb *Make* with an Infinitive". *SN* 57.133-43.

1327. Thomas, Russell. 1931. *Syntactical Processes Involved in the Development of the Adnominal Periphrastic Genitive in the English Language.* Michigan diss. [No further information available.]

1328. ———. 1935. "The Use of the Superlative Degree for the Comparative". *EJ* (college ed.) 24.821-29. [Examples from the Lindisfarne MS of the Gospel to the present time.]

1329. Thornburg, Linda Louise. 1984. *Syntactic Reanalysis in Early English.* Univ. of Southern California diss. (no pagination available). [Abstr. in *DA* 45.2513A (1985). Covers the period 900-1500.]

1330. ———. 1985. "The History of the Prepositional Passive in English". *Proceedings of the 11th Annual Meeting of the Berkeley Linguistics Society*, 327-36.

1331. Traugott, Elizabeth Closs. 1969. "Toward a Grammar of Syntactical Change". *Lingua* 23.1-27. [Concerns changes from OE to ModE.]

1332. ———. 1972. *A History of English Syntax: A Transformational Approach to the History of English Sentence Structure.* New York: Holt, Rinehart and Winston, viii + 216 pp.

Reviews: Ernst Burgschmidt in *Anglia* 92.194-98 (1974); Charles W. Kreidler in *FL* 12.429-38 (1974/75).

1333. Vallins, George Henry. 1956. *The Pattern of English*. (The Language Library.) London: André Deutsch; Fair Lawn, NJ: Essential Books, 188 pp. [Deals with the development of the construction of the sentence.]

Reviews: Margaret M. Bryant in *AS* 32.197-99 (1957); S. Gerson in *MSpr* 51.479-80 (1957); James Sledd in *Language* 33.81 (1957); G.W. Turner in *AUMLA* 8.40 (1958).

1334. Van der Gaaf, Willem. 1928. "The Predicative Passive Infinitive". *ES* 10.107-14.

1335. ———. 1928. "The Post-Adjectival Passive Infinitive". *ES* 10.129-38.

1336. ———. 1930. "The Passive of a Verb Accompanied by a Preposition". *ES* 12.1-24.

1337. ———. 1930. "Some Notes on the History of the Progressive Form". *Neophil* 15.201-15.

1338. ———. 1934. "The Connection between Verbs of Rest (*lie*, *sit*, and *stand*) and Another Verb, Viewed Historically". *ES* 16.81-99.

1339. Visser, Frederikus Theodorus. 1948. *Enige opmerkingen betreffende de studie van de historische syntaxis van het Engels*. Nijmegen & Utrecht: Dekker & Van de Vegt, 18 pp.

1340. ———. 1950. "Two or More Auxiliaries with a Common Verbal Complement". *ES* 31.11-27. [From OE to ModE.]

1341. ———. 1963. *An Historical Syntax of the English Language. Part I: Syntactical Units with One Verb*. Leiden: E.J. Brill, lxxi + 657 pp.

Reviews: Torben Kisbye in *SN* 37.418-21 (1965); Ernst Leisi in *GRM* 46.318-21 (1965); Samuel R. Levin in *JEGP* 64.143-46 (1965); Simeon Potter in *MLR* 60.234-36 (1965); A.A. Prins in *LT* 1965, 275-78; Norman Davis in *RES* n.s. 17.73-75 (1966); O. Funke in *ES* 47.47-56 (1966); Ewald Standop in *Anglia* 84.76-83 (1966); J. Boswinkel in *Neophil* 50.291-93 (1966); Broder Carstensen in *NS* N.F. 16.323-27 (1967); Alfred Reszkiewicz in *KN* 16.411-19 (1969).

1342. ———. 1966. *An Historical Syntax of the English Language. Part II: Syntactical Units with One Verb (continued)*. Leiden: E.J. Brill, xxxii + 659-1305 pp.

Reviews: Torben Kisbye in *SN* 39.196-99 (1967); (I&II) Martin Lehnert in *ZAA* 15.68-71 (1967); J. Boswinkel in *Neophil* 52.458-61 (1968); O. Funke in *ES* 49.51-61 (1968); A.A. Prins in *LT* 1968, 714-16; Broder Carstensen in *NS*

N.F. 18.98-99 (1969); Norman Davis in *RES* n.s. 20.196-200 (1969); Ewald Standop in *Anglia* 88.104-14 (1970); Simeon Potter in *YES* 1.200-02 (1971).

1343. ———. 1969. *An Historical Syntax of the English Language. Part III, First Half: Syntactical Units with Two Verbs.* Leiden: E.J. Brill, xxx + 1307-1858 pp.

Reviews: K.C. Phillipps in *ES* 51.344-49 (1970); A.A. Prins in *LT* 1970, 720-23; Norman Davis in *RES* n.s. 22.64-66 (1971); Torben Kisbye in *SN* 43.329-31 (1971); Samuel R. Levin in *JEGP* 70.649-51 (1971); Simeon Potter in *YES* 1.200-02 (1971); Broder Carstensen in *NS* N.F. 22.44-45 (1973); Heinz W. Viethen in *Anglia* 91.371-78 (1973).

1344. ———. 1973. *An Historical Syntax of the English Language. Part III, Second Half: Syntactical Units with Two and with More Verbs.* Leiden: E.J. Brill, xxviii + 1859-2470 pp.

Reviews: John Algeo in *AS* 49.272-77 (1974); Martin Lehnert in *ZAA* 22.202-05 (1974); K.C. Phillipps in *ES* 55.586-87 (1974); Norman Davis in *RES* n.s. 26.454-58 (1975); Torben Kisbye in *SN* 50.141-44 (1978).

1345. Von Schon, Catherine Virginia. 1977. *The Origin of Phrasal Verbs in English.* Univ. of New York at Stony Brook diss., 262 pp. [Abstr. in *DA* 38.1365A (1977). The period covered is from 600 A.D. to the 15th century.]

1346. Wallum, Mary Karen. 1973. *The Syntax and Semantics of the English Modal Verbs from the Late Tenth to the Fifteenth Century.* Michigan diss., 224 pp. [Abstr. in *DA* 35.437A (1974).]

1347. West, Fred. 1969. *The Cumulative Sentence in Old and Middle English.* Univ. of Nevada diss., 129 pp. [Abstr. in *DA* 31.749A (1970).]

1348. ———. 1973/74. "Some Notes on Word Order in Old and Middle English". *MP* 71.48-53. [See Dolan's criticism [no. 1215].]

1349. Whitaker, Harry A. 1968. "Negation in Old and Middle English". *UCLA Graduate Journal* 2.55-67.

1350. Wiegand, Nancy. 1982. "From Discourse to Syntax: *For* in Early English Causal Clauses". *PICHL*/5, 385-93.

1351. Wik, Berit. 1973. *English Nominalizations in '-ing': Synchronic and Diachronic Aspects.* (= SAU, 12) Uppsala: Universitetsbiblioteket; Stockholm: Almqvist & Wiksell, 158 pp. [Umeå diss.]

1352. Yngve, Victor H. 1975. "Depth and the Historical Change of the English Genitive". *JEngL* 9.47-57.

1353. Zimmermann, Rüdiger. 1973. "Structural Change in the English Auxiliary System: On the Replacement of *Be* by *Have*". *FoL* 6.107-17.

B. Old English

1354. Abruzzo, Donald J. 1969. "A Transformational Analysis of the Old English Attributive Genitive Construction". *PIL* 1.399-406.

1355. Allen, Cynthia Louise. 1975. "Case Marking and the NP Cycle in Old English". *LingA* 1.389-403.

1356. ———. 1975. "Old English Modals". *Grimshaw Papers*, 89-100.

1357. ———. 1980. "Movement and Deletion in Old English". *LingI* 11.261-323.

1358. ———. 1980. "*Whether* in Old English". *LingI* 11.789-93.

1359. ———. 1986. "Dummy Subjects and the Verb-Second 'Target' in Old English". *ES* 67.465-70.

1360. Anderson, George Kulmer. 1925. *A Study of Case Syntax in Some Old Northumbrian Texts*. Harvard diss. (no pagination available). [Abstr. in *Harvard Univ. Summaries of Theses Accepted . . . in 1925*, 5-9.]

1361. ———. 1935. "Some Irregular Uses of the Instrumental Case in Old English". *PMLA* 50.946-56.

1362. ———. 1958. "The Fifth Case in Old English". *JEGP* 57.21-26. [A reconsideration of the OE 'instrumental' case.]

1363. Anderson, John (Mathieson). 1985. "The Case System of Old English: A Case for Non-Modularity". *SL* 39.1-22.

1364. ———. 1986. "A Note on Old English Impersonals". *JL* 22.167-77.

1365. Andrew, Samuel Ogden. 1934. "Some Principles of Old English Word-Order". *MAE* 3.167-88.

1366. ———. 1936. "Relative and Demonstrative Pronouns in Old English". *Language* 12.283-93. [Especially with regard to word-order.]

1367. ———. 1940. *Syntax and Style in Old English*. Cambridge: Cambridge Univ. Press; New York: Macmillan, x + 112 pp. [Repr., New York: Russell & Russell, 1966.]

Reviews: Anon. in *TLS*, Dec. 14, 1940, p. 635; A. Macdonald in *RES* 17.499-50 (1941); Howard Merony in *MP* 39.99-100 (1941/42); S. Potter in *MLR* 36.252-55 (1941); Henning Larsen in *JEGP* 41.85-88 (1942); G.V. Smithers in *MAE* 12.104-06 (1943).

1368. ———. 1948. *Postscript on 'Beowulf'*. Cambridge: Cambridge Univ. Press, viii + 158 pp. [Repr., New York: Russell & Russell, 1969. Aims to show that the conclusions reached regarding prose syntax in Andrew [no. 1367] hold good also with regard to verse.]

Reviews: Anon. in *N&Q* 193.373-74 (1948); F. Mossé in *BSL* 45.170-71 (1949); M.L. Samuels in *MAE* 18.60-64 (1949); C.L. Wrenn in *RES* n.s. 1.353-56 (1950); K. Malone in *ES* 32.116-19 (1951).

1369. Bacquet, Paul. 1962. *La Structure de la Phrase Verbale à l'Époque Alfrédienne*. (= Pubs. de la Faculté de Lettres de l'Université de Strasbourg, 145.) Paris: Les Belles Lettres, 775 pp. [Paris diss.]

Reviews: Gero Bauer in *Anglia* 82.209-12 (1964); A. Campbell in *RES* n.s. 15.190-93 (1964); Westbrook Barritt in *Language* 41.146-51 (1965); S.R.T.O. d'Ardenne in *EA* 18.169-71 (1965); Bruce Mitchell in *MAE* 34. 244-45 (1965) and *NM* 67.86-97 (1966); Gerhard Nickel in *Archiv* 202.129-32 (1965/66); Torben Kisbye in *SN* 38.399-402 (1966); Kenneth R. Brooks in *MLR* 62.107 (1967); Charles Jones in *ES* 48.62-65 (1967); A. Reszkiewicz in *SAP* 3.143-52 (1970).

1370. ———. 1975. "From Doubt to Negativity: Remarks on the Particle *ne* in Old English". *Joly & Fraser Studies*, 13-15.

1371. Bammesberger, Alfred. 1978. "Zum syntaktischen Aufbau von Bedas Sterbespruch". *MSS* 37.5-9.

1372. ———. 1979. "Die syntaktische Analyse von *Exodus* 1-7a". *Pinsker Festschrift*, 6-15.

1373. Barasch, Monique. 1979. "A Study of the Anglo-Saxon Subjunctive in the *Lindisfarne Gospels*". *USFLQ* 18:1/2.16-18 and 52.

1374. Barela, Robert Edward. 1971. *A Descriptive Syntax of King Alfred's 'Soliloquies'*. Univ. of Southern California diss., 144 pp. [Abstr. in *DA* 32.3280-81A (1972).]

1375. Barrett, Charles Robin. 1953. *Studies in the Word-Order of Ælfric's 'Catholic Homilies' and 'Lives of the Saints'*. (= The Dept. of Anglo-Saxon, Cambridge Univ., Occasional Papers, 3.) Cambridge: Heffer, ix + 135 pp. [Bern diss.]

Reviews: M.L. Samuels in *RES* n.s. 5.401-03 (1954); A.A. Prins in *ES* 37.170-73 (1956).

1376. ———. 1967. "Aspects of the Placing of the Accusative Object in Ælfric". *AUMLA* 28.178-202.

1377. Bauer, Gero. 1963. "Über Vorkommen und Gebrauch von ae. *Sin*". *Anglia* 81.323-34. [On the use of the reflexive possessive *sīn* in OE.]

1378. Baxter, Andy. 1985. "The Old English Moods: Problems of Markedness, Morphosyntax and Speech-Act Theory". *Current Research 1984*, 1-18.

1379. Baxter, Lewis and Michael Cummings. 1983. "Computerized Analysis of Systemic Tree Diagrams in Old English". *LACUS*/9, 540-48.

1380. Bean, Marian Callaway. 1976. *A Study of the Development of Word Order Patterns in Old English in Relation to Theories of Word Order Change*. Univ. of California, Los Angeles, diss., 270 pp. [Abstr. in *DA* 37.7112A (1977).]

1381. ———. 1983. *The Development of Word Order Patterns in Old English*. (Croom Helm Linguistics Ser.) London & Canberra: Croom Helm; Totowa, NJ: Barnes & Noble Books, 150 pp. [A rev. version of no. 1380.]

Reviews: Edwin Battistella in *Language* 60.455-56 (1984); Paloma Tejada in *RCEI* 8.179-81 (1984); Cynthia L. Allen in *Australian Journal of Linguistics* (St. Lucia, Queensland) 5.131-34 (1985); M. Gouet in *Linguisticae Investigationes* (Amsterdam) 9.179 (1985); Geoffrey Russom in *JEGP* 84.117-18 (1985).

1382. Behre, Frank. 1934. *The Subjunctive in Old English Poetry*. (= GHÅ, 40:2.) Göteborg: Wettergren and Kerber, iv + 320 pp. [Göteborg diss.]

Reviews: A.O. B[elfour] in *MLR* 30.129 (1935); K. Jost in *IF* 53.162-63 (1935); F. Klaeber in *Archiv* 168.105-07 (1935); S.B. Liljegren in *Anglia B* 51.28-35 (1940).

1383. ———. 1934. "The Perceptive Subjunctive in Old English". *GHÅ* 40.37-42. [Repr. in *Behre Papers*, 83-88.]

1384. Bliss, Alan. 1980. "Auxiliary and Verbal in *Beowulf*". *ASE* 9.157-82.

1385. Bourcier, Georges. 1977. *Les Propositions Relatives en Vieil-Anglais*. (Pubs. de l'Université de Paris X Nanterre.) Paris: Champion, iv + 626 pp.

Reviews: A. Crépin in *BSL* 74.238-40 (1979); Juliette De Calwé-Dor in *EA*

32.223-26 (1979); Martin Huld in *Language* 55.483-84 (1979); B. Mitchell in *MAE* 48.121-22 (1979).

1386. Breivik. Leiv Egil. 1984. "The Diachrony of Introductory *There*: A Rejoinder". *FLH* 5.313-29. [Mainly concerned with the role of introductory *there* in OE.]

1387. Bremmer, Rolf H., Jr. 1984. "'Substantival Adverbs' and 'Prepositionalization' in Old Frisian, Compared with Old English in Particular". *NM* 85.411-21.

1388. Brown, William Hutchinson, Jr. 1970. *A Syntax of King Alfred's 'Pastoral Care'*. (= JanL, Ser. Practica, 101.) The Hague & Paris: Mouton, 91 pp. [An entirely rev. version of Michigan diss. 1963; Abstr. in *DA* 24.5396-97 (1964) and *Linguistics* 11.93-94 (1965).]

Reviews: Elizabeth Closs Traugott in *Language* 48.182-84 (1972); David L. Shores in *ES* 54.163-66 (1973).

1389. Burkhart, Russell S. 1935. *The Syntax of Place in Old English Prose*. Univ. of Pittsburg diss. (no pagination available). [Abstr. in *Univ. of Pittsburg Bulletin, The Graduate School, Abstracts of Theses* 11.63-70.]

1390. Butler, Milton Chadwick. 1976. "Verb Complementation in the *Anglo-Saxon Chronicle* to 891". *The Journal of the Linguistic Association of the Southwest* (Austin, TX) 1:3/4.53-68.

1391. Cable, Thomas M. 1970. "Rules for Syntax and Metrics in *Beowulf*". *JEGP* 69.81-88.

1392. Callaway, Morgan, Jr. 1931. *The Temporal Subjunctive in Old English*. Austin, TX: Univ. of Texas Press, xvi + 222 pp.

Reviews: H. Glunz in *Anglia B* 43.72-77 (1932); E.E. Ericson in *RES* 9.369-71 (1933); F. Holthausen in *LGRP* 55.223-24 (1934).

1393. ———. 1933. *The Consecutive Subjunctive in Old English*. (= The Modern Language Association of America, Monograph Ser., 4.) Boston: D.C. Heath; London: Oxford Univ. Press, viii + 110 pp.

Reviews: G.O. Curme in *JEGP* 33.462-63 (1934); J.R. H[ulbert] in *MP* 32.107 (1934); A.O. Belfour in *MLR* 30.71-72 (1935); H. Glunz in *Anglia B* 46.193-97 (1935).

1394. Canale, (William) Michael. 1976. "Implicational Hierarchies of Word Order Relationships". *PICHL*/2, 39-69. [Concerned with word order changes which took place in the development of OE from Proto-Germanic.]

1395. ———. 1978. *Word Order Change in Old English: Base Reanalysis in Generative Grammar*. McGill Univ. diss. (no pagination available). [Abstr. in *DA* 39.2223A (1978).]

1396. Capek, Michael Joseph. 1968. *A Commentary on the Syntax of 'Genesis B'*. Wisconsin diss., 86 pp. [Abstr. in *DA* 30.313A (1969).]

1397. ———. 1971. "The Nationality of a Translator: Some Notes on the Syntax of *Genesis B*". *Neophil* 55.89-96.

1398. Carkeet, David Corydon. 1973. *An Old English Syntactic Constraint*. Indiana Univ. diss., 215 pp. [Abstr. in *DA* 34.5941-42A (1974).]

1399. ———. 1976. "Old English Correlatives: An Exercise in Internal Syntactic Reconstruction". *Glossa* 10.44-63.

1400. Carleton, Charles. 1963. "Word Order of Noun Modifiers in Old English Prose". *JEGP* 62.778-83.

1401. ———. 1970. *Descriptive Syntax of the Old English Charters*. (= JanL, Ser. Practica, 111.) The Hague: Mouton, 200 pp. [A rev. version of Michigan diss. 1958; Abstr. in *DA* 19.1372-73 (1958/59).]

Reviews: C.J.E. Ball in *RES* n.s. 22.467-68 (1971); Bruce Mitchell in *MAE* 40.181-84 (1971); Ursula Oomen in *Anglia* 90.524-25 (1972); Patrizia Lendinara in *AION-SG* 15:1.191-93 (1972); David L. Shores in *ES* 53.166-67 (1973); Aleksander Szwedek in *Linguistics* 99.115-18 (1973); E.A. Ebbinghaus in *GL* 13.53-56 (1973).

1402. Cassidy, Frederic Gomes. 1938. *The Backgrounds in Old English of the Modern English Substitutes for the Dative-Object in the Group Verb + Dative-Object + Accusative-Object*. Michigan diss. [No further information available.]

1403. Červenkova, Pepa. 1979. "The Functions of the Prepositions in the Parker Manuscript of the *Anglo-Saxon Chronicle* up to 924". *Aspirantski sbornik na Velikotarnovskija Universitet 'Kiril i Metodij'* (Tărnovo, Bulgaria) 6.115-27.

1404. Cobb, George W. 1949. "The Subjunctive Mood in Old English Poetry". *Malone Festschrift*, 43-55.

1405. Collins, Janet Duthie. 1980. "An Hypothesis for Old English Object Noun Case Alternation". *LACUS*/6, 125-31.

1406. ———. 1981. "The Old English Nominal Form/Function Configuration". *LACUS*/7, 368-73.

1407. ———. 1985. "Old English: A Language Indo-European in Form but not in Function". *LACUS*/11, 392-403. [Based on an analysis of the verb system.]

1408. Coombs, Virginia M. 1975. "*Beowulf* Negative Indefinites: The Klima Hypothesis Tested". *Orbis* 24.417-25.

1409. Cosmos, Spencer. 1976. "Kuhn's Law and the Unstressed Verbs in *Beowulf*". *TSLL* 18.306-28. [Makes a distinction between finites, which are unmarkedly stressed, and non-lexical finites, which are unmarkedly unstressed.]

1410. Cummings, Michael J. 1975. "Scale-and-Category Analysis of Old English Verbal Groups". *CJL* 20.23-58.

1411. ———. 1980. "Paired Opposites in Wulfstan's *Sermo Lupi ad Anglos*". *Proceedings of the Ottawa-Carleton Medieval-Renaissance Club*, 5 = *University of Ottawa Quarterly* 50.233-43.

1412. ———. 1980. "Systemic Analysis of Old English Nominal Groups". *LACUS*/6, 228-42.

1413. ———. 1981. "Systemic Phoricity in the Old English Nominal Group". *LACUS*/ 7, 348-58.

1414. ———. 1982. "A Systemic-Functional Model for Old English". *LACUS*/8, 196-206.

1415. ———. 1985. "Sequence and Function in the Old English Nominal Group". *LACUS*/11, 422-31.

1416. Dančev, Andrej. 1967. "The Syntactic Functions of the Preposition *mid* in Old English Poetry and Prose. Part I". *GSU-ZF* 61:2.51-130.

1417. ———. 1969. "The Parallel Use of the Synthetic Dative-Instrumental and Periphrastic Prepositional Constructions in Old English". *GSU-ZF* 63:2.39-99.

1418. Daron, Carol Fields. 1974. *The Positions of Adverbials in a Selected Corpus of Early Old English Prose*. Auburn Univ. diss., 144 pp. [Abstr. in *DA* 35.1642A (1974).]

1419. De la Cruz, Juan M. 1972. "The Latin Influence on the Germanic Development of the English Phrasal Verb". *EPS* 13.1-42.

1420. Denison, David. 1985. "Why Old English had no Prepositional Passive". *ES* 66.189-204.

1421. Diamond, Celia Bidwell. 1970. *Alliterative Figurations, Syntax, and Meaning in Old English Poetry*. Pennsylvania diss., 291 pp. [Abstr. in *DA* 31.5395A (1971).]

1422. Dolcetti Corazza, Vittoria. 1978. "Le preposizioni in inglese antico: contributo all'analisi di un sistema". *Atti della Accademia delle Scienze di Torino, Classe di scienze morali, storiche e filologiche* (Torino) 112.89-116.

1423. Downs, Lynwood G. 1939. "Notes on the Intensive Use of Germanic *te, *to, 'to: too'". *JEGP* 38.64-68.

1424. Dowsing, Anita. 1976. "Some Apsects of Old English Syntax". *The Computer in Literary and Linguistic Studies* (Papers from the Third International Symposium on the Use of the Computer in Linguistic Literary Research, Cardiff, April 1974), ed. Alan Jones & R.F. Churchhouse, 285-92. Cardiff: Univ. of Wales Press.

1425. ———. 1979. "Some Syntactic Structures Relating to the Use of Relative and Demonstrative *þæt* and *se*, in Late Old English Prose". *NM* 80.289-303.

1426. ———. 1979. *A Computer Investigation of Active Periphrases Involving 'habban', 'beon', 'wesan' and 'weordan' and the Second Participle in Old English Prose*. Univ. of Wales (Swansea) diss. [No further information available.]

1427. Doyle, Debra. 1981. *Coordination, Subordination, and Sentence Structure in Old English Poetry: An Inquiry into Aspects of the Interplay between Syntax and Style*. Pennsylvania diss., 137 pp. [Abstr. in *DA* 42.2662-63A (1981).]

1428. Engberg, Norma Joyce. 1969. *Structure and Style in Alfredian Prose: A Linguistic Description of Late Ninth-Early Tenth Century Old English Sentence Structure and Word Order Based on Comparison of Selected Prose Texts*. Pennsylvania diss., 485 pp. [Abstr. in *DA* 31.1249A (1970).]

1429. ———. 1975. "Form and Function of the Infinitive in Alfredian Prose". *JEngL* 9.1-17.

1430. Erazmus, Edward Thomas. 1962. *Some Features of Morpheme Recurrence in Middle English Syntax*. Michigan diss., 290 pp. [Abstr. in *DA* 23.628-29 (1962).]

1431. Erickson, Jon L. 1973. "*An* and *na þæt an* in Late Old English Prose: Some Theoretical Questions of Derivation". *ArchL* n.s. 4.75-88.

1432. ———. 1975. "The *Deor* Genitives". *ArchL* n.s. 6.77-84.

1433. ———. 1977. "Subordinator Topicalization in Old English". *ArchL* n.s. 8.99-111.

1434. Ericson, Eston Everett. 1930. "The Use of Old English *swa* in Negative Clauses". *Studies in Honor of Hermann Collitz*, 159-75. Baltimore: The Johns Hopkins Press.

1435. ———. 1931. "Old English *swa* in Worn-down Correlative Clauses". *EStn* 65.343-50.

1436. ———. 1931. "The Use of Old English *swa* as a Pseudo-Pronoun". *JEGP* 30.6-20; 473.

1437. ———. 1932. *The Use of 'Swa' in Old English*. (= Hesperia. Ergänzungsreihe: Schriften zur englischen Philologie, 12.) Baltimore: The Johns Hopkins Press; Göttingen: Vandenhoeck & Ruprecht, 89 pp.

   Review: G.W. Small in *MLN* 49.537-39 (1934).

1438. Faraci, Mary Elizabeth. 1972. *A Syntactic Description of the Mood in the Old English Complement Clause*. Univ. of Florida diss., 195 pp. [Abstr. in *DA* 34.298A (1973).]

1439. ———. 1980. "The Modally Marked Form in Old English Subordinate Clauses: A Structure Signal". *NM* 81.378-84.

1440. Firbas, Jan. 1957. "Some Thoughts on the Function of Word Order in Old English and Modern English". *Sborník Prací Filosofické Fakulty Brněnské University* (Brno) 6 (A5).72-100.

1441. Fischer, Olga C.M. and Frederike C. van der Leek. 1983. "The Demise of the Old English Impersonal Construction". *JL* 19.337-68.

1442. Fourquet, Jean. 1938. *L'Ordre des Éléments de la Phrase en Germanique Ancien: Études de Syntaxe de Position*. (= Pubs. de la Faculté des Lettres de l'Univ. de Strasbourg, 86.) Paris: Les Belles Lettres, vi + 299 pp. [Strasbourg diss. Contains three sections concerned with OE: (1) the Anglo-Saxon Chronicle up to 891; (2) after 891; (4) *Beowulf* and the *Hêliand*.]

   Reviews: K. Schneider in *Anglia B* 50.225-33 (1939); Stefán Einarsson in *JEGP* 40.277-79 (1941).

1443. Frary, Louise Grace. 1929. *Studies in the Syntax of the Old English Passive with Special Reference to the Use of 'Wesan' and 'Weorðan'*. (= Language Dissertations of the Linguistic Society of America, 5.) Baltimore: Wavery Press, 80 pp. [Minnesota diss.]

   Reviews: G.O. Curme in *JEGP* 29.271-72 (1930); J.R. Hulbert in *MP* 27.372 (1930); A.J.F. Zieglschmid in *PQ* 10.91-93 (1931); F. Karpf in *Anglia B* 43.129-30 (1932); K. Jost in *IF* 50.299-301 (1932).

1444. Fraser, Thomas. 1985. "Did Old English Have a Middle Voice?" *PICHL*/6, 129-38.

1445. Fröhlich, Jürg. 1951. *Der indefinite Agens im Altenglischen, unter besonderer Berücksichtigung des Wortes 'Man'*. (= SAA, 25.) Bern: Francke, 145 pp. [Zürich diss.]

   Reviews: N.E. Eliason in *MLN* 68.569-70 (1953); R. Vleeskruyer in *Lingua* 4.436-38 (1954/55); R. Quirk in *MLR* 51.87-88 (1956); B.J. Timmer in *ES* 37.140-42 (1956); R.M. Wilson in *Erasmus* 9.346-48 (1956); R. Derolez in *RBPH* 35.422-25 (1957); A. Rynell in *SL* 11.61-63 (1957); F. Schubel in *DLZ* 78.613-16 (1957); S. Wyler in *Kratylos* 4.55-65 (1959).

1446. Fujiwara, Hiroshi. 1983. "The OE Relative Particle *þe*". *Poetica* 15/16.49-56.

1447. Funke, Otto. 1956. "Some Remarks on Late O.E. Word-Order, with Special Reference to Aelfric and the Maldon Poem (about 991)". *ES* 37.99-104.

1448. Gardner, Faith Folger. 1971. *An Analysis of Syntactic Patterns of Old English*. (= JanL, Ser. Practica, 140.) The Hague: Mouton, 85 pp. [Originally Wayne State Univ. diss. 1967; Abstr. in *DA* 29.245-46A (1969).]

   Reviews: Bruce Mitchell in *RES* n.s. 23.461-63 (1972); A.R. Tellier in *BSL* 68.258-59 (1973).

1449. Gattiker, Godfrey Leonard. 1962. *The Syntactic Basis of the Poetic Formula in 'Beowulf'*. Wisconsin diss., 223 pp. [Abstr. in *DA* 23.2114-15 (1962).]

1450. Glunz, Hans. 1929. *Die Verwendung des Konjunktivs im Altenglischen*. (= BEP, 11.) Leipzig: Tauchnitz, xvi + 144 pp. [Repr., New York: Johnson Reprint, 1968.]

   Reviews: F. Klaeber in *Anglia B* 41.261-63 (1930); H. Dehmer in *NS* 39.299 (1931); F. Fiedler in *ZFEU* 30.331-32 (1931); A.H. Smith in *MLR* 27.98-99 (1932); K. Jost in *IF* 51.82-84 (1933); W. van der Gaaf in *ES* 15.222-25 (1933). Cf. also *ES* 16.25 (1934).

1451. Goldman, Stephen Henry. 1970. *Basic and Marked Sentence Patterns in the Vercelli Homilies*. Wisconsin diss., 240 pp. [Abstr. in *DA* 31.5382-83A (1971).]

1452. ———. 1971. "Toward a Base for Late Old English". *Papers from the Fifth Kansas Linguistics Conference* [Univ. of Kansas Oct. 30-31, 1970], ed. Frances Ingemann, 35-53. Lawrence, KS: The Linguistics Dept., Univ. of Kansas. [A description of the phrase-structure rules for the base component of 10th-century OE. The data is taken from the Vercelli Homilies.]

1453. ——. 1972. "Rhetorical Transformations and the Old English *Vercelli Homilies*" *PMALC*/1971, 135-41.

1454. ——. 1972. "The Old English *Vercelli Homilies*: Rhetoric and Transformational Analysis". *JEngL* 6.20-27.

1455. Gray, Louis H. 1945. "*Man* in Anglo-Saxon and Old High German Bible-Texts". *Word* 1.19-32. [On the use of *man* as an indefinite pronoun.]

1456. Green, Donald Charles. 1967. *The Syntax of the Poetic Formula in a Cross-Section of Old English Poetry*. Wisconsin diss., 768 pp. [Abstr. in *DA* 28.629A (1968).]

1457. ——. 1971. "Formulas and Syntax in Old English Poetry: A Computer Study". *CHum* 6.85-93.

1458. Greene, Jesse Laurence. 1982. "Object-Verb and Verb-Object Sequences in *Beowulf*". *JIES* 10.71-115.

1459. Greenfield, Stanley Brian. 1963. "Syntactic Analysis and Old English Poetry". *NM* 64.373-78. [With a sample analysis of *The Wanderer* 19-29a.]

1460. ——. 1967. "Grendel's Approach to Heorot: Syntax and Poetry". *Old English Poetry: Fifteen Essays*, ed. Robert P. Creed, 275-84. Providence, RI: Brown Univ. Press.

1461. Groussier, Marie-Line. 1984. "Le Système des prépositions dans la prose en vieil-anglais". *Bulletin des Anglicistes Médiévistes* (Paris: L'Association des Médiévistes Anglicistes) 26.375-84.

1462. Guerrieri, Anna Maria. 1982. "La congiunzione *ond* nel *Beowulf*: Problemi di dizione, di sintassi e di stile". *AION-SG* 25.7-55.

1463. ——. 1983. "Ags. *cyst* col genitivo: un'analisi grammaticale ed estetica". *AION-SG* 26.7-27.

1464. Hacikyan, Agop. 1966. *A Linguistic and Literary Analysis of Old English Riddles*. Montreal: Mario Casalini, viii + 94 pp. [Includes 26 pages of tables analysing the uses of the definite article and demonstratives in the *Riddles*.]

Review: E.G. Stanley in *N&Q* n.s. 14.202 (1967).

1465. Hahn, E. Adelaide. 1961. "*Wæs Hrunting nama*". *Language* 37.476-83. [On *Beowulf* 1457 and the construction "a man X in name" in Indo-European languages.]

1466. Hall, J.R. 1981. "Duality and the Dual Pronoun in *Genesis B*". *PLL* 17.139-45.

1467. Harbert, Wayne. 1983. "A Note on Old English Free Relatives". *LingI* 14.549-53.

1468. Helming, Emily M. 1930. "The Absolute Participle in the *Apollonius of Tyre*". *MLN* 45.175-78.

1469. Heltveit, Trygve. 1969. "The Old English Appositional Construction Exemplified by *sume his geferan*: A Forerunner of the Modern Construction *a friend of mine*". *ES* 50.225-35.

1470. ———. 1977. "Aspects of the Syntax of Quantifiers in Old English". *NJL* 31.47-94.

1471. Hess, H. Harwood. 1970. "Old English Nominals". *PLL* 6.302-13. [Limited to an analysis of the nominals in "St Oswald, King and Martyr" from Ælfric's *Lives of Three English Saints*.]

1472. Hickey, Raymond. 1984. "A Valency Framework for the Old English Verb". *Historical Syntax*, 199-216.

1473. Hill, Leslie Alexander. 1960. "Diachronic Study of Word-Order in CCCC MS A of the Anglo-Saxon Chronicle". *ZPhon* 13.199-334.

1474. Hillard, Robert. 1972. *A Re-Examination of the Separable Verb in Selected Anglo-Saxon Prose Works*. Memorial Univ. of Newfoundland diss. (no pagination available). [Abstr. in *DA* 34.7192A (1974).]

1475. ———. 1972. "The Old English Separable Verb". *RLS: Regional Language Studies Newfoundland* (St. John's) 4.15-18.

1476. Hollmann, Else Germania. 1937. *Untersuchungen über Aspekt und Aktionsarten unter besonderer Berücksichtigung des Altenglischen*. Würzburg: Triltsch, x + 62 pp. [Jena diss.]

1477. Ingersoll, Sheila Most. 1976. "The Comparative Absolute in Old English". *NM* 77.177-89.

1478. ———. 1978. *Intensive and Restrictive Modification in Old English*. (= AF, 124.) Heidelberg: Carl Winter, x + 245 pp. [A rev. version of Northwestern diss. 1969 (submitted under her maiden name Sheila Marie Most); Abstr. in *DA* 30.2992-93A (1970).]

Review: E.G. Stanley in *Archiv* 219.419-20 (1982).

1479. Jacobson, Sven. 1978. "Adverb Generation in a Historical Perspective". *Rynell Festschrift*, 64-73. [A comparison between the generation of some Present-day English adverbs and that of the OE words from which they originate.]

1480. Johnson, Judith Anne. 1975. *A Transformational Analysis of the Syntax of Ælfric's 'Lives of Saints'*. (= JanL, Ser. Practica, 212.) The Hague: Mouton, 111 pp. [Originally Michigan diss. 1969; Abstr. in *DA* 31.2367A (1970).]

1481. Joly, André. 1972. "La Négation Dite 'Explétive' en Vieil Anglais et dans d'autres Langues Indo-Européennes". *EA* 25.30-44.

1482. Jones, Charles. 1967. "The Functional Motivation of Linguistic Change: A Study of the Development of the Grammatical Category of Gender in the Late Old English Period". *ES* 48.97-111. [The materials are taken from the *Lindisfarne Gospels* and the *Durham Ritual*.]

1483. ———. 1969. "A Further Note on the Use of *This* in the Gloss to the *Lindisfarne Gospels* and the *Durham Ritual*". *N&Q* n.s. 16.122-25.

1484. ———. 1970. "Some Features of Determiner Usage in the Old English Glosses to the *Lindisfarne Gospels* and the *Durham Ritual*". *IF* 75.198-219.

1485. Kageyama, Taro. 1974. "The Old English Genitive and Role Transposition Phenomena". *SEL* English No. 1974, 89-113.

1486. Kahlas, Leena. 1980. "Old English *everyone*". *Syntactic Variation* I, 125-32. [Studies OE indefinites for 'every' and 'each'.]

1487. Kahlas-Tarkka, Leena. 1983. "On the Variation of the Words Meaning 'Every' and 'Each' in Old English". *Current Topics in EHL*, 279-89.

1488. ———. 1984. "On the Syntactic Types 'Every Man' and 'Each of Men' in Old English". *Proceedings from the Second Nordic Conference for English Studies* (= MSAAF, 92), ed. Håken Ringbom and Matti Rissanen, 11-21. Åbo: Åbo Akademi Forskningsinstitut.

1489. Khomiakov, V.A. 1964. "A Note on the So-Called 'Passive Participles with Active Meaning' in Old English". *JEGP* 63.675-78.

1490. Kisbye, Torben. 1965. "Zur pronominalen Anrede bei Ælfric: Anmerkung zu Th. Finkenstaedts *You* und *Thou*". *Archiv* 201.432-35.

1491. Klaeber, Frederick. 1923. "Eine Bemerkung zum altenglischen Passivum". *EStn* 57.187-95.

1492. ———. 1929. "Eine germanisch-englische Formel: Ein stilistisch-syntaktischer Streifzug". *Förster Festschrift*, 1-22. [Analyses the clauses introduced by *þær* both in OE and in the Old High German and Old Norse parallel constructions.]

1493. ———. 1931. "Eine Randbemerkung zum Schwund von altengl. *weorðan*". *Anglia B* 42.348-52.

1494. ———. 1934. "Zwei Anmerkungen zur Wortstellung im Altenglischen". *Studia Germanica, tillägnade Ernst Albin Kock*, 107-15. Lund: Blom.

1495. ———. 1941. "Eine Randbermerkungen zur Nebenordnung und Unterordnung im Altenglischen". *Anglia B* 52.216-19. .

1496. Klingebiel, Josef. 1937. *Die Passivumschreibungen im Altenglischen*. Bottrop i. W.: Wilhelm Postberg, x + 115 pp. [Berlin diss.]

Reviews: G. L[inke] in *Archiv* 172.243-44 (1937); Karl Jost in *Anglia B* 49.356-57 (1938); E.L. Deuschle in *ES* 21.15-17 (1939)

1497. Kohonen, Viljo. 1976. "A Note on Factors Affecting the Position of Accusative Objects and Complements in Ælfric's *Catholic Homilies I*". *Reports on Text Linguistics*, 175-96.

1498. Koopman, Willem F. 1984. "Some Thoughts on Old English Word Order". *Current Research 1983*, 2-20.

1499. Krzyszpień, Jerzy. 1979. "The Periphrastic Subjunctive with *Magan* in Old English". *SAP* 11.49-64.

1500. Kurtz, Georg. 1931. *Die Passivumschreibungen im Englischen*. Breslau diss., ix + 114 pp.

1501. Lagerquist, Linnea M. 1985. "The Impersonal Verb in Context: Old English". *PICHL*/4, 123-36.

1502. Lehmann, Winfred Philipp. 1972. "Comparative Constructions in Germanic of the OV Type". *Haugen Festschrift*, 323-30. [Considers *Beowulf* 696, *Exodus* 369-73, and *Elene* 646b-48a.]

1503. Levin, Samuel R. 1956. *Negative Contraction with Old English Verbs*. Pennsylvania diss., 93 pp. [Abstr. in *DA* 16.1679 (1956).]

1504. Liggins, Elizabeth M. 1960. "The Clause of 'Denied Reason' in Old English". *JEGP* 59.457-62. [A study of OE subordinate clauses of the 'not because...' type.]

1505. ———. 1970. "The Authorship of the Old English *Orosius*". *Anglia* 88.289-322. [Examines a number of points of syntax.]

1506. ———. 1985 [1986]. "Syntax and Style in the Old English *Orosius*". *Studies in Earliest Old English Prose*, ed. Paul E. Szarmach, 245-73. Albany, NY: State Univ. of New York Press.

1507. Lovelady, Elgar John. 1974. *A Tagmemic Analysis of Ælfric's 'Life of St Oswald'*. Purdue Univ. diss., 336 pp. [Abstr. in *DA* 35.3713-14A (1974).]

1508. Malone, Kemp. 1953. "A Note on *Beowulf* 377ff". *MLN* 68.354-56. [On the syntax of the passage.]

1509. Malsch, Derry L. 1976. "Clauses and Quasi-clauses: VO Order in Old English". *Glossa* 10.28-43.

1510. Manabe, Kazumi. 1976. "Syntactic and Stylistic Analysis of Finite and Nonfinite Clauses in Four Texts of Alfred's Time". *SEL* English No. 1976, 89-103.

1511. Mann, Gerd. 1939. *Konjunktionen und Modus im konsekutiven und finalen Nebensatz des Altenglischen*. (= Sprache und Kultur der germanischen und romanischen Völker, A. Anglistische Reihe, 33.) Breslau: Priebatsch, v + 58 pp. [Berlin diss.]

Reviews: Herbert Koziol in *Archiv* 178.47-48 (1941); W. Preusler in *Anglia B* 52.248-50.

1512. Marcq, Philippe. 1973. "Structure du Système des Prépositions Spatiales dans le *Beowulf*". *EGerm* 28.1-19.

1513. Matsuda, Tokuichiro. 1965. *A Transformational Analysis of the Old English 'Pastoral Care'*. Indiana Univ. diss., 317 pp. [Abstr. in *DA* 26.2736-37 (1965).]

1514. Matsunami, Tamotsu. 1958. "On the Old English Participles". *SEL* 34.161-80.

1515. ———. 1966. "Functional Development of the Present Participle in English. Part I: Native Syntactic Functions of the OE Present Participle (I)". *Collected Papers in Commemoration of the 40th Anniversary of the Faculty of Literature, Kyushu University*, 315-48. Fukuoka, Japan: Faculty of Literature, Kyushu Univ.

1516. ———. 1966. "Functional Development of the Present Participle in English. Part I: Native Syntactic Functions of the OE Present Participle (II)". *Bungaku Kenkyu* [Studies in Literature] (Kyushu Univ., Fukuoka) 63.1-81.

1517. McLaughlin, John. 1983. *Old English Syntax: A Handbook.* (= Sprachstrukturen, A: Historische Sprachstrukturen, 4.) Tübingen: Max Niemeyer, xii + 105 pp.

Reviews: Carmela Rizzo in *Schede Medievali* 5.504-05 (1983); Enrique Bernárdez in *RCEI* 8.177-78 (1984); Bruce Mitchell in *RES* n.s. 35.217-18 (1984); Robert D. Stevick in *JEGP* 83.551-53 (1984); X. Dekeyser in *LB* 73.260 (1984); Corinna Weiss in *SAP* 17.293-97 (1984); Matti Kilpiö in *Speculum* 61.442-44 (1986).

1518. McNally, Charles Edward. 1975. *'Beowulf mapelode ..': Text Linguistics and Speech Acts.* State Univ. of New York at Binghamton diss., 217 pp. [Abstr. in *DA* 36.1476A (1975).]

1519. McRae, Michael Hartwell. 1974. *The Syntactic Basis of Anglo-Saxon Poetry.* Univ. of Wisconsin-Madison diss., 318 pp. [Abstr. in *DA* 35.5381-82A (1975).]

1520. Meroney, Howard. 1945. "The Early History of *Down* as an Adverb". *JEGP* 44.378-86. [Discusses the use in OE of *ofdune* as compared with *niðer*.]

1521. Micillo, Valeria. 1982. "Osservazioni sulla determinazione in antico inglese". *AION-SG* 25.161-202.

1522. Millward, Celia McCullough. 1971. *Imperative Constructions in Old English.* (= JanL, Ser. Practica, 124.) The Hague: Paris, 75 pp. [Originally Brown diss. 1966: Abstr. in *DA* 28.216-17A (1967).]

Reviews: Janet Bately in *Anglia* 92.198-200 (1974); Bruce Mitchell in *ES* 55.387-89 (1974).

1523. Mitchell, Bruce. 1959. *Subordinate Clauses in Old English Poetry.* Oxford diss., xxxi + 648; i + 649-894 pp.

1524. ———. 1963. "Old English Syntactical Notes". *N&Q* n.s. 10.326-28. [Deals with three passages from the *Cura Pastoralis*, and with *Daniel* 598.]

1525. ———. 1963. "Adjective Clauses in Old English Poetry". *Anglia* 81.298-322.

1526. ———. 1964. "Pronouns in Old English Poetry: Some Syntactical Notes". *RES* n.s. 15.129-41.

1527. ———. 1965. "Some Problems of Mood and Tense in Old English". *Neophil* 49.44-57.

1528. ———. 1965. "The Status of *Hwonne* in Old English". *Neophil* 49.157-60.

1529. ———. 1967. "An Old English Syntactical Reverie: *The Wanderer*, Lines 22 and 34-36". *NM* 68.139-49.

1530. ———. 1967. "*Swa* in Cædmon's *Hymn*, Line 3". *N&Q* n.s. 14.203-04.

1531. ———. 1968. "More Musings on Old English Syntax". *NM* 69.53-63. [On linguistic problems in the interpretation of certain passages of OE.]

1532. ———. 1968. "Some Syntactical Problems in *The Wanderer*". *NM* 69.172-98.

1533. ———. 1968. "Two Syntactical Notes on *Beowulf*". *Neophil* 52.292-99. [Discusses. ll. 1141 and 2035.]

1534. ———. 1969. "Five Notes on Old English Syntax". *NM* 70.70-84. [Concerns *Genesis* 241, *Exodus* 326, the use of *swa* in *Andreas*, *Andreas* 271, and *Paris Psalter*.]

1535. ———. 1972. "The Narrator of *The Wife's Lament*: Some Syntactical Problems Reconsidered". *Mustanoja Festschrift* = *NM* 73.222-34.

1536. ———. 1974. "Bede's Account of the Poet Cædmon: Two Notes". *Maxwell Festschrift*, 126-31.

1537. ———. 1976. "The Expression of Extent and Degree in Old English". *NM* 77.25-31.

1538. ———. 1976. "Some Problems Involving Old English Periphrases with *beon/wesan* and the Present Participle". *NM* 77.478-91.

1539. ———. 1976. "No 'House Is Building' in Old English". *ES* 57.385-89.

1540. ———. 1977. "Old English *Ac* as an Interrogative Particle". *NM* 78.98-100.

1541. ———. 1978. "Old English "Oð þæt" Adverb?". *N&Q* n.s. 25.390-94.

1542. ———. 1978. "Prepositions, Adverbs, Prepositional Adverbs, Postpositions, Separable Prefixes, or Inseparable Prefixes, in Old English?". *NM* 79.240-57. [Discusses a terminological problem of OE. Cf. also no. 33.]

1543. ———. 1979. "F.Th. Visser, *An Historical Syntax of the English Language*: Some Caveats concerning Old English". *ES* 60.537-42.

1544. ———. 1979. "Old English *Self*: Four Syntactical Notes". *NM* 80.39-45.

1545. ———. 1982. "Old English *Man* 'One': Two Notes". *McIntosh Festschrift* (A),

277-84. [1. Problems of classification, 2. *Man* + an active verb form as a periphrasis for the passive voice.]

1546. ———. 1983. "*Old English Syntax* (OUP): A Preview". *MESN* 8.3-7. [Repr. in *RCEI* 7.155-58 (1983).]

1547. ———. 1983. "A Note on Negative Sentences in *Beowulf*". *Poetica* 15/16.9-12. [Apropos of l. 949.]

1548. ———. 1984. "The Origin of Old English Conjunctions: Some Problems". *Historical Syntax*, 271-99. [Chiefly concerned with Carkeet [no. 1399].]

1549. ———. 1985. "The Syntax of *The Seafarer*, Lines 50-52". *RES* n.s. 36.535-37.

1550. ———. 1985. *Old English Syntax*. 2 Vols. Oxford: Clarendon Press; New York: Oxford Univ. Press. Vol. I: Concord, the Parts of Speech, and the Sentence, lxiv + 820 pp.; Vol. II: Subordination, Independent Elements, and Element Order, xlv + 1080 pp.

Reviews: T.A. Shippey in *TLS*, 28 June 1985, p. 716; N.F. Blake in *Lore&L* 4:1.113 (1985); Shigeru Ono in *SEL* English No. 1986, 99-104 (1986); E.G. Stanley in *RES* n.s. 37.234-37 (1986); Willem Koopman in *Neophil* 71.460-66 (1987).

1551. Mitchell, John Lawrence. 1972. "Old English as an SVO Language: Evidence from the Auxiliary". *PIL* 5.183-201.

1552. Miyabe, Kikuo. 1974. "Some Notes on Negative Sentences in *Beowulf*". *Poetica* 2.25-35.

1553. Möllmer, Hans. 1937. *Konjunktionen und Modus im Temporalsatz des Altenglischen.* (= Sprache und Kultur der germanischen und romanischen Völker, A. Anglistische Reihe, 24.) Breslau: Priebatsch, xii + 118 pp. [Berlin diss.]

Reviews: G. L[inke] in *Archiv* 171.258-59 (1937); Walther Preusler in *Anglia B* 49.225-26 (1938); B.J. Timmer in *ES* 23.154 (1941).

1554. Nagucka, Ruta. 1979 [1980]. "The Grammar of OE *Hatan*". *SAP* 11.27-39.

1555. ———. 1979. "Syntax and Semantics of *Hatan* Compounds". *KN* 26.19-28. [On *behatan* and chiefly *gehatan*.]

1556. ———. 1980. "Directionality and the Verb of Motion". *BPTJ* 37.13-27.

1557. ———. 1985. "Some Remarks on Complementation in Old English". *PICEHL/* 4, 195-204.

1558. Nevanlinna, Saara. 1986. "Variation in the Syntactic Structure of Simile in OE Prose". *Syntactic Variation* III, 89-98.

1559. Nichols, Ann Eljenholm. 1964. *A Syntactical Study of Ælfric's Translation of Genesis*. Univ. of Washington diss., 242 pp. [Abstr. in *DA* 25.5270-71 (1965) and *Linguistics* 20.112-14 (1966).]

1560. Nickel, Gerhard. 1966. *Die Expanded Form im Altenglischen: Vorkommen, Funktion und Herkunft der Umschreibung 'beon'/'wesan'* + Partizip Präsens. (= KBAA, 3.) Neumünster: Karl Wachholtz, 400 pp. [Friedrich-Alexander-Universität Habilitationsschrift.]

   Reviews: A. Campbell in *RES* n.s. 18.443-44 (1967); Barbara Butte in *ZAA* 15.292-94 (1967); Nils Erik Enkvist in *SN* 39.194-95 (1967); Herbert E. Brekle in *Kratylos* 12.181-85 (1967); Reinhard Koch in *Wissenschaftliche Zeitschrift der Martin Luther-Universität* (Halle-Wittenberg) 16.106-12 (1967); Christian Rohrer in *IF* 72.359-65 (1967/68); Manfred Scheler in *BGDSL*(T) 89.72-75 (1967/68); M.C. Seymour in *Lingua* 19.223-24 (1967/68); Alfred Bammesberger in *NS* N.F. 17.416-17 (1968); Kurt Otten in *ZMaf* 35.347-48 (1967); H.E. Pinsker in *Sprache* 14.182-83 (1967); Jacek Fisiak in *SAP* 2.109-10 (1968); J. Scheffer in *Neophil* 52.461-62 (1968); Ewald Standop in *Archiv* 205.53-56 (1968/69); Eric P. Hamp in *FL* 5.297-300 (1969); Bohumil Trnka in *PP* 12.179-81 (1969); C.J.E. Ball in *JL* 6.157-58 (1970); Herbert Koziol in *ES* 51.349-52 (1970); Thomas Gardner in *Anglia* 89.121-25 (1971); Simeon Potter in *YES* 1.202-03 (1971).

1561. ———. 1967. "An Example of a Syntactic Blend in Old English". *IF* 72.261-74. [On such constructions as *he is feohtende* 'he is fighting'.]

1562. Ogawa, Hiroshi. 1979. "Modal Verbs in Noun Clauses after Volitional Expressions in the Old English *Orosius*". *SEL* English No. 1979, 115-37.

1563. Ogura, Michiko. 1984. "OE Temporal Conjunctions Denoting 'When' or 'While': with Special Regard to the Gospels and the Psalter". *NM* 85.273-90.

1564. ———. 1986. "Old English 'Impersonal Periphrasis', or the Construction 'Copula + Past Participle' of 'Impersonal' Verbs". *Poetica* 23.16-52.

1565. ———. 1986. *Old English 'Impersonal' Verbs and Expressions*. (= Anglistica, 24.) Copenhagen: Rosenkilde and Bagger, 310 pp.

1566. O'Neil, Wayne. 1977. "Clause Adjunction in Old English". *GL* 17.199-211.

1567. Ordeman, D. Thos. 1932. "Position of Adverbs". *JEGP* 31.228-33. [Analyses adverb-positions in *Beowulf*.]

1568. Page, Raymond Ian. 1958. "Northumbrian *æfter* (= in memory of) + Accusative". *SN* 30.145-52.

1569. Peltola, Niilo. 1959. "On the 'Identifying' *Swa (Swa)* Phrase in Old English". *NM* 60.156-73.

1570. ———. 1960. "On Appositional Constructions in Old English Prose". *NM* 61.159-203.

1571. Penhallurick, J.M. 1975. "Old English Case and Grammatical Theory". *Lingua* 36.1-29.

1572. Pflueger, Solveig Mary Vadheim. 1970. *Syntax and Verse in 'Beowulf' and Selected Passages of Germanic Poetry*. Univ. of Texas at Austin diss., 207 pp. [Abstr. in *DA* 31.6037-38A (1971).]

1573. Pilch, Herbert. 1970. "Syntactic Prerequisites for the Study of Old English Poetry". *Lang&S* 3.51-61.

1574. ———. 1970. "Matrix der altenglischen Satztypen". *Buyssens Festschrift*, 161-67.

1575. Pillsbury, Paul W. 1967. *Descriptive Analysis of Discourse in Late West Saxon Texts*. (= JanL, Ser. Practica, 44.) The Hague: Mouton, 91 pp. [Originally Michigan diss. 1961; Abstr. in *DA* 22.2788 (1962).]

Reviews: Elizabeth Closs Traugott in *Language* 45.138-40 (1969); F.G. Cassidy in *JEngL* 4.97-98 (1970); R.E. Palmer, Jr. in *Lingua* 26.96-112 (1970/71); M. Nowakowski in *SAP* 3.165-68 (1970); Broder Carstensen in *Anglia* 89.246-48 (1971).

1576. Post, Thomas Charles. 1979. *Syntax and Narrative Habit in 'Beowulf'*. Univ. of California, Berkeley, diss., 354 pp. [Abstr. in *DA* 41.242-43A (1980).]

1577. Poussa, Patricia. 1986. "Historical Implications of the Distribution of the Zero-Pronoun Relative Clause in Modern English Dialects: Looking Backwards towards OE from Map S5 of *The Linguistic Atlas of England*". *Syntactic Variation* III, 99-117.

1578. Purdy, D.W. 1972. "Did Old English Have a Definite Article?". *YPL* 2.121-24.

1579. Quirk, Randolph. 1951. "Expletive or Existential *there*". *LMS* 2.32. [Gives a short note on the 'expletive' use of *þær* which S.O. Andrew regarded as 'a late prosaism', and rare in early OE.]

1580. ———. 1954. *The Concessive Relation in Old English Poetry*. (= YSE, 124.) New Haven, CT: Yale Univ. Press, x + 148 pp. [Originally London diss. 1951. Repr., with minor corrections and a new preface, as an Archon Book. Hamden, CN: The Shoe String Press, 1973.]

Reviews: K.R. Brooks in *MLR* 50.518-19 (1955); M.M. Bryant in *Language* 31.147-50 (1955); L. Blakeley in *ArchL* 8.70-73 (1956); A. Culioli in *EA* 9.39-40 (1956); B. Mitchell in *MAE* 25.36-40 (1956); A Campbell in *RES* n.s. 7.64-68 (1956); O. Funke in *ES* 37.212-17 (1956); R.W. Zandvoort in *Speculum* 32.199-202. [The original diss. (1951) is also reviewed by H.H. Meier in *ES* 34.296-97 (1953).]

1581. Raith, Josef. 1951. *Untersuchungen zum englischen Aspekt. I: Grundsätzliches Altenglisch*. (= Studien und Texte zur englischen Philologie, 1.) München: Max Hueber, vi + 116 pp. [A discussion of the expanded forms of the verb in OE.]

Reviews: C.A. Bodelsen in *ES* 32.258-62 (1951); G. Dietrich in *DLZ* 72.255-58 (1951); V. Pisani in *Paideia* 6.182 (1951); E. Otto in *NZ* 4.213-16 (1952); Carrol E. Reed in *MLQ* 13.110-11 (1952); B.J. Timmer in *MLR* 47.421 (1952); G. Kirchner in *ZAA* 1.87-89 (1953); C.L. Wrenn in *Erasmus* 6.81-83 (1953); W. Preusler in *IF* 61.326-27 (1954).

1582. Reddick, Robert John. 1975. *A Transformational-Generative Analysis of Negative Concord in Early West Saxon*. Minnesota diss., 103 pp. [Abstr. in *DA* 36.2178-79A (1975).]

1583. ———. 1981. "Reason Adverbials and Syntactic Constraints in Early West Saxon". *Glossa* 15.17-52.

1584. ———. 1982. "On the Underlying Order of Early West Saxon". *JL* 18.37-56.

1585. Reszkiewicz, Alfred. 1966. *Ordering of Elements in Late Old English Prose in Terms of their Size and Structural Complexity*. Wrocław: Komitet Neofilologiczny Polskiej Akademii Nauk/Zaklad Narodowy Imienia Ossolińskich, 125 pp. [Based on Ælfric.]

Reviews: Charles Jones in *ES* 48.64-65 (1967); J. Šimko in *JČ* 18.196-98 (1967); G. Storms in *Neophil* 51.99 (1967); Klaus Faiss in *Linguistics* 48.99-103 (1969); Siegfried Wyler in *Erasmus* 28.229-32 (1976).

1586. ———. 1966. "Split Constructions in Old English". *Schlauch Festschrift*, 313-26.

1587. Retelewska, Teresa. 1975. "On the Performative Analysis of Imperatives". *SAP* 6.83-90. [Based on a corpus of OE sentences.]

1588. Riffer-Maček, Dora. 1981. "On Interpreting a Type of Ambiguity in an Old English Text". *SRAZ* 26.281-95.

1589. Rissanen, Matti. 1967. "Old English *þæt an* 'only'". *NM* 68.409-28.

1590. ———. 1985. "Expression of Exclusiveness in Old English and the Development of the Adverb *Only*". *PICEHL*/4, 253-67.

1591. ———. 1986. "*Sum* in Old English Poetry". *Greenfield Festschrift*, 197-225. [Shows how *sum* and *an* compete as pronouns of indefinite, non-generic reference in OE poetry.]

1592. Robbins, Susan Wolfe. 1976. *Relative Clauses in Old English*. State Univ. of New York at Stony Brook diss., 229 pp. [Abstr. in *DA* 37.4330A (1977). Analysed within the framework of generative grammar.]

1593. Roberts, Jane. 1970. "Traces of Unhistorical Gender Congruence in a Late Old English Manuscript". *ES* 51.30-37. [Uses a prose transl. of Felix's *Vita sancti Guthlaci*.]

1594. Robinson, Fred Colson. 1973. "Syntactical Glosses in Latin Manuscripts of Anglo-Saxon Provenance". *Speculum* 48.443-75.

1595. Ross, Alan Strode Campbell. 1936. "Sex and Gender in the *Lindisfarne Gospels*". *JEGP* 35.321-30.

1596. Rudanko, (Martti) Juhani. 1981. "A Note on Word Order in Old English". *NM* 82.155-58.

1597. ———. 1983. *Towards Classifying Verbs and Adjectives Governing the Genitive in 'Beowulf'*. Tampere: Dept. of English and German, Tampere Univ., v + 111 pp.

1598. Russom, Jacqueline Haring. 1982. "An Examination of the Evidence for OE Indirect Passives". *LingI* 13.677-80.

1599. Rybarkiewicz, Włodzimierz. 1977. "The Word Order in Old English Prose and the Functional Sentence Perspective". *SAP* 9.87-93.

1600. Rynell, Alarik. 1952. *Parataxis and Hypotaxis as a Criterion of Syntax and Style, especially in Old English Poetry*. (= LUÅ, N.F. Avd. 1, Bd. 48, Nr. 3.) Lund: Gleerup, 60 pp.

    Reviews: B.M.H. Carr in *ES* 34.30-32 (1953); S.B. Liljegren in *SN* (1953); A.A. Prins in *Museum* 59.58-59 (1953); H. Pilch in *Anglia* 73.368-71 (1955); A. Culioli in *BSL* 52.148-49 (1956).

1601. Saitz, Robert Leonard. 1955. *Functional Word Order in Old English Subject-Object Patterns*. Univ. of Washington diss., 930 pp. [Abstr. in *Summaries of Doctoral Dissertations, Univ. of Washington* 16.555-56 (1956).]

1602. Samuels, Michael Louis. 1949/50. "The Elder Edda and the Lindisfarne Gloss: A Syntactic Parallel". *EGS* 3.37-41.

1603. Sandved, Arthur Olav. 1981. "Some Notes on the Syntax of Prepositions in Ælfric's Homilies". *Christophersen Festschrift*, 117-35.

1604. Scaffidi Abbate, Augusto. 1974. *Le proposizioni introdotte dalla congiunzione 'þæt' nel 'Beowulf'*. (= Quanderni degli *AION-SG* 7.) Naples: Instituto Universitario Orientale, 135 pp.

   Review: Gabriella Del Lungo Camiciotti in *BN* 10.453-55 (1975).

1605. Scheler, Manfred. 1961. *Altenglische Lehnsyntax: Die syntaktischen Latinismen im Altenglischen*. Berlin: Privately printed, 143 pp. [Freie Univ. Berlin diss.]

   Reviews: A. Campbell in *RES* n.s. 14.218 (1963); E.G. Stanley in *MLR* 58.150-51 (1963); E. Mayer in *Archiv* 201.205 (1964).

1606. Scherer, Philip. 1958. "Aspect in the Old English of the Corpus Christi MS". *Language* 34.245-51.

1607. Schulz, Muriel Ripley. 1973. *A Case Grammar of the Parker Manuscript of the 'Anglo-Saxon Chronicle' from 734 to 891*. Univ. of Southern California diss., 318 pp. [Abstr. in *DA* 33.5156-57A (1973).]

1608. Shannon, Ann. 1964. *A Descriptive Syntax of the Parker Manuscript of the Anglo-Saxon Chronicle from 734 to 891*. (= JanL, Ser. Practica, 14.) The Hague: Mouton, 68 pp. [Originally Michigan diss. 1962; Abstr. in *DA* 23.231 (1962).]

   Reviews: R.E. Diamond in *Linguistics* 17.88-89 (1965); E.V.K. Dobbie in *Language* 42.649-51 (1966); Jacek Fisiak in *LPosn* 11.156-58 (1966); Robert A. Peters in *Linguistics* 25.81-84 (1966); Peter H. Salus in *ES* 49.140-41 (1966).

1609. Short, Douglas D. 1983. "Another Look at a Point of Old English Grammar: *Elene* 508 and *Psalm* 77:27". In *Geardagum* 5.39-46. [Concerns subject-verb agreement.]

1610. Simpson, Dale Wilson. 1983. *Word Order and Style in the Old English 'Apollonius of Tyre'*. North Texas State Univ. diss., 301 pp. [Abstr. in *DA* 44.2468A (1984).]

1611. Small, George William. 1926. "The Syntax of *The* with the Comparative". *MLN* 41.300-13. [On the OE construction '*þon* (or *þȳ*, or *þē*) + comparative + *þe* (relative particle)'.]

1612. ———. 1929. *The Germanic Case of Comparison with a Special Study of English*. (= LM, 4.) Philadelphia: Linguistic Society of America, 121 pp.

   Reviews: W. Preusler in *Anglia B* 42.359-62 (1931); P. Gurrey in *RES* 8.366-68 (1932).

1613. ———. 1930. "The Syntax of *the*, and OE *þon mā þe*". *PMLA* 45.368-91.

1614. ———. 1936. "On the Study of Old English Syntax". *PMLA* 51.1-7.

1615. Solo, Harry Jay. 1973. "The Twice-Told Tale: A Reconsideration of the Syntax and Style of the Old English *Daniel*, 245-429". *PLL* 9.347-64.

1616. Standop, Ewald. 1957. *Syntax und Semantik der modalen Hilfsverben im Altenglischen: 'Magan', 'Motan', 'Sculan', 'Willan'*. (= BEP, 38.) Bochum-Langendreer: Pöppinghaus, 178 pp. [Münster Habilitationsschrift.]

   Reviews: Martin Lehnert in *ZAA* 6.302-03 (1958); A.R. Tellier in *EA* 11.241-43 (1958); H. Marcus in *Archiv* 195.208 (1958/59); A. Campbell in *RES* n.s. 10.186-87 (1959); Bruce Mitchell in *N&Q* n.s. 7.273-74 (1960); B.J. Timmer in *ES* 41.104-06 (1960); Herbert Pilch in *Anglia* 80.165-68 (1962).

1617. Stewart, Ann Harleman. 1973. "The Old English 'Passive' Infinitive". *JEngL* 7.57-68.

1618. Stockwell, Robert P. 1977. "Motivation for Exbraciation in Old English". *Mechanisms of Syntactic Change*, ed. Charles N. Li, 291-314. Austin, TX: Univ. of Texas Press.

1619. Strauss, Otto. 1925. "Beiträge zur Syntax der im Codex Junius enthaltenen altenglischen Dichtungen". *Luick Festschrift*, 172-82.

1620. Swan, Toril. 1984. "Adverbial Usage in Ælfric's *Lives of Saints*". *Nordlyd: Tromsø Univ. Working Papers on Language and Linguistics* (Tromsø) 9.7-70.

1621. Tandy, Keith Alan. 1976. *Aspect and 'Ælfric'*. Univ. of California, Berkeley, diss., 128 pp. [Abstr. in *DA* 37.5812A (1977). Examines patterns of aspectual features of verbs in Ælfric's *Lives of Saints*.]

1622. Taylor, M.V. 1973. "Another Look at Old English Word Order". *Edinburgh Working Papers in Linguistics* 3.93-99.

1623. Tengstrand, Erik. 1965. "A Special Use of Old English ōþer after swilce". SN 37.382-92. [On the use of swilce ōþer in the meaning 'like any'.]

1624. Terasawa, Jun. 1984. "The Function of the Passive in Old English and Present-Day English". SEL 61.287-304.

1625. Timmer, Benno Johan. 1934. *Studies in Bishop Wærferth's Translation of the 'Dialogues' of Gregory the Great.* Wageningen: Venman, 122 pp. [Groningen diss. Deals with: I. The order of words; II. The use of prepositions; III. The use of *wearð* and *wæs* in the passive.]

1626. ———. 1939. "The Place of the Attributive Noun-Genitive in Anlgo-Saxon with Special Reference to Gregory's *Dialogues*". ES 21.49-72. [A study of OE word-order.]

1627. Turner, Kathleen. 1985. *Categorization, Meaning, and Change in the English Modal System.* Univ. of Alabama diss., 184 pp. [Abstr. in DA 46.1926A (1986). Mainly concerned with OE.]

1628. Van Beek, Peter. 1932. *The Prefix 'be-' in King Alfred's Translation of Boethius' De Consolatione Philosophiae.* Univ. of Iowa diss. (no pagination available). [Abstr. in *Univ. of Iowa Doctoral Dissertation Abstracts and References (1900-1937)* 1.161-75 (1940).]

1629. Van Dam, Johannes. 1957. *The Causal Clause and Causal Prepositions in Early Old English Prose.* Groningen: J.B. Wolters, xii + 93 pp. [Municipal Univ. of Amsterdam diss.]

   Review: O. Funke in ES 41.380-82 (1960).

1630. Van der Gaaf, Willem. 1931. "*Beon* and *Habban* connected with an Inflected Infinitive". ES 13.176-88.

1631. Van der Leek, Frederike. 1982. "De syntacticus als anglist: de Oudengelse onpersoonlijke constructie". *Handelingen van het zeven en dertigste Nederlandse Filologencongres,* ed. René Stuip and Wiecher Zwanenburg, 149-58. Amsterdam: APA-Holland Universiteits Pers.

1632. Van Kemenade, Ans. 1984. "Verb Second and Clitics in Old English". *Linguistics in the Netherlands 1984,* ed. Hans Bennis and W.U.S. van Lessen Kloeke, 101-09. Dordrecht & Cinnaminson, NJ: Foris Publications.

1633. ———. 1984. "On the Clitic Status of Old English Personal Pronouns". *Current Research 1983,* 21-28.

1634. ———. 1985. "Old English Infinitival Complements and West-Germanic V[erb]-Raising". *PICEHL*/4, 73-84.

1635. Vat, Jan [pseudonym]. 1978. "On Footnote 2: Evidence for the Pronominal Status of *þær* in Old English Relatives". *LingI* 9.695-716.

1636. Visser, Frederikus Theodorus. 1954. "*Beowulf* 991-992". *ES* 35.116-20. [Discusses examples, from OE and later, of the type *he was* plus two past participles (e.g. *he was said killed*).]

1637. Vogt, Andreas. 1930. *Beiträge zum Konjunktivgebrauch im Altenglischen*. Borna: Noske, 80 pp. [Erlangen diss.]

1638. Von Schaubert, Else. 1954. *Vorkommen, Gebietsmässige Verbreitung und Herkunft altenglischer absoluter Partizipialkonstruktionen in Nominativ und Akkusativ*. Paderborn: Ferdinand Schöningh, 200 pp.

Reviews: H. Marcus in *Archiv* 191.94-95 (1954/55); R. Quirk in *Speculum* 31.214-15 (1956); Carroll E. Reed in *MLQ* 17.174-75 (1956); Rudolf Keller in *ES* 38.116-18 (1957).

1639. Wagner, Karl Heinz. 1969. *Generative Grammatical Studies in the Old English Language*. (= Wissenschaftliche Bibliothek, 11.) Heidelberg: Julius Groos Verlag, viii + 298 pp. [Kiel diss.]

Reviews: Dieter Kastovsky in *Anglia* 89.482-92 (1971); Herbert E. Brekle in *FL* 8.449-55 (1972); Elizabeth Closs Traugott in *JL* 8.297-301 (1972).

1640. Wahlén, Nils. 1925. *The Old English Impersonalia. Part I: Impersonal Expressions Containing Verbs of Material Import in the Active Voice*. Göteborg: Elander, iii + 224 pp. [Göteborg diss.]

Review: H.M. Flasdieck in *Anglia B* 37.198-99 (1926).

1641. Waterhouse, Ruth. 1976. "The Two-to-One Construction in Ælfric's *Lives of Saints*". *Working Papers of the Speech and Language Research Centre* (Macquarie Univ., Australia) 1.173-200. [Studies the types and positioning of subordinate clauses.]

1642. ———. 1980. *Some Syntactic and Stylistic Aspects of Ælfric's 'Lives of Saints'*. Macquarie Univ. (Australia) diss., 482 pp. [Abstr. in *DA* 42.2666A (1981).]

1643. ———. 1982. "Modes of Address in Ælfric's *Lives of Saints* Homilies". *SN* 54.3-24.

1644. ———. 1983. *The Triangular Clause Relationship in Ælfric's 'Lives of Saints' and in Other Works.* (= American Univ. Studies, 4: Anglo-Saxon Language and Literature, 1.) New York-Frankfurt am Main-Bern: Peter Lang, vii + 112 pp. [The final version of Waterhouse's 1976 working paper [no. 1641].]

Review: E.G. Stanley in *N&Q* n.s. 31.436-37 (1984).

1645. ———. 1983. "'If You Can Talk with Crowds': Ælfric's Placement of *Gif*-Clauses in *Lives of Saints*". *AUMLA* 59.48-65.

1646. ———. 1984. "Sentence Determination in Ælfric's *Lives of Saints*". *NM* 85.257-72.

1647. ———. 1984. "'And Have They Fixed the Where and the When?': Temporal Clause Placement in Ælfric's *Lives of Saints*" *Parergon* n.s. 2.25-55.

1648. Wattie, J.M. 1930. "Tense". *E&S* 16.120-43. [A survey of the tense system of OE.]

1649. Wedel, Alfred R. 1978. "Participial Construction in High German and West Saxon of the Eleventh and Twelfth Centuries: Latin and Germanic Differences". *JEGP* 77.383-97. [Uses the OE *Apollonius*.]

1650. Wełna, Jerzy. 1978. "Complex Gender in Old English Loanwords". *Acta Philologica* (Warsaw) 7.143-64.

1651. ———. 1980. "On Gender Change in Linguistic Borrowing (Old English)". *Historical Morphology*, 399-420.

1652. Whitman, Frank H. 1979. "Constraints on the Use of the Relative Pronoun Forms in *Beowulf*". *TSLL* 21.1-16.

1653. Whittier, Phyllis Gage. 1968. *Syntax and Poetry in Four Old English Elegies.* Oregon diss., 298 pp. [Abstr. in *DA* 29.2232A (1969).]

1654. Wilde, Hans-Oskar. 1939-40. "Aufforderung, Wunsch und Möglichkeit. Die englische Sprache und die Grundlagen englischer Lebenshaltung". *Anglia* 63.209-391; 64.10-105. [Considers the problem of meaning and expression in situations involving invitation, wish, and possibility.]

1655. Woodell, Thomas McMillan, II. 1968. *Selected Syntactical Aspects of the 'Worcester Chronicle' from 1054 through 1079.* Univ. of Florida diss., 87 pp. [Abstr. in *DA* 30.309A (1969). Focuses on the clause.]

1656. Woolf, Henry Bosley. 1943. "Subject-Verb Agreement in *Beowulf*". *MLQ* 4.49-55.

1657. Wright, Virginia Dieckman. 1972. *Syntax as a Tool for Determining Authorship: A Linguistic Investigation of the Old English 'Christ'*. Indiana Univ. diss., ii + 276 pp. [Abstr. in *DA* 33.4396A (1973).]

1658. Wyss, Simone. 1977. *Le Système du genre en vieil-anglais jusqu'à la Conquête*. Univ. de Paris III Doctrat d'État diss., 615 pp. [Pub. in 1982, Lille: Service de reproduction des thèses, Univ. de Lille III, 637 pp.]

   Review: Anon. in *EA* 31.245-46 (1978).

1659. ———. 1977. "L'anaphorique neutre en vieil-anglais". *Linguistique et Philologique*, 119-33.

1660. ———. 1978. "Sexe et genre dans la pronominalisation des noms de personne en vieil-anglais (1)'. *Confluents* (Lyon) 4.177-98.

1661. Yerkes, David. 1982. *Syntax and Style in Old English: A Comparison of the Two Versions of Wærferth's Translation of Gregory's Dialogues*. (= Medieval and Renaissance Texts and Studies, 5.) Binghamton, NY: Center for Medieval and Early Renaissance Studies, State Univ. of New York at Binghamton, 109 pp.

   Reviews: Daniel G. Calder in *Speculum* 59.246 (1984); Patrizia Lendinara in *Schede Medievali* 6/7.297 (1984); Celia Sisam in *RES* n.s. 36.393-94 (1985); E.G. Stanley in *MAE* 54.133-34 (1985); Peter S. Baker in *MLR* 81.438-39 (1986).

1662. Young, George Arthur. 1965. *Sentence Patterns in Alfred's 'Orosius' and the Latin Original: A Comparative Study*. Texas Technological College diss., 107 pp. [Abstr. in *DA* 26.1034 (1965).]

1663. Zieglschmid, A.J. Friedrich. 1929. "Is the Use of *wesan* in the Periphrastic Actional Passive in the Germanic Languages Due to Latin Influence?" *JEGP* 28.360-65.

1664. Zuck, Louis Victor. 1966. *The Syntax of the Parker Manuscript of the Anglo-Saxon Chronicle from the Year 892 through 1001*. Michigan diss., 123 pp. [Abstr. in *DA* 27.2143A (1967).]

C. Middle English

1665. Åkerlund, Alfred. 1936/37. "I go a-fishing". *SN* 9.3-13. [Illustrations of the *a*-phrase in its active significance, from 1290 to the present time in literary, dialectal and vulgar English.]

1666. Akkartal, T. 1953. "A Point of Syntax in *Sir Gawain and the Green Knight*". *N&Q* 198.322. [Discusses the meanings of *þeroute* and *þerwyth*.]

1667. Baghdikian, S. 1979. "*NE* in ME and EModE". *ES* 60.673-79. [A survey of expletive *ne* in Chaucer's *Boece* (cl386) and Queen Elizabeth's *Englishing of Boethius* (1593).]

1668. Bald, Wolf-Dietrich. 1984. "Form and Functions of ONE: Diachronic Aspects". *MSC Aachen 1983*, 143-53. [From late ME to Shakespearean English.]

1669. ———. 1985. "On the Diachrony of English Linking Verb". *Gerritsen Festschrift*, 175-89. [A comparison of the distribution of linking and nonlinking constructions of verbs like *go*, *run*, *turn* in ModE and ME, esp. Chaucer.]

1670. Bauer, Gero. 1967. "Historisches Präsens und Vergegenwärtigung des epischen Geschehens: Ein erzähltechnischer Kunstgriff Chaucers". *Anglia* 85.138-60.

1671. ———. 1970. *Studien zum System und Gebrauch der 'Tempora' in der Sprache Chaucers und Gowers*. (= WBEP, 73.) Wien: Wilhelm Braumüller, viii + 165 pp.

Reviews: R. Zimmermann in *Sprache* 17.185 (1971) and *Archiv* 210.174-76 (1973); K.C. Phillipps in *ES* 53.456-58 (1972).

1672. Bauschatz, Paul C. 1972. *The Modal Auxiliaries of English, Middle to Modern: Their Semantics*. Columbia diss., 593 pp. [Abstr. in *DA* 33.5701A (1973).]

1673. Behre, Frank. 1950. "The Origin and Early History of Meditative-Polemic *should* in *that*-clauses". *GHÅ* 56.273-309. [Traces the use of *should* in *that*-clauses back to the late 13th century. Repr. with postscript (pp. 122-24) in *Behre Papers*, 89-127.]

1674. Benson, Larry D. 1961. "Chaucer's Historical Present: Its Meaning and Uses". *ES* 42.65-77.

1675. Block, David N. 1974. *The Structure of Relative Clauses in the Early Scots 'Legends of the Saints'*. New York Univ. diss., 193 pp. [Abstr. in *DA* 35.1075A (1974).]

1676. Brinton, Laurel Jean. 1983. "Criteria for Distinguishing the Non-Aspectual Functions of ME *Ginnen*". *GL* 23.235-45.

1677. Brose, Brigitte. 1939. *Die englischen Passivkonstruktionen vom Typus 'I am told a story' und 'I am sent for': Ein Beitrag zur englischen Syntax des 14. bis 16. Jahrhunderts*. Würzburg: Triltsch, 119 pp. [Berlin diss.]

Review: G. Linke in *Archiv* 177.55 (1940).

1678. Buchholz, Erich. 1936. *Das Verbum substantivum im Mittelenglischen*. Bottrop i. W.: Wilhelm Postberg, x + 70 pp. [Berlin diss.]

Review: H. Koziol in *EStn* 72.272-73 (1937/38).

1679. Butler, Milton Chadwick. 1976. "The Reanalysis of Middle English Impersonal Constructions and the Characterization of 'Subject of a Sentence'". *Texas Linguistic Forum* (Austin, TX) 4.1-19.

1680. ———. 1977. "Reanalysis of Object as Subject in Middle English Impersonal Constructions". *Glossa* 11.155-70.

1681. ———. 1977. "Grammaticalization of Topical Elements in Middle English". *Proceedings of the Annual Meeting of the Berkeley Linguistics Society*, (Berkeley, CA) 3.626-36.

1682. Caldwell, Sarah J.G. 1974. *The Relative Pronoun in Early Scots*. (= MSNH, 42.) Helsinki: Société Néophilologique, 80 pp. [The period covered is c1375-c1500. Originally Part One of the Univ. of Edinburgh diss. 1967.]

1683. Carstensen, Broder. 1956. *Syntax des Nomens und des Pronomens in den 'Paston Letters'*. Kiel Habilitationsschrift, vii + 368 pp.

1684. ———. 1959. *Studien zur Syntax des Nomens, Pronomens und der Negation in den 'Paston Letters'*. (= BEP, 42.) Bochum-Langendreer: Heiner Pöppinghaus, viii + 328 pp.

Reviews: R.M. Wilson in *N&Q* n.s. 7.398 (1960); Karl Brunner in *NS* 1961, 440-43; N.E. Eliason in *JEGP* 60.165-66 (1961); Alison Hanham in *RES* n.s. 12.183-85 (1961); Ewald Standop in *Archiv* 198.191-93 (1961/62); A.R. Tellier in *EA* 14.357-59 (1961); F.Th. Visser in *ES* 42.376-79 (1961); M. Lehnert in *ZAA* 9.291-94 (1961); Norman Davis in *MAE* 31.229-32 (1962); M. Rissanen in *NM* 63.76-79 (1962).

1685. Chatman, Seymour Benjamin. 1956. *Structural and Lexical Distributions of Function Words with Substantives in the Paston Letters (1440-1460)*. Michigan diss., 271 pp. [Abstr. in *DA* 16.1440-41 (1956).]

1686. Chevillet, François. 1981. *Les Relatifs au Début du Moyen-anglais*. 2 vols. Lille: Univ. de Lille III; Paris: Librairie Honoré Champion. Vol. I: v [+1] + 462 pp.; Vol. II: 463-813 pp. + 151 pp. (appendix of quotations). [Univ. de Paris X diss. 1977.]

Review: E.G. S[tanley] in *N&Q* n.s. 30.386 (1983).

1687. ———. 1983. "A propos des relatifs en anglais médiéval". *MLing* 5.141-54. [Covers the period 1100-1299.]

1688. Clark, Cecily. 1957. "Gender in *The Peterborough Chronicle, 1070-1154*". *ES* 38.109-15.

1689. Connoly, J.H. 1977. *A Method of Analysing Syntactic Change, Exemplified with Reference to Six Middle English Texts*. Reading Univ. diss. [No further information available.]

1690. Cosper, Russell. 1948. *The English Question Patterns from 1100-1600*. Michigan diss., 230 pp. [Abstr. in *Microfilm Abstracts* 8:1.85-86 (1948).]

1691. Cross, James E. 1952. "A Point of Chaucer's Syntax". *N&Q* 197.468. [Discusses '*of* + noun' as an adjective.]

1692. Curme, George Oliver. 1930. "The Gerund Preceded by the Common Case Again". *ES* 12.111. [Cf. Van der Gaaf [no. 1884].]

1693. ———. 1930. "Origin of the Accusative Often Used as Subject of the Gerund". *ES* 12.180-82. [Cf. Van der Gaaf [no. 1886].]

Review: F. Karpf in *EStn* 65.333-34 (1930/31).

1694. Davis, Norman. 1961. "The Earliest *Do Not*". *N&Q* n.s. 8.48-49.

1695. ———. 1972. "Margaret Paston's Uses of *Do*". *Mustanoja Festschrift* = *NM* 73.55-62.

1696. Deakins, Alice Hanna. 1975. *A Sector Analysis of the Language of Margaret Paston*. Columbia diss., 355 pp. [Abstr. in *DA* 36.8023-24A (1976).]

1697. ———. 1985. "The Informal English Sentence: Change since 1450". *Word* 36.109-35. [A 'sector analysis' of word order, based on Margaret Paston's letters (1441-1478) and Florence Mary Eaton's letters (1894-1957).]

1698. Dean, Christopher. 1964. "Chaucer's Use of Function Words with Substantives". *CJL* 9.67-74. [The classification of the use of function words follows C.C. Fries (*American English Grammar* [New York: Appleton-Century-Crofts, 1940], pp. 108 ff.).]

1699. Dekeyser, Xavier. 1983. "Relative Markers in the *Peterborough Chronicle*: 1070-1154, or, Linguistic Change Exemplified". *Steenbergen Festschrift*, 95-107.

1700. Dekker, Arie. 1932. *Some Facts concerning the Syntax of Malory's Morte Darthur* (according to the edition of H. Oskar Sommer). Amsterdam: Portielje, x + 205 pp. [Amsterdam diss.]

Review: E. Ekwall in *Anglia B* 45.139-40 (1934).

1701. ———. 1935. "Some Observations in Connection with B. Trnka: *On the Syntax of the English Verb from Caxton to Dryden*". *Neophil* 20.113-20.

1702. De la Cruz, Juan M. 1972. "Transference and Metaphor in Middle English: Verbs Accompanied by a Locative Particle". *Orbis* 21.114-35.

1703. ———. 1973. "A Late 13th Century Change in English Structure". *Orbis* 22.161-76. [Discusses the change from synthetic structures of 'prefix + verb' to analytical structures of 'verb + preposition'.]

1704. Denison, David. 1985. "The Origins of Periphrastic *Do*: Ellegård and Visser Reconsidered". *PICEHL*/4, 45-60.

1705. Dillon, Bert. 1969. "Formal and Informal Pronouns of Address in Malory's *Le Morte Darthur*". *AnM* 10.94-103.

1706. Donaldson, Ethelbert Talbot. 1966. "The Grammar of Book's Speech in *Piers Plowman*". *Schlauch Festschrift*, 103-09. [Examines in the light of contemporary usage the syntactic problems in *PPl.B* XVIII.252-57. Repr., with some revisions, in *Style and Symbolism in Piers Plowman: A Modern Critical Anthology*, ed. Robert J. Blanch, 264-70. Knoxville, TN: The Univ. of Tennessee Press, 1969.]

1707. Donner, Morton. 1986. "The Gerund in Middle English". *ES* 67.394-400.

1708. Ekwall, Eilert. 1943. *Studies on the Genitive of Groups in English*. (= K. Humanistiska Vetenskaps-Samfundets i Lund, Årsberättelse 1942-1943, 1.) Lund: Gleerup, 104 pp. [Based on the ME material.]

Reviews: S.B. Liljegren in *SN* 16.151-52 (1943/44); R.W. Zandvoort in *ES* 27.59-62 (1946); F. Mossé in *BSL* 44.121-22 (1947/48).

1709. Elmer, Willy. 1983. "Semantic-Syntactic Patterning: The Lexical Valency of *Seem* in Middle English". *ES* 64.160-68.

1710. Emonds, Joseph. 1973. "The Derived Nominals, Gerunds, and Participles in Chaucer's English". *Issues in Linguistics: Papers in Honor of Henry and Renée Kahane*, ed. Braj B. Kacharu, et al., 185-98. Chicago: Univ. of Chicago Press.

1711. Engblom, Victor. 1938. *On the Origin and Early History of the Auxiliary 'Do'*. (= LundSE, 6.) Lund: Gleerup, 171 pp. [Lund diss.]

Reviews: G. Linke in *Archiv* 174.256 (1938); Hans Marchand in *ES* 21.121-25

(1939); F. Mossé in *EA* 3.371-72 (1939); A. Dekker in *Museum* 46.269 (1939); H. Koziol in *EStn* 74.218-19 (1940/41); Kemp Malone in *MLN* 57.127-28 (1942).

1712. Evans, William W., Jr. 1959. The Second-Person Pronoun in 'Sir Gawain and the Green Knight'. Univ. of Florida diss., 151 pp. [Abstr. in *DA* 24.4184 (1964).]

1713. ———. 1967. "Dramatic Use of the Second Person Singular Pronoun in *Sir Gawain and the Green Knight*". *SN* 39.38-45.

1714. Fisiak, Jacek. 1976. "Subjectless Sentences in Middle English". *KN* 23.263-70.

1715. Fridén, Georg. 1948. *Studies on the Tenses of the English Verbs from Chaucer to Shakespeare, with Special Reference to the Late Sixteenth Century.* (= Essays and Studies on English Language and Literature, 2.) Uppsala: Almqvist & Wiksell, 222 pp. [Uppsala diss.]

Reviews: B.M. Charleston in *MSpr* 43.216-19 (1949); F. Mossé in *BSL* 45.175-76 (1948/49) and *EA* 5.69-70 (1952); F. Schubel in *SN* 21.300-02 (1948/49); J. Sledd in *MP* 47.208-09 (1949/50); W.E. Collinson in *SL* 4.113-17 (1950); S.M. Kuhn in *JEGP* 49.104-06 (1950); S. Potter in *MLR* 45.77-78 (1950); A.A. Hill in *SIL* 9.98-99 (1951).

1716. ———. 1957. "On the Use of Auxiliaries to Form the Perfect and the Pluperfect in Late Middle English and Early Modern English". *SL* 11.54-56. [Repr. in *Archiv* 196.152-53 (1959).]

1717. Fries, Udo. 1968. *Zur Syntax der Chester Plays.* (= Dissertationen der Univ. Wien, 6.) Wien: Notring, iv + 208 pp. [Wien diss. 1965.]

Review: Broder Carstensen in *Anglia* 89.538-40 (1971).

1718. ———. 1968. "Demonstrativum und bestimmter Artikel". *NM* 69.209-22. [On variations between *the* and *this/that* in late ME and early ModE texts.]

1719. Gage, Phyllis C. 1966. "Syntax and Poetry in Chaucer's *Prioress's Tale*". *Neophil* 50.252-61. [Syntactic analysis.]

1720. González Escribano, José Luis. 1981. "Observaciones sobre la posición de los complementos circunstanciales en la prose de Los Paston, 1425-1450". *RCEI* 3.14-15.

1721. Goodman, John Stuart. 1962. *The Syntax of the Verb 'To Be' in Malory's Prose.* Michigan diss., 216 pp. [Abstr. in *DA* 23.3363-64 (1963).]

1722. Grad, Anton. 1956. *Notes about the Origin of the 'For + Subject + Infinitive' Construction in English.* Ljubljana: Slovenska Akademija, 11 pp. [= *Razprave* 2:4.93-101.]

1723. Grimshaw, Jane B. 1975. "Evidence for Relativization by Deletion in Chaucerian Middle English". *Grimshaw Papers*, 35-43.

1724. Harris, David Payne. 1964. "The Development of Word-Order in Twelfth-Century English". *Fries Festschrift*, 187-98.

1725. Häusermann, Hans Walter. 1930. *Studien zu den Aktionsarten im Frühmittelenglischen.* (= WBEP, 54.) Wien: Braumüller, viii + 86 pp.

Reviews: W. Preusler in *Anglia B* 43.82-84 (1932); A.H. Smith in *MLR* 27.98-99 (1932); H. Heuer in *LGRP* 54.307-08 (1933); W. van der Gaaf in *ES* 15.65-67 (1933).

1726. Heuer, Hermann. 1932. *Studien zur syntaktischen und stilistischen Funktion des Adverbs bei Chaucer und im Rosenroman.* (= AF, 75.) Heidelberg: Carl Winter, viii + 168 pp.

Reviews: John Koch in *EStn* 67.391-95 (1933); H. Koziol in *DLZ* 54.1889-90 (1933); O. Funke in *Anglia B* 45.141-47 (1934); H.C. Matthes in *GRM* 22.409 (1934) and *LGRP* 56.164-66 (1935); C.S. Northup in *JEGP* 34.105-07 (1935).

1727. Hill, L.A. 1978. *A Detailed Analysis of the Word-Order of 102 Letters Dictated by Margaret Paston to Members of her Family, with Notes on Ways in which this Word-Order Differs from that of MS CCCC A of the Anglo-Saxon Chronicle and Present-day Educated English.* London (External) diss., 731 pp.

1728. Hittmair, Rudolf. 1923. *Das Zeitwort 'Do' in Chaucers Prosa.* (= WBEP, 51.) Wien & Leipzig: Braumüller, vi + 126 pp.

Review: G.C. Moore Smith in *MLR* 19.256 (1924).

1729. ———. 1935. "Zu den Aktionsarten im Mittelenglischen". *EStn* 70.81-91. [Apropos of Häusermann [no. 1725].]

1730. Homann, Elizabeth R. 1954. "Chaucer's Use of *Gan*". *JEGP* 53.389-98.

1731. Hungerford, Harold Roe, Jr. 1963. *Comparative Constructions in the Works of Sir Thomas Malory: A Synchronic Study.* Univ. of California, Berkeley, diss., 190 pp. [Abstr. in *DA* 24.5399 (1964) and *Linguistics* 11.101-02 (1965).]

1732. Huntsman, Jeffrey Forrest. 1976. "Celts and Saxons: Creolization and Syntactic

Change in Historical Linguistics". *Lektos: Interdisciplinary Working Papers in Language Sciences* (Louisville, KY) 4.79-92.

1733. ———. 1977. "Creolization and Syntactic Change in Early Middle English". *Papers from the 1975 Mid-American Linguistics Conference*, ed. Frances Ingemann, 141-54. Lawrence, KS: Dept. of Linguistics, Univ. of Kansas.

1734. Irvine, Annie Sowell. 1929. "The Participle in Wycliffe, with Especial Reference to his Original English Works". *Univ. of Texas Bulletin: Studies in English* 9.5-68.

1735. ———. 1930. "The *To Comyng(e)* Construction in Wyclif". *PMLA* 45.468-500.

1736. Ito, Eiko Tamano. 1971. *Sentential Complementation in Middle English and Early Modern English: A Study of Linguistic Change*. Michigan diss., 129 pp. [Abstr. in *DA* 33.2354-55A (1972).]

1737. ———. 1978. "Reflexive Verbs in Chaucer". *SEL* English No. 1978, 65-89.

1738. Iwasaki, Haruo. 1968. "A Peculiar Feature in the Word-Order of Layamon's *Brut*". *Gengo Kenkyu* (Tokyo: The Linguistic Society of Japan) 25.64-77.

1739. Jack, George Barr. 1975. "Relative Pronouns in Language AB". *ES* 56.100-07. [AB = the Corpus MS of the *Ancrene Riwle* (A) and the Bodley MS of the *Katherine Group* (B).]

1740. ———. 1978. "Negative Adverbs in Early Middle English". *ES* 59.295-309.

1741. ———. 1978. "Negation in Later Middle English Prose". *ArchL* n.s. 9.58-72.

1742. ———. 1978. "Negative Concord in Early Middle English". *SN* 50.29-39.

1743. ———. 1981. "The Prepositional Plural in the AB Language". *NM* 82.175-80.

1744. Jacobson, Rodolfo. 1970. *The London Dialect of the Late Fourteenth Century: A Transformational Analysis in Historical Linguistics*. The Hague: Mouton, 193 pp. [Originally Michigan diss. 1966; Abstr. in *DA* 27.2141A (1967). Corpus: Chaucer, Wyclif, and some ordinances, chronicles, and charters.]

Reviews: Maria Lipińska in *SAP* 4.214-18 (1972); Klaus Faiss in *Linguistics* 102.108-11 (1973); Bertil Sundby in *ES* 54.308-12 (1973); Elizabeth Closs Traugott in *JEngL* 8.78-80 (1974).

1745. Johannesson, Nils-Lennart. 1986. "Variable Subject Deletion in Late Middle English Topic Constructions". *Syntactic Variation* III, 119-29.

1746. Johnson, Judith A. 1977. "*Ye* and *Thou* among the Canterbury Pilgrims". *Michigan Academician* (Ann Arbor, MI) 10.71-76. [Discusses the social nuances implied by the use of *ye* and *thou*.]

1747. Johnston, Everett C. 1967. "The Significance of the Pronoun of Address in *Sir Gawain and the Green Knight*". *LangQ* 5:3/4.34-36. [Cf. Evans [no. 1713] and Metcalf [no. 1787].]

1748. Joly, André. 1982. "The System of Negation in Later Middle English Prose". *PICHL*/5, 176-89.

1749. Jones, Charles. 1967. "The Grammatical Category of Gender in Early Middle English". *ES* 48.289-305. [An extension of Jones [no. 1482].]

1750. ———. 1983. "Determiners and Case Marking in Middle English: A Localist Approach". *Lingua* 59.331-43.

1751. Jud-Schmid, Elisabeth. 1956. *Der indefinite Agens von Chaucer bis Shakespeare: Die Wörter und Wendungen für 'Man'*. (= SAA, 39.) Bern: Francke, 128 pp. [Zürich diss.]

Reviews: R.M. Wilson in *Erasmus* 9.346-48 (1956); Ingrid Brunner in *Word* 13.382-86 (1957); R. Derolez in *RBPH* 35.422-25 (1957); A. Rynell in *SL* 11.61-63 (1957); F. Schubel in *DLZ* 78.613-16 (1957); Ewald Standop in *Archiv* 194.236 (1957/58); R. Quirk in *MLR* 53.458 (1958); S. Wyler in *Kratylos* 4.55-65 (1959); H.C. Matthes in *Anglia* 78.480-81 (1960); H. Hartmann in *IF* 67.320-22 (1962); E.G. Stanley in *EPS* 8.58-59 (1963).

1752. Kaartinen, Anja and Tauno Frans Mustanoja. 1958. "The Use of the Infinitive in *A Book of London English 1384-1425*". *NM* 59.179-92.

1753. Karakida, Shigeaki. 1983. "The Grammatical Category of Gender in *Vices and Virtues*: Evidence of Gender Change in Middle English". *SEL* English No. 1983, 83-99.

1754. Keyser, Samuel Jay. 1975. "A Partial History of the Relative Clause in English". *Grimshaw Papers*, 1-33. [From ME through ModE.]

1755. Kisbye, Torben. 1967. "On the So-called Imperative with Preposed Pronominal Subject (1489-1695)". *Archiv* 203.438-43.

1756. Kivimaa, Kirsti. 1966. *'þe' and 'þat' as Clause Connectives in Early Middle English with Especial Consideration of the Emergence of the Pleonastic 'þat'*. (= CHL, 39:1.) Helsinki: Societas Scientiarum Fennica, 271 pp. [Helsinki diss.]

Reviews: T.F. Mustanoja in *NM* 68.327-30 (1967); Charles Jones in *MAE*

37.328-32 (1968); Broder Carstensen in *Archiv* 207.300-01 (1970/71); K.C. Phillipps in *ES* 52.160-62 (1971).

1757. ———. 1966. *The Pleonastic 'That' in Relative and Interrogative Constructions in Chaucer's Verse.* (= CHL, 39:3.) Helsinki: Societas Scientiarum Fennica, 40 pp.

Reviews: T.F. Mustanoja in *NM* 68.329-30 (1967); Broder Carstensen in *Archiv* 207.300-01 (1970/71).

1758. ———. 1968. *Clauses in Chaucer Introduced by Conjunctions with Appended 'That'.* (= CHL, 43:1.) Helsinki: Societas Scientiarum Fennica, 75 pp.

Review: Uwe Carls in *ZAA* 20.203-05 (1972) (also on two other books [nos. 1756 and 1757.]).

1759. ———. 1972. "*Betwix and* in *Cursor Mundi*". *Mustanoja Festschrift* = *NM* 73.134-42.

1760. ———. 1975. "Notes on Sentence Patterns and Style in *Purity* and *Patience*". *Enkvist Festschrift*, 202-11.

1761. Klammer, Thomas P. 1971. "Multihierarchical Structure in a Middle English Breton Lay — A Tagmemic Analysis". *Lang&S* 4.3-23. [*Sir Orfeo*.]

1762. Kolinsky, Muriel. 1967. "Pronouns of Address and the Status of Pilgrims in the *Canterbury Tales*". *PLL* 3 (Summer Supplement).40-48.

1763. Kovatcheva, Mira. 1982. "An Aspect of the Transition towards Analytical Sentence Structure in English". *FLH* 3.109-19. [Mainly concerned with ME syntax.]

1764. Koziol, Herbert. 1932. *Grundzüge der Syntax der mittelenglischen Stabreimdichtungen.* (= WBEP, 58.) Wien & Leipzig: Braumüller, xvi + 172 pp.

Reviews: J. Koch in *EStn* 68.249-50 (1933); W. Franz in *DLZ* 54.1606-09 (1933); M. Callaway, Jr. in *Language* 10.212-17 (1934); H. Marcus in *Archiv* 165.254-55 (1934); H.C. Matthes in *GRM* 22.409 (1935); H. Heuer in *LGRP* 56.17-19 (1935); K. Jost in *Anglia B* 46.363-64 (1935); C.S. Northup in *JEGP* 34.440-41 (1935); C.L. W[renn] in *RES* 12.246 (1936).

1765. ———. 1936. "Die Entstehung der Umschreibung mit 'to do'". *GRM* 24.460-66. [A historical study of the periphrastic construction with *do*.]

1766. ———. 1938. "Zur Syntax der englischen Urkundensprache des 14. und 15. Jahrhunderts". *Anglia* 62.100-15.

1767. Kubouchi, Tadao. 1982. "Word Order in Richard Rolle's English Epistles". *In Geardagum* 4.19-31.

1768. Langenfelt, Gösta. 1931. "Uppkomsten av omskrivning med *do* i engelskan". *MSpr* 25.148-59. [On the origin of periphrastic *do*.]

1769. ———. 1946. "The Roots of the Propword *One*". *SMS* 16.97-138. [Provides material from the ME and ModE periods for the study of this problem.]

1770. Lawton, David A. 1980. "Larger Patterns of Syntax in Middle English Unrhymed Alliterative Verse". *Neophil* 64.604-618.

1771. Lee, Donald Woodward. 1948. *Functional Change in Early English*. Menasha, WI: George Banta, ix + 128 pp. [A study of functional change between nouns and verbs, and adjectives and verbs, in English (1200-1600). Originally Columbia diss.]

   Reviews: Anon. in *N&Q* 193.329 (1948); Stefán Einarsson in *MLN* 64.498-500 (1949); N.E. Eliason in *Language* 25.68-69 (1949); A.A. Hill in *AS* 24.59-61 (1949); P.M. Kean in *MAE* 18.78-80 (1949); R. Quirk in *MLR* 44.591-92 (1949); H.T. Price in *JEGP* 48.151-52 (1949); J.H. Fisher in *Word* 6.190-92 (1950); C.T. Hodge in *SIL* 8.13-14 (1950); A.A. Prins in *ES* 32.31-32 (1951).

1772. Lenerz, Jürgen. 1979. "Zur Beschreibung eines syntaktischen Wandels: das periphrastische *do* im Englischen". *Sprachstruktur, Individuum und Gesellschaft. Akten des 13. Linguistischen Kolloquiums, Gent 1978*, ed. Marc van de Velde and Willy Wandeweghe, I, 93-102. Tübingen: Max Niemeyer.

1773. Lewandowska, Barbara. 1972. "Direct Alternative Questions in Late Middle English". *ZNUŁ* 91.7-21.

1774. ———. 1973. "Indirect Questions in the English of the Fifteenth Century". *SAP* 5.57-66.

1775. ———. 1973. "Direct Special Questions in Late Middle English". *ZNUŁ* 100.87-97.

1776. Lightfoot, David. 1976. "The Base Component as a Locus of Syntactic Change". *PICHL*/2, 17-37. [Concentrates on the change from the ME type *for to love* to Early ModE *for John to love*.]

1777. Maček, Dora. 1972/73. "A Draft for the Analysis of Verbal Periphrases in the *Canterbury Tales*". *SRAZ* 33-36.695-708.

1778. MacLeish, Andrew. 1969. *The Middle English Subject-Verb Cluster*. (= JanL, Ser. Practica, 26.) The Hague: Mouton, 276 pp. [Originally Wisconsin diss. 1961; Abstr. in *DA* 22.865(1961).]
Reviews: J.R. Simon in *EA* 25.59-62 (1972); Götz Wienold in *DLZ* 93.106-08 (1972); Rüdiger Zimmermann in *Anglia* 90.370-72 (1972); Ruta Nagucka in *Linguistics* 106.121-25 (1973).

1779. Maling, Joan M. 1978. "The Complementizer in Middle English Appositives". *LingI* 9.719-25.

1780. Marchand, Hans. 1939. "Syntaktische Homonymie: das umschreibende *do*". *EStn* 73.227-52. [On the origin of the periphrastic *do*.]

1781. Mausch, Hanna. 1986. "A Note on Late Middle English Gender". *SAP* 18.89-100.

1782. McClean, R.J. 1934. "The Deictic Use of *ein* in Middle High German". *MLR* 29.336-39. [Contains references to ME *oon the best*, etc.]

1783. McIntosh, Angus. 1947/48. "The Relative Pronoun *þe* and *þat* in Early Middle English. *EGS* 1.73-87.

1784. Meier, Hans Heinrich. 1953. *Der indefinite Agens im Mittelenglischen (1050-1350): Die Wörter und Wendungen für 'Man'*. (= SAA, 34.) Bern: Francke, 256 pp.
Reviews: Hans Marcus in *Archiv* 192.72-73 (1956); Heinrich Christoph Matthes in *Anglia* 74.462-70 (1956); B.J. Timmer in *ES* 37.140-42 (1956); R. Derolez in *RBPH* 35.422-25 (1957) and *ZDP* 78.320-21 (1959); F. Schubel in *DLZ* 78.613-16 (1957); E.G. Stanley in *EGS* 6.107-09 (1957); A. Rynell in *SL* 11.61-63 (1957); W. Preusler in *IF* 64.327 (1959); S. Wyler in *Kratylos* 4.55-56 (1959).

1785. ———. 1967. "The Lag of Relative *Who* in the Nominative". *Neophil* 51.277-88.

1786. Meissgeier, Ernst. "Der Untergang des grammatischen Geschlechts im Frühmittelenglischen". *Anglia* 47.193-212.

1787. Metcalf, Allan A. 1971. "Sir Gawain and *You*". *ChauR* 5.165-78. [Discusses the implications of a speaker's choice between *you* and *thou*.]

1788. Mitchell, Bruce. 1964. "Syntax and Word-Order in *The Peterborough Chronicle* 1122-1154". *NM* 65.113-44.

1789. ———. 1970. "The Subject-Noun Object-Verb Pattern in *The Peterborough Chronicle*: A Reply". *NM* 71.611-14. [Reply to Shores [no. 1851].]

1790. Mittermann, Harald. 1973. "Zur sogennanten 'bildlichen Verneinung' im Mittelenglischen". *Koziol Festschrift*, 193-203. [On 'not worth a fly', etc.]

1791. ———. 1975. *Untersuchungen zum historischen Präsens und Perfekt in frühen mittelenglischen Romanzen.* (= Dissertationen der Univ. Wien, 119.) Wien: VWGÖ, 209 pp. [Wien diss. 1973; Abstr. in *EASG* 1973, 12-14 (1974).]

Review: R. Zimmermann in *Anglia* 96.471-74 (1978).

1792. Miyabe, Kikuo. 1968. "On Some Features of Negative Sentences of Early Middle English". *SEL* English No. 1968, 83-103.

1793. Moessner, Lilo. 1984 [1985]. "Impersonal Constructions in Early Middle English". *SAP* 17.29-38.

1794. Mossé, Fernand. 1952. "Un Cas d'Ambiguité syntactique en Moyen-Anglais: Le Type *I was wery forwandred*". *EA* 5.289-308.

1795. ———. 1957. "Réflexions sur la genèse de la 'forme progressive'". *Studies in English Language and Literature Presented to Professor Dr. Karl Brunner on the Occasion of his Seventieth Birthday* (= WBEP, 65), ed. Siegfried Korninger, 155-74. Wien & Stuttgart: Wilhelm Braumüller. [Gives examples of the falling together in ME and early ModE of *-ind* and *-ing* in *-in*.]

1796. Mustanoja, Tauno Frans. 1955. "Middle English *Wery of Wandred*: A Variant of *Wery for Wandred*". *NM* 56.90-94. [On the construction discussed by Mossé [no. 1794] and Spitzer [no. 1863]. Cf. also Samuels [no. 1849].]

1797. ———. 1955. "*Troilus and Criseyde*, IV, 607: *Of Fered*". *NM* 56.174-77.

1798. ———. 1958. *The English Syntactical Type 'One the Best Man' and Its Occurrence in Other Germanic Languages.* (= MSNH, 20:5.) Helsinki: Société Néophilologique, 55 pp.

Reviews: Ewald Standop in *Anglia* 77.498-99 (1959); M.L. Samuels in *MAE* 29.147-48 (1960); R.W. Zandvoort in *ES* 41.62 (1960); Hans Marcus in *Archiv* 197.210 (1961); Eric Buyssens in *RBPH* 39.121-22 (1961).

1799. ———. 1959. "The Middle English Syntactical Type *His Own Hand(s)* 'With His Own Hands, Himself', with Reference to Other Similar Expressions". *NM* 60.267-86.

1800. ———. 1960. *A Middle English Syntax. Part I: Parts of Speech.* (= MSNH, 23.) Helsinki: Société Néophilologique, 702 pp. [Repr., Tokyo: Meicho-fukyu-kai, 1985.]

SYNTAX 189

Reviews: Broder Carstensen in *NS* 1961, 294-96; Jacek Fisiak in *KN* 8.451-54 (1961); M. Lehnert in *ZAA* 9.294-96 (1961); V. Pisani in *Paideia* 16.362 (1961); A.R. Tellier in *EA* 14.357-59 (1961); R.M. Wilson in *MLR* 56.573-74 (1961); Karl Brunner in *Anglia* 80.309-11 (1962); Elliot V.K. Dobbie in *AS* 37.141 (1962); Pamela Gradon in *RES* n.s. 13.164-66 (1962); G. Kirchner in *DLZ* 83.131-32 (1962); G. Scheurweghs in *LB* 51. Bijblad 121-23 (1962); M.L. Samuels in *MAE* 31.147-51 (1962); B. Trnka in *PP* 5.177 (1962); P.J. Verhoeff in *Neophil* 46.242-43 (1962); S. Einarsson in *RBPH* 41.532-33 (1963); Morton Y. Jacobs in *MLQ* 24.414 (1963); Samuel R. Levin in *JEGP* 62.359-62 (1963); B.D.H. Miller in *N&Q* n.s. 10.468-71 (1963); Gerhard Nickel in *Archiv* 200.374-75 (1963/64); H. Pilch in *IF* 68.127-29 (1963); O. Funke in *ES* 46.57-61 (1965); Torben Kisbye in *SN* 37.222-27 (1965)

1801. ———. 1981. "Some Reflections on Lawman's Poetical Syntax". *McIntosh Festschrift* (E), 335-40.

1802. ———. 1983. "Chaucer's Use of *Gan*: Some Recent Studies". *Davis Festschrift*, 59-64.

1803. ———. 1985. "Some Features of Syntax in Middle English Main Clauses". *Gerritsen Festschrift*, 73-75. [Discusses (1) the repetition of the subject and (2) the placing of the infinitive and its object in main clauses.]

1804. Mutt, Oleg. 1964. "The Adjectivization of Nouns in English". *ZAA* 12.341-49. [Covers ME and Early ModE.]

1805. ———. 1968. "The Use of Substantives in the Common Case as Prepositive Attributes in Middle English". *Töid Romaani-Germaani Filologia Alalt*, ed. K. Kann and O. Mutt, 43-67. Tartu: Univ. of Tartu.

1806. Nagucka, Ruta. 1968. *The Syntactic Component of Chaucer's 'Astrolabe'*. (= Zeszyty Naukowe Uniwersytetu Jagiellońskiego, 199: Prace Językoznawcze Zeszyt, 23.) Cracow: Uniwersytet Jagielloński, 123 pp.

Review: Horst Weinstock in *Anglia* 92.201-03 (1974).

1807. ———. 1968. "An Interpretation of the *Because* Construction in Middle English". *SAP* 1.63-70.

1808. ———. 1978 [1979]. "A Note on ME Subjectless Sentences". *SAP* 10.49-53.

1809. ———. 1980. "Grammatical Peculiarities of the Contact-Clause in Early Modern English". *FLH* 1.171-84. [Despite the title, the author examines 14th- and 15th-century English usage, especially *there is/are* subject contact clauses.]

1810. Nakashima, Kunio. 1983. "Present Participle in the *Cely Letters*". *Poetica* 15/16.160-73.

1811. Nathan, Norman. 1956. "Pronouns of Address in the *Friar's Tale*". *MLQ* 17.39-42.

1812. ———. 1959. "Pronouns of Address in the *Canterbury Tales*". *MS* 21.193-201.

1813. Nummenmaa, Liisa. 1972. "The Quasi-Pronominal *So* in Corroborative and Additive Sentences in EME". *NM* 73.675-81.

1814. ———. 1973. *The Uses of 'So', 'Al So' and 'As' in Early Middle English*. (= MSNH, 39.) Helsinki: Société Néophilologique, 194 pp.

   Reviews: Matti Rissanen in *NM* 74.764-67 (1973); Torben Kisbye in *SN* 49.342-45 (1977).

1815. O'Grady, William D. 1982. "The Subject Relation in Middle English". *SAP* 14.87-90.

1816. O'Hearn, Carolyn Jean. 1982. *Syntactic Variation and Change in Later Middle English Negation*. Arizona State Univ. diss., 317 pp. [Abstr. in *DA* 43.3309A (1983).]

1817. Ohlander, Urban. 1936. *Studies on Coordinate Expressions in Middle English*. (= LundSE, 5.) Lund: Gleerup; London: Williams and Norgate, 213 pp.

   Reviews: W. Héraucourt in *Anglia B* 48.264-66 (1937); H. Koziol in *LGRP* 58.394-96 (1937); G. L[inke] in *Archiv* 171.259-60 (1937); W. Preusler in *IF* 55.318 (1937); F. Behre in *ES* 20.140-44 (1938); A. Sale in *MLR* 33.276-77 (1938); G.W. Small in *JEGP* 37.291-95 (1938); R.W. Zandvoort in *Museum* 46.175 (1939).

1818. ———. 1941/42. "A Study on the Use of the Infinitive Sign in Middle English". *SN* 14.58-66.

1819. ———. 1950. "*A Passage in Cleanness* (ll. 1562 ff.): A Note on Middle English Construction-Change". *GHÅ* 56.311-23.

1820. ———. 1981. "Notes on the Non-Expression of the Subject-Pronoun in Middle English". *SN* 53.37-49.

1821. ———. 1984. "Predicative Complements and Predicative Attributes: A Note on Middle English Usage in Coordinate Structures". *NM* 85.438-44.

1822. Ono, Shigeru. 1969. "Chaucer's Variants and What They Tell Us: Fluctuation in the Use of Modal Auxiliaries". *SEL* English No. 1969, 51-74.

1823. ———. 1975. "A Statistical Study of *Shall* and *Will* in Chaucer's *Canterbury Tales* and Its Relevance to Style". *Poetica* 3.35-44.

1824. Palmatier, Robert Allen. 1969. *A Descriptive Syntax of the 'Ormulum'*. (= JanL, Ser. Practica, 74.) The Hague: Mouton, 137 pp. [Originally Michigan diss. 1965; Abstr. in *DA* 26.2199-2200 (1965).]

   Reviews: A.H. Marckwardt in *JEngL* 5.145-49 (1971); Ursula Oomen in *Anglia* 89.528-32 (1971); Elizabeth Closs Traugott in *Language* 48.182-84 (1972); Ruta Nagucka in *Linguistics* 135.125-28 (1974).

1825. Partridge, Astley Cooper. 1969. *Tudor to Augustan English: A Study in Syntax and Style from Caxton to Johnson*. (The Language Library.) London: André Deutsch, 242 pp.

   Reviews: Anon. in *TLS*, 8 Jan. 1970, p. 40; Vivian Salmon in *YES* 2.247-48 (1972).

1826. Paschke, Elisabeth. 1934. *Der Gebrauch des bestimmten Artikels in der spätmittelenglischen Prosa (1380-1500)*. Emsdetten: Lechte, xvi + 272 pp. [Münster diss.]

   Review: G.T. Flom in *JEGP* 38.472-73 (1939).

1827. Pervaz, D. 1958. *The Survival of Grammatical Gender in 'Laʒamon's Brut', 'The Southern Legendary', and 'Robert of Gloucester's Chronicle'*. Edinburgh diss. [No further information available.]

1828. Peters, Gerhard. 1937. *Der syntaktische Gebrauch des unbestimmten Artikels im Zentral- und Spätmittelenglischen*. Braunschweg: Vieweg und Sohn, xii + 65 pp. [Göttingen diss.]

   Review: W. Preusler in *Anglia B* 50.193-95 (1939).

1829. Phillipps, Kenneth C. 1954. "Contamination in Late Middle English". *ES* 35.17-20.

1830. ———. 1956. "Contamination in Late Middle English, II". *ES* 37.12-14.

1831. ———. 1965. "Asyndetic Relative Clauses in Late Middle English". *ES* 46.323-29.

1832. ———. 1966. "Absolute Constructions in Late Middle English". *NM* 67.282-90.

1833. ———. 1966. "Adverb Clauses in the Fifteenth Century". *ES* 47.355-65.

1834. Pirkhofer, Anton. 1935/36. "Zum syntaktischen Gebrauch des bestimmten Artikels bei Caxton". *EStn* 70.92-101.

1835. Preusler, Walther. 1938. "Keltischer Einfluss im Englischen". *IF* 56.178-91. [Discusses a number of possible influences of the Celtic languages on English syntax, from the 13th century down.]

1836. ———. 1939. "Zu: Keltischer Einfluss im Englischen (*IF* 56, S. 178 ff.)". *IF* 57.140-41. [Some addenda to Preusler [no. 1835].]

1837. Rantavaara, Irma. 1962. "On the Development of the Periphrastic Dative in Late Middle English Prose". *NM* 63.175-203.

1838. Rebsamen, Frederick Raymond. 1962. *The Position of the English Adverb in Relation to Subject, Verb, and Object, 1400-1600*. Columbia diss., 138 pp. [Abstr. in *DA* 23.3366-67 (1963).]

1839. Reichl, Karl. 1982. "Zur syntaktischen Interferenz im Mittelenglischen". *Sprachtheorie und angewandte Linguistik: Festschrift für Alfred Wollmann zum 60. Geburtstag* (= TBL, 195), ed. Werner Welte, 221-34. Tübingen: Gunter Narr.

1840. Rennhard, Siegfried. 1962. *Das Demonstrativum im Mittelenglischen 1200-1500, unter besonderer Berücksichtigung der geographischen Verteilung der Formen*. Winterthur: Keller, 124 pp. [Zürich diss.]

Review: Siegfried Wyler in *ES* 48.438-39 (1967).

1841. Reszkiewicz, Alfred. 1962. *Main Sentence Elements in 'The Book of Margery Kempe': A Study in Major Syntax*. Wrocław-Warszawa-Kraków: Zakład Narodowy imienia Ossolińskich; London: Collet's, 100 pp.

Reviews: Johan Gerritsen in *ES* 44.452-55 (1963); R.M. Wilson in *MLR* 58.455 (1963); Robert P. Stockwell in *Language* 41.155-66 (1965); Sherman M. Kuhn in *Linguistics* 35.106-10 (1967); J. Šimko in *JČ* 18.196-98 (1967).

1842. Reuter, Ole. 1937. "Some Notes on the Origin of the Relative Combination *the which*". *NM* 38.146-88.

1843. Roberts, W.J.F. 1937. "Ellipsis of the Subject Pronoun in Middle English". *LMS* 1.107-15.

1844. Romaine, Suzanne. 1984. "Some Historical and Social Dimensions of Syntactic Change in Middle Scots Relative Clauses". *Blake & Jones*, 101-22. [The term 'Middle Scots' here refers to the period c1450-1650.]

1845. Roscow, Gregory H. 1981. *Syntax and Style in Chaucer's Poetry*. (= Chaucer Studies, 6.) Cambridge: D.S. Brewer; Totowa, NJ: Roman & Littlefield, x + 158 pp.

Reviews: Valerie Adams in *TLS*, Oct. 15, 1982, p. 1135; Joyce Bazire in *MAE* 52.131-32 (1983); N.F. Blake in *ES* 64.75-77 (1983); André Crépin in *EA* 37.184 (1984); W. Elmer in *Anglia* 101.224-28 (1983); Mark Lambert in *Speculum* 58.811-13 (1983); Edward Wilson in *N&Q* n.s. 30.70-71 (1983);

David C. Fowler in *MP* 81.407-14 (1984); Charles A. Owen, Jr. in *SAC* 5.200-02 (1983); Manfred Markus in *Archiv* 223.394-98 (1986).

1846. Russom, Geoffrey R. 1976. "A Syntactic Key to a Number of *Pearl*-Group Cruxes". *JEngL* 10.21-29. [Concerns relative constructions.]

1847. Rydén, Mats. 1983. "The Emergence of *Who* as Relativizer". *SL* 37.126-34.

1848. Rynell, Alarik. 1964. "On Alleged Constructions like *did wrote*". *SMSpr* n.s. 2.132-47. [Suggests that examples of this construction attested in late ME are the result of scribal error.]

1849. Samuels, Michael Louis. 1955. "Middle English *wery forwandred*: A Rejoinder". *ES* 36.310-13. [A rejoinder to Mossé [no. 1794]. Cf. also Mustanoja [no. 1796].]

1850. Schmidt, Dieter. 1975. "Das Anredepronomen in Chaucers *Troilus and Criseyde*". *Archiv* 212.120-24.

1851. Shores, David Lee. 1969. "The Subject — Noun Object — Verb Pattern in the Peterborough Chronicle". *NM* 70.623-26. [Apropos of Mitchell [no. 1788]. See also Mitchell's reply [no. 1789].]

1852. ———. 1971. "Morphosyntactic Relations in *The Peterborough Chronicle*, 1122-1154". *ES* 52.1-13.

1853. ———. 1971. *A Descriptive Syntax of the 'Peterborough Chronicle' from 1122 to 1154*. (= JanL, Ser. Practica, 103.) The Hague: Mouton, 225 pp. [Originally George Peabody College for Teachers diss. 1966; Abstr. in *DA* 27.3859-60A (1967).]

Reviews: Thomas M. Woodell in *AS* 45.134-38 (1970); Robert D. Stevick in *Speculum* 48.789-93 (1973); Cecily Clark in *MAE* 43.47-50 (1974); Margret Popp in *Anglia* 93.172-76 (1975).

1854. Šimko, Ján. 1956. "A Linguistic Analysis of the Winchester Manuscript and William Caxton's Edition of Sir Thomas Malory's *Morte Darthur*". *Philologica* (Supplement to *ČMF*) 8.1-2. [Abstr. of Šimko [no. 1855].]

1855. ———. 1957. *Word-Order in the Winchester Manuscript and in William Caxton's Edition of Thomas Malory's 'Morte Darthur' (1485) — A Comparison*. Halle/Saale: Max Niemeyer, xii + 122 pp.

Reviews: Rolf Berndt in *ZAA* 7.77-82 (1959); A.A. Hill in *Language* 35.561-64 (1959); H. Pilch in *Anglia* 77.496-98 (1959); Priscilla Preston in *MLR* 54.252-53 (1959); B. Trnka in *ČMF* 41.51-52 (1959); T.F. Mustanoja in *NM* 61.391-92 (1960); Gerd Mann in *Archiv* 197.213-14 (1960/61).

1856. ———. 1968. "Some Aspects of the Transition from the Impersonal to the Personal Construction in English". *RLB* 2.108-23. [A revised version of the chapter "Impersonal-Personal Verbs" in Šimko [no. 1855].]

1857. Simon-Vandenbergen, A.M. 1983. "On the Decline of Dynamic *May*". *SN* 55.143-45. [A study on the use of *can* and *may* from the 15th to the 19th century. The 15th-century sources are Malory (*The Tale of King Arthur*) and *The Paston Letters*.]

1858. ———. 1983. "'Subjunctive' *May*: A Fossilizing Pattern". *SAP* 16.71-76. [Deals with the development in late ME as well as the present-day situation.]

1859. Siporin, Rae Lee. 1968. *Negation in Late Middle English: A Transformational-Generative Approach*. Univ. of California, Los Angeles, diss., 141 pp. [Abstr. in *DA* 29.3600A (1968).]

1860. Smyser, Hamilton M. 1967. "Chaucer's Use of *Gin* and *Do*". *Speculum* 42.68-83.

1861. Snortum, Niel Klendenon. 1956. *'Apo Koinou' and Allied Constructions in Middle English*. Stanford diss., 189 pp. [Abstr. in *DA* 16.749 (1956).]

1862. Snouffer, Eugene J. 1971. *Verbal Syntax of 'Cursor Mundi' (Cotton MS. Vespasian A III)*. Univ. of North Carolina at Chapel Hill diss., 268 pp. [Abstr. in *DA* 32.6960A (1972).]

1863. Spitzer, Leo. 1954. "Le type moyen anglais *I was weary for wandred* et ses parallèles romans". *NM* 55.161-77. [Apropos of Mossé [no. 1794].]

1864. Stahl, Leon, 1927. "Der adnominale Genitiv und sein Ersatz im Mittelenglischen und Frühneuenglischen". *Giessener Beiträge zur Erforschung der Sprache und Kultur Englands und Nordamerikas* (Breslau) 3.1-32.

1865. Steinki, Johannes. 1932. *Die Entwicklung der englischen Relativpronomina in spätmittelenglischer und frühneuenglischer Zeit*. Ohlau i. Schl.: Eschenhagen, 97 pp. [Breslau diss.]

1866. Stevick, Robert David. 1965. "Historical Selection of Relative *þat* in Early Middle English". *ES* 46.29-36.

1867. Sundby, Bertil. 1957. "The Independent Genitive in English". *Vetenskaps-Societetens i Lund, Årsbok/Yearbook of the New Society of Letters at Lund* (Lund) 1957, 5-17. [On a type of genitive met with in certain official documents dated from the 14th to the 16th centuries.]

1868. ———. 1970. "A Note on Causative Verbs in 15th Century English". *NM* 71.101-04.

1869. Svartvik, Jan and Randolph Quirk. 1970. "Types and Uses of Non-Finite Clause in Chaucer". *ES* 51.393-411.

1870. Świeczkowski, Walerian. 1962. *Word Order Patterning in Middle English: A Quantitative Study Based on 'Piers Plowman' and Middle English Sermons*. (= JanL, 19.) The Hague: Mouton, 114 pp.

   Reviews: Johan Gerritsen in *ES* 44.452-55 (1963); J. Firbas in *SFFBU* 14(AB).244-45 (1965).

1871. Tajima, Matsuji. 1975. "The *Gawain*-Poet's Use of *Con* as a Periphrastic Auxiliary". *NM* 76.429-38.

1872. ———. 1978. "Additional Syntactical Evidence against the Common Authorship of MS. Cotton Nero A.x". *ES* 59.193-98.

1873. ———. 1985. *The Syntactic Development of the Gerund in Middle English*. Tokyo: Nan'un-do (distributed outside Japan by John Benjamins, Amsterdam & Philadelphia), xii + 154 pp. [Originally Univ. of Ottawa diss. 1983.]

   Reviews: Eiichi Suzuki in *Eigo Seinen* (Tokyo) 131.474 (1985); W.F. Bolton in *Diachronica* 2.259-62 (1985 [1986]); François Chevillet in *EA* 40.332-33 (1987); W. Elmer in *Anglia* 105.423-26 (1987); G. Jack in *MAE* 56.152-53 (1987).

1874. ———. 1985. "The Gerund in Chaucer, with Special Reference to the Development of its Verbal Character". *Poetica* 20/21.106-20.

1875. Terasawa, Yoshio. 1974. "Some Notes on ME *Gan* Periphrasis". *Poetica* 1.89-105.

1876. Trnka, Bohumil. 1930. *On the Syntax of the English Verb from Caxton to Dryden*. (= TCLP, 3.) Prague (: no publisher mentioned). 98 pp. [Repr., New York: Klaus, 1974.]

   Reviews: K. Jost in *IF* 50.309-10 (1932); F. Karpf in *Archiv* 162.242-43 (1932); W. van der Gaaf in *ES* 14.159-65 (1932).

1877. Ueda, Minoru. 1966. *A Study of the Order of Clause Elements in the Later Parts of the Peterborough Chronicle, with Special Reference to Constructional Types*. Univ. of Texas diss., 321 pp. [Abstr. in *DA* 27.469A (1966).]

1878. Urwin, Kenneth. 1941. "The Progressive Tense in Early English and Old French". *Comparative Literature Studies* 3.13-16. ["Early English" here means ME.]

1879. Utley, Francis Lee. 1972. "Syntactical Problems in Middle English". *Mustanoja Festschrift* = *NM* 73.456-71. [Apropos of Mustanoja [no. 1800].]

1880. Van Beeck, Frans Jozef. 1985. "A Note on *ther* in Curses and Blessings in Chaucer". *Neophil* 69.276-83.

1881. Van der Auwera, Johan. 1983. "On the Delay of the Nominative *Who* as Relativizer". *Steenbergen Festschrift*, 21-28.

1882. ———. 1984. "More on the History of the Subject Contact Clause in English". *FLH* 5.171-84. [From ME through ModE.]

1883. Van der Gaaf, Willem. 1924. "Three Remarkable Infinitives". *Neophil* 9.190-94. [On the origin of *to blame* in 'he is to blame' and *to say* and *to wit* in similar constructions in ME.]

1884. ———. 1928. "The Gerund Preceded by the Common Case: A Study in Historical Syntax". *ES* 10.33-41 and 65-72. [Cf. Curme's rejoinder [no. 1692].]

1885. ———. 1929. "The Conversion of the Indirect Personal Object into the Subject of a Passive Construction". *ES* 11.1-11 and 58-67.

1886. ———. 1930. "The Gerund Preceded by the Common Case Again". *ES* 12.111. [Reply to Curme [no. 1692].]

1887. ———. 1930. "Origin of the Accusative Often Used as Subject of the Gerund". *ES* 12.183-84. [Reply to Curme [no. 1693].]

1888. ———. 1932. "The Absolute Genitive". *ES* 14.49-65. [Traces the history of forms like *St Paul's* from the late 13th century to the middle of the 15th century.]

1889. ———. 1933. "The Split Infinitive in Middle English". *ES* 15.15-20.

1890. Van der Meer, Hindrikus Johannes. 1929. *Main Facts concerning the Syntax of Mandeville's Travels*. Utrecht: Kemink en Zoon, xii + 176 pp. [Amsterdam diss.]

1891. Visser, Frederikus Theodorus. 1964. "The 'Historical Present' in Middle English Verse Narratives". *Zandvoort Festschrift = ES* 45 Supplement.135-42.

1892. Visser, Gerard J. 1955. "Celtic Influence in English". *Neophil* 39.276-93. [Discusses (1) the prepositional object with infinitive construction and (2) the use of *to go* as a copula in the light of Welsh syntax, the first of which is concerned with ME.]

1893. Walcutt, Charles C. 1935. "The Pronoun of Address in *Troilus and Criseyde*". *PQ* 14.282-87.

1894. Warner, Anthony R. 1975. "Infinitive Marking in the Wycliffite Sermons". *ES* 56.207-14.

1895. ———. 1982. *Complementation in Middle English and the Methodology of Historical Syntax: A Study of the Wyclifite Sermons*. London: Croom Helm; University Park, PA: Pennsylvania State Univ. Press, [xii +] 266 pp. [A revised and shortened version of Edinburgh diss. 1978.]

Reviews: Suzanne Romaine in *JL* 19.478-80 (1983); Edwin Battistella in *Language* 60.456-57 (1984); B.G. Hewitt in *Lingua* 62.157-62 (1984); J.T. Faarlund in *SLang* 9.297-304 (1985).

1896. Watts, Richard J. 1982. "The Conjunction *that*: a Semantically Empty Particle?". *SAP* 15.13-27. [The text studied is the *Peterborough Chronicle*.]

1897. Way, Annette. 1970. "Old English Prenominal Modifiers in Noun-Headed Objects of Prepositions in the First and Second Continuations of the *Peterborough Chronicle* (1122-54)". *JEngL* 4.90-94.

1898. Wegner, Alicja. 1976. "The Derivation of Infinitive Forms in Mirk's *Festial*". *SAP* 7.71-93.

1899. ———. 1977. "Some Aspects of Predicate Relations in the Fifteenth Century English". *SAP* 9.43-53. [Based on Mirk's *Festial*.]

1900. ———. 1977. "Some Remarks on Infinitival Nominalization in Late Middle English". *KN* 24.63-68.

1901. Winkler, Gerda. 1933. *Das Relativum bei Caxton und seine Entwicklung von Chaucer bis Spenser*. Saalfeld: Günther, xii + 82 pp. [Berlin diss.]

1902. Yonekura, Hiroshi. 1985. *The Language of the Wycliffite Bible: The Syntactic Differences between the Two Versions*. Tokyo: Aratake Shuppan, xviii + 525 pp.

Review: Knud Sørensen in *ES* 67.78-80 (1986).

1903. Zettler, Howard George. 1971. *Word Order in Late Middle English: An Analysis of 'Revelations of Divine Love'*. Ohio Univ. diss., 532 pp. [Abstr. in *DA* 32.6409-10A (1972).]

1904. Zimmermann, Rüdiger. 1968. *Untersuchungen zum frühmittelenglischen Tempussystem: Perfect, Preterite und Pluperfect um 1200*. (= Wissenschaftliche Bibl., 8.) Heidelberg: Groos, ii + 265 pp. [Kiel diss.]

XI. LEXICOLOGY, LEXICOGRAPHY, AND WORD-FORMATION

A. General

1905. Aijmer, Karin. 1985. "The Semantic Development of *Will*". *Historical Semantics*, 11-21.

1906. Aitken, Adam Jack. 1971. "Historical Dictionaries and the Computer". *The Computer in Literary and Linguistic Research* (= Pubs. of the Literary and Linguistic Computing Centre, Univ. of Cambridge, 1), ed. R.A. Wisbey, 3-17. Cambridge: Cambridge Univ. Press.

1907. ———. 1986. "The Period Dictionaries". *Studies in Lexicography*, 94-116. [Includes reference to *MED*, *DOST*, and *The Dictionary of Old English* (in progress).]

1908. Alanne, Eero. 1957 [1959]. *Observations on the Development and Structure of English Wine-Growing Terminology.* (= MSNH, 20:3.) Helsinki: Société Néophilologique, 55 pp. [Lists in turn the survivals from OE into ME and ModE and those which have been lost.]

1909. Alexander, Henry. 1953. "The French Element in the English Vocabulary". *Culture: A Quarterly Review* (Montreal) 14.274-80. [A survey of the continuous infiltration of French words into English from the time of Edward the Confessor to the present.]

1910. Bacquet, Paul. 1974. *Le vocabulaire anglais.* (= Collection «Que sais-je?» 1574.) Paris: Presses Universitaires de France, 126 pp. [An account of the development of the English vocabulary.]

1911. Bähr, Dieter. 1959. *Ae. 'æpele' und 'freo': Ihre Ableitungen und Synonyma im Ae. und Me. Wortgeschichtliche Studien zum Wandel des englischen Freiheitsbegriffes im Mittelalter.* Freie Univ. Berlin diss., 135 pp.

1912. Bald, Wolf-Dietrich. 1985. "On the Diachrony of English Linking Verbs". *Gerritsen Festschrift*, 175-89.

1913. Barfield, Owen. 1926. *History in English Words*. Introduction by George Philip Krapp. New York: George H. Doran, xii + 223 pp. [2nd ed. 1933.; New ed., London: Faber & Faber, 1954.]

    Reviews: Katherine Buxbaum in *AS* 3.75-77 (1927); J.H.G. G[rattan] in *RES* 3.120 (1927); Edith C. Batho in *History* (London) 13.47-49 (1928); George T. Flom in *JEGP* 27.143 (1928).

1914. Bengtsson, Elna. 1927. *Studies on Passive Nouns with a Concrete Sense in English*. Lund: Gleerup, 164 pp. [Discusses the problem of the passive meaning of concrete nouns in OE, ME and ModE. Lund diss.]

    Reviews: W.E. Collinson in *Litteris* (Lund) 6.38-39 (1928); G. Stern in *SN* 2.101-04 (1929); W. Fischer in *Anglia B* 41.77-80 (1930); G.T. Flom in *Language* 6.94-96 (1930); E. Kruisinga in *ES* 12.235-36 (1930); A. Dekker in *Neophil* 23.65-66 (1938).

1915. Brorström, Sverker. 1971. "A Historical Survey of Prepositions Expressing the Sense 'for the duration of'". *ES* 52.105-16.

1916. Brown, Alan K. 1978. "The English Compass Points". *MAE* 47.221-46. [Discusses compass, i.e. directional terms.]

1917. Burchfield, Robert William. 1985. "An Outline History of Euphemisms in English". *Fair of Speech: the Use of Euphemism*, ed. Dennis Joseph Enright, 13-31. Oxford & New York: Oxford Univ. Press.

1918. Collier, Leslie William and Christian J. Kay. 1980/81. "The Historical Thesaurus of English". *Dictionaries* 2/3.80-89.

1919. Denison, David. 1985. "The Origins of Completive *up* in English". *NM* 86.37-61. [On the lexical history of completive *up*.]

1920. Deutschbein, Max. 1935. "Die Bedeutungsentwicklung von *road* bei Shakespeare". *Anglia* 59.368-75. [An investigation of the semantic development of *road* from Anglo-Saxon to the present day.]

1921. Dike, Edwin Berck. 1933. "Obsolete Words". *PQ* 12.207-19. [Discusses obsolete words and affixes: *-aster, -logue, -ess, -age, -ment, -ate*.]

1922. ———. 1935. "Obsolete English Words: Some Recent Views". *JEGP* 34.351-65. [Bibliographical.]

1923. Ehrensperger, Edward C. 1931. "Dream Words in Old and Middle English". *PMLA* 46.80-89.

1924. Einarsson, Stefán. 1937. "Old and Middle English Notes". *JEGP* 36.183-87. [Discusses OE *dæg* 'dawn', *begæð* 'confesses or professes', ME *all and some*, and ME *lake* 'fine linen'.]

1925. Ellinger, Johann. 1939. "Die mit Präpositionen zusammengesetzten Adverbien *here, there, where*". *EStn* 73.334-43. [An historical study of adverbs of the form *thereby, hereafter*, etc. from OE to the 20th century.]

1926. Faiss, Klaus. 1978. *Verdunkelte Compounds im Englischen: Ein Beitrag zu Theorie und Praxis der Wortbildung.* (= TBL, 104.) Tübingen: Gunter Narr, 241 pp.

Reviews: W. Hüllen in *Archiv* 217.402-04 (1980); K. Sprengel in *Anglia* 98.450-54 (1980).

1927. Fischer, Olga. 1979. "A Comparative Study of Philosophical Terms in the Alfredian and Chaucerian Boethius". *Neophil* 63.622-39.

1928. Flasdieck, Hermann Martin. 1951. "Studien zur Laut- und Wortgeschichte". *Anglia* 70.225-84. [Discusses 'I. Die Schicksale der tektalen Media aspirata; II. Das älteste französische Lehngut; III. Ae. Reflexe idg. Wurzelvariationen bei tektaler Erweiterung'.]

1929. Fleenor, Terry Richard. 1972. *The Martyr Figure in the Dramatic Literature of the West, Preceded by an Essay on the Evolution of the Word 'Martyr'*. Univ. of California, Riverside, diss., 400 pp. [Abstr. in *DA* 34.271-72A (1973). Contains a linguistic evaluation of the word *martyr* from its Indo-European origin as *smer 'to remember' to ModE.]

1930. Fraser, Thomas K.H. 1982. "The System of Verbs Involving a Speaker-Hearer Relationship: Come/Go, Bring/Take in Old and Middle English". *PICHL/5*, 54-61.

1931. Frey, Edgar. 1967. *Die Verben des Transportfeldes bei Chaucer und König Alfred dem Grossen: Untersuchung über das nebeneinander sprachlicher Begriffe im semantischen Feld.* Zürich: Keller, xi + 288 pp. [Zürich diss.]

1932. Götz, Dieter. 1971. *Studien zu den verdunkelten Komposita im Englischen.* (= Erlanger Beiträge zur Sprach- und Kunstwissenschaft, 40.) Nürnberg: Hans Karl, x + 137 pp. [Erlangen diss.]

Review: Gabriele Stein in *Anglia* 93.205-10 (1975).

1933. Grinda, Klaus R. 1983. "Englands Holzwerker in altenglischer und nachaltenglischer Zeit. Beobachtungen an Schriftquellen und Wortgut". *Das Handwerk in vor- und frühgeschichtlicher Zeit. Teil II: Archäologische und philologische Beiträge*, ed. Herbert Jankuhn, et al., 670-716. Göttingen: Vandenhoeck & Ruprecht. [An attempt to define the vocabulary and behaviour of "woodworkers" in the OE and ME periods.]

1934. Groom, Bernard. 1934. *A Short History of English Words*. London: Macmillan, vii + 221 pp. [Surveys the development of the English vocabulary from the earliest times to the present day.]

Reviews: Anon. in *TLS*, Sept. 27, 1934, p. 658; R. Church in *Spectator*, Feb. 15, No. 154, p. 257 (1935).

1935. Hiltunen, Risto. 1984. "On the Semantic and Lexical Development of the 'Phrasal Verb' in Old and Early Middle English". *Crépin LSSME*/10, 47-61.

1936. Hlebec, Boris. 1986. "Sources of Shared Polysemy in English Spatial Adjectives". *SAP* 18.205-22.

1937. Holthausen, Ferdinand. 1951. "Beiträge zur englischen Etymologie". *Anglia* 70.1-21. [Consists of etymological notes on 165 words, mainly OE, but some ME and ModE.]

1938. Jaeschke, Kurt. 1931. *Beiträge zur Frage des Wortschwundes im Englischen*. (= Sprache und Kultur der germanischen und romanischen Völker, Anglistische Reihe, 6.) Breslau: Priebatsch, 103 pp. [Continues the work done by Emil Hemken (1906), Johannes Offe (1908), W. Oberdörffer (1908) and Friedrich Teichert (1912) on the same subject (cf. Kennedy [no. 11]). The monographs of these four writers dealt with words from *A* to *S*. Jaeschke discusses and classifies words from *T* to *Y* which have disappeared from English, especially during the ME period.]

Reviews: W. Fischer in *DLZ* 53.981-85 (1932); Fritz Fiedler in *Archiv* 163.289-90 (1933).

1939. Kay, Christian J. 1984. "The Historical Thesaurus of English". *LEXeter '83*, 87-91.

1940. König, Ekkehard and Elizabeth Closs Traugott. 1982. "Divergence and Apparent Convergence in the Development of *Yet* and *Still*". *Proceedings of the Eighth Annual Meeting of the Berkeley Linguistics Society, 13-15 February 1982*, ed. Monica Maccauley, et al., 170-79. Berkeley: Berkeley Linguistics Society.

1941. Koskenniemi, Inna. 1968. *Repetitive Word Pairs in Old and Early Middle English Prose: Expressions of the Type 'Whole and Sound' and 'Answered and Said', and Other Parallel Constructions*. (= AUT, B. 107.) Turku: Turun Yliopisto, 170 pp.

Reviews: Matti Kilpiö in *NM* 72.374-75 (1971); Fred C. Robinson in *Anglia*

90.166-68 (1972).

1942. Koziol, Herbert. 1937. *Handbuch der englischen Wortbildungslehre.* (= GB, Grammatiken, 21.) Heidelberg: Carl Winter, xv + 260 pp. [Covers the whole extent from the oldest times.]

Reviews: Wilhelm Horn in *Archiv* 173.235-39 (1938); S.B. Liljegren in *Anglia B* 49.37-47 (1938); W. Schmidt in *ZNU* 37.317-20 (1938); W. Héraucourt in *NS* 46.332-33 (1938); F. Holthausen in *EStn* 73.70-71 (1938/39); S. Potter in *MLR* 33.621 (1938); R.W. Zandvoort in *ES* 26.151-52 (1944/45).

1943. ———. 1972. *Handbuch der englischen Wortbildungslehre. Zweite, neubearbeitete Auflage.* Heidelberg: Carl Winter, 329 pp.

Reviews: R.W. Zandvoort in *ES* 54.402 (1973); Manfred Görlach in *Archiv* 212.169-73 (1975).

1944. Krieg, Martha Lenore Fessler. 1976. *Semantic Fields of Color Words in Old French, Old English, and Middle English.* Michigan diss., 198 pp. [Abstr. in *DA* 37.1517A (1976).]

1945. Last, W. 1925. *Das Bahuvrîhi-Compositum im Altenglischen, Mittelenglischen und Neuenglischen, mit einem Geleitwort von Prof. Dr. Heinrich Spies.* Greifswald: H. Adler, 124 pp. [Originally Greifswald diss. 1921.]

Reviews: W. Preusler in *ZFEU* 25.377 (1926); W. Franz in *EStn* 61.283-84 (1926/27).

1946. Leake, Jane Acomb. 1962. "Middle English Glosses in the *Beowulf*-Codex". *MLQ* 23.229-32.

1947. Lenaghan, R.T. 1961. "A Note on OE. *Melcan*" *N&Q* n.s. 8.6. [On a survival of the past participle *molken* in Caxton's edition of *Aesop's Fables* (1483-84).]

1948. Lockwood, William Burley. 1973. "More English Etymologies". *ZAA* 21.414-23. [Discusses *ganot*, *stearn*, etc.]

1949. ———. 1979. "Some Expressions for the Setting Sun". *MAE* 48.102-04. [Concerned with OE, ON, and ME.]

1950. Lohmander, Ingegerd. 1981. *Old and Middle English Words for 'Disgrace' and 'Dishonour'.* (= GothSE, 49.) Göteburg: Acta Universitatis Gothburgensis, 228 pp. [Göteborg diss.]

Reviews: Norman F. Blake in *ES* 64.175-76 (1983); Klaus Hansen in *ZPhon* 36.485-86 (1983); Gertrud Hülsmann in *Archiv* 221.361-62 (1984); Sölve Ohlander in *SN* 57.119-21 (1985).

1951. Lotspeich, C.M. 1938. "The Type O.E. *lōca hwā*, M.E. *looke who*". *JEGP* 37.1-2. [On various OE and ME indefinite pronouns, meaning 'whoever'.]

1952. Magoun, Francis Peabody, Jr. 1925. "Two Lexicographical Notes". *MLN* 40.408-12. [On ME *büsten* and *beten*, and OE *lōf* and *grīn*.]

1953. Majut, Rudolf. 1973. "Zur geschichte der Verzehr-Wörter im Englischen. Vom Altenglischen bis zum Beginn der Neuzeit". *GRM* N.F. 23.423-49.

1954. Marckwardt, Albert Henry. 1967. "Lexical Redistribution in Modern English *Say* and *Tell*". *Papers in Linguistics in Honor of Léon Dostert* (= JL, Ser. Maior, 25), ed. William M. Austin, 118-22. The Hague: Mouton.

1955. Marcus, Hans. 1939. "Morgenländisches Lehngut im Englischen". *Neuphilologische Monatsschrift* 10.289-300. [A list of Arabic and other oriental words in English, with notes on the chronology of the borrowings.]

1956. Morris, Kenneth Michael. 1973. *'Blue', 'Green', 'Yellow', 'Red': A Study of their Sense Development in English*. Columbia diss., 405 pp. [Abstr. in *DA* 34.5113A (1974). Traces the sense development of these four color words from their earliest applications in OE to current use in idiom, jargon, and slang.]

1957. Onions, Charles Talbut. 1938. "The Phrase *end of one's kin*". *MAE* 7.118-19. [On occurrences of the phrase in OE and ME, apparently with the meaning 'part of one's kindred'.]

1958. Pilch, Herbert. 1951. *Der Untergang des Präverbs 'ʒe-' im Englischen*. Kiel diss. (1952), xx + 227 pp.

  Review: G.S. Waldo in *Word* 11.488-91 (1955).

1959. ———. 1959. "Der Untergang des Präverbs ʒe- im Englischen". *Anglia* 73.37-64.

1960. Potter, Simeon. 1952. "On the Etymology of *Dream*". *ArchL* 4.148-54. [Deals with the semantic history of the word from IE to ModE.]

1961. Raith, Josef. 1931. *Die englischen Nasalverben*. (= BEP, 17.) Leipzig: B. Tauchnitz, 128 pp. [München diss.; repr., New York: Johnson Reprint, 1968. Deals mainly with nasal suffix OE *-nian*, ME *-nen*, ModE *-en*.]

  Reviews: F. Holthausen in *Anglia B* 43.88-89 (1932); H. Dehmer in *NS* 41.465-66 (1933); M. Schubiger in *ES* 18.91-94 (1936).

1962. Riddle, Elizabeth M. 1985. "A Historical Perspective on the Productivity of Suffixes *-ness* and *-ity*". *Historical Semantics*, 435-61.

1963. Robinson, Fred Colson. 1967. "European Clothing Names and the Etymology of *Girl*". *Lane Festschrift*, 233-40. [Suggests that Late OE *gyrela* 'garment' may be the etymon of ME *girle*, ModE *girl*.]

1964. Romaine, Suzanne. 1985. "Variability in Word Formation Patterns and Productivity in the History of English". *PICHL*/6, 451-65. [Chiefly concerned with the suffix *-ness*.]

1965. Ross, Alan Strode Campbell. 1958. *Etymology, with Special Reference to English.* (The Language Library.) London: André Deutsch, 169 pp. [New ed. 1965.]

Reviews: Ewald Standop in *IF* 64.325-26 (1959); R.M. Wilson in *ArchL* 11.74-75 (1959); Norman E. Eliason in *MLR* 55.257 (1960); Hans Schabram in *Anglia* 78.449-61 (1960).

1966. ———. 1963. "Three Lexicographical Notes". *EPS* 8.30-35. [Discusses: 1. Some obscure "Grocers'" words (1345-1463); 2. An early occurrence of the word *kerbing*; 3. *Rune Poem* 77-78.]

1967. ———. 1965. "Fox". *EPS* 9.1-46. [Discusses the history and etymology of *fox* and related words.]

1968. Salmon, Vivian. 1959. "Some Connotations of *Cold* in Old and Middle English". *MLN* 74.314-22.

1969. Samuels, Michael Louis. 1981. "Historical Thesaurus of English: Annual Report, July 1981". *OEN* 15:1.13-14.

1970. ——— (et al.). 1982. "Historical Thesaurus of English: Annual Report 1981-82". *OEN* 16:1.20-21.

1971. ———. 1985. "Historical Thesaurus of English: Annual Report 1985". *OEN* 19:1.26-28.

1972. Sandred, Karl Inge. 1966. "On the Terminology of the Plough in England". *SN* 38.323-38. [A historical study, with a glossary of terms.]

1973. Savory, Theodore Horace. 1953. *The Language of Science: Its Growth, Character and Usage.* (The Language Library.) London: André Deutsch, 184 pp. [Rev. ed. 1967, 173 pp. Deals with the development of the scientific vocabulary of English from OE through ModE.]

1974. Schäfer, Jürgen. 1982. "Alt- und Mittelenglisch in der lexikographischen Tradition des 17. Jahrhunderts". *Schneider Festschrift*, 169-85.

1975. Scheler, Manfred. 1972. "Zum Bedeutungswandel des englischen 'to show': ('schauen' > 'zeigen')". *Archiv* 209.357-60.

1976. ———. 1977. *Der englische Wortschatz*. (= Grundlagen der Anglistik und Amerikanistik, 9.) Berlin: Erich Schmidt, 177 pp.

Review: Bernhard Diensberg in *Anglia* 97.183-86 (1979).

1977. Schlepper, Erich. 1936. *Die Neubildung von Substantiven in den Übersetzungen König Alfreds mit einem Ausblick auf Chaucer*. Gütersloh i. Westf.: Thiele, vi + 136 pp. [Münster diss.]

1978. Serjeantson, Mary Sydney. 1935. *A History of Foreign Words in English*. London: Routledge & Kegan Paul, ix + 354 pp. [Repr., New York: Barnes & Noble, 1961.]

Reviews: Anon. in *TLS*, July 4, 1935, p. 429; Anon. in *N&Q* 169.36 (1935); R. Macaulay in *Spectator* 155.63-64 (1935); E. Weekley in *Observer*, Dec. 29, 1935; M. Ashdown in *MLR* 31.225-26 (1936); J.B. Dudek in *SRL* 14.16 (1936); J.A. Kerns in *Classical Weekly* 30.214-15 (1937); T.A. Knott in *AS* 12.140-41 (1937); G. Weber in *Anglia B* 48.8-13 (1937).

1979. ———. 1936. "The Vocabulary of Folklore in Old and Middle English". *Folklore* 47.42-73.

1980. Sheard, John Albert. 1954. *The Words We Use*. (The Language Library.) London: André Deutsch, 344 pp. [A study of the growth and development of the English vocabulary. Also repr. in 1966 as *The Words of English*. New York: Norton.]

Reviews: Ernest Gowers in *Sunday Times*, July 11, 1954, p. 5; James Reeves in *Observer*, July 18, 1954, p. 9; Robert W. Albright in *QJS* 41.83-84 (1955); K.R. Brooks in *MLR* 50.517-18 (1955); Margaret M. Bryant in *JEGP* 54.394-97 (1955); A.C. Baugh in *Language* 31.309-11 (1955); N.E. Eliason in *AS* 30.127-28 (1955); Anon. in *English Language Teaching* (London) 9.68-69 (1954/55); Gerhard Graband in *ZAA* 3.486-88 (1955); F. Wölcken in *Archiv* 192.204-05 (1955/56); A. Culioli in *EA* 10.242-44 (1957); Thomas Pyles in *MLN* 72.66-71 (1957).

1981. Sievers, Eduard. 1927. "Ae. me. *wel* und *wēl*". *BGDSL* (H) 51.304-05.

1982. Sihler, Andrew L. 1981. "Early English Feminine Agent Nouns in *-ild*: a PIE relic". *Sprache* 27.35-42.

1983. Sprengel, Konrad. 1977. *A Study in Word-Formation: The English Verbal Prefixes 'Fore-' and 'Pre-' and their German Counterparts*. (= TBL, 89.) Tübingen: Gunter Narr, xviii + 292 pp. [Compares the history of the prefixes in English. TH Aachen diss.; Abstr. in *EASG* 1977 (1978), 15-16.]

Reviews: K. Faiss in *Linguistics* 17.935-39 (1979); E. Burgschmidt in *Anglia* 99.167-69 (1981); E. Pennanen in *ES* 62.187-94 (1981).

1984. Stanley, Eric Gerald. 1982. "The Prenominal Prefix *ge-* in Late Old English and Early Middle English". *TPS* 1982, 25-66.

1985. Steinberg, Clarence Bernard. 1969. *Some Medieval Traditions of Etymological Characterization*. Pennsylvania diss., 417 pp. [Abstr. in *DA* 30.2500-01A (1969).]

1986. Strang, Barbara M.H. 1969. "Aspects of the History of the *-er* Formative in English". *TPS* 1969, 1-30.

1987. Thun, Nils. 1968. "Germanic Words for Deer". *SN* 40.94-113.

1988. Ufimzewa, A.A. 1960. "Zur Geschichte der semantischen Entwicklung des Wortes *land* (am Material der englischen Sprache)". *ZAA* 8.272-88.

1989. Vallins, George Henry. 1935. *Words in the Making*. London: Adam and Charles Black; New York: Macmillan, 96 pp.

Review: Anon. in *TLS*, Mar. 28, 1935, p. 214.

1990. ———. 1949. *The Making and Meaning of Words: A Companion to the Dictionary*. London: Adam and Charles Black, vii + 216 pp.

1991. Visser, Frederikus Theodorus. 1949. *Some Causes of Verbal Obsolescence*. Nijmegen & Utrecht: Dekker & Van de Vegt, 26 pp.

Reviews: F. Mossé in *ES* 31.180-81 (1950); A.A. Prins in *LT* 1950, 69-71 (1950); Angus McIntosh in *RES* n.s. 3.188-90 (1952).

1992. von Lindheim, Bogislav. 1949. "O.E. *drēam* and its Subsequent Development". *RES* 25.193-209. [Discusses also OE *spēd* and OE *gamen*.]

1993. von Rüden, Michael. 1978. *'Wlanc' und Derivate im Alt- und Mittelenglischen: eine wortgeschichtliche Studie*. (= EurH, 14; Angelsachsischen Sprache und Literatur, 61.) Frankfurt/Main-Bern-Las Vegas: Peter Lang, 324 pp. [Göttingen diss.; Abstr. in *EASG* 1978 (1979), 27-28.]

Reviews: E.G. Stanley in *MAE* 48.271 (1979); Klaus Bitterling in *Archiv* 220.148-49 (1983).

1994. Wahrig, Gerhard. 1953. *Die Ausdrücke des Lachens und des Spottens im Alt- und Mittelenglischen*. Leipzig diss., 142 pp.

1995. ———. 1955. "Das Lachen im Altenglischen und Mittelenglischen (I-II)". *ZAA* 3.274-304 and 389-418.

1996. Waldron, Ronald A. 1967. *Sense and Sense Development*. (The Language Library.) London: André Deutsch, 224 pp.

> Reviews: Daniel J. Casey in *MSpr* 62.305-06 (1968); Klaus Hansen in *ZAA* 16.405-08 (1968); Robert Henry Robins in *Bulletin of the School of Oriental and African Studies* (London) 31.442-43 (1968).

1997. Winter, Wolfgang. 1955. *'Aeht', 'Wela', 'Gestreon', 'Sped' und 'Ead' im Alt- und Mittelenglischen. Eine bedeutungsgeschichtliche Untersuchung*. Freie Univ. Berlin diss., 285 pp.

1998. Wolff, Edward J. 1966. *Chaucer's Normalized Diction: A Comparison of Recurring Phrases in Chaucer and 'Beowulf' to Determine the Validity of the Magoun Thesis*. Michigan State Univ. diss., 122 pp. [Abstr. in *DA* 27.3022-23A (1967).]

1999. Zieglschmidt, A.J. Friedrich. 1930. "The Disappearance of *werdan* in English". *PQ* 9.111-15. [Investigates the causes of the disappearance of OE *weorðan*.]

B. Old English

2000. Addy, Sidney Oldall. 1927. "The *stapol* in *Beowulf*: Hall and Chambers". *N&Q* 152.363-65.

2001. Amos, Ashley Crandell. 1978. "Dictionary of Old English: 1977 Progress Report". *OEN* 11:2.12-14.

2002. ———. 1979. "Dictionary of Old English: 1978 Progress Report". *OEN* 12:2.13-15.

2003. ———. 1980. "Dictionary of Old English: 1979 Progress Report". *OEN* 13:2.21-22.

2004. ———. 1981. "Dictionary of Old English: 1980 Progress Report". *OEN* 14:2.11-12.

2005. ———. 1982. "Dictionary of Old English: 1981 Progress Report". *OEN* 15:2.12-14.

2006. ———. 1983. "Dictionary of Old English: 1982 Progress Report". *OEN* 16:2.18-20.

2007. ———. 1984. "Dictionary of Old English: 1983 Progress Report". *OEN* 17:2.12-13. [Continued in Healey [no. 2275] and Holland [no. 2294].]

2008. ——— and Antonette diPaolo Healey. 1985. "The Dictionary of Old English: The Letter "D"". *Cameron Studies*, 13-38.

2009. Anderson, Olof Sigfrid. 1941/42. "An Etymological Note". *SN* 14.247-51. [On the etymology of OE *lȳþre* 'evil, base, mean', ModE *lither*.]

2010. Anderson, Earl R. 1972. "*Sæmearh* and Like Compounds: A Theme in Old English Poetry". *Comitatus* 3.3-11.

2011. Anon. 1931. "The Study of Words in *Beowulf*". *Word Study* 7.1.

2012. Århammar, Nils. 1964. "Altsächsisch *skion* m. 'Wolke' und altengl. *scēo* (?), mit einem Beitrag zur Textkritik von *Genesis* 16ff. und des altenglischen Rätsels vom Gewittersturm". *Jahrbuch des Vereins für niederdeutsche Sprachforschung* (Neumünster) 87.24-28.

2013. Bäck, Hilding. 1934. *The Synonyms for 'Child', 'Boy', 'Girl' in Old English: An Etymological-Semasiological Investigation.* (= LundSE, 2.) Lund: Gleerup, xvi + 273 pp. [Lund diss.]

   Reviews: O. Anderson in *Anglia B* 46.291-94 (1935); K. Malone in *ES* 17. 225-27 (1935); S. Potter in *MLR* 31.461-62 (1936); C.L. W[renn] in *RES* 12.490-92 (1936); R.G. Kent in *Language* 13.325-26 (1937); K. Jost in *IF* 56.74 (1939); Gwyn Jones in *MAE* 9.111-14 (1940).

2014. Bähr, Dieter. 1971. "Altenglisch *īsig* (*Beowulf*, Zeile 33)". *ZAA* 19.409-12.

2015. Baird, Joseph Lee. 1968. "*for metode: Beowulf* 169". *ES* 49.418-23.

2016. Bak, Walter. 1970. "A Concordance to MS Hatton 20". *Computers and OE Concordances*, 61-65.

2017. Ball, Christopher J.E. 1960. "*Incge Beow.* 2577". *Anglia* 78.403-10.

2018. ———. 1970. "Questions of Old English Lexicography". *Computers and OE Concordances*, 89-94.

2019. ———. 1985. "Homonymy and Polysemy in Old English: A Problem for Lexicographers". *Cameron Studies*, 39-46.

2020. ——— and Angus Fraser Cameron. 1973. "Some Specimen Entries for the *Dictionary of Old English*". *Kurath Festschrift*, 46-64. [Also printed in *DOE Plan*, 329-47.]

2021. Bammesberger, Alfred. 1965. *Deverbative 'jan'-Verba des Altenglischen. Vergleichend mit den übrigen altgermanischen Sprachen dargestellt.* München: Mikrokopie G.m.b.H., x + 147 pp. [München diss.]

2022. ———. 1965. "Old English *gycer* and Gothic *jukuzi*". *Language* 41.416-19.

2023. ———. 1967. "Old English *brecþa* and *-brecþ*". *Language* 43.452-56.

2024. ———. 1967. "Altenglisch *blectha* 'Aussatz'". *MSS* 22.5-6.

2025. ———. 1968. "Altenglisch *suht* und *-siht*". *MSS* 23.5-6.

2026. ———. 1968. "Altenglisch *frēo* 'frei'". *NS* N.F. 17.257-58.

2027. ———. 1969. "Das Genus von ae. *-swyrd* 'Schwur'". *MSS* 25.5-6.

2028. ———. 1969. "Der Ansatz ae. *feogað* 'Hass'". *Sprache* 15.62.

2029. ———. 1969. "Gibt es ae. *fyllað* m. 'Fülle'?". *Anglia* 87.392-93.

2030. ———. 1970. "Av. *mimara-*, lat. *memor* und ae. *gemimor*". *MSS* 28.5-8.

2031. ———. 1971. "Zu altenglisch *-faerae* in Bedas Sterbespruch". *ZVS* 85.276-79.

2032. ———. 1972. "Altenglisch *geoht* und *geiht*". *IF* 77.100-02.

2033. ———. 1972. "Zur Vorgeschichte von westsächsisch *-sīene/-sȳne* und anglisch *gesēne*". *Anglia* 90.427-36.

2034. ———. 1972. "Altenglisch *gedægeþ* in Napier XLIV". *ZVS* 86.190-92.

2035. ———. 1972. "Altenglisch *hlæfþe*". *ZVS* 86.307-11.

2036. ———. 1972. "Altenglish *hligan*". *MSS* 30.5-7.

2037. ———. 1973. "Zu altenglischen *berofan* in Genesis 2078b". *Sprache* 19.205-07.

2038. ———. 1973. "Altenglisch *gethyngu*". *MSS* 31.5-9.

2039. ———. 1973. "Altenglisch *brosnian* und *molsnian*". *MSS* 31.11-13.

2040. ———. 1973. "Das anglische Verb *lioran/leoran*". *ZVS* 87.272-82.

2041. ———. 1974. "Einige versteckte Weiterbildungen von altenglisch *æwisc(e)*". *Sprache* 20.130-33.

2042. ———. 1974. "Altenglisch *gedræg* und *gedreag*". *ZVS* 88.139-46.

2043. ———. 1975. "Gotisch *hnasqus** und altenglisch *hnesce*". *Sprache* 21.188-91.

2044. ———. 1975. "Altenglisch *stulor*". *MSS* 33.5-6.

2045. ———. 1975. "Altenglisch *agetan*". *Archiv* 212.313-16.

2046. ———. 1976. "Gotisch *awepi*". *MSS* 34.5-7. [Includes reference to OE *eode*.]

2047. ———. 1976. "Zum Ansatz von altenglisch *bedæcc(e)an*". *MSS* 35.5-6.

2048. ———. 1976. "Altenglisch *sneowan/snowan* und gotisch *sniwan*". *ZVS* 90.258-61.

2049. ———. 1976. "Altenglisch *gamban* 'Tribut'". *Sprache* 22.53-54.

2050. ———. 1977. "Zur Herkunft von ae. *ondrædan* und *andrysne*". *BGDSL*(T) 99.206-12.

2051. ———. 1977. "Two Old English Glosses". *ES* 58.1-3. [Discusses *blefla* and *flycge*.]

2052. ———. 1978. "On the Gloss to Matthew 26.8 in the *Lindisfarne Gospels*". *Linguistic and Literary Studies in Honor of Archibald A. Hill, III: Historical and Comparative Linguistics*, ed. M.A. Jazayery, et al., 9-12. The Hague: Mouton. [On the word *abloncgne*.]

2053. ———. 1978. "Old English *broc* and Middle Irish *broc(c)*". *Bulletin of the Board of Celtic Studies* (Cardiff) 27.552-54.

2054. ———. 1979. "Vieil irlandais *sacart* et vieil anglais *sacerd*". *Études Celtiques* (Paris) 16.187-89.

2055. ———. 1979. "Zum Vokalismus von altenglisch *-næman*". *Anglia* 97.420-28.

2056. ———. 1980. "Altenglische Komposita mit *hild(e)-*". *MSS* 39.5-10.

2057. ———. 1981. "Vier altenglische Interpretamenta des Épinal-Erfurt Glossars". *Anglia* 99.383-89. [Discusses *fex, gitiungi, satul*, and *suollaen*.]

2058. ———. 1982. "A Note on *Beowulf* 83b". *NM* 83.24-25. [Maintains that on syntactic grounds *lenge* in *Beowulf* 83b cannot be interpreted as the comparative of the adverb *lange*.]

2059. ———. 1983. "Das etymologische Wörterbuch des Altenglischen: Probleme und Methoden". *Anglistentag 1981*, 29-34.

2060. ———. 1983. "The Old English Adjective *Ambryre*". *ES* 64.97-101.

2061. ———. 1985. "Old High German *Bretan* and Old English *(A)bre(o)dwian*". *GL* 25.4-7.

2062. ———. 1986. *Linguistic Notes on Old English Poetic Texts*. (= AF, 189.) Heidelberg: Carl Winter, 124 pp. [A collection of lexical and interpretative notes.]

2063. ———. 1986. "On Old English *gefrægnod* in *Beowulf* 1333a". *Linguistics across Historical and Geographical Boundaries. Vol.I: Linguistic Theory and Historical Linguistics*, ed. Dieter Kastovsky and Aleksander Szwedek, 193-97. Berlin-New York-Amsterdam: Mouton de Gruyter.

2064. ———. 1987. "Altenglisch *gewif*". *Anglia* 105.115-20.

2065. Barley, Nigel F. 1974. "Old English Colour Classification: Where Do Matters Stand?" *ASE* 3.15-28.

2066. Barnes, Richard. 1960. "Horse Colors in Anglo-Saxon Poetry". *PQ* 39.510-12. [Deals with *fealwe* and *æppel-fealwe* used to describe horses in *Beowulf*.]

2067. Barry, Phillips. 1936. "Old English *priusa* 'tabanus bovinus'". *MLN* 51.331-35.

2068. Bately, Janet Margaret. 1978. "The Compilation of the Anglo-Saxon Chronicle, 60 BC to AD 890: Vocabulary as Evidence". *PBA* 64.93-129.

2069. ———. 1982. "Lexical Evidence for the Authorship of the Prose Psalms in *Paris Psalter*". *ASE* 10.69-95. [Concerning the vocabulary of 'Alfredian' OE.]

2070. ———. 1985. "On Some Words for Time in Old English Literature". *Cameron Studies*, 47-64.

2071. Bauschatz, Paul C. 1977. "Old English Conjunctions: Some Semantic Considerations". *In Geardagum* 2.18-30.

2072. Beck, Heinrich. 1968. "Waffentanz und Waffenspiel". *Festschrift für Otto Höfler zum 65. Geburtstag*, ed. Helmut Birkhan, et al., I, 1-16. Wien: Notring. [Discusses OE *lāc* and its cognates.]

2073. Beckers, Hartmut. 1968. *Die Wortsipp '*hail-' und ihr sprachliches Feld im älteren Westgermanischen (Altenglischen und Altdeutschen))*. Münster diss., xxxviii + 592 pp.

2074. Beer, Herbert. 1939. *Führen und Folgen, Herrschen und Beherrschtwerden im Sprachgut der Angelsachsen*. (= Sprache und Kultur der germanischen und romanischen Völker, A. Anglistische Reihe, 31.) Breslau: Priebatsch, 327 pp. [A study of OE words denoting the acts of leading and following, ruling and being ruled.]

2075. Bennet, Jack Arthur Walter. 1942. "Old English *hrohian*". *MAE* 11.90. [Notes the possible existence of the derivative *hrohung* from this rare OE verb.]

2076. Benning, Helmut A. 1961. *'Welt' und 'Mensch' in der altenglischen Dichtung: Bedeutungsgeschichtliche Untersuchungen zum germanisch-altenglischen Wortschatz*. (= BEP, 44.) Bochum & Langendreer: Pöppinghaus, viii + 241 pp. [Münster diss., 1958.]

   Reviews: A.C. Bouman in *ES* 43.498-501 (1962); K. Grinda in *Anglia* 79.451-57 (1962); J.L. Rosier in *JEGP* 61.631-33 (1962); C.L. Wrenn in *MAE* 31.140-41 (1962); C.A. Ladd in *N&Q* n.s. 9.394-96 (1962); A. Campbell in *RES* n.s. 14.99 (1963); B. Carstensen in *NS* 12.283-84 (1963); Klaus Ostheeren in *Archiv* 205.56-60 (1968/69).

2077. Berkhout, Carl T. 1974. "The Problem of OE *holmwudu*". *MS* 36.429-33.

2078. Bessinger, Jess Balsor, Jr. 1970. "A Concordance to *Beowulf*". *Computers and OE Concordances*, 35-39.

2079. Bierbaumer, Peter. 1974. "Ae. *fornetes folm* — eine Orchideenart". *Anglia* 92.172-76.

2080. ———. 1975. *Der botanische Wortschatz des Altenglischen*. I. Teil: *Das Læcebōc*. (= GBEP, 1.) Bern: Herbert Lang; Frankfurt am Main: Peter Lang, xvi + 168 pp. [Abstr. of Pt. I in *EASG* 1975 (1976), pp. 22-24.]

2081. ———. 1976. *Der botanische Wortschatz des Altenglischen*. II. Teil: *'Lācnunga', 'Herbarium Apuleii', 'Peri Didaxeon'*. (= GBEP, 2.) Bern: Herbert Lang; Frankfurt am Main: Peter Lang, xvii + 160 pp.

   Review: E.G. Stanley in *N&Q* n.s. 24.561-63 (1977).

2082. ———. 1977. "Zu J.V. Goughs Ausgabe einiger altenglischer Glossen". *Anglia* 95.115-21. [Cf. Gough [no. 2239].]

2083. ———. 1979. "Aspekte der altenglischen Glossenforschung". *Pinsker Festschrift*, 33-50.

2084. ———. 1979. "Zu den altenglischen Psalterglossen *hwit stow* und *hwit tor*". *Anglia* 97.168-71.

2085. ———. 1979. "Altenglisch *seonuwealtian* — ein 'ghost-word'". *Anglia* 97.429-30.

2086. ———. 1979. *Der botanische Wortschatz des Altenglischen*. III. Teil: *Der botanische Wortschatz in altenglischen Glossen.* (= GBEP, 3.) Frankfurt am Main-Bern-Las Vegas: Peter Lang, xlviii + 341 pp. [Abstr. in *EASG* 1978 (1979), pp. 24-27.]

   Review: E.G. Stanley in *N&Q* n.s. 26.566 (1979).

2087. ———. 1983. "Aktuelle Probleme der altenglischen Wortforschung". *Anglistentag 1981*, 22-28.

2088. ———. 1985. "Research into Old English Glosses: A Critical Survey". *Cameron Studies*, 65-78.

2089. Blake, Norman Francis. 1962. "Two Notes on the Exeter Book". *N&Q* n.s. 9.45-47. [Discusses 1. *gehwore* (*Phoenix* 336 & *Christ* 928) and 2. *toheanes* (*Phoenix* 124, 421).]

2090. Bloomfield, Leonard. 1929. "Notes on the Preverb *ge-* in Alfredian English". *Klaeber Festschrift*, 79-102.

2091. ———. 1930. "O.H.G. *eino*, O.E. *ana* 'solus'". *Curme Volume of Linguistic Studies*, edited on the Occasion of his Seventieth Birthday, by James Taft Hatfield, et al., (= LM, 7), 50-59. Philadelphia: Linguistic Society of America.

2092. Bonser, Wilfrid. 1951/52. "Anglo-Saxon Medical Nomenclature". *EGS* 4.13-19.

2093. Bouman, A.C. 1951. "Een Drietal Etymologieën: *Aibr, Eolete, Garsecg*". *Neophil* 35.238-41. [The first of the three words discussed is Gothic, the last two Old English.]

2094. Boyd, W.J.P. 1967. "Aldrediana VII: Hebraica". *EPS* 10.1-32. [On Biblical words and names in Aldred's gloss to the *Lindisfarne Gospels*.]

2095. ———. 1975. "Aldrediana XXV: *Ritual* Hebraica". *EPS* 14.1-57.

2096. ———. 1975. *Aldred's Marginalia: Explanatory Comments in the Lidisfarne Gospels*. (= Exeter Mediaeval English Texts and Studies, 4.) Exeter: Univ. of Exeter, x + 62 pp. [Comments on 71 hard glosses in the *Lindisfarne Gospels*.]

2097. Brady, Caroline. 1952. "The Synonyms for 'Sea' in *Beowulf*". *Studies in Honor of Albert Morey Sturtevant* (= Univ. of Kansas Pubs., Humanstic Studies,

29), 22-46. Lawrence: Univ. of Kansas Press. [Continued by Woodward [no. 2820].]

2098. ———. 1952. "The Old English Nominal Compounds in -*rád*". *PMLA* 67.538-71.

2099. ———. 1979. "'Weapons' in *Beowulf*: An Analysis of the Nominal Compounds and an Evaluation of the Poet's Use of Them". *ASE* 8.79-141.

2100. ———. 1983. "'Warriors' in *Beowulf*: An Analysis of the Nominal Compounds and an Evaluation of the Poet's Use of Them". *ASE* 11.199-246. [Includes 'Index Locutionum', compiled by Jonathan Wilcox, pp. 245-46.]

2101. Bratley, Paul and Serge Lusignan. 1976. "Information Processing in Dictionary Making: Some Technical Guidelines". *CHum* 10.133-43. [Concerns the *Dict. of Old English* (in progress).]

2102. Bremmer, Rolf H., Jr. 1983. "Old English *feoh and feorh*, Old Norse *fé ok fjor*, ergo: Old Frisian *fiā and ferech* 'money and life'". *Us Wurk* 32.55-62.

2103. Bridier, Yvonne. 1972. "La fonction sociale du *Horn* chez les Anglo-Saxons". *EA* 25.74-77.

2104. Brøndegaard, Vagn Jorgensen. 1979. "Ein Angelsächsischen Pflanzenname: *openars(e)*". *Sudhoffs Archiv: Zeitschrift für Wissenschaftgeschichte* 63.190-93.

2105. Brooks, Kenneth R. 1948/49. "Old English *woþes hring*". *EGS* 2.68-74.

2106. ———. 1952/53. "Old English *ēa* and Related Words". *EGS* 5.15-66. [An etymological study of OE *ēa* 'river, water' and other words of similar form and meaning.]

2107. Brown, Alan K. 1973. "*Neorxnawang*". *NM* 74.610-23.

2108. Bryan, William Frank. 1930/31. "*Ǣrgold* in *Beowulf*, and Other Old English Compounds of *ǣr*". *MP* 28.157-61. [Cf. Swaen [no. 2742].]

2109. Büchner, Günter. 1968. *Vier altenglische Bezeichnungen für Vergehen und Verbrechen ('Firen', 'Gylt', 'Man', 'Scyld')*. Berlin: Dissertations-Druckstelle, 205 pp. [Freie Univ. Berlin diss.]

2110. Buckhurst, Helen Thérèse McMillan. 1929. "Terms and Phrases for the Sea in Old English Poetry". *Klaeber Festschrift*, 103-19.

2111. Burchfield, Robert William. 1955. "*Beowulf* 219: *ymb an tid*". *MLR* 50.485-87.

2112. Butler, Sharon. 1980. "Problems with Headwords in Old English". *Theory and Method in Lexicography: Western and Non-Western Perspectives*, ed. Ladislav Zgusta, 105-14. Columbia, SC: Hornbeam.

2113. ——— and Bruce Mitchell. 1985. "Some Lexicographical Problems Posed by Old English Grammar Words". *Cameron Studies*, 79-89.

2114. Byerly, Gayle Kimbrel A. 1966. *Compounds and Other Elements of Poetic Diction Derived from an Oral-Formulaic Poetic Tradition: A Comparison of Aeschylus and the Beowulf Poet*. Pennsylvania diss., 204 pp. [Abstr. in *DA* 27.1333A (1966).]

2115. Cameron, Angus Fraser. 1968. *The Old English Nouns of Colour: A Semantic Study*. Oxford [B.Litt.] diss., iii + 391 pp.

2116. ———. 1969. "Old English *unbleoh* Again". *Neophil* 53.299-302. [Apropos of Whitbread [no. 2812].]

2117. ———. 1977. "The Dictionary of Old English and the Computer". *Computing in the Humanities: Proceedings of the Third International Conference on Computing in the Humanities*, ed. Serge Lusignan and John S. North, 101-06. Waterloo, Ontario: Univ. of Waterloo Press.

2118. ———. 1983. "On the Making of the *Dictionary of Old English*". *Poetica* 15/16.13-22.

2119. ——— and Ashley Crandell Amos. 1978. "The Dictionary of Old English: A Turning Point". *ES* 59.289-94.

2120. ——— and Antonette diPaolo Healey. 1979. "The Dictionary of Old English". *Dictionaries* 1.87-96.

2121. Campbell, Alistair. 1933. "Old English *Reord*". *MLR* 28.231-33.

2122. Campbell, Jackson J. 1951. "The Dialect Vocabulary of the OE Bede". *JEGP* 50.349-72.

2123. ———. 1952. "The OE Bede: Book III, Chapters 16 to 20". *MLN* 67.381-86. [Based on an examination of Anglian words in the TB version.]

2124. ———. 1955. "The Harley Glossary and 'Saxon Patois'". *PQ* 34.71-74. [Doubts the validity of K.D. Büldring's term *Saxon Patois*.]

2125. Carr, Charles Telford. 1939. *Nominal Compounds in Germanic*. (= St Andrews Univ. Pubs., 41.) London: Oxford Univ. Press/Milford, xxxvi + 497 pp. [Treats of the nominal compounds in the Old Germanic dialects (Gothic, ON, OE, OS, OHG and OFris).]

Reviews: Edward H. Sehrt in *MLN* 54.618-22 (1939); C.E.B. in *MAE* 9.26-30 (1940); M.F. Richey in *RES* 17.121-24 (1941).

2126. Cassidy, Frederic Gomes. 1970. "A Symbolic Word-Group in *Beowulf*". *Utley Festschrift*, 27-34. [Examines *sunne, leoht, beacen,* and *tacen*.]

2127. ———. 1972. "*Beowulf*: *Icge* and *Incge* Once More". *Haugen Festschrift*, 115-18.

2128. ———. 1972. "Old English *gārsecg* — An Eke-Name?". *Names* 20.95-100.

2129. Cawley, Arthur Clare. 1948/49. "Notes on Old English". *EGS* 2.75-80. [Discusses 1. *scennum* (*Beowulf*, 1694), 2. *strǣt* (*Beowulf*, 164), 3. *hit* (Ælfric's *Colloquy*, 94).]

2130. Chase, Denis Elwyn. 1976. *A Semantic Study of Old English Words for 'Warrior'*. New York Univ. diss., 412 pp. [Abstr. in *DA* 37.5807-08A (1977).]

2131. Christiani, Brigitte. 1938. *Zwillingsverbindungen in der altenglischen Dichtung*. Königsberg diss., v + 76 pp. Würzburg. [A study of word-pairs (e.g. *innan and utan, wordum and dædum*) in OE poetry.]

2132. Clark, Cecily. 1969. "'France' and 'French' in the *Anglo-Saxon Chronicle*". *LSE* n.s. 3.35-45.

2133. Clipsham, David. 1974. "*Beowulf* 168-169". *In Geardagum* 1.19-24. [Discusses the *gifstol* crux.]

2134. Colgrave, B. 1937. "*Scūrheard*". *MLR* 32.281. [Suggests a possible meaning for the adjective.]

2135. Collinder, Björn. 1932. "Wortgeschichtliches aus dem Bereich der Germanisch-Finnischen und Germanisch-Lappischen Lehnbeziehungen". *APS* 7.193-225. [References to OE *āgan, āgend, unāga, grindan, lifer, mægþ, mos, norþ, tācn,* and *ðēon*.]

2136. Collins, Rowland L. 1963. "A Reexamination of the Old English Glosses in the *Blickling Psalter*". *Anglia* 81.124-28.

2137. ———. 1970. "Six Words in the *Blickling Homilies*". *Meritt Festschrift*, 137-41. [Deals with *cyningan, ungereclic, m[ar]þon, unwitweorc, onaþrycte,* and *þystrogeniþum*.]

2138. Colman, Fran. 1985 [1987]. "On Some Morphological Formatives in Old English". *FLH* 6:2.267-83. [Refers in particular to L. Bauer's *English Word-Formation* (Cambridge Univ. Press, 1983).]

2139. Condren, Edward I. 1973. "*Unnyt* Gold in *Beowulf* 3168". *PQ* 52.296-99.

2140. Cook, Albert Stanburrough. 1926. "The Beowulfian *maðelode*". *JEGP* 25.1-6.

2141. Cooke, W.G. 1971. "*Hronas* and *Hronfixas*". *N&Q* n.s. 18.245-47. [Suggests that the *Beowulf* reference is to porpoises of the type familiar in English harbours.]

2142. ———. 1980. "Firy Drakes and Blazing-Bearded Light". *ES* 61.97-103. [Argues that the *fyrenne dracan* of the *Anglo-Saxon Chronicle* for 793 was recognized as a meteor.]

2143. Corso, Louise. 1980. "Some Considerations of the Conquest "Nið" in *Beowulf*". *Neophil* 64.121-26.

2144. Cosmos, Spencer. 1975. "Old English *Limwæstm* (*Christ and Satan* 129)". *N&Q* n.s. 22.196-98.

2145. Cowgill, Warren. 1960. "Gothic *iddja* and Old English *ēode*". *Language* 36.483-501.

2146. Cronan, Dennis. 1987. "Old English *gelad*: 'A Passage across Water'". *Neophil* 71.316-19.

2147. Crosby, H. Lamar, Jr. 1940. "Two Notes on *Beowulf*". *MLN* 45.605-06. [On ll. 212 and 216.]

2148. Cross, James E. 1957. "On Sievers-Brunner's Interpretation of *The Ruin*, Line 7, *forweorone geleorene*". *EGS* 6.104-06.

2149. ———. 1971. "Lexicographical Notes on the Old English *Life of St. Giles and the Life of St. Nicholas*". *N&Q* n.s. 18.369-72.

2150. ———. 1974. "Mainly on Philology and the Interpretative Criticism of *Maldon*". *Pope Festschrift*, 235-53. [Re-examines the range of meaning of *lytegian* and *ofermōd*.]

2151. ———. 1981. "Old English *leasere*". *N&Q* n.s. 28.484-86.

2152. ———. 1981. "*Passio Symphoriani* and OE *Cund(d)*: for the Revision of the Dictionary". *NM* 82.269-75.

2153. Crozier, Alan. 1986. "Old West Norse *íþrótt* and Old English *indryhtu*". *SN* 58.3-10.

2154. Curtis, Jay L. 1946. *The Vocabulary of Medical 'Craftas' in the Old English 'Leechbook of Bald'*. Univ. of North Carolina at Chapel Hill diss., 292 pp. [Abstr. in *Univ. of North Carolina Record*, No. 464 (1946), Research in Progress, 184-85.]

2155. Daunt, Marjorie. 1966. "Some Modes of Anglo-Saxon Meaning". *In Memory of John Rupert Firth*, ed. Charles Ernest Bazell, et al., 66-78. London: Longmans. [An investigation of passages from *Beowulf*, *Andreas*, *Elene*, and *Guthlac I*.]

2156. Davis, Norman. 1953. "*Hippopotamus* in Old English". *RES* n.s. 4.141-42.

2157. De Caluwé-Dor, Juliette. 1977. "A propos de l'étymologie du verbe anglais 'to come'". *Linguistics in Belgium/Linguistiek in België/Linguistique en Belgique*, ed. S. de Vriendt & C. Peeters, I, 14-22. Brussels: Didier.

2158. De la Cruz, Juan M. 1975. "Old English Pure Prefixes: Structure and Function". *Linguistics* 145.47-81.

2159. Dempsey, George T. 1982. "Legal Terminology in Anglo-Saxon England: *Trimoda Necessitas* Charter". *Speculum* 57.843-49.

2160. Dent, Anthony. 1965. "OE. *Hors-ōme*". *N&Q* n.s. 12.446.

2161. Derolez, René L.M. 1946. "— And That Difficult Word *Garsecg* (Gummere)". *MLQ* 7.445-52.

2162. ———. 1948. "Some Notes on OE *firgenstream*". *Album Prof. Dr. Frank Baur*, den jubilaris bij zijn zestigsten verjaardag als huldeblijk aangeboden door collega's, vakgenoten en oud-leerlingen, I, 182-91. Antwerp-Brussels-Gent-Leuven: Standaard-Boekhandel.

2163. ———. 1960. "Aldhelms Glosatus IV: Some 'Hapax Legomena' among the Old English Aldhelm Glosses". *SGG* 2.81-95.

2164. ———. 1985. "Aldhelm and the Lexicographer". *Cameron Studies*, 91-106.

2165. ——— and Ute Schwab. 1980/81. "*Logðor*, ein altenglisches Glossenwort". *SGG* 21.95-125.

2166. De Roo, C. Harvey. 1980. "Old English *Sele*". *Neophil* 64.113-20.

2167. ———. 1982. "*Beowulf* 2223b: A Thief by Any Other Name?". *MP* 79.297-304. [Argues for *þegn* in *Beowulf* 2223b, drawing on lexical investigations.]

2168. De Tollenaere, F. 1981. "Nochmals ahd. *săn(o)*, ae. *sŏna*, got. *suns*". *ZVS* 95.309-10.

2169. Deutschbein, Max. 1941. "Geographie der Wortbildung der germanischen Völkernamen nach angelsächsischer Überlieferung". *ZMaF* 16.113-22.

2170. Dick, Ernst S. 1965. *Ae. 'dryht' und seine Sippe: Eine wortkundliche, kultur- und religionsgeschichtliche Betrachtung zur altgermanischen Glaubensvorstellung vom wachstümlichen Heil*. (= NBEP, 3.) Münster: Aschendorff, xv + 579 pp.

  Reviews: A. Campbell in *RES* n.s. 18.297-99 (1967); R. Faeber in *EA* 20.183-85 (1967); E. H[ofmann] in *ZVS* 80.284 (1966); W. Meid in *IF* 72.219-20 (1967); F. Norman in *MAE* 37.66-70 (1968); K. Ostheeren in *Archiv* 205.60-63 (1968); E. Ploss in *Anzeiger für deutsches Altertum* 83.121-23 (1972); B.A. Rosenberg in *JAF* 80. 401-02 (1967). [Cf. also Hallander [no. 2262].]

2171. ———. 1982. "Ae. *drēam*: Zur Semantik der Verbalbeziehungen in der Dichtung". *Schneider Festschrift*, 121-35.

2172. Dietz, Klaus. 1985. "Ae. *bēocere* 'Imker', me. *bīke* 'Bienennest' und die Ortsnamen auf *Bick-*". *Anglia* 103.1-25.

2173. ———. 1985. "Ae. *tasol — te(o)sol* 'Würfel'". *Anglia* 103.90-95.

2174. Doane, A.N. 1973. "The Green Street of Paradise: A Note on Lexis and Meaning in Old English Poetry". *NM* 74.456-65. [Examines the meaning of *green* in OE poetry.]

2175. Downs, Lynwood Gifford. 1931. *Intensive Adverbs and Intensive Prefixes in the West Germanic Dialects: A Lexical and Semantic Investigation*. Minnesota diss. (no pagination available). [Abstr. in *Univ. of Minnesota Summaries of Ph.D. Theses* 1.168-72 (1940).]

2176. Droege, Geart B. 1975. "OE *grindan* — OFris. **grinda* 'to grind': An English-Frisian Isogloss within Germanic". *Us Wurk* 24.12-18.

2177. Duckert, Audrey R. 1972. "*Erce* and Other Possibly Keltic Elements in the Old English Charm for Unfruitful Land". *Names* 20.83-90.

2178. Ebbinghaus, Ernst Albrecht. 1976. "Old English *Agu* 'Pica'". *GL* 16.187-90.

2179. ———. 1977. "The Etymology of OE *mælsceafa*". *GL* 17.92-93.

2180. Ehrhart, Margaret J. 1975. "Tempter as Teacher: Some Observations on the Vocabulary of the Old English *Genesis B*". *Neophil* 59.435-46.

2181. Einarsson, Stefán. 1949. "*Beowulf* 249: *Wlite* = Icelandic *Litr*". *MLN* 64.347. [Both words signify 'looks, appearance'.]

2182. ———. 1952. "Old English *Ent*: Icelandic *Enta*". *MLN* 67.554-55.

2183. ———. 1960. "*Kyning-Wuldor* and *Mann-Skratti*". *MLN* 75.193-94. [On compounds of this type in OE and OIcel.]

2184. Ekwall, Eilert. 1943. "Old English *ambyrne wind*". *Mélanges de philologie offerts à M. Jehan Mélander*, 275-84. Uppsala: A.-B. Lundequistska Bokhandeln.

2185. ———. 1943. "Old English *forræpe*". *SN* 16.33-38.

2186. Eliason, Norman Ellsworth. 1935. "*Wulfhlið* (*Beowulf*, 1. 1358)". *JEGP* 34.20-23.

2187. Elliot, Constance O. and Alan Strode Campbell Ross. 1972. "Aldrediana XXIV: The Linguistic Peculiarities of the Gloss of St. John's Gospel". *EPS* 13.49-72.

2188. Erades, Pieter Abraham. 1967. "A Romance Congener of O.E. *symbel*". *ES* 48.25-27.

2189. Evans, Ruth. 1979. "Worcester Glosses in an Old English Homily". *N&Q* n.s. 26.393-95.

2190. Faiss, Klaus. 1967. '*Gnade*' *bei Cynewulf und seiner Schule: Semasiologisch-onomasiologische Studien zu einem semantischen Feld*. (= SEP, N.F. 12.) Tübingen: Niemeyer, vi + 146 pp. [Tübingen diss.]

Reviews: R.C. Alston in *MAE* 37.373-74 (1968); Raffaella Del Pezzo in *AION-SG* 11.512-14 (1968); Wolfgang Kühlwein in *GRM* 19.345-46 (1969); Marianne Latendorf in *Anglia* 89.513-16 (1971); Hans Schabram in *IF* 80.290-95 (1975).

2191. ———. 1969. "Old English Verbs in *-sian*: Bemerkungen zu Lars-G. Hallanders Studie". *Lang&S* 2.233-43. [Review article on L.-G. Hallander [no. 2260].]

2192. ———. 1970. "'Gnade' und seine Kontexte in der altenglischen *Genesis*: Ein Beitrag zum Problem der altenglischen Dichtersprache". *Linguistics* 56.5-30.

2193. Faull, Margaret Lindsey. 1975. "The Semantic Development of Old English *Wealh*". *LSE* n.s. 8.20-44.

2194. Feldman, Thalia Phillies. 1975. "Terminology for 'Kingship and God' in *Beowulf*". *LOS* 2.100-15.

2195. Fell, Christine E. 1975. "Old English *beor*". *LSE* n.s. 8.76-95.

2196. ———. 1981. "A Note on Old English Wine Terminology: The Problem of *cæren*". *NMS* 25.1-12.

2197. ———. 1982/83 "*Unfrið*: An Approach to a Definition". *Saga-Book* 21.85-100.

2198. Fischer, Andreas. 1986. *Engagement, Wedding and Marriage in Old English*. (= AF, 176). Heidelberg: Carl Winter, 196 pp. [Studies the OE marriage vocabulary.]

2199. Fischer, Walther. 1944. "Zur Etymologie von ae. *docga*, ne. *dog* und einigen anderen Tiernamen". *Anglia* 67/68.321-38.

2200. Flasdieck, Hermann Martin. 1923. "Zu ae. *onʒean* u. ä". *Anglia B* 34.271-72.

2201. ———. 1929. "Anglosaxonica" *Anglia B* 40.342-45. [Discusses the problems involved in the OE *crēcas, crēacas* and the Anglian *bernan*.]

2202. ———. 1933. "Ae. *ēow*". *Anglia* 57.208-15.

2203. ———. 1950. "OE *nefne*: a Revaluation". *Anglia* 69.135-71. [On the history of this Anglian form and its significance for the chronology of OE texts.]

2204. ———. 1951. "Nochmals ae. *nefne*". *Anglia* 70.46.

2205. Fletcher, Alan J. 1984. "*Cald Wæter, Scir Wæter*: A Note on Lines 91 and 98 of *The Battle of Maldon*". *NM* 85.435-37.

2206. Fogelman, Roger Harry. 1965. *Semantic Systems in Anglo-Saxon Poetry*. Univ. of Virginia diss., 141 pp. [Abstr. in *DA* 26.7304 (1966).]

2207. Forsberg, Rune. 1961. "Old English *scipsteall*". *SN* 33.128-32.

2208. Förster, Max. 1923. "Herrn Otto Schlutter zur Antwort". *Anglia* 47.185-88. [On OE *cīne, bed, toroc, gafolrind*.]

2209. ———. 1923. "Das *Whītlēad-tēauer*-Rezept". *Anglia B* 34.115-16.

2210. ———. 1935. "Altenglisch *stōr*, ein altirisches Lehnwort". *EStn* 70.49-54.

2211. ———. 1937. "Ae. *hrinder, hriddern* und *hriddel* im Lichte altbritischer Entlehnungen". *Anglia* 61.341-50.

2212. ———. 1942. "Die Bedeutung von ae. *gebisceopian* und seiner Sippe" *Anglia* 66.255-62.

2213. ———. 1942. "Zu ae. *beard* und *bearm*". *Anglia B* 53.141-42.

2214. ———. 1942. "Die liturgische Bedeutung von ae. *traht*". *Anglia B* 53.180-84.

2215. Frank, Roberta. 1986. "*Mere* and *Sund*: Two Sea-Changes in *Beowulf*". *Greenfield Festschrift*, 153-72.

2216. Franson, J. Karl. 1975 [1976]. "An Anglo-Saxon Etymology for Milton's *Haemony*". *AN&Q* 14.18-19.

2217. Fraser, Thomas (K.H.) 1975. "The Preverbs *for-* and *fore-* in Old English". *Joly & Fraser Studies*, 19-28.

2218. ———. 1977. "Les rôles du préverbe en vieil-anglais". *Linguistique et Philologie*, 79-94.

2219. ———. 1980. "The Preverb *to-* in Old English". *Langage et psychomécanique du langage: études dédiées à Roch Valin*, ed. André Joly and W.H. Hirtle, 185-94. Lille: Presses Univ. de Lille; Québec: Presses de l'Univ. Laval.

2220. ———. 1985. "Etymology and the Lexical Semantics of the Old English Preverb *be-*" *Historical Semantics*, 113-26.

2221. Fulk, R.D. 1978. "Old English *Icge* and *Incge*". *ES* 59.255-56.

2222. Funke, Otto. 1958. "Altenglische Wortgeographie (eine bibliographische Überschau)". *Wild Festschrift*, 39-51. [Bibliographical survey.]

2223. Gade, Kari Ellen. 1985. "Skjalf". *ANF* 100.59-71. [*Scylf, scylfe*, etc.]

2224. Gardner, Thomas J. 1966. "Old English *gārsecg*". *Archiv* 202.431-36.

2225. ———. 1968. *Semantic Patterns in Old English Substantival Compounds*. Heidelberg diss. 1967, 366 pp. Heidelberg: no publisher available.

2226. ———. 1969. "*preaniedla* and *preamedla*: Notes on Two Old English Abstracta in *-la(n)*". *NM* 70.255-61.

2227. Gillam, Doreen M.E. 1961. "The Use of the Term *æglæca* in *Beowulf* at Lines 893 and 2592". *SGG* 3.145-69. [Cf. Olsen [no. 2535].]

2228. ———. 1962. "The Connotations of O.E. *fæge*: With a Note on *Beowulf* and *Byrhtnoth*". *SGG* 4.165-202.
Review: K.H. Göller in *Anglia* 83.90-91 (1965).

2229. ———. 1964. "A Method for Determining the Connotations of OE Poetic Words". *SGG* 6.85-101.

  Review: Karl Heinz Göller in *Anglia* 85.70-71 (1967).

2230. Gneuss, Helmut. 1955. *Lehnbildungen und Lehnbedeutungen im Altenglischen*. Berlin-Biefeld-München: Erich Schmidt, viii + 184 pp. [Freie Univ. Berlin diss. 1953. Deals with Latin loans in the gloss of the *Vespasian Psalter*.]

  Reviews: K. Schneider in *Archiv* 192.201 (1955/56); Gerhard Graband in *ZAA* 3. 369-71 (1955); E.G. Stanley in *MLR* 50.565 (1955); E. Polomé in *Latomus* (Bruxelles) 14.583-84 (1955); Carrol E. Reed in *MLQ* 17.371 (1956); E. Haugen in *Language* 32.761-66 (1956); S. Einarsson in *MLN* 71.207-08 (1956); R. Quirk in *BGDSL*(T) 78.315-17 (1956); K. Brunner in *Anglia* 75.347-48 (1957); E.V.K. Dobbie in *Word* 13.172-75 (1957); R. Girvan in *RES* 8.45-51 (1957); O. Funke in *ES* 39.130-31 (1958); A. Rynell in *SN* 30.111-12 (1958); S.M. Kuhn in *JEGP* 57.329-31 (1958).

2231. ———. 1962. "Ergänzungen zu den ae. Wörterbuchen". *Archiv* 199.17-24.

2232. ———. 1973. "Vorarbeiten und Vorüberlegungen zu einem neuen Wörterbuch des Altenglischen". *Koziol Festschrfit*, 105-15.

2233. ———. 1982. "Some Problems and Principles of the Lexicography of Old English". *Schneider Festschrift*, 153-68.

2234. ———. 1985. "Linguistic Borrowing and Old English Lexicography: Old English Terms for the Books of the Liturgy". *Cameron Studies*, 107-30.

2235. Godden, Malcolm R. 1980. "Ælfric's Changing Vocabulary". *ES* 61.206-23.

2236. Goepp, Philip H., II. 1949. "Verstegan's 'Most Ancient Saxon Words'". *Malone Festschrfit*, 249-55. [An analysis of the list of 'Saxon' words given in Richard Verstegan's *Restitution of Decayed Intelligence* (1605).]

2237. Golden, John. 1969. "An Onomastic Allusion in Cædmon's *Hymn*?". *NM* 70.627-29. [Discusses the West Saxon *eorðan bearnum* for 'children of Adam'.]

2238. Gottzmann, Carola L. 1977. "Sippe". *Sprachw* 2.217-58. [Includes OE kinship terms.]

2239. Gough, John Vaughan. 1974. "Some Old English Glosses". *Anglia* 92.279-90. [Cf. Bierbaumer [no. 2082].]

2240. Gradon, Pamela. 1947/48. "A Contribution to Old English Lexicography". *SN* 20.199-202. [Lists the extant OE forms of the word *Sion*.]

2241. Gramm, Willi. 1938. *Die Körperpflege der Angelsachsen*. Heidelberg: Carl Winter, 137 pp. [A study of OE words dealing with the ideal of bodily beauty and with the care of the body.]

2242. Grandinger, Maria Margareta. 1933. *Die Bedeutung des Adjektivs 'good' in der religiösen Literatur der Angelsachsen*. Landshüt: Thomann, xii + 83 pp. [München diss.]

2243. Green, Dennis Howard. 1968. "Old English *Dryht*: A New Suggestion". *MLR* 63.392-406. [Criticizes Dick [no. 2170].]

2244. Greenfield, Stanley Brian. 1977. "Old English Words and Patristic Exegesis — *hwyrftum scriþað*: A Caveat". *MP* 75.44-48.

2245. Grinda, Klaus R. 1975. *'Arbeit' und 'Mühe': Untersuchungen zur Bedeutungsgeschichte altenglischer Wörter*. München: Wilhelm Fink, 319 pp. [Originally Heidelberg diss. 1965.]

Reviews: E.G. Stanley in *N&Q* n.s. 24.481 (1977); Michael Pflaum in *Erasumus* 30.269-72 (1978); R. Sch[ützeichel] in *BN* N.F. 13.70 (1978); Ashley Crandell Amos in *N&Q* n.s. 26.245-46 (1979); C.T. Berkhout in *Speculum* 54.807-08. (1979); Angus Cameron in *MAE* 49.163-64 (1980); Klaus Bitterling in *IF* 86.365-67 (1981).

2246. ———. 1979. "Die Hide und verwandte Landmasse im Altenglischen". *Untersuchungen zur Flur* I, 92-133.

2247. ———. 1985. "Altenglischen *ceap*: zur Verwendung von Simplex, Komposita und Ableitungen". *Untersuchungen zu Handel und Verkehr der vor- und frühgeschichtlichen Zeit in Mittel- und Nordeuropa, III: Der Handel des frühen Mittelalters*, ed. Klaus Düwel, et al. (= Abhandlungen der Akademie der Wissenschaften in Göttingen, Philologisch-historische Klass, 3: 150), 347-80.

2248. Grube, Frank W. 1963. "Old English Food and Food Names". *Northwest Missouri State College Studies* (Maryville, MO) 27: February. 3-28.

2249. ———. 1963. "Old English Vegetable Terms". *Northwest Missouri State College Studies* 27: May. 3-30.

2250. Gruber, Loren C. 1974. "Motion, Perception, and *oþþæt* in *Beowulf*". *In Geardagum* 1.31-37.

2251. Grüner, Rolf. 1972. *Die Verwendung der unbestimmten substantivischen Zeitbegriffswörter in der altenglischen Dichtersprache*. Zürich: Juris, 195 pp. [Zürich diss.]

2252. Günther, Veronika and Walther von Wartburg. 1960. "Das angelsächsiche Element im französischen Wortschatz". *Flasdieck Festschrift*, 113-28.

2253. Gusmani, Roberto. 1972. "Anglosassone *myltestre* 'meretrix'". *SGerm* n.s. 10.157-67.

2254. Gutch, Ulrike. 1979. *Altenglisch 'cnawan', 'cunnan', 'witan', neuenglisch 'know': eine bedeutungsgeschichtliche Untersuchung*. Freie Univ. Berlin diss., 254 pp. [Abstr. in *DA* 46.4104C (1985).]

2255. Gutenbrunner, Siegfried. 1936. "Der Malvenname ags. *geormanlēaf*" *ZMaF* 12.40-42.

2256. Haessler, Luise. 1935. "Old English *bebeodan* and *forbeodan*". *Language* 11.211-15.

2257. Hall, J.R. 1976. "*Friðgedal*: Genesis A 1142". *N&Q* n.s. 23.207-08.

2258. ———. 1977. "Perspective and Wordplay in the Old English *Rune Poem*". *Neophil* 61.453-60. [Discusses the double meaning of such words as *oferhyrned* in the poem.]

2259. ———. 1982. "*Mansceaðan*: Old English *Exodus* 37". *Neophil* 66.145-47.

2260. Hallander, Lars-Gunnar. 1966. *Old English Verbs in '-sian': A Semantic and Derivational Study*. (= SSE, 15.) Stockholm: Almqvist & Wiksell, 619 pp.

   Reviews: Conrad Lindberg in *SN* 38.402-05 (1966); Manfred Schentke in *ZAA* 16.79-80 (1968); C.J.E. Ball in *RES* n.s. 21.187-89 (1970); Kenneth Brooks in *MAE* 39.368-70 (1970); Herbert Koziol in *Archiv* 207.119-21 (1970/71); Simeon Potter in *MLR* 65.861-62 (1970); Hans Schabram in *Anglia* 93.454-58 (1975).

2261. ———. 1970. "Contributions to Old English Lexicography I: *Hwamm* ~ *Hwemm*". *ES* 51.497-507.

2262. ———. 1973. "Old English *dryht* and its Cognates". *SN* 45.20-31. [Apropos of Dick [no. 2170].]

2263. Halvorson, Nelius O. 1932. *Doctrinal Terms in Ælfric's Homilies*. (= Univ. of Iowa Studies, Humanistic Ser. 5:1.) Iowa City: Univ. of Iowa Press, 98 pp.

   Reviews: E.V. Gordon in *RES* 9.87-89 (1933); F. Delatte in *RBPH* 12.1147-48 (1933).

2264. Hamp, Eric P. 1976. "Etymologies: OE *feower*, OHG *niun*" *MGS* 2.1-2.

2265. ———. 1977. "Old English *lēod-*". *ES* 58.97-100.

2266. ———. 1979. "*Horst* and Method". *Penzl Festschrift*, 175-81. [On OE *hyrst*.]

2267. ———. 1985. "German *Bein*, Old English *bān*; Slavic *kostь*". *NOWELE* 6.67-70.

2268. Harbert, Bruce. 1974. "King Alfred's *æstel*". *ASE* 3.103-10.

2269. Harder, Hermann. 1935. "Ein ags. Sternbildname". *Archiv* 168.235-37. [Explains the OE gloss of *Hyadas* as *Raedgasram*.]

2270. ———. 1940. "Zur Herkunft von ahd. *thuris*, ags. *þyrs*, aisl. *þurs*". *Archiv* 175.90.

2271. Harmer, Florence E. 1950. "*Chipping* and *Market*: A Lexicographical Investigation". *The Early Cultures of North-West Europe* (H.M. Chadwick Memorial Studies), ed. Cyril Fox and Bruce Dickins, 333-60. Cambridge: Cambridge Univ. Press. [In certain texts purporting to belong to the pre-Conquest period.]

2272. Harris, Joseph. 1976. "*Stemnettan*: *Battle of Maldon*, line 122a". *PQ* 55.113-17.

2273. ———. 1977. "A Note on *eorðscræf/eorðsele* and Current Interpretations of *The Wife's Lament*". *ES* 58.204-08.

2274. Hatto, Arthur T. 1957. "Snake-Swords and Boar-Helms in *Beowulf*". *ES* 38.145-60 and 257-59. [On some terms used of swords in *Beowulf*.]

2275. Healey, Antonette diPaolo. 1985. "Dictionary of Old English: 1984 Progress Report". *OEN* 18:2.20-21. [For previous reports see Amos [nos. 2001-2007].]

2276. ———. 1985. "The Dictionary of Old English and the Final Design of its Computer System". *CHum* 19.245-49.

2277. Helbig, Ludwig. 1960. *Altenglische Schlüsselbegriffe in den Augustinus- und Boetius-Bearbeitungen Alfreds des Grossen*. Frankfurt diss., 131 pp.

2278. Heller, L.G. 1973. "Late Indo-European Water Deity as Spearman: Greek *triton* and Old English *gārsecg*". *Names* 21.75-77.

2279. Hendrickson, John R. 1948. *Old English Prepositional Compounds in Relationship to Their Latin Originals* (= LM, 43.) Baltimore: Linguistic Society of America, 73 pp. [Pennsylvania diss.]

2280. Hetherington, Mary Sue. 1973. *Old English Lexicography 1550-1659*. Univ. of Texas at Austin diss., 417 pp. [Abstr. in *DA* 35.2969A (1974).]

2281. ———. 1975. "Sir Simonds D'Ewes and Method in Old English Lexicography". *TSLL* 17.75-92.

2282. ———. 1979. "Old English Lexicography: The First Eleven Decades, 1550-1659".. *Papers on Lexicography in Honor of Warren N. Cordell*, ed. James Edmund Congleton, John Edward Gates, and Donald Hobar, 125-39. Terre Haute, IN: Dictionary Society of North America, Indiana State Univ.

2283. ———. 1980. *The Beginnings of Old English Lexicography*. Spicewood, Texas: privately printed., vii + 344 pp. [Copies available from the author, College of Charleston, Charleston, SC.]

Reviews: Gilda Cilluffo in *Schede Medievali* 2.127-29 (1982); Basil Cottle in *RES* n.s. 33.446-47 (1982); Manfred Görlach in *Colloquia Germanica* 15.257-58 (1982); E.G. Stanley in *N&Q* n.s. 29.238-40 (1982); Martin Lehnert in *ZAA* 31.53-54 (1983); Fred C. Robinson in *Speculum* 58.1121 (1983); Johan Kerling in *ES* 65.174 (1984); Angelika Lutz in *Archiv* 221.160-63 (1984); Henry Woudhuysen in *YES* 14.302-03 (1984); Susan Cooper in *MAE* 54.291-92 (1985).

2284. ———. 1982. "The Recovery of the Anglo-Saxon Lexicon". *Anglo-Saxon Scholarship: The First Three Centuries*, ed. Carl T. Berkhout & Milton McC. Gatch, 79-89. Boston: Hall.

2285. Hietsch, Otto. 1955. "On the Authorship of the Old English *Phoenix*". *Anglo-America: Festschrift zum 70. Geburtstag von Professor Dr. Leo Hibler-Lebmannsport*, ed. Karl Brunner (= WBEP, 62), 72-79. Wien & Stuttgart: W. Braumüller. [Based on the frequency of nominal compounds.]

2286. Hill, Betty. 1955. "Notes on Five Difficult Glosses to the *Lindisfarne Gospels*". *MLR* 50.487-88.

2287. ———. 1957. "Four Anglo-Saxon Compounds". *RES* n.s. 8.162-66. [*All-efne, fifteig-dæg, hwit-corn*, and *lar-cnæht*, all found in the *Lindisfarne Gospels*.]

2288. Hill, Joyce. 1983. "On the Semantics of Old English *cempa* and *campian*". *Neophil* 67.273-76. [Cf. Morrison [no. 2513].]

2289. Hill, Thomas D. 1974. "The *fyrst ferhðbana*: Old English *Exodus*, 399". *N&Q* n.s. 21.204-05.

2290. Hille, Arnoldus. 1963. "OE *Seoluini* and ON *Sjóli*". *ES* 44.28-35.

2291. Hoad, T.F. 1985. "The Reconstruction of Unattested Old English Lexical Items". *Cameron Studies*, 131-50.

2292. Hofmann, Josef. 1963. "Altenglische und althochdeutsche Glossen aus Würzburg und dem weiteren angelsächsischen Missionsgebiet". *BGDSL*(H) 85.27-131.

2293. Hofstetter, Walter. 1979. "Der Erstbeleg von ae. *pryte/pryde*". *Anglia* 97.172-75.

2294. Holland, Joan. 1986. "Dictionary of Old English: 1985 Progress Report". *OEN* 19:2.21-22. [For previous reports, see Amos [no. 2001-2007] and Healey [no. 2275].]

2295. Hollowell, Ida Masters. 1978. "*Scop* and *Woðbora* in OE Poetry". *JEGP* 77.317-29.

2296. Holmes, Urban T., Jr. 1938. "Old French *Mangon*, Anglo-Saxon *Mancus*, Late Latin *Mancussus*, *Mancosus*, *Mancessus*, etc.". *PMLA* 13.34-37.

2297. Holthausen, Ferdinand. 1930. "Wortdeutungen" [Altenglische etymologien]. *IF* 48.254-67. [On OE *æg*, *bēam*, *behēfe*, *bīwan*, *blagettan*, *borettan*, *budda*, *būla*, *eafor*, *fadian*, *funta*, and fifty other words.]

2298. ———. 1933. "Angelsächsisches Allerlei". *Anglia B* 44.349-50.

2299. ———. 1934. "Altenglisches". *Anglia B* 45.19 [Discusses OE *blio(h)*; *strapul*; etc.]

2300. Hoops, Johannes. 1924. "Angelsächsisch *blæd*". *NM* 25.109-17.

2301. ———. 1929. "Altenglisch *gēap*, *horngēap*, *sǣgēap*". *EStn* 64.201-11.

2302. ———. 1930/31. "Altenglisch *ealuscerwen*, *meoduscerwen*". *EStn* 65.177-80. [Concerns *Beowulf* 769a.]

2303. ———. 1931/32. "Altenglisch *ealuscerwen* und kein Ende". *EStn* 66.3-5.

2304. ———. 1933. "Nochmals ae. *orc*". *Anglia* 57.110-11.

2305. Hoops, Reinald. 1936. "Ae. *nefa* (Zur Sachsenchronik a. 534)". *EStn* 70.429-31.

2306. Hopper, H.P. 1956. *A Study of the Function of the Verbal Prefix 'ge-' in the Lindisfarne Gospel of St. Matthew*. George Washington Univ. diss. [No further information available.]

2307. Horgan, A.D. 1963. "*Beowulf*, Lines 224-25". *EPS* 8.24-29. [Discusses the word *eoletes*.]

2308. Horgan, Dorothy M. 1980. "Patterns of Variation and Interchangeability in Some Old English Prefixes". *NM* 81.127-30.

2309. Horn, Wilhelm. 1929. "Ae. *tō*". *Archiv* 155.249.

2310. ———. 1935. "Altenglisch *hwæþere* 'dennoch'". *EStn* 70.46-48.

2311. Hotchner, Cecilia A. 1942. "A Note on *Dux Vitae* and *Lifes Lattiow*". *PMLA* 57.572-75. [Considers the phrase more likely to have been taken over by continental Latin writers from OE than vice versa.]

2312. Howlett, D.R. 1975. "Alfred's *æstel*". *EPS* 14.65-74.

2313. Huffines, Marion Lois. 1974. "OE *āglæce*: Magic and Moral Decline of Monsters and Men". *Semasia* (Amsterdam) 1.71-81.

2314. Hulbert, James Root. 1932. "A Note on Compounds in *Beowulf*". *JEGP* 31.504-08.

2315. Hunt, Tony. 1981. "The Old English Vocabularies in MS. Oxford, Bodley 730". *ES* 62.201-09.

2316. Ingersoll, Sheila Most. 1971. "*Scūr-heard*: A New Dimension of Interpretation". *MLN* 86.378-80.

2317. Jacobs, Nicholas. 1971. "OE. *wered* 'drink', *werod* 'sweet'". *N&Q* n.s. 18.404-07.

2318. Jankowsky, Kurt R. 1982. "On OE Time Concepts and Their Germanic and IE Cognates". *Schneider Festschrift*, 95-110. [Discusses 1. *fæc*, 2. *first*, 3. *hwīl*.]

2319. Jennings, Louis Girton. 1968. *The Old English Noun in Present English*. Pennsylvania diss., 245 pp. [Abstr. in *DA*, 29.2243-44A (1969).]

2320. Jiriczek, Otto L. 1930. "Zur Bedeutung von ae. *stedeheard* (*Judith*, 223)". *EStn* 64.212-18.

2321. Johannisson, Ture. 1941/42. "Altenglisch *incūð* und *oncȳð(ð)*". *Ekwall Festschrift* = *SN* 14.214-20.

2322. Johnson, William C., Jr. 1976. "Pushing and Shoving in *Beowulf*: A Semantic

Inquiry". *ELN* 14.81-87.

2323. Jolliffe, J.E.A. 1935. "The Old English Term *Snade*". *Antiquity* 9.220-22.

2324. Joly, André. 1967. "*Ge-* préfixe lexical en vieil anglais" *CJL* 12.78-89. [A semantic study of the OE prefix *ge-*, in both verbal and nominal use.]

2325. Juzi, Gertrud. 1939. *Die Ausdrücke des Schönen in der altenglischen Dichtung: Untersuchung über ein sprachliches Feld.* Zürich: Aschmann & Scheller, 139 pp. [Zürich diss.]

   Review: E. Schwentner in *IF* 59.344-45 (1949).

2326. Kartschoke, Dieter. 1977. "*Selfsceaft*". *ZDA* 106.73-82. [On the crux in *Genesis B* 523. Cf. Vickrey [no. 2776].]

2327. Kastovsky, Dieter. 1968. *Old English Deverbal Substantives Derived by Means of a Zero Morpheme.* Esslingen/N.: Bruno Langer Verlag, xv + 639 pp. [Tübingen diss.]

   Reviews: Ewald Standop in *IF* 75.356-59 (1970); Wolf-Peter Funk in *ZAA* 20.415-17 (1972).

2328. ———. 1971. "The Old English Suffix *-er(e)*". *Anglia* 89.285-325.

2329. ———. 1985. "Deverbal Nouns in Old and Modern English: from Stem-formation to Word-formation". *Historical Semantics*, 221-61.

2330. Keefer, Sarah Larratt. 1979. *The Influence of Glossing Traditions in the Vocabulary of the Old English Metrical Psalter.* Univ. of Toronto diss. (no pagination available). [Abstr. in *DA* 40.840A (1979).]

2331. Kellermann, Günter. 1954. *Studien zu den Gottesbezeichnungen der angelsächsischen Dichtung: Ein Beitrag zum religionsgeschichtlichen Verständnis der Germanenbekehrung.* Münster diss., xv + 411 pp.

2332. Ker, Neil R. 1932. "Old English *scægan*". *MAE* 1.137-38.

2333. ———. 1932. "Old English *hrohian*". *MAE* 1.208.

2334. Kern, Johan Hendrik. 1923. "A Ghostword". *Neophil* 8.301-03. [On *ofʒerād*.]

2335. Kiessling, Nicholas K. 1967/68. "Grendel: A New Aspect". *MP* 65.191-201. [On the meaning of *mære* in ll.103 and 762 of *Beowulf*.]

2336. Kirby, I.J. 1974. "Old English *ferð*". *N&Q* n.s. 21.443.

2337. Kirschner, Josef. 1975. *Die Bezeichnungen für Kranz und Krone im Altenglischen*. München diss., xix + 305 pp. [Abstr. in *EASG* 1975 (1976), 20-22.]

Review: E.G. Stanley in *N&Q* n.s. 24.97-98 (1977).

2338. Klaeber, Frederick. 1929. "Altenglische wortkundliche Randglossen". *Anglia B* 40.21-32. [Discusses *ent, sendan* (*Beowulf* 600), *belifan, (ge)wrecan*, etc.]

2339. ———. 1929. "*Belūcan* in dem altenglischen Reisesegen". *Anglia B* 40.283-84.

2340. ———. 1931/32. "Altenglisch *ealuscerwēn* und kein Ende". *EStn* 66.1-3.

2341. ———. 1935. "Altenglisch *begæð* 'bekennt', 'behauptet'". *Archiv* 166.81-82.

2342. Klegraf, Josef. 1971/72. "*Beowulf* 769: *ealuscerwen*". *Archiv* 208.108-12.

2343. Kleman, M. Maurice. 1953. "Three Old English Verbs for 'Cleanse, Purge'". *IALR* 1.179-84.

2344. Koban, Charles. 1963. *Substantive Compounds in Beowulf*. Univ. of Illinois diss., 329 pp. [Abstr. in *DA* 24.4175-76 (1964); *Linguistics* 9.110-11 (1964).]

2345. Kökeritz, Helge. 1963. "The Anglo-Saxon Unicorn". *Smith Festschrift*, 120-26. [On the OE glosses to *unicornus* to be found in the glosses of *Psalters*.]

2346. Kolb, Eduard. 1962. "English Light on the Scand. Assimilation of *ht* > *tt*". *ES* 43.307-10. [On Scandinavian loan words in English of the tenth and eleventh centuries.]

2347. ———. 1969. "The Scandinavian Loanwords in English and the Date of the West North Change MP > PP, NT > TT, NK > KK". *ES* 50.129-40.

2348. König, Günter. 1957. *Die Bezeichnungen für Farbe, Glanz und Helligkeit im Altenglischen*. Mainz: Universitätsdruckerei, 247 pp. [Mainz diss.]

Reviews: Erkki Penttilä in *NM* 62.118-21 (1961); Herbert Pilch in *IF* 67.121-22 (1962).

2349. Korhammer, Michael. 1985. "Viking Seafaring and the Meaning of Ohthere's *ambyrne wind*". *Cameron Studies*, 151-74.

2350. Kotzor, Günter. 1985. "Wind and Weather: Semantic Analysis and the Classification of Old English Lexemes". *Cameron Studies*, 175-96.

2351. Krämer, Peter. 1968. "Altenglisch *dyde* und altfriesisch *dwā*". *Festschrift für*

Otto Höffer zum 65. Geburtstag, ed. Helmut Birkhan & Otto Gschwantler, II, 315-26. Wien: Notring.

2352. ——. 1984. "Neuenglisch *to die* — ein skandinavisches Lehnwort? Überlegungen zu *Beowulf* 850a". *Linguistica et Philologica: Gedenkschrift für Björn Collinder (1894-1983)* (= Philologica Germanica, 6), ed. Otto Gschwantler, et al., 279-86. Wien: Braumüller.

2353. Kranz, Marie. 1973. *A Semantic Analysis of the Verbs Denoting Speech in the Anglo-Saxon Poem, 'Daniel'*. Catholic Univ. of America diss., 212 pp. [Abstr. in *DA* 33.6336A (1973).]

2354. Kristensson, Gillis. 1969. "Old English *gēol, *golu". *SN* 41.130-34.

2355. ——. 1971. "An Etymological Note: Old English *drȳgan* 'to make dry'". *SN* 43.257-59.

2356. ——. 1972. "A Note on Old English *slagu* 'slag, dross'". *SN* 44.274-77.

2357. ——. 1984. "Old English *glīse* 'a bright place' and Cognates". *N&Q* n.s. 31.149.

2358. ——. 1984. "Old English *cēo* 'a Clearing'". *NM* 85.59-60.

2359. Kroesch, Samuel. 1929. "The Semantic Development of OE *cræft*". *MP* 26.433-43.

2360. ——. 1929. "Semantic Borrowing in Old English". *Klaeber Festschrift*, 50-72.

2361. Krogmann, Willy. 1929. "Ags. *neorxenawang*". *Anglia* 53.337-44.

2362. ——. 1931. "Ae. *geneorð*". *Anglia* 55.397-99.

2363. ——. 1931/32. "Ae. *scerwan*". *EStn* 66.346.

2364. ——. 1932. "Ae. *orcnēas*". *Anglia* 56.40-42.

2365. ——. 1932. "Ae. *īsig*". *Anglia* 56.438-39.

2366. ——. 1932. "*Ealuscerwen* und *meoduscerwen*". *EStn* 67.15-23.

2367. ——. 1933. "Ae. *orc*". *Anglia* 57.112.

2368. ——. 1933. "Ae. *gang*". *Anglia* 57.216-17.

2369. ———. 1933. "Ae. *dyde*". *Anglia* 57.377-95.

2370. ———. 1933. "*Orc* und *orcnēas*". *Anglia* 57.396.

2371. ———. 1933/34. "Got. *iddja* und ae. *ēode*". *EStn* 68.155-57.

2372. ———. 1934. "Ae. *neorx[e]nawang* 'Paradies'". *Anglia* 58.28-29.

2373. ———. 1934. "Ae. *strosle* 'Drossel'". *Anglia* 58.448.

2374. ———. 1934. "Ae. *geormanlēaf* und der Name der Germanen". *EStn* 69.161-79.

2375. ———. 1934. "Ae. *ēolet (Beowulf* 224)". *Anglia* 58.351-58.

2376. ———. 1935. "Ae. *tō-sōcnung*". *Anglia* 59.271-72.

2377. ———. 1935. "Altengl. *āntīd* und seine Sippe". *EStn* 70.40-45.

2378. ———. 1935/36. "Ae. *defu*". *EStn* 70.321-22.

2379. ———. 1935/36. "Ae. *georman-, geormen-*". *EStn* 70.322-23.

2380. ———. 1935. "Hoch- und tiefstufige Doubletten in Zusammensetzungen". *BGDSL*(H) 59.313-16. [Discusses OE *fullest* and *fylst*, *ofost* and *ofst*.]

2381. ———. 1936. "Zwei ae. Wortdeutungen". *Anglia* 60.33-38. [Discusses *þēofentu* and *ēowend*.]

2382. ———. 1936. "Ae. Wortdeutungen". *Anglia* 60.369-73. [Discusses 1. *ambeht, ymbeaht, embeht*, 2. *gullisc*, 3. *swicn*.]

2383. ———. 1936. "Ae. *geormanlēaf*". *ZMaF* 12.173-81.

2384. ———. 1937. "Altenglisches". *Anglia* 61.351-60. [Comparative philological notes on OE *glemn*; *gewesan*; *eg(e)sa*; *gangan*; *dyst, dyþ*.]

2385. ———. 1939. "Altenglisches". *Anglia* 63.67-72 and 398-99. [The former (pp. 67-72) discusses 1. **drocen* 'trocken'; 2. *byrig*; 3. *haranhīge* und *higre*, and the latter (pp. 398-99) 1. *Beowulf* 3114f.; 2. Ae. *ȳst*.]

2386. ———. 1940/41. "Ae. *(n)eorx(e)nawang*". *EStn* 74.1-18.

2387. ———. 1954/55. "*Neorxna wang* und *Iða vǫllr*". *Archiv* 191.31-43. [On the OE name of the paradise.]

2388. Kryger Kabell, Inge. 1987. "The Old English *rēodmuþa* and the Bird Today Called the Pheasant". *SN* 59.3-6.

2389. Kuhn, Hans. 1962. "Angelsächsisch *cōp* 'Kappe' und seinesgleichen". *Festgabe für L.L. Hammerich: Aus Anlass seines siebzigsten Geburtstags*, 113-24. Copenhagen: Naturmodens Sproginstitut.

2390. Kuhn, Sherman McAllister. 1947. "Synonyms in the Old English *Bede*". *JEGP* 46.168-76.

2391. ———. 1979. "Old English *aglæca* — Middle Irish *óclach*". *Penzl Festschrift*, 213-30.

2392. ———. 1986. "Old English *macian*, Its Origin and Dissemination" *JEngL* 19.49-93.

2393. Kühlwein, Wolfgang. 1967. *Die Verwendung der Feindseligkeitsbezeichnungen in der altenglischen Dichtersprache* (= KBAA, 5.) Neumünster: Karl Wachholtz, 316 pp.

Reviews: Ewald Standop in *Anglia* 87.73-80 (1969); Nils Erik Enkvist and Håkan Ringbom in *SN* 41.457-59 (1969); Ulf Bartholomae in *BGDSL*(T) 91.401-04 (1969); Stephen Ullmann in *Archiv* 206.372-74 (1969/70); Klaus Faiss in *Linguistics* 59.108-13 (1970); Aleš Svoboda in *SFFBU* 19.142-43 (1970) and *ČMF* 52.142-43 (1971); E.G. Stanley in *IF* 75.352-56 (1970); Klaus Hansen in *ZAA* 19.417-19 (1971).

2394. ———. 1968. *Modell einer operationellen lexikologischen Analyse: Altenglisch 'Blut'* (= AF, 95.) Heidelberg: Carl Winter, 79 pp.

Reviews: Nils Erik Enkvist and Håkan Ringbom in *SN* 41.457-59 (1969); Hartmut Beckers in *Archiv* 208.122-23 (1971/72).

2395. ———. 1969. "Andreascrux 1241 und Beowulfcrux 849". *BGDSL*(T) 91.77-81. [Discusses *hat of heolfre* (*Andrea* 1241) and *haton heolfre* (*Beowulf* 849).]

2396. ———. 1971. "Entropie und Redundanz in der Angelsächsischen Poesie". *Linguistics* 68.13-28.

2397. Kylstra, H.E. 1974. "Ale und Beer in Germanic". *Maxwell Festschrift*, 7-16. [Corroborates the thesis of Fell [no. 2195].]

2398. Lane, George S. 1933. "Two Germanic Etymologies". *JEGP* 32.293-95. [Contains one section dealing with OE *mētan*.]

2399. Langenfelt, Gösta. 1931. "The OE. Paradise Lost". *Anglia* 55.250-65. [Discusses *neorxnawang*.]

2400. ———. 1936. "The OE. Paradise Lost: *neorxnawang*". *Anglia* 60.374-76.

2401. Lapidge, Michael. 1982. "Some Old English Sedulius Glosses for BN Lat. 8092". *Anglia* 100.1-17. [Prints a number of OE glosses with annotations.]

2402. Law, Vivien. 1977. "The Latin and Old English Glosses in the *Ars Tatuini*". *ASE* 6.77-89.

2403. Leavitt, Jay A., John Lawrence Mitchell, and Eric Inman. 1980. "KIT and the Investigation of Old English Prose". *ALLCB* 8.1-14. [Contains an investigation of variants of *cyning* in the Parker and Laud Anglo-Saxon Chronicle.]

2404. Leisi, Ernst. 1959. "Aufschlussreiche altenglische Wortinhalte". *Sprache: Schlüssel zur Welt. Festschrift für Leo Weisgerber*, ed. Helmut Gipper, 309-18. Düsseldorf: Pädagogischer Verl. Schwann.

2405. Lendinara, Patrizia. 1976. "Ags. *wlanc*: Alcune Annotazioni". *AION-SG* 19.53-81.

2406. Lerner, L.D. 1951. "Colour Words in Anglo-Saxon". *MLR* 46.246-49.

2407. Leyerle, John. 1971. "*The Dictionary of Old English*: A Progress Report". *CHum* 5.279-83. [Also printed in *OEN* 4:2.3-9 (1971).]

2408. Liebermann, Felix. 1924. "Angelsächsisch *lidwicas*". *Archiv* 147.249-50.

2409. ———. 1927. "Ags. *oððe* 'und'". *Archiv* 151.79-80.

2410. ———. 1927. "Ags. *hydesace* 'Fellsack'". *Archiv* 151.80.

2411. ———. 1927. "Ælfreds *dulmun* aus Isidor". *Archiv* 151.80.

2412. Lindeman, Fredrik O. 1967. "Gotisch *iddja* und altenglisch *ēode*". *IF* 72.275-86.

2413. Lindemann, John William Richard. 1957. '*Ge-*' *as a Preverb in Late Old English Prose: Its Meaning and Function as Suggested by a Collation of West-Saxon, Mercian, and Northumbrian Versions of 'The Gospel According to Saint Matthew'*. Wisconsin diss., 460 pp. [Abstr. in *DA* 17.2004-05 (1957).]

2414. ———. 1965. "Old English Preverbal *Ge-*: A Re-examination of Some Current Doctrines". *JEGP* 64.65-83.

2415. ———. 1970. *Old English Preverbal 'Ge-': Its Meaning*. Charlottesville: The Univ. Press of Virginia, x + 71 pp.

Reviews: R.W. Z[andvoort] in *ES* 52.302 (1971); M.M. Makovskij in *VJa* 1972, 153-56 (1972); Norman Eliason in *SAB* 37:2.93-95 (1972); M.L. Samuels in

MAE 41.289-92 (1972); E.G. Stanley in *Anglia* 91.493-94 (1973); Ruta Nagucka in *Linguistics* 137.108-11 (1974); David L. Shores in *AS* 49.281-83 (1974 [1976]); Klaus Bitterling in *BGDSL*(T) 97.105-07 (1975); Udo Fries in *Archiv* 213.168-70 (1976).

2416. Lindkvist, Harald. 1926. "A Study on Early Medieval York". *Anglia* 50.345-94. [A survey of the principal topographical nomenclature in York during the 10th-11th centuries.]

2417. Linke, G. 1937. "Zu ae. *blægettan* = blöken, schreien". *Archiv* 172.64-65.

2418. ———. 1938. "Zur Präposition *betweoh* und zum Zahlwort *tuwa* im ags. Beda". *Archiv* 173.71-72.

2419. ———. 1939. "Grammatische und phraseologische Tautologie im ae. Beda". *Archiv* 175.98-101.

2420. Löfvenberg, Mattias T. 1945. "An Etymological Note". *SN* 17.259-64. [On OE *cȳte*, *cēte*.]

2421. ———. 1956. "Old English *twicele*". *SMSpr* 19.125-28. [On the word found in a late 12th century transcript of an OE charter of 1005.]

2422. Lotspeich, C.M. 1941. "Old English Etymologies". *JEGP* 40.1-4. [Discusses *āglǣca*, *eoletes*, *nerhsnawang*, *tintrega*, *endebyrdnes*, and *lǣwede*.]

2423. Lucas, Peter J. 1969. "*Exodus* 480: *mod gerymde*". *N&Q* n.s. 16.206-07.

2424. Ludlum, Charles Daniel, Jr. 1954. *A Critical Commentary on the Vocabulary of the Canterbury Psalter*. Stanford diss., 129 pp. [Abstr. in *DA* 14.979-80 (1954).]

2425. Lühr, Rosemarie. 1976. "Die Wörter für 'oder' in den germanischen Sprachen". *MSS* 34.77-94.

2426. Luick, Karl. 1924. "Zu ae. *onʒēan*". *Anglia B* 35.190-92.

2427. Lumiansky, Robert Mayer. 1947. "Old English *onbyrð* in Wærferð's *Dialogues of Gregory*". *MLR* 42.358.

2428. ———. 1949. "The Contexts of O.E. *Ealuscerwen* and *Meoduscerwen*". *JEGP* 48.116-26.

2429. Lynch, Eileen Dorothy. 1972. *A Statistical Study of the Collocations in 'Beowulf'*. Univ. of Massachusetts diss., vi + 558 pp. [Abstr. in *DA* 33.2898A (1972).]

2430. Madden, John F. 1953. "A Frequency Word-Count of Anglo-Saxon Poetry". *MS* 15.221-25.

2431. Magoun, Francis Peabody, Jr. 1929. "Recurring First Elements in Different Nominal Compounds in *Beowulf* and the *Elder Edda*". *Klaeber Festschrift*, 73-78.

2432. ———. 1945. "The Domitian Bilingual of the Old-English Annals: Notes on the F-Text". *MLQ* 6.371-80. [Provides corrections to the published text and lexical notes on eight words.]

2433. ———. 1948. "OE *ealle þrage*". *MLN* 63.127-28. [On the meaning of the phrase.]

2434. Maisenhelder, Karl. 1935. *Die altenglische Partikel 'and', mit Berücksichtigung anderer germanischer Sprachen*. Königsfeld: Herbert Stolz, 87 pp. [Heidelberg diss.]

2435. Malone, Kemp. 1928. "The Kenning in *Beowulf* 2220". *JEGP* 27.318-24.

2436. ———. 1930. "Old English *(ge)hȳdan* 'heed'". *Jespersen Festschrift*, 45-54.

2437. ———. 1933. "The Suffix of Appurtenance in *Widsith*". *MLR* 28.315-25.

2438. ———. 1937. "Old English *Cáre, Cáser, Cásere*". *Anglia B* 48.221-22. [Accounts for the loss of *s* in the first form.]

2439. ———. 1941. "Old English *bēagas*". *Anglia B* 52.179-80.

2440. ———. 1947. "Old English *gār* 'storm'". *ES* 28.42-45.

2441. ———. 1951. "A Note on *Beowulf* 2466". *JEGP* 50.19-21. [On the epithet *heaðoric*.]

2442. Marckwardt, Albert Henry. 1942. "The Verbal Suffix *-ettan* in Old English". *Language* 18.275-81.

2443. ———. 1947. "Nowell's *Vocabularium Saxonicum* and Somner's *Dictionarium*". *PQ* 26.345-51. [Points out Somner's dependence on Nowell's manuscript dictionary of OE.]

2444. ———. 1947. "An Unnoted Source of English Dialect Vocabulary". *JEGP* 46.177-82. [On Laurence Nowell's MS dictionary *Vocabularium Saxonicum* (c1565).]

2445. ———. 1948. "The Sources of Laurence Nowell's *Vocabularium Saxonicum*". *SP* 45.21-36.

2446. Marquardt, Hertha. 1938. *Die altenglischen Kenningar: Ein Beitrag zur Stilkunde altgermanischer Dichtung.* (= Schriften der Königsberger Gelehrten Gesellschaft, 14: 3.) Hall/S.: Niemeyer, xvi + 238 pp.
Reviews: Fr. Klaeber in *Anglia B* 49.321-26 (1938); G. Linke in *Archiv* 174.251-52 (1938); F.R. Schröder in *GRM* 26.467 (1938); Jan de Vries in *Museum* 46.296 (1939); S. Potter in *MLR* 34.128 (1939); J.W. Rankin in *JEGP* 38.282-85 (1939); A.G. van Hamel in *ES* 21.12 (1939); Anne Holtsmark in *ANF* 55.284-87 (1940); K. Malone in *MLN* 55.73-74 (1940); D.W. Reed in *LGRP* 62.196-97 (1941) and *Names* 6.241-47 (1958).

2447. Martz, Otto. 1939. *Die Wiedergabe biblischer Personenbezeichnungen in der altenglischen Missionssprache* (= BEP, 33.) Bochum-Langendreer: H. Pöppinghaus, xxi + 79 pp.

2448. Marynissen, C. 1977. "Een Oudengels -*cin* suffix?". *Nku* 9.51-78. [Especially on personal names.]

2449. McCord, Laura Ruth. 1979. *A Study of the Meanings of 'Hliehan' and 'Hleahtor' in Old English Literature.* Univ. of Missouri-Columbia diss., 173 pp. [Abstr. in *DA* 41.2101A (1980).]

2450. ———. 1980. "Morris's Translation of *Hleahtras* in *Blickling Homily IV*". *N&Q* n.s. 27.488-89.

2451. McGovern, John F. 1971. "The Meaning of *Gesette Land* in Anglo-Saxon Land Tenure". *Speculum* 46.589-96.

2452. McLintock, D.R. 1959. "O.E. *Wīs* and *(Ge)wiss*". *ArchL* 11.18-20.

2453. McNair, John R. 1984. "An Early Hard Word List: Stephen Batman's "A Note of Saxon Wordes"". *Neophil* 68.317-19.

2454. Meid, Wolfgang. 1966. "Die Königsbezeichnung in den germanischen Sprachen". *Sprache* 12.182-89. [On OE *rīca*, *þēoden*, *cyning*, *dryhten*, and their Germanic cognates.]

2455. Meissner, P. 1934-35. "Studien zum Wortschatz Ælfrics". *Archiv* 165.11-19; 166.30-39; 166.205-15. [A systematic study of Ælfric's vocabulary. Criticized by Schabram [no. 2657].]

2456. Menner, Robert J. 1944. "Two Old English Words". *MLN* 59.106-12. [Discusses Old Anglian *(ge)strynd* and OE *gullisc*.]

2457. ———. 1947. "The Vocabulary of the Old English Poems on Judgement Day". *PMLA* 62.583-97.

2458. ———. 1948. "Anglian and Saxon Elements in Wulfstan's Vocabulary". *MLN* 63.1-9.

2459. ———. 1949. "The Anglian Vocabulary of the *Blickling Homilies*". *Malone Festschrift*, 56-64.

2460. Meritt, Herbert Dean. 1933. "Old English Scratched Glosses in Cotton MS. Tiberius C. ii". *AJP* 54.305-22.

2461. ———. 1936. "Old English Sedulius Glosses". *AJP* 57.140-50.

2462. ———. 1938. "Possible Elliptical Compounds in Old English Glosses". *AJP* 59.209-17.

2463. ———. 1941. "Some Minor Ways of Word-Formation in Old English". *Stanford Studies in Language and Literature for the 50th Anniversary of Stanford University*, ed. Hardin Craig, 74-80. Stanford, CA: Stanford Univ. Press.

2464. ———. 1941. "Three Studies in Old English". *AJP* 62.331-39. [1. The context for some Latin words in the Harleian glossary. 2. An Old English term for waled ornamentation. 3. A ghost-word (*oferwyrþe*) and a dark gloss.]

2465. ———. 1944. "The Old English Glosses *deðæ* and *minnæn*: A Study in Ways of Interpretation". *JEGP* 43.434-46. [The two words dicussed are in Eadwine's *Canterbury Psalter*, glossing *manipulos*.]

2466. ———. 1945. *Old English Glosses (A Collection)* (= The Modern Language Association of America Ser., 16.) New York: Modern Language Association of America; London: Oxford Univ. Press, xx + 135 pp. [Contains about 2300 glosses from Latin MSS of the 8th to the 12th centuries.]

Reviews: S.M. Kuhn in *JEGP* 45.344-46 (1946); Howard Meroney in *MLN* 62.566-68 (1947); Phyllis Hodgson in *RES* 23.155-56 (1947); J.T.P. in *MAE* 17.57-59 (1948).

2467. ———. 1947. "Studies in Old English Vocabulary". *JEGP* 46.413-27. [Discusses 60 words known only from glosses, about half of which the author suggests are ghost words.]

2468. ———. 1950. "Twenty Hard Old English Words". *JEGP* 64.231-41.

2469. ———. 1954. *Fact and Lore about Old English Words* (= Stanford Univ. Pubs., Language and Literature, 13.) Stanford, CA: Stanford Univ. Press; London: Oxford Univ. Press, xiv + 226 pp. [Lexicographical notes on nearly 700 words entered in OE dictionaries, 204 of which are marked as 'ghost words'.]

Reviews: J.R. Hulbert in *MP* 53.58 (1955/56); Robert A. Caldwell in *JEGP* 55.636-37 (1956); Sherman M. Kuhn in *Speculum* 31.392-95 (1956).

2470. ———. 1957. "Old English Glosses to Gregory, Ambrose and Prudentius". *JEGP* 56.65-68.

2471. ———. 1961. "Old English Glosses, Mostly Dry Point". *JEGP* 60.441-50.

2472. ———. 1962. "The Leiden Gloss to *Histrionibus*". *Anglia* 80.379-83.

2473. ———. 1963. "Strange Sauce from Worcester". *Brodeur Festschrift*, 152-54. [On the OE gloss *sweorsaga*.]

2474. ———. 1968. "The Old English Ghost Word *Drisne*". *NM* 69.47-53.

2475. ———. 1968. *Some of the Hardest Glosses in Old English*. Stanford, CA: Stanford Univ. Press, xiii + 130 pp.

Reviews: A. Campbell in *MAE* 38.306-08 (1969); M.M. Makovskij in *Ètimologija* (Moskva) 1970, 387-93; Sherman M. Kuhn in *JEGP* 70.651-54 (1971).

2476. ———. 1968. "*Thestisuir* in the Leiden Glossary". *Anglia* 86.155-57.

2477. ———. 1969. "Old English *Hūnsporan*". *Willard Festschrift*, 70-72.

2478. ———. 1972. "Conceivable Clues to Twelve Old English Words". *ASE* 1.193-205.

2479. Meroney, Howard M. 1942. "Old English ðær 'if'". *JEGP* 41.201-09. [With particular reference to *Christ and Satan* 107 and *Beowulf* 2573.]

2480. ———. 1943. *Old English 'upp', 'uppe', 'uppan', and 'uppon'*. Chicago diss., 95 pp.

2481. ———. 1945. "Irish in the Old English Charms". *Speculum* 20.172-82. [Discusses the non-Anglo-Saxon words in these charms.]

2482. Metcalf, Allan A. 1973. *Poetic Diction in the Old English Meters of Boetius* (= De Proprietatibus Litterarum, Ser. Practica, 50.) The Hague: Mouton, x + 166 pp.

Reviews: Patrizia Lendinara in *AION-SG* 17.254-57 (1974); Nicholas Jacobs in *MAE* 44.282-84 (1975); Fred C. Robinson in *Speculum* 52.714-15 (1977); E.G. Stanley in *N&Q* n.s. 24.1-2 (1977).

2483. Meyer, Willy. 1942. "Die Bedeutung des altenglischen Wortes *hūru*". *Anglia B* 53.87-90.

2484. Mezger, Fritz. 1931. "Old English *ersc* (stubble-field)". *PMLA* 46.90-92.

2485. ———. 1931. "Ae. *fæsl*, n. 'Nachkommenschaft' und ae. *cnósl* 'Nachkommenschaft, Geschlecht, Familie, Vaterland'". *Archiv* 160.91-92.

2486. ———. 1932. "Ae. *forecynren*, n. 'Nachkommenschaft' — *mægcynren*, n. 'Familie, Linie' — *cynren*, n. 'Art, Gattung, Familie, Verwandtschaft, Generation, Nachkommenschaft'". *Archiv* 161.228-29.

2487. ———. 1933. "Ae. *cræftiga* 'artifex' — ae. *byrdicga* 'plumaria'". *Archiv* 163.42-46.

2488. ———. 1935. "Ae. *fleard* n. = aisl. *flárád* n. — ae. *reord* < **rereð*?". *Archiv* 167.66-67.

2489. ———. 1935. "Ae. *tintreg(a)* < **tind-treg(a)*?". *Archiv* 167.252-53.

2490. ———. 1935. "Der germanische Kult und die ae. Feminia auf *-icge* und *-estre*". *Archiv* 168.177-84.

2491. ———. 1937. "Ae. *eart*, *earð*, *arð* 'du bist' und got. *sijum* 'wir sind'". *ZVS* 64.137-41.

2492. ———. 1938. "Gehört ae. *earwunga* 'gratis', got. *arwjo*, ahd. *arw(ing)un* zu got. *arjan* . . . 'pflügen'?". *Archiv* 173.209-10.

2493. ———. 1938. "Got. *niuklahs* 'wie ein Kind, unmündig', *niuklahei* 'Kleinmut, Unverstand': ae. *cild*; got. *kalkjom*". *Archiv* 174.78-79.

2494. ———. 1939. "Ae. *genæstan* 'streiten': ae. *hæst* 'Heftigkeit, Streit'". *Archiv* 175.97-98.

2495. ———. 1939. "OE *gehygd, hyht, hlyst, geþyld*". *ANF* 54.229-34.

2496. ———. 1941. "O.E. *tán*: Idg. *$d\underset{\smile}{u}\bar{o}u$; *$d\underset{\smile}{u}oi$-?". *JEGP* 40.348.

2497. ———. 1942. "The Formation of Old High German *diorna*, Old Saxon *thiorna*, Gothic *widwairna*, and Old English *níwerne*". *MLN* 57.432-33.

2498. ———. 1943. "Two Etymologies" *Language* 19.261-63. [The first considers OE *swicn*, 'clearance from a criminal charge'.]

2499. ———. 1946. "Gothic *aglaiti*, OE *aglæc*". *Word* 2.66-71.

2500. ———. 1951. "Two Notes on *Beowulf*". *MLN* 66.36-38. [On l. 446 *hafalan hȳdan* and l. 253 *lēasscēaweras*.]

2501. ———. 1951. "OE *Hāmweorðung*, *Beowulf* 2998". *JEGP* 50.243-45. [Argues against regarding the word as a compound.]

2502. ———. 1954. "Zu einigen idg. g- und l-Bildungen: Zur Bildung von ae. *þeowen*, *þeowincel* neben ahd. *huoniklin*". *ZVS* 72.103.

2503. ———. 1958. "Ae *intinga*, got. *inilō*". *ZVS* 75.210.

2504. ———. 1965. "Ae. *ǣnett*: ahd. *einōti*: mnd. *einihte*". *ZVS* 79.41-46.

2505. Miedema, Henricus Theodorus Jacobus. 1972. "De oudengelse muntnaam *sceat* en het oudfriese diminutivum *skeisen* 'duit'". *Nku* 4.320-32.

2506. Mills, Carl R. 1976. "Stylistic Applications of Ethnosemantics: Basic Color Terms in *Brunanburh* and *Maldon*". *Lang&S* 9.164-70.

2507. Miller, Miriam Youngerman. 1975. *The Concept of Deprivation in Old English Poetry*. Pennsylvania diss., 326 pp. [Abstr. in *DA* 36.2851A (1975). Explores the expression and function of the concept.]

2508. Mincoff, Marco K. 1933. *Die Bedeutungsentwicklung der ags. Ausdrücke für 'Kraft' und 'Macht'* (= Palaestra, 188.) Leipzig: Mayer und Müller, 156 pp. [Berlin diss.]

Reviews: J. Daniels in *ES* 17.22 (1935); H. Marcus in *Archiv* 166.292-93 (1935); F. M[ossé] in *RG* 26.378 (1935); Arthur Szogs in *Anglia B* 45.353-55 (1935).

2509. Mitchell, Bruce. 1965. "Bede's *Habere* = Old English *Magan*?". *NM* 66.107-11.

2510. Molinari, Maria Vittoria. 1983. "Per un'analisi tipologica della kenning anglosassone". *AION-SG* 26.29-52.

2511. Moore, Bruce. 1976. "*Eacen* in *Beowulf* and Other Old English Poetry". *ELN* 13.161-65.

2512. Morris, William Still. 1968. *Possible Solutions to Some Old English Words of Uncertain Etymology*. Stanford diss., 229 pp. [Abstr. in *DA* 29.587A (1968).]

2513. Morrison, Stephen. 1979. "OE *cempa* in Cynewulf's *Juliana* and the figure of the *miles Christi*". *ELN* 17.81-84. [cf. Hill [no. 2288].]

2514. ———. 1980. "*Beowulf* 698a, 1273a: *frōfor ond fultum*". *N&Q* n.s. 27.193-96 [On the meaning of the phrase.]

2515. ———. 1987. "On Some Noticed and Unnoticed Scratched Glosses". *ES* 68.209-13.

2516. Most, Sheila Marie. 1970. *Intensive and Restrictive Modification in a Select Corpus of Old English Poetry and Prose*. Northwestern diss., 344 pp. [Abstr. in *DA* 30.2992-93A (1970). See also Ingersoll [no. 1478]]

2517. Munske, Horst H. 1970 [1971]. "Angelsächsisch-altfriesische Beziehungen in der Rechtsterminolgie für Missetaten". *Flecht op 'e koai: Stúdzjes oanbean oan Prof. Dr. W.J. Buma to syn sechstichste jierdei*, ed. Teake Hoekema, et al. (= Fryske Akademy, 382), 40-52. Groningen: Wolters-Noordhoff.

2518. Murtagh, Marie B. 1985. *Some Words for 'lord' in Old English Poetry: an Investigation of Word Meaning and Use*. Boston diss., 303 pp. [Abstr. in *DA* 46.420A (1985).]

2519. Must, Gustav. 1960. "English *holy*, German *heilig*". *JEGP* 59.184-89. [Traces the meaning of OE *hālig* from its pre-Christian sense of 'whole' to its Christian one.]

2520. Mustanoja, Tauno Frans. 1950. "Notes on Some Old English Glosses in Aldhelm's *De Laudibus Verginitatis*". *NM* 51.49-50. [Deals with nineteen of the glosses.]

2521. Neuhaus, Hans Joachim. 1985. "Design Options for a Lexical Database of Old English". *Cameron Studies*, 197-209.

2522. Nichols, Ann Eljenholm. 1964. "*Awendan*: A Note on Ælfric's Vocabulary". *JEGP* 63.7-13.

2523. Nickel, Gerhard. 1966. "Operational Procedures in Semantics, with Special Reference to Medieval English". *Problems in Semantics, History of Linguistics, Linguistics and English*, ed. Francis P. Dinneen (= *Monograph Series on Languages and Linguistics: Report of the 17th Annual Round Table Meeting on Linguistics and Language Studies*, 19), 34-43. Washington, D.C.: Georgetown Univ. Press. [Discusses OE *guð*, *fæhðe*, *hild*, etc.]

2524. Niwa, Yoshinobu. 1966. "The Preverb *ge-* Added to *niman* in the OE Gloss to the *Lindisfarne Gospels*". *SEL* English No. 1966, 65-79.

2525. ———. 1974. "On the Collective Meaning of OE Preverb *ge-*". *SEL* English No. 1974, 155-67.

2526. Nowakowski, Mirosław. 1978. *A Study in Generative Historical Linguistics. On Language Change: Some Aspects of Old English Nominalizations*. (= *Uniwersytet im. Adama Mickiewicza w Poznaniu; Seria Filologia Angielska*,

9.) Poznań: Wydawnictwo Naukowe UAM, 122 pp. [Originally Poznań diss. 1973. Deals with nominal compounds in OE from a generative point of view.]

Review: Christopher Greene in *SAP* 11.205-07 (1979).

2527. O'Dwyer, P.F. 1967. "Old English *Unwitweorc*: A Ghost Word". *ELN* 5.79-80.

2528. Oehl, W. 1941. "Ags. *mamor* 'Schlaf' und Elementar-Paralleles". *IF* 57.1-24.

2529. Ogura, Michiko. 1986. "OE Verbs of Thinking". *NM* 87.325-41.

2530. Okasha, Elisabeth. 1976. "*Beacen* in Old English Poetry". *N&Q* n.s. 23.200-07.

2531. Oliphant, Robert (Thompson). 1962. *The Latin-Old English Glossary in British Museum MS Harley 3376*. Stanford diss., 392 pp. [Abstr. in *DA* 23.4345 (1963).]

2532. ———. 1963. "*Ætnes* and *Ytend*: Two Rare Old English Glossary Words". *PQ* 42.249-50.

2533. ———. 1964. "Two Questionable Old English Compounds: *Dungræg* and *Tīdscriptor*". *PQ* 43.123-25.

2534. ———. 1965. "Dark Lemmata Documented for Common Old English Words". *JEGP* 64.489-95.

2535. Olsen, Alexandra Hennessey. 1982. "The Aglæca and the Law". *AN&Q* 20:5/6.66-68. [On the OE word *æglæca*. Cf. Gillam [no. 2227].]

2536. O'Neill, Patrick. 1981. "Old English *Brondeguī*". *ES* 62.2-4.

2537. Onions, Charles Talbut. 1933. "Old English *hrohian*". *MAE* 2.73.

2538. Ono, Shigeru. 1975. "The Old English Verbs of Knowing". *SEL* English No. 1975, 33-60.

2539. ———. 1979 [1981]. "Supplementary Notes on *ongietan*, *undergietan* and *understandan*". *Poetica* 12.94-97.

2540. Osborn, Marijane and Stella Longland. 1980. "A Celtic Intruder in the Old English *Rune Poem*". *NM* 81.385-87.

2541. Ostheeren, Klaus. 1964. *Studien zum Begriff der 'Freude' und seinen Ausdrucksmitteln in altenglischen Texten (Poesie, Alfred, Ælfric)*. Freie Univ. Berlin diss., 289 pp. Heidelberg.

> Reviews: E.G. Stanley in N&Q n.s. 13.399-400 (1966); A. Campbell in RES n.s. 18.177-78 (1967); K.R. Brooks in MAE 37.71 (1968).

2542. Overholser, Lee Charles. 1971. *A Comparative Study of the Compound Use in 'Andreas' and 'Beowulf'*. Michigan diss., ix + 253 pp. [Abstr. in DA 32.1498A (1971).]

2543. Owen, Gale R. 1979. "Wynflæd's Wardrobe". ASE 8.195-222. [Deals with a large number of terms for women's clothing as they appear in a probably tenth-century will.]

2544. Page, Raymond Ian. 1968. "The Old English Rune *eoh*, *ih*, 'Yew Tree'". MAE 37.125-36.

2545. ———. 1969. "Old English *cyningstan*". LSE n.s. 3.1-5.

2546. ———. 1975. "'The Proper Toil of Artless Industry': Toronto's Plan for an Old English Dictionary". N&Q n.s. 22.146-55. [Review article on DOE Plan (1973).]

2547. ———. 1979. "OE. *Fealh* 'Harrow'". N&Q n.s. 26.389-93.

2548. ———. 1979. "More Old English Scratched Glosses". Anglia 97.27-45.

2549. ———. 1981. "New Work on Old English Scratched Glosses". Christophersen Festschrift, 105-15.

2550. ———. 1983. "Four Rare Old English Words". N&Q n.s. 30.2-8. [1. flæð, 2. cimbiren, 3. *cant(e)l, 4. *readlesc.]

2551. ———. 1985. "*Gerefa*: Some Problems of Meaning". Cameron Studies, 211-28.

2552. ———. 1985. "Two Problematic Old English Words". Cross Festschrift = LSE n.s. 16.198-207. [Discusses *byrding and *mexscofl.]

2553. Parker, Roscoe E. 1956. "*Gyd, Leoð,* and *Sang* in Old English Poetry". Univ. of Tennessee Studies in the Humanities (Nashville) 1.59-63.

2554. Paues, A.C. 1931. "*Cincdaðenan* in the Will of Wynflæd". MLR 26.168-69.

2555. Pedersen, Holger. 1930. "Oldengelsk *fæmne*". Jespersen Festschrift, 55-68.

2556. ———. 1941/42. "Angl. *wife* et *woman*". Ekwall Festschrift = SN 14.252-54. [Discusses the origin of OE *wif*, OHG *wib*.]

2557. Peeters, Christian. 1970. "Ahd. *sān(o)*, ae. *sōna*, got. *suns*". ZVS 84.231-32.

2558. ———. 1973. "On English *lie*, Old English *lēogan*, 'mentiri'". *ES* 54.58-59.

Review: R. D[erolez] in *ES* 55.494-95 (1974).

2559. Pelteret, David A.E. 1978. "Expanding the Word Hoard: Opportunities for Fresh Discoveries in Early English Vocabulary". *Indiana Social Studies Quarterly* (Muncie, IN) 31:1.56-65.

2560. Peltola, Niilo. 1971. "Observations on Intensification in Old English Poetry". *NM* 72.649-90.

2561. Penttilä, Erkki. 1956. *The Old English Verbs of Vision: A Semantic Study* (= MSNH, 18: 1.) Helsinki: Société Néophilologique, 209 pp. [Also deals with their development in early ME.]

Reviews: H. Gneuss in *BGDSL*(T) 79.399-402 (1957); Randolph Quirk in *MAE* 26.211-13 (1957); A. Culioli in *BSL* 53:2.165-67 (1957/58); A.A. Prins in *Museum* 64.246-48 (1958); H.A. Benning in *Anglia* 79.448-50 (1962).

2562. Peters, Robert Anthony. 1960. "OE *Ceargest*". *N&Q* n.s. 7.167. [On the word in *Guthlac* 393.]

2563. ———. 1961. *A Study of Old English Words for 'Demon' and 'Monster' and Their Relation to Englsih Place-Names*. Pennsylvania diss., 293 pp. [Abstr. in *DA* 22.253 (1961).]

2564. ———. 1963. "OE *ælf, -ælf, ælfen, -ælfen*". *PQ* 42.250-57. [Analyses the OE nouns *ælf, ælfen*, and nouns compounded with them.]

2565. Phillips, Michael Joseph. 1985. *Heart, Mind and Soul in Old English: A Semantic Study*. Univ. of Illinois at Urbana-Champaign diss., 325 pp. [Abstr. in *DA* 46.1925A (1986). Treats nine OE soul-terms: *hyge, sefa, ferhð, hreðer, breost, heorte, mod, sawol*, and *gast*.]

2566. Pilch, Herbert. 1952/53. "Das ae. Präverb ʒe-". *Anglia* 71.129-39.

2567. ———. 1968. "Modelle der englischen Wortbildung". *Marchand Festschrift*, 160-78. [Produces examples from Old and Modern English to illustrate his 'Modelle'.]

2568. Pillsbury, Paul W. 1970. "A Concordance to *The West Saxon Gospels*". *Computers and OE Concordances*, 48-56.

2569. Plank, Frans. 1982. "Coming into Being Among the Anglo-Saxons". *FoL* 16.73-118. [A lexical and morphosyntactic analysis of OE expressions for talking about having children, and especially about begetting them. Also printed in *Current Topics in EHL*, 239-78.]

2570. Pope, John Collins. 1955. "*Beowulf* 3150-3151: Queen Hygd and the Word *Geomeowle*". *MLN* 70.77-87.

2571. ———. 1986. "*Beowulf* 505, *gehedde*, and the Pretensions of Unferth". *Greenfield Festschrift*, 173-87.

2572. Pottle, Frederick A. 1931. "*Næs gīt yfel wīf* in the Old English *Apollonius*". *JEGP* 30.21-25.

2573. Price, Jocelyn. 1983. "Theatrical Vocabulary in Old English: A Preliminary Survey (1)". *METh* 5.58-71.

2574. ———. 1984. "Theatrical Vocabulary in Old English (2)". *METh* 6.101-25.

2575. Quinn, John J. 1961. "Ghost Words, Obscure Lemmata, and Doubtful Glosses in a Latin-Old English Glossary". *PQ* 40.313-18. [Discusses 16 words found in MS Cotton Cleopatra A. iii in the British Museum.]

2576. ———. 1966. "Some Puzzling Lemmata and Glosses in MS. Cotton Cleopatra A III". *PQ* 45.434-37. [Discusses 11 words in the MS.]

2577. Quirk, Randolph. 1963. "Poetic Language and Old English Metre". *Smith Festschrift*, 150-71. [Suggests that the alliterative linkage of words in OE sets up a semantic as well as a prosodic connection between them. Repr. in *Quirk Essays*, 1-19.]

2578. Rauch, Irmengard. 1964. "A Problem in Historical Synonymy". *Linguistics* 6.92-98. [On the words *ofermōd, -es, -a*; *ofermēde*; *oferhygd*; and *ofermētto* in the OE *Genesis B*.]

2579. Rauh, Hildegard. 1936. *Der Wortschatz der altenglischen Übersetzungen des Matthaeus-Evangeliums untersucht auf seine dialektische und zeitliche Gebundenheit*. Berlin: Funk, 75 pp. [Berlin diss.]

   Review: G. Linke in *Archiv* 170.245-46 (1936).

2580. Raw, Barbara. 1961. "A Latin-English Word-List in MS. Arundel 60". *EGS* 7.37-42. [Written in a mid-14th-century hand in the margins of ff.8-11 of the MS.]

2581. Redbond, W.J. 1932. "Notes on the Word *gar-secg*". *MLR* 27.204-06.

2582. ———. 1935. "The Old English Word *sætilcas*". *MLR* 30.210-11.

2583. ———. 1936. "Notes on the word *eolhx*". *MLR* 31.55-57.

2584. Reddick, R.J. 1985. "Old English *unlæd*: A Note on *Andreas*". *ELN* 22:4.1-10.

2585. Redwine, Bruce. 1982. ""Ofost is selest": The Pragmatics of Haste in *Beowulf*". *SN* 54.209-16. [Analyses the variety of words relating to 'haste' in *Beowulf*.]

2586. Reibel, David A. 1963. *A Grammatical Index to the Compound Nouns of Old English Verse (Based on the Entries in Grein-Köhler, 'Sprachschatz der angelsächsischen Dichter')*. Indiana diss., 212 pp. [Abstr. in *DA* 25.465-66 (1964); *Linguistics* 12.117-18 (1965). Cf. Christian Grein, *Sprachschatz der angelsächsischen Dichter*, rev. J. Köhler (Heidelberg, 1912).]

2587. Reinhard, Mariann. 1976. *On the Semantic Relevance of the Alliterative Collocations in 'Beowulf'*. (= SAA, 92.) Bern: Francke, 277 pp.

Reviews: E.G. Stanley in *Anglia* 96.502-03 (1978); F.C. Robinson in *Speculum* 53.839-41 (1978).

2588. Rice, Robert C. 1974/75. "*Hreowcearig* 'Penitent, Contrite'". *ELN* 12.243-50.

2589. Riehle, Wolfgang. 1966. "Über einige neuentdeckte altenglische Glossen". *Anglia* 84.150-55. [Discusses *halsberigold, cyniuiddan, steopsunu, uuf, hrooc, ciae*, and *osle* from the MS BN. lat. 1750.]

2590. Ritter, Otto. 1927. "Beiträge zur altenglischen Wort- und Namenkunde". *EStn* 62.106-12.

2591. Roberts, Jane. 1978. "Towards an Old English Thesaurus". *Poetica* 9.56-72.

2592. ———. 1980. "Old English *Un*- 'Very' and Unferth". *ES* 61.289-92.

2593. ———. 1985. "Some Problems of a Thesaurus Maker". *Cameron Studies*, 229-44.

2594. ———. 1985. "A Preliminary 'heaven' Index for Old English". *Cross Festschrift* = *LSE* n.s. 16.208-19.

2595. ——— and Christian Kay. 1986. "An Old English Thesaurus: A Progress Report". *MESN* 15.1-3.

2596. Robinson, Fred Colson. 1965. "Old English Lexicographical Notes". *PP* 8.303-07. [Five notes on OE words.]

2597. ———. 1968. "The American Element in *Beowulf*". *ES* 49.508-16. [Notes passages in which the phraseology of *Beowulf* corresponds to American English rather than to Present-day British English.]

2598. ———. 1970. "Lexicography and Literary Criticism: A Caveat". *Meritt Festschrift*, 99-110. [The examples are all taken from OE dictionaries.]

2599. ———. 1973. "Old English *Awindan, Of,* and *Sinhere*". *Koziol Festschrift*, 266-71.

2600. ———. 1985. "Metathesis in the Dictionaries: A Problem for Lexicographers". *Cameron Studies*, 245-66.

2601. Roe, Harald A. 1967. "A Note on Loanwords from Old Norse". *ES* 48.409-10. [On the OE spelling *-ht-*.]

2602. Rogers, H.L. 1984. "*Beowulf*, line 804". *N&Q* n.s. 31.289-92. [Discusses the meaning of *forsworen hæfde.*]

2603. Rosenberg, Bruce A. 1966. "The Meaning of *Æcerbot*". *JAF* 79.428-36.

2604. Rosier, James L. 1960. "Old English Glosses to an Epistle of Boniface". *JEGP* 59.710-13.

2605. ———. 1960. "The Sources of John Joscelyn's Old English-Latin Dictionary". *Anglia* 78.28-39.

2606. ———. 1963/64. "Contributions to OE Lexicography: Some Boethius Glosses". *Archiv* 200.197-98. [Lists 28 words not hitherto recorded.]

2607. ———. 1964. "Ten Old English Psalter Glosses". *JEGP* 63.1-6.

2608. ———. 1966. "Lexicographical Genealogy in Old English". *JEGP* 65.295-302. [Some observations on the 16th- and 17th-century MS dictionaries of Old English.]

2609. ———. 1970. "*Hrincg* in *Genesis A*". *Anglia* 88.334-36.

2610. ———. 1974. "What Grendel Found: *heardan hæle*". *NM* 75.40-49. [*Beowulf* 719a.]

2611. ———. 1977. "A New Old English Glossary: Nowell upon Huloet". *SN* 49.189-94. [Huloet's *Abcedarium Anglico Latinum* (1552).]

2612. ———. 1977. "Generative Composition in *Beowulf*". *ES* 58.193-203. [Discusses various methods of word-formation, esp. compounding in *Beowulf.*]

2613. ———. 1978. "Four Old English Psalter Glosses". *PP* 21.44-45.

2614. ———. 1978. "A Different Hyssop: Old English *Hlenortear*". *Word* 29.110-13. [On the gloss in the *Lambeth Psalter* 50.9.]

2615. ———. 1983. "Old English *egeswin*". *ES* 64.344.

2616. ———. 1983. "Old English *cofan*, Latin *cremium*". *Sprache* 29.53-54.

2617. Ross, Alan Strode Campbell. 1932. "Old English *gebidæþ*". *MLN* 47.377.

2618. ———. 1932. "Notes on Some Words in the *Lindisfarne Gospels*". *MLR* 27.451-53.

2619. ———. 1933. "Notes on Some Old English Words". *EStn* 67.344-49. [**āncum*; *-spere* 'reed'; OE *fæger, fǣger*; Northumbrian *gedeða*.]

2620. ———. 1933. "Northumbrian *Forwost*". *APS* 8.146-49.

2621. ———. 1934. "OE. *wēofod*". *LSE* 3.2-6.

2622. ———. 1940 [1942]. "Four Examples of Norse Influence in the Old English Gloss to the *Lindisfarne Gospels*". *TPS* 1940, 39-52. [1. *Ambeht*, etc. 2. *floege* 3. *groefa*, 4. forms of 'tree' (and 'straw').]

2623. ———. 1949/50. "Miscellaneous Notes on *Cædmon's Hymn* and *Bede's Death Song*". *EGS* 3.88-96.

2624. ———. 1957. "Aldrediana III: *Sniueð*". *NM* 58.144-47. [On the word in Alfred's Anglo-Saxon gloss to the *Lindisfarne Gospels*.]

2625. ———. 1959. *Aldrediana I: Three Suffixes*. (= *Moderna Språk*, Language Monographs, 3.) Saltsjö & Duvnäs: *Moderna Språk* (The Mod. Lang. Teachers' Association of Sweden).

2626. ———. 1961. "Aldrediana II: Observations upon Certain Words of the Lindisfarne Gloss". *ZVS* 77.258-95.

2627. ———. 1961. "Aldrediana XIV: *Felle-Read*". *NM* 62.1-10.

2628. ———. 1968. "Aldrediana XVII: *Ritual* Supplement". *EPS* 11.1-43.

2629. ———. 1968. "Notes on Some Words in the Anglo-Saxon Gloss to the *Durham Ritual*". *N&Q* n.s. 15.405-07. [= Aldrediana IIA.]

2630. ———. 1968. "The Earliest Occurrence of *riding*?" *N&Q* n.s. 15.444. [Suggests that a form *ðirde* (altered from *ðirdung*) in the gloss to the *Durham Ritual* (c.970) is the Scandinavian word from which English *riding*, as in West *Riding*, developed.]

2631. ———. 1972. "Notes on Some Further Words in the Anglo-Saxon Gloss to the *Durham Ritual*". *Mustanoja Festschrift* = *NM* 73.372-80. [= Aldrediana IIB.]

2632. ———. 1974. "Old English *Secgan*". *N&Q* n.s. 21.284.

2633. ———. 1975. "OE *Leoht* 'World'". *N&Q* n.s. 22.196.

2634. ———. 1976. "OE. nap. *broðro*, etc". *IF* 81.180.

2635. ———. 1978. "A Point of Comparison between Aldred's Two Glosses". *N&Q* n.s. 25.197-99. [Concludes that the major difference between the two glosses lies in the vocabulary used.]

2636. ———. 1979. "The Rare Words of Rushworth One". *N&Q* n.s. 26.495-98.

2637. ———. 1979. "Lindisfarne and Rushworth One". *N&Q* n.s. 26.194-98. [Considers the relationship between two sets of glosses.]

2638. ———. 1980. "The Correspondent of West Saxon *Cweþan* in late Northumbrian and Rushworth One". *NM* 81.24-33.

2639. ———. 1982. "Rare Words in Northumbrian". *N&Q* n.s. 29.196-98. [Quoted from *Lindisfarne Gospels* and *Rushworth Gospels*.]

2640. ——— and Harold W. Bailey. 1934. "OE. *afigen*: Ossete *fezonag, fizonag*". *LSE* 3.7-9.

2641. ——— and Rodney L. Thomson. 1979. "An Early Occurrence of *Brooch*". *N&Q* n.s. 26.498. [Points to an occurrence of *broche* in the Old Cornish version of Ælfric's *Glossary*.]

2642. Rubke, Henning. 1953. *Die Nominalkomposita bei Ælfric: Eine Studie zum Wortschatz Ælfrics in seiner zeitlichen und dialektischen Gebundenheit*. Göttingen diss. 1954, 171 pp.

2643. Rudolph, Robert Samuel. 1967. *The Old English Synonyms for 'Brave'*. Wisconsin diss., 257 pp. [Abstr. in *DA* 28.658A (1967).]

2644. Salus, Peter H. 1963. "OE *eoletes*". *Lingua* 12.429-30.

2645. ———. 1965. "OE *eoletes* Once More". *Lingua* 13.451.

2646. Samuels, Michael Louis. 1949. "The *ge-* prefix in the Old English Gloss to the *Lindisfarne Gospels*". *TPS* 1949, 62-116.

2647. Sanderlin, George. 1938. "A Note on *Beowulf* 1142". *MLN* 53.501-03. [On the meaning of *worold rædenne*.]

2648. Sauer, Hans. 1985. "Die Darstellung von Komposita in altenglischen Wörterbüchern". *Cameron Studies*, 267-316.

2649. Scaffidi Abbate, Augusto. 1975. "*Stod on Stapole e stapul ǣren*". *AION-SG* 18.143-58.

2650. Schaar, Claes. 1962. "*Brondhord* in the Old English Rhyming Poem". *ES* 43.490-91.

2651. Schabram, Hans. 1956. "Zur Bedeutung von ae. *cēne*". *Anglia* 74.181-87.

2652. ———. 1957. "Zur Bedeutung und Etymologie von ae. *rof*". *Anglia* 75.259-74.

2653. ———. 1958. "Ae. *þ(r)istra* 'coniuncla'". *Anglia* 76.411-21.

2654. ———. 1960. "Die Bedeutung von *gal* und *galscipe* in der ae. *Genesis B*". *BGDSL*(T) 82.265-74.

2655. ———. 1965. *Superbia: Studien zum altenglischen Wortschatz. Teil I: Die dialektale und zeitliche Verbreitung des Wortguts*. München: Wilhelm Fink, 140 pp. [Studies all the occurrences of words connected with the idea of pride.]

   Reviews: J.J. Campbell in *JEGP* 65.705 (1966); Otto Funke in *Anglia* 84.407-09 (1966); Kurt Otten in *ZMaF* 33.361 (1966); Hanspeter Schelp in *IF* 71.151-54 (1966); R.E. Kaske in *Speculum* 41.762-64 (1966); G. Storms in *Neophil* 50.293-94 (1966); A. Campbell in *RES* n.s. 18.177-79 (1967); Herbert Koziol in *GRM* 17.100-03 (1967); Manfred Schentke in *ZAA* 15.76-77 (1967); Hans Käsman in *BGDSL*(T) 89.348-51 (1967/68); E.G. Stanley in *Archiv* 204.380-82 (1967/68); H.D. Chickering, Jr. in *MLR* 63.160 (1968); Rolf Kaiser in *GGA* 220.309-12 (1968); Gotz Wienold in *Sprache* 14.66-67 (1968); C.J.E. Ball in *MAE* 38.208-10 (1969); C.A. Ladd in *N&Q* n.s. 18.187 (1971); Lars-G. Hallander in *SN* 45.171-72 (1973).

2656. ———. 1968. "Ae. *beohata, Exodus* 253". *Marchand Festschrift*, 203-09.

2657. ———. 1969. "Kritische Bemerkungen zu Angaben über die Verbreitung altenglischer Wörter". *Festschrift für Edgar Mertner*, ed. Bernhard Fabian and Ulrich Suerbaum, 89-102. München: Wilhelm Fink. [Focuses on *galness* and *wlanc*. Criticizes Meissner [no. 2455].]

2658. ———. 1970. "Bemerkungen zu den ae. Nomina agentis auf *-estre* und *-icge*". *Anglia* 88.94-98. [Additions to two articles by von Lindheim [nos. 2782 & 2784].]

2659. ———. 1970. "Etymologie und Kontextanalyse in der altenglischen Semantik". *ZVS* 84.233-53. [Uses examples from *Paris Psalter* and *Whale*.]

2660. ———. 1973. "Das altenglische *superbia*-Wortgut: Eine Nachlese". *Koziol Festschrift*, 272-79.

2661. ———. 1974. "Ae. *Wlanc* und Ableitungen: Vorarbeiten zu einer wortgeschichtlichen Studie". *Papajewski Festschrift*, 70-88.

2662. ———. 1975. "Bezeichnungen für 'Bauer' im altenglischen". *Wort und Begriff Bauer*, ed. R. Wenskus, et al. (= Abhandlungen der Akademie der Wissenschaften in Göttingen, Philologisch-historische Klasse, 3:89), 73-88. Göttingen, Vandenhoeck und Ruprecht.

2663. ———. 1980. "Bezeichnungen für den Pflug und seine Teile im Altenglischen". *Untersuchungen zur Flur* II, 99-125.

2664. ———. 1985. "Ae. *smylting* 'electrum': Polysemie lat. Wörter als Problem der ae. Lexikographie". *Cameron Studies*, 317-30.

2665. Schelp, Hanspeter. 1956. *Der geistige Mensch im Wortschatz Alfreds des Grossen*. Göttingen diss., 186 pp.

2666. Scherer, Günther. 1928. *Zur Geographie und Chronologie des angelsächsischen Wortschatzes im Anschluss an Bischof Wærferths Übersetzung der 'Dialoge' Gregors*. Leipzig: Mayer und Müller, v + 63 pp. [Berlin diss.]

Reviews: R. Spindler in *Archiv* 158.144-45 (1930); F. Klaeber in *Anglia B* 42.3-6 (1931); A.E.H. Swaen in *Neophil* 16.68 (1931); C.A. Weber in *Anzeiger der Zeitschrift für deutsches Altertum und deutsche Literatur* 50.66-67 (1931); A.H. Smith in *MLR* 27.98-99 (1932); A. Szogs in *LGRP* 53.16-19 (1932).

2667. Schibsbye, Knud. 1969. "*þæs oferēode, þisses swā mæȝ*". *ES* 50.380-81. [An interpretation of the phrase in *Deor*.]

2668. Schlutter, Otto B. 1923-28. "Weitere Beiträge zur altenglischen Wortforschung". *Anglia* 47.34-52, 244-63, 287-88, 383-84; 48.101-04, 375-92; 49.92-96, 183-92, 376-83; 51.156-63; 52.83-87, 183-91. [Discusses various OE words.]

2669. ———. 1923. "OE *Pillsápe* 'soap for removing hair'". *Neophil* 8.204-05.

2670. ———. 1923. "Is There Any Evidence for OE. *Weargincel* 'butcher-bird'?". *Neophil* 8.206-08.

2671. ———. 1923. "Is There Any Real Evidence for an Alleged OE. *Whytel* 'quail'?". *Neophil* 8.303-04.

2672. ———. 1924. "Some Further Remarks on Toller's Supplement to B.-T." *Neophil* 9.194-99.

2673. ———. 1927. "Is There an OE. Plant-Name *twínihte*?". *Neophil* 12.117-18.

2674. ———. 1927. "OE (Anglian) *gégan* 'arsare' = ON *geya* 'bellen, ausschelten'". *Neophil* 12.118-19.

2675. ———. 1930. "Is There Any Evidence on Which to Base the Assumption That OE. *hólinga* is Equivalent in Meaning with *dearnunga* or *geresta* with *láf*?" *Neophil* 15.262-63.

2676. ———. 1930. "Further Remarks on Toller's Supplement to Bosworth-Toller". *Neophil* 15.271-74.

2677. Schmoock, Peter. 1965. *Patientia: Die Terminologie des Duldens in der Leid-Synonymik der altenglischen und altsächsischen Epik: Semasiologische Studien zum Christianisierungsprozess des germanischen Wortschatzes*. Kiel diss., iii + 719 pp.

2678. ———. 1976. "*Patientia*: Zum Christianisierungsprozess des Wortschatzes der altenglischen und altsächsischen Epik". *Festschrift für Gerhard Cordes zum 65. Geburtstag*, ed. Friedhelm Debus and Joachim Hartig, II, 322-53. Neumünster: Wachholtz.

2679. Schneider, Karl. 1969. "Zu den ae. Zaubersprüchen *wið wennum* und *wið wæterælfädle*". *Anglia* 87.282-302.

2680. Schubel, Friedrich. 1952/53. "Zur Bedeutungskunde altenglischer Wörter mit christlichem Sinngehalt". *Archiv* 189.289-303.

2681. ———. 1961. "Die Bedeutungsnuancen von *bealu* in *Christ I-III*". *Festschrift zum 75. Geburtstag von Theodor Spira*, ed. Helmut Viebrock and Willi Erzgräber, 328-34. Heidelberg: Carl Winter.

2682. Schücking, Levin Ludwig. 1929. "*Sōna* im *Beowulf*". *Förster Festschrift*, 85-88.

2683. Schulze, Wilhelm. 1933. "Zur Blattfüllung: Ags. *nænigra <nanra> þinga*". *ZVS* 60.144.

2684. Schwammberger, E. 1945. *Die Entwicklung der altenglischen Verben 'beodan' und 'biddan' zu neuenglisch 'to bid': Eine lautliche, syntaktische und semantische Untersuchung.* Zürich: Aschmann & Scheller, 105 pp. [Zürich diss.]

2685. Schwentner, Ernst. 1940. "Alts. *dref*, ags. *drep, dreb*". *ZVS* 66.128-29.

2686. ———. 1940. "Ags. *wuducocc*, altind. *vanakukkuta*". *IF* 57.142.

2687. ———. 1943. "Ae. *hlōse*, ne. *looze* 'Schweinestall'". *Archiv* 183.122.

2688. Scragg, Donald George. 1966. "Old English *bryt* in the *Vercelli Book*". *N&Q* n.s. 13.168-69.

2689. ———. 1977. "Old English *Forhtleasness, Unforhtleasness*". *N&Q* n.s. 24.399-400.

2690. Seebold, Elmer. 1968. "Ae. *twegen* und ahd. *zwēne* 'Zwei'". *Anglia* 86.417-36.

2691. ———. 1974. "Die ae. Entsprechungen von lat. *Sapiens* und *Prudens*: eine Untersuchung über die mundartliche Gliederung der ae. Literatur". *Anglia* 92.291-333.

2692. Severynse, Marion. 1980. *Three Old English Verbs of 'Turning': A Semantic Study of 'wendan', 'cierran', and 'hweorfan'*. Harvard diss. [No further information available.]

2693. Shook, Lawrence Kennedy. 1939. *Ælfric's Latin Grammar: A Study in Old English Grammatical Terminology*. Harvard diss., iii + 322 pp. [Abstr. in *Harvard Univ. Summaries of Theses* 1940, 360-63.]

2694. ———. 1940. "A Technical Construction in Old English: Translation Loans in *-lic*". *MS* 2.253-57. [On renderings in OE of Latin technical terms in *-ivus*, as they appear in Ælfric's *Grammar*.]

2695. Sievers, Eduard. 1926. "Ags. *hlæfdige*". *BGDSL*(T) 50.16-17.

2696. Simmonds, Paula. 1984. "Nautical Terms in the Brussels Glossary". *Literature and Learning in Medieval and Renaissance England: Essays Presented to Fitzroy Pyle*, ed. John Scattergood, 41-58. Dublin: Blackrock.

2697. Sisam, Kenneth. 1962. "O.E. *stefn, stefna* 'stem'". *RES* n.s. 13.282-83. [Discusses the phrase *steoran ofer stæfnan* (*Andreas* 495).]

2698. Sklute, Larry M. 1970. "*Freoðuwebbe* in Old English Poetry". *NM* 71.534-41.

2699. Sledd, James. 1954. "Nowell's *Vocabularium Saxonicum* and the Elyot-Cooper Tradition". *SP* 51.143-48.

2700. Smith, Garland Garvey. 1931. *Recurring First Elements of Anglo-Saxon Nominal Compounds: A Study in Poetic Style*. Harvard diss. (no pagination available). [Abstr. in *Harvard Univ. Summaries of Thesis* 1931, 244-46.]

2701. Smith, Henry Lee, Jr. 1938. "Some Germanic Developments of IE **ĝeneu and **ĝen-*, **ĝenē". *Language* 14.95-103. [Contains a discussion of various OE words, especially of OE *cnossian*, *cnyssan* 'beat, strike'.]

2702. Smith, Roger. 1987. "*Garsecg* in Old English Poetry". *ELN* 24:3.14-19. [An etymological study.]

2703. Smithers, Geoffrey Victor. 1966. "Four Cruces in *Beowulf*". *Schlauch Festschrift*, 413-30. [Discusses *nēodlaðu* (1320), *wyrmfāh* (1698), *Mōdþrȳðo* (1931), *dryhtbearn* (2035).]

2704. Sokolova, M.N. 1973. "Signification des Termes *ham* et *tun* dans les Documents Anglo-Saxons". *CCM* 16.123-32.

2705. Soland, Margrit. 1979. *Altenglische Ausdrücke für 'Leib' und 'Seele': Eine semantische Analyse*. Zürich: Juris, 139 pp.

2706. Solo, Harry Jay. 1977. "The Meaning of *Motan: A Secondary Denotation of Necessity in Old English?". *NM* 78.215-32.

2707. Specht, Franz. 1935. "Ags. *scrúd*". *ZVS* 62.242-43.

2708. Spolsky, Ellen. 1977. "Old English Kinship Terms and *Beowulf*". *NM* 78.233-38.

2709. Stanley, Eric Gerald. 1969. "Old English *-calla*, *ceallian*". *Garmonsway Festschrift*, 94-99.

2710. ———. 1971. "Studies in the Prosaic Vocabulary of Old English Verse". *NM* 72.385-418.

2711. ———. 1979. "Two Old English Poetic Phrases Insufficiently Understood for Literary Criticism: *ðing gehegan* and *seonoþ gehegan*". *Old English Poetry: Essays on Style*, ed. Daniel G. Calder (= Contributions of the UCLA Center for Medieval & Renaissance Studies, 10), 67-90. Berkeley, CA: Univ. of California Press. [On *Beowulf* 419-26 and *Phoenix* 491-94.]

2712. ———. 1985. "OE *tō-gedēgled*: A Ghost-word". *N&Q* n.s. 32.10.

2713. ———. 1985. "The Treatment of Late, Badly Transmitted and Spurious Old English in a Dictionary of that Language". *Cameron Studies*, 331-68.

2714. ———. 1986. "Old English in *The Oxford English Dictionary*". *Studies in Lexicography*, 19-35.

2715. Stanley, Julia Penelope and Cynthia McGowan. 1979. "*Woman* and *Wife*: Social and Semantic Shifts in English". *PIL* 12.491-502. [Considers the history of the term *woman* in the context of related vocabulary change in OE.]

2716. Stapelkamp, Christiaan. 1947. "Oude Engelse Plantnamen". *ES* 28.111-14. [The words treated are *bismalwe*, *lemkehleomoc-lumeke*, and *erbe water*.]

2717. Štech, Svatopluk. 1969. "A Few Remarks on the Etymology of OE *ǣdre* 'vein'". *BSE* 8.179-81.

2718. Stern, Gustaf. 1933/34. "Old English *fuslic* and *fus*". *EStn* 68.161-73.

2719. ———. 1944/45. "On Methods of Interpretation". *SN* 17.35-41. [On equivocal meanings of OE words, and dangers in the usual present-day intepretation of them.]

2720. Steuernagel, Konrad. 1924. *Der Wortschatz des Old English Martyrology unter besonderer Berücksichtigung des Gebrauchs der Präpositionen und Konjunktionen sowie einer ausführlichen Darstellung des syntaktischen Gebrauchs der Präpositionen*. Frankfurt am Main: no publisher available, 335 pp.

2721. Stibbe, Hildegard. 1935. *'Herr' und 'Frau' und verwandte Begriffe in ihren altenglischen Äquivalenten*. (= AF, 80.) Heidelberg: Carl Winter, xvi + 105 pp. [Heidelberg diss.]

Review: K. Malone in *MLN* 53.32-34 (1938).

2722. Strachan, L.R.M. 1931. "Hernia among the Anglo-Saxons". *N&Q* 160.192-93.

2723. ———. 1936. "Old Vocabulary of Weaving". *N&Q* 171.409-10. [List of words related to 'weaving' in Bosworth-Toller's *Anglo-Saxon Dictionary*.]

2724. Stracke, John Richard. 1970. *Studies in the Vocabulary of the 'Lambeth Psalter' Glosses*. Pennsylvania diss., 175 pp. [Abstr. in *DA* 32.987A (1971).]

2725. ———. 1974. "Eight *Lambeth Psalter*-Glosses". *PQ* 53.121-28.

2726. ———. 1976/77. "*Eþelboda*: *Guthlac B*, 1003". *MP* 74.194-95.

2727. Strang, Barbara M.H. 1961. "Two Wulfstan Expressions". *N&Q* n.s. 8.166-67. [1. *bec*; 2. *stric*.]

2728. Strauss, Jürgen. 1974. *Eine Komponentenanalyse im verbal- und situationskontextuellen Bereich: die Bezeichnungen für 'Herr' und 'Gebieter' in der altenglischen Poesie.* (= AF, 103.) Heidelberg: Carl Winter, 352 pp.

2729. ———. 1980. "Compounding in Old English Poetry". *FLH* 1.305-16.

2730. Strite, Victor Lindsey. 1970. *Old English Sea-Terms: A Word-List and a Study of Definitions.* Univ. of Missouri diss., 153 pp. [Abstr. in *DA* 31.4147A (1971).]

2731. ———. 1983. "Semantic-Field Analysis for Old English Poetry Using Computers and Semantic Features to Find Meaning". *In Geardagum* 5.29-38.

2732. Stryker, William G. 1952. *The Latin-Old English Glossary in MS. Cotton Cleopatra A III.* Stanford diss., 199 pp. [Abstr. in *Stanford Univ. Abstracts of Diss.* 27.238-42 (1953).]

2733. ———. 1953. "Old English Glossary Gleanings". *JEGP* 52.372-77. [Discusses ten OE words found in Latin-OE glossaries.]

2734. Stuart, C.I.J.M. 1964. "Wulfstan's Use of *leofan men*". *ES* 45.39-42.

2735. Stuart, Heather. 1972. "The Meaning of OE **ælfsciene*". *Parergon* 2.22-26.

2736. ———. 1975. "Some Old English Medical Terms" *Parergon* 13.21-35.

2737. ———. 1976. "The Anglo-Saxon Elf". *SN* 48.313-20.

2738. ———. 1977. "*Spider* in Old Englsih". *Parergon* 18.37-42.

2739. Sundby, Bertil. 1958. "Old English *Gumstōl* > Modern English *Gumble-Stool*: An Etymological-Semasiological Problem". *ES* 39.110-16.

2740. Sutherland, Raymond Carter. 1955. "The Meaning of *Eorlscipe* in *Beowulf*". *PMLA* 70.1133-42.

2741. Swaen, A.E.H. 1923. "Contributions to Old English Lexicography". *EStn* 57.1-7. [Discusses *andfengstōw, belimp, dēad, forþweard, fugoldæg, gedrecness, gemynd, gerisene, grētan, hand, inn tō, insting, nōnhring, onborgian, onstandan, rǣd, strīd, tōlōcian, upphefedness, ungēaplice*.]

2742. ———. 1930/31. "*Æræt*". *EStn* 65.471-73.

2743. ———. 1931. "Anglo-Saxon Lexicography". *Anglia* 55.8-9. [Additions to Willard [no. 2815].]

2744. ———. 1936. "Is *seo hiow*='fortune' a Ghost-word?". *EStn* 71.153-54.

2745. ———. 1943. "Contributions to Anglo-Saxon Lexicography". *Neophil* 28.42-49. [Some lexicographical notes on passages in Whitelock's *Anglo-Saxon Wills* (1930).]

2746. Szogs, Arthur. 1931. *Die Ausdrücke für 'Arbeit' und 'Beruf' im Altenglischen.* (= AF, 73.) Heidelberg: Carl Winter, xv + 143 pp. [Giessen diss. 1930.]

> *Reviews*: A. B[randl] in *Archiv* 161.301 (1932); F.H. Braulin in *Language* 8.238 (1932); F. Holthausen in *Anglia B* 43.330 (1932); C. van Spaendonck in *ES* 14.25-27 (1932); F. Klaeber in *EStn* 67.247-49 (1932/33); F. Fiedler in *ZFEU* 32.44-45 (1933); H. Papajewski in *DLZ* 54.1757-59 (1933); F. Stroh in *LGRP* 65.234-36 (1933).

2747. Talentino, Arnold Victor. 1971. *A Study of Compound 'Hapax Legomena' in Old English Poetry.* State Univ. of New York at Binghamton diss., 196 pp. [Abstr. in *DA* 31.6025A (1971).]

2748. ———. 1979. "Fitting *guðgewæde*: Use of Compounds in *Beowulf*". *Neophil* 63.592-96.

2749. Taylor, Paul Beekman. 1964/65. "OE *eoletes* Again". *Lingua* 13.196-97. [Comments on Salus [no. 2644]; Answered by Salus [no. 2645].]

2750. ———. 1986. "The Traditional Language of Treasure in *Beowulf*". *JEGP* 85.191-205.

2751. Temple, Winifred M. 1955. "OE *Hlædfæt*—Welsh *Lletwad*". *RES* n.s. 6.63-65.

2752. Thacker, A.T. 1981. "Some Terms for Noblemen in Anglo-Saxon England, c.650-900". *ASSAH* 2.201-36.

2753. Thomson, Rodney L. 1957. "Three Etymological Notes". *EGS* 6.79-91. [1. OE *eolet*; 2. OE *hrān* and *hran/hron*; 3. The dental preterite in Germanic and Celtic.]

2754. ———. 1961. "Aldrediana V: Celtica". *EGS* 7.20-36. [On words in the Aldredian texts, in which some trace of Celtic influence may be suspected.]

2755. ———. 1981. "Ælfric's Latin Vocabulary". *LSE* n.s. 12.155-61. [= *Essays in Honour of A.C. Cawley.*]

2756. Timmer, Benno Johan. 1957. "De Laet's Anglo-Saxon Dictionary". *Neophil* 41.199-202.

2757. Tinkler, John Douglas. 1971. *Vocabulary and Syntax of the Old English Version in the 'Paris Psalter'*. (= JanL, Ser. Practica, 67.) The Hague & Paris: Mouton, 92 pp. [Originally Stanford diss. 1964; Abstr. in *DA* 25.1900-01 (1964) and *Linguistics* 14.121-22 (1965).]

   Review: Klaus R. Grinda in *Anglia* 91.494-99 (1973).

2758. Toon, Thomas Edward. 1978. "Lexical Diffusion in Old English", *Papers from the Parasession on the Lexicon*, ed. Donka Farkas, et al., 357-64. Chicago: Chicago Linguistic Society.

2759. ———. 1985. "Preliminaries to the Linguistic Analysis of Old English Glosses and Glossaries". *PICEHL*/4, 319-29.

2760. Torkar, Roland. 1985. "Zehn altenglische 'Ghost-Words'". *Cameron Studies*, 369-92.

2761. Toth, Karl. 1986. "Ae. *lǣ* 'Haupthaar'". *Anglia* 104.94-103.

2762. Tremaine, Hadley P. 1969. "*Beowulf's Ecg Brun* and Other Rusty Relics". *PQ* 48.145-50. [On the meaning of the word *brun* in several OE poems.]

2763. Trnka, Bohumil. 1982. "The Old English Diminutive Suffix *-INCEL*". *Trnka Papers*, 253-57. [The original, Czech version appeared in *ČMF* 38.1-5 (1956).]

2764. Tuso, Joseph Frederick. 1966. *An Analysis and Glossary of Dialectal Variations in the Vocabularies of Three Late Tenth-century Old English Texts, the 'Corpus', 'Lindisfarne', and 'Rushworth Gospels'*. Univ. of Arizona diss., 86 pp. [Abstr. in *DA* 27.1357-58A (1966).]

2765. ———. 1968. "An Analysis and Glossary of Dialectal Synonymy in the *Corpus*, *Lindisfarne*, and *Rushworth Gospels*". *Linguistics* 43.89-118. [Based on the above item.]

2766. Uhler, Karl. 1926. *Die Bedeutungsgleichheit der altenglischen Adjectiva und Adverbia mit und ohne '-lic (-lice)'*. (= AF, 62.) Heidelberg: Carl Winter, ix + 68 pp.

   Reviews: Kemp Malone in *JEGP* 25.586-88 (1926); S.L.P.W. in *MLR* 21.344 (1926); Morgan Callaway, Jr. in *MLN* 43.203-04 (1928).

2767. Van Beek, Peter. 1932. *The Prefix 'be-' in King Alfred's Translation of Boethius' De Consolatione Philosophiae*. Iowa diss. (no pagination available). [Abstr.

in *Univ. of Iowa Doctoral Dissertation Abstracts and References (1900-1937)* I, 161-75 (1940).]

2768. V[an] d[er] G[aaf], W[illem]. 1934. "*Forlorn hope* (Ælfric's *Homilies I*, p. 342)". *ES* 16.25.

2769. Van der Merwe Scholtz, Hendrik. 1927. *The Kenning in Anglo-Saxon and Old Norse Poetry*. Utrecht: N.V. Dekker & van de Vegt, 180 p.

   Reviews: H.A.C. Green in *MLR* 25.196-97 (1930); F. M[ossé] in *RG* 22.220 (1931).

2770. Velten, Harry V. 1931. "A Note on Semantic Borrowing in Old English". *JEGP* 30.494-97.

2771. Venezky, Richard Lawrence. 1970. "Concordances to the Rushworth Matthew and the Vercelli Homilies". *Computers and OE Concordances*, 43-46.

2772. ———. 1970. "Computer Processing of Old English Texts". *Computers and OE Concordances*, 65-75.

2773. ———. 1973. "Computational Aids to Dictionary Compilation". *DOE Plan*, 307-27. [Concerns computer concordances to OE texts.]

2774. Verdonck, Jan. 1975. "Taalkundige problemen bij de uitgave en studie van de Oudengelse glossen". *Handelingen van de Koninklijke Zuidnederlandse Maatschappij voor Taal- en Letterkunde en Geschiedenis* (Brussels) 29.287-92.

2775. ———. 1976. "Notes on Some Problematic Glosses in the *Liber Scintillarum* Interlineation (MS. London, BM Royal 7C. iv)". *ES* 57.97-102.

2776. Vickrey, John F. 1965. "*Selfsceaft* in *Genesis B*". *Anglia* 83.154-71.

2777. ———. 1970. "A Note on *Genesis* Lines 242-44". *NM* 71.191-92. [Discusses the meaning of *nyston* (242b), referring to Mitchell [no. 1534].]

2778. ———. 1981. "Some Further Remarks on *selfsceaft*". *ZDA* 110.1-14. [Reply to Kartschoke [no. 2326].]

2779. Vleeskruyer, R. 1952. "Old English Vocabulary Research". *Handelingen van het twee en twintigste Nederlands Philologen-Congres, Utrecht* (Groningen) 22.46-47.

2780. Vočadlo, Otakar. 1933. "Anglo-Saxon Terminology". *PSE* 4.61-85.

2781. von Lindheim, Bogislav. 1951. "Traces of Colloquial Speech in OE". *Anglia* 70.22-42. [Discusses three groups of words in the OE vocabulary which may well be colloquial.]

2782. ———. 1958. "Die weiblichen Genussuffixe im Altenglischen". *Anglia* 76.479-504.

2783. ———. 1964. "Problems of Old English Semantics". *English Studies Today*, 3rd ser., ed. G.I. Duthie, 66-77. Edinburgh: Edinburgh Univ. Press. [Concerns semantic change.]

2784. ———. 1969. "Die weiblichen Genussuffixe im Altenglischen: Korrekturen und Nachträge". *Anglia* 87.64-65. [Errata and addenda to his article of 1958 [no. 2782].

2785. ———. 1970. "Das altenglische Deminutivsuffix *-incel*". *BGDSL*(T) 92.43-50.

2786. ———. 1971. "Das Suffix *-bære* im Altenglischen". *Archiv* 208.310-20.

2787. Von Schaubert, Else. 1949. *Bedeutung und Herkunft von altenglischen 'feormian' und seiner Sippe*. (= Hesperia: Ergänzungsriehe: Schriften zur englischen Philologie, 13) Göttingen: Vandenhoeck und Ruprecht; Baltimore: Johns Hopkins Press. 120 pp.

Reviews: John E. Housman in *MLR* 45.421 (1950); H.C. Matthes in *Archiv* 187.132-33 (1950); E.A. Philippson in *JEGP* 49.103 (1950); R. Fricker in *ES* 32.256-58 (1951); A.A. Prins in *Museum* 56.111-12 (1951); F. Mossé in *BSL* 49.112 (1953).

2788. Wadstein, Elis. 1925. "Le mot *viking*, Anglo-Saxon *wicing*, frison *wising*, etc.". *Mélanges de philologie offerts à M. Johan Vis17ing*, 381-86. Göteborg: Blanders Boktryckeri.

2789. Waite, Gregory George. 1984. *The Vocabulary of the Old English Version of Bede's 'Historia Ecclesiastica'*. Univ. of Toronto diss. (no pagination available). [Abstr. in *DA* 46.1276a (1985).]

2790. Wakelin, Martyn Francis. 1971. "OE *bræȝen, braȝen*". *Neophil* 55.108.

2791. ———. 1979. "OE. *brægen, bragen*: A Further Note". *Orbis* 28.369-71.

2792. Waldorf, Norman Omar. 1953. *The 'Hapex Legomena' in the Old English Vocabulary: A Study Based upon the Bosworth-Toller Dictionary*. Stanford diss., 582 pp. [Abstr. in *DA* 13.558 (1953).]

2793. Walker, James Albert. 1948. *Adjective Suffixes in Old English*. Harvard diss., 115 pp.

2794. ———. 1948. "The Rank-Number Relationship of Adjectival Suffixes in Old English". *PQ* 27.264-72.

2795. Walker, Warren S. 1952. "The *Brūnecg* Sword". *MLN* 67.516-20. [On the meaning of *brūn* in Old English descriptions of metal.]

2796. Waterhouse, Ruth. 1973. "Semantic Development of Two Terms within the Anglo-Saxon *Chronicle*". *SGG* 14.95-106. [Traces the distinction between *fyrd* and *here*.]

2797. Weimann, Klaus. 1966. *Der Friede im Altenglischen: Eine bezeichnungsgeschichtliche Untersuchung*. Bonn diss., 296 pp.

   Review: Roland Torkar in *Göttingen Gelehrte Anzeigen* (Göttingen) 221.234-38 (1969).

2798. Weisweiler, Josef. 1923. "Beiträge zur Bedeutungsentwicklung germanischer Wörter für sittliche Begriffe". *IF* 41.13-75 and 304-68. [Discusses many words in various OE texts.]

2799. Weman, Bertil. 1933. *Old English Semantic Analysis and Theory with Special Reference to Verbs Denoting Locomotion*. (= LundSE, 1) Lund: Lindstedt, 188 pp. [Lund diss.]

   Reviews: A. Kihlbom in *SN* 7.62-72 (1934); K. Jost in *LGRP* 57.25-26 (1936); C.L. W[renn] in *RES* 12.490-92 (1936); B. von Lindheim in *Anglia B* 50.35-40 (1939).

2800. Wenisch, Franz. 1976. "Sächsische Dialektwörter in *The Battle of Maldon*". *IF* 81.181-203. [Especially on *gehende* and *ætforan*]

2801. ———. 1978. "Kritische Bemerkungen zu Angaben über die Verbreitung einiger angeblich westsächsischer Dialektwörter". *Anglia* 96.5-44. [Reclassifies nine words once thought to be West-Saxon as 'common OE'.]

2802. ———. 1979. *Spezifisch anglisches Wortgut in den nordhumbrischen Interlinearglossierungen des Lukasevangeliums*. (= AF, 132.) Heidelberg: Carl Winter, 352 pp. [Giessen diss.]

   Reviews: Hans Sauer in *Anglia* 99.420-24 (1982); Angus Cameron in *Speculum* 57.956-57 (1982).

2803. ———. 1982. "*Judith*—eine westsächsische Dichtung?". *Anglia* 100.273-300. [Analyses the vocabulary of *Judith* from the viewpoint of dialectal relationships.]

2804. ———. 1985. "*(ge)fægnian*: zur dialektalen Verbreitung eines altenglischen Wortes". *Cameron Studies*, 393-410.

2805. Wentersdorf, Karl P. 1972. "The Semantic Development of O.E. *dreorig* and *dreorigian*". *SN* 44.278-88.

2806. ———. 1973. "On the Meaning of O.E. *Dreorig* in *Brunanburh* 54". *NM* 74.232-37.

2807. ———. 1973. "On the Meaning of O.E. *heorodreorig* in *The Phoenix* and Other Poems". *SN* 45.32-46.

2808. ———. 1975. "*The Wanderer*: Notes on Some Semantic Problems". *Neophil* 59.287-92. [Discusses *drēorig, drēorighlēor, seledrēorig, seledrēamas*.]

2809. Wetzel, Claus-Dieter. 1985. "Ae. *īsīðes*". *IF* 90.213-26.

2810. Whitbread, Leslie. 1963. "Old English and Old High German: A Note on *Judgement Day II*, 292-293". *SP* 60.514-24. [Accepts *drūt* and *frōwe* as feminine substantives derived from a dialect of OHG, and used in the poem more or less with their German meanings.]

2811. ———. 1965. "An Old English Gloss". *ELN* 2.245-47. [Comments on *ongrynt oððe ongratað* in Bede's *Versus de die iudicii* in MS Cotton Domitian A i.]

2812. ———. 1966. "Old English *Unbleoh*". *Neophil* 50.447-48. [Cf. Cameron [no. 2116].]

2813. Wiersma, Stanley Marvin. 1961. *A Linguistic Analysis of Words Referring to Monsters in 'Beowulf'*. Wisconsin diss., 512 pp. [Abstr. in *DA* 22.570 (1961).]

2814. Wietelmann, Inge. 1952. *Die Epitheta in den 'Caedmonischen' Dichtungen*. Göttingen diss., v + 207 pp.

2815. Willard, Rudolph. 1930. "Gleanings in Old English Lexicography". *Anglia* 54.8-24. [Cf. Swaen [no. 2741].]

2816. ———. 1951. "O.E. *Oma* 'Rust'". *MLN* 66.261-63.

2817. Williams, Edna Rees. 1958. "Ælfric's Grammatical Terminology". *PMLA* 73.453-62. [Shows that Ælfric's grammatical terminology is essentially Latin, not English, and that the English terms were mainly intended to interpret, not to replace the Latin.]

2818. Wolf-Rottkay, W.H. 1953. "Zur Etymologie von ae. *bāt*". *Anglia* 71.140-47.

2819. Wood, Francis A. 1926. "Some Revised Etymologies". *MP* 24.215-20. [Contains several OE items.]

2820. Woodward, Robert H. 1954. "*Swanrod* in *Beowulf*". *MLN* 69.544-46. [Continues Brady [no. 2097].]

2821. Wüst, Walther. 1955. "Zur Deutung und Herkunft des ae. *Bāt*, m.f. 'Boot, Schiff'". *Anglia* 73.262-75. [Cf. Wolf-Rottkay [no. 2818].]

2822. Wyler, Siegfried. 1984. "Old English Colour Terms and Berlin and Kay's Theory of Basic Colour Terms". *Modes of Interpretation: Essays Presented to Ernst Leisi on the Occasion of His 65th Birthday* (= TBL, 260), ed. Richard J. Watts and Urs Weidmann, 41-57. Tübingen: Gunter Narr.

2823. Wyss, Simone. 1981. "Un Cas de 'filiation fonctionnelle': Le Suffixe *-a* du vieil-anglais et le suffixe *-er* de l'anglais moderne". *Confluents* 7:2.5-22.

2824. Yerkes, David. 1976. "Dugdale's Dictionary and Somner's *Dictionarium*". *ELN* 14.110-12. [Discusses the debt of Somner's *Dictionarium Saxonico-Latino-Anglicum* of 1659 to Dugdale's MS dictionary of 1644 (Bodleian, MS Dugdale 29).]

2825. ———. 1979. *The Two Versions of Wærferth's Translation of Gregory's Dialogues: An Old English Thesaurus*. (= TOES, 4.) Toronto: Univ. of Toronto Press/Centre for Medieval Studies, Univ. of Toronto, xxvi + 100 pp. [A highly annotated ed.]

Reviews: Geoffrey Russom in *Speculum* 55.878-79 (1980); Ernst A. Ebbinghaus in *GL* 21.30-31 (1981); Jane Roberts in *N&Q* n.s. 28.179-81 (1981); Patrizia Lendinara in *Schede Medievali* 2 (1982) [page nos. illegible]; R.I. Page in *MAE* 51.115-19 (1982).

2826. ———. 1979. "Twelve New Old English Words". *Sprache* 25.171-73. [Taken from the OE translation of Bili's *Life of Machutees* in British Library, Cotton Otho A. viii.]

2827. Yorke, Barbara A.E. 1981. "The Vocabulary of Anglo-Saxon Overlordship". *ASSAH* 2.171-200.

2828. Zettersten, Arne. 1969. "The Source of **mocritum* in Old English". *SN* 41.375-77. [On the word in the OE *Lapidary*.]

C. Middle English

2829. Ackerman, Robert W. 1941. "*Dub* in the Middle English Romances". *Research Studies of the State College of Washington* 9.109-14.

LEXICOLOGY, LEXICOGRAPHY, AND WORD-FORMATION 267

2830. Aertsen, H. 1981. "Lexical Variation in Three Middle English Romances". *Current Research 1980*, 17-30.

2831. Aitken, Adam Jack. 1973. "Sense-analysis for a Historical Dictionary". *Kurath Festschrift*, 5-16. [On *DOST*.]

2832. Allen, Hope Emily. 1935. "'Little King', 'Sow', 'Lady-Cow'". *JAF* 48.191-93. [Indicates that these three folk-names come into literature as names for the wren, the woodlouse, and the lady-bird, in c.1450-80, 1580, 1630, respectively.]

2833. ———. 1936. "The Fifteenth-Century 'Associations of Beasts, of Birds, and of Men': The Earliest Text with 'Language for Carvers'". *PMLA* 51.602-06. [List of phrases such as *flock of sheep*, *bevy of quail*, *school of clerks*, etc.]

2834. Anon. 1956. "Robert of Gloucester's *Chronicle*: Some Additions to the O.E.D.". *N&Q* n.s. 3.279-81.

2835. Anttila, Raimo. 1963. "Loanwords and Statistical Measures of Style in the *Towneley Plays*". *Statistical Methods in Linguistics* (Stockholm) 2.73-93.

2836. Appenzeller-Gassmann, Verena. 1961. *Mittelenglische Bekräftigungsformeln*. Zürich: Juris-Verlag, 156 pp. [Zürich diss. Discusses emphasizing words, phrases and formulas in ME.]

Review: Siegfried Wyler in *ES* 49.242-43 (1968).

2837. Archer, Jerome Walter. 1942. *Latin Loan-Words in Early Middle English*. Northwestern diss., 416 pp. [Abstr. in *Summaries of Doctoral Diss., Northwestern Univ.*, 10.5-11 (1943).]

2838. Arngart, Olof. 1943. "English *Craft* 'a vessel' and Some Other Names for Vessels". *ES* 25.161-69. [Deals with a number of ME ships' names.]

2839. ———. 1947. "*Al hende ase hak in chete*: A Note on a Middle English Alliterative Poem". *ES* 28.77-79.

2840. ———. 1951. "M.E. *ladel* 'a by-path'". *ES* 32.252.

2841. ———. 1957. "Two Lexical Query-Marks". *ES* 38.206-08. [1. ME *dewes* 'damp places'; 2. ME *iusted* 'joined, allied oneself'.]

2842. ———. 1959. "Middle English *wold*, *awold*". *ES* 40.376-78.

2843. ———. 1979. "*Egest swilc*, *Genesis and Exodus* 143". *NM* 80.229-30.

2844. ———. 1980. "Middle English *Hogt*". *NM* 81.258-59. [Apropos of the form *hogt* occurring in *Genesis and Exodus* 2119.]

2845. Bailey, Harold W. and Alan Strode Campbell Ross. 1957. "*Wastel*". *EGS* 6.1-29. [On the etymology of the word.]

2846. Bailey, Richard Weld. 1978. *Early Modern English: Additions and Antedatings to the Record of English Vocabulary 1475-1700*. Hildesheim & New York: Georg Olms, xv + 367 pp.

Review: Jürgen Schäfer in *Anglia* 99.427-30 (1981).

2847. Baldinger, Kurt. 1960. "Lexikalische Auswirkungen der englischen Herrschaft in Südwestfrankreich (1152-1453)". *Flasdieck Festschrift*, 11-50.

2848. Baldwin, Mary. 1976. "Some Difficult Words in the *Ancrene Riwle*". *MS* 38.268-90. [Discusses *bihalden*, *cnost* & *dolc*, *woh*, *schrift*, *fleschliche sawlen*, *worltliche*, *loke cape*.]

2849. Ball, Christopher J.E. 1960. "Old Kentish *Wig* and Middle English *Owy*". *RES* n.s. 11.52-53.

2850. Barnickel, Klaus-Dieter. 1975. *Farbe, Helligkeit und Glanz im Mittelenglischen: Bedeutungsstruktur und literarische Erscheinungsform eines Wortschatzbereichs*. (= Düsseldorfer Hochschulreihe, 1.) Düsseldorf: Janssen, 306 pp. [Abstr. in *EASG* 1975 (1976), 24-26.]

Review: D. Nehls in *IF* 86.367-71 (1981 [1982]).

2851. Baron, W.R.J. 1965. "*Luf-daungere*". *Vinaver Festschrift*, 1-18. [Discusses the meaning of *luf-daungere* in *Pearl* and of OF *dangier*.]

2852. Barstow, Allen Merrill. 1970. *A Lexicographical Study of Heraldic Terms in Anglo-Norman Rolls of Arms: 1300-1350*. Pennsylvania diss., 682 pp. [Abstr. in *DA* 31.2866-67A (1970).]

2853. Baugh, Albert Croll. 1935. "The Chronology of French Loan-Words in English". *MLN* 50.90-93. [Classifies 1000 arbitrarily chosen loan-words from French according to the period of borrowing.]

2854. ———. 1961. "Two Middle English Lexical Notes". *Language* 37.539-43. [1. *embose*; 2. *double worstede*.]

2855. Bazire, Joyce. 1952. "The Vocabulary of *The Metrical Life of St. Robert of Knaresborough*". *LSE* 7/8.39-44.

2856. Bean, J. Malcolm W. 1972. "'Bachelor' and Retainer". *M&H* n.s. 3.117-31.

[Analyses the meaning of the term 'bachelor' in the late 13th and the 14th centuries.]

2857. Behre, Frank. 1938. "A Middle English Noun *lede*". *ES* 20.49-57. [Repr. in *Behre Papers*, 1-14.]

2858. ———. 1938. "Middle English *rochine*". *SN* 11.251-56. [Repr. in *Behre Papers*, 15-19.]

2859. ———. 1939. "Middle English *hāk*, a Scandinavian Loan-Word". *MASO* 2.25-37. [Repr. in *Behre Papers*, 20-31.]

2860. ———. 1941/42. "Two Middle English Words of Scandinavian Origin". *SN* 14.221-37. [Discusses *stroke* and *in waght* occurring in Thomas Castleford's *Chronicle* (?a1350 [*MED*]). Repr. in *Behre Papers*, 32-49.]

2861. ———. 1944/45. "English *gal(e)*, *gol*, *goal*". *SN* 17.265-83. [Repr. in *Behre Papers*, 50-67, with postscript (66-67).]

2862. ———. 1959. "A Middle English Rhyme-Pair: Further Studies in Scandinavian Origins". *ES* 40.353-58. [Deals with the rhyme *ouse:trouse* in Castleford's *Chronicle*. Repr. in *Behre Papers*, 68-74.]

2863. ———. 1959. "Three Dialect Words in Middle English Verse". *Septentrionalia et Orientalia: Studia Bernhardo Karlgren a.d. III Non. Oct. anno MCMLIX Dedicata* (= Kungl. Vitterhets- Historie- och Antikvitetsakademiens handlingar, 91), 43-50. Stockholm: Almqvist & Wiksell. [The words discussed are *staite*, *gā*, and *etheer*. Repr. in *Behre Papers*, 75-82.]

2864. Bell, Alexander. 1948. "Glossarial and Textual Notes on Gaimar's *Estoire des Engleis*". *MLR* 43.39-46. [Mainly concerns OF, but contains two notes on ME: *cyules* 'long ships' and *here* 'lord'.]

2865. Berger, Sidney. 1973. "A Method for Compiling a Concordance for a Middle English Text". *SB* 26.219-28.

2866. Bergner, Heinz. 1978. "*Miles*: A Crux in MS. Harley 2253 f.71v". *NM* 79.354-58.

2867. Berndt, Rolf. 1981. "The 'Ivanhoe' Legend and Changes in the English Lexicon after the Norman Conquest". *Linguistische Arbeitsberichte* (Tübingen) 35.10-23.

2868. Besserman, Lawrence L. 1976. "Merisms in Middle English Poetry". *AnM* 17.58-69. [Discusses set phrases like *fer and ner*, *grete and smal*, *old and yong*, etc.]

2869. Biggins, Dennis. 1966. "A Chaucerian Crux: *Spiced Conscience, CT* 1(A) 526, III(D) 435". *ES* 47.169-80.

2870. Bishop, Helen. 1972. "The Vocabulary of the English Translation of *Speculum Humanae Salvationis*". *ES* 53.105-09. [MS Date: late 14th-century.]

2871. Bitterling, Klaus. 1973. "Middle English *Hornet* 'A Beetle'?". *N&Q* n.s. 20.326-27.

2872. ———. 1975. "*Till* 'While' in Barbour's *Bruce*". *NM* 76.428.

2873. ———. 1975. "Middle English *Glouberd* 'A Dormouse'". *N&Q* n.s. 22.388.

2874. ———. 1979. "*Anoyntyng* in Robert Mannyng's *Handlyng Synne*". *N&Q* n.s. 26.8-9.

2875. ———. 1980. "Three Middle English Ghost-Forms of Names for Precious Stones". *N&Q* n.s. 27.495.

2876. ———. 1981. "A ME Treatise on Angling from BL MS Sloane 1698". *ES* 62.110-14. [Prints the text of *De arte piscandi* (dated the middle of the 15th century) and discusses fishing terms in it.]

2877. ———. 1983. "The *Proverbs of Alfred* and the *Middle English Dictionary*". *NM* 84.344-46. [Questions Moessner's suggestions [no. 3194] for additions to the *MED*.]

2878. Blake, Norman Francis. 1968. "Word Borrowings in Caxton's Original Writings". *ELN* 6.87-90. [Disagrees with Donner [no. 2992].]

2879. ———. 1969. "Some Low Dutch Loan-Words in Fifteenth-Century English". *N&Q* n.s. 16.251-53.

2880. ———. 1979. "*Astromye* in 'The Miller's Tale'". *N&Q* n.s. 26.110-11. [Cf. Huntsman [no. 3074] and Ross [no. 3288].]

2881. ———. 1983. "Aspects of Syntax and Lexis in *The Canterbury Tales*". *RCEI* 7.1-19. [The passage discussed is the General Prologue 118-62.]

2882. Blanch, Robert J. 1983. "The Legal Framework of "a Twelmonyth and a Day" in *Sir Gawain and the Green Knight*". *NM* 84.347-52. [Deals with legal terms in *Sir Gawain and the Green Knight*.]

2883. Blenner-Hassett, Roland. 1941/42. "A Nature-Name Puzzle in Lawman's *Brut*". *SN* 14.53-57. [On the origin and identity of the *mære swiðe muchel* (l. 22017).]

2884. ———. 1953. "Middle English *Muggles, Muglinges*". *PMLA* 68.917-20. [On the origin of these forms, which appear in Layamon's *Brut* 29588-90.]

2885. Bliss, Alan J. 1963. "Imparisyllabic Nouns in English". *EPS* 8.1-5. [Deals with those ME words borrowed from French of which the original Latin has more syllables in the oblique cases than in the nominative.]

2886. Bloomfield, Morton Wilfred. 1962. "Middle English *Gladly*: An Instance of Linguisticism". *NM* 63.167-74. [On the interpretation of ME *gladly* in various contexts.]

2887. ———. 1969. "Some Notes on *Sir Gawain and the Green Knight* (Lines 374, 546, 752, 1236) and *Pearl* (Lines 1-2, 61, 775-776, 968)". *Willard Festschrift*, 300-02. [Interprets difficult words on the lines specified.]

2888. ——— and Benjamin A. Eilbott. 1957. "A Diachronic Approach to Lexical Number: Middle and Modern English". *AS* 32.170-75. [Deals with mass-words and countables in ME and ModE.]

2889. Bøgholm, Niels. 1937. "Vocabulary and Style of the Middle English *Ancrene Riwle*". *ES* 19.113-16.

2890. Bone, Gavin. 1937. "A Note on *Pearl* and *The Buke of the Howlat*". *MAE* 6.169-70. [On the interpretation of *myrþes* in *Pearl* 140.]

2891. Borroff, Marie. 1976. "*It wern fowre letterys of purposy*: A New Interpretation". *N&Q* n.s. 23.294-95. [On the meaning of *purposy*.]

2892. Boys, Richard C. 1937. "An Unusual Meaning of *Make* in Chaucer". *MLN* 52.351-53. [Notes Chaucer's use of *make* in the sense of 'match' in *Troilus and Criseyde*, V. 1788.]

2893. Braddy, Haldeen. 1966. "Chaucer's Bawdy Tongue". *SFQ* 30.214-22. [Contains numerous examples of Chaucer's bawdy vocabulary.]

2894. ———. 1968. "Chaucer's Bilingual Idiom". *SFQ* 32.1-6. [Discusses bawdy slang from French and Aglo-Saxon.]

2895. Brault, Gerard J. 1972. *Early Blazon: Heraldic Terminology in the Twelfth and Thirteenth Centuries, with Special Reference to Arthurian Literature*. Oxford: Clarendon Press, 327 pp.

Reviews: Dafydd Evans in *N&Q* n.s. 20.61-70 (1973); Constance Bullock-Davies in *MAE* 43.314-16 (1974); M.A. Stones in *Speculum* 49.319-20 (1974); P. Spufford in *Neophil* 58.82 (1974); Lilo Paoletti in *SMed* 17.435 (1976); Anne Iker-Gittleman in *RP* 29.372-74 (1976).

2896. Brekle, Herbert Ernst. 1963. *Semantische Analyse von Wertadjektiven als Determinanten persönlicher Substantive in William Caxtons Prologen und Epilogen.* Tübingen: Privately printed [Buchdruckerei H. Laupp], 100 pp. [Tübingen diss. Discusses 12 adjectives in all: *vulnerable, worshipful, noble, redoubted, mighty, puissant, virtuous, wise, excellent, sovereign, simple,* and *rude.*]

Reviews: Arne Rudskoger in *SN* 36.380-81 (1964); Harry Spitsbardt in *ZZA* 12.405-08 (1964); Ewald Standop in *IF* 69.92-93 (1964); W.A. Koch in *Anglia* 84.420-23 (1966).

2897. Britton, Geoffrey C. 1960. "A Note on the Word *Thing* in *Havelok the Dane*". *NM* 61.77-79.

2898. Brook, George Leslie. 1934. "Recipes from Harley 2253". *LSE* 3.17-19. [Lists the words used in the MS but not recorded elsewhere earlier than the late 14th or 15th centuries.]

2899. Brorström, Sverker. 1965. *Studies on the Use of the Preposition 'of' in 15th-Century Correspondence, with Special Reference to Constructions Differing from Present-day Usage.* (= SSE, 14.) Stockholm: Almqvist & Wiksell, 74 pp.

Reviews: E. Vorlat in *LB* 55.Bijblad 230 (1966); Herbert Koziol in *Archiv* 204.286-87 (1967/68); Horst Weinstock in *Anglia* 86.369-70 (1968).

2900. Brown, Emerson, Jr. 1980. "Word Play in the Prologue to the *Manciple's Tale*, 98: "T'acord and love and many a wrong apese"". *ChauN* 2:2.11-12. [On the meaning of *apese.*]

2901. Burch, J.C. Horton. 1934. "Notes on the Language of John Gower". *ES* 16.209-15. [Presents a comparison of information drawn from Burch's *A Combined Lexicon and Concordance of the English Works of John Gower* (Duke Univ. diss., 1933) with that furnished by *OED*.]

2902. Burchfield, Robert William. 1952. "Two Misreadings of the *Ormulum* Manuscript". *MAE* 21.37-39. [On the origin and meaning of the word *apperrmod.*]

2903. ———. 1962. "*Ormulum*: Words Copied by Jan van Vliet from Parts now Lost". *Tolkien Festschrift*, 94-111. [Notes some new or rare words preserved in Jan van Vliet's transcriptions from that text in MS Lambeth 783.]

2904. Burgschmidt, Ernst. 1976. *Koexistenz, Distribution, Äquivalenz, Synonymie: Studien zur Beschreibung der mittelenglischen Lokal- und Temporalpräpositionen.* Nürnberg: E. Burgschmidt, xi + 713 pp. [Erlangen diss. Discusses *to/till, fro/from, before/tofore/afore, in/on,* etc. in six periods from 1200-1450.]

2905. Burnley, John David. 1972. *Aspects of Patterning in the Vocabulary of Chaucer, with Particular Reference to His Courtly Terminology*. Durham diss., 593 pp.

2906. ———. 1972. "Chaucer's Art of Verbal Allusion: Two Notes". *Neophil* 56.93-99.

2907. ———. 1976. "Middle English Colour Terminology and Lexical Structure". *LingB* 41.39-49.

2908. ———. 1976. "Proude Bayard: *Troilus and Criseyde*, I. 218". *N&Q* n.s. 23.148-52.

2909. ———. 1977. "Chaucer's *Termes*". *YES* 7.53-67. [Explores the word's meanings and implications.]

2910. ———. 1979. *Chaucer's Language and the Philosophers' Tradition*. (= Chaucer Studies, 2.) Cambridge: D.S. Brewer; Totowa, NJ: Roman & Littlefield, x + 196 pp. [Explores the various kinds of association found in Chaucer's lexical usage.]

Reviews: Bill Quinn in *Style* 15.499-501 (1981); A.V.C. Schmidt in *MAE* 50.344-46 (1981); Pillipa Hardman in *RES* n.s. 33.71-73 (1982); Peter Mack in *MLR* 77.404-05 (1982); Götz Schmitz in *Anglia* 100.183-85 (1982); David Staines in *SN* 55.206-09 (1983).

2911. ———. 1980. "*Fine Amor*: Its Meaning and Context". *RES* n.s. 31.129-48.

2912. ———. 1982. "Criseyde's Heart and the Weakness of Women: An Essay in Lexical Interpretation". *SN* 54.25-38.

2913. ———. 1984. "Picked Terms". *ES* 65.195-204. [Discusses the importance of verbal selection to style in late ME authors.]

2914. ———. 1985. "Chaucer Through His Language". *ChauN* 7:1.1 & 5.

2915. ———. 1986. "Some Terminology of Perception in the *Book of the Duchess*". *ELN* 23:3.15-22.

2916. Burrow, John Anthony. 1980. "Laʒamon's *Brut* 10,642: *Wleoteð*". *N&Q* n.s. 27.2-3.

2917. Burton, Tom L. 1973. "Fifteenth- and Sixteenth-Century Antedatings, Postdatings and Additions to *O.E.D.*, *M.E.D.* and *D.O.S.T.* from *Sidrak and Bokkus*". *N&Q* n.s. 20.369-75.

2918. ———. 1978. "Late Fifteenth-Century 'Terms of Association' in MS. Pepys 1047". *N&Q* n.s. 25.7-12.

2919. ———. 1987. "Some Unnoticed ME Idioms Involving Chiefly *Reason* and *Skill*, *Showing* and *Telling*". *ES* 68.122-28.

2920. Busse, W.G. 1980. "*Pearl* 1104: An Unnecessary Emendation". *N&Q* n.s. 27.3-4. [Discusses the MS reading *wythouten delyt* (l. 1104).]

2921. Butler, Marilyn S. 1983. "Early Middle English *Budde*: A Ghost Word". *N&Q* n.s. 30.104-05.

2922. Caldwell, Robert A. 1943. "An Elizabethan Chaucer Glossary". *MLN* 58.374-75. [On a glossary (c.1600) by Joseph Holand in the Chaucer Codex now known as MS Gg. 4.27, Cambridge Univ. Library.]

2923. Camden, Carroll, Jr. 1932. "Chauceriana". *MLN* 47.360-62. [Notes on *worthy* (A 43, etc.), *sangwyn* (A 333), *moral vertu* (A 307, etc.), and *Wel coude he fortunen the ascendent Of his images for his pacient* (A 417-418).]

2924. Cassidy, Frederic Gomes. 1943. "Chaucer's 'Broken Harm'". *MLN* 58.23-27. [On the meaning of "broken in the *Merchant's Tale*, 1425.]

2925. ———. 1958. "'Don Thyn Hood' in Chaucer's *Troilus*". *JEGP* 57.739-42. [Questions F.N. Robinson's note to *TC* II. 954.]

2926. Casson, Leslie F. 1934. "Studies in the Diction of the *Confessio Amantis*". *EStn* 69.184-207. [On Gower's vocabulary.]

2927. Clark, Cecily. 1952/53. "Studies in the Vocabulary of the *Peterborough Chronicle*, 1070-1154". *EGS* 5.67-89.

2928. ———. 1966. "*Ancrene Wisse* and *Katherine Group*: A Lexical Divergence". *Neophil* 50.117-24.

2929. Clark, G.N. 1935. *The Dutch Influence on the English Vocabulary*. Oxford: Clarendon Press; London: Milford, 14 pp. [= *S.P.E. Tract* 44.161-72.]

2930. Clark, John Williams. 1941. "The Authorship of *Sir Gawain and the Green Knight, Pearl, Cleanness, Patience,* and *Erkenwald* in the Light of the Vocabulary". Minnesota diss., 425 pp. [Abstr. in *Summaries of Ph.D. Theses, Univ. of Minnesota* 4.107-12 (1949).]

2931. ———. 1949. "Observations on Certain Differences in Vocabulary between *Cleanness* and *Sir Gawain and the Green Knight*". *PQ* 28.261-73.

2932. ———. 1950. "'The *Gawain*-poet' and the Substantival Adjective". *JEGP* 49.60-66.

2933. ———. 1950. "Paraphrases for "God" in the Poems Attributed to 'The *Gawain*-Poet'". *MLN* 65.232-36.

2934. ———. 1951. "On Certain 'Alliterative' and 'Poetic' Words in the Poems Attributed to 'The *Gawain*-Poet'". *MLQ* 12.387-98.

2935. Clark, Roy Peter. 1976. "*Alfin*: Invective in the Alliterative *Morte Arthure*". *ELN* 13.165-68.

2936. Clough, Andrea. 1985. "The French Element in *Sir Gawain and the Green Knight*: with Special Reference to the Description of Bertilak's Castle in ll.785-810". *NM* 86.187-96. [Discusses the nature of the French loan words in *SGGK*.]

2937. Coates, Richard. 1978. "Etymologica: Three Mismatches with the Goshawk". *Neophil* 62.131-34. [Includes discussion on ME *ostreger/ostringer*.]

2938. Cochran, Leonard. 1984. "Chaucer's Fish". *Verbatim* (Essex, CT) 10:4.8.

2939. Colledge, Eric. 1958. "*Aliri*". *MAE* 27.111-13. [On the meaning and etymology of ME *aliri*.]

2940. Collins, Fletcher, Jr. 1932. "*Solas* in the *Miller's Tale*". *MLN* 47.363-64. [*Solas*=*sol-la's* in the hexachord scale series *ut, re, mi, fa, sol, la*.]

2941. Conley, John. 1964. "Scholastic Neologisms in Usk's *Testament of Love*". *N&Q* n.s. 11.209.

2942. ———. 1982. "*Everyman* 504: *Ase, Beholde*, or 'Ah, See'?". *N&Q* n.s. 29.339-400.

2943. Cooper, Geoffrey. 1980. "'Sely John' in the 'Legende' of the *Miller's Tale*". *JEGP* 79.1-12. [Discusses Chaucer's use of the adjective.]

2944. Corner, Rachel. 1962. "More Fifteenth-Century 'Terms of Association'". *RES* n.s. 13.229-44.

2945. Craigie, William Alexander. 1923. "Two Middle-English Ghost-Words". *N&Q* 145.228. [On †*angrom* and †*angromed*.]

2946. ———. 1932. "The Older Scottish and American English Dictionaries". *PMLA* 47.891-93.

2947. ———. 1935. "Older Scottish and English: A Study in Contrasts". *TPS* 1935, 1-15.

2948. Cross, James E. 1951. "On the Meaning of *a-blakeberyed (Canterbury Tales*, C 406)". *RES* n.s. 2.372-74.

2949. Crowell, T.L. 1955. "Predating 'Have To,' 'Must'?". *AS* 30.68-69. [Suggests an early example in the *Paston Letters*.]

2950. Dahl, Torsten. 1949/50. "Middle English *seint, seinte*". *SN* 22.15. [Comments on Donaldson [no. 2991].]

2951. Dahood, Roger. 1978. "A Lexical Puzzle in *Ancrene Wisse*". *N&Q* n.s. 25.1-2. [On *locunges-efter*.]

2952. d'Ardenne, Simonne T.R.O. 1946 [1948]. "The Devil's Spout". *TPS* 1946, 31-55. [An inquiry into the meaning of the noun *tutel* and the related verb *tutelin*, found in early ME, only in the *Ancrene Wisse*.]

2953. ———. 1974. "**Bratewil (Katerine*, 1690)". *ES* 55.282-83; 497 (addendum).

2954. ———. 1978. "Additional Note to SW *Iseh towart*, EMEVP, 286". *ES* 59.114-15 [The line quoted is *Sawles Warde* 286 in J.A.W. Bennett and G.V. Smithers (eds.), *Early Middle English Verse and Prose*, 2nd ed. (Oxford: Clarendon Press, 1968). The author argues that the prefix *i-* still has a perfective sense in the AB dialect.]

2955. ———. 1978. "*Beatewil* (R *batewil*, T *swetewil*), MS Bodley 34, fol. 11/20". *Mélanges de philologie et de littératures romanes offerts à Jeanne Wathelet-Willem*, ed. Jacques de Caluwé, 1-4. Liège: Cahiers de l'A.R.U. Lg.

2956. ———. 1982. "Two Words for *Ancrene Wisse* and the Katherine Group". *N&Q* n.s. 29.3. [Discusses *utnume* in *Ancrene Wisse* and *bur* in *St. Margaret*.]

2957. Dareau, Margaret Grace and Angus McIntosh. 1971. "A Dialect Word in Some West Midland Manuscripts of the *Prick of Conscience*". *Edinburgh Studies*, 20-26. [On the word *goben*.]

2958. d'Aronco, Maila. 1974 [1979]. "Medio inglese *false*". *InLi* 1.83-88.

2959. Davenport, W.A. 1977. "The Word *Norne* and the Temptation of Sir Gawain". *NM* 78.256-63. [Discusses the meaning of the verb *norne*.]

2960. Davis Norman. 1966. "*Sir Gawain and the Green Knight* 611-12". *N&Q* n.s. 13.448-51. [Emends the MS reading *pernyng* (l.611) to *peruyng* 'periwinkle' and interprets *trulofez* (l.612) as 'quatrefoils', not 'true lover's knots'.]

2961. ———. 1969. "Sheep-Farming Terms in Medieval Norfolk". *N&Q* n.s. 16.404-05. [On three sheep-farming terms in the *Paston Letters*.]

2962. ———. 1970. "*Sir Gawain and the Green Knight* 2073". *N&Q* n.s. 17.163-64. [Discusses the syntax and meaning of *Gef hym God and goud day*.]

2963. ———. 1974. "A Ghostly Middle English Forms of *leopard*". *N&Q* n.s. 21.210.

2964. De Caluwé-Dor, Juliette. 1977. "Divergence lexicale entre le *Katherine Group* et l'*Ancrene Riwle*: valeur statistique des premières attestations de mots d'origine français en anglais". *EA* 30.463-72.

2965. ———. 1979. "The Chronology of the Scandinavian Loan-Verbs in the *Katherine Group*". *ES* 60.680-85.

2966. ———. 1979. "Le Diable dans les *Contes de Cantorbéry*: Contribution à l'étude sémantique du terme *devil*". *Le Diable au Moyen Age: Doctrine problèmes moraux, représentations* (= Sénéfiance, 6), 97-116. Aix-en-Provence: Pubs. du CUER MA, Univ. de Provence.

2967. ———. 1982. *Forms and Meaning of the Verbs Contained in M.S. Bodley 34.* (= Publ. de l'assoc. des médiévistes anglicistes de l'enseignement supérieur, 7). Paris & Amiens: Assoc. des Médiévistes anglicistes de l'Enseignement Supérieur, 432 pp. [Thèse Liege 1981. MS Bodley 34 = the *Katherine Group*.]

2968. ———. 1982. "La Convergence Étymologique et le Bilinguisme". *Linguistics in Belgium/Linguistiek in België/Linguistique en Belgique* (= Proceedings of the 1980 Cercle Belge de Linguistique Conference) 5.66-80. [Apropos of the *Katherine Group*.]

2969. ———. 1983. "Chaucer's Contribution to the English Vocabulary: A Chronological Survey of French Loan-Words". *NOWELE* 2.73-91.

2970. ———. 1983. "Etymological Convergence in the Katherine Group". *Current Topics in EHL*, 211-23.

2971. ———. 1984. "Chaucer's Derivational Morphemes Revisited". *Crépin LSSME/* 10, 63-79.

2972. De la Cruz, Juan M. 1978 [1980]. "The Construction of a Specialized Corpus-Glossary Showing Syntactic Patterning (A Contribution to Middle English Lexicography and Syntax)". *Orbis* 27.287-311.

2973. Dent, Anthony Austen. 1959. "Chaucer and the Horse". *Proceedings of the Leeds Philosophical and Literary Society* 9:4.1-12. [Deals with the technical vocabulary used by Chaucer to describe horses, riding equipment, etc.]

2974. Derolez, René. 1969. "A Chronic Case of Linguistic Indigestion?". *RLV* 35.481-89. [Examines some aspects of that large-scale borrowing of French words which some scholars have considered as one of the most momentous, not to say the most disastrous, consequences of the Norman Conquest.]

2975. De Weever, Jacqueline. 1983. "*Lufly* and Its Variants in *Sir Gawain and the Green Knight*". *Journal of the Rocky Mountain Medieval and Renaissance Association* (Northern Arizona Univ., Flagstaff) 4.33-43.

2976. Dieckmann, Emma P.M. 1929. "The Meaning of *burdoun* in Chaucer". *MS* 26.279-82.

2977. Diensberg, Bernhard. 1978. "*Ancrene Wisse/Riwle surquide, caue, creauant/creaunt, trusse, bereget* und *babanliche*". *Archiv* 215.79-82.

2978. ———. 1978. "Westsächsische Lehnwörter im Merzischen AB-Dialekt?" *Anglia* 96.447-50.

2979. ———. 1985. "The Lexical Fields 'Boy/Girl-Servant-Child' in Middle English". *NM* 86.328-36.

2980. Dietz, Klaus. 1985. "Alte und neue Wege der Erschliessung des mittelenglischen Wortschatzes". *Symposium on Lexicography II: Proceedings of the Second International Symposium on Lexicography, May 16-17, 1984 at the University of Copenhagen* (= Lexicographica, Ser. Maior, 5), ed. Karl Hyldgaard-Jensen and Arne Zettersten, 199-222. Tübingen: Niemeyer.

2981. Dike, Edwin Berck. 1934. "Our Oldest Obsoletisms". *EStn* 68.339-50. [Discusses a number of groups of words which went out of use during the ME period.]

2982. ———. 1937. "The Suffix *-ess*, etc". *JEGP* 36.29-34. [On the history and development of the feminine suffix *-ess* in words of agency.]

2983. DiMarco, Vincent and Leslie Perelman. 1977. "Noteworthy Lexical Evidence in the Middle English *Letter of Alexander to Aristotle*". *Neophil* 61.297-303.

2984. Dobson, Eric John. 1940. "The Etymology and Meaning of *Boy*". *MAE* 9.121-54. [Includes a discussion of the word in ME, the period of the word's importation and popularization.]

2985. ———. 1943. "Middle English and Middle Dutch *Boye*". *MAE* 12.71-76. [Concludes that in spite of the resemblance, the words are unrelated.]

2986. ———. 1974. "Two Notes on Early Middle English Texts". *N&Q* n.s. 21.124-26. [Discusses *weoli* in *Ancrene Wisse* and *deoren* in Layamon's *Brut*.]

2987. Dodgson, John McNeal. 1968. "ME. *Cronebery*". *N&Q* n.s. 15.88-89.

2988. Dodson, Sarah. 1932. "The Glosses in *The Earliest Complete English Psalter*". *[Univ. of Texas] Studies in English* 12.5-26.

2989. Dolan, T.P. 1979. "'Riote" in *Ancrene Wisse*". *ELN* 16.198-200.

2990. Döll, Helene. 1932. *Mittelenglische Kleidernamen im Spiegel literarischer Denkmäler des 14. Jahrhunderts*. Giessen: Glasgow, 163 pp. [Giessen diss.]

Review: E. von Erhardt-Siebold in *Anglia B* 44.337-40 (1933).

2991. Donaldson, Ethelbert Talbot. 1948/49. "Middle English *Seint, Seinte*". *SN* 21.222-30. [Attempts to account historically for the alternation of the two forms before proper names in Chaucer. Cf. Dahl [no. 2950].]

2992. Donner, Morton. 1966. "The Infrequency of Word Borrowings in Caxton's Original Writings". *ELN* 4.86-89.

2993. ———. 1978. "Derived Words in Chaucer's Language". *ChauR* 13.1-15.

2994. ———. 1984. "Derived Words in Chaucer's *Boece*: The Translator as Wordsmith". *ChauR* 18.187-203.

2995. ———. 1987. "Agent Nouns in *Piers Plowman*". *ChauR* 21.374-82.

2996. Draper, John W. 1925/26. "Chaucer's 'Wardrobe'". *EStn* 60.238-51.

2997. Dunlap, Arthur Ray. 1934. *A Study of the Vocabulary and the Dialect of the Middle English Romances in Tail-Rhyme Stanza*. Yale diss., 143 pp. [Abstr. in *DA* 31.1783-84A (1970).]

2998. ———. 1941. "The Vocabulary of the Middle English Romances in Tail-Rhyme Stanza". *Delaware Notes* (14th series), 36.1-42.

2999. Dustoor, Phiroze Edulji. 1937. "Chaucer's Use of *discreet*". *RES* 13.206-09. [On the word *discreet* in Chaucer in the sense of 'civil, courteous', etc.]

3000. Ebin, Lois. 1977. "Lydgate's Views on Poetry". *AnM* 18.76-105. [In the first part (pp. 76-88), the author discusses eight words: *enlumyn, adourne enbelissche, aureate, goldyn, surgrid, rethorik,* and *elloquence,* which Lydgate popularized or developed with new meanings.]

3001. Einarsson, Stefán. 1938. "Two Scandinavianisms in the *Peterborough Chronicle*". *JEGP* 37.18-20. [On *þoþ* and *innen*.]

3002. Ekwall, Eilert. 1938/39. "English *fond*: An Etymological and Semasiological Study". *SN* 11.289-317. [Discusses 1. ME *fon* adj., 2. ME *fon* sb., 3. ME *fonne* vb.]

3003. ———. 1939. "Middle English *o bon*". *MASO* 2.16-24.

Review: A. B[randl] in *Archiv* 174.256.

3004. ———. 1947. "A Twelfth Century Lollard?". *ES* 28.108-10. [Notes in a Ramsay document the name *Elfred Lollere* which provides evidence for an English *lollere*, an agent-noun formed from a verb *lollen*.]

3005. ———. 1949. "Two Middle English Etymologies". *Malone Festschrift*, 144-53. [Discusses *fōn* 'few, a few' and *sēn* 'to happen'.]

3006. Ellenberger, Bengt. 1974. "On Middle English *Mots Savants*". *SN* 46.142-50.

3007. ———. 1977. *The Latin Element in the Vocabulary of the Earlier Makars Henryson and Dunbar*. (= LundSE, 51.) Lund: LieberLäromedel/C.W.K. Gleerup, 163 pp. [Lund diss.]

Reviews: Priscilla Bawcutt in *N&Q* n.s. 25.168-70 (1978); Jürgen Schäfer in *Anglia* 97.187-89 (1979); J. Norton-Smith in *MAE* 49.151-53 (1980); Manfred Görlach in *Archiv* 217.410-12; J. Derrick McClure in *Scottish Literary Journal* (Aberdeen Univ.), Supplement 16.4-6 (1982).

3008. Elliot, Ralph Warren Victor. 1974. "Some Northern Landscape Features in *Sir Gawain and the Green Knight*". *Maxwell Festschrift*, 132-43. [An examination of the topographical vocabulary.]

3009. ———. 1977. "Staffordshire and Cheshire Landscapes in *Sir Gawain and the Green Knight*". *North Staffordshire Journal of Field Studies* 17.20-49.

3010. ———. 1978. "Hills and Valleys in the *Gawain* Country". *LSE* n.s. 10.18-41. [An examination of the topographical vocabulary of ME alliterative poetry.]

3011. ———. 1979. "Woods and Forests in the *Gawain* Country". *NM* 80.48-64. [A study of the topographical vocabulary of the *Gawain*-poet.]

3012. ———. 1982. "Streams and Swamps in the *Gawain* Country". *LSE* n.s. 13.56-73. [Investigates the *Gawain*-poet's fluvial and paludal vocabulary.]

3013. ———. 1984. *The Gawain Country: Essays on the Topography of Middle English Alliterative Poetry*. (= Leeds Texts and Monographs, New Ser., 8.) Leeds: School of English, Univ. of Leeds, v + 165 pp.

3014. 'Espinasse, Margaret. 1976. "Chaucer's *fare-carte*". *N&Q* n.s. 23.295-96. [*Troilus and Criseyde* V. 1162]

3015. Everett, Dorothy and Naomi D. Hurnard. 1947. "Legal Phraseology in a Passage in *Pearl*". *MAE* 16.9-15. [The passage is ll.697-708.]

3016. Faust, George P. 1932. "Two Notes on Chaucer". *MLN* 47.365-67. [Notes on *tonyght* and *undern*.]

3017. Feist, Robert. 1934. *Studien zur Rezeption des französischen Wortschatzes im Mittelenglischen*. (= BEP, 25). Leipzig: Tauchnitz, 87 pp. [München diss. Repr., New York: Johnson Reprint, 1968.]

    Reviews: H.C. Matthes in *GRM* 23.393-94 (1935); A.H. Brand in *ES* 24.62-64 (1942).

3018. Fettig, Adolf. 1934. *Die Gradadverbien im Mittelenglischen*. (= AF, 79.) Heidelberg: Carl Winter, viii + 222 pp. [Heidelberg diss.]

    Reviews: G.-K. Bauer in *GRM* 23.311 (1935); H. Heuer in *Anglia B* 46.197-201 (1935); H. Koziol in *EStn* 71.244-47 (1936); O. Anderson in *ES* 19.176-77 (1937); J.L.N. O'Loughlin in *MAE* 8.166-67 (1939).

3019. Finkelstein, Dorothee. 1970/71. "The Code of Chaucer's 'Secree of Secrees': Arabic Alchemical Terminology in *The Canon's Yeoman's Tale*". *Archiv* 207.260-76.

3020. Fisher, John Hurt. 1951. "Chaucer's Use of *Swete* and *Swote*". *JEGP* 50.326-31. [Shows that the two forms are as a rule used by Chaucer in different senses.]

3021. Flasdieck, Hermann Martin. 1923. "Zu me. *made*". *EStn* 57.139-41.

3022. Fleck, Elga. 1973. *Ausgewählte mittelenglische Speisennamen*. Graz diss., 250 pp. [Abstr. in *EASG* 1973 (1974), 16-18.]

3023. Fogg, Wendell F. 1928. "O.E. *mæȝeþ* in *Hali Meidenhad*". *MLN* 43.527-28.

3024. Foster, Frances A. 1940. "Some English Words from the *Fasciculus Morum*". *Essays and Studies in Honor of Carleton Brown*, 149-57. New York: New York Univ. Press; London: Oxford Univ. Press. [The corpus is a collection of exempla for the use of preachers, dated c.1320.]

3025. Fowler, David Covington. 1954. "An Unusual Meaning of *Win* in Chaucer's *Troilus and Criseyde*". *MLN* 69.313-15. [Argues that the verb *wynne* (*TC* I. 390) means 'to complain'.]

3026. Frankis, Percy John. 1960. "A Middle English Crux, *nere*: With a Note on Initial Consonant Mutation in English". *NM* 61.373-87.

3027. ———. 1963. "Flemish Words in a Fifteenth-Century English Poem". *N&Q* n.s. 10.12-13.

3028. ———. 1983. "Word Formation by Blending in the Vocabulary of Middle English Alliterative Verse". *Dobson Festschrift*, 29-38. [Discusses *clynterand*, *maskel/maskelles*, *runisch/renisch/roynisch*, *skelten*, *sniteren*, *stryppe*, and *Gawain* 2461.]

3029. Funke, Otto. 1945. "Zur Wortgeschichte der französischen Elemente im Englischen". *Wege und Ziele* by Otto Funke, 99-121. Bern: Francke. [An examination of the history of some French loan-words in early ME.]

3030. Galway, Margaret. 1942. "A Basque Word in Chaucer". *TLS*, Oct. 3, 1942, p. 492. [The word is *phislyas*, in the *Man of Law*'s endlink (B 1189). Replies by K. Sisam, *TLS*, Oct. 24, 1942, p. 525, and R. Gallop, *TLS*, Nov. 14, 1942.]

3031. ———. 1943. "A Basque Word in Chaucer?". *TLS*, Apr. 10. 1943, p. 180. [An answer to critics of her original article [no. 3030].]

3032. Ganguli, Sukumar. 1940. *A Study of Chaucer's Diction and Terms for Womanly Beauty*. Univ. College and King's College, London, diss., 529 pp.

Review: Hans Heinrich Meier in *ES* 34.293 (1953).

3033. Gerhard, George Brinsley. 1961. '*A Dictionary of Middle English Musical Terms*', by Henry Holland Carter, Late Professor of English at Indiana University. Indiana diss. (no pagination available). [Abstr. in *DA* 22.2383-84 (1962). For the dictionary, see Carter [no. 117].]

3034. Gerould, Gordon H. 1933. "New Evidence for Middle English *þef*". *MLN* 48.525-27.

3035. Gerritsen, Johan. 1961. "A Ghost-Word: *crucet-hūs*". *ES* 42.300-01. [On the word in the *Peterborough Chronicle*.]

3036. Gerson, Stanley. 1981. "Adjectival Compounds in *-looking*: A Diachronic Survey". *SN* 53.51-61. [Covers the period from the second half of the 14th century to the present.]

3037. Gillmeister, Heiner. 1975. "The Origin of Imperative Constructions and Chaucer's Nonce-words *viritoot*, *virytrate*, and *phislyas*". *Poetica* 4.24-49.

3038. ———. 1978. "Chaucer's *Kan Ke Dort* (*Troilus*, II, 1752), and the 'Sleeping Dogs' of the Trouvères". *ES* 59.310-23.

3039. Gilmour, J. 1956. "Notes on the Vocabulary of Richard Rolle [c.1300-1349]". *N&Q* n.s. 3.94-95. [Addenda to *OED*.]

3040. Golden, Samuel A. 1970. "Chaucer in Minsheu's *Guide into the Tongues*". *ChauR* 4.49-54. [Discusses Minsheu's more than fifty citations of Chaucer in his work of 1617.]

3041. Gordon, Ian A. 1955. "*The Owl and the Nightingale* 258: The Semantic Development of *Spell* (= 'Rest')". *MLN* 70.5-8.

3042. Grant, Clyde Murrell. 1956. *A Vocabulary Study of Skeat's Edition of the A-Text of 'Piers Plowman'*. Univ. of Oklahoma diss., 645 pp. [Abstr. in *DA* 17.850 (1957).]

3043. Griffith, Dudley David. 1949. "On Word-Studies in Chaucer". *Malone Festschrift*, 195-99.

3044. Gross, Laila. 1968. "The Meaning and Oral-Formulaic Use of *Riot* in the Alliterative *Morte Arthure*". *AnM* 9.98-102.

3045. Hammerschlag, Johannes. 1937. *Dialekteinflüsse im frühneuenglischen Wortschatz, nachgewiesen an Caxton und Fabyan*. (= BSEP, 31.) Bonn: Peter Hanstein, 142 pp.

3046. Hanham, Alison. 1961. "The Cely Papers and the *Oxford English Dictionary*". *ES* 42.129-52. [*Cely Papers* (1472-c.1490 [1488]).]

3047. Hargreaves, Henry. 1956. "The Vocabulary of the *Surtees Psalter*". *MLQ* 17.326-39. [Apparently of the second half of the 13th century.]

3048. ———. 1961. "The Marginal Glosses to the Wycliffite New Testament". *SN* 33.285-300.

3049. Harvey, Patricia A. 1968. "ME. Point (*Troilus and Criseyde* III. 695)". *N&Q* n.s. 15.243-44.

3050. Haworth, Mary. 1959. "*Barlay* — *Sir Gawain and the Green Knight* (Line 296)". *N&Q* n.s. 6.104.

3051. Haworth, Paul. 1967. "*Warthe* in *Sir Gawain and the Green Knight*". *N&Q* n.s. 14.171-72.

3052. Heltveit, Trygve. 1964. "Dialect Words in *The Seven Sages of Rome*". *Zandvoort Festschrift* = *ES* 45 Supplement. 125-34.

3053. Hench, Atcheson L. 1973. "*Game* in *Havelok* 996". *ChauR* 7.297-98.

3054. Héraucourt, Will. 1939. "Das Hendyiadyoin als Mittel zur Hervorhebung des Werthaften bei Chaucer". *EStn* 73.190-201. [On syntactical word-pairs (*errour and folye*, *vexed and travailled*, etc.) in Chaucer.]

3055. ———. 1940. "Das sprachliche Feld der *goodes* und seine Gliederung bei Chaucer". *NMon* 11.9-21. [Deals with the terms used by Chaucer for the goods of nature, of fortune, and of grace.]

3056. Herdan, Gustav. 1956. "Chaucer's Authorship of *The Equatorie of the Planetis*: The Use of Romance Vocabulary as Evidence". *Language* 32.254-59.

3057. Heyworth, Peter Lorriman. 1967. "ME *alumere* and *snowcrie*: Two Ghosts". *EPS* 10.57-61.

3058. Higuchi, Masayuki. 1983. "On the Counterfactual Force of *Wenen*: With Special Reference to Chaucer's Use". *SEL* English No. 1983, 101-25.

3059. Hille, Arnoldus. 1969. "Exit Middle English *micclelic*, 'multitude' — Enter *þe micclelic* 'leprosy'". *ES* 50.284-90.

3060. Hillman, Mary Vincent. 1943. "*The Pearl*: *west ernays* (307); *Fasor* (432 [sic])". *MLN* 58.42-44. [The word *fasor* is actually found in l. 431.]

3061. Hoad, T.F. 1984. "English Etymology: Some Problematic Areas in the Vocabulary of the Middle English Period". *TPS* 1984, 27-57.

3062. Hoffman, Donald L. 1970. "*Renischsche Renkes* and *Runisch Sauez*". *N&Q* n.s. 17.447-49. [Examines 12 occurrences of *runish/renish* in ME alliterative poems.]

3063. Holman, C. Hugh. 1951. "*Marereʒ mysse* in *The Pearl*". *MLN* 66.33-36.

3064. Holmes, Urban T., Jr. 1937. "Chaucer's *tydif* 'a small bird'". *PQ* 16.65-67.

3065. Holthausen, Ferdinand. 1925/26. "Mittelengl. *me* 'aber'; Ne *sta(u)nch*; Ne. *skew*". *EStn* 60.119-20.

3066. Howlett, David R. 1974. "The Meaning of Middle English *borgener, burgener*". *N&Q* n.s. 21.205-06.

3067. Hudson, Anne. 1981. "A Lollard Sect Vocabulary". *McIntosh Festschrift* (E), 15-30.

3068. ———. 1983. "Observations on a Northerner's Vocabulary". *Dobson Festschrift*, 74-83.

3069. Hughes, Geoffrey Ian. 1978. "Gold and Iron: Semantic Change and Social Change in Chaucer's Prologue". *Standpunte* (Stellenbosch, Republic of South Africa) 31:5.1-5.

3070. ———. 1979. *Semantic Change in English: An Investigation into the Relation between Semantic Change and the Forces of Social, Economic and Political Change from the Norman Conquest to the Present Day*. Univ. of South Africa diss. (no pagination available). [Abstr. in DA 41.1565A (1980).]

3071. Hulbert, James R. 1936. "English in Manorial Documents of the Thirteenth and Fourteenth Centuries". *MP* 34.37-61. [A study of occasional English words embedded in the Latin manuscripts.]

3072. ———. 1947. "Chaucer's Romance Vocabulary". *PQ* 26.302-06. [Questions the conclusions of Mersand [no. 3186] concerning the extent of Chaucer's romance innovations.]

3073. Hunt, Tony. 1981. "The Trilingual Vocabulary in MS. Westminster Abbey 34/11". *N&Q* n.s. 28.14-15. [Prints the text of a 14th-century Latin-French-English vocabulary.]

3074. Huntsman, Jeffrey Forrest. 1976. "Caveat Editor: Chaucer and Medieval English Dictionaries". *MP* 73.276-79. [Discusses *stot* (*CT* III, 1630); *nakers* (*CT* I, 2511); *astromye* (*CT* I, 3451, 3457).]

3075. ———. 1978. "Computers and Medieval English Lexicography". *CHum* 12.53-60. [Also printed in *Medieval Studies and the Computer* (A Special Issue of *Computers and the Humanities*, vol. 12), ed. Anne Gilmour-Bryson, 53-60. New York & Oxford: Pergamon, 1979.]

3076. ———. 1981. "The State of Lexicography and Lexicology in Plantagenet England: A Data Base". *Data Bases in the Humanities and Social Sciences*, ed. Joseph Raben and G. Marks, 197-201. Amsterdam-New York-Oxford: North-Holland. [The House of Plantagenet (1154-1399).]

3077. ———. 1982. "*Astromye* in the *Miller's Tale* Yet Again". *N&Q* n.s. 29.237. [See Huntsman [no. 3074], Blake [no. 2880], and Ross [no. 3288].]

3078. ———. 1983. "Definitions and Glossing Procedures in Medieval English

Lexicology". *Papers of the Dictionary Society of North America 1981*, ed. Yeatman Anderson III, 57-60. Terre Haute, IN: Indiana State Univ. Press.

3079. Huppé, Bernard F. 1948. "The Translation of Technical Terms in the Middle English *Romaunt of the Rose*". *JEGP* 47.334-42. [Calls attention to the inadequacy of the translation of Jean de Meun's scholastic terminology.]

3080. Ikegami, Yoshihiko. 1964. *ME 'Dight': A Structural Study in the Obsolescence of Words*. (= Proceedings of the Dept. of Foreign Languages and Literatures, College of Gen. Education, Univ. of Tokyo, 1963, 11:4.) Tokyo: Tokyo Univ. Press, 63 pp.

3081. Immaculate, Sr. Mary. 1941. "'Sixty' as a Conventional Number and Other Chauceriana". *MLQ* 2.59-66.

3082. Irwin, P.J. 1934. "Some Emendations in the Chronology of the N.E.D." *JEGP* 33.502-05. [From Anglo-Irish documents of the 1200-1600 period.]

3083. Jacobs, Nicolas. 1977. "The Ottoman *Porte* in Middle English". *N&Q* n.s. 24.306-07. [On the meaning of *porte* in the *Morte Arthure*.]

3084. Jenkins, T. Atkinson. 1928. "*Vitremyte*: mot latin-français employé par Chaucer". *Mélanges de Linguistique et de Littérature, offerts à M. Alfred Jeanroy*, 141-47. Paris: Droz. [Repr., Genève: Slatkine Reprints, 1972.]

3085. Jespersen, Otto. 1939. "The History of a Suffix". *ALH* 1.48-56. [On the verb-suffix *-en*, as in *sharpen*, etc. in ME and ModE.]

3086. Johnston, Grahame K.W. 1957. "A Prayer of the Five Joys". *N&Q* n.s. 4.508. [On the word *tuet* found in no. 18 of *English Lyrics of the XIIIth Century*, ed. Carleton Brown (Oxford: Clarendon Press, 1932).]

3087. ———. 1959. "Northern Idiom in *Pearl*". *N&Q* n.s. 6.347-48. [Argues that *mysse* (l. 382) is a noun.]

3088. Jonsson, T. 1975. *On the Formation and Use of Preparticle Compounds in Middle English: A Study in Grammatical Interference*. Nottingham diss. [No further information available.]

3089. K., A.R. 1927. "Parked". *AS* 2.215. [Apropos of *Y-parked* in *Piers Plowman* C 7.144.]

3090. Kabell, Aage. 1971. "Mittelenglisch *bryniges*". *Anglia* 89.117-18.

3091. Kaiser, Rolf. 1937. *Zur Geographie des mittelenglischen Wortschatzes*. (=

Palaestra, 205.) Leipzig: Mayer und Müller, [viii +] 318 pp. [Originally Berlin diss. 1936.]

Reviews: G.T. Flom in *JEGP* 36.569-72 (1937); G. Linke in *Archiv* 171.80-82 (1937); Karl Brunner in *Anglia B* 49.7-10 (1938); E. Ekwall in *ES* 20.257-59 (1938); E.L. Deuschle in *Museum* 45.147-48 (1938); S.B. Meech in *Speculum* 13.107-10 (1938); J.L.N. O'Loughlin in *MAE* 8.164-66 (1939); Hans Marcus in *EStn* 74.217-18 (1940).

3092. Kalb, Hans. 1937. *Die Namen der Säugetiere im Mittelenglischen.* Bottrop: Postberg, 87 pp. [Berlin diss.]

Review: G. L[inke] in *Archiv* 172.248 (1937).

3093. Källner, R. 1934. *Die Bezeichnungen für Geldwerte im Mittelenglischen.* Breslau diss., 56 pp.

3094. Kaplan, Theodore J. 1932. "Gower's Vocabulary". *JEGP* 31.395-402. [Points out that Gower's English vocabulary numbers 4648 words of which about 38 per cent are French and 55 per cent native.]

3095. Kaske, Robert E. 1952. "A Note on *Bras* in *Piers Plowman*, A, III, 189: B, III, 195". *PQ* 31.427-30.

3096. Käsman, Hans. 1958. "Zur Rezeption französischer Lehnwörter im Mittelenglischen". *Anglia* 76.285-98.

3097. ———. 1959. "Anmerkungen zum *Middle English Dictionary*". *Anglia* 77.65-74. [A number of comments on specific words.]

3098. ———. 1961. *Studien zum kirchlichen Wortschatz des Mittelenglischen 1100-1350: Ein Beitrag zum Problem der Sprachmischung.* (= Buchreihe der *Anglia*, 9.) Tübingen: Niemeyer, viii + 380 pp. [Freie Univ. Berlin Habilitationsschrift.]

Reviews: Herbert Koziol in *Anglia* 79.457-60 (1961); Morton W. Bloomfield in *Archiv* 199.49-51 (1962/63); P. M[ertens]-F[onck] in *RLV* 28.565-66 (1962); K. Baldinger in *ZRP* 78.610-11 (1962); O. Funke in *BGDSL* (T) 83.348-54 (1962); H. Marchand in *IF* 68.235-39 (1963); Gilbert De Smet in *LB* 57. Bijblad 140-42 (1968); A.A. Prins in *ES* 49.241-42 (1968).

3099. Keiser, George R. 1978. ""Epwort": A Ghost Word in the *Middle English Dictionary*". *ELN* 15.163-64.

3100. Kenyon, B. 1961. "A Note on Two Expressions contained in the Manuscript B.M. Royal 13 A xviii: *En le mene temps, en poynt devis*". *MLR* 56.381-89. [The expressions occur in an Anglo-Norman chess treatise.]

3101. Kerling, Johan. 1979. *Chaucer in Early English Dictionaries: The Old-Word Tradition in English Lexicography down to 1721 and Speght's Chaucer Glossaries.* (= Germanic and Anglistic Studies of the Univ. of Leiden, 18.) Leiden: Leiden Univ. Press, xv + 360 pp.

   Review: H.H. Meier in *DQR* 12.153-56 (1982).

3102. ———. 1979. "English Old-Word Glossaries 1553-1594". *Neophil* 63.136-47. [Deals with glossaries of 'Chaucerian' words which were compiled before the publication of Thomas Speght's edition of Chaucer (1598).]

3103. ———. 1984. "Franciscus Junius, 17th-Century Lexicography and Middle English". *LEXeter '83*, 92-100.

3104. Kihlbom, Asta. 1929. "Some Words in N.E.D. Antedated". *SN* 2.70-74. [The examples are taken from 15th-century letters such as the *Cely Papers*, the *Paston Letters*, etc.]

3105. ———. 1934. "Notes on Some Words in N.E.D." *Studia Germanica, tillägnade Ernst Albin Kock*, 97-106. Lund: Carl. Blom. [Quotes some words from the *Paston Letters*.]

3106. Kinkade, Berte L. 1934. *The English Translations of Higden's 'Polychronicon'.* Univ. of Illinois diss. (no pagination available). [Contains a valuable table of 687 words introduced into English by the anonymous translator.]

3107. Kittner, Heinz. 1937. *Studien zum Wortschatz William Langlands.* Halle diss., xiv + 131 pp. [A systematic study of the words found in *Piers Plowman* but not in Chaucer.]

3108. Kjellmer, Göran. 1971. *Context and Meaning: A Study of Distributional and Semantic Relations in a Group of Middle English Words.* (= GothSE, 22.) Stockholm: Almqvist & Wiksell, 201 pp. [Göteborg diss.; Abstr. in *DA* 35.5379-80A (1975). Discusses ME words covering the same semantic ground as ModE 'people': *folk, leod, man, nation, people,* and *þeod.*]

   Reviews: Nils Erik Enkvist in *SN* 45.439-43 (1973); Richard M. Hogg in *Lingua* 31.79-82 (1973); Wolfgang Kühlwein in *Anglia* 94.469-73 (1976); Udo Fries in *Archiv* 211.423-24 (1974).

3109. ———. 1973. *Middle English Words for 'People'.* (= GothSE, 27.) Stockholm: Almqvist & Wiksell, 307 pp.

   Reviews: Arne Rudskoger in *MSpr* 68.174-76 (1974); Nils Erik Enkvist in *SN* 47.169-70 (1975); Dieter Bähr in *Anglia* 95.182-87 (1977).

3110. Kloss, Robert James. 1968. *The Verbs of Being and Becoming in Middle English and Early Modern English*. Columbia diss., 193 pp. [Abstr. in *DA* 29.2697A (1969). A descriptive analysis.]

3111. Knight, Stephen Thomas. 1968. "*Almoost a Spanne Brood*". *Neophil* 52.178-80. [Explains *Almoost a Spanne Brood* (Chaucer's *General Prologue* 155) as 'almost four inches high'.]

3112. Knott, Thomas A. 1942. "The Middle English Dictionary". *Michigan Alumnus Quarterly Review* (Ann Arbor, MI) 48.127-32.

3113. Koch, John. 1934. "Der anglonormannische Traktat des Walter von Bibbesworth in seiner Bedeutung für die Anglistik". *Anglia* 58.30-77. [Contains useful information about the meanings and distribution of ME words.]

3114. Kökeritz, Helge. 1943. "*Sir Gawain and the Green Knight*, 1954". *MLN* 58.373-74. [Translates *with loteȝ of bordes* as 'with the gay chatter of the maidens'.]

3115. ———. 1947. "The Wyf of Bathe and *al hire secte*". *PQ* 26.147-51. [Points out that the word *secte* in *CT* IV 1171 means 'sex'.]

3116. ———. 1949. "*Out born* in *Ludus Coventriae*". *MLN* 64.88-90.

3117. Koskenniemi, Inna. 1975. "On the Use of Repetitive Word Pairs and Related Patterns in *The Book of Margery Kempe*". *Enkvist Festschrift*, 212-18.

3118. ———. 1983. "Semantic Assimilations in Middle English Binominals". *Studies in Classical and Modern Philology Presented to Y.M. Biese on the Occasion of his 80th Birthday 4.1.1983* (= AASF, B 223), 77-84. Helsinki: Suomalainen Tiedeakatemia.

3119. Koziol, Herbert. 1940. "Die romanischen Lehnwörter in Chaucers Werken". *EStn* 74.270-71.

3120. ———. 1942. "He was whit so þe flur, Rose red was his colur". *Archiv* 181.44-45.

3121. Krebs, Karl. 1933. *Der Bedeutungswandel von me. 'clerk' und damit zusammenhängende Probleme*. (= BSEP, 21.) Bonn: Hanstein, 162 pp.

Reviews: A. B[randl] in *Archiv* 165.301 (1934); F.R. Schröder in *GRM* 22.488 (1934); F. Fiedler in *ZNU* 34.124 (1935); C. van Spaendonck in *ES* 17.73-76 (1935); L. Stettner in *Neue Jahrbücher f. Wissenschaft und Jugendbildung* 12.375 (1936).

3122. Krieg, Martha Fessler. 1979. "The Influence of French Color Vocabulary on Middle English". *MichA* 11.431-37.

3123. Krishna, Valerie. 1975. "Archaic Nouns in the Alliterative *Morte Arthure*, 208-09". *NM* 76.439-45. [Cf. Suzuki [no. 3362].]

3124. Kristensson, Gillis. 1970. "Middle English *scuter signe*". *NM* 71.211-12. [On the word *scuter* occurring in the *Ancrene Wisse*.]

3125. Kuhn, Sherman McAllister. 1975. "On the Making of the *Middle English Dictionary*". *Poetica* 4.1-23. [Repr. in *Dictionaries: Journal of the Dictionary Society of North America* 4.14-41 (1982).]

3126. ———. 1977 [1980]. "Middle English *Don* and *Maken*: Some Observations on Semantic Patterning". *AS* 52.5-18.

3127. ———. 1979. "A Report on the *Middle English Dictionary*". *ChauN* 1:2.19-20.

3128. ———. 1980. "A Second Report on the *Middle English Dictionary*". *ChauN* 2:2.18.

3129. ———. 1984. "Chaucer's ARMEE: Its French Ancestors and Its English Poetry". *MSC Aachen 1983*, 85-102.

3130. Kurath, Hans. 1960. "Some Comments on Professor Visser's Notes on the *Middle English Dictionary*". *ES* 41.253-54. [With Visser's reply in *ES* 41.254-55 (1960). For Visser's original notes on the *MED*, see no. 3385.]

3131. ——— and Sherman McAllister Kuhn. 1951. "Statement on the *Middle English Dictionary*". *Language* 27.207-09.

3132. Lambert, Eugene. 1957. *French Vocabulary Influences in Some Thirteenth-Century English Works*. Univ. of Illinois at Urbana-Champaign diss., 262 pp. [Abstr. in *DA* 18.585 (1958).]

3133. Langenfelt, Gösta. 1953. "The Type *A Talbot!*". *SMSpr* 18.55-64. [On the history of *A Talbot!* and similar war-cries. Cf. Onions [no. 3236].]

Review: G.W.S.F. in *MAE* 26.49-51 (1957).

3134. Larsen, Swen A. 1949. "The Boat of Chaucer's *Connyng*: Troilus and Criseyde, II. 3-4". *N&Q* 194.332. [Suggests that *connyng* is derived from *con* 'to steer (a ship)'.]

3135. Lawson, Sarah. 1975. "*Well and truly*: A Durable Cliché". *N&Q* n.s. 22.290-91. [Notes the use of this cliché in a notice printed by Caxton in 1477.]

3136. Lehmann, Winfred Philipp. 1952. "A Rare Use of Numerals in Chaucer". *MLN* 67.317-21. [Interprets ll. 163-64 of the General Prologue as referring to three persons only — two nuns and one priest.]

LEXICOLOGY, LEXICOGRAPHY, AND WORD-FORMATION 291

3137. Leisi, Ernst. 1947. *Die tautologischen Wortpaare in Caxton's 'Eneydos': Zur synchronischen Bedeutungs- und Ursachenforschung*. Cambridge, MA: Murray; New York: Hafner, vi + 139 pp. [Zürich diss. 1945.]

3138. Lenaghan, Robert Thomas. 1963. "*Bytwene playn rude and curyous*: A Note on Caxton's Use of *Park*". *PQ* 42.95-97. [On Caxton's use of *park* in the sense of 'flock'.]

3139. Lewis, Robert Enzer. 1985. "The Middle English Dictionary: Present and Future". *ChauN* 4:1.1, 4, 5, and 6. [A condensation of the report read at the "Work in Progress" session of the 1984 New Chaucer Society Congress, York.]

3140. Liebermann, Felix. 1927. "Mittelengl. *baseling*". *Archiv* 151.82-83.

3141. Lindberg, Conrad. 1985. "A Note on the Vocabulary of the Middle English Bible". *SN* 57.129-31.

3142. Lindelöf, Uno. 1930. "Late Middle English *waffore*". *NM* 31.93.

3143. ———. 1937. *English Verb-Adverb Groups Converted into Nouns*. (= SSF-CHL, 9:5.) Helsingfors: Akademische Buchhandlung; Leipzig: Otto Harrassowitz, 41 pp. [Beginning with Langland's gad-about preacher, the *Robert renne-aboute* of the B-text of *Piers Plowman*, he ends with the *frame-up, getaway, spread-over, laze-off,* and *black-out* of today.]

Reviews: Johan Ellinger in *Anglia B* 50.65-66 (1939); S. Potter in *MLR* 34.582-84 (1939); G. Linke in *Archiv* 177.54 (1940); Herbert Penzl in *EStn* 75.78-80 (1942).

3144. Lindström, Bengt. 1974. "Four Middle English Passages". *SN* 46.151-58. [Interpretative notes on *Aʒenbite of Inwyt*, *Gospel of Nicodemus*, and Chambers and Daunt's *A Book of London English 1384-1425* (Oxford, 1931).]

3145. Linke, G. 1935. *Der Wortschatz des mittelenglischen Epos Genesis und Exodus*. (= Palaestra, 197.) Leipzig: Mayer und Müller, 165 pp.

3146. Livingston, Charles H. 1925. "Middle English *Askances*". *MLR* 20.71-72.

3147. ———. 1960. "Middle English *chewette, chawette*". *RP* 14.14-18.

3148. Llewellyn, Evan Clifford. 1936. *The Influence of Low Dutch on the English Vocabulary*. (= Pubs. of the Philological Society, 12.) London: Oxford Univ. Press/Milford, xii + 223 pp.

Reviews: F. Holthausen in *Anglia B* 47.357-58 (1936); Anon. in *TSL*, Mar. 6, 1937, p. 167; J.F. Bense in *ES* 19.165-72 (1937); A. B[randl] in *Archiv* 171.118-

19 (1937); H. Lange in *DLZ* 58.1419-20 (1937); G.T. Flom in *JEGP* 37.118-20 (1938).

3149. Lockwood, William Burley. 1961. "A Note on the Middle English 'Sunset on Calvary'". *ZAA* 9.410-12. [On the phrase *Nou goth sunne under wode*.]

3150. Löfvenberg, Mattias T. 1941/42. "Notes on Middle English *aubel* and English dialectal *ebble*". *SN* 14.86-88.

3151. ———. 1946. *Contributions to Middle English Lexicography and Etymology*. (= LUÅ, N.F. Avd. I. 41:8.) Lund: Gleerup, xxiii + 110 pp.

Reviews: A.A. Prins in *ES* 28.159 (1947); K. Malone in *MLN* 64.557 (1949); H.T. Price in *JEGP* 48.149-50 (1949); Hilda M. Hulme in *MLR* 44.292 (1949); G.V. Smithers in *RES* n.s. 2.67-68 (1951).

3152. Lucas, Peter J. 1976. "Some Words for Irish Yarn and Cloth in Late Middle English". *Journal of the Royal Society of Antiquaries of Ireland* (Dublin) 106.118-19.

3153. ———. 1979. "John Capgrave's *Chronicle*: Additions, Antedatings, Postdatings and Corrections to *OED* and *MED*, A-L". *NM* 80.231-37. [Capgrave's *Chronicle* (al464).]

3154. Lumiansky, Robert Mayer. 1951. "Chaucer's *for the nones*". *Neophil* 35.29-36. [Distinguishes four senses of the phrase in Chaucer's works: (1) 'for that purpose'; (2) 'for this occasion'; (3) 'at that time'; (4) 'for that position'.]

3155. Luttrell, C.A. 1955. "The *Gawain* Group: Cruxes, Etymologies, Interpretations". *Neophil* 39.207-17. [The words discussed are *bale, bele, carye, raged, rout, scarre, skyly, skwe, sour* and *wawe*.]

3156. ———. 1956. "The *Gawain* Group: Cruxes, Etymologies, Interpretations, II". *Neophil* 40.290-310. [Deals with *sweʒe, nay, barbe, dumpe, lauce (-se), swey, skyl(l)y* (again).]

3157. ———. 1962. "A *Gawain* Group Miscellany". *N&Q* n.s. 9.447-50. [Discusses 1. *dayly* (*Pearl* 313), 2. *freles* (*Pearl* 431), 3. *þrod* (*Cleanness* 751), 4. *childgered* (*Gawain* 86), 5. *tan hym bytwene hem* (*Gawain* 977).]

3158. Machan, Tim William. 1982. "Etymology of *Helde* in the English Harley Lyric". *Comments on Etymology* 11:11/12.2-4. [Cf. Watts [no. 3393].]

3159. ———. 1984. "*Forlynen*: A Ghost Word Rematerializes". *N&Q* n.s. 31.22-24. [On the word in Chaucer's *Boece*, Book III, Prosa 6.]

3160. Magoun, Francis Peabody, Jr. 1976. "The Cook's *Jakke of Dovere*: *CT* A 4347-48". *NM* 77.79.

3161. ———. 1977. "Two Chaucer Items". *NM* 78.46. [Examines the meaning of *at the townes ende* (*CT* II[D], 1285, 1537) and *estres* of the place, etc. (*Knight's Tale*, *Reeve's Tale*, *LGW*).]

3162. Malone, Kemp. 1935. "Herlekin and Herlewin". *ES* 17.141-44.

3163. ———. 1955. "On the Etymology of *Filch*". *MLN* 70.165-68.

3164. Mandel, Jerome. 1975. "'Boy' as Devil in Chaucer". *PLL* 11.407-11.

3165. Manzalaoui, M.A. 1962. "*Derring-do*". *N&Q* n.s. 9.369-70. [On the expression in Chaucer's *Troilus and Cryseyde* and Lydgate's *Troy Book*.]

3166. Marcus, Hans. 1936. "Zum neuen mittelenglischen Wörterbuch". *Archiv* 169.30-35.

3167. Marshall, John. 1975. "The Chester Coopers' Pageant: *selles* and *cathedral*". *LSE* n.s. 8.120-28.

3168. Marshall, Mary Hatch. 1950. "'Theatre' in the Middle Ages: Evidence from Dictionaries and Glosses". *Symposium* (Syracuse Univ.) 4.1-39 and 366-89. [On medieval concepts of the theatre.]

3169. Martin, Lynn Simpson. 1966. *Sir Thomas Malory's Vocabulary in 'The Tale of Arthur and Lucius', 'The Tale of Sir Gareth', and 'The Tale of the Sankgreal': A Comparative Study*. Pennsylvania diss., 270 pp. [Abstr. in *DA* 27.1376A (1966).]

3170. Matheson, Lister M. 1978. "A Middle English Antedating of 'Protocol'". *N&Q* n.s. 25.204-05.

3171. ———. 1979. "*Troilus and Criseyde*, III, 1460 *pourynge*". *N&Q* n.s. 26.203.

3172. ———. 1983. "The Middle English Verb *sane*: A Probable Ghost Word". *N&Q* n.s. 30.199-202.

3173. ———. 1986. "*Licere*: A Ghost Word in the *Middle English Dictionary*". *N&Q* n.s. 33.9.

3174. Matsunami, Tamotsu. 1985. "The Middle English Verbs of Motion". *Poetica* 20/21.71-105.

3175. Matthes, Heinrich Christoph. 1931. "*Wel* und *well* in *Orrmulum*". *Anglia* 55.10-56.

3176. Matthews, William. 1975. "*bi lag mon*: A Crux in *Sir Gawayn and the Grene Knyʒt*". *M&H* n.s. 6.151-55.

3177. McCarren, V.P. 1985. "ME *Plaunting*, Latin *Plantarium*". *MAE* 54.270-71.

3178. McClure, Peter. 1983. "The ME. Occupational Term *Ringere*". *Nomina* 7.102.

3179. McGee, Alan Van Keuren. 1940. *The Geographical Distribution of Scandinavian Loan-Words in Middle English, with Special Reference to the Alliterative Poetry*. Yale diss., 597 pp. [Abstr. in *DA* 31.1785A (1970).]

3180. McIntosh, Angus. 1966. "Middle English *upon schore* and Some Related Matters". *Schlauch Festschrift*, 255-60. [Apropos of the phrase in *Sir Gawain and the Green Knight* 2332.]

3181. ———. 1972. "Some Words in the *Northern Homily Collection*". *Mustanoja Festschrift* = *NM* 73.196-208. [Discusses some 150 words and phrases.]

3182. Meier, Hans Heinrich. 1969. "Lexicography as Applied Linguistics". *ES* 50.141-51. [Concerning the *Dictionary of the Older Scottish Tongue*.]

3183. Menner, Robert J. 1923. "An Etymology for ME. *Olypraunce*, AN. *Oriprance*". *MLN* 38.348-52.

3184. ———. 1931. "Middle English *Lagman* (*Gawain* 1729) and Modern English 'Lag'". *PQ* 10.163-68.

3185. Mersand, Joseph. 1934. *Scientific Studies in Chaucer's Romance Vocabulary*. New York Univ. diss., 768 pp.

3186. ———. 1937. *Chaucer's Romance Vocabulary*. Brooklyn, NY: The Comet Press, xii + 173 pp. [2nd ed. 1939, xii + 179 pp.; Repr., Port Washington, NY: Kennikat Press, 1968.]

Reviews: Anon. in *TSL*, Sept. 18, 1937, p. 677; John S.P. Tatlock in *Romantic Review* (Chicago) 28.274 (1937); Anon. in *EJ* 27.877 (1938); W. Héraucourt in *Anglia B* 49.231-32 (1938) and *EA* 3.259 (1939); R.G. Kent in *Language* 14.301-02 (1938); H. Koziol in *EStn* 72.270-72 (1938); J.P. Oakden in *MLR* 33.576-77 (1938); S.H.B. in *PQ* 18.91-92 (1939); Karl Brunner in *LGRP* 61.213 (1939); F. Delatte in *RBPH* 18.142-44 (1939); Rolf Kaiser in *Archiv* 176.117-18 (1939); Martin B. Ruud in *MLN* 54.140-42 (1939); E.L. Deuschle in *ES* 22.119-21 (1940); J.R. Hulbert in *PQ* 26.302-06 (1947).

LEXICOLOGY, LEXICOGRAPHY, AND WORD-FORMATION 295

3187. Miller, B.D.H. 1961. "'Dame Sirith' and the O.E.D.". *N&Q* n.s. 8.129-32. [Quotes some 50 words from the ME fabliau.]

3188. ———. 1961. "Mala Medicamenta, viz. Yele Syne". *N&Q* n.s. 8.205-07. [On the meaning of *yele syne*.]

3189. Mills, Anthony David. 1963. "Some Middle English Occupational Terms". *N&Q* n.s. 10.249-57.

3190. ———. 1964. "Some Late Middle English Fish Names". *N&Q* n.s. 11.170-71. [From a document of 1427.]

3191. ———. 1968. "Notes on Some Middle English Occupational Terms". *SN* 40.35-48.

3192. Mitchell, A.G. 1944. "Worth Both His Ears". *MLN* 59.222. [Takes issue with Spencer's gloss of *Piers Plowman* B Prol. 78-79 [no. 3340].]

3193. Moe, Phyllis. 1965. "A Fifteenth-Century Manuscript: New Words and Antedatings". *N&Q* n.s. 12.450.

3194. Moessner, Lilo. 1982. "Some Remarks on the *MED*". *NM* 83.150-51. [Suggests additions or changes for the five entries *alothen*, *bilongen*, *coveren* (2), *don*, and *forleren*. Cf. Bitterling [no. 2877].]

3195. Moore, Arthur K. 1947. "The Eyen Greye of Chaucer's Prioress". *PQ* 26.307-12. [Studies the meaning of ME *greye* as applied to eye-color.]

3196. ———. 1949. "*Somer* and *Lenten* as Terms for Spring". *N&Q* 194.82-83.

3197. Moore, Samuel, Sanford Brown Meech, and Harold Whitehall. 1933. "The Middle English Dictionary". *PMLA* 48.281-88.

3198. Mossé, Fernand. 1943. "On the Chronology of French Loan-words in English". *ES* 25.33-40.

3199. Muir, A. Laurence. 1948. "Some Observations on the Early English Psalters and the English Vocabulary". *MLQ* 9.273-76. [On various ways of translating the same Latin expression in the ME Psalters.]

3200. Muir, Margaret A. and Peter John Christopher Field. 1971. "French Words and Phrases in Sir Thomas Malory's *Le Morte Darthur*". *NM* 72.483-500.

Review: Felix Lecoy in *Romania* (Paris) 95.421 (1974).

3201. Murison, David. 1971. "The Dutch Element in the Vocabulary of Scots". *Edinburgh Studies*, 159-76. [Provides a detailed list of Dutch and Flemish loanwords in Scots, recorded from the 14th century onwards.]

3202. Murtaugh, Daniel M. 1971. "*Pearl* 462: þe *Mayster of myste*". *Neophil* 55.191-94. [Discusses the meaning of *myste*.]

3203. Mustanoja, Tauno Frans. 1954. "Two Lexical Notes: *at random* and *cyprine*". *NM* 55.56-59. [Points out an early instance of *at random* in a manuscript of *Piers Plowman*.]

3204. ———. 1955. "Middle English *With an O and an I*, with a Note on Two Shakespearean *O-I* Puns". *NM* 56.161-74.

3205. ———. 1956. "'Chalking' Furs". *NM* 57.126-28. [Notes the occurrence of the phrase in the accounts of Henry, earl of Derby (1391).]

3206. Nevanlinna, Saara. 1972. "On the Origin of the Middle English Adverbs *bedene* and *albedene*". *Mustanoja Festschrift = NM* 73.245-47.

3207. ———. 1980. "*To Make Merry*: Notes on the Origin and Meaning of the Idiomatic Expression *to Make Merry* in Middle English". *NM* 81.34-41.

3208. Nichols, Pierrepont Herrick. 1932. "Lydgate's Influence on the Aureate Terms of the Scottish Chaucerians". *PMLA* 47.516-22.

3209. Nicholson, Lewis E. 1981. "Chaucer's "Com pa me": A Famous Crux Reexamined". *ELN* 19.98-102.

3210. Norwood, J.E. 1968. "Lexical Changes in the Preposition during the Middle English Period as Related to Modern Problems in Definition". *PP* 11.171-73.

3211. Oliphant, Robert. 1962. "Middle English *Bāner*". *PQ* 41.518-19.

3212. Ong, Walter J. 1950. "The Green Knight's Harts and Bucks". *MLN* 65.536-39. [On hunting terms in *Sir Gawain and the Green Knight*. Answered by Savage [no. 3313].]

3213. Olszewska, E.S. 1935. "Types of Norse Borrowing in Middle English". *Saga-Book* 11.153-60.

3214. ———. 1936. "Alliterative Phrases in the *Ormulum*". *LSE* 5.50-67.

3215. ———. 1937. "ME. *isked* 'longed'". *LSE* 6.65-66.

3216. ———. 1945. "Some English and Norse Alliterative Phrases". *Saga-Book* 12.238-45. [Discusses ME *yeme and gete*, *help and hald*, *raynande ryg*, and also ModE dialectal *rug and rive*.]

3217. ———. 1945. "Friend and fellow". *Saga-Book* 12.272-76. [On the currency of the phrase in ME and early ModE.]

3218. ———. 1947/48. "Middle English *trigg 7 trowwe*". *EGS* 1.88-90. [On the phrase in the *Ormulum*.]

3219. ———. 1962. "Alliterative Phrases in the *Ormulum*: Some Norse Parallels". *Tolkien Festschrift*, 112-27.

3220. ———. 1973. "Middle English *setten spel on ende*". *N&Q* n.s. 20.2-3.

3221. ———. 1973. "ME *takenn 7 trowwenn*". *N&Q* n.s. 20.83.

3222. ———. 1973. "Middle English *fader and frendes*". *N&Q* n.s. 20.205-07.

3223. ———. 1973. "Middle English *gold and gōd*". *N&Q* n.s. 20.243-44.

3224. ———. 1974. "ME. *brittene & brenne*". *N&Q* n.s. 21.207-09.

3225. ———. 1974. "Middle English *tonge 7 tothe*". *N&Q* n.s. 21.323-25.

3226. ———. 1974. "Middle English *trowe 7 traist*". *N&Q* n.s. 21.325.

3227. ———. 1974. "Middle English *wille 7 walde*". *N&Q* n.s. 21.325-26.

3228. Onions, Charles Talbut. 1928. "Middle English: (i) *Wite God*, *Wite Crist*, (ii) *God it Wite*". *RES* 4.334-37.

3229. ———. 1929. "Middle English *Ord and Ende*". *MLR* 24.389-93.

3230. ———. 1930. "*Breche* in *The Owl and the Nightingale*, Line 14". *Jespersen Festschrift*, 105-08.

3231. ———. 1932. "Middle English *Alod*, *Olod*". *MAE* 1.206-08.

3232. ———. 1933. "Middle English *Alod*, *Olod*". *MAE* 2.73. [Addition to no. 3231].

3233. ———. 1941. "Middle English *Wrabbe*, *Wrobbe*". *MAE* 10.159-60.

3234. ———. 1952. "Middle English *Gawne*". *MAE* 21.39.

3235. ———. 1953. "Middle English *Gawne*: A Correction, with Some Notes". *MAE* 22.111-13.

3236. ———. 1957. "The Type *A Talbot*". *MAE* 26.114. [Examples from *Morte Arthure* 1791. Cf. Langenfelt [no. 3133].]

3237. Ortego, Philip Darraugh. 1974. "Chaucer's 'Phislyas': A Problem in Paleography and Linguistics". *ChauR* 9.182-89. [Supports a sense of 'medicine' for *phislyas* at *CT* II 1189.]

3238. Orton, P.R. 1985. "Chaucer's General Prologue, A 673 *Burdoun* and Some Sixteenth-Century Puns". *ELN* 23.3-4.

3239. Ostheeren, Klaus. 1971. "Toposforschung und Bedeutungslehre: Die Glanzvorstellung im Schönheitskatalog und die mittelenglischen Farbadjektive *blak* und *brown*". *Anglia* 89.1-47.

3240. Otto, Gertrand. 1938. *Die Handwerkernamen im Mittelenglischen*. Berlin diss., 98 pp. [A study of ME words denoting manual laborers.]

Review: G. Linke in *Archiv* 174.253-54 (1938).

3241. Palmgren, Carl. 1923. *A Chronological List of English Formations of the Types 'Alive', 'Aloud', 'Aglow'*. (= Norrköpings Högre Allm. Läroverks Redogörelse, 1923.) Norrköping: A.-B. Trycksaker, 38 pp.

3242. ———. 1924. *A Study on the History of English Words Formed by the Prefix 'a-' < 'on (in)-'*. (= Norrköpings Högre Allm. Laroverks Redogörelse, 1924.) Norrköping: A.-B. Trycksaker, 22 pp.

3243. Pearcy, Roy J. 1975. "A Pun in *The Franklin's Tale* 942: *Withouten coppe he drank al his penaunce*". *N&Q* n.s. 22.198. [On the word *coppe*.]

3244. Pennanen, Esko V. 1971. *On the Introduction of French Loan-Words into English* (= Acta Universitatis Tamperensis, A:38.) Tampere: Tampereen Yliopisto, 59 pp. [Covers the period from 1000 to 1900.]

Review: R.W. Zandvoort in *ES* 52.400 (1971).

3245. Penttilä, Erkki. 1958. "A Sense-Development of Verbs Denoting Emission of Light". *NM* 59.161-72.

3246. Peters, Hans. 1983. *Das mittelenglische Wortfeld 'schlecht'/'böse': synchronisch-diachronische Darstellung seiner semantischen Struktur*. (= EurH, Reihe 14, 115.) Frankfurt am Main-Bern-New York: Peter Lang, [viii +] 227 pp. [Freie Univ. Berlin diss., 1982.]

Review: E.G. Stanley in N&Q n.s. 31.419 (1984).

3247. Peverett, Michael. 1986. "*Quod* and *Seide* in *Piers Plowman*". *NM* 87.117-27.

3248. Phelan, Walter Steven. 1977. "Beyond the Concordance: Semantic and Mythic Structures in Gower's Tale of Florent". *Neophil* 61.461-79.

3249. ———. 1978. "The Study of Chaucer's Vocabulary". *CHum* 12.61-69.

3250. Pilch, Herbert. 1955. "Der Untergang des Präverbs *ge-* im Englischen". *Anglia* 73.37-64.

3251. ———. 1955/56. "Me. *I*-beim Participium Präteriti". *Anglia* 73.279-91. [Deals with the distribution of the prefix in the ME dialects.]

3252. Pontifex, E.L. 1924. "Fifteenth Century Words from Records". *N&Q* 146.79-80.

3253. Potter, Simeon. 1962. "Gallicisms Past and Present". *E&S* n.s. 15.1-12. [Surveys Fowler's treatment of Gallicisms, indicates the different periods of borrowing, and shows something of their impact on English.]

3254. ———. 1972. "Chaucer's Untransposable Binominals". *Mustanoja Festschrift* = *NM* 73.309-14. [On *hous and hoom*, etc.]

3255. Prins, Anton Adriaan. 1941-42. "On the Loss and Substitution of Words in Middle English". *Neophil* 26.280-98 and 27.49-59.

3256. ———. 1948. "French Phrases in English, I-II". *Neophil* 32.28-39 and 73-83.

3257. ———. 1951. "Further Notes on the *Canterbury Tales*". *ES* 32.250-51. [On the phrases *in muwe* and *in stuwe* (*CT* I. 349-50).]

3258. ———. 1952. *French Influence in English Phrasing*. Leiden: Univ. Pers Leiden, vii + 320 pp. [Based upon a number of ME and ModE texts.]

Reviews: John Orr in *EA* 5.340-42 (1952); S.B. Liljegren in *SN* 25.185 (1952/53); H.M. Flasdieck in *Anglia* 71.466-68 (1953); [R.W.] Z[andvoort] in *ES* 34.192 (1953); Eric Buyssens in *RBPH* 31.608-10 (1953); A. van Wijngaarden in *LT* 1953, 81-83 (1953); A.A. Hill in *Language* 30.171-73 (1954); Norman Davis in *Neophil* 38.154 (1954); Fernand Mossé in *ES* 35.218-22 (1954); Tauno F. Mustanoja in *NM* 55.318-19 (1954); J.A. Sheard in *MLR* 50.519-21 (1955); E.G. Stanley in *EGS* 5.118-19 (1952/53); Angus McIntosh in *Museum* 58.164-67 (1953).

3259. ———. 1956. "*As fer as last Ytaille*". *ES* 37.111-16. [On the meaning of *last* in Chaucer (*Clerk's Tale* 266) and in translations from the French.]

3260. ———. 1959. "Notes on Some Middle English Texts". *Mossé Festschrift*, 413-22. [Contains lexical notes on *The Owl and the Nightingale* 37, 57, 1724 & 1070, and *The Towneley Play of Noah* 225.]

3261. ———. 1959. "French Influence in English Phrasing: A Supplement". *ES* 40.27-32. [See no. 3258.]

3262. ———. 1960. "French Influence in English Phrasing (Continued)". *ES* 41.1-17.

3263. ———. 1962. "*Loke who, what, how, when*". *ES* 43.165-69 and 497. [Gives a number of 14th-century instances, mainly from Chaucer.]

3264. Pyles, Thomas. 1942. "'Dan Chaucer'". *MLN* 57.437-39. [On the use of the title *dan* with the surname instead of the Christian name.]

3265. Quirk, Randolph. 1953. "Langland's Use of *kind wit* and *inwit*" *JEGP* 52.182-88. [Repr. in *Quirk Essays*, 20-26.]

3266. ———. 1954. "Vis Imaginativa". *JEGP* 53.81-83. [On Langland's use of the term *Imaginatif*. Repr. in *Quirk Essays*, 27-29.]

3267. Reuter, Ole. 1934. *On the Development of English Verbs from Latin and French Past Participles*. (= SSF-CHL, 6:6.) Helsingfors: Societas Scientiarum Fennica, vi + 171 pp. [From the 13th century to the present day.]

Reviews: A.O.B. in *MLR* 30.267-68 (1935); G.T. Flom in *JEGP* 34.250-53 (1935); M.S. Serjeantson in *ES* 20.42-44 (1938).

3268. ———. 1936. *Verb Doublets of Latin Origin in English*. (= SSF-CHL, 8:4.) Helsingfors: Societas Scientiarum Fennica, 45 pp. [Refers to Chaucer, Caxton, and Shakespeare.]

Reviews: G. L[inke] in *Archiv* 170.288 (1936); W. Preusler in *Anglia B* 48.299-300 (1937).

3269. ———. 1937. *A Study of the French Words in the Earliest Complete English Prose Psalter*. (= SSF-CHL, 9:4.) Helsingfors: Societas Scientiarum Fennica, 60 pp.

Reviews: G. Linke in *Archiv* 174.254 (1938); Brice Harris in *JEGP* 37.448-49 (1938); W. Héraucourt in *Anglia B* 50.163 (1939); Simeon Potter in *MLR* 34.582-84 (1939); Herbert Penzl in *EStn* 75.82 (1942).

3270. Revard, Carter. 1962. "A Note on *Stonden, Pearl* 113". *N&Q* n.s. 9.9-10.

3271. Rickenbach, Max. 1963. *Die Dimensionalwörter im Mittelenglischen (1250-1500)*. Winterthur: Keller, vii + 142 pp. [Zürich diss.]

Review: Siegfried Wyler in *ES* 48.545-46 (1967).

3272. Rigg, A.G. 1983. "Clocks, Dials, and Other Terms". *Davis Festschrift*, 255-74. [Explores the vocabulary used in time-reckoning in ME.]

3273. Rioux, Robert N. 1959. "Sir Thomas Malory, Créateur Verbal". *EA* 12.193-97. [Assesses the influence of French on Malory's vocabulary.]

3274. Robertson, Durrant Waite, Jr. 1977. "Some Disputed Chaucerian Terminology". *Speculum* 52.571-81. [Concerns Chaucer's portraits of humbler folk.]

3275. Robertson, Stuart. 1933. "The Chaucerian-American *I guess*". *MLN* 48.37-40.

3276. Rønberg, Gert. 1976. "A Note on *Endorde* in *Pearl* (368)". *ES* 57.198-99.

3277. Ross, Alan Strode Campbell. 1939. "German *dirne*: Icelandic *perna*: Middle English *perne*". *Proceedings of the Leeds Philos. and Lit. Society, Lit. and Hist. Section*, 5:2.113-24.

3278. ———. 1947/48. "The Vocabulary of the Records of the Grocers' Company". *EGS* 1.91-100. [Provides lexicographical material from the archives of the Company of Grocers of the City of London, 1345-1463.]

3279. ———. 1970. "The Rare Words of the *Ormulum*". *EPS* 12.42-47.

3280. ———. 1970. "Some Alliterative Phrases in the *Bodley Homilies*". *N&Q* n.s. 17.46-48.

3281. ———. 1970. "Conservatism in the Anglo-Saxon Gloss to the Durham Ritual". *N&Q* n.s. 17.363-66.

3282. ———. 1973. "To Go A-Blackberrying". *N&Q* n.s. 20.284-85. [On forms and senses of the phrase in Chaucer and Mrs. Henry Wood (1874) not accounted for in *OED*.]

3283. ———. 1974. "Middle English *Covent*". *N&Q* n.s. 21.83.

3284. ———. 1974. "*Dub*". *N&Q* n.s. 21.209-10.

3285. ———. 1975. "*Run and Reve* and Similar Alliterative Phrases". *NM* 76.571-82.

3286. ———. 1978. "*Morse*". *N&Q* n.s. 25.533. [On the word *morse* which appears in 1482 (in *The Chronicles of England*).]

3287. Ross, Thomas W. 1980. "ME *Meving*". *ChauN* 2:2.11.

3288. ———. 1981. "*Astromye* in the *Miller's Tale* Again". *N&Q* n.s. 28.202. [Answer to Blake [no. 2880].]

3289. ———. 1984. "Taboo-Words in Fifteenth-Century English". *Fifteenth-Century Studies*, 137-60.

3290. Rothwell, William. 1980. "Lexical Borrowing in a Medieval Context". *Bulletin of the John Rylands Library* (Manchester) 63.118-43.

3291. Roucaute, Danielle. 1972. "Champs sémantique de l'erotique dans les *Contes de Canterbury* de Chaucer". *Cahiers Élisabéthains: Études sur la Pré-Renaissance et la Renaissance Anglaises* (Univ. Paul Valéry, Montpellier) 1.3-24.

3292. Rupp, Henry R. 1955. "Word-Play in *Pearl*, 277-278". *MLN* 70.558-59. [Suggests that the word *geste* may mean not only 'guest' but 'story, tale'.]

3293. Russ, Jon R. 1969. "For the *MED* and *OED* from the *Song of Roland*". *AN&Q* 8.37-38. [Dated about 1400.]

3294. Russell-Smith, Joy. 1953. "*Keis* in *Sawles Warde*". *MAE* 22.104-10. [Connects the word *keis* with the *keys* of the Welsh legal documents.]

3295. ———. 1957. "Ridiculosae Sternutationes (*o nore* in *Ancrene Wisse*)". *RES* n.s. 8.266-69.

3296. Ryan, William M. 1959. "Modern Idioms in *Piers Plowman*". *AS* 34.67-69.

3297. Rynell, Alarik. 1948. *The Rivalry of Scandinavian and Native Synonyms in Middle English, Especially 'taken' and 'nimen'. With an Excursus on 'nema' and 'taka' in Old Scandinavian.* (= LundSE, 13.) Lund: C.W.K. Gleerup, 431 pp. [Lund diss.]

> Reviews: A.A. Prins in *Museum* 53.194-95 (1948); E. Schubel in *SN* 21.303-05 (1948/49); F.P. Magoun, Jr. in *Speculum* 24.140-41 (1949); K. Malone in *MLN* 64.560-61 (1949); Angus McIntosh in *RES* 25.258-59 (1949); F. Mossé in *BSL* 45.174-75 (1949); Simeon Potter in *MLR* 44.258-59 (1949); John H. Fisher in *Word* 6.247-48 (1950); H.T. Price in *JEGP* 49.579-81 (1950); E.V.K. Dobbie in *GR* 26.140-42 (1951); E. Polomé in *RBPH* 29.188-90 (1951); M.L. Samuels in *MAE* 20.70-75 (1951); Bogislav von Lindheim in *Anglia* 70.108-12 (1951); A. Macdonald in *ES* 35.23-24 (1954).

3298. ———. 1953. "On the Origin of Middle English *rinnen*". *SMSpr* 18.113-32.

3299. ———. 1956. "A Note on *lynde(s)* in Robert Mannyng's *Chronicle*". *SMSpr* 19.153-59.

3300. ———. 1959. "On the Meaning of *foyn* and *fo* in the *Towneley Plays*". *ES* 40.379-81.

3301. ———. 1960. "On Middle English *take(n)* as an Inchoative Verb". *SMSpr* n.s. 1.115-31. [On constructions of the type *taken to counseil, taken to rede* 'to take counsel'.]

3302. Salter, F.M. 1945. "John Skelton's Contribution to the English Language". *Transactions of the Royal Society of Canada* (Ottawa), 3rd ser., Sect. II, 39.119-217. [Lists some 800 words from Skelton's transl. of Diodorus Siculus which are earlier than the earliest recorded instances in *OED*.]

   Review: Kemp Malone in *MLN* 64.564-65 (1949).

3303. Salu, Mary. 1952/53. "Some Obscure Words in *Ancrene Wisse* (MS. C.C.C.C. 402)". *EGS* 5.100-02. [Discusses 1. *criblin*, 2. *taueles*, 3. *riuin, riuunges*.]

3304. Samuels, Michael Louis. 1953. "*Ancrene Riwle* Studies". *MAE* 22.1-9. [Includes discussion of alliteration, proverbs, word-play, vocabulary, mistranslation, and style.]

3305. Sandahl, Bertil. 1951. *Middle English Sea Terms. I: The Ship's Hull.* (= Uppsala E&S, 8.) Uppsala: A.-B. Lundequistska Bokhandeln; Copenhagen: Munksgaard; Cambridge, MA: Harvard Univ. Press, 235 pp. [Uppsala diss.]

   Reviews: A.A. Hill in *SIL* 9.99-100 (1951); E. Ekwall in *SN* 24.211-13 (1951/52); D.S. Bland in *ES* 33.126-27 (1952); A. Macdonald in *RES* n.s. 4.276-78 (1953); F. Mossé in *EA* 8.148-49 (1955).

3306. ———. 1958. *Middle English Sea Terms. II: Masts, Spars and Sails.* (= Uppsala E&S, 20.) Uppsala: A.-B. Lundequistska Bokhandeln; Copenhagen: Munksgaard; Cambridge, MA: Harvard Univ. Press, 151 pp.

   Review of I & II; John Leyerle in *MAE* 34.68-73 (1965).

3307. ———. 1982. *Middle English Sea Terms. III: Standing and Running Rigging.* (= SAU, 42.) Uppsala: Acta Universitatis Upsaliensis; Stockholm: Almqvist & Wiksell, [xvi +] 194 pp.

3308. Sauer, Hans. 1985. "Laȝamon's Compound Nouns and their Morphology". *Historical Semantics*, 483-532.

3309. Savage, Henry Lyttleton. 1940. "A Note on *Sir Gawain* 1795". *MLN* 55.604. [On the word *may* 'woman'.]

3310. ———. 1943. "*Methles* in *Sir Gawain and the Green Knight*, 2106". *MLN* 58.46-47. [Argues that the word denotes 'without principle'.]

3311. ———. 1945. "*Lote, Lote3* in *Sir Gawain and the Green Knight*". *MLN* 60.492-93. [Discusses the use of these words in *Pearl* and *Patience* as well as in *Sir Gawain*.]

3312. ———. 1949. "The Green Knight's *Molaynes*". *Malone Festschrift*, 166-78. [On the etymology of the word in *Sir Gawain* 169.]

3313. ———. 1951. "Hunting Terms in Middle English". *MLN* 66.216. [Answer to Ong [no. 3212].]

3314. ———. 1965. "'Hang Up Thine Axe'". *N&Q* n.s. 12.375-76. [On the proverbial expression in *Sir Gawain* 477.]

3315. ———. 1966. "*Fare*, Line 694 of *Sir Gawain and the Green Knight*". *Schlauch Festschrift*, 373-74. [On the meaning of *fare*.]

3316. Schäfer, Jürgen. 1982. "Chaucer in Shakespeare's Dictionaries: The Beginning". *ChauR* 17.182-92. [Stresses the importance of the glossary of Speght's edition of Chaucer (1602) to 17th- and 18th-century dictionaries.]

3317. Scheler, Manfred. 1968. "Zur Etymologie des me. *Burde*". *Archiv* 205.189-91.

3318. Schelp, Hanspeter. 1965. "*Nurture*: Ein mittelenglischer Statusbegriff". *Anglia* 83.253-70.

3319. Schendl, Herbert. 1984. "Me. *randon* in *Sir Bevis of Hamtoun*". *Anglia* 102.101-07.

3320. Scheps, Walter. 1979. "Chaucer's Use of Nonce Words, Primarily in the *Canterbury Tales*". *NM* 80.69-77.

3321. Schmidt, A.V.C. 1968. "A Note on the Phrase *Free Wit* in the C-text of *Piers Plowman* (Passus XI.51)". *N&Q* n.s. 15.168-69.

3322. Sedgwick, W.B. 1929. "An Unworked Vein in Middle-English Lexicography?". *Speculum* 4.91-92.

3323. Serjeantson, Mary Sydney. 1938. "The Vocabulary of Cookery in the Fifteenth Century". *E&S* 23.25-37.

3324. Shaw, Judith Davis. 1985. "An Etymology of the Middle English *Coise*". *ELN* 22:4.11-13.

3325. Simmons, Autumn. 1968. "A Contribution to the *Middle English Dictionary*: Citations from the English Poems of Charles, Duc d'Orléans". *JEngL* 2.43-56. [The poems are dated at about mid-15th century.]

3326. Simpson, J.A. 1981. "Notes on Some Norse Loans, Real or Supposed, in *Sir Gawain and the Green Knight*". *MAE* 50.301-04. [Discusses 1. *draȝt*, 2. *droupyng*, *drowping*, 3. *faltered*, 4. *slentyng*, 5. *þryve*, 6. *welcum*, *-com*.]

3327. Sisam, Celia. 1962. "Notes on Middle English Texts". *RES* n.s. 13.385-90. [Comments on the interpretation of words and phrases in the *Peterborough Chronicle*, *The Owl and the Nightingale*, *Sir Orfeo*, The Towneley *Noah*, and Barbour's *Bruce*.]

3328. ———. 1983. "*Redy* and *Unredy* in Middle English". *Dobson Festschrift*, 137-43.

3329. ———. 1983. "Early Middle English *Drihtin*". *Davis Festschrift*. 245-54.

3330. Sisam, Kenneth. 1956. "Middle English *oliue*, *o-liue*, *o liue*". *N&Q* n.s. 3.317.

3331. Slettengren, Emrik. 1932. *Contributions to the Study of French Loan-Words in Middle English*. I. *OF ö < ue and its Variants in Anglo-French and ME*. Örebro: Lindhska Boghandeln, v + 136 pp. [Only Part I appeared. Repr., College Park, MD: McGrath, 1970.]

  Review: E. Fischer in *LGRP* 55.100-02 (1934).

3332. ———. 1941/42. "On the Origin of the ME Variant *diol*, OF *due(i)l* and the Pronunciation of OF *-uel* in the Anglo-French Dialect". *SN* 14.369-85.

3333. Smith, Charles Campbell. 1971. *Noun + Noun Compounds in the Works of Geoffrey Chaucer*. New York Univ. diss., 156 pp. [Abstr. in *DA* 32.5769A (1972).]

3334. Smith, Merete. 1982. "Literary Loanwords from Old French in *The Romaunt of the Rose*: A Note". *ChauR* 17.89-93.

3335. Smithers, Geoffrey Victor. 1947/48. "A Middle English Idiom and its Antecedents". *EGS* 1.101-13. [On *bidde* as used in Chaucer's *Troilus* II. 406.]

3336. ———. 1954. "Some English Ideophones". *ArchL* 6.73-111. [Mainly concerned with ME.]

3337. ———. 1964. "*Nahhi*: A Middle English Ideophonic Word". *N&Q* n.s. 11.371-73.

3338. Spargo, John Webster. 1940. "Chaucer's Love-Days". *Speculum* 15.36-56. [Studies the linguistic history and meaning of *love-day*.]

3339. ———. 1949. "Chaucer's *kankedort* (*Troilus and Criseyde* II, 1752)". *MLN* 64.264-66. [Cf. Spitzer [no. 3341].]

3340. Spencer, Hazelton. 1943. "Worth Both His Ears". *MLN* 58.48. [On the phrase found in *Piers Plowman* B Prol. 78. Refuted by Mitchell [no. 3192].]

3341. Spitzer, Leo. 1949. "*Kanke(r)dort* 'a State of Suspense, a Difficult Position'". *MLN* 64.502-04. [Cf. Spargo [no. 3339].]

3342. ———. 1950. "A Chaucerian Hapax Legomenon: *upon the viritoot*". *Language* 26.389-93. [On the word *viritoot* in *CT* I. 3770.]

3343. Stanley, Eric Gerald. 1957. "Some Notes on *The Owl and the Nightingale*". *EGS* 6.30-63. [Discusses several passages and words in the poem.]

3344. ———. 1983. "Early Middle English *Oc*, 'but, and'". *Dobson Festschrift*, 144-50.

3345. Stapelkamp, Christiaan. 1951. "Notes on *Ein mittelenglisches Medizinbuch*". *ES* 32.24-29 and 77 (Corrigenda). [Lexical notes on some words of a 'leechbook', ed. Fr. Heinrich (1896).]

3346. Steadman, John M., Jr. 1923. "Notes on *Wynnere and Wastoure*". *MLN* 38.308-11. [Illustrates and defines some of the rarer and more difficult words in the poem.]

3347. Stein, Gabriele. 1981. "The English Dictionary in the 15th Century". *Coseriu Festschrift* I, 313-22.

3348. Stewart, George R., Jr. 1934. "The Meaning of *Bacheler* in Middle English". *PQ* 13.40-47.

3349. Stieve, Edwin. 1987. "A New Reading of The Host's *in terme* (*Canterbury Tales* VI, line 311)". *N&Q* n.s. 34.7-10.

3350. Stiles, Patrick V. 1985. "EME (AB) *wes*: A Reflex of IE **wes-* 'to pasture, tend (livestock)'?". *ZVS* 98.295-301. [On the word in *St Margaret*.]

3351. Storms, G. 1952. "The Middle English Dictionary". *ES* 33.257-59. [A note on organization and scope.]

3352. Strickland, Eleanor C. 1971. *The Poetic Diction of William Dunbar*. Arizona State Univ. diss., 215 pp. [Abstr. in *DA* 32.2654A (1971).]

3353. Strohm, Paul. 1975. "*Passioun, Lyf, Miracle, Legend*: Some Generic Terms in Middle English Hagiographical Narrative". *ChauR* 10.62-75 and 154-71.

3354. Sundby, Bertil. 1952. "Some Middle English Occupational Terms". *ES* 33.18-20.

3355. ———. 1955. "A Note on Middle English *sley(e)* (< Old English *slege)*". *SN* 27.105-07.

3356. Sundén, Karl Frithiof. 1925. "The Origin of the English Affirmative Particle *aye* 'yes'". *Mélanges de Philologie offerts à M. Johan Vising*, 202-10. Göteborg: Gumperts; Paris: Champion. [Argues that it is ultimately the first syllable of ME *i-wisse*.]

3357. ———. 1925. "Three Middle English Verbs of Scandinavian Origin". *Minneskrift utgiven av Filologiska Samfundet i Göteborg*, 75-84. [1. *chymble*, 2. *nurne*, 3. *skruke*.]

3358. ———. 1929. "The Etymology of ME. *trayþ(e)ly* and *runisch, renisch*". *SN* 2.41-55.

3359. ———. 1930. "The Etymology of the ME. Verbs *Rope, Ropele*, and *Rupe*". *Jespersen Festschrift*, 109-22.

3360. ———. 1941/42. "Notes on the Vocabulary of Layamon's *Brut*". *SN* 14.281-300.

3361. Suzuki, Eiichi. 1977. "A Note on the Age of the Green Knight". *NM* 78.27-30. [Argues that *of hyghe eldee* (l. 844) should be glossed 'old, advanced in age'.]

3362. ———. 1979. "Archaic Nouns in *Morte Arthure*: A Reconsideration". *Poetica* 12.134-41. [Apropos of Krishna [no. 3123].]

3363. ———. 1981. "Another Note on *hyghe* in *Sir Gawain*". *MESN* 5.1-2. [Cf. Suzuki [no. 3361].]

3364. Taglicht, J. 1970. "Notes on *Ywain and Gawain*". *NM* 71.641-47. [Intended to correct the errors in the text and to correct and supplement the linguistic notes and the glossary of the EETS edition of the poem, ed. A.B. Friedman and N.T. Harrington (1964).]

3365. Tengstrand, Erik. 1949. "Three Middle English Bahuvrīhi Adjectives". *SMSpr* 17.210-26. [The adjectives discussed are *nesshe-wombe, harde-wombe*, and *clere-syghte*, all found in ME medical books.]

3366. Tester, Sue K. 1970. "The Use of the Word *Lee* in *Sir Gawain and the Green Knight*". *Neophil* 54.184-90.

3367. Thun, Nils. 1966. "Chevin, Chavender and Club: Notes on English Fish-Names". *SN* 38.117-30. [Points out the occurrences of the words in ME.]

3368. Thuresson, Bertil. 1950. *Middle English Occupational Terms*. (= LundSE, 19.) Lund: Gleerup; Copenhagen: Munksgaard, xix + 285 pp.

Reviews: H.T. Price in *JEGP* 50.540-42 (1951); B.M.H. Carr in *RES* n.s. 3.65-67 (1952); R. Derolez in *RBPH* 30.255-57 (1952); E.V.K. Dobbie in *Word* 8.188 (1952); Sherman M. Kuhn in *Language* 28.135-39 (1952); F.P. Magoun, Jr. in *Speculum* 27.431-32 (1952); F. Mossé in *BSL* 48.90 (1952); Bertil Sundby in *ES* 33.20-24 (1952); A.A. Prins in *Museum* 58.124-25 (1953); Henry Bosley Woolf in *MLN* 68.577-78 (1953); Heinrich C. Matthes in *Anglia* 73.92-97 (1955).

3369. Tilander, Gunnar. 1969. "Moyen anglais *gauntycule* (écrit *gountycule*)". *Lombard Festschrift*, 216-19.

3370. Tilgner, Elfriede. 1936. *Die Aureate Terms als Stilelement bei Lydgate*. (= Germanische Studien, 182.) Berlin: Ebering, 91 pp. [Berlin diss. Discusses Lydgate's 'aureate terms' and their relation to Chaucerian language and to the 15th century in general.]

Reviews: W. Héraucourt in *Anglia B* 48.169-70 (1937); Simeon Potter in *MLR* 32.658-59 (1937).

3371. Tolkien, John Ronald Reuel. 1925. "Some Contributions to Middle-English Lexicography". *RES* 1.210-15. [Notes on ME *long home* & *burde* and also on the glossary to the EETS edition of *Hali Meidenhad* (1922).]

3372. ———. 1925. "The Devil's Coach-Horses". *RES* 1.331-36. [Notes on ME *eauer*.]

3373. ———. 1953. "Middle English *losenger*: Sketch of an Etymological and Semantic Enquiry". *Essais de Philologie moderne (1951)* (= Bibliothèque de la Faculté de Philosophie et Lettres de l'Univ. de Liège, 129), 63-76. Paris: Les Belles Lettres.

3374. Toll, Johann M. 1926. *Niederländisches Lehngut im Mittelenglsichen: Ein Beitrag zur englischen Wortgeschichte*. (= SEP, 69.) Halle/S.: Niemeyer, xxii + 102 pp.

Reviews: Karl Luick in *DLZ* 48.802-04 (1927); C.B. van Haeringen in *ES* 10.183-85 (1928); Fritz Karpf in *NS* 37.170-71 (1929).

3375. Townsend, Brenda. 1973. "The Word *Pyn* in the Harley Lyric "Ichot a Burde in a Bour ase Beryl so Bryht"". *ELN* 11.89-91.

3376. Tucker, Susie I. 1949. "Sixty as an Indefinite Number in Middle English". *RES* 25.152-53.

3377. ———. 1958. "Reginald Pecock: Additions to the Dictionary". *N&Q* n.s. 5.477-79. [A number of citations from Pecock's *Reule of Crysten Religioun* (c1443) which antedate *OED*.]

3378. Turville-Petre, Joan. 1969. "Two Etymological Notes: Ancrene Wisse *eskibah*, *hond þet ilke*". *SN* 41.156-61.

3379. Turville-Petre, Thorlac. 1978. "Two Notes on Words in Alliterative Poems". *N&Q* n.s. 25.295-96. [On *porte* (*Wars of Alexander*) and *tried* (*Sir Gawain*).]

3380. Van der Gaaf, Willem. 1927. "Contributions to the History of English". *Neophil* 12.194-99. [1. Christian; 2. Jeames, the flunkey; 3. A ME instance of *would sooner*; 4. The short vowel in *let* (= Du. *laten*); 5. The origin of *to sigh*; 6. The rhyme *syghte: scumfyghte* in Brunne's *Handlyng Synne* 4979f.]

3381. ———. 1932. "*To laugh to scorn*". *ES* 14.20-21. [On the idiomatic phrase in ME and early ModE.]

3382. Van Roosbroeck, Gustave L. 1923. "*Under the Sonne he loketh*". *MLN* 38.59. [On the line found in Chaucer *CT* I 1697.]

3383. Visser, Frederikus Theodorus. 1955. "Three Suggested Emendations of the *Middle English Dictionary*". *ES* 36.23-24. [The words discussed are *ensercher*, *fairneshed* (= splendor, beauty), and *feinednes*.]

3384. ———. 1958. "*Pearl* 609-611". *ES* 39.20-23. [On the interpretation of the word *dared* as 'dared to go'.]

3385. ———. 1959. "The *Middle English Dictionary* (Parts A, B1-4, E and F)". *ES* 40.18-27. [Gives additions, mainly from Barbour's *Bruce*.]

3386. ———. 1962. "Middle English *leten for* = 'to regard as'". *ES* 43.491.

3387. Wallace, Kathryn Y. 1974. "A French Source for an English Word Not in the *O.E.D.* or *M.E.D.*". *N&Q* n.s. 21.123-24. [On the word *denscot* 'danegeld'.]

3388. Wallenberg, Johannes K. 1923. *The Vocabulary of Dan Michael's 'Ayenbite of Inwyt': A Phonological, Morphological, Etymological, Semasiological and Textual Study*. Uppsala: Appelberg, xviii + 348 pp. [Uppsala diss.]

Reviews: Richard Jordan in *EStn* 59.100-01 (1925); Etsko Kruisinga in *ES* 8.84 (1926); Karl Jost in *Anglia B* 37.172-75 (1926).

3389. Wallner, Björn. 1959. "The Distribution and Frequency of Scandinavian and Native Synonyms in *Kyng Alisaunder* and *Arthour and Merlin*". *ES* 40.337-52.

3390. ———. 1964. "Lexical Matter in the Middle English Translation of *Guy de Chauliac*". *Zandvoort Festschrift* = *ES* 45 Supplement.151-56.

3391. ———. 1969. "A Note on Some Middle English Medical Terms". *ES* 50.499-503.

3392. Wandl, Enna. 1974. *Der Wortschatz Chaucers: Seine Gliederung nach Herkunft und Bedeutung: Ein Beitrag zur Forschungsgeschichte*. Wien diss., v + 290 pp.

3393. Watts, V.E. 1983. "The Etymology of *Helde* Again". *Comments on Etymology* 12:7/8.2-4. [On the word found in the eighth Harley Lyric "In a fryht". Cf. Machan [no. 3158].]

3394. Webster, Mildred. 1938. "The Vocabulary of "An Holy Medytacion"". *PQ* 17.359-64. [A statistical study furnishing support for the theory of Chaucerian authorship.]

3395. Wehrle, Otto. 1935. *Die hybriden Wortbildungen des Mittelenglischen (1050-1400): Ein Beitrag zur englischen Wortgeschichte*. Freiburg: Weis, Mühlhans & Räpple, iii + 62 pp. [Freiburg diss.]

3396. Wermser, Richard. 1976. *Statistische Studien zur Entwicklung des englischen Wortschatzes*. (= SAA, 91.) Bern: Francke, 141 pp. [Zürich diss. Deals with over 16,000 words newly recorded between 1450-1900 on the basis of *A Chronological English Dictionary*, ed. T. Finkenstaedt, et al. (Heidelberg: Carl Winter, 1970).]

Reviews: Manfred Görlach in *Archiv* 216.401-03 (1979); Hans Käsmann in *Anglia* 97.491-96 (1979).

3397. Westergaard, Elisabeth. 1924. *Studies in Prefixes and Suffixes in Middle Scottish*. London: Oxford Univ. Press/Milford, xii + 135 pp. [Copenhagen diss.]

Reviews: Anon. in *Archiv* 148.300 (1925); C.B. in *MLR* 20.497 (1925); J.H.G.G. in *RES* 3.119 (1927); F.P. Magoun, Jr. in *MLN* 42.196-97 (1927); J. Marik in *Anglia B* 37.299-303 (1926).

3398. White, Beatrice. 1953. "Two Notes on Middle English". *Neophil* 37.113-15. [Discusses: 1. the forms *camaille* and *aventaille* in Chaucer CT IV 1196, 1204; 2. *barlay* in *Sir Gawain and the Green Knight* 295.]

3399. Whitehall, Harold. 1939. "On the Etymology of *Lad*". *PQ* 18.19-24 [On ME *ladde*.]

3400. ———. 1939. "The Etymology of Middle English *Myse*". *PQ* 18.314-16. [On the word in *York Plays* XI.273.]

3401. ———. 1941. "Interim Etymologies: L.". *PQ* 20.25-37. [Deals with 15 ME words beginning with *l-*.]

3402. Whiting, Bartlett Jere. 1948. "A Colt's Tooth". *Medieval Studies in Honor of Jeremiah Denis Matthia Ford*, ed. U.T. Holmes and A.J. Demony, 319-31. Cambridge, MA: Harvard Univ. Press. [Provides French instances of the phrase which occurs first in English in Chaucer.]

3403. Whitteridge, Gweneth. 1949/50. "The Word *archaungel* in Chaucer's *Romaunt of the Rose*". *EGS* 3.34-36.

3404. Wilcockson, Colin. 1983. "A Note on *Riflynge* in *Piers Plowman* B. v. 234". *MAE* 52.302-05.

3405. Willard, Rudolph. 1947. "Chaucer's *holt and heeth*". *AS* 22.196-98. [*CT*, General Prol. 6.]

3406. Williams, Arnold. 1948. "Middle English *Questmonger*". *MS* 10.200-04.

3407. Williams, Edna R. 1944. *The Conflict of Homonyms in English*. New Haven, CT: Yale Univ. Press, 127 pp. [With numerous examples from ME and ModE.]

3408. Wilson, Edward. 1971. "*Gromylyoun* (Gromwell) in *Pearl*". *N&Q* n.s. 18.42-44. [*Pearl* 43.]

3409. Wilson, Janet. 1975. "A Note on the Use of the Word *kny3t* in Fitt 4 of *Sir Gawain and the Green Kny3t*". *Parergon* 13.49.

3410. Wright, Herbert G. 1959. "Thomas Speght as a Lexicographer and Annotator of Chaucer's Works". *ES* 40.194-208.

3411. Wyatt, A.J. 1928. "Chaucer's *In Termes*". *RES* 4.439.

3412. Wyld, Henry Cecil. 1930-37. "Studies in the Diction of Layamon's *Brut*". *Language* 6.1-24; 9.47-71 and 171-91; 10.149-201; 13.29-59 and 194-237. [Deals with 'Points of Difference between the Earlier and Later Text', 'The Vocabulary of Layamon in Relation to the Old English Poetical Usage', 'The Voice, Speech, Shouting, Singing', and 'Words Expressing Movement'.]

3413. Wyler, Siegfried. 1944. *Die Adjektive des mittelenglischen Schönheitsfeldes, unter besonderer Berücksichtigung Chaucers: Ein Begriff in seiner sprachlichen Gestaltung*. Biel: Schüler, 187 pp. [Zürich diss.]

3414. Yamaguchi, Hideo. 1965. "A Lexical Note on the Language of *Sir Gawain and* the *Green Knight". PP* 8.372-80. [Discusses OF and ON influence on the poet's language.]

3415. Yerkes, David. 1975. "*Sir Gawain and the Green Knight* 211: *Grayn*". *N&Q* n.s. 22.4.

3416. Young, Karl. 1943. "Chaucer's *Vitremyte*". *SP* 40.494-501. [On the origin and meaning of the word in *CT* VII 2372.]

3417. Zandvoort, Reinard Willem. 1942. "Een middel-engelse parallel van een opmerkelijk gebruik van ander". *De Nieuwe Taalgids* (Groningen) 36.236. [On a ME parallel of the particular use of Dutch *ander* 'other'.]

3418. Zettersten, Arne. 1964. *Middle English Word Studies.* (= LUÅ N.F. I, 56:1.) Lund: Gleerup, 47 pp. [Discusses etymologies for 16 words in the *Ancrene Riwle.*]

Review: E.G. Stanley in *N&Q* n.s. 11.203 (1964).

3419. ———. 1969. "French Loan-Words in the *Ancrene Riwle* and Their Frequency". *Lombard Festschrift*, 227-50.

3420. ———. 1979. "On the Aureate Diction of William Dunbar". *Schibsbye Festschrift*, 51-68.

XII. ONOMASTICS

A. General

3421. Allen, Mark Edward. 1982. *Personal Names in Old and Middle English Poetry*. Univ. of Illinois at Urbana-Champaign diss., 268 pp. [Abstr. in *DA* 43.784A (1982).]

3422. Biddle, Martin and D.J. Keene, with contributions by Kenneth Cameron, Olof von Feilitzen, and J.E.B. Gower. 1976. "The Early Place-Names of Winchester". *Winchester Studies*, 231-39. [1. Street-names; 2. Place-names other than street-names.]

3423. Ewen, Cecil Henry L'Estrange. 1931. *A History of Surnames of the British Isles: A Concise Account of Their Origin, Evolution, Etymology, and Legal Status*. London: K. Paul, Trench, Trubner, xx + 508 pp. [Repr., Detroit: Gale Research Co., 1968.]

3424. Fellows Jensen, Gillian. 1968. *Scandinavian Personal Names in Lincolnshire and Yorkshire*. (= Navnestudier udgivet af Inst. for Navneforskning, 7.) Copenhagen: Akademisk Forlag, cviii + 374 pp. [Covers the period from the time of the first Scandinavian settlements until the end of the 13th century. Copenhagen diss.]

3425. ———. 1972. *Scandinavian Settlement Names in Yorkshire*. (= Navnestudier udgivet af Inst. for Navneforskning, 11.) Copenhagen: Akademisk Forlag, xx + 276 pp. [Collects all the place-names in Yorkshire recorded in the *Domesday Book*.]

Reviews: Bertil Ejder in *ANF* 88.256-57 (1973); Margaret Gelling in *N&Q* n.s. 20.144-46 (1973).

3426. ———. 1978. *Scandinavian Settlement Names in the East Midlands*. (= Navnestudier udgivet af Inst. for Navneforskning, 16.) Copenhagen: Akademisk Forlag, xxiv + 406 pp.

Reviews: Margaret Gelling in *Nomina* 4.79-83 (1980); Peter McClure in *Lincolnshire Hist. and Archaeol.* 15.93-94 (1980); Fred C. Robinson in *Speculum* 55.117-18 (1980); V.E. Watts in *Northern History* 17.285-86 (1981); A.M.J. Perrott in *Saga-Book* 20.325-28 (1981).

3427. Gillespie, George T. 1973. *A Catalogue of Persons Named in Germanic Heroic Literature, 700-1600, Including Named Animals and Objects and Ethnic Names.* Oxford: Clarendon Press, 203 pp.

3428. Hill, Betty. 1965. "Problems in the "Clee" Place-Names of Shropshire". *N&Q* n.s. 12.242-45.

3429. Kristensson, Gillis. 1974. "English Name-Studies". *EDB på navnearkiverne Redigeret af John Kousgård Sørensen* (= NORNA rapporter, 4), 29-37. Uppsala: Nordiska samarbetskommittén för namnforskning. [A project aiming at an inventory of OE and ME personal names.]

3430. ———. 1986. "The Place-Name *Scugger Ho* (Cumberland)". *N&Q* n.s. 33.2-3.

3431. Reaney, Percy Hide. 1961. *The Origin of English Place-Names.* London: Routledge and Kegan Paul; New York: Hillary House, x + 277 pp.

3432. ———. 1967. *The Origin of English Surnames.* London: Routledge and Kegan Paul; New York: Barnes and Noble, xix + 415 pp. [Gives a general account of the development of English surnames, changes in pronunciation and spelling, and the gradual growth of hereditary family names.]

Reviews: Roger Lass in *FL* 9.392-402 (1973); Kelsie B. Harder in *Names* 16.305-07 (1968).

3433. von Feilitzen, Olof. 1945. "Some Unrecorded Old and Middle English Personal Names". *NoB* 33.69-98.

3434. ———. 1976. "The Personal Names and Bynames of the Winton Domesday". *Winchester Studies*, 143-229.

3435. Watts, V.E. 1983. "Medieval Fisheries in the Wear, Tyne and Tweed: The Place-Name Evidence". *Nomina* 7.35-45.

3436. Whitelock, Dorothy. 1940. "Scandinavian Personal Names in the Liber Vitae of Thorney Abbey". *Saga-Book* 12:2.127-53. [On Scandinavian names in England during the 11th and 12th centuries.]

3437. Wrander, Nils. 1983. *English Place-Names in the Dative Plural.* (= LundSE, 65.) Lund: Gleerup; Stockholm: Almqvist & Wiksell, 172 pp. [Lund diss.; Abstr. in *DA* 46.10/132C (1985).]

Reviews: Margaret Gelling in *Nomina* 8.101 (1984); E.G. S[tanley] in *N&Q* n.s. 31.437 (1984).

B. Old English

3438. Arngart, Olof. 1972. "On the *Ingtūn* Type of English Place Name". *SN* 44.263-73.

3439. ———. 1979. "Domus *Godebiete*". *SN* 51.125-26. [Apropos of von Feilitzen's mention of the name [no. 3434].]

3440. ———. 1979. "Old English *hund*: 'A Territorial Hundred'?". *NoB* 67.26-33.

3441. ———. 1979. "The Place-Name *Oundle*". *N&Q* n.s. 26.4-5.

3442. ———. 1979. "Again the Place-Name *Oundle*". *N&Q* n.s. 26.389.

3443. ———. 1979. "The Word *Wolverine*". *N&Q* n.s. 26.494-95. [Suggests that the word is derived from OE **wulf(a)-ryne*.]

3444. ———. 1979. "*Gertre, Gartee, Garstang*". *Sydsvenska Ortnamnssällskapets Årsskrift* (Lund) 1979, 50-53.

3445. Bäck, Hilding. 1932. "Der ae. Eigenname *It(h)amar*". *Anglia B* 43.355.

3446. Barley, Nigel F. 1974. "Perspectives on Anglo-Saxon Names". *Semiotica* 11.1-31.

3447. Beeaff, Dianne Ebertt. 1978. "Aelfraed and Haranfot: Anglo-Saxon Personal Names". *History Today* (London) 28.688-90.

3448. Bell, Alexander. 1977. "Zu ae. *Anche*". *BN* N.F. 12.419.

3449. Böhler, Maria. 1930. *Die altenglischen Frauennamen.* (= Germanische Studien, 98.) Berlin: Ebering, 261 pp.

    Reviews: F. Holthausen in *LGRP* 52.356-57 (1931); J.K. Wallenberg in *Anglia B* 42.356-59 (1931); A. B[randl] in *Archiv* 164.128-29 (1933); H. Dehmer in *NS* 41.465 (1933); G.T. Flom in *JEGP* 32.133-34 (1933); E. Schröder in *Anzeiger für deutsches Altertum und deutsche Literatur* (Wiesbaden) 53.216-17 (1934).

3450. Bolton, Whitney French. 1962. "The Background and Meaning of *Guthlac*". *JEGP* 61.595-603. [Concerning the rendering of the saint's name.]

3451. Brandl, Alois. 1930. "Einige Tatsachen betreffend Scyld Siefing". *Jespersen Festschrift*, 31-37.

3452. Brandon, Peter. 1978. "The South Saxon *Andredesweald*". *South Saxons*, 138-59.

3453. Bryan, William Frank. 1929. "Epithetic Compound Folk-Names in *Beowulf*". *Klaeber Festschrift*, 120-34.

3454. Cameron, Kenneth. 1965. *Scandinavian Settlement in the Territory of the Five Boroughs: The Place-Name Evidence*. Nottingham: Nottingham Univ., 24 pp.

3455. ———. 1968. "*Eccles* in English Place-Names". *Barley & Hanson*, 87-92.

3456. ———. 1970. "Scandinavian Settlement in the Territory of the Five Boroughs: The Place-Name Evidence, Part II, Place-Names in Thorp". *Mediaeval Scandinavia* (Odense, Denmark) 3.35-49. [For Part I, see Cameron [no. 3454].]

3457. ———. 1971. "Scandinavian Settlement in the Territory of the Five Boroughs: The Place-Name Evidence, Part III, the Grimston-Hybrids". *Whitelock Festschrift*, 147-63.

3458. ———. 1978. "The Scandinavian Settlement of Eastern England: The Place-Name Evidence". *Ortnamnssällskapets i Uppsala Årsskrift* 1978, 7-17.

3459. ———. 1979/80. "The Meaning and Significance of Old English *walh* in English Place-Names". *JEPNS* 12.1-46.

3460. Campbell, J. 1979. "Bede's Words for Places". *Names, Words, and Graves: Early Medieval Settlement* (Lectures Delivered in the Univ. of Leeds, May 1978), 34-54. Leeds: School of History, Univ. of Leeds.

3461. Coates, Richard. 1979. "Old English *steorf* in Sussex Place-names". *BN* N.F. 14.320-24.

3462. ———. 1980. "A Phonological Problem in Sussex Place-names". *BN* N.F. 15.299-318.

3463. ———. 1981. "On *cumb* and *denu* in Place-Names of the English South-East". *Nomina* 5.29-38.

3464. Cockburn, J.H. 1931. *The Battle of Burnanburh and its Period elucidated by Place-Names*. London & Sheffield: Leng and Co., xiv + 300 pp.

Review: F.P. Magoun, Jr. in *Speculum* 8.85-87.

3465. Cole, Ann. 1982. "Topography, Hydrology, and Place-Names in the Chalklands of Southern England: *cumb* and *denu*". *Nomina* 6.78-87. [Disputes Coates [no. 3463].]

3466. Colman, Fran. 1981. "The Name-Element *Æðel-* and Related Problems". *N&Q* n.s. 28.295-301.

3467. Cox, Barrie. 1976. "The Place-Names of the Earliest English Records". *JEPNS* 8.12-66.

3468. ———. 1980. "Aspects of Place-Name Evidence for Early Medieval Settlement in England". *Viator* 11.35-50.

3469. Dickins, Bruce. 1934. "English Names and Old English Heathenism". *E&S* 19.148-60.

3470. ———. 1973. "*Fagaduna* in Orderic (A.D. 1075)". *von Feilitzen Festschrift*, 44-45.

3471. Dodgson, John McNeal. 1967. "Various Forms of OE *-ing* in English Place-Names". *BN* N.F. 2.325-96.

3472. ———. 1968. "Various English Place-Name Formations Containing OE *-ing*". *BN* N.F. 3.141-89.

3473. ———. 1973. "Place-Names from *hām*, Distinguished from *hamm* Names, in Relation to the Settlement of Kent, Surrey and Sussex". *ASE* 2.1-50.

3474. ———. 1973. "Two Coals to Newcastle". *von Feilitzen Festschrift*, 46-48.

3475. ———. 1978. "Place-Names in Sussex: The Material for a New Look". *South Saxons*, 54-88.

3476. Dolley, Michael. 1973. "The Forms of the Proper Names Appearing on the Earliest Coins Struck in Ireland". *von Feilitzen Festschrift*, 49-65.

3477. Ekblom, Richard. 1940/41. "Der Volksname *Osti* in Alfreds des Grossen Orosius-Übersetzung". *SN* 13.161-73.

3478. Ekwall, Eilert. 1925. "On Some Old English Charters". *Luick Festschrift*, 152-57. [Examines place-names in five charters.]

3479. ———. 1925. "An Old English Sound-Change and Some English Forest Names". *Anglia B* 36.146-51.

3480. ———. 1928. "Notes on the Inflexion of Old English Place-Names". *NoB* 16.59-77.

3481. ———. 1936. "The Scandinavian Settlement". *An Historical Geography of Eng-*

land before A.D. 1800, ed. H.C. Darby, 133-64. Cambridge: Cambridge Univ. Press. [Deals with place-names.]

3482. ———. 1964. *Old English 'wic' in Place-Names*. (= Nomina Germanica: Arkiv för Germansk Namnforskning, 13.) Uppsala: Lundequistska Bokhandeln; Copenhagen: Munksgaard, 70 pp.

Reviews: O. Arngart in *NoB* 53.63-65 (1965); Paul Bacquet in *EA* 18.407-08 (1965); Wolfgang Laur in *BN* 16.211-12 (1965); R.W. Zandvoort in *ES* 46.51-52 (1965); Herbert Voitl in *Anglia* 86.363-64 (1968). Cf. also Tengstrand [no. 3598].

3483. ———. 1965. "A Note on O.E. *Bece* 'brook, valley' in Place-names". *NoB* 53.22-25.

3484. Fellows Jensen, Gillian. 1969. "The Scribe of the Lindsey Survey". *NoB* 57.58-74. [Studies place-names of Lindsey.]

3485. ———. 1975. "The Vikings in England: A Review". *ASE* 4.181-206. [Discusses place-names as evidence for Scandinavian settlement.]

3486. ———. 1975. "Personal Name or Appellative? A New Look at Some Danelaw Place-Names". *Onoma* 19.445-58.

3487. ———. 1976. "Some Problems of a Maverick Anthroponymist". *Erlangen Proceedings*, 43-61.

3488. ———. 1977. "Place-Names and Settlement History: A Review, with a Select Bibliography of Works Mostly Published since 1960". *Northern History* 13.1-26.

3489. ———. 1978. "Place-Names and Settlement in the North Riding of Yorkshire". *Northern History* 14.19-46.

3490. ———. 1978. "Topography, Toponymy and Topographical Toponyms". *Nomina* 2.14-19.

3491. ———. 1978. "Place-Name Evidence for Scandinavian Settlement in the Danelaw: A Reassessment". *The Vikings*, 89-98.

3492. ———. 1980. "Conquests and the Place-Names of England, with Special Reference to the Viking Settlements". *Ortnamn och Språkkontakt: Handlingar från NORNA: S sjätte Symposium i Uppsala 5-7 maj 1978*, ed. Thorsten Andersson, et al., 192-210. Uppsala: Nordiska samarbetskommittén för namnforskning.

3493. ———. 1981. "Scandinavian Settlement in the Danelaw in the Light of the Place-Names of Denmark". *Proceedings of the Eighth Viking Congress Århus 24-31 August 1977*, ed. Hans Bekker-Nielsen, et al., 133-45. Odense: Odense Univ. Press.

3494. Flom, George T. 1924. "Place Name Tests of Racial Mixture in Northern England". *MLN* 39.203-12. [Concerned with the OE period.]

3495. Forsberg, Rune. 1950. *A Contribution to a Dictionary of Old English Place-Names*. (= Nomina Germanica: Arkiv för Germansk Namnforskning, 9.) Uppsala: Almqvist & Wiksell, xlvi + 225 pp. [Uppsala diss.]

 Reviews: Roland Blenner-Hassett in *Speculum* 26.388-90 (1951); K.R. Brooks in *MLR* 46.546-47 (1951); E.C. Ehrensperger in *JEGP* 50.111 (1951); H. Flasdieck in *BN* 2.216 (1950/51); F.Th. Visser in *Museum* 56.142-44 (1951); F.E. Harmer in *RES* n.s. 3.275-76 (1952); E. Bonsack in *SIL* 9.77-78 (1951); Otto Ritter in *Anglia* 71.481-88 (1952/53).

3496. ———. 1960. "English *wormsteall*". *NoB* 48.120-39.

3497. ———. 1970. "On Old English *ād* in English Place-Names". *NoB* 58.20-82.

3498. ———. 1973. "*Æstealles beorh*: A Place-Name Crux Reconsidered". *SN* 45.3-19.

3499. ———. 1984. "Old English *burnstōw* and *merestōw*: Two Appelative Compounds in *-stow* with a Topographical First Element". *SN* 56.3-20.

3500. Förster, Max. 1941. *Der Flussname Theme und seine Suppe: Studien zur Anglisierung keltischer Eigennamen und zur Lautchronologie des Altbritischen*. München: Beck, xii + 951 pp. [Part I "Allgemeiner Teil" (pp. 1-366) includes a chapter "Flexion und Genus der ae. Flussnamen".]

 Reviews: K. Brunner in *Anglia B* 54/55.53-58 (1943/44); K. Malone in *MLN* 64.538-41 (1949).

3501. Gelling, Margaret. 1973. "Further Thoughts on Pagan Place-Names". *von Feilitzen Festschrift*, 109-28.

3502. ———. 1974. "The Chronology of English Place-Names". *Anglo-Saxon Settlement and Landscape* (= British Archaeological Reports, 6), ed. Trevor Rowley, 93-101. Oxford: British Archaeological Reports.

3503. ———. 1976. "The Evidence of Place-Names". *Sawyer Med.Settlement*, 200-11.

3504. ———. 1977. "Latin Loan-Words in Old English Place-Names". *ASE* 6.1-13.

3505. ———. 1978. *Signposts to the Past: Place-Names and the History of England.* London: J.M. Dent & Sons, 256 pp. + 21 maps. [Ranges chronologically from the Romano-British era through the Anglo-Saxon and Viking settlements to the early Norman period.]

Reviews: Ronald Blythe in *Listener* 99.505-06 (1978); Basil Cottle in *British Book News* 1978, p. 584; Eugene B. Vest in *Names* 26.423-24 (1978); Alexander Rumble in *Nomina* 2.61-62 (1978); Gillis Kristensson in *N&Q* n.s. 26.52-53 (1979); Peter McClure in *Lincolnshire History and Archaeology* 14.62 (1979); John McNeal Dodgson in *Journal of Historical Geography* 5.222-23 (1979); Tim Tatton-Brown in *Journal of the British Archaeological Association* 132.102-03 (1979); V.E. Watts in *History* 64.78 (1979); Gillian Fellows Jensen in *Midland History* 5.93-94 (1979/80); A.D. Mills in *MAE* 49.167-70 (1980); H.S. Fox in *Geographical Review* 71.231-32 (1981); C.V. Phythian-Adams in *Northern History* 18.287-88 (1982).

3506. Gerould, Gordon Hall. 1934. "Thunor in Kent". *MLN* 49.238-39.

3507. Ginsberg, Warren. 1977. "Cynewulf and His Sources: *The Fates of the Apostles*". *NM* 78.108-14. [Interprets the names of the apostles.]

3508. Goffart, Walter. 1981. "*Hetware* and *Hugas*: Datable Anachronisms in *Beowulf*". *Dating Beowulf*, 83-100.

3509. Gray, Louis Herbert. 1935. "The Origin of the Name of Glastonbury". *Speculum* 10.46-53.

3510. Green Carleton. 1936. *The Place-Names in the 'Historia Ecclesiastica' of Bede.* Harvard diss. (no pagination available). [Abstr. in *Harvard Univ. Summaries of Theses* 1936, 326-28.]

3511. Grundy, George Beardoe. 1936. *Saxon Charters and Field-Names of Gloucestershire.* Gloucester: Council of the British and Gloucester Archaeological Society, 306 pp.

Review: Anon. in *N&Q* 171.342 (1936).

3512. ———. 1943. "The Development of the Meanings of Certain Anglo-Saxon Terms". *The Archaeological Journal* (London) 99.67-98. [Deals with the use and distribution of such place-name elements as *-ing*, *-tun*, *-ham*, etc.]

3513. Herben, Stephen J., Jr. 1935. "Heorot". *PMLA* 50.933-45. [On the site in *Beowulf*.]

3514. Hooke, Della. 1979. "Anglo-Saxon Landscapes of the West Midlands". *JEPNS* 11.3-23.

3515. ———. 1981. "Burial Features in West Midlands Charters". *JEPNS* 13.1-40. [Discusses such elements as *beorg*, *hlæw*, and *crug*.]

3516. ———. 1982. *Anglo-Saxon Landscapes of the West Midlands: the Charter Evidence*. (= BAR, British Ser., 95.) Oxford: British Archaeological Reports, 380 pp. + 77 plates.

   Reviews: J.D. Hamshere in *Nomina* 6.111-12 (1982); D.J.H. Michelmore in *Landscape History* 4.71-72 (1984).

3517. Janzén, Assar. 1972. "The Viking Colonization of England in the Light of Place-Names". *Names* 20.1-25.

3518. Johansson, Christer. 1975. *Old English Place-Names and Field-Names Containing 'lēah'*. (= SSE, 32.) Stockholm: Almqvist & Wiksell, 170 pp. [Stockholm diss.]

   Reviews: Gillis Kristensson in *SN* 48.369-72 (1976); Klaus Dietz in *BN* 13.42-47 (1978).

3519. ———. 1977. "The Place-Names in a Herefordshire Charter". *SN* 49.185-87. [The charter is listed as No. 1462 in Sawyer's *Anglo-Saxon Charters* (London, 1968).]

3520. Karlström, Sigurd. 1927. *Old English Compound Place-Names in '-ing'*. (= UUÅ, 1927:2.) Uppsala: A.-B. Lundequistska Bokhandeln, xxiii + 196 pp. [Uppsala diss.]

   Review: J.K. Wallenberg in *ZON* 4.282-92 (1927/28).

3521. Kaske, Robert E. 1963. "*Hygelac* and *Hygd*". *Brodeur Festschrift*, 200-06. [Names in *Beowulf*.]

3522. Kisbye, Torben. 1975. "Sardina — Sarþina: über die Wiedergabe einiger griechisch-lateinischer Namensformen im altenglischen *Orosius*". *SN* 47.301-12.

3523. ———. 1979. "*Osgod/Osgot* on Early Anglo-Danish Coins: the Provenance of Some Names in *-god* Reassessed in the Light of Numismatic Evidence". *Schibsbye Festschrift*, 12-26.

3524. ———. 1982. *Vikingerne i England: sproglige spor*. Copenhagen: Akademisk Forlag, 145 pp.

3525. Kökeritz, Helge. 1943. "*Wihtgaraburh*". *MLN* 58.181-91. [Explanation of the place-name in the Anglo-Saxon Chronicle, 530-544.]

3526. Langenfelt, Gösta. 1961. "Foreign Names in Old English: A Comparison between Alfred's *Orosius* and *Widsith*". *NM* 62.10-22.

3527. Laur, Wolfgang. 1964. "Namenübertragungen im Zuge der angelsächsischen Wanderungen". *BN* 15.287-97.

3528. ———. 1965. "Ortsnamen in England und in den festländischen Stammlanden der Angelsachsen". *Namenforschung: Festschrift für Adolf Bach zum 75. Geburtstag am 31. Januar 1965*, ed. Rudolf Schützeichel and Matthias Zender, 300-12. Heidelberg: Carl Winter.

3529. Lehiste, Ilse. 1958. "Names of Scandinavians in *The Anglo-Saxon Chronicle*". *PMLA* 73.6-22.

3530. Lund, Niels. 1976. "*Thorp*-Names". *Sawyer Med.Settlement*, 223-25.

3531. Magoun, Francis Peabody, Jr. 1935. "Territorial, Place-, and River-Names in the Old-English Chronicle, A-Text (Parker MS.)". *Harvard Studies and Notes in Philology and Literature* 18.69-111.

3532. ———. 1938. "Territorial, Place-, and River-Names in the Old English Annals, D-Text (MS. Cotton Tiberius B. iv)". *Harvard Studies and Notes in Philology and Literature* 20.147-80.

3533. ———. 1944. "King Alfred's Hálgoland and Old Norwegian Syncope". *Scandinavian Studies* (Lincoln, NB) 18.163-64. [Argues that the name of the district represents an instance of syncope of the unstressed medial vowel in ON.]

3534. Malone, Kemp. 1927. "A Note on Brunanburh". *MLN* 42.238-39. [On the length of the first *u*.]

3535. ———. 1928. "Hunlafing". *MLN* 43.300-04. [On the name in *Beowulf* 1143.]

3536. ———. 1928. "King Alfred's "Gōtland"". *MLR* 23.336-39.

3537. ———. 1931. "On Wulfstan's Scandinavia". *SP* 28.574-79. [Discusses some place-names in *Orosius*.]

3538. ———. 1931/32. "Hliþe and Hlöðr". *APS* 6.328-31. [On the names in *Widsith*.]

3539. ———. 1932. "The Frumtings of *Widsith*". *ES* 14.154-58. [On the tribal name.]

3540. ———. 1932. "Notes on *Beowulf*: VI". *Anglia* 56.436-37. [On *Ecgwela* (l. 1710).]

3541. ———. 1932. "Two Notes on *Widsith*". *MLN* 47.367-71. [Notes on the tribal names *Amopingas* (1.86) and *Geflegan* (1.60).]

3542. ———. 1933. "*Ic wæs mid Eolum*". *EStn* 67.321-24. [On the tribal name *Eolum* in *Widsith* 87.]

3543. ———. 1937. "The Lidwicings of *Widsith*". *MAE* 6.213. [On the tribal name.]

3544. ———. 1940. "The Myrgingas of *Widsith*". *MLN* 55.141-42. [On the tribal name.]

3545. ———. 1940. "The Meaning of Bede's *Iutae*". *Anglia B* 51.262-64.

3546. ———. 1940. "Freawaru". *ELH* 7.39-44. [Discusses the name in *Beowulf*.]

3547. ———. 1947. "The Name of the Wends". *MLN* 62.556-57.

3548. ———. 1953. "Royal Names in Old English Poetry". *Names* 1.153-62.

3549. ———. 1954. "Epithet and Eponym". *Names* 2.109-12. [Reply to Ramsay [no. 3559].]

3550. Mawer, Allen. 1925. "Some Place-Name Identifications in the Anglo-Saxon Chronicles". *Anglica: Untersuchungen zur englischen Philologie; Alois Brandl zum 70. Geburtstage überreicht*, 19-40. Leipzig: Mayer & Müller.

3551. Miedema, Henricus Theodorus Jacobus. 1979. "Anglo-Frisian Relations and the Map of *Breg* and *(H)reg*, Especially in English, Dutch and Frisian Place Names". *Nomina* 3.78-80.

3552. Nicolaisen, W.F.H. 1967. "Scottish Place-Names, 28. Old English *wīc*". *ScoS* 11.75-84.

3553. Orrick, Allan Howard. 1956. *A History of the Generic Names for the Germanic Settlers in the British Isles*. Johns Hopkins diss. [No further information available.]

3554. Pearce, Thomas M. 1966. "Name Patterns in Ælfric's *Catholic Homilies*". *Names* 14.150-56.

3555. Peters, Hans. 1981. "Zum skandinavischen Lehngut im Altenglischen". *Sprachw* 6.85-124.

3556. ———. 1981. "Onomasiologische Untersuchungen: zum skandinavischen Lehngut im Altenglischen". *Sprachw* 6.169-85.

3557. Ploegstra, Robert A. 1974. *The Historicity of 'Beowulf': An Onomastic and Comparative Study*. Michigan State Univ. diss., 440 pp. [Abstr. in *DA* 35.6106A (1975).]

3558. Pogatscher, Alois. 1925. "Altenglisch *Grendel*". *Luick Festschrift*, 151.

3559. Ramsay, Robert Lee. 1953. "Scyldings and Shields". *Names* 1.274-76. [Reply to Malone [no. 3548]; reply by Malone [no. 3549].]

3560. Reaney, Percy Hide. 1952. "Three Unrecorded O.E. Personal Names of a Late Type". *MLR* 47.374. [On the type of OE personal name in which the first theme is descriptive of a locality.]

3561. Richards, Melville. 1973. "Welsh Influences on Some English Place-Names in North East Wales". *von Feilitzen Festschrift*, 216-20.

3562. Robinson, Fred Colson. 1968. "The Significance of Names in Old English Literature". *Anglia* 86.14-58. [On name-etymologizing among the Anglo-Saxons.]

3563. ———. 1968. "Some Uses of Name-Meanings in Old English Poetry". *NM* 69.161-71.

3564. ———. 1970. "Personal Names in Medieval Narrative and the Name of Unferth in *Beowulf*". *Essays in Honor of Richebourg Gaillard McWilliams*, ed. Howard Creed, 43-48. Birmingham, AL: Birmingham-Southern College.

3565. ———. 1973. "Anglo-Saxon Onomastics in the Old English *Andreas*". *Names* 21.133-36.

3566. Rositzke, Harry A., ed. 1940. *The C-Texts of the Old English Chronicles*. (= BEP, 34.) Bochum-Langendreer: Pöppinghaus, 100 pp. [Contains a number of new identifications of place-names in the Chronicle.]

3567. Ross, Alan Strode Campbell. 1978. "The *Este*". *N&Q* n.s. 25.100-04. [On the etymology of the tribal name which appears in the *Orosius*.]

3568. Rumble, Alexander. 1977. "*Hrepingas* Reconsidered". *Mercian Studies*, ed. Ann Dornier, 169-72. Leicester: Leicester Univ. Press.

3569. Sandred, Karl Inge. 1967. "Notes on English Compound Place-Names in *-hamstede*". *NoB* 55.72-84.

3570. ———. 1971. "New Light on an Old English Landmark". *NoB* 59.37-39. [On the landmark *huiæinhamstedi*.]

3571. ———. 1979. "Scandinavian Place-Names and Appellatives in Norfolk: A Study of the Medieval Field-Names of Flitcham". *NoB* 67.98-122.

3572. ———. 1982. "Scandinavian Place-Names and Appellatives in Norfolk: A Study of the Medieval Field-Names of Flitcham". *Proceedings of the Thirteenth International Congress of Onomastic Sciences*, ed. Kazamierz Rymut, Vol. 2, 357-63. Cracow: Nakładem Uniwersytetu Jagiellońskiego: Warsaw: PWN.

3573. Schnetz, Joseph. 1936. "Fiktion und Tatsache". *ZON* 12.27-33. [On the name *geormanlēaf.*]

3574. ———. 1937. "Der altenglische Malvenname *geormant *leab* und deutsche Ortsnamen". *ZON* 13.122-33.

3575. Schröder, Edward. 1932. "Beowulf". *Anglia* 56.316-17. [On the name *Beowulf.*]

3576. ———. 1933. "Nochmals Beowulf = 'Bienenwolf'". *Anglia* 57.400.

3577. ———. 1934. "Der Name *Healfdene*". *Anglia* 58.345-50. [In *Beowulf.*]

3578. Schwartz, Ernst. 1950. "Das angelsächsische Landnahmeproblem". *GRM* N.F. 1.35-55. [A critical evaluation of recent historical, linguistic and onomastic publications.]

3579. Silber, Patricia. 1980. "Unferth: Another Look at the Emendation". *Names* 28.101-11. [On *(H)unferth* in *Beowulf.*]

3580. Slover, Clark H. 1936. "A Note on the Names of Glastonbury". *Speculum* 11.129-32. [Apropos of Gray [no. 3509].]

3581. Smart, Veronica. 1973. "Cnut's York Moneyers". *von Feilitzen Festschrift*, 221-31.

3582. ———. 1979. "Moneyers' Names on the Anglo-Saxon Coinage". *Nomina* 3.20-28.

3583. ———. 1983. "Variation between *Aethel-* and *Aegel-* as a Name-Element on Coins". *Nomina* 7.91-96.

3584. Smith, Albert Hugh. 1957. *Place-Names and the Anglo-Saxon Settlement.* London: Oxford Univ. Press, 21 pp. [Gollancz Memorial Lecture, British Academy, for 1956.]

Review: Karl Brunner in *MLR* 53.226 (1958).

3585. Smith, Colin. 1980. "The Survival of Romano-British Toponymy". *Nomina* 4.27-40.

3586. Stanley, Eric Gerald. 1979. "*Geoweorþa*: 'Once Held in High Esteem'". *J.R.R. Tolkien, Scholar and Storyteller: Essays in Memoriam*, ed. Mary Salu and Robert T. Farrell, 99-119. Ithaca, NY: Cornell Univ. Press.

3587. Steinberg, Clarence. 1978. "For a Servian Reading of *Beowulf*: Further Studies in Old English Onomastics". *NM* 79.321-29.

3588. Stenton, Frank M. 1939. "The Historical Bearing of Place-Name Studies: England in the Sixth Century". *TRHS* 4th ser. 21.1-19.

3589. ———. 1940. "The Historical Bearing of Place-Name Studies: The English Occupation of Southern Britian". *TRHS* 4th ser. 22.1-22.

3590. ———. 1941. "The Historical Bearing of Place-Name Studies: Anglo-Saxon Heathenism". *TRHS* 4th ser. 23.1-24.

3591. ———. 1942. "The Historical Bearing of Place-Name Studies: The Danish Settlement of Eastern England". *TRHS* 4th ser. 24.1-24.

3592. ———. 1943. "The Historical Bearing of Place-Name Studies: The Place of Women in Anglo-Saxon History". *TRHS* 4th ser. 25.1-13.

3593. Stewart, George R. 1962. "*Lēah*, Woods, and Deforestation as an Influence on Place-Names". *Names* 10.11-20. [On OE *lēah* meaning both 'a wood' and 'a clearing in a wood'.]

3594. Storms, Godfrid. 1957. *Compounded Names of Peoples in 'Beowulf': A Study in the Diction of a Great Poet*. Utrecht & Nijmegen: Dekker en Van de Vegt, 26 pp.

Reviews: A. van Wijngaarden in *LT* 1958, 293-94; K. Malone in *ES* 41.200-05 (1960); H.C. Matthes in *Anglia* 80.168-70 (1962).

3595. Strachan, L.R.M. 1935. "*-flæd* in Feminine Anglo-Saxon Names". *N&Q* 168.247.

3596. Ström, Hilmer. 1939. *Old English Personal Names in Bede's History: An Etymological-Phonological Investigation*. (= LundSE, 8.) Lund: Gleerup; London: Williams and Norgate, xliv + 181 pp.

Reviews: N.E. Eliason in *Language* 17.271-73 (1941); O.S. Arngart in *ES* 25.18-20 (1942); Kemp Malone in *MLN* 57.128-29 (1942).

3597. Tengstrand, Erik. 1940. *A Contribution to the Study of Genitival Composition in Old English Place-Names*. (= Nomina Germanica, 7.) Uppsala: Almqvist & Wiksell, lxvii + 354 pp.

Reviews: F. Holthausen in *LGRP* 63.20-21 (1941); F. Klaeber in *Archiv* 179.60 (1941); S.B. Liljegren in *Anglia B* 52.10-20 (1941); S. Potter in *MLR* 36.427-28 (1941); Eilert Ekwall in *SN* 16.147-51 (1942); Kemp Malone in *MLN* 57.130-31 (1942).

3598. ———. 1965. "Det fornengelska ortnamnselementet *wīc*". *NoB* 53.111-21. [Review article on Ekwall [no. 3482].]

3599. Tengvik, Gösta. 1938. *Old English Bynames*. (= Nomina Germanica, 4.) Uppsala: Almqvist & Wiksell, xxii + 407 pp.

Reviews: F. Holthausen in *Anglia B* 49.354-56 (1938); A. Macdonald in *MLR* 35.76-77 (1940); H.B. Woolf in *EStn* 74.89-91 (1940/41).

3600. Tolkien, John Ronald Renel. 1932 & 1934. "*Sigelwara land*". *MAE* 1.183-96 and 3.95-111. [On the name *Sigelwara* in *Exodus* 69, etc.]

3601. Unwin, P.T.H. 1982. "The Anglo-Saxon and Scandinavian Occupation of Nottinghamshire". *JEPNS* 14.1-31. [Based on place- and personal name distribution.]

3602. Unwin, Tim. 1978. "Some Perspectives on the Place-Name Evidence for Nottinghamshire's Early Settlement". *Nomina* 2.22-25.

3603. Vaughan, M.F. 1976. "A Reconsideration of *Unferð*". *NM* 77.32-48. [On the name in *Beowulf*.]

3604. von Feilitzen, Olof. 1937. *The Pre-Conquest Personal Names of Domesday Book*. Uppsala: Almqvist & Wiksell, xxxii + 430 pp.

Reviews: F. Holthausen in *Anglia B* 49.137 (1938); Helge Kökeritz in *NoB* 26.25-41 (1938); G. Linke in *Archiv* 174.252 (1938); Anon. in *N&Q* 174.53 (1938); D. Whitelock in *History* (London) 23.68-70 (1938); H.B. Woolf in *MLN* 53.542-43 (1938); G.T. Flom in *JEGP* 38.443-44 (1939); F. M[ossé] in *RG* 30.82-83 (1939); G. Neckel in *DLZ* 60.770-71 (1939); F.R. Schröder in *GRM* 26.174 (1938); E. Schroeder in *Anzeiger für die Altertumswissenschaft* (Wien) 57.54-55 (1938).

3605. ———. 1939. "Notes on Old English Bynames". *NoB* 27.116-30.

3606. ———. 1947. "Old Welsh *Enniaun* and the Old English Personal Name Element *Wen*". *MLN* 62.155-65.

3607. ———. 1968. "Some Old English Uncompounded Personal Names and Bynames". *SN* 40.5-16.

3608. ———. 1976. "Planning a New Old English Onomasticon". *Erlangen Proceedings*, 16-42.

3609. ——— and Christopher Blunt. 1971. "Personal Names on the Coinage of Edgar". *Whitelock Festschrift*, 183-214.

3610. Wadstein, Elis. 1925. "*Beowulf*: Etymologie und Sinn des Namens". *Sievers Festschrift*, 323-26.

3611. Wallenberg, Johannes K. 1928. "Studies in Old Kentish Charters". *SN* 1.34-44. [Includes a discussion of the possible identification of the place-name *Hyringdænn*.]

3612. ———. 1931. *Kentish Place-Names: A Topographical and Etymological Study of the Place-Name Material in Kentish Charters dated before the Conquest*. (= UUÅ, 1931:2.) Uppsala: A.-B. Lundequistska Bokhandeln, xix + 378 pp.

Review: R.E. Zachrisson in *SN* 5.77-83 (1932/33).

3613. Watts, V.E. 1978. "The Earliest Anglian Names in Durham". *Nomina* 2.30-33.

3614. ——— and E.F.M. Prince. 1981/82. "OE *walh* in English Place-Names: an Addendum". *JEPNS* 14.32-36.

3615. Welch, Martin G. 1978. "Early Anglo-Saxon Sussex: From Civitas to Shire". *South Saxons*, 13-35.

3616. Whatley, E. Gordon. 1975. "Old English Onomastics and Narrative Art: *Elene* 1062". *MP* 109-20.

3617. Woolf, Henry Bosley. 1937/38. "The Name of Beowulf". *EStn* 72.7-9.

3618. ———. 1938. "The Personal Names in *The Battle of Maldon*". *MLN* 53.109-12.

3619. ———. 1938/39. "The Naming of Women in Old English Times". *MP* 36.113-20.

3620. ———. 1939. *The Old Germanic Principles of Name-Giving*. Baltimore: The Johns Hopkins Press; London: Milford, xii + 300 pp. [Examines the OE genealogies and also the early genealogies of the continental Germanic nations.]

Reviews: N.E. Eliason in *SFQ* 4.256 (1940); S.J. Herben, Jr. in *American Historical Review* 46.183-84 (1940); F.M. S[tenton] in *History* (London) 25.88

(1940); A. Campbell in *MAE* 10.43-46 (1941); Eilert Ekwall in *ES* 23.83-87 (1941); S.B. Liljegren in *SN* 13.159-60 (1941); S. Potter in *MLR* 36.249-52 (1941); G.V. S[mithers] in *RES* 20.93 (1944).

3621. Wright, Louise E. 1980. "*Merewioingas* and the Dating of *Beowulf*: A Reconsideration". *NMS* 24.1-6.

3622. Yerkes, David. 1982. "Ælfric's *thesalla*". *N&Q* n.s. 29.397-99.

3623. Zachrisson, Robert Eugen. 1924. *English Place-Names in '-ing' of Scandinavian Origin*. Uppsala: Almqvist & Wiksell, 130 pp.

Reviews: G. Binz in *Anglia B* 37.22-25 (1926); E.V. Gordon in *MLR* 21.76-77 (1926)

3624. ———. 1927. *Romans, Kelts and Saxons in Ancient Britain: An Investigation into the Two Dark Centuries (400-600) of English History*. (= Skrifter utgivna av K. Humanistiska Vetenskapssamfundet i Uppsala, 24:12.) Uppsala: Almqvist & Wiksell, 95 pp. [Chapter II deals with place-names containing *weall*, *wealh*, *weala-* and *breta-*; distribution of Celtic place-names in England; the survival of Romano-British towns and settlements.]

Reviews: Kemp Malone in *MLN* 43.481-84 (1928); Reginald A. Smith in *Antiquaries' Journal* 8.533 (1928); G. Binz in *Anglia B* 40.289-93 (1929); J. Mansion in *ES* 11.207-08 (1929); J.H.G. Grattan in *RES* 6.88-89 (1930); J. Vendryes in *Revue Celtique* (Paris) 1931, 387-90.

3625. ———. 1927. "Six Groups of English River-Names". *ZON* 2.134-47. [Includes '3. OE *Sceldes heafda*, Warw.']

Review:Gustav Binz in *Anglia B* 40.293-96 (1929).

3626. ———. 1928. "Germanic Personal Names Supposed to Contain an *r*-suffix: III. Old English Place-Names". *ZON* 4.247-55.

3627. ———. 1928. "Notes on Early Germanic Personal Names". *SN* 1.74-77.

3628. ———. 1930. "Grendel in *Beowulf* and in Local Names". *Jespersen Festschrift*, 39-44.

3629. ———. 1932. "O.E. *Citel*, *Cytel*, *Cetel* and O. Scand. *Ketill* in English Place-Names". *Germanska Namnstudier tillägnade Evald Lidén = NoB* 21.1-7.

3630. ———. 1932/33. "O.E. *Wise*, *Usan*, *Wassan*, *Wær-*, *Ur-*". *SN* 5.70-76.

3631. ———. 1934/35. "Descriptive Words or Personal Names in Old English Place-Name Compounds". *SN* 7.30-39.

Reviews: Karl Brunner in *LGRP* 57.244-45 (1936); F. Holthausen in *Anglia B* 47.67 (1936).

3632. ———. 1935. "Some Identifications of Place-Names in Old English Charters". *NoB* 23.149-53.

3633. ———. 1935/36. "Full-Names and Short-Names in Old English Place-Names". *SN* 8.82-98.

3634. ———. 1936/37. "Studies on the *-ing* Suffix in Old English Place-Names with some Etymological Notes". *SN* 9.66-129.

C. Middle English

3635. Blanchet, Marie-Claude. 1970. "L'Argante de Layamon". *Mélanges de langue et de littérature du Moyen Âge et de la Renaissance offerts à Jean Frapper par ses collègues, ses élèves et ses amis* (= Pubs. Romanes et Français, 112), ed. J.C. Payen and C. Regnier, I.133-44.

3636. Blenner-Hassett, Roland. 1940. "The English River-Names in Lawman's *Brut*". *MLN* 55.373-78.

3637. ———. 1942. "*Gernemuðe*: A Place-Name Puzzle in Lawman's *Brut*". *MLN* 57.179-81.

3638. ———. 1950. *A Study of the Place-Names in Lawman's 'Brut'*. (= Stanford Univ. Ser. in Language and Literature, 9:1.) Stanford, CA: Stanford Univ. Press, 77 pp. [Originally Harvard diss. 1940. Repr., New York: AMS Press, 1967.]

Reviews: E.C. Ehrensperger in *JEGP* 50.116 (1951); Arthur E. Hutson in *Speculum* 26.375-76 (1951); A. Macdonald in *RES* n.s. 4.276-78 (1953).

3639. Brown, Emerson, Jr. 1983. "Chaucer and a Proper Name: January in *The Merchant's Tale*", *Names* 31.79-87.

3640. Clark, Cecily. 1976. "Some Early Canterbury Surnames". *ES* 57.294-309. [Uses records spanning the period from the mid-twelfth century to the early thirteenth.]

3641. ———. 1978. "Women's Names in Post-Conquest England: Observations and Speculations". *Speculum* 53.223-51.

3642. ———. 1978. "Thoughts on the French Connections of Middle-English Nicknames". *Nomina* 2.38-44.

3643. ———. 1979. "Clark's First Three Laws of Applied Anthroponymics". *Nomina* 3.13-19.

3644. ———. 1980. "Battle c. 1100: An Anthroponymist Looks at an Anglo-Norman New Town". *Proceedings of the Battle Conference on Anglo-Norman Studies II, 1979*, ed. R. Allen Brown, 21-41. Woodbridge, Suffolk: Boydell & Brewer. [Also available from Rowman & Littlefield, Totowa, NJ.]

3645. ———. 1981. "The Middle English Nickname *Kepeharm*". *Nomina* 5.94.

3646. ———. 1982. "The Early Personal Names of King's Lynn: An Essay in Socio-Cultural History, I: Baptismal Names". *Nomina* 6.51-72. [The period covered is 1100-1299.]

3647. ———. 1983. "The Early Personal Names of King's Lynn: An Essay in Socio-Cultural History, II: By-Names". *Nomina* 7.65-89.

3648. Clark, Roy Peter. 1977. "A Possible Pun on Chaucer's Name". *Names* 25.49-50. [Argues that the word *soutere* 'shoemaker' in *CT* I.3904 may possibly be a pun on *Chaucer* (Fr. *Chaussier* 'shoemaker').]

3649. Cameron, Kenneth. 1973. "Early Field-Names in an English-Named Lincolnshire Village". *von Feilitzen Festschrift*, 38-43.

3650. Cassidy, Frederic Gomes. 1948. "The Merit of Malkyn". *MLN* 63.52-53. [A gloss on *Piers Plowman* B I.182.]

3651. De Weever, Jacqueline. 1980. "Chaucerian Onomastics: The Formation and Use of Personal Names in Chaucer's Works". *Names* 28.1-31.

3652. Dietz, Klaus. 1985. "Me. *berse 'Jagdrevier'". *Anglia* 103.271-81.

3653. Dunn, Charles W. 1965. "Havelok and Anlaf Cuaran". *Magoun Festschrift*, 244-49. [On the etymology of the name *Havelok*.]

3654. Dunn, F.I. and Diana Deterding. 1978. "*Diana*, an Early Occurrence of the Name". *N&Q* n.s. 25.532-33. [On its occurrences in the 13th century.]

3655. East, W.G. 1977. "Lollius". *ES* 58.396-98. [On the name in Chaucer.]

3656. Ekwall, Eilert. 1938. "The Middle English *ā/ō* Boundary". *ES* 20.147-68. [A place-name study.]

3657. ———. 1940. "Some Notes on Place-Names in Middle English Writings". *Studies for William A. Read: A Miscellany Presented by Some of His Col-*

leagues and Friends, ed. Nathaniel M. Caffee and Thomas A. Kirby, 16-28. University, LA: Louisiana State Univ. Press.

3658. ———. 1945. *Variation in Surnames in Medieval London*. (= Kungl. Humanistiska Vetenskapssamfundet i Lund Årsberättelse 1944-1945, 6.) Lund: Gleerup, 56 pp. [Covers the period 1270-1350.]

Review: A. Macdonald in *ES* 32.80-81 (1951).

3659. ———. 1947. *Early London Personal Names*. (= Skrifter utgivna av Kungl. Humanistiska Vetenskapssamfundet i Lund, 43.) Lund: Gleerup, xx + 208 pp. [An exhaustive examination of the personal names of OE origin in post-Conquest London.]

Reviews: Karl Brunner in *Erasmus* 2.280-83 (1948/49); K. Malone in *MLN* 64.542-43 (1949): A.A. Prins in *Museum* 53.111-12 (1951); A. Macdonald in *ES* 32.80-81 (1951); R. Quirk in *SN* 24.162-63 (1951/52).

3660. ———. 1956. *Studies on the Population of Medieval London*. (= Kungl. Vitterhets-, Historie- och Antikvitetsakademiens Handlingar: Filologisk-Filosofiska Serien, 2.) Stockholm: Almqvist & Wiksell, lxxii + 334 pp. [Mainly a list of London citizens from the Midlands and North with local surnames.]

3661. ———. 1957. "Some Cases of Initial Variation in Medieval Surnames". *MSpr* 51.21-27.

3662. ———. 1965. "Some Early London Bynames and Surnames". *ES* 46.113-18. [Adds further twenty such names to those in Ekwall [no. 3659].]

3663. Eliason, Norman Ellsworth. 1973. "Personal Names in the *Canterbury Tales*". *Names* 21.137-52.

3664. Emery, Richard W. 1952. "The Use of the Surname in the Study of Medieval Economic History". *M&H* 7.43-50.

3665. Fellows Jensen, Gillian. 1973. "The Names of the Lincolnshire Tenants of the Bishop of Lincoln c.1225". *von Feilitzen Festschrift*, 86-95.

3666. ———. 1975. "The Surnames of the Tenants of the Bishop of Lincoln in Nine English Counties c.1225". *Binamn och släktnamn: Avgränsning och ursprung* (= NORNA-rapporter, 8), ed. Thorsten Andersson, 39-65. Uppsala: Nordiska samarbetskommittén för namnforskning.

3667. Ferris, Summer. 1983. "*His Barge Ycleped Was the Maudelayne: Canterbury Tales* A 410". *Names* 31.207-10. [On the naming of ships.]

3668. Field, Peter John Christopher. 1985. "Malory's Place-Names: Roone and the Low Country". *N&Q* n.s. 32.452-53.

3669. Flom, George T. 1924. "Der Name des Green Knight". *Archiv* 147.194-96.

3670. Fransson, Gustav. 1935. *Middle English Surnames of Occupation, 1100-1350, with an Excursus on Toponymical Surnames.* (= LundSE, 3.) Lund: Gleerup; London: Williams and Norgate, xx + 217 pp.

   Reviews: O. Anderson in *ES* 18.77-81 (1936); J.R. H[ulbert] in *MP* 33.440 (1936); G. L[inke] in *Archiv* 169.295 (1936); P. Fijn van Draat in *Museum* 44.39-40 (1936); G.T. Flom in *JEGP* 36.577-79 (1937); F. Holthausen in *LGRP* 58.26-27 (1937); W. Preusler in *Anglia B* 48.4-5 (1937); R.M. Wilson in *MLR* 32.331 (1937).

3671. French, Walter Hoyt. 1940. *Essays on King Horn.* Ithaca, NY: Cornell Univ. 204 pp. [Contains 'The personal names' (pp. 115-46).]

3672. Harley, Marta Powell. 1981. "The Derivation *Hawkin* and Its Application in *Piers Plowman*". *Names* 29.97-99.

3673. Hulbert, James Root. 1923. "The Name of the Green Knight". *The Manly Anniversary Studies in Language and Literature*, 12-19. Chicago: Univ. of Chicago Press.

3674. Hutson, Arthur E. 1940. *British Personal Names in the 'Historia Regum Britanniae'.* (= UCPE, 5:1.) Berkeley: Univ. of California Press, 160 pp. [The text is dated 1137.]

3675. Jacobs, Nicolas. 1974. "Middle English "Cleo" Hill". *N&Q* n.s. 21.44-46. [Cf. Hill [no. 3428].]

3676. ———. 1978. "*Clanvowe*". *N&Q* n.s. 25.292-95. [On the etymology of the name which appears first in Herefordshire in the 14th century.]

3677. Jönsjö, Jan. 1979. *Studies on Middle English Nicknames. I: Compounds.* (= LundSE, 55.) Lund: LiberLäromedel/Gleerup, 227 pp. [Lund diss.: Abstr. in *DA* 41.1516C (1980/81).]

   Reviews: Gillian Fellows Jensen in *NoB* 68.102-15 (1980); Karl Schneider in *BN* N.F. 15.202-03 (1980); Eldson C. Smith in *Names* 28.89-90 (1980); Eric Christiansen in *EHR* 96.197-98 (1981); Peter McClure in *Nomina* 5.95-104 (1981); Jerzy Wełna in *LB* 70.214-17 (1981); Cecily Clark in *ES* 63.168-70 (1982); Basil Cottle in *RES* n.s. 33.68-69 (1982); Peter Erlebach in *Archiv* 219.430-32 (1982); C. Marynissen in *Nku* 11.239-51 (1979).

3678. Kelly, Susan. 1979. "Place-Names in the *Awntyrs off Arthure*". *LOS* 6.162-99.

3679. Kristensson, Gillis. 1969. "Studies on Middle English Local Surnames Containing Elements of French Origin". *ES* 50.465-68.

3680. ———. 1970. *Studies on Middle English Topographical Terms*. (= AUL, 1:13.) Lund: Gleerup, 122 pp.

Reviews: E.G. Stanley in *N&Q* n.s. 18.188-89 (1971); Kenneth Cameron in *MAE* 41.161-64 (1972); Klaus Dietz in *BN* N.F. 7.194-97 (1972); Margaret Gelling in *YES* 2.232-33 (1972); Herbert Voitl in *Archiv* 210.177-79 (1973).

3681. ———. 1976. "Computer-Processing of Middle English Personal-Name Materials". *Erlangen Proceedings*, 62-74.

3682. Löfvenberg, Mattias T. 1942. *Studies on Middle English Local Surnames*. (= LundSE, 11.) Lund: Gleerup; Copenhagen: Munksgaard; London: Williams and Norgate, xlviii + 255 pp. [Lund diss.]

Reviews: O.S. Arngart in *ES* 25.20-23 (1943) and *SN* 16.144-46 (1943/44); F. Holthausen in *Anglia B* 53.203-04 (1942); K. Malone in *MLN* 64.558-59 (1949); H.T. Price in *JEGP* 48.150-51 (1949).

3683. Loomis, Roger Sherman. 1957. "Onomastic Riddles in Malory's *Book of Arthur and his Knights*". *MAE* 25.181-90.

3684. Lucas, Peter J. 1986. "Hautdesert in *Sir Gawain and the Green Knight*". *Neophil* 70.319-20. [On the name in *SGGK* 2445.]

3685. Lyle, E.B. 1969. "A Reconsideration of the Place-Names in *Thomas the Rhymer*". *ScoS* 13.65-71.

3686. McClure, Peter. 1974. "Three Plant Names in ME Place-Names and Surnames: *Breme, Rounce, Bilbery*". *N&Q* n.s. 21.42-44.

3687. McIntosh, Angus. 1940. "Middle English *Gannokes* and Some Place-Name Problems". *RES* 16.54-61.

3688. McKinley, Richard Alexander. 1975. *Norfolk and Suffolk Surnames in the Middle Ages*. With a Foreword by Alan Everitt. (= English Surnames Ser., 2.) London: Phillimore, for the Marc Fitch Fund, xiii + 175 pp.

Review: Peter McClure in *Nomina* 1.46-47 (1977).

3689. Mustanoja, Tauno Frans. 1970. "The Suggestive Use of Christian Names in Middle English Poetry". *Utley Festschrift*, 51-76. [A number of the examples are taken from Chaucer's works.]

3690. Nicholaisen, Wilhelm F.H. 1971. "Early Spellings and Scottish Place-Names". *Edinburgh Studies*, 210-33.

3691. ———. 1980. "Tension and Extension: Thoughts on Scottish Surnames and Medieval Popular Culture". *Journal of Popular Culture* (Bowling Green State Univ., Bowling Green, OH) 14.119-30.

3692. Nitze, William A. 1949. "Arthurian Names: *Arthur*". *PMLA* 64.585-96 and 64.1235.

3693. ———. 1950. "Additional Note on Arthurian Names (*PMLA*, LXIV, 585 ff.)". *PMLA* 65.1287-88.

3694. Reaney, Percy Hide. 1953. "Notes on the Survival of Old English Personal Names in Middle English". *SMSpr* 18.84-112.

3695. Seltén, Bo. 1965. "Some Notes on Middle English By-Names in Independent Use". *ES* 46.165-81.

3696. ———. 1969. *Early East-Anglian Nicknames: 'Shakespeare' Names*. (= Scripta Minora 1968-1969, 3.) Lund: Gleerup, 27 pp.

3697. ———. 1972. *The Anglo-Saxon Heritage in Middle English Personal Names: East Anglia 1100-1399.* (= LundSE, 43.) Lund: Gleerup, 187 pp. [Lund diss. 1973.]

Reviews: Karl Inge Sandred (review article) in *NoB* 61.83-92 (1973) and *SN* 46.262-67 (1974); Hartmut Beckers in *BN* N.F. 9.278-79 (1974); Herbert Voitl in *Anglia* 93.176-80 (1975); C. Marynissen in *LB* 65.202-03 (1976); C.M. Carnes in *JEPNS* 9.26-31 (1976/77); Egon Felder in *ZDL* 44.97-98 (1977); M. Lehnert in *ZAA* 25.180-84 (1977); Cecily Clark in *ES* 59.257-60 (1978).

3698. ———. 1975. *Early East-Anglian Nicknames: Bahuvrihi Names*. (= Scripta Minora 1974-1975, 3.) Lund: LiberLäromedel/Gleerup, 69 pp.

Reviews: Elsdon C. Smith in *Names* 23.303-04 (1975); C. Marynissen in *LB* 65.405-06 (1976); Egon Felder in *ZDL* 44.355 (1977); Cecily Clark in *ES* 59.257-60 (1978); Martin Lehnert in *ZAA* 28.66-67 (1980); Karl Schneider in *BN* N.F. 15.102-03 (1980).

3699. ———. 1979. *The Anglo-Saxon Heritage in Middle English Personal Names: East Anglia 1100-1399, II.* (= Acta Regiae Societatis Humaniorum Litterarum Lundensis, 73.) Lund: Liberläromedel/Gleerup, 223 pp. [A sequel to Seltén [no. 3697].]

Reviews: Gillian Fellows Jensen in *N&Q* n.s. 27.546-47 (1980); Elsdon C. Smith in *Names* 28.158 (1980); Cecily Clark in *ES* 62.473 (1981); M. Lehnert in

ZAA 29.70-74 (1981); C. Marynissen in *LB* 70.211-14 (1981); Karl Schneider in *BN* N.F. 15.102-03 (1981); Peter Erlebach in *Archiv* 219.427-29 (1982); (together with I) Peter McClure in *Antiquaries Journal* 64.180-81 (1984); Herbert Voitle in *Anglia* 105.426-29 (1987).

3700. Steinberg, Clarence. 1970. "*Kemp Towne* in the Townley *Herod* Play: A Local Wakefield Allusion?". *NM* 71.253-60.

3701. Sundby, Bertil. 1972. "A Middle English Example of Alliteration as a Principle of Name-Giving". *Mustanoja Festschrift* = *NM* 73.437-47.

3702. Swanton, Michael J. 1980. "Middle English *Leteworthi*: An Unnoticed Tenement-Descriptor". *Nomina* 4.75-77.

3703. Tengstrand, Erik. 1977. "The Middle English Surname *atte Bewe*". *SN* 49.131-34.

3704. Utley, Francis Lee. 1941. "The One Hundred and Three Names of Noah's Wife". *Speculum* 16.426-52.

3705. ———. 1975. "The Names of the Knights of the Round Table". *Names* 23.194-214.

3706. von Feilitzen, Olof. 1965. "Notes on Some Scandinavian Personal Names in English 12th-Century Records". *Anthroponymica Suecana* (Stockholm) 6.52-68.

3707. Wakelin, Martyn Francis. 1978. "The Place-Name *Helford*". *Neophil* 62.294-96. [On the name in west Cornwall which first appears in 1230.]

3708. Wilson, Robert H. 1943. "Malory's Naming of Minor Characters". *JEGP* 42.364-85.

XIII. DIALECTOLOGY

A. General

3709. Brook, George Leslie. 1963. *English Dialects*. (The Language Library.) London: André Deutsch, 232 pp. [Deals briefly with the Old and Middle English dialects.]

   Reviews: Basil Cottle in *JEGP* 63.835-37 (1964); B. Hunter Smeaton in *AN&Q* 3.29-30 (1964).

3710. Kristensson, Gillis. 1983. "Dialectology and Historical Linguistics". *Current Topics in EHL*, 29-35. [Argues that onomastics should play a more important role in OE and ME dialectology.]

3711. Levin, Samuel R. 1958. "Negative Contraction: An Old and Middle English Dialect Criterion". *JEGP* 57.492-501.

3712. Samuels, Michael Louis. 1985. "The Great Scandinavian Belt". *PICEHL*/4, 269-81. [Chiefly concerned with ModE dialects.]

B. Old English

3713. Crowley, Joseph Patrick. 1980. *The Study of Old English Dialects*. Univ. of North Carolina at Chapel Hill diss., 399 pp. [Abstr. in *DA* 42.1125A (1981).]

3714. ———. 1986. "The Study of Old English Dialects". *ES* 67.97-112.

3715. DeCamp, David. 1958. "The Genesis of the Old English Dialects: A New Hypothesis". *Language* 34.232-44.

3716. Horgan, Dorothy M. 1982. "The Distribution of West Saxon Dialect Criteria in the Extant Manuscripts of the *Pastoral Care*". *SN* 54.217-35.

3717. Kirsten, Hans. 1969. "Die angelsächsische Besiedlung Britanniens in ihrer Bedeutung für die Herausbildung der altenglischen Sprache und deren Dialektgeographie". *ZAA* 17.239-51.

3718. Korhammer, Michael. 1980. "Altenglische Dialekte und der *Heliand*". *Anglia* 98.85-94.

3719. Kuhn, Sherman McAllister. 1938. *A Grammar of the Mercian Dialect*. Chicago: Univ. of Chicago, i + 40 pp. [Part of Kuhn's Chicago diss. 1935.]

3720. ———. 1939. "The Dialect of the Corpus Glossary". *PMLA* 54.1-19. [Argues against the theory of dialect mixture.]

3721. Menner, Robert J. 1934. "Farman Vindicatus: The Linguistic Value of *Rushworth I*". *Anglia* 58.1-27. [Analyses Farman's practice in *Rushworth I* and shows that the text represents a genuine form of the Mercian dialect.]

3722. ———. 1951. "The Date and Dialect of *Genesis A* 852-2936 (Part III)". *Anglia* 70.285-94. [Based upon an examination of the vocabulary.]

3723. Nielsen, Hans Frede. 1979. *The Old English Dialects and the Continental Germanic Languages: A Survey of Morphological and Phonological Interrelations*. (= Mindre Skrifter udgivet af Laboratorium for Folkesproglig Middelalderlitteratur, 3.) Odense: Odense Univ., 40 pp.

3724. ———. 1981. "Old Frisian and the Old English Dialects". *Us Wurk* 30.49-66.

3725. Peterson, Paul W. 1953. "Dialect Grouping in the Unpublished Vercelli Homilies". *SP* 50.559-65.

3726. Rypins, Stanley I. 1923. "The Old English *Epistola Alexandri ad Aristotelem*". *MLN* 38.216-20. [On the dialectal characteristics of the text.]

3727. Salmen, Herbert. 1936. *'W' + westgermanisches 'ē' und 'ī' im Angelsächsischen: Ein Beitrag zur ags. Dialektgeographie*. Berlin diss., 122 pp.

Review: G. L[inke] in *Archiv* 171.116-17 (1937).

3728. Sisam, Kenneth. 1953. "Dialect Origins of the Earlier Old English Verse". *Studies in the History of Old English Literature*, 119-39. Oxford: Clarendon Press. [Discusses the dialect of the poetic vocabulary.]

3729. Snyder, Lee Lamar. 1969. *The Old English Dialect Boundaries: Some Place-Name Evidence*. Pennsylvania diss., 677 pp. [Abstr. in *DA* 30.4971A (1970).]

3730. Wilson, Richard Middlewood. 1959. "The Provenance of the Vespasian Psalter Gloss: The Linguistic Evidence". *Dickins Festschrift*, 292-310. [Compares the dialect with that of various other OE texts.]

C. Middle English

3731. Aitken, Adam Jack. 1981. "The Scottish Vowel-Length Rule". *McIntosh Festschrift* (E), 131-57. [An account of the history of the phenomenon.]

3732. Arngart, Olof. 1949. "Middle English Dialects". *SMSpr* 17.17-29. [Comments on the use of place names and personal names in ME dialectology.]

3733. Basilius, H.A. 1937. "The Rhymes in *Eger and Grime*". MP 35.129-33. [Uses rhymes for estimating the original dialect.]

3734. Bazire, Joyce. 1957. "The Dialects of the Manuscripts of *The Chastising of God's Children*". *EGS* 6.64-78. [The *Chastising* is a homiletic treatise of about 1400.]

3735. Beadle, Richard. 1977. *The Medieval Drama of East Anglia: Studies in Dialect, Documentary Records and Stagecraft*. Univ. of York (UK) diss., 381 pp. [Abstr. in *DA* 38.1494C (1977/78).]

3736. Bennett, Jacob. 1970. "The Middle English Dialect of the Northeast Midlands". *Orbis* 19.324-36. [Discusses characteristics of the language of the Macro *Castle of Perseverance*.]

3737. Benskin, Michael. 1977. "Local Archives and Middle English Dialects". *JSA* 5.500-14.

3738. ———. 1981. "A Linguistic Atlas for Late Medieval English". *MESN* 4.5-13.

3739. ———. 1981. "The Middle English Dialect Atlas". *McIntosh Festschrift* (E), xxvii-xli.

3740. ———. 1982. "Marian Verses from a Hedon Manuscript: Some New Materials for the Middle English Dialectology of the East Riding". *RCEI* 5.27-58.

3741. ——— and Margaret Laing. 1981. "Translations and *Mischsprachen* in Middle English Manuscripts". *McIntosh Festschrift* (E), 55-106.

3742. ——— and Angus McIntosh. 1972. "A Mediaeval English Manuscript of Irish Provenance". *MAE* 41.128-31. [Locates MS HM 129 in the Huntington Library, an early 15th-century version of the *Northern Homily Collection*.]

3743. Blake, Norman Francis. 1976. "Born in Kent". *Lore&L* 2:5.5-9. [Reviews the status of Kentish at the end of the 15th century.]

3744. ———. 1977. "Another Northernism in *The Reeve's Tale*". *N&Q* n.s. 24.400-01. [Indicates two examples of a Northern uninflected genitive.]

3745. ———. 1979. "The Northernisms in *The Reeve's Tale*". *Lore&L* 3:1.1-8. [Argues that despite Tolkien [no. 436] Chaucer's knowledge of Northern dialect was in no way exceptional and that many of the Northern speech characteristics of the two students were added by later scribes.]

3746. Bliss, Alan J. 1952/53. "A Note on 'Language AB'". *EGS* 5.1-6. [On the dialect of MS Corpus Christi College, Cambridge, 402 (MS "A") of the *Ancrene Wisse* and MS Bodley 34 (MS "B") of the *Katherine Group*.]

3747. Bohman, Hjördis. 1944. *Studies in the Middle English Dialects of Devon and London*. Göteborg: Pehrsson, xvi + 364 pp. [Göteborg diss.]

Reviews: Simeon Potter in *MLR* 40.219-20 (1945); O. Arngart in *ES* 27.77-81 (1946).

3748. Brunner, Karl. 1959. "Die Herkunft der anglischen Elemente in der frühen englischen Schriftsprache". *Mossé Festschrift*, 49-55.

3749. Cavers, Dorothy L. 1977. "In Support of the Use of Place-Names as an Aid to the Study of Middle English Dialects". *An English Miscellany Presented to W.S. Mackie*, ed. Brian S. Lee, 54-71. Cape Town & London: Oxford Univ. Press.

3750. Clark, Cecily. 1981. "Another Late-Fourteenth-Century Case of Dialect-Awareness". *ES* 62.504-05.

3751. Conner, J.E. 1957. "Phonemic Discrimination of Middle English Dialects". *Rice Institute Pamphlets* 44.17-32.

3752. Crow, Martin M. 1938. "*The Reeve's Tale* in the Hands of a Northern Scribe". *Studies in English 1938* (= Univ. of Texas Pubs., 3826), 14-24. [A study of the speech of the Northern students.]

3753. Cubbin, G.P. 1981. "Dialect and Scribal Usage in Medieval Lancashire: A New Approach to Local Documents". *TPS* 1981, 67-117.

3754. Dietz, Klaus. 1978. "Zur mittelenglischen ā/ǭ-Grenze in Lincolnshire". *BN* 13.185-93.

3755. Donahue, Thomas Scott. 1968. *The Present State of Middle English Dialect Studies*. Ohio State Univ. diss., 215 pp. [Abstr. in *DA* 29.3119-20A (1969).]

3756. Duncan, Thomas Gibson. 1968. "Notes on the Language of the Hunterian MS. of the *Mirror*". *NM* 69.204-08. [Discusses the date and dialect of the MS.]

3757. ———. 1981. "A Middle English Linguistic Reviser". *NM* 82.162-74. [A study of a contemporary revision of MS Glasgow Univ. Library 250 (one of the six surviving MSS of the *Mirror*) by a southern scribe.]

3758. Fisiak, Jacek. 1982. "Isophones or Isographs? A Problem in Historical Dialectology". *McIntosh Festschrift* (A), 117-28. [Chiefly concerned with ME.]

3759. ———. 1983. "Some Problems in Historical Dialectology". *SAP* 16.5-14. [A rev. version of Fisiak [no. 3758].]

3760. ———. 1983. "English Dialects in the Fifteenth Century: Some Observations concerning the Shift of Isoglosses". *FLH* 4.195-217.

3761. Freeman, Lawrence Hilton. 1973. *Dialect Characteristics of Late Middle English Prepositions in Two Parallel Prose Works: 'Ayenbite of Inwyt' and 'Book of Vices and Virtues'*. Univ. of Oregon diss., 389 pp. [Abstr. in *DA* 34.3371-72A (1973).]

3762. French, Walter Hoyt. 1946. "Dialects and Forms in Three Romances". *JEGP* 45.125-32. [The three romances discussed are *Arthour and Merlin*, *King Alisaunder*, and *Richard Coeur de Lion*.]

3763. Geist, Robert J. 1948. "Notes on *The King of Tars*". *JEGP* 47.173-78. [Notes on the relationship of the MSS and on the dialect.]

3764. Hooper, A.G. 1935. "*The Awntyrs of Arthure*: Dialect and Authorship". *LSE* 4.62-74.

3765. Jones, Charles. 1968. "The Computer in Middle English Studies: A Note". *CJL* 14.58-62. [Criticizes Logan [no. 3775].]

3766. Kline, Edward A. 1969. "The Computer, Graphemics and Middle English Dialectology". *Computer Studies in the Humanities and Verbal Behavior* (The Hague) 2.57-81.

3767. Kniezsa, Veronika. 1981. "An Attempt at the Study of Early Scots in the Fourteenth Century". *HSE* 14.109-14.

3768. Kristensson, Gillis. 1965. "Another Approach to Middle English Dialectology". *ES* 46.138-56. [On the linguistic value of the spellings of proper names in the Lay Subsidy Rolls from 1290 to 1350.]

3769. ———. 1967. *A Survey of Middle English Dialects 1290-1350: The Six Northern Counties and Lincolnshire*. (= LundSE, 35.) Lund: Gleerup, xxii + 299 pp.

Reviews: Basil Cottle in *JEGP* 67.694-95 (1968); Norman Davis in *N&Q* n.s. 15.270-72 (1968); Manfred Schentke in *ZAA* 16.408-09 (1968); Anne Hudson in *RES* n.s. 20.68-69 (1969); H.E. Kijlstra in *Linguistics* 54.113-14 (1969); Angus McIntosh in *MAE* 38.210-16 (1969); Arne Zettersten in *SN* 41.218-21 (1969); Bo Seltén in *ES* 51.445-48 (1970); Herbert Koziol in *Archiv* 207.299-300 (1970/71); Simeon Potter in *YES* 1.204-05 (1971); Horst Weinstock in *GRM* N.F. 22.448-50 (1972); Christopher Moss in *ZDL* 40.224-25 (1973); Klaus Dietz in *BN* 10.457-58 (1975) and *Anglia* 94.463-69 (1976); Sherman M. Kuhn in *Speculum* 50.134-39 (1975).

3770. ———. 1976. "Lay Subsidy Rolls and Dialect Geography". *ES* 57.51-59. [Reply to McClure [no. 3780].]

3771. ———. 1977. *Studies on the Early 14th-Century Population of Lindsey (Lincolnshire)*. (= Scripta Minora 1976/77, 2.) Lund: LiberLäromedel/Gleerup, 39 pp. [On the distribution of OE /a:/ in the Lincolnshire dialects of ME.]

Reviews: B.L. Collins in *Names* 26.121-22 (1978); C. Marynissen in *LB* 69.54-55 (1980).

3772. ———. 1979. "A Piece of Middle English Word Geography". *ES* 60.254-60. [Deals with ME words for 'brook, stream'.]

3773. ———. 1981. "On Middle English Dialectology". *McIntosh Festschrift* (E), 3-14.

3774. Lambert, Jacob J. 1954. *The Dialect of 'Cursor Mundi' (Cotton MS. Vespasian A III)*. Michigan diss., 130 pp. [Abstr. in *DA* 14.678 (1954).]

3775. Logan, H.M. 1967. "The Computer and Middle English Dialectology". *CJL* 13.37-49. [Refuted by Jones [no. 3765].]

3776. Mackenzie, Barbara Alida. 1926/27. "A Special Dialectal Development of $\bar{e}a$ in Middle English". *EStn* 61.386-92.

3777. ———. 1928. *The Early London Dialect: Contributions to the History of the Dialect of London during the Middle English Period*. Oxford: Clarendon Press, 151 pp. [Repr., Folcroft, PA: Folcroft Library Editions, 1974.]

Reviews: Anon. in *TLS*, Sept. 20, 1928, p. 665; Anon. in *N&Q* 155.288 (1928); Percy H. Reany in *RES* 5.470-71 (1929); H.M. Flasdieck in *Anglia B* 42.33-47 (1931).

3778. Macrae-Gibson, O. Duncan. 1971. "The Auchinleck MS: Participles in *-and(e)*". *ES* 52.13-20.

3779. ———. 1979. "*Of Arthour and of Merlin* in Sussex?". *ELN* 17.7-10. [Cf. Sklar [no. 3807].]

3780. McClure, Peter. 1973. "Lay Subsidy Rolls and Dialect Phonology". *von Feilitzen Festschrift*, 188-94. [Apropos of Kristensson [nos. 3768 and 3769]. For Kristensson's reply to McClure, see no. 3770.]

3781. McIntosh, Angus. 1963. "A New Approach to Middle English Dialectology". *ES* 44.1-11. [Repr. in *Lass EHL*, 392-403.]

3782. ———. 1973. "Word Geography in the Lexicography of Medieval English". *Lexicography in English* (= Annals of the New York Academy of Sciences, 211), ed. Raven I. McDavid, Jr. and Audrey R. Duckert, 55-66. New York: New York Academy of Sciences.

3783. ———. 1978. "The Middle English Poem 'The Four Foes of Mankind': Some Notes on the Language and the Text". *NM* 79.137-44. [An examination of its vocabulary from a word-geographical point of view.]

3784. ———. 1978. "The Dialectology of Mediaeval Scots: Some Possible Approaches to Its Study". *Scottish Literary Journal* (Aberdeen Univ.) Supplement 6 (= Language Supplement, 1). 38-44.

3785. ———. 1978. "Middle English Word-Geography: Its Potential Role in the Study of the Long-Term Impact of the Scandinavian Settlements upon English". *The Vikings*, 124-30.

3786. ———. 1979. "Some Notes on the Language and Textual Transmission of the Scottish Troy Book". *ArchL* n.s. 10.1-19.

3787. ———. 1983. "Present Indicative Plural Forms in the Later Middle English of the North Midlands". *Davis Festschrift*, 235-44.

3788. ——— and Michael Louis Samuels. 1968. "Prolegomena to a Study of Mediaeval Anglo-Irish". *MAE* 37.1-11.

3789. ——— and Martyn Francis Wakelin. 1982. "John Mirk's *Festial* and Bodleian MS Hatton 96". *NM* 83.443-50.

3790. ———, Michael Louis Samuels, and Michael Benskin, with the assistance of Margaret Laing and Keith Williamson. 1987. *A Linguistic Atlas of Late Mediaeval English*. 4 vols. Aberdeen: Aberdeen Univ. Press. Vol. I: General Introduction, Index of Sources, Dot Maps, x + 569 pp.; Vol. II: Item Maps. xxiii + 388 pp.; Vol. III: Linguistic Profiles, xxiv + 700 pp; Vol. IV: County Dictionary, xxii + 345 pp.

3791. Meech, Sanford Brown. 1934. "Nicholas Bishop, an Exemplar of the Oxford Dialect of the Fifteenth Century". *PMLA* 49.443-59.

3792. Menner, Robert J. 1926. "Four Notes on the West Midland Dialect". *MLN* 41.454-58. [Discusses four phonological developments characteristic of West Midland.]

3793. Moore, Samuel, Sanford Brown Meech, and Harold Whitehall. 1935. "Middle English Dialect Characteristics and Dialect Boundaries. Preliminary Report of an Investigation Based Exclusively on Localized Texts and Documents". *Michigan Essays and Studies*, 1-60.

3794. Peitz, Agnes. 1933. *Der Einfluss des nördlichen Dialektes im Mittelenglischen auf die entstehende Hochsprache.* (= BSEP, 20.) Bonn: Hanstein, 133 pp. [Bonn diss.]

 Reviews: A. B[randl] in *Archiv* 164.294-95 (1933); G.T. Flom in *JEGP* 33.468-70 (1934); H.C. Matthes in *GRM* 22.409-10 (1934); O. Boerner in *NS* 44.308-10 (1936); F. Fiedler in *ZNU* 35.201-02 (1936); F. Wild in *LGRP* 57.311-13 (1936).

3795. Proctor, John William. 1966. *A Description of the Fifteenth Century Scots Dialect of Robert Henryson Based on a Complete Concordance of His Works.* Univ. of Missouri, Columbia, diss., 558 pp. [Abstr. in *DA* 27.3444A (1967).]

3796. Reaney, Percy Hide. 1926/27. "The Dialect of London in the Thirteenth Century". *EStn* 61.9-23. [Discusses some phonological features.]

3797. Rubin, Sven. 1951. *The Phonology of the Middle English Dialect of Sussex.* (= LundSE, 21.) Lund: Gleerup; Copenhagen: Munksgaard, 235 pp. [Lund diss.]

 Reviews: A. Rynell in *SL* 5.44-50 (1951); E.V.K. Dobbie in *Word* 8.187-88 (1952); H.C. Matthes in *Anglia* 71.234-37 (1952/53); E. Polomé in *RBPH* 30.257-59 (1952); A.A. Hill in *Language* 28.276-78 (1952); Henry Alexander in *MLN* 69.138-39 (1954); A.A. Prins in *Museum* 59.212-13 (1954); B.M.H. Carr in *ES* 36.67-69 (1955).

3798. Samuels, Michael Louis. 1963. "Some Applications of Middle English Dialectology". *ES* 44.81-94. [A companion article to McIntosh [no. 3781].]

3799. ———. 1969. "The Dialect of MS Bodley 959". *MS Bodley 959: Genesis-Baruch 3.20 in the Earlier Version of the Wycliffite Bible. Vol. 5: Ecclesiasticus 48.6 — Baruch 3.20* (= SSE, 20), ed. Conrad Lindberg, 329-39.

3800. ———. 1971. "Kent and the Low Countries: Some Linguistic Evidence". *Edinburgh Studies*, 3-19.

3801. ———. 1981. "Spelling and Dialect in the Late and Post-Middle English Periods". *McIntosh Festschrift* (E), 43-54.

3802. ———. 1985. "Langland's Dialect". *MAE* 54.232-47.

3803. ——— and Jeremy John Smith. 1981. "The Language of Gower". *NM* 82.295-304. [An examination of how Gower's language exemplifies a combination of two entirely separate regional dialects.]

3804. Serjeantson, Mary Sydney. 1924. "The Dialect of the Earliest Complete English Prose Psalter". *ES* 6.177-99.

3805. ———. 1925. *Distribution of Dialect Characters in Middle English*. Amsterdam: Swets and Zeitlinger, 34 pp. [Cf. *ES* 4.93-109, 191-98, and 223-33 (1922).]

Review: E. Ekwall in *Anglia B* 38.46-48 (1927).

3806. ———. 1927. "The Dialects of the West Midlands in Middle English". *RES* 3.54-67, 186-203, and 319-31. [Discusses some phonological features.]

3807. Sklar, Elizabeth S. 1977. "The Dialect of *Arthour and Merlin*". *ELN* 15.88-94. [Cf. Macrae-Gibson [no. 3779].]

3808. Sundby, Bertil. 1950. *The Dialect and Provenance of the Middle English Poem 'The Owl and the Nightingale': A Linguistic Study*. (= LundSE, 18.) Lund: Gleerup; Copenhagen: Munksgaard, 218 pp. [Lund diss.]

Reviews: N. Davis in *MAE* 20.64-70 (1951); E.V.K. Dobbie in *Word* 7.263-64 (1951); Sherman M. Kuhn in *Language* 27.420-23 (1951); H.C. Matthes in *Anglia* 70.242-44 (1951); R.J. Menner in *JEGP* 50.263-65 (1951); A.C. Cawley in *RES* n.s. 3.167-68 (1952); Kathryn Huganir in *Speculum* 27.425-27 (1952); F. Schubel in *SN* 25.196-99 (1952/53); A.A. Prins in *Museum* 58.167-68 (1953); Claes Schaar in *ES* 34.168-71 (1953).

3809. ———. 1963. *Studies in the Middle English Dialect Material of Worcestershire Records*. (= NSE, 10.) Bergen & Oslo: Norwegian Universities Press; New York: Humanities Press, viii + 280 pp.

Reviews: C.J.E. Ball in *Le Maître Phonétique* (London) 122.27-29 (1964); M.L. Samuels in *N&Q* n.s. 11.351-52 (1964); Anne Hudson in *RES* n.s. 16.186-88 (1965); Hilda M. Hulme in *MLR* 60.239-40 (1965); Assar Janzén in *JEGP* 64.758-61 (1965); Herbert Koziol in *Archiv* 202.137-38 (1965/66); Sherman M. Kuhn in *Speculum* 40.160-66 (1965); T.F. Mustanoja in *NM* 66.260-62 (1965); Klaus Dietz in *Anglia* 84.201-08 (1966); Hans Kurath in *Phonetica* (Basel & New York) 14.108-09 (1966); Veronika Kniezsa in *ALH* 16.417-19 (1966); M.C. Seymour in *Lingua* 16.435-37 (1966); Wolfgang Viereck in *Zeitschrift für Mundartforschung* (Wiesbaden) 33.85-88 (1966); Zygmunt Klimek in *Onomastica* (Wrocław) 11.362-64 (1966); Horst Weinstock in *SN* 39.206-08 (1967); Gillis Kristensson in *ES* 48.338-42 (1967); S. Ellis in *MAE* 37.92-93 (1968).

3810. ———. 1970. "Present-day Trends in Middle English Dialectology". *RLV* 36.566-81.

3811. Vogel, Bertram. 1941. "The Dialect of *Sir Tristrem*". *JEGP* 40.538-44.

3812. ———. 1942. "Wortgeographische Belege and *Sir Tristrem*". *JEGP* 41.478-81.

3813. Wakelin, Martyn Francis. 1981. "Mediaeval Written English at Bodmin". *McIntosh Festschrift* (E), 237-49. [Attempts to define a number of features of the ME dialect of Cornwall (more specifically Bodmin).]

3814. ———. 1983. "Later Middle English from Bodmin". *NM* 84.353-56. [Based on official documents written in Bodmin, Cornwall between 1489 and 1498.]

XIV. STYLISTICS

A. General

3815. Baker, Carole Frances. 1975. *The Rags and Bones of Fictive Worlds: Ontological Implications of Syntax in Early English Prose and Poetry.* Bryn Mawr College diss., 227 pp. [Abstr. in *DA* 36.6109A (1976).]

3816. Chambers, Raymond Wilson. 1932. *On the Continuity of English Prose from Alfred to More and his School.* (= EETS 191A.) London: Oxford Univ. Press, xlv-clxxiv pp. [An extract from the Introduction to Nicholas Harpsfield's *Life of Saint Thomas More*, ed. E.V. Hitchcock and R.W. Chambers, EETS 186 (1931), xlv-clxxiv.]

   Reviews: W. Plomer in *Spectator* 149.922 (1932); F.P. Magoun, Jr. in *MLN* 49.477-80 (1934).

3817. Gordon, Ian A. 1966. *The Movement of English Prose.* With Foreword by Randolph Quirk. (English Language Series.) London: Longmans, ix + 182 pp. [Surveys the development of English prose from Anglo-Saxon to the present day.]

   Reviews: Anon. in *TLS*, June 23, 1966, p. 533; G. Celati in *LeSt* 1.432-33 (1966); Susie I. Tucker in *N&Q* n.s. 13.428-29 (1966); Niels Jørgen Skydsgaard in *ES* 49.83-85 (1968); G.W. Turner in *AUMLA* 30.291-92 (1968).

3818. Gradon, Pamela. 1971. *Form and Style in Early English Literature.* London: Methuen, x + 398 pp. [Covers the period from OE to the 15th century. Repr. as paperback, 1974.]

   Reviews: R.M. Wilson in *English* 21.23 (1972); J.D.A. Ogilvy in *ELN* 10.140-41 (1972/73); J.J. Anderson in *Critical Quarterly* (Manchester) 15.186-87 (1973); A.J. Bliss in *RES* n.s. 24.197-99 (1973); D.S. Brewer in *Anglia* 91.388-92 (1973); Dieter Mehl in *Erasmus* 25.222-28 (1973); E.G. Stanley in *YES* 3.265-67 (1973); J. Stephens in *Southern Review* 6.180-86 (1973); P.B. Taylor in *ES* 54.383-85 (1973); Anon. in *TLS*, 8 Nov. 1974, p. 1265: P. Rogers in *HAR* 25.248-50 (1974); B. Rowland in *MAE* 43.286-89 (1974).

3819. Toor, Sidney David. 1965. *Euphuism in England Before John Lyly.* Oregon diss., 197 pp. [Abstr. in *DA* 26.4642 (1966). Begins with the OE period.]

B. Old English

3820. Anderson, Orval J. 1951. "Once More—the Old English Simile". *West Virginia Univ. Philological Papers* (Morgantown, WV) 8.1-12.

3821. Bethurum, Dorothy. 1932. "The Form of Ælfric's *Lives of Saints*". *SP* 29.515-33. [Minimizes Ælfric's indebtedness to Lain stylistic tradition.]

3822. ———. 1932. "Stylistic Features of the Old English Laws". *MLR* 27.263-79.

3823. Campbell, Alistair. 1962. "The Old English Epic Style". *Tolkien Festschrift*, 13-26.

3824. Carkeet, David. 1977. "Aspects of Old English Style". *Lang&S* 10.173-89. [Based on syntactic considerations.]

3825. Clement, Richard Wolcott. 1978. "An Analysis of Non-Finite Verb Forms as an Indication of the Style of Translation in Bede's *Ecclesiastical History*". *JEngL* 12.19-28.

3826. Clemoes, Peter. 1985. "Language in Context: *Her* in the 890 *Anglo-Saxon Chronicle*". *LSE* n.s. 16.27-36.

3827. Cornell, Muriel. 1981. "Varieties of Repetition in Old English Poetry, Especially in *The Wanderer* and *The Seafarer*". *Neophil* 65.292-307. [Considers the repetition of phonological, syntactic, and lexical patterns.]

3828. Enkvist, Nils Erik. 1972. "Old English Adverbial *þā*: An Action Marker?". *Mustanoja Festschrift* = *NM* 73.90-96. [On the use of adverbial *þā* 'then' as a style marker.]

3829. Fanagan, John M. 1978. "An Examination of Tense-Usage in Some of the Shorter Poems of *The Exeter Book*". *Neophil* 62.290-93.

3830. Fowler, Roger. 1966. "Some Stylistic Features of the *Sermo Lupi*". *JEGP* 65.1-18. [A grammatical study of Wulfstan's homily.]

3831. Funke, Otto. 1962. "Some Remarks on Wulfstan's Prose Rhythm". *ES* 43.311-18. [A critique of McIntosh [no. 3840].]

3832. Gardner, Thomas. 1969. "The Old English Kenning: A Characteristic Feature of Germanic Poetical Diction?". *MP* 67.109-17.

3833. Gerould, Gordon Hall. 1925. "Abbot Ælfric's Rhythmic Prose". *MP* 22.353-66.

3834. Harmatiuk, Sandra J. 1975. *A Statistical Approach to Some Aspects of Style in the Signed Poems of Cynewulf: A Computer-Assisted Study*. Notre Dame diss., 251 pp. [Abstr. in *DA* 36.1492A (1975).]

3835. ———. 1980. "A Statistical Approach to Some Aspects of Style in Six Old English Poems: A Computer-Assisted Study". *Glottometrika* 2, ed. R. Grotjahn, 89-107. Bochum: Brockmeyer.

3836. Hollowell, Ida Masters. 1972. *Wulfstan's Style: A Linguistic Analysis*. Univ. of North Carolina at Chapel Hill diss., 217 pp. [Abstr. in *DA* 34.299A (1973). Chap. I examines clauses, dealing with their length, type, and function. II involves a count of verbs, nouns, adjectives, and adverbs in all four homilies. III deals with rhythm.]

3837. ———. 1977. "Linguistic Factors Underlying Style Levels in Four Homilies of Wulfstan". *Neophil* 61.287-96.

3838. Kerling, Johan. 1982. "A Case of 'Slipping': Direct and Indirect Speech in Old English Prose". *Neophil* 66.286-90.

3839. Kintgen, Eugene R. 1974. "Echoic Repetition in Old English Poetry, Especially *The Dream of the Rood*". *NM* 75.202-23.

3840. McIntosh, Angus. 1949. "Wulfstan's Prose". (Sir Israel Gollancz Memorial Lecture for 1948 [delivered 11 May 1949].) *PBA* 35.109-42. [Pub. separately in 1950, London: Geoffrey Cumberlego, 36 pp. Approaches the writings of Wulfstan from a metrical point of view. Cf. Funke [no. 3831].]

Reviews: B.J. Timmer in *ES* 32.162-63 (1951); A. Campbell in *RES* n.s. 3.166-67 (1952); Hilda Hulme in *MLR* 47.271 (1952).

3841. Metcalf, Allan Albert. 1966. *The Poetic Language of the Old English 'Meters of Boethius'*. Univ. of California, Berkeley, diss., 244 pp. [Abstr. in *DA* 27.3876A (1967).]

3842. Metes, George Sorin. 1972. *Word-Order Variation as a Stylistic Feature in the Old English 'Andreas'*. Wisconsin diss., 123 pp. [Abstr. in *DA* 33.3621A (1973).]

3843. Minkoff, Harvey. 1977. "An Example of Latin Influence on Ælfric's Translation Style". *Neophil* 61.127-42. [Focuses on the placement of the past participle in the past participle + auxiliary verb construction.]

3844. Moloney, Bernadette. 1982. "Another Look at Ælfric's Use of Discourse in Some Saints' Lives". *ES* 63.13-19. [Cf. Waterhouse [no. 3857].]

3845. Myrvaagnes, Naomi S. 1970. *A Stylistic Study of the Old English 'Meters of Boethius'*. New York Univ. diss., 178 pp. [Abstr. in *DA* 31.4131A (1971).]

3846. Niles, John D. 1981. "Compound Diction and the Style of *Beowulf*". *ES* 62.489-503.

3847. Olsan, Lea Thompson. 1973. *The Style of the West Saxon Gospels*. Tulane Univ. diss., 259 pp. [Abstr. in *DA* 34.2574A (1973).]

3848. Richman, Gerald. 1986. "Artful Slipping in Old English". *Neophil* 70.279-91. [On the shift from indirect to direct discourse within a single speech.]

3849. Robinson, Fred Colson. 1982. "Latin for Old English in Anglo-Saxon Manuscripts". *McIntosh Festschrift* (A), 395-400.

3850. ———. 1985. *Beowulf and the Appositive Style*. (The Hodges Lectures.) Knoxville, TN: The Univ. of Tennessee Press, ix + 106 pp.

Reviews: Roberta Frank in *Speculum* 61.992-94 (1986); M.C. Seymour in *ES* 67.363-64 (1986).

3851. Schaar, Claes. 1949. *Critical Studies in the Cynewulf Group*. Lund: C.W.K. Gleerup, 337 pp. [Textual and stylistic studies.]

Reviews: F. Schubel in *SN* 22.217-19 (1949/50); S.M. Kuhn in *JEGP* 49.391-94 (1950); H.C. Matthes in *Archiv* 187.132 (1950); A.A. Prins in *Museum* 55.391-94 (1950); K. Malone in *Anglia* 70.444-50 (1951/52); S.R.T.O. d'Ardenne in *RBPH* 30.259-63 (1952); G.N. Garmonsway in *MLR* 47.382-83 (1952); B.J. Timmer in *ES* 33.71-72 (1952).

3852. Shaheen, Abdel-Rahman. 1981. "The Style of *Beowulf*: A Study of Diction and Rhetorical Devices". *SAP* 13.149-62.

3853. Sheets, Louis Arden. 1964. *Wulfstan's Prose: A Reconsideration*. Ohio State Univ. diss., 164 pp. [Abstr. in *DA* 25.6611 (1965).]

3854. Spamer, James Blakeman. 1977. *The Kenning and the Kend Heiti: A Contrastive Study of Periphrasis in Two Germanic Poetic Traditions*. Brown diss., 220 pp. [Abstr. in *DA* 38.4859A (1978).]

3855. Wall, Carolyn. 1968. "Stylistic Variation in the Old English *Exodus*". *ELN* 6.79-84.

3856. Wärtli, H. 1935. *Stilistische Dämpfung als Mittel der Ausdruckssteigerung und der Ausdrucksmilderung im Altenglischen und im Neuenglischen (Litotes und Understatement)*. Zürich diss., 193 pp.

3857. Waterhouse, Ruth. 1976. "Ælfric's Use of Discourse in Some Saints' Lives". *ASE* 5.83-103. [Cf. Moloney [no. 3844].]

C. Middle English

3858. Arrathoon, Leigh A. 1984. "Antinomic Cluster Analysis and the Boethian Verbal Structure of Chaucer's *Merchant's Tale*". *Lang&S* 17.92-120.

3859. Aurner, Robert Ray. 1923. "Caxton and the English Sentence". *Univ. of Wisconsin Studies in Language and Literature* 18.23-59. [Discusses Caxton's sentence structure.]

3860. ———. 1923. "The History of Certain Aspects of the Structure of the English Sentence". *PQ* 2.187-208. [From Caxton to Macauley.]

3861. Baum, Paull Franklin. 1946. "Chaucer's Metrical Prose". *JEGP* 45.38-42. [Deals almost exclusively with *The Tale of Melibee*.]

3862. Bennett, Henry Stanley. 1945. "Fifteenth Century Secular Prose". *RES* 21.257-63. [Qualifies Chambers [no. 3816].]

3863. Bethurum, Dorothy. 1935. "The Connection of the Katherine Group with Old English Prose". *JEGP* 34.553-64. [On Ælfric's influence on ME literature.]

3864. Blake, Norman Francis. 1968. "Caxton and Courtly Style". *E&S* n.s. 21.29-45.

3865. Bosse, Roberta Jeanne Bux. 1971. *Early Middle English Prose Style: 'Sawles Warde'*. St. Louis Univ. diss., 186 pp. [Abstr. in *DA* 32.4554A (1972).]

3866. Clark, Cecily. 1977. "As Seint Austin Seith". *MAE* 46.212-18. [Stresses the stylistic importance, not only for the *Ancrene Wisse* but also for all serious medieval writing in a vernacular, of the Latin studies underlying it.]

3867. ———. 1978. "*Wiþ Scharpe Sneateres*: Some Aspects of Colloquialism in *Ancrene Wisse*". *NM* 79.341-53.

3868. Cleve, Gunnel. 1984. "Some Remarks on Richard Rolle's Prose Style". *NM* 85.115-21. [Points to the relevance of the passive in passages that describe mystical experience.]

3869. Davis, Norman. 1961. "Styles in English Prose of the Late Middle and Early Modern Period". *Langue et Littérature: Actes du VIIIe Congrès de la Fédération Internationale des Langues et Littératures Modernes* (= Bibliothèque de la Faculté de Philosophie et Lettres de l'Université de Liége, 161), 165-81. Paris: Société d'édition "Les Belles Lettres". [Argues against Chambers [no. 3816].]

3870. ———. 1967. "Style and Stereotype in Early English Letters". *LSE* n.s. 1.7-17. [Concerning the *Paston Letters*.]

3871. Donaldson, Ethelbert Talbot. 1981. "Adventures with the Adversative Conjunction in the General Prologue to the *Canterbury Tales*: or, What's before the *But*?". *McIntosh Festschrift* (E), 355-66.

3872. Eliason, Norman Ellsworth. 1972. *The Language of Chaucer's Poetry: An Appraisal of the Verse, Style, and Structure*. (= Anglistica, 17.) Copenhagen: Rosenkilde and Bagger, 250 pp.

Reviews: T.F. Hoad in *N&Q* n.s. 21.230-32 (1974); Dieter Mehl in *Anglia* 92.451-54 (1974); Charles A. Owen, Jr. in *Speculum* 49.727-30 (1974); C. Schaar in *SN* 46.547-51 (1974); Theodore A. Stroud in *MP* 72.60-70 (1974); Ralph W.V. Elliott in *ES* 56.153-54 (1975); Heiner Gillmeister in *Archiv* 212.366-69 (1975).

3873. Field, Peter John Christopher. 1971. *Romance and Chronicle: A Study of Malory's Prose Style*. London: Barrie & Jenkins, 202 pp.

Reviews: Ellyn Olefsky Bache in *JEGP* 71.109-11 (1972); Brian Vickers in *ELN* 10.291-95 (1973).

3874. Gilbert, Anthony James. 1979. *Literary Language from Chaucer to Johnson*. London: Macmillan; Totowa, NJ: Barnes and Noble, ix + 224 pp.

Review: Basil Cottle in *TLS*, March 14, 1980, p. 300.

3875. Green, Maureen Flanagan. 1973. *Verbal and Structural Repetition as Devices of Representation in the York Cycle*. Univ. of Wisconsin-Madison diss., 203 pp. [Abstr. in *DA* 34.4201-02A (1974).]

3876. Hastings, George Sands, Jr. 1965. *Two Aspects of Style in the AB Dialect of Middle English*. Pennsylvania diss., 80 pp. [Abstr. in *DA* 26.5425 (1966). Discusses alliteration and pronoun reference.]

3877. Humbert, Agnes Margaret. 1944. *Verbal Repetition in the 'Ancren Riwle'*. Washington, DC: Catholic Univ. of America Press, xxii + 137 pp. [Catholic Univ. of America diss.]

3878. Hynes-Berry, Mary. 1976. "Language and Meaning: Malory's Translation of the Grail Story". *Neophil* 60.309-19.

3879. Jambeck, Thomas J. 1975. "Characterization and Syntax in the *Miller's Tale*". *JNT* 5.73-85.

3880. Keiser, George R. 1977. "Language and Meaning in Chaucer's *Shipman's Tale*". *ChauR* 12.147-61. [On the swearing.]

3881. Kliman, Bernice W. 1977. "John Barbour and Rhetorical Tradition". *AnM* 18.106-35. [Discusses Barbour's diction, using as aids *OED*, *MED* and *DOST*.]

3882. Knapp, Peggy Ann. 1971. "John Wyclif as Bible Translator: The Texts of the English Sermons". *Speculum* 46.713-20. [A stylistic comparison between Wyclif's translations of texts from St. Matthew in his sermons and the two versions of the Wycliffite Bible.]

3883. ———. 1977. *The Style of John Wyclif's English Sermons*. (= De Proprietatibus Litterarum, Ser. Practica, 16.) The Hague: Mouton, x + 116 pp. [Originally Pittsburg diss. 1966.]

Reviews: Anne Hudson in *N&Q* n.s. 25.359 (1978); John H. Fisher in *Speculum* 54.161-62 (1979).

3884. Knight, Stephen Thomas. 1974. "Style and the Effects of Style in Malory's Arthuriad". *Parergon* 9.3-24.

3885. Lawton, David A. 1980. "*The Destruction of Troy* as Translation from Latin Prose: Aspects of Form and Style". *SN* 52.259-70.

3886. Markus, Manfred. 1981. "The Language and Style: The Paradox of Heroic Poetry". *The Alliterative 'Morte Arthure': A Reassessment of the Poem* (= Arthurian Studies, 2), ed. Karl Heinz Göller, 57-69. Cambridge: D.S. Brewer.

3887. Martin, L.S. 1969/70. "An Essay in Middle English Stylistics". *PICL*/10, 3:489-91. Bucarest: Ed. Acad. R.S.R.

3888. Meier, Hans Heinrich. 1974. "Middle English Styles in Action". *ES* 55.193-204. [The passages analysed are from *Sir Gawain and the Green Knight*, Henryson, Layamon, and *þe wohunge of Ure Lauerd*.]

3889. ———. 1979. "Middle English Styles in Translation: A Note on *Everyman* and Caxton's *Reynard*". *From Caxton to Beckett: Essays Presented to W.H. Toppen*, ed. B.H. Ablas and R. Todd, 13-30. Amsterdam: Rodopi.

3890. ———. 1981. "Middle English Styles in Translation: The Case of Chaucer and Charles". *McIntosh Festschrift* (E), 367-76. [Charles = Charles d'Orléans.]

3891. Millet, Bella. 1983. "*Hali Meiðhad*, *Sawles Warde* and the Continuity of English Prose". *Dobson Festschrift*, 100-08.

3892. Morgan, Margery M. 1952. "*A Talking of the Love of God* and the Continuity of Stylistic Tradition in Middle English Prose Meditations". *RES* n.s. 3.97-116.

3893. Muir, Laurence. 1935. "The Influence of the Rolle and Wyclifite Psalters upon the Psalter of the Authorised Version". *MLR* 30.302-10. [Discusses primarily the literary influence, but touches on linguistic developments as well.]

3894. Mustanoja, Tauno Frans. 1974. "Verbal Rhyming in Chaucer". *Robbins Festschrift*, 104-10.

3895. Nattinger, James Ralph. 1969. *A Linguistic Study of William Caxton as a Translator*. Michigan diss., 240 pp. [Abstr. in *DA* 31.2351A (1970).]

3896. Nelson, Veatrice Claudia. 1979. *Historical Present and Mixed Discourse in Sir Thomas Malory's 'Morte Darthur': An Analysis of Abrupt Shifts in Deixis*. Georgia State Univ. diss., 332 pp. [Abstr. in *DA* 40.4025A (1980).]

3897. Ness, Lynn and Caroline Duncan-Rose. 1982. "A Syntactic Correlate of Style Switching in *The Canterbury Tales*". *PICHL*/3, 293-322.

3898. Novelli, Cornelius. 1957. "The Demonstrative Adjective *This*: Chaucer's Use of a Colloquial Narrative Device". *MS* 19.246-49. [Comments on the narrative and dramatic effects produced by Chaucer's use of *this*.]

3899. Olmes, Antonie. 1933. *Sprache und Stil der englischen Mystik des Mittelalters unter besonderer Berücksichtigung des Richard Rolle von Hampole*. (= SEP, 76.) Halle/Saale: Max Niemeyer, viii + 100 pp. [Almost exclusively concerned with the language and style of Richard Rolle's Latin and English prose.]

3900. Rygiel, Dennis. 1981. "*Ancrene Wisse* and 'Colloquial' Style: A Caveat". *Neophil* 65.137-43.

3901. Schlauch, Margaret. 1950. "Chaucer's Prose Rhythms". *PMLA* 65.568-89.

3902. ———. 1952. "Chaucer's Colloquial English: Its Structural Traits". *PMLA* 67.1103-16.

3903. ———. 1966. "The Art of Chaucer's Prose". *Chaucer and Chaucerians: Critical Studies in Middle English Literature*, ed. D.S. Brewer, 140-63. London: Nelson; University, AL: Univ. of Alabama Press. [Examines the language and style of Chaucer's prose.]

3904. Stokes, Myra. 1980. "Recurring Rhymes in *Troilus and Criseyde*". *SN* 52.287-97.

3905. Stone, Robert Karl. 1970. *Middle English Prose Style: Margery Kempe and Julian of Norwich*. (= Studies in English Literature, 36.) The Hague: Mouton, 220 pp. [Originally Univ. of Illinois diss. 1963; Abstr. in *DA* 24.288 (1963).]

Reviews: P.J.C. Field in *Speculum* 48.182-85 (1973); S.S. Hussey in *N&Q* n.s. 20.302 (1973); R.M. Wilson in *MAE* 42.183-84 (1973); Gero Bauer in *Anglia* 92.462-64 (1974).

3906. Tatlock, John Strong Perry, 1923. "Laʒamon's Poetic Style and Its Relations". *The Manly Anniversary Studies in Language and Literature*, 3-11. Chicago: Univ. of Chicago Press.

3907. Terasawa, Yoshio. 1968. "A Rhetorical Spoken Style of M.E.: The Case of Wyclif's Sermon Translation". *SEL* English No. 1968, 61-81.

3908. Weese, Walter Eugene. 1950. *Word-Order as a Factor of Style in Chaucer's Poetry*. Yale diss., 218 pp. [Abstr. in *DA* 31.4138A (1971).]

3909. Whiting, Bartlett Jere. 1934. *Chaucer's Use of Proverbs*. (= Harvard Studies in Comparative Literature, 11.) Cambridge, MA: Harvard Univ. Press, xii + 297 pp. [Repr., New York: AMS Press, 1973. Shows that the use of proverbs is a distinctive and important feature of Chaucer's style.]

3910. Wilson, Richard Middlewood. 1959. "On the Continuity of English Prose". *Mossé Festschrift*, 486-94.

3911. Workman, Samuel K. 1940. *Fifteenth Century Translation as an Influence on English Prose*. (= Princeton Studies in English, 18.) Princeton, NJ: Princeton Univ. Press, x + 210 pp.

Reviews: E.E.H. in *RES* 17.249-50 (1941); A.A. Prins in *ES* 24.120-21 (1942).

3912. Zeeman, Elizabeth. 1955. "Nicholas Love — A Fifteenth Century Translator". *RES* n.s. 6.113-27.

3913. Zimmermann, Rüdiger. 1973. "Verbal Syntax and Style in *Sir Gawain and the Green Knight*". *ES* 54.533-43. [A stylistic analysis of the poet's use of tense, voice, and mood.]

INDEX OF NAMES*

This index lists all authors, editors, collaborators, revisers, translators, assistants and reviewers mentioned in the bibliography. Arabic numbers refer to item numbers in the main body, while Roman numerals indicate page numbers in the list of abbreviations. The symbol R after an item number shows that it is a review.

Aarts, F.G.A.M., 169R
Abels, R., 329R
Ablas, B.H., 3889
Abruzzo, D.J., 1354
Ackerman, R.W., 111, 118R, 126R, 462R, 2829
Acobian, R., xxx
Adams, G.B., 521
Adams, J.D., 200R
Adams, V., 1845R
Adamska-Sałaciak, A., 145R, 896
Addy, S.O., 2000
Aertsen, H., 2830
Ahlgren, A., 1174
Aijmer, K., 1905
Aiken, J.R., 142, 610
Aitken, A.J., xxvii, 120, 564, 897, 1906, 1907, 2831, 3731
Åkerlund, A., 1665
Akkartal, T., 1666
Alanne, E., 1908
Albright, R.W., 1980R
Alexander, H., 143, 192R, 1909, 3797R
Alexander, J.D., 611
Alfonsin, E.J., 37R
Algeo, J., 156R, 188R, 193R, 206, 792R, 1344R
Allen, C.L., 1175, 1355, 1356, 1357, 1358, 1359, 1381R

Allen, H.B., 1, 2
Allen, H.E., 2832, 2833
Allen, M.E., 3421
Alston, R.C., 244, 245, 1305R, 2190R
Amis, K., 78R
Amos, A.C., 29, 334, 448, 2001, 2002, 2003, 2004, 2005, 2006, 2007, 2008, 2119, 2245R
Anderson, E.R., 2010
Anderson, G.K., 444, 1360, 1361, 1362
Anderson, J.J., 121R, 3818R
Anderson, James M., 309
Anderson, John (M.), xxix, 612, 613, 667, 668, 669, 708, 792, 1176, 1363, 1364
Anderson, M., 246
Anderson, O. (S.), 2009, 2013R, 3018R, 3670R
Anderson, O.J., 3820
Anderson, Y., III, 3078
Andersson, T., xxxii, 3492, 3666
Andrew, M., 40
Andrew, S.O., 1135, 1365, 1366, 1367, 1368
Ångström, M., 670
Anon., 9R, 11R, 46R, 49R, 51R, 81R, 82R, 86R, 88R, 90R, 101R, 120R, 126R, 140R, 141R, 147R, 148R, 154R, 160R, 194R, 199R, 207R,

*Prepared by Sukeaki Matsuda and revised by Matsuji Tajima

230R, 234R, 246R, 256R, 274R, 279R, 284R, 286R, 301R, 314R, 336R, 415R, 416R, 461R, 531R, 666R, 913R, 1031R, 1367R, 1368R, 1658R, 1771R, 1825R, 1934R, 1978R, 1980R, 2011, 2834, 3148R, 3186R, 3397R, 3511R, 3604R, 3777R, 3817R, 3818R
Antonsen, E.H., 535, 556R, 614, 671
Antilla, R., 2835
Appenzeller-Gassmann, V., 2836
Appleby, M.J., 1177
Arakelian, P.G., 565
Arcamone, M.G., 265R
Archer, J.W., 2837
Arend, Z.M., 898
Arhammar, N., 2012
Armalytė, O., 672
Armborst, D., 673, 674
Armentrout, R.E., 1178
Armour, J.S., 144
Arn, M.-J., xxviii
Arndt. W.W., xxix
Arngart, O. (S.), 163R, 228R, 335, 1067R, 1179, 1180, 2838, 2839, 2840, 2841, 2842, 2843, 2844, 3438, 3439, 3440, 3441, 3442, 3443, 3444, 3482R, 3596R, 3682R, 3732, 3747R
Arrathoon, L.A., 3858
Ashdown, M., 1978R
Attreed, L., 84R
Atwood, E.B., xxxii, 1324R
Aurner, R.R., 3859, 3860
Austin, W.M., 1954
Awedyk, W., 675, 676, 677, 1136
Ayres, H.M., 207R
B., A.O., 3267R
B., C., 229R, 666R, 1315R, 3397R
B., C.E., 2125R
B., S.H., 3186R
Baader, T., 899
Bache, E.O., 3873R
Bachmann, W., 900
Bäck, H., 2013, 3445
Bäckman, S., 520R

Bacquet, P., 46R, 249R, 274R, 1369, 1370, 1910, 3482R
Baghdikian, S., 1667
Bahnick, K.R., 336
Bähr, D., 287, 1911, 2014, 3109R
Bailey, C.-J.N., 901
Bailey, H.W., 2640, 2845
Bailey, R.W., 26, 2846
Baird, I., 314R
Baird, J.L., 2015
Baird, L.Y., 41
Bak, W., 2016
Baker, C.F., 3815
Baker, D.C., 49R, 78R
Baker, P.S., 1661R
Baker, R.T., 148R
Bald, W.-D., xxx, 1668, 1669, 1912
Baldinger, K., 2847, 3098R
Baldner, R.W., 683
Baldwin, M., 2848
Ball, C.R., 678
Ball, C.J.E., 89R, 193R, 445, 679, 680, 1401R, 1560R, 2017, 2018, 2019, 2020, 2260R, 2655R, 2849, 3809R
Ball, R.H., 115
Bammesberger, A., xxvi, 85, 102R, 145, 153R, 310, 562R, 1033, 1053, 1054, 1055, 1056, 1141R, 1371, 1372, 1560R, 2021, 2022, 2023, 2024, 2025, 2026, 2027, 2028, 2029, 2030, 2031, 2032, 2033, 2034, 2035, 2036, 2037, 2038, 2039, 2040, 2041, 2042, 2043, 2044, 2045, 2046, 2047, 2048, 2049, 2050, 2051, 2052, 2053, 2054, 2055, 2056, 2057, 2058, 2059, 2060, 2061, 2062, 2063, 2064
Barasch, M., 1373
Barber, C.C., 681
Barber, C.(L.), 146, 147, 204R
Barela, R.E., 1374
Barfield, O., 1913
Barker, C.R., 56
Barley, M.W., xxvi
Barley, N.F., 2065, 3446
Barnes, R., 2066

INDEX OF NAMES

Barnett, L., 148
Barney, S.A., 86, 121R
Barnickel, K.-D., 2850
Baron, D.E., 1181
Baron, N.S., 1182, 1183
Baron, W.R.J., 2851
Barquist, C.R., 682
Barrack, C.M., 683, 684, 685
Barrett, C.R., 271R, 1033R, 1375, 1376
Barritt, (C.)W., 862, 863, 864, 1248R, 1369R
Barron, W.R.J., 134R
Barry, P., 2067
Barstow, A.M., 2852
Bartholomae, U., 2393R
Bashe, E.J., 10, 1157R
Basilius, H.A., 3733
Başkan, Ö., 615
Bately, J.M., 337, 338, 593R, 1086R, 1522R, 2068, 2069, 2070
Bateson, F.W., 3, 566, 599
Batho, E.C., 1913R
Battistella, E., 1381R, 1895R
Bauer, Gerd, 686
Bauer, Gero, xxviii, 155R, 295R, 307R, 332R, 687, 688, 1033R, 1295R, 1305R, 1369R, 1377, 1670, 1671, 3905R
Bauer, G.-K., 3018R
Bauer, L., 638R
Baugh, A.C., 42, 43, 141R, 149, 150, 151, 306R, 1980R, 2853, 2854
Baum, P.F., 3861
Bauschatz, P.C., 1672, 2071
Bawcutt, P., 3007R
Baxter, A., 1378
Baxter, L., 1379
Bazell, C.E., 251R, 254R, 689, 1034, 1057, 1058, 1059, 1060, 2155
Bazire, J., 454R, 902, 903, 1845R, 2855, 3734
Beade, P., 684R, 792R, 904
Beadle, R., 3735
Beale, W.H., 4
Bean, J.M.W., 2856

Bean, M.C., 1380, 1381
Beck, H., xxxii, 2072
Becker, R., 27
Beckers, H., 2073, 2394R, 3697R
Beeaff, D.E., 3447
Beer, H., 2074
Behre, F., 1184, 1382, 1383, 1673, 1817R, 2857, 2858, 2859, 2860, 2861, 2862, 2863
Beichner, P.E., 138R
Bekker-Nielsen, H., 3493
Benardete, D., 610R
Benchley, N., 148R
Bengtsson, E., 1914
Bennett, Hobart., 690
Bennett, Henry S., 3862
Bennett, Jack A.W., 51R, 105R, 111R, 430, 2075
Bennett, Jacob, 457, 458, 3736
Bennett, J.R., 28
Bennett, P.A., 1185
Bennett, W.H., 616, 691
Benning, H.A., 2076, 2561R
Bennis, H., 1218R, 1632
Belfour, A.O., 1382R, 1393R
Bell, A., 2864, 3448
Bellamy, S.E., 217R
Bense, J.F., 112, 311, 3148R
Benskin, M., xxix, 567, 3737, 3738, 3739, 3740, 3741, 3742, 3790
Benson, L.D., 89R, 128R, 1674
Benson, R.G., 372
Bergener, C., 1186
Berger, S.(E.), 113, 2866
Berghaus, F.-G., 651R
Bergman, M.M., 87
Bergner, H., 2866
Berkhout, C.T., 9R, 329R, 562R, 2077, 2245, 2284
Berman, A., 1187
Bernárdez, E., 1517R
Berndt, R., 51R, 152, 162R, 168R, 218R, 288, 312, 373, 374, 375, 1061, 1062, 1855R, 2867
Besserman, L.L., 2868

Bessinger, J.B., Jr., xxix, 88, 89, 90, 128R, 339, 2078
Bethurum, D., 452R, 3821, 3822, 3863
Bibire, P., 340
Biddle, M., xxxii, 3422
Bierbaumer, P., 368, 732R, 2079, 2080, 2081, 2082, 2083, 2084, 2085, 2086, 2087, 2088
Biese, Y.M., 1188
Biggins, D., 2869
Binnick, R.I., 1313R
Binz, G., 296R, 3623R, 3624R, 3625R
Birkhan, H., 2072, 2351
Bishko, C.J., 5
Bishop, H., 2870
Bitterling, K., 114, 1141R, 1993R, 2245R, 2415R, 2871, 2872, 2873, 2874, 2875, 2876, 2877
Björk, A., xxxi
Blake, N.F., xxvi, 44, 165R, 313, 314, 376, 377, 459, 460, 461, 486R, 501R, 509R, 510R, 536, 1063, 1064, 1550R, 1580R, 1845R, 1950R, 2089, 2878, 2879, 2880, 2881, 3743, 3744, 3745, 3864
Blakely, L., 247
Blanch, R.J., 45, 2882
Blanchet, M.-C., 3635
Bland, D.S., 3305R
Blansitt, E.L., Jr., 875
Blenner-Hassett, R., 2883, 2884, 3495R, 3636, 3637, 3638
Bliss, A.(J.), 9R, 314R, 332R, 528R, 568, 692, 905, 906, 1003, 1033R, 1384, 2885, 3746, 3818R
Block, D.N., 1675
Blockley, M.E., 341
Bloomfield, L., 1065, 2090, 2091
Bloomfield, M.W., 150R, 153, 168R, 2886, 2887, 2888, 3098R
Blumbach, W., 179R, 315R, 651R, 693
Blunt, C., 3609
Blythe, R., 3505R
Bock, H., 1189
Bodden, M.C., 342

Bodelsen, C.A., 234R, 1289R, 1581R
Boerner, O., 297R, 3794R
Bøgholm, N., xxviii, 154, 462, 2889
Böhler, M., 3449
Bohman, H., 3747
Boisson, C., 617
Bolognesi, G., 569
Bolton, W.F., 89R, 155, 156, 378, 1873R, 3450
Bond, G., 907
Bone, G., 2890
Bonebrake, V., 908
Bonnerot, L., 115R
Bonsack, E., 3495R
Bonser, W., 2092
Borden, A.R., Jr., 91
Bornstein, D., 379
Borowski, B., 286R, 694
Borroff, M., 2891
Bosker, A., 1315R
Bosse, R.J.B., 3865
Boswinkel, J., 293R, 1143R, 1220R, 1341R, 1342R
Bouman, A.C., 2076R, 2093R
Bourcier, É., 25R
Bourcier, G., 25R, 157, 158, 481R, 522, 1130R, 1218R, 1385
Bourquin, G., 153R, 495R
Bowers, F., 888
Bowman, E., 198R
Bowman, W.P., 115
Boyd, W.J.P., 2094, 2095, 2096
Boys, R.C., 2982
Braasch, T., 92
Braddy, H., 2893, 2894
Bradley, H., 80, 159
Bradley, R.J., 909
Brady, C., 2097, 2098, 2099, 2100
Brahmer, M., xxxi
Braidwood, J., 120R, 274R
Brand, A.H., 3017R
Brandl, A., 10R, 81R, 92R, 140R, 260R, 297R, 415R, 733R, 1036R, 1164R, 2746R, 3121R, 3148R, 3449R, 3451, 3794R

INDEX OF NAMES 361

Brandon, P., xxxi, 3452
Bratley, P., 2101
Braulin, F.H., 2746R
Brault, G.J., 2895
Breivik, L.E., 651R, 1190, 1191, 1192, 1242R, 1386
Brekle, H.E., xxix, 38R, 980R, 1560R, 1639R, 2896
Bremmer, R.H., Jr., 9R, 29R, 268R, 343, 363R, 1387, 2102
Brett, C., 296R
Brewer, D.J., 90R
Brewer, D.(S.), 386, 3818R, 3903
Bridier, Y., 2103
Bright, J.W., 248
Brink, D., 145R, 695
Brinton, L.J.(T.), 1193, 1676
Britton, D.A., 218R, 332R
Britton, G.C., 45R, 446, 465R, 696, 697, 1137, 2897
Bromwich, J., 380, 447
Brøndegaard, V.J., 2104
Brook, G.L., 153R, 160, 249, 251R, 289R, 344, 570, 618, 619, 1323R, 2898, 3709
Brooks, K.R., 249R, 263R, 274R, 1049R, 1151R, 1369R, 1580R, 1980R, 2105, 2106, 2260R, 2541R, 3495R
Brorström, S., 1915, 2899
Brose, B., 1677
Brosnahan, L.F., 698
Brounts, A., 450R
Brown, Alan K., 503R, 1916, 2107
Brown, Arthur, xxxi
Brown, C., 3086
Brown, E., Jr., 2900, 3639
Brown, Peter, 54R
Brown, Phyllis R., xxviii
Brown, R.A., 3644
Brown, U., 51R
Brown, W.H., Jr., 1388
Brunner, K., xxxii, 161, 162, 182R, 196R, 232R, 238R, 243R, 250, 251R, 262R, 274R, 282, 283, 289, 290, 415R, 416R, 463, 517R, 537, 698R, 699, 700, 944R, 1039R, 1248R, 1684R, 1751R, 1800R, 2230R, 2285, 3091R, 3186R, 3500R, 3584R, 3631R, 3659R, 3748
Bruten, A., 218R
Bryan, W.F., 236R, 281R, 666R, 2108, 3453
Bryant, M.M., 163, 164, 1333R, 1580R, 1980R
Buchholz, E., 1678
Buchloh, P.G., xxx
Büchner, G., 2109
Buck, C.D., 523
Buckhurst, H.T.M., 2110
Buehler, P.G., 116
Bühler, C.F., 381
Bullock-Davies, C., 2895R
Bungenstab, E., 1194
Bunting, C.L., 117R
Burch, J.C.H., 2901
Burchfield, R.W., xxxi, 78, 165, 464, 1917, 2111, 2902, 2903
Burgess, A., 78R
Burgschmidt, E., 315, 1218R, 1332R, 1983R, 2904
Burkhart, R.S., 1389
Burlin, R.B., xxx
Burnley, (J.)D., 9R, 226R, 465, 481R, 510R, 1138, 1313R, 2905, 2906, 2907, 2908, 2909, 2910, 2911, 2912, 2913, 2914, 2915
Burrow, J.A., 2916
Burton, D.M., 26
Burton, T.L., 2917, 2918, 2919
Buschinger, D., xxix
Busse, W.G., 2920
Butler, M.C., 1195, 1390, 1679, 1680, 1681
Butler, M.S., 2921
Butler, S., 110, 448, 2112, 2113
Butte, B., 1560R
Buxbaum, K., 1913R
Buyssens, E., 219R, 270R, 300R, 462R, 1039R, 1798R, 3258R

Byerly, G.K.A., 2114
C., G.H., 143R
Cable, T.(M.), 151, 334R, 382, 1391
Caffee, N.M., 3657
Calder, D.G., 268R, 1661R, 2711
Caldwell, R.A., 2469R, 2922
Caldwell, S.J.G., 1682
Callaway, M., Jr., 666R, 1196, 1315R, 1392, 1393, 1764R, 2766R
Camden, C., Jr., 2923
Cameron, A. (F.), xxvi, xxvii, 29, 193R, 277R, 316, 448, 2020, 2115, 2116, 2117, 2118, 2119, 2120, 2245R, 2802R
Cameron, K., 3422, 3454, 3455, 3456, 3457, 3458, 3459, 3649, 3680R
Campbell, A., 88R, 89R, 93, 106R, 251, 454R, 1369R, 1560R, 1580R, 1605R, 1616R, 2076R, 2121, 2170R, 2475R, 2541R, 2655R, 3620R, 3823, 3840R
Campbell, J., 3460
Campbell, J.J., 161R, 2122, 2123, 2124, 2655R
Canale, (W.)M., 1394, 1395
Cannon, G., 166
Capek, M.J., 1396, 1397
Carkeet, D.C., 1398, 1399, 3824
Carleton, C., 1400, 1401
Carls, U., 1130R, 1758R
Carlson, A.M., 1197
Carlton, C., 193R
Carnes, C.M., 3697R
Carnoy, A., 666R
Carr, B.M.H., 698R, 1600R, 3368R, 3797R
Carr, C.T., 2125
Carr, G.F., xxx, 684R
Carr, W.L., 213
Carrell, J.C., 100, 101
Carson, H.L., 115R
Carstensen, B., 162R, 204R, 218R, 240R, 509R, 1305R, 1341R, 1342R, 1343R, 1575R, 1683, 1684, 1717R, 1756R, 1757R, 1800R, 2076R
Carter, H.H., 117
Carter, R., 910

Casey, D.J., 1996R
Casieri, S., 252
Cassidy, F.G., 208, 253, 1402, 1575R, 2126, 2127, 2128, 2924, 2925, 3650
Casson, L.F., 2926
Catalini Fennel, C., 231
Cavers, D.L., 3749
Cawley, A.C., 466, 571, 2129, 3808R
Cecioni, C.G., 279R, 291
Celati, G., 3817R
Cerasano, S.P., 345
Cercignani, F., 701, 951R
Cervenkova, P., 1403
Chambers, R.W., 3816
Chapman, C.O., 118
Chapman, R.W., 215
Charleston, B.M., 1715R
Chase, C., xxvii
Chase, D.E., 2130
Chatman, S.(B.), 274R, 702, 1685
Chestnut, M., xxxi
Chevillet, F., 158R, 1686, 1687, 1873R
Chickering, H.D., Jr., 2655R
Chourová, V., 146R
Christensen, I.G., 1139
Christiani, B., 2131
Christiansen, E., 3677R
Christophersen, P., 234
Church, R., 1934R
Churchhouse, R.F., 1424
Cilluffo, G., 334R, 2283R
Claiborne, R., 167
Clark, C., 157R, 158, 314R, 383, 479R, 520R, 1688, 1853R, 2132, 2927, 2928, 3640, 3641, 3642, 3643, 3644, 3645, 3646, 3647 3677R, 3697R, 3698R, 3699R, 3750, 3866, 3867
Clark, G.W., 2929
Clark, J.W., 168, 169, 225, 531, 532, 2930, 2931, 2932, 2933, 2934
Clark, R.P., 2935, 3648
Clement, R.W., 3825
Clemoes, P., xxvii, xxxii, 524, 3826
Cleve, G., 3868
Clipsham, D., 2133

Clogan, P.M., 89R
Closs, (O.E.)E., 449, 1198
Clough, A., 2936
Coates, R., 620, 703, 911, 2937, 3461, 3462, 3463
Cobb, G.W., 1404
Cochburn, J.H., 3464
Cochran, L., 2938
Coffey, J., 465R
Coghill, N., 139
Colaianne, A.J., 47
Colburn, W.E., 12
Cole, A., 3465
Colgrave, B., 2134
Colledge, E., 467, 2939
Collier, L.W., 294R, 1031R, 1220R, 1918
Collinder, B., 2135
Collins, B.L., 3771R
Collins, F., Jr. 2940
Collins, H.E., 203R
Collins, J.D., 468, 1405, 1406, 1407
Collins, R.L., 2136, 2137
Collinson, W.E., 185R, 234R, 1715R, 1914R
Colman, F., 268R, 704, 705, 706, 707, 708, 2138, 3466
Condren, E.I., 2139
Congleton, J.E.P., 2282
Conley, J., 2941, 2942
Conner, J.E., 525, 912, 3751
Connoly, J.H., 1689
Conroy, K.C., 119
Cook, A.B., III, 170
Cook, A.S., 2140
Cook, D., 251R
Cooke, W.G., 1035, 2141, 2142
Cooley, M., 621, 950, 1031R
Cooley, R.E., 1107
Coombs, V.M., 1408
Cooper, G., 2943
Cooper, S., 29R, 2283R
Copeland, J.E., xxix
Coppola, M.A., 283
Cornell, M., 3827

Corner, R., 2944
Corso, L., 2143
Cosmos, S., 1409, 2144
Cosper, R., 1690
Cottle, (A.)B., 78R, 82R, 121R, 165R, 300R, 384, 509R, 520R, 2283R, 3505R, 3677R, 3709R, 3769R, 3874R
Coulson, J., 81
Covella, F.D., 385
Cowgill, W.(C.), 1066, 2145
Cox, B., 3467, 3468
Craig, H., 2463
Craigie, W.A., 80, 120, 469, 2945, 2946, 2947
Crampton, G.R., xxviii
Crawford, J., 980R
Crawford, W.R., 46
Creed, H., 3564
Creed, R.P., xxix, 1460
Crépin, A., xxvi, 86R, 107R, 155R, 157R, 171, 172, 173, 465R, 303R, 1385R, 1845R
Cronan, D., 2146
Crook, E.J., 295R, 299
Crosby, E.U., 5
Crosby, H.L., Jr., 2147
Crossley-Holland, K., 329R
Cross, J.E., 9R, 266R, 1691, 2148, 2149, 2150, 2151, 2152, 2948
Cross, S.H., 346
Crow, M.M., 3752
Crowell, T.L., 2949
Crowley, J.P., 3713, 3714
Crozier, A., 2153
Cruse, D.A., 1181R
Cubbin, G., 86R
Cubbin, G.P., 3753
Culioli, A., 82R, 249R, 274R, 656R, 1039R, 1199, 1580R, 1600R, 1980R, 2561R
Cummings, M.(J.), 1379, 1410, 1411, 1412, 1413, 1414, 1415
Curme, G.O., 234R, 1200, 1393R, 1443R, 1692, 1693
Curtis, J.L., 2154

Cusack, B., 572
Daems, Fr., xxxi
Dahl, I., 1067, 1202
Dahl, T., 1201, 2950
Dahood, R., 2951
Dal, I., 709, 1114R
Dančev [Danchev], A., 710, 711, 1416, 1417
Daniels, J., 92R, 2508R
Danielsson, B., 1217R
Danron, C.F., 1418
Darby, H.C., 3481
D'Ardenne, S.R.T.O., 289R, 1008R, 1325R, 1369R, 2952, 2953, 2954, 2955, 2956, 3851R
Dareau, M.G., 2957
d'Aronco, M., 2958
Daunt, M., 712, 713, 2155
Davenport, M., xxvii
Davenport, W.A., 2959
Davidsen-Nielsen, N., 714, 715
Davies, C., 913
Davies, R.T., 130R, 134R
Davis, A.L., 163R
Davis, N., xxxii, 8R, 121, 128R, 141R, 153R, 284, 386, 387, 388, 430, 465R, 470, 471, 472, 473, 474, 475, 476, 477, 486R, 510R, 573, 574, 1084R, 1143R, 1174R, 1341R, 1342R, 1343R, 1344R, 1684R, 1694, 1695, 2156, 2960, 2961, 2962, 2963, 3258R, 3769R, 3808R, 3869, 3870
Davis, P.W., xxix
Davis, R.C., 625
Davis, R.T., 372R
Davison, P., 25R
Dawson, R.M., 88R
Day, M., 409R
Deakins, A.H., 1696, 1697
Dean, C., 244R, 1698
Debus, F., 2678
de Caluwé, J., 2955
De Caluwé-Dor, J., 172R, 173R, 1140, 1385R, 2157, 2964, 2965, 2966, 2967, 2968, 2969, 2970, 2971

DeCamp, D., 3715
De Garcia, E.C., 1203
Dehmer, H., 1450R, 1961R, 3449R
Dekeyser, X., 292R, 315R, 622, 1204, 1205, 1268, 1310R, 1517R, 1699
Dekker, A., 1206, 1700, 1701, 1711R, 1914R
De la Cruz, J.M., 1207, 1208, 1209, 1210, 1211, 1419, 1702, 1703, 2158, 2972
Delatte, F., 234R, 2263R, 3186R
Delcourt, J., 174
Del Lungo Camiciotti, G., 179R, 291R, 1604R
Demony, A.J., 3402
Dempsey, G.T., 2159
Denison, D., 1212, 1420, 1704, 1919
Dent, A.(A.), 2160, 2973
De Pezzo, R., 2190R
Derolez, R.(L.M.), 8R, 19R, 38R, 79R, 103R, 161R, 251R, 347, 348, 389, 390, 539R, 698R, 740R, 1445R, 1751R, 1784R, 2161, 2162, 2163, 2164, 2165, 2974, 3368R
De Roo, C.H., 2166, 2167
De Smet, G., 3098R
Deterding, D., 3654
De Tollenaere, F., 2168
Deuschle, E.L., 289R, 1496R, 3091R, 3186R
Deutschbein, M. 1920, 2169
DeVito, J.A., 218R
de Vriend, H.J., 454R
de Vriendt, S., 2157
de Vries, F.C., 307R
de Vries, J., 2446R
De Weever, J.(E.), 122, 2975, 3651
Diamond, C.B., 1421
Diamond, R.E., 254, 1608R
Dick, E.S., xxxi, 2170, 2171
Dickins, B., xxvi, 120R, 391, 2271, 3469, 3470
Dieckmann, E.P.M., 2976
Diekstra, F.(N.M.), xxvii, 487R, 1213
Diensberg, B., 102R, 493R, 914, 915,

916, 1141, 1214, 1976R, 2977, 2978, 2979
Dierickz, J., xxvi, 79R
Dieth, E., 234R, 1142
Dietrich, G., 1581R
Dietz, K., 298, 307R, 317, 651R, 684R, 716, 917, 918, 919, 920, 951R, 2172, 2173, 2980, 3518R, 3652, 3680R, 3754, 3769R, 3809R
Dike, E.B., 1921, 1922, 2981, 2982
Diller, H.J., 176R
Dillon, B., 123, 1705
DiMarco, V., 2983
Dimler, G.R., 717
Dinneen, F.P., 2523
diPaolo Healey, A., see Healey, A. diP.
Di Pietro, R.J., 875
Doane, A.N., 2174
Dobbie, E.V.K., 8R, 82R, 105R, 196R, 239R, 270R, 281R, 740R, 980R, 1039R, 1144R, 1217R, 1608R, 1800R, 2230R, 3297R, 3368R, 3797R, 3808R
Dobson, E.J., 211R, 650R, 921, 2984, 2985, 2986
Dobson, T.P., 267R
Dobyns, M.F., 94
Dodgson, J.M., 2987, 3471, 3472, 3473, 3474, 3475
Dodson, S., 2988
Dolan, T.P., 1215, 2989
Dolcetti Corazza, V., 1422
Döll, H., 2990
Dolley, M., 3476
Domingue, N.Z., 392
Domínguez, P., 2R, 78R
Donahue, D., 175
Donahue, T.S., 3755
Donaldson, E.T., 1706, 2991, 3871
Donner, M., 1707, 2992, 2993, 2994, 2995
Dornier, A., 3568
Downs, L.G., 1423, 2175
Dowsing, A., 1424, 1425, 1426
Doyle, D., 1427
Draper, J.W., 2996

Dresher, B.E., 718, 719, 720, 792R
Dressler, W.U., 825
Droege, G.B., 2176
Duckert, A.R., 2177, 3782
Dudek, J.B., 1978R
Duncan, T.G., 218R, 3756, 3757
Duncan-Rose, C., 3897
Dunlap, A.R., 2997, 2998
Dunn, C.W., 3653
Dunn, F.I., 3654
Durand, M., 623
Dürmüller, U., 255, 292, 393
Dušková, L., 1295R
Dustoor, P.E., 2999
Duthie, G.I., 2783
Düwel, K., 556R, 2247
East, W.G., 3655
Eaton, R., xxx
Ebbinghaus, E.A., 85R, 170R, 1401R, 2178, 2179, 2825R
Ebin, L., 3000
Eble, C.C., 349, 1068
Eckhardt, E., 297R, 624, 721, 1323R
Edwards, A.S.G., 44R
Ehrensperger, E.C., 1923, 3495R, 3638R
Ehrhart, M.J., 2180
Eichler, A., 973R
Eilbott, B.A., 2888
Einarsson, S., 196R, 256R, 270R, 274R, 300R, 539R, 1442R, 1771R, 1800R, 1924, 2181, 2182, 2183, 2330R, 3001
Einenkel, E., 1216
Eisenring, A.J.T., 161R
Ejder, B., 3425R
Ek, K.-G., 923, 924
Ekblom, R., 3477
Ekselius, P., 925
Ekwall, E., xxvii, 149R, 230R, 232, 233, 234R, 236R, 243R, 296R, 308R, 318, 478, 722, 723, 926, 931R, 1700R, 1708, 2184, 2185, 3002, 3003, 3004, 3005, 3091R, 3305R, 3478, 2379, 3480, 3481, 3482, 3483, 3597R, 3620R, 3656, 3657, 3658, 3659, 3660,

3661, 3662, 3805R
Elgin, S.H., 1242R
Eliason, N.E., 8R, 160R, 192R, 199R, 251R, 263R, 301R, 625, 656R, 724, 1069, 1174R, 1248R, 1445R, 1684R, 1771R, 1965R, 1980R, 2186, 2415R, 3596R, 3620R, 3663, 3872
Ellengård, A., xxvi, 1217
Ellenberger, B., 3006, 3007
Ellinger, J., 1925, 3143R
Elliot, C.O., 2187
Elliott, R.W.V., 274R, 479, 538, 539, 540, 3008, 3009, 3010, 3011, 3012, 3013, 3872R
Ellis, S., 3809R
Elmer, W., 1218, 1709, 1845R, 1873R
Embleton, S.M., 158R, 1033R
Emerson, O.F., 541
Emery, R.W., 3664
Emonds, J., 1710
Emsley, B., 194
Engberg, N.J., 1428, 1429
Engblom, V., 1711
Enkvist, N.E., xxxi, 134R, 1031R, 1259, 1560R, 2393R, 2394R, 3108R, 3109R, 3828
Enright, D.J., 1917
Erades, P.A., 656R, 1248R, 2188
Erazmus, E.T., 1430
Erdmann, P.(H.), 575, 626, 927, 1070, 1219
Erickson, J.L., xxxi, 1431, 1432, 1433
Erickson, K., 928
Ericson, E.E., 256R, 415R, 1392R, 1434, 1435, 1436, 1437
Erlebach, P., 3677R, 3699R
Erzgräber, W., 2681
'Espinasse, M., 299R, 3014
Esser, J., 1191R
Evans, B., 160R
Evans, Dafydd, 2895R
Evans, D.A.H., 19R
Evans, R., 2189
Evans, W.W., Jr., 1712, 1713
Everett, D., 979R, 3015

Everitt, A., 3688
Ewen, C.H., 2423
F., G.W.S., 3133R
Faarlund, J.T., 1895R
Fabian, B., 2657
Fadda, A.M.L., 255R
Faeber, R., 2170R
Faiss, K., 176, 509R, 520R, 1585R, 1744R, 1926, 1983R, 2190, 2191, 2192, 2393R
Fanagan, J.M., 2829
Faraci, M.(E.), 350, 1438, 1439
Farish, J., 576
Farkas, D., 2758
Farrell, R.T., 3586
Faulkner, D.R., 725
Faull, M.L., 2193
Fausbøll, E., 929
Faust, G.P., 3016
Feist, R., 3017
Felder, E., 3697R, 3698R
Feldman, T.P., 2194
Fell, C.E., 2195, 2196, 2197
Fellows Jensen, G., 319R, 3424, 3425, 3426, 3484, 3485, 3486, 3487, 3488, 3489, 3490, 3491, 3492, 3493, 3505R, 3665, 3666, 3677R, 3699R
Felperin, M.P., 520R
Fenster, V., 9R
Fenton, A., 120R
Fernandez, F., 177
Ferris, S., 3667
Fettig, A., 3018
Fetting, H.F., 627, 930
Field, P.J.C., 3200, 3668, 3873, 3905R
Fiedler, F., 98R, 223R, 234R, 236R, 297R, 1450R, 1938R, 2746R, 3121R, 3794R
Fill, A., 158R
Finger, H., 1295R
Finkelstein, D., 3019
Finkenstaedt, T., 79, 130R, 211R, 1220
Finnie, W.B., 121R
Firbas, J., 1440, 1870R
Firchow, E.S., xxviii

Fischer, A., 924R, 2198
Fischer, E., 236R, 931, 932, 949R, 1127R, 3331R
Fischer, O.(C.M.), 1441, 1927
Fischer, W., 140R, 184R, 282R, 289R, 1914R, 1938R, 2199
Fisher, J.H., 48, 394, 395, 396, 542, 1771R, 3020, 3297R, 3883R
Fisher, J.L., 124
Fisher, J.R., 153R
Fisiak, J., xxviii, 6, 7, 153R, 204R, 293, 294, 397, 628, 726, 933, 934, 1143, 1560R, 1608R, 1714, 1800R, 3758, 3759, 3760
Flasdieck, H.(M.), 8R, 11R, 51R, 105R, 191R, 230R, 238R, 249R, 256R, 263R, 274R, 284R, 286R, 301R, 398, 399, 629, 694R, 698R, 727, 728, 889R, 935, 936, 937, 938, 949R, 1071, 1072, 1073, 1074, 1075, 1076, 1640R, 1928, 2200, 2201, 2202, 2203, 2204, 3021, 3258R, 3495R, 3777R
Fleck, E., 3022
Fleener, T.R., 1929
Fletcher, A.J., 2205
Flom, G.T., 11R, 256, 262R, 286R, 729, 733R, 1224R, 1323R, 1826R, 1913R, 1914R, 3091R, 3148R, 3267R, 3449R, 3494, 3604R, 3669, 3670R, 3794R
Fogelman, R.H., 2206
Fogg, W.F., 3023
Foley, J.M., 30
Foote, P.G., xxxi
Forsberg, R., 2207, 3495, 3496, 3497, 3498, 3499
Forsström, G., 1144
Förster, M., 730, 1077, 1078, 2208, 2209, 2210, 2211, 2212, 2213, 2214, 3500
Forsythe, R.S., 194R
Foster, F.A., 3024
Foster, R., 1221
Fosty, A., 178

Fourquet, J., 731, 1079, 1325R, 1442
Fowler, D.C., 1845R, 3025
Fowler, H.W., 81
Fowler, R., 218R, 3830
Fox, C., xxvi, 2271
Fox, H.S., 3505R
Francis, W.N., 165R, 377R, 577
Francovich Onesti, N., 480, 1145
Frank, R., xxvi, xxvii, 9R, 2215, 3850R
Frankis, P.J., 3026, 3027, 3028
Franson, J.K., 2216
Fransson, G., 3670
Franz, W., 234R, 1764R, 1945R
Frappier, J., 111R
Frary, L.G., 1443
Fraser, T.(K.H.), xxviii, 255R, 1444, 1930, 2217, 2218, 2219, 2220
Freeman, D.C., 197R, 198R, 200R
Freeman, L.H., 3761
French, W.H., 3671, 3762
Frey, E., 1931
Fricker, R., 1174R, 2787R
Fridén, G., 1715, 1716
Fried, V., xxxii
Friederici, H., 939
Friedrichsen, G.W.S., 81
Friend, A.C., 141R
Fries, C.C., 1222
Fries, U., 368, 481, 510R, 917R, 1717, 1718, 2415R, 3108R
Fröhlich, J., 1445
Fry, D.K., 9R, 49, 109R
Fucilla, J.G., 51R
Fujiwara, H., 1446
Fulcher, R., 976
Fulk, R.D., 2221
Füller, L., 1146
Fullerton, G.L., 1080
Fullmer, D.H., 1081
Funk, W.-P., 2327R
Funke, O., xxviii, 8, 249R, 251R, 274R, 1223, 1341R, 1342R, 1447, 1580R, 1629R, 1726R, 1800R, 2222, 2230R, 2655R, 3029, 3098R, 3831

G., C., 913R
G., J.H.G., 3397R
Gabrielson, A., 11R
Gade, K.E., 2223
Gage, P.C., 1719
Gaines, B., 54R
Gallup, W., 216
Galway, M., 3030, 3031
Ganguli, S., 3032
Garcia, E.C., 153R, 1147
Gardner, E.F., 1448
Gardner, T.(J.), 153R, 201R, 204R, 1560R, 2224, 2225, 2226, 3832
Garmonsway, G.N., 3851R
Gatch, M.M., 2284
Gates, J.E., 2282
Gattiker, G.L., 1449
Gburek, H., 125, 630, 1148
Geckeler, H., xxvi
Gehse, H., 1224
Geipel, J., 319
Geist, R.J., 3763
Gelling, M., 3425R, 3426R, 3437R, 3501, 3502, 3503, 3504, 3505, 3680R
Gerhard, G.B., 117, 3033
Gericke, B., 1036, 1082
Gerould, G.H., 3034, 3506, 3833
Gerritsen, J., 25R, 1841R, 1870R, 3035
Gerson, S., 1333R
Geschiere, L., 219R
Giffhorn, B., 940
Giffhorn, J., 732, 941
Gilbert, A.J., 3874
Gilbert, T.Mª., 190R
Gillam, D.M.E., 2227, 2228, 2229
Gillespie, G.T., 3427
Gillmeister, H., 3037, 3038, 3872R
Gilmour, J., 3039
Gilmour-Bryson, A., 3075
Gimson, A.C., 522R
Ginsberg, W.,3507
Gipper, H., 2404
Girvan, R., 92R, 98R, 257, 2230R
Gleissner, R., 1149
Glunz, H., 1392R, 1393R, 1450

Gneuss, H., 1R, 9R, 19R, 95, 117R, 134R, 141R, 218R, 338, 351, 450, 2230, 2231, 2232, 2233, 2234, 2561R
Godden, M.(R.), 9R, 268R, 334R, 2235
Goebl, H., 421R
Goedhals, B., 314R
Goedsche, C.R., 1225
Goepp, P.H., II, 2236
Goffart, W., 3508
Göhler, T., 733
Golden, J., 2237
Golden, S.A., 3040
Goldman, S.H., 1451, 1452, 1453, 1454
Göller, K.H., 2228R, 2229R, 3886
Golson, E.O., 578
González Escribano, J.L., 1720
Gonzo, S.T., 631
Goodman, J.S., 1721
Goodman, P., 153R
Goossens, L., xxxi, 734, 735, 1226
Gordon, E.V., 2263R, 3623R
Gordon, I.A., 3041, 3817
Görlach, M., 86R, 125R, 179, 287R, 292R, 304R, 315R, 368R, 421R, 482, 487R, 1052R, 1181R, 1295R, 1313R, 1943R, 2283R, 3007R, 3396R
Gottzman, C.L., 2238
Götz, D., 315, 1932
Gouet, M., 1381R
Gougenheim, G., 1217R
Gough, J.V., 1083, 2239
Gower, J.E.B., 3422
Gowers, E., 1980R
Goyvaerts, D.L., xxvii, 193R
Graband, G., 89R, 531R, 698R, 1039R, 1220R, 1980R, 2230R
Grad, A., 1227, 1722
Gradon, P., 58R, 288R, 290R, 509R, 520R, 579, 736, 1800R, 2240, 3818
Gramm, W., 2241
Grandinger, M.M., 2242
Grant, C.M., 737, 3042
Grattan, J.H.G., 243R, 1315R, 1913R, 3624R
Gray, D., xxvii, 121, 134R, 388

Gray, L.H., 1455, 3509
Green, Carleton, 3510
Green, D.C., 1456, 1457
Green, D.H., 2243
Green, H.A.C., 2769R
Green, M.F., 3875
Greenbaum, S., 322
Greene, C.(L.), 632, 2526R
Greene, J.L., 1458
Greene, R.L., 117
Greenfield, S.B., xxvi, 9, 168R, 1459, 1460, 2244
Greet, W.C.,103R
Grenzel, P., 19R
Gretsch, M., 121R, 264R, 299R
Greul, W., 1036, 1150
Griffhorn, J., 503R
Griffith, D.D., 50, 51, 3043
Grimshaw, J.B., xxviii, 1723
Grinda, K.(R.), 36R, 88R, 106R, 1933, 2076R, 2245, 2246, 2247, 2757R
Groom, B., 1934
Grootaers, L., 181R, 185R
Gross, L., 3044
Grosse, E., 526
Grotjahn, R., 3835
Groussier, M.-L., 1461
Grube, F.W., 2248, 2249
Gruber, L.C., 2250
Grumbach, D., 214R
Grüner, R., 2251
Grundt, A.W., 738
Grundy, G.B., 3511, 3512
Grzebieniowski, T., 211R
Gschwantler, O., 2351, 2352
Guerrieri, A.M., 1462, 1463
Guimier, C., 31
Guinn, L.E., 543
Gumbert, J.P., 580
Günther, V., 2252
Gurrey, P., 1612R
Gusmani, R., 455R, 732R, 2253
Gutch, U., 2254
Gutenbrunner, S., 2255
Guy, E.F., 314R

H., E.E., 3911R
H., G.B., 308R
Habicht, W., 67, 372R
Hacikyan, A., 1464
Haessler, L., 2256
Hagenbüchle, R., 509R
Hagerman, B.E., 14
Hahn, E.A., 1465
Haislund, N., 234
Hald, K., 739
Hall, J.R., 1466, 2257, 2258, 2259
Hall, John R.C., 96, 97
Hall, R.A., xxix
Hallander, L.-G., 271R, 2260, 2261, 2262, 2655R
Haller, R.S., 1249
Hallqvist, H., 740
Halvorson, N.O., 2263
Hamer, R. (F.S.), 581, 741, 1130R
Hammerschlag, J., 3045
Hamp, E.P., 1560R, 2264, 2265, 2266, 2267
Hamshere, J.D., 3516R
Handley, R., 407R
Hanham, A., 1684R, 3046
Hansen, B.H., 352
Hansen, K., 38R, 79R, 171R, 187R, 240R, 241R, 271R, 289R, 302R, 307R, 315R, 951R, 1950R, 1996R, 2393R
Hanson, R.P.C., xxvi
Harbert, B., 2268
Harbert, W., 1467
Harder, B.D., 1228
Harder, H., 2269, 2270
Harder, K.B., 3432R
Hardman, P., 2910R
Hargreaves, H., 314R, 3047, 3048
Harl, W., 742
Harley, M.P., 3672
Harlow, C.G., 524R, 544
Harmatiuk, S.J., 3834, 3835
Harmer, F.E., 168R, 2271, 3495R
Harris, B., 3269R
Harris, D.P., 633, 1724

Harris, J., 2272, 2273
Harris, R., 78R
Harsh, W., 1229
Hart, P., 400
Hart, T.E., 90R
Hartig, J., 2678
Harting, P.N.U., 260R
Hartmann, H., 1751R
Hartmann, R.R.K., xxix
Hartung, A.E., 20
Harvey, P.A., 3049
Hasler, J., xxvi
Hastings, G.S., Jr., 3876
Hatfield, J.T., 412, 2091
Hatto, A.T., 2274
Haugen, E., 2230R
Häusermann, H.W., 1725
Hausmann, R.B., 1230
Havely, N.R., 411R
Haworth, M., 3050
Haworth, P., 3051
Hayes, R., 1231
Hays, D.G., xxx
Heald, A.R.B., 743
Healey, A. diP., 109, 2008, 2120, 2275, 2276
Hedberg, J., 78R, 130R, 165R, 205R, 1084
Heidemann, G., 1085
Heilmann, L., 171R, 263R
Heinrich, H., 78R
Helbig, L., 2277
Helgander, J., 1232
Heller, L.G., 1037, 2278
Helming, E.M., 1468
Heltveit, T., 1038, 1039, 1469, 1470, 3052
Hench, A., 3053
Hendrickson, J.R., 2279
Héraucourt, W., 289R, 1817R, 1942R, 3054, 3055, 3186R, 3269R, 3370R
Herben, S.J., Jr., 3513, 3620R
Herdan, G., 3056
Herold, C.P., 1086
Herzog, P., 334R

Hess, H.H., 1471
Hetherington, M.S., 2280, 2281, 2282, 2283, 2284
Heuer, H., 1217R, 1323R, 1725R, 1726, 1764R, 3018R
Heusinkveld, A.H., 10
Hewitt, B.G., 1895R
Heyworth, P.L., xxvi, 582, 583, 3057
Hickey, R., 368R, 744, 745, 1472
Hieatt, C.B., 29R, 258
Hietsch, O., 1149, 2285
Higuchi, M., 3058
Hill, A.A., xxxii, 161R, 324, 942, 1049R, 1095R, 1715R, 1771R, 1855R, 3258R, 3305R, 3797R
Hill, B., 2286, 2287, 3428
Hill, J., 259, 2288
Hill, L.A., 1473, 1727
Hill, T.D., 86R, 2289
Hillard, R., 1474, 1475
Hille, A., 2290, 3059
Hillman, M.V., 3060
Hiltunen, R., 1233, 1234, 1235, 1935
Hinckley, H.B., 401
Hirtle, W.H., 2219
Hittmair, R., 1728, 1729
Hjelmslev, L., 154R
Hladký, J., 528R, 1236
Hlebec, B., 1936
Hoad, T.F., 264R, 309R, 1047R, 2291, 3061, 3872R
Hobar, D., 2282
Hock, H.H., 7R
Hockett, C.F., 746
Hodge, C.T., 1771R
Hodgson, P., 2466R
Hoekema, T., 2517
Hoenigswald, H.M., 332R
Hoffman, D., 353
Hoffman, D.L., 3062
Hoffman, R.L., 20R
Hoffmann, E., 2170R
Hoffmann, G., 1237
Hofmann, J., 2292
Hofstetter, W., 2293

Hogan, J.J., 320
Hogg, R.M., 638R, 651R, 747, 748, 749, 750, 751, 752, 753, 754, 755, 756, 792R, 877R, 1087, 3108R
Holden, A.J., 421R
Holland, J., 2294
Hollifield, H., 757
Hollmann, E.G., 1476
Hollowell, I.M., 2295, 3836, 3837
Holman, C.H., 3063
Holmes, U.T., Jr., 2296, 3064, 3402
Holoien, R.A., 360
Hols, E.J., 1238
Holthausen, F., 92R, 96R, 98, 99, 112R, 236R, 257R, 308R, 321, 533R, 681R, 758, 943, 1088, 1392R, 1937, 1942R, 1961R, 2297, 2298, 2299, 2746R, 3065, 3148R, 3449R, 3597R, 3599R, 3604R, 3631R, 3670R, 3682R
Holtsmark, A., 2446R
Homann, E.R., 1730
Hook, J.N., 180
Hooke, D., 3514, 3515, 3516
Hooper, A.G., 3764
Hoops, J., 10R, 140R, 2300, 2301, 2302, 2303, 2304
Hoops, R., 2305
Hopper, H.P., 2306
Horgan, A.D., 2307
Horgan, D.M., 451, 545, 2308, 3716
Horn, W., 174R, 282R, 944, 1188R, 1239, 1942R, 2309, 2310
Horner, P.J., 402
Hotchner, C.A., 2311
Houghton, H.S., 372R
Housman, J.E., 2787R
Howell, R.B., 759
Howlett, D.R., 2312, 3066
Howren, R., 1086R, 1089
Huang Do, M.T.-L., 52
Hubmayer, K., 760
Huchon, R., 181, 182, 207R, 1289R
Hudson, A., 20R, 403, 3067, 3068, 3769R, 3809R, 3883R
Huffines, M.L., 2313

Huganir, K., 3808R
Hughes, G.I., 3069, 3070
Hughes, K., xxxii
Hughes, S.E.S., 404, 405
Hughes, S.F.D., 166R
Hulbert, J.R., 192R, 194R, 248, 300R, 406, 415R, 416R, 1393R, 1443R, 2314, 2469R, 3071, 3072, 3186R, 3670R, 3673
Huld, M., 1385R
Hüllen, W., 1926R
Hulme, H.(M.), 3151R, 3809R, 3840R
Hülsmann, G., 1950R
Hultzén, L.S., 150R, 163R, 199R
Humbert, A.M., 3877
Hungerford, H.R., Jr., 1731
Hunt, T., 2315, 3073
Huntsman, J.F., 226R, 1732, 1733, 3074, 3075, 3076, 3077, 3078
Huppé, B.F., 3079
Hurnard, N.D., 3015
Hussey, M., 511
Hussey, S.S., 3905R
Hutson, A.E., 3638R, 3674
Hyldgaard-Jensen, K., 1041, 2980
Hynes-Berry, M., 3878
Iarovici, E., 183
Ikegami, M.T., 946
Ikegami, T., 45R
Ikegami, Y., 3080
Iker-Gittleman, A., 2895R
Immaculate, Sr. M., 3081
Ingargiola, N., 1151
Ingemann, F., 1452, 1733
Ingersoll, S.M., 1477, 1478, 2316
Ingham, P., 121
Ingram, E.G., 238R, 654R
Inman, E., 2403
Innes, E.R., 416
Irvine, A.S., 483, 1734, 1735
Irving, E.B., Jr., xxx
Irwin, B.J., 1240
Irwin, P.J., 3082
Iser, W., xxvii, 2847
Ito, E.T., 1736, 1737

Ivanova, I.P., 761
Ivy, G.S., 314R
Iwasaki, H., 1152, 1738
Izzo, H.J., xxix
Jack, G.(B), 484, 584, 1141R, 1153, 1241, 1739, 1740, 1741, 1742, 1743, 1873R
Jacobs, M.Y., 1800R
Jacobs, N. 2317, 2482R, 3083, 3675, 3676
Jacobs, R.A., 1191R
Jacobsen, B., 1191R
Jacobson, R., 1744
Jacobson, S., xxxi, 1242, 1260R, 1479
Jacobson, U., 520R
Jaeschke, K., 1938
Jambeck, T.J., 1243, 3879
Janda, R.D., 1040
Janelle, P., 251R
Jankowsky, K.(R.), xxxi, 2318
Jankuhn, H., 1933
Jazayery, M.A., 2052
Jansen, H., xxviii
Janzén, A., 3517, 3809R
Jember, G.K., 100, 101, 102
Jenkins, T.A., 3084
Jennings, L.G., 2319
Jespersen, O., 181R, 184, 223R, 234, 235, 947, 3085
Jiriczek, O.L., 2320
Johannesson, N.-L., 1244, 1745
Johannisson, T., 2321
Johansson, C., 3518, 3519
Johansson, (K.A.)S., 426, 1245
Johnson, J.A., 193R, 1480, 1746
Johnson, W.C., Jr., 2322
Johnston, E.C., 1747
Johnston, G.K.W., 290, 3086, 3087
Jolliffe, J.E.A., 2323
Joly, A., xxviii, 1246, 1247, 1481, 1748, 2219, 2324
Jones, A., 1424
Jones, C., xxvi, 295, 613, 634, 762, 763, 1369R, 1482, 1483, 1484, 1585R, 1749, 1750, 1756R, 3765

Jones, D.A.N., 78R
Jones, G., 2013R
Jönsjö, J., 3677
Jonsson, T., 3088
Jordan, R., 296, 297, 298, 299, 3388R
Jost, D., 941R
Jost, K., 98R, 452, 1164R, 1201R, 1382R, 1443R, 1450R, 1496R, 1764R, 1876R, 2013R, 2799R, 3388R
Jud, J., 417R
Jud-Schmid, E., 1751
Judson, L.S., 213R
Juilland, A.(G.), 32, 826
Jungandreas, W., 185
Juntune, T.W., 1080R
Juzi, G., 2325
K., A.R., 3089
Kaartinen, A., 1752
Kabell, A., 3090
Kacharu, B.B., 1710
Kageyama, T., 1485
Kahlas, L., 1486
Kahlas-Tarkka, L., 1487, 1488
Kaiser, R., 289R, 416R, 2655R, 3091, 3186R
Kalb, H., 3092
Kalifa, S., 172R, 173R
Källner, R., 3093
Kane, G., 417R
Kane, H., 193R
Kann, K., 1805
Kaplan, T.J., 3094
Karakida, S., 1753
Karlberg, G., 1248
Karlgren, H., 79R
Karlström, S., 3520
Karpf, F., 184R, 191R, 1196R, 1443R, 1693R, 1876R, 3374R
Karstien, C., 764
Kartschoke, D., 2326
Kaske, R.E., 2655R, 3095, 3521
Käsmann, H., 79R, 125R, 165R, 421R, 2655R, 3096, 3097, 3098, 3396R
Kastovsky, D., 1041, 1639R, 2063,

INDEX OF NAMES

2327, 2328, 2329
Kato, T., 126
Kaufman, T.S., 1017
Kay, C.(J.), 1918, 1939, 2595
Kean, P.M., 47R, 407R, 1771R
Keefer, S.L., 2330
Keel, W.D., 1249
Keenan, H., 49R
Keene, D.J., 3422
Keiser, G.R., 3099, 3880
Keller, R., 1202R, 1638R
Keller, W., 1042, 1090
Kellermann, G., 2331
Kellog, A.B., 485
Kellog, R.L., 5
Kelly, F.M., Jr., 948
Kelly, S., 3678
Kemmler, F., 102
Kennedy, A.G., 11, 12, 140, 194R, 234R, 257R, 1186R
Kent, R.G., 149R, 2013R, 3186R
Kenyon, B., 3100
Ker, N.R., 2332, 2333
Kerkhof, J., 486, 487
Kerling, J., xxvi, 295R, 2283R, 3101, 3102, 3103, 3838
Kern, J.H., 2334
Kerns, J.A., 1978R
Kesselring, W., 79R
Keyser, S., 765, 766, 1091, 1754
Khomiakov, V.A., 1489
Kieckers, E., 260
Kiessling, N.K., 2335
Kiffer, T.E., 1250
Kihlbom, A., 949, 1251, 2799R, 3104, 3105
Kijlstra, H.E., 3769R
Killough, G.B., 585, 586
Kilpiö, M., 1517R, 1941R
Kim, S., 587, 767, 768, 769, 770, 771
King, R.D., 950
Kingsmill, A., 29, 33
Kinkade, B.L., 3106
Kinneavy, G.B., 127
Kintgen, E.R., 3839
Kiparsky, P., 772

Kirby, I.J., 2336
Kirby, T.A., xxix, 118R, 495R, 3657
Kirch, M.S., 1252
Kirchner, G., 161R, 196R, 211R, 228R, 1581R, 1800R
Kirk, J.M., 179R
Kirschner, J., 2337
Kirsten, H., 3717
Kisbye, T., 186, 209R, 241R, 635, 773, 1220R, 1253, 1254, 1255, 1256, 1257, 1305R, 1341R, 1342R, 1343R, 1344R, 1369R, 1490, 1755, 1800R, 1814R, 3522, 3523, 3524
Kispert, R.J., 261
Kittner, H., 3107
Kivimaa, K., 951, 1756, 1757, 1758, 1759, 1760
Kjellmer, G., 407, 3108, 3109
Kjerrström, B., 488
Klaeber, F., 10R, 92R, 96R, 182R, 250R, 296R, 533R, 1285R, 1382R, 1450R, 1491, 1492, 1493, 1494, 1495, 2338, 2339, 2340, 2341, 2446R, 2666R, 2746R, 3597R
Klammer, T.P., 1761
Klar, K., 738
Klegraf, J., 2342
Kleman, M.M., 2343
Kleparski, G., 152R
Kliman, B.W., 3881
Klimek, Z., 3809R
Kline, E.A., 546, 588, 3766
Klingebiel, J., 1496
Kloss, R.J., 3110
Knapp, G.P., 685
Knapp, P.A., 3882, 3883
Kniezsa, V., 153R, 218R, 332R, 636, 774, 775, 776, 777, 952, 953, 954, 3767, 3809R
Knight, S.T., 3111, 3884
Knispel, E., 1258
Knott, T.A., 269, 1978R, 3112
Knowles, G., 649R
Knowlton, E.C., 416R
Knuth, A.M.L., 266R
Koban, C., 2344

Kobayashi, E., 1154
Koch, J., 50R, 1726R, 1764R, 3113
Koch, R., 1560R
Koch, W.A., 2896R
Kohl, N., 13
Kohler, K.J., 957
Kohonen, V., xxxi, 1259, 1260, 1261, 1497
Kökeritz, H., 143R, 670R, 944R, 955, 956, 2345, 3114, 3115, 3116, 3525, 3604R
Kolb, E., 271R, 2346, 2347
Kolinsky, M., 1762
König, E., 1262, 1940, 2348
Kooper, E.(S.), xxvi
Koopman, W.F., 638R, 778, 792R, 1263, 1498, 1550R
Korhammer, M., 2349, 3718
Korninger, S., xxxii, 1795
Koskenniemi, I., 1941, 3117, 3118
Kossick, S.G., 329R
Kottler, B., 128
Kotzor, G., 503R, 2350
Kovatcheva, M., 1763
Koziol, H., xxxii, 171R, 187, 209, 234R, 236, 271R, 409R, 656R, 733R, 779, 939R, 944R, 958, 1217R, 1264, 1289R, 1511R, 1560R, 1678R, 1711R, 1726R, 1764, 1765, 1766, 1817R, 1942, 1943, 2260R, 2655R, 2899R, 3018R, 3098R, 3119, 3120, 3186R, 3769R, 3809R
Krämer, P., 2351, 2352
Kranz, M., 2353
Krapp, G.P., 11R, 142, 188, 194R, 1913
Krebs, K., 3121
Kreidler, C.W., 1332R
Kretzschmar, W.A., Jr., 322
Krieg, M.(L.)F., 1944, 3122
Krishna, V., 3123
Kristensson, G., 152R, 299R, 314R, 407R, 589, 637, 780, 941R, 959, 960, 961, 962, 2354, 2355, 2356, 2357, 2358, 3124, 3429, 3430, 3505R, 3518R, 3679, 3680, 3681, 3710, 3768,
3769, 3770, 3771, 3772, 3773, 3809R
Kroesch, S., 2359, 2360
Krogmann, W., 2361, 2362, 2363, 2364, 2365, 2366, 2367, 2368, 2369, 2370, 2371, 2372, 2373, 2374, 2375, 2376, 2377, 2378, 2379, 2380, 2381, 2382, 2383, 2384, 2385, 2386, 2387
Kruisinga, E., 229R, 234R, 235R, 243R, 250R, 308R, 323, 354, 994R, 1186R, 1265, 1914R, 3388R
Krupatkin, Y., 781, 782, 783
Krutch, J.W., 199R
Kryger Kabell, I., 2388
Krzyszpień, J., 1266, 1499
Kubouchi, T., 1767
Kučera, H., 26R
Kühlwein, (H.A.)W., 1246R, 2190R, 2393, 2394, 2395, 2396, 3108R
Kuhn, H., 2389
Kuhn, O., 920
Kuhn, S.M., 82R, 106R, 129, 274R, 408, 489, 698R, 740R, 784, 785, 786, 787, 788, 1715R, 1841R, 2230R, 2390, 2391, 2392, 2466R, 2469R, 2475R, 3125, 3126, 3127, 3128, 3129, 3131, 3368R, 3719, 3720, 3769R, 3808R, 3809R, 3851R
Kuno, S., 1187
Kunsmann, P., 920
Kupetz, R., 1295R
Kurath, H., 129, 324, 963, 3130, 3131, 3809
Kurban, N., 325
Kurtz, G., 1500
Kurvinen, A., 11R
Kuryłowicz, J., 964
Kyes, R.L., 14
Kylstra, H.E., 2397
LaBrum, R.W., 1267
Ladd, C.A., 490, 2076R, 2655R
Lagerquist, L.M., 1501
Laing, M., 3790
Lalley, J.M., 200R
Lambert, E., 3132
Lambert, J.J., 3774

INDEX OF NAMES

Lambert, M., 1845R
Lance, D.M., xxx
Lane, G.S., 2398
Lange, H., 3148R
Langenfelt, G., 355, 409, 1768, 1769, 2399, 2400, 3133, 3526
Långfors, A., 184R
Lanzisera, F., 189
Lapidge, M., 338, 2401
Larsen, H., 112R, 270R, 1367R
Larsen, S.A., 3134
Lass, R., xxix, 510R, 638, 639, 789, 790, 791, 792, 965, 3432R
Lassaut, J., 1268
Last, R., 56
Last, W., 1945
Latendorf, M., 2190
Laur, W., 3482R, 3527, 3528
Lauttamus, T., 640
Law, V., 2402
Lawson, D.D., 1155
Lawson, S., 3135
Lawton, David, 930
Lawton, D.A., 1770, 3885
Leake, J.A., 1946
Leavitt, J.A., 2403
Lebow, D.B., 1269
Lebrun, Y., xxvi
Lecoy, F., 3200R
Lee, B.G., 491
Lee, B.S., 3749
Lee, D.W., 197R, 1771
Lehiste, I., 3529
Lehmann, R.P.M., 792R
Lehmann, W.P., 793, 794, 1092, 1502, 3136
Lehnert, M., 78R, 82R, 89R, 103, 114R, 125R, 160R, 228R, 262, 263, 280R, 301R, 303R, 314R, 454R, 455R, 740R, 944, 1156, 1270, 1342R, 1344R, 1616R, 1684R, 1800R, 2283R, 3697R, 3698R, 3699R
Lehto, L., 951
Leinbaugh, T.H., 29R
Leisi, E., 8R, 79, 1341R, 2404, 3137

Leith, D., 190
Lenaghan, R.T., 1947, 3138
Lendinara, P., 9R, 19R, 29R, 86R, 264R, 283R, 562R, 1218R, 1401R, 1661R, 2405, 2482R, 2825R
Lenerz, J., 1772
Leone, C., 480R
Leopold, W.F., 185R
Lerer, S., 156R
Lerner, L.D., 2406
Lester, M.P., 795
Levin, S.R., 26R, 288R, 1093, 1341R, 1343R, 1503, 1800R, 3711
Lewandowska, B., 219R, 247R, 1773, 1774, 1775,
Lewis, R.E., 129, 3139
Leyerle, J., xxvi, 53, 2407, 3306R
Li, C.N., 1618
Liberman, A.S., 966, 967
Lieber, R., 968
Liebermann, F., 2408, 2409, 2410, 2411, 3140
Liedholm, A., 969
Life, P.W., 54
Liggins, E.M., 1086R, 1504, 1505, 1506
Lightfoot, D.(W.), 1218R, 1271, 1272, 1273, 1776
Liljegren, S.B., 8R, 105R, 163R, 182R, 184R, 196R, 250R, 263R, 925R, 969R, 1156R, 1382R, 1600R, 1708R, 1942R, 3258R, 3597R, 3620R
Lindberg, C., 492, 2260R, 3141, 3799
Lindelöf, U., 191, 527, 3142, 3143
Lindeman, F.O., 2412
Lindemann, J.W.R., 2413, 2414, 2415
Lindkvist, K.-G., 1274, 1275, 2416
Lindström, B., 3144
Linke, G., 262R, 526R, 547, 796, 797, 1094, 1114R, 1496R, 1553R, 1677R, 1711R, 1817R, 2417, 2418, 2419, 2446R, 2579R, 3091R, 3092R, 3143R, 3145, 3240R, 3268R, 3269R, 3604R, 3670R, 3727R
Lipińska, M., 1744R
Lipka, L., xxix

Little, W., 81
Livingston, C.H., 3146, 3147
Llewellyn, E.C., 3148
Locherbie-Cameron, M.A.L., 268R
Lockwood, W.B., 798, 1948, 1949, 3149
Löfstedt, B., 1310R
Löfvenberg, M.T., 1084R, 1095, 2420, 2421, 3150, 3151, 3682
Logan, H.M., 493, 3775
Lohmander, I., 1950
Long, M.M., 1144R, 1157
Long, P.W., 120R
Longland, S., 2540
Loomis, R.S., 111R, 3683
Lotspeich, C.M., 144R, 194R, 1096, 1591, 2422
Loyn, H.R., 356
Lovelady, E.J., 1507
Lucas, P.J., 86R, 590, 591, 592, 2423, 3152, 3153, 3684
Ludlum, C.D., Jr., 2424
Lühr, R., 2425
Luick, K., 236, 296R, 415R, 2426, 3374R
Lumiansky, R.M., 196R, 2427, 2428, 3154
Lund, N., 3530
Lundquist, R.P., 100, 101
Lusignan, S., 2101, 2117
Luttrell, C.A., 3155, 3156, 3157
Lutz, A., 548, 549, 550, 732R, 2283R
Lyle, E.B., 3685
Lynch, E.D., 2429
Macaulay, R., 1978R
Maccaulay, M., 1940
MacDonald, Alasdair A., 372R
Macdonald, A[ngus], 118R, 120R, 196R, 270R, 300R, 301R, 418R, 1289R, 1367R, 3297R, 3305R, 3599R, 3638R, 3658R, 3659R
Maček, D., 194R, 1777
Macháček, J., 171R, 1276
Machan, T.W., 410, 411, 3158, 3159
Mack, P., 2910R
Mackenzie, B.A., 970, 971, 3776, 3777

Mackenzie, J.L., 1274R
Macleish, A., 1778
Macrae-Gibson, O.D., 3778, 3779
Macris, J., 148R, 1037
Madden, J.F., 104, 2430
Magers, M.K., 1277
Magnusson, U., 651R, 972
Magoun, F.P., Jr., 10R, 96R, 98R, 104, 105R, 130, 284R, 326, 494, 1157R, 1952, 2431, 2432, 2433, 3160, 3161, 3297R, 3368R, 3397R, 3464R, 3531, 3532, 3533, 3816R
Mahling, C., 973
Maisenhelder, K., 2434
Majut, R., 1953
Makkai, A., 595
Makovskij, M.M., 2415R, 2475R
Maling, J.M., 799, 1779
Malone, K., xxviii, 10R, 11R, 230R, 234R, 239R, 286R, 296R, 357, 412, 641, 666R, 740R, 800, 801, 974, 975, 1084R, 1097, 1144R, 1368R, 1508, 1509, 1711R, 2013R, 2435, 2436, 2437, 2438, 2439, 2440, 2441, 2446R, 2721R, 2766R, 3151R, 3162, 3163, 3297R, 3302R, 3500R, 3534, 3535, 3536, 3537, 3538, 3539, 3540, 3541, 3542, 3543, 3544, 3545, 3546, 3547, 3548, 3549, 3594R, 3596R, 3597R, 3624R, 3659R, 3682R, 3851R
Malsch, D.L., 642, 643, 802, 976
Manabe, K., 1278, 1510
Mandel, J., xxxii, 3164
Mann, G., 1279, 1511, 1855R
Mann, J., 123R
Mann, M.F., 184R
Manning, S., 49R
Mansion, J., 182R, 296R, 3624R
Manzalaoui, M.A., 3165
Marchand, H., 1220R, 1280, 1281, 1711R, 1780, 3098R
Marckwardt, A.H., xxviii, 105, 168R, 188, 192, 239, 264, 979R, 1043, 1098, 1282, 1824R, 1954, 2442, 2443, 2444, 2445

INDEX OF NAMES

Marcq, P., 1512
Marcus, H., 103R, 263R, 282R, 289R, 301R, 604R, 1036R, 1324R, 1616R, 1638R, 1764R, 1784R, 1798R, 1955, 2508R, 3091R, 3166
Marik, J., 3397R
Marino, C., 102R
Marino, M., 358
Markey, T.L., 14, 363R, 1158
Markman, A.M., 128
Marks, G., 3076
Markus, M., 190R, 413, 465R, 1845R, 3886
Marquardt, H., 2446
Marrack, C.M., 924R
Marshall, J., 3167, 3168
Martin, J.S., xxix
Martin, L.S., 3169, 3887
Martin, W., 79R
Martin, W.E., Jr., 55
Martorelli, M., 232R
Martz, O., 2447
Marynissen, C., 2448, 3677R, 3697R, 3698R, 3699R, 3771R
Masui, M., 495
Matheson, L.M., 3170, 3171, 3172, 3173
Mathews, M.M., 78R
Matsuda, T., 1513
Matsunami, T., 1283, 1514, 1515, 1516, 3174
Matthes, H.C., 8R, 161R, 250R, 297, 298, 462R, 977, 1084R, 1127R, 1144R, 1726R, 1751R, 1764R, 1784R, 2787R, 3017R, 3175, 3368R, 3594R, 3794R, 3797R, 3808R, 3851R
Matthews, W., 15, 978, 3176
Mausch, H., 1781
Mawer, A., 120R, 181R, 3550
Mayer, E., 650R, 655R, 1605R
Mazzuoli Porru, G., 265
McCalla, K., 803
McCarren, V.P., 3177
McCarthy, J., 198R
McCawley, N.A., 1284
McClean, R.J., 1782
McClure, J.D., 3007R

McClure, P., 3178, 3426R, 3505R, 3677R, 3686, 3688R, 3699R, 3780
McClusky, D., 26R
McColly, W., 414
McCord, L.R., 2449, 2450
McCormack, W.C., xxix
McCracken, R.E., 551
McCue, G.S., 644
McDavid, R.I., Jr., 148R, 153R, 199R, 3782
McGee, A.V.K., 3179
McGovern, D.S., 552
McGovern, J.F., 2451
McGowan, C., 2715
McIntosh, A., xxvii, 417R, 452R, 496, 497, 593, 594, 595, 980R, 1783, 1991R, 2957, 3180, 3181, 3258R, 3297R, 3687, 3769R, 3781, 3782, 3783, 3784, 3785, 3786, 3787, 3788, 3789, 3790, 3840
McJimsey, R.B., 979
McKelvey, R.L., 129
McKerrow, R.B., 11R
McKinley, R.A., 3688
McKnight, G.H., 194
McLaughlin, J., 1517
McLaughlin, J.C., 193, 218R, 804 980
McLintock, D.R., 2452
McMillan, J.T., 805
McNair, J.R., 2453
McNally, C.E., 1518
McNeal, J., 3505R
McRae, M.H., 1519
Measham, D.C., 195
Meech, S.B., 163R, 3091R, 3197, 3791, 3793
Mehl, D., 41R, 3818R, 3872R
Meid, W., xxx, 2170R, 2454
Meier, H.H., 120R, 466R, 486R, 651R, 980R, 1305R, 1784, 1785, 3101R, 3182, 3888, 3889, 3890
Meillett, A., 98R
Meissgeier, E., 1786
Meissner, P., 2455
Meling, K., 553
Mendilow, A.A., 515

Menner, R.J., 34, 140R, 296R, 740R, 1084R, 2456, 2457, 2458, 2459, 3183, 3184, 3721, 3722, 3792, 3808R
Meritt, H.D., 97, 503R, 1157R, 1285, 2460, 2461, 2462, 2463, 2464, 2465, 2466, 2467, 2468, 2469, 2470, 2471, 2472, 2473, 2474, 2475, 2476, 2477, 2478
Meroney, H.(M.), 1520, 1367R, 2466R, 2479, 2480, 2481
Mersand, J., 3185, 3186
Mertens-Fonck, P., 103R, 106, 147R, 454R, 522R, 1099, 1100, 3098R
Metcalf, A.A., 201R, 1787, 2482, 3841
Metes, G.S., 3842
Meyer, P.G., 64
Meyer, W., 2483
Mezger, F., 161R, 1044, 1159, 2484, 2485, 2486, 2487, 2488, 2489, 2490, 2491, 2492, 2493, 2494, 2495, 2496, 2497, 2498, 2499, 2500, 2501, 2502, 2503, 2504
Michelmore, D.J.H., 3516R
Micillo, V., 1521
Miedema, H.T.J., 2505, 3551
Miller, A.D., 290R
Miller, B.D.H., 156R, 158R, 1039R, 1220R, 1800R, 3187, 3188
Miller, M.Y., 2507
Millet, B., 3891
Milroy, J., 327, 645
Mills, A.D., 3189, 3190, 3191, 3505R
Mills, C.R., 2506
Millward, C.M., 1522
Mincoff, M.K., 237, 2508
Mindt, D., 131
Minkoff, H., 3843
Minkova, D., 242R, 981, 982, 983, 984, 985, 986
Mitchell, A.G., 3192
Mitchell, B., 9R, 33, 90R, 101R, 266, 267, 268, 359, 455R, 554, 1274R, 1369R, 1385R, 1401R, 1448R, 1517R, 1522R, 1523, 1524, 1525, 1526, 1527, 1528, 1529, 1530, 1531, 1532, 1533, 1534, 1535, 1536, 1537, 1538, 1539, 1540, 1541, 1542, 1543, 1544, 1545, 1546, 1547, 1548, 1549, 1550, 1580R, 1616R, 1788, 1789, 2113, 2509
Mitchell, J.L., 253R, 254R, 261R, 360, 498, 1286, 1551, 2403
Mittermann, H., 1790, 1791
Miyabe, K., 1552, 1792
Moessner, L., 218R, 304, 481R, 1130R, 1181R, 1218R, 1287, 1793, 3193, 3194
Mohr, E.V., 499
Molinari, M.V., 2510
Möllmer, H., 1553
Moloney, B., 3844
Mönkkönen, I., 29R
Monteser, F., 328
Moore, A.K., 3195, 3196
Moore, B., 2511
Moore, S., 238, 239, 269, 1160, 1161, 3197, 3793
Morgan, M.M., 3892
Morris, K.M., 1956
Morris, W.S., 2512
Morrisson, S., 2513, 2514, 2515
Morse, J.M., 222R
Moss, C., 3769R
Mossé, F., 8R, 51R, 81R, 98R, 161R, 184R, 196, 225R, 234R, 250R, 256R, 263R, 270, 284R, 300, 301, 302, 303, 462R, 531R, 740R, 829R, 1067R, 1084R, 1114R, 1157R, 1188R, 1224R, 1288R, 1289, 1368R, 1708R, 1711R, 1715R, 1794, 1795, 1991R, 2508R, 2769R, 2787R, 3198, 3258R, 3297R, 3305R, 3368R, 3604R
Most, S.M., 2516
Motherwell, G.M., 1101
Muinzer, L.A., 97R, 249R, 263R
Muir, (A.)L., 3199, 3893
Muir, E., 199R
Muir, M.A., 3200
Muller-Schwefe, G., 16
Mulryan, J., 25R
Munderloh, H., 500
Munske, H.H., 2517
Murison, D., 3201

INDEX OF NAMES 379

Murphy, M., 361
Murray, J.A.H., 80
Murtagh, D.M., 3202
Murtagh, M.B., 2518
Must, G., 2519
Mustanoja, T.F., 103R, 130R, 161R, 162R, 196R, 249R, 289R, 300R, 301R, 495R, 955R, 1061R, 1156R, 1290, 1305R, 1752, 1756R, 1757R, 1796, 1797, 1798, 1799, 1800, 1801, 1802, 1803, 1855R, 2520, 3203, 3204, 3205, 3258R, 3689, 3809R, 3894
Mutt, O., 1291, 1804, 1805
Myers, L.M., 197
Myrvaagnes, N.S., 3845
Nagucka, R., 7R, 1143R, 1292, 1293, 1294, 1554, 1555, 1556, 1557, 1778R, 1806, 1807, 1808, 1809, 1824R, 2415R
Nakao, T., 987, 988
Nakao, Y., 126R
Nakashima, K., 501, 1810
Nathan, N., 1811, 1812
Nattinger, J.R., 3895
Neckel, G., 3604R
Negro, P.G., 453
Nehls, D., 1295, 2850R
Nelson, V.C., 3896
Ness, L., 3897
Neuhaus, H.J., 2521
Neuman, E., 806
Nevanlinna, S., 1296, 1558, 3206, 3207
Newfield, M., 807
Newmark, L., 153
Ney, J.W., 808
Nichols, A.E., 1559, 2522
Nichols, P.H., 3208
Nicholson, L.E., 3209
Nickel, G., 187R, 1369R, 1560, 1561, 1800R, 2523
Nicolaisen, W.F.H., 3552, 3690, 3691
Nida, E.A., 1313R
Nielsen, H.F., 362, 363, 364, 809, 810, 3723, 3724
Niles, J.D., 3846
Nieuwint, P.J.G.M., 989

Nist, J.(A.), 198, 561R, 811
Nitze, W.A., 3692, 3693
Niwa, Y., 2524, 2525
Norman, F., 2170R
North, J.S., 2117
Northup, C.S., 140R, 1726R, 1764R
Norton-Smith, J., 3007R
Norwood, J.E., 3210
Nosek, J., 240R, 271R
Novelli, C., 3898
Nowakowski, M., 1575R, 2526
Nucciarelli, F.I., 265R
Nummenmaa, L., 1813, 1814
Oakden, J.P., 415, 416, 3186R
Oda, T., 107
O'Donoghue, B., 329R
O'Dwyer, P.F., 2527
Oehl, W., 2528
Öfverberg, W., 1162
Ogawa, H., 334R, 1562
Ogden, M.S., 129
Ogura, Michiko, 1563, 1564, 1565, 2529
Ogura, Mieko, 990
Ogilvy, J.D.A., 3818R
O'Grady, W.D., 1815
O'Hearn, C.J., 1816
Ohlander, S., 1950R
Ohlander, U., 132, 1248R, 1297, 1817, 1818, 1819, 1820, 1821
Oizumi, A., 17, 18, 479R
Okasha, E., 2530
O'Keeffe, K.O., 268R
Olds, B.M., 100, 101
Oliphant, R.(T.), 2531, 2532, 2533, 2534, 3211
Olmes, A., 3899
O'Loughlin, J.L.N., 249R, 3018R, 3091R
Olsan, L.T., 3847
Olsen, A.H., 2535
Olson, Y., xxvi
Olszewska, E.S., 3213, 3214, 3215, 3216, 3217, 3218, 3219, 3220, 3221, 3222, 3223, 3224, 3225, 3226, 3227
O'Neil, W.(A.), 646, 766, 772, 812, 813,

1045, 1091, 1566
O'Neill, P., 2536
Ong, W.J., 3212
Onions, C.T., 80, 81, 297R, 415R, 1957, 2537, 3228, 3229, 3230, 3231, 3232, 3233, 3234, 3235, 3236
Ono, S., 1550R, 1822, 1823, 2538, 2539
Oomen, U., 1401R, 1824R
Ordeman, D.T., 1567
Orr, J., 417, 3258R
Orrick, A.H., xxvii, 104R, 3553
Ortego, P.D., 3237
Orton, H., 941
Orton, P.R., 3238
Ørum, H., 715
Osborn, M., 2540
Osselton, N.E., 528R
Ostheeren, K., 2076R, 2170R, 2541, 3239
Otten, K., 1560R, 2655R
Otto, E., 1581R, 3240
Overholser, L.C., 2542
Owen, C.A., Jr., 1845R, 3872R
Owen, G.R., 2543
P., J.T., 836R, 2466R
Page, R.I., 93R, 266R, 365, 366, 503R, 555, 556, 1568, 2544, 2545, 2546, 2547, 2548, 2549, 2550, 2551, 2552, 2825R
Pak, T.-Y., 814, 815, 816
Palmatier, R.A., 1163, 1824
Palmer, C.E., 129
Palmer, R.E., Jr., 204R, 218R, 1575R
Palmgren, C., 3241, 3242
Palsson, H., xxvii
Pamp, B., 36R
Paoletti, L., 2895R
Papajewski, H., 2746R
Paradis, M., 349
Parker, F., 1102
Parker, R.E., 2553
Partridge, A.C., 329, 1825
Paschke, E., 1826
Pasicki, A., 1298
Patch, H.R., 34, 51R

Patton, P.C., 360
Pauchard, J., 165R
Paues, A.C., 2554
Payen, J.C., 3635
Pearce, T.M., 82R, 3554
Pearcy, R.J., 3243
Pearsall, D.(A.), xxviii, 20R, 429, 465
Pedersen, H., 2555, 2556
Peeters, C., 817, 1103, 1181R, 2157, 2557, 2558
Pei, M., 199, 200
Peinovich, M.P., 1046, 1047
Peitz, A., 3794
Peteret, D.A.E., 2559
Peltola, N., 1299, 1569, 1570, 2560
Penhallurick, J.M., 1104, 1571
Pennanen, E.(V.), 1983R, 3244
Penttilä, E., 2348R, 2561, 3245
Penzl, H., 152R, 161R, 162R, 462R, 770R, 818, 819, 820, 944R, 3143R, 3269R
Perelman, L., 2983
Perrelet-Bridges, M., 271R
Peters, G., 1828
Peters, H., 268R, 3246, 3555, 3556
Peters, M., 1033R
Peters, R.A., 86R, 151R, 201, 502, 821, 1048, 1105, 1106, 1608R, 2562, 2563, 2564
Peterson, P.W., 3725
Perrott, A.M.J., 3426R
Pervaz, D., 1827
Peverett, M., 3247
Pezzini, D., 202, 314R
Pflaum, M., 2245R
Pfleiderer, J.D., 133, 135
Pflueger, S.M.V., 1572
Pheifer, J.D., 503
Phelan, W.S., 502R, 3248, 3249
Philippson, E.A., 2787R
Phillipps, K.C., 218R, 314R, 479R, 486R, 1343R, 1344R, 1671R, 1756R, 1829, 1830, 1831, 1832, 1833
Phillips, B.S., 647, 648, 792R, 822, 823, 824, 825, 991, 1047R

Phillips, M.J., 2565
Phythian-Adams, C.V., 3505R
Pickford, C.E., 56
Pierce, J.E., 200R
Pilch, H., 271, 272, 303, 367, 644R, 826, 827, 1573, 1574, 1600R, 1616R, 1800R, 1855R, 1958, 1959, 2348R, 2566, 2567, 3250, 3251
Pillsbury, P.W., 1575, 2568
Pinsker, H.(E.), 240, 241, 368, 1560R
Pirkhofer, A., 1834
Pisani, V., 8R, 196R, 300R, 1581R, 1800R
Plank, F., 2569
Ploegstra, R.A., 3557
Plomer, W., 3816R
Ploss, E., 2170R
Plotkin, V.J., 201R
Plotkin, V.Y., 649, 992
Počepcov, G.G., 244R
Pogatscher, A., 3558
Polomé, E.C., 1084R, 2230R, 3297R, 3797R
Pons, E., 666R, 1289R
Pontifex, E.L., 3252
Pope, J.C., 2570, 2571
Popp, M., 307R, 917R, 1853R
Post, T.C., 1576
Potter, S., 78R, 147R, 159, 161R, 203, 211R, 234R, 288R, 471R, 979R, 1084R, 1114R, 1157R, 1220R, 1248R, 1300, 1301, 1305R, 1341R, 1342R, 1343R, 1367R, 1560R, 1715R, 1942R, 1960, 2013R, 2260R, 2446R, 3143R, 3253, 3254, 3269R, 3297R, 3370R, 3597R, 3620R, 3747R, 3769R
Pottle, F.A., 2572
Pound, L., 11R
Poussa, P., 330, 993, 1577
Premsingh, S.K., 1129
Preston, M.J., 133, 134, 135
Preston, P., 1855R
Preusler, W., 229R, 234R, 260R, 1039R, 1302, 1303, 1323R, 1511R, 1553R, 1581R, 1612R, 1725R, 1784R, 1817R, 1828R, 1835, 1836, 1945R, 3268R, 3670R
Prewitt, T., 1107
Price, H.T., 418, 1157R, 1771R, 3297R, 3368R, 3682R
Price, J., 2573, 2574
Prince, E.F.M., 3614
Prince, H.T., 3151R
Prins, A.A., 8R, 161R, 174R, 234R, 250R, 282R, 289R, 300R, 462R, 650, 651, 733R, 740R, 944R, 994, 995, 996, 997, 1003R, 1324R, 1341R, 1342R, 1343R, 1375R, 1600R, 1771R, 1991R, 2561R, 2787R, 3098R, 3151R, 3255, 3256, 3257, 3258, 3259, 3260, 3261, 3262, 3263, 3297R, 3368R, 3659R, 3797R, 3808R, 3851R, 3911R
Proctor, J.W., 3795
Prokosch, E., 273, 1108
Prudent, R., 369
Pullum, G.K., xxvii
Purdy, D.W., 1578
Pyles, T., 204, 205, 206, 828, 955R, 1980R, 3264
Quick, A., 53
Quinn, J.J., 2575, 2576
Quirk, R., xxx, 8R, 103R, 105R, 161R, 196R, 184, 203R, 274, 284R, 301R, 740R, 787, 788, 1095R, 1109, 1144R, 1248R, 1445R, 1579, 1580, 1638R, 1751R, 1771R, 1869, 2230R, 2561R, 2577, 2910R, 3265, 3266, 3659R, 3817
Raben, J., 3076
Rainbow, R.S., Jr., 46R, 504
Raiter, G.W., 505
Raith, J., 98R, 161R, 681R, 1114R, 1581, 1961
Ramsay, R.L., 3559
Rankin, J.W., 2446R
Rantavaara, I., 1837
Rau, F., 282R
Rau, R., 998
Rauch, I., xxx, 2578

Rauh, H., 2579
Raw, B.(C.), 47R, 275, 2580
Reaney, P.H., 999, 1000, 3431, 3432, 3560, 3694, 3777R, 3796
Rebsamen, F.R., 1838
Recktenwald, R.P., 1304
Redbond, W.J., 2581, 2582, 2583
Reddick, R.J., 91R, 1582, 1583, 1584, 2584
Redin, M., 234R
Redwine, B., 2585
Reed, A.W., 418R
Reed, C.E., 1581R, 1638R, 2230R
Reed, D.W., 1049, 1144R, 2446R
Reevers, J., 531R, 1980R
Regnier, C., 3635
Reibel, D.A., 2586
Reichl, K., 114R, 1839
Reidy, J., xxviii, 117R
Reinhard, M., 2587
Reinhardt, W., 1281R
Reiss, E., 372R
Relihan, M.P., 506
Rennhard, S., 1840
Renoir, A., 244R
Reszkiewicz, A., 251R, 274R, 276, 277, 278, 288R, 294R, 829, 830, 831, 1341R, 1369R, 1585, 1586, 1841
Reteleweska, T., 1587
Rettger, J.F., 1164
Reuter, O., 1842, 3267, 3268, 3269
Revard, C., 3270
Reynell, A., 1144R
Reynolds, H., 199R
Rice, R.C., 2588
Richards, Melville, 3561
Richards, Michael D., 832
Richardson, M., II, 419, 420
Richey, M.F., 2125R
Richman, G., 3848
Richter, M., 421, 422
Rickenbach, M., 3271
Riddle, E.M., 1962
Riehle, W., 423, 2589
Riffer-Maček, D., 1588
Rigby, M., 254R

Rigg, A.G., 141R, 3272
Ringbom, H., xxvii, 1488, 2393R, 2394R
Ringler, R.N., 253
Rioux, R.N., 3273
Rissanen, M., 9R, 268R, 334R, 1814R, 1305, 1306, 1307, 1310R, 1488, 1589, 1590, 1591, 1684R
Ritter, O., 833, 2590, 3495R
Rizzo, C., 268R, 1130R, 1517R
Roach, B.V., 136
Robb, K.A., 834
Robbins, R.H., 40R, 46R, 450R
Robbins, S.W., 1168, 1592
Robins, R.H., 1996R
Roberge, P.T., 14, 263R, 1080R
Roberts, J., 268R, 334R, 1593, 2591, 2592, 2593, 2594, 2595
Roberts, R.J., 35
Roberts, W.J.F., 1843
Robertson, D.W., Jr., 955R, 3274
Robertson, S., 207, 208, 3275
Robinson, F.C., xxviii, 9, 19, 25R, 78R, 109R, 268, 450R, 1594, 1941R, 1963, 2283R, 2482R, 2587R, 2596, 2597, 2598, 2599, 2600, 3426R, 3562, 3563, 3564, 3565, 3849, 3850
Robinson, M., 137
Roe, H.A., 2601
Rogers, H.L., 2602
Rogers, P.(W.), 141R, 3818R
Rohr, A., 1127R
Rohrer, C., 1560R
Romaine, S., 1001, 1308, 1844, 1895R, 1964
Rønberg, G., 507, 596, 3276
Root, R., 148R
Rooth, E., 1050
Roscow, G.H., 1845
Rosenberg, B.A., xxxii, 2170R, 2603
Rosenborough, M.M., 305
Rosier, J.L., xxix, 88R, 89R, 106R, 264R, 2076R, 2604, 2605, 2606, 2607, 2608, 2609, 2610, 2611, 2612, 2613, 2614, 2615, 2616
Rositzke, H.A., 370, 3566

Ross, A.S.C., 279, 340, 446, 539R, 557, 558, 652, 835, 836, 837, 838, 839, 1061R, 1110, 1111, 1112, 1113, 1114, 1115, 1116, 1117, 1118, 1119, 1120, 1121, 1122, 1123, 1124, 1595, 1965, 1966, 1967, 2187, 2617, 2618, 2619, 2620, 2621, 2622, 2623, 2624, 2625, 2626, 2627, 2628, 2629, 2630, 2631, 2632, 2633, 2634, 2635, 2636, 2637, 2638, 2639, 2640, 2641, 2845, 3277, 3278, 3279, 3280, 3281, 3282, 3283, 3284, 3285, 3286, 3567
Ross, T.W., 138, 3287, 3288, 3289
Rossi, S., 450R
Rot, S., 280, 952, 1309
Rothwell, W., 424, 3290
Roucaute, D., 3291
Rousse, J., 840
Rowland, B., xxxi, 46R, 3818R
Rowley, T., 3502
Royster, J.F., 11R, 140R
Rubin, S., 3797
Rubke, H., 2642
Rudanko, (M.)J., 1596, 1597
Rudolph, R.S., 2643
Rudskoger, A., 2896R, 3109R
Rumble, A., 3505R, 3568
Rupp, H.R., 3292
Russ, J.R., 3293
Russell-Smith, J., 3294, 3295
Russom, G.(R.), 1381R, 1846, 2825R
Russom, J.H., 1598
Ruud, M.B., xxviii, 50R, 207R, 234R, 238R, 243R, 1165, 3186R
Ryan, J.S., 78R
Ryan, W.M., 3296
Rybarkiewicz, W., 1599
Rydén, M., xxxi, 1310, 1311, 1847
Rydland, K., 841
Rygiel, D., 3900
Rymut, K., 3572
Rynell, A., 218R, 274R, 1445R, 1600, 1751R, 1784R, 1848R, 2230R, 3297, 3298, 3299, 3300, 3301, 3797R
Rypins, S.I., 3726

S., R., 223R
Sabatini, R.N., 1312
Saitz, R.L., 1601
Sale, A., 1817R
Salmen, H., 3727
Salminen, T.F., 174R
Salmon, V., 425, 528R, 1825R, 1968
Salter, F.M., 3302
Salu, M., 3303, 3304, 3586
Salus, P.H., 509R, 1608R, 2644, 2645
Samuels, M.L., xxix, 8R, 9R, 93R, 165R, 249R, 263R, 284R, 310R, 331, 332, 465R, 597, 741R, 842, 1061R, 1217R, 1305R, 1368R, 1375R, 1602, 1798R, 1800R, 1849, 1969, 1970, 1971, 2415R, 2646, 3297R, 3304, 3712, 3788, 3790, 3798, 3799, 3800, 3801, 3802, 3803, 3809R
Sand, D.B., 78R
Sandahl, B., 1002, 3305, 3306, 3307
Sanderlin, G., 2647
Sandgren, F., xxxii
Sandred, K.I., xxxii, 1972, 3569, 3570, 3571, 3572, 3697R
Sands, D.B., 12, 598
Sandved, A.O., 426, 427, 508, 509, 510, 1603
Sauer, H., 334R, 1052R, 2648, 2802R, 3308
Savage, H.(L.), 118R, 416R, 3309, 3310, 3311, 3312, 3313, 3314, 3315
Savory, T.H., 1973
Sawyer, P.H., xxxi
Scaffidi Abbate, A., 1604, 2649
Scaglione, A., 382
Scargill, M.H., 843
Scattergood, J., 2696
Schaar, C., 452R, 2650, 3808R, 3851, 3872R
Schabram, H., xxvii, 97R, 162R, 240R, 241R, 263R, 503R, 1965R, 2190R, 2260R, 2651, 2652, 2653, 2654, 2655, 2656, 2657, 2658, 2659, 2660, 2661, 2662, 2663, 2664
Schaefer, U., 304

Schäfer, J., 1974, 2846R, 3007R, 3316
Scheffer, J., 1313, 1560R
Scheler, M., 179R, 732R, 1560R, 1605, 1975, 1976, 3317
Schelp, H., 2655R, 2665, 3318
Schendl, H., 693R, 844, 3319
Schentke, M., 1220R, 2260R, 2655R, 3769R
Scheps, W., 3320
Scherer, G., 2666
Scherer, P., 1606
Scheurweghs, G., 161R, 196R, 300R, 1039R, 1095R, 1220R, 1800R
Schibsbye, K., 209, 234, 2667
Schirmer, W.F., 50R
Schlauch, M., 163R, 210, 211, 288R, 495R, 3901, 3902, 3903
Schlepper, E., 1977
Schlutter, O.B., 2668, 2669, 2670, 2671, 2672, 2673, 2674, 2675, 2676
Schmeja, H., xxx
Schmidt, A.V.C., 599, 2910R, 3321
Schmidt, Deborah A., 1314
Schmidt, Dieter, 1850
Schmidt, G., 212
Schmidt, U., 1003
Schmidt, W., xxvii, 1942R
Schmidt-Hidding, W., 161R, 263R, 1156R
Schmierer, R.J., 845
Schmitt, L.E., 272
Schmitz, G., 2910R
Schmoock, P., 2677, 2678
Schneider, K., 232R, 539R, 556R, 559, 944R, 1039R, 1442R, 2230R, 2679, 3677R, 3698R, 3699R
Schnetz, J., 3573, 3574
Scholler, H., xxviii
Schram, O.K., 112R
Schröder, E., 3449R, 3575, 3576, 3577
Schröder, F.R., 2446R, 3121R, 3604R
Schroeder, E., 3604R
Schubel, E., 3297R
Schubel, F., 263R, 846, 1445R, 1715R, 1751R, 1784R, 2680, 2681, 3808R, 3851R
Schubiger, M., 1961R
Schücking, L.L., 81R, 2682
Schultz, Manfred, 847
Schultz, Muriel R., 1607
Schulze, W., 2683
Schützeichel, R., 2245R, 3528
Schwab, U., 2165
Schwake, H.P., 491R
Schwammberger, E., 2684
Schwartz, E., 3578
Schwentner, E., 2325R, 2685, 2686, 2687
Scott, A.F., 139
Scott, C.T., xxxi, 653
Scott, F.S., 848
Scott, H.F., 213
Scott, J.R., 1051
Scragg, D.G., 528, 532, 849, 2688, 2689
Sebeok, T.A., 437
Sedgwick, W.B., 3322
Seebold, E., 732R, 1125, 1126, 2690, 2691
Seeling, F., 1127
Sehrt, E.H., 2125R
Seiffert, L., 266R
Seltén, B., 3695, 3696, 3697, 3698, 3699, 3769R
Senff, H., 1166
Serjeantson, M.S., 666R, 850, 931R, 1004, 1005, 1036R, 1164R, 1978, 1979, 3267R, 3323, 3804, 3805, 3806
Setzler, E.B., 281
Setzler, E.L., 281
Setzler, H.H., 281
Seuren, P.A.M., 1246R
Severs, J.B., 20
Severynse, M., 2692
Seymour, M.C., 600, 980R, 1151R, 1560R, 3809R, 3850R
Seymour, R.K., 36
Shaheen, A.-R., 3852
Shalvi, A., 515
Shannon, A., 1608
Shaw, J.D., 3324

INDEX OF NAMES 385

Sheard, J.A., 529, 1980, 3258R
Sheehy, E.P., 9R
Sheets, L.A., 3853
Sheldon, E.K., 1006
Shepherd, G., 1039R, 1248R
Shields, K., Jr., 1128
Shipley, J.T., 82, 214
Shippey, T.A., 121R, 1550R
Shook, L.K., 88R, 2693, 2694
Shores, D.L., 253R, 428, 1388R, 1401R, 1851, 1852, 1853, 2415R
Short, D.D., 57, 1609
Short, I., 421R
Sievers, E., 282, 283, 1981, 2695
Siewert, U., 303
Sihler, A.L., 851, 1982
Sikora, R., 293R, 980R
Silber, P., 3579
Silvertsen, E., 347
Silvestre, H., 524R
Simko, J., 263R, 333, 509R, 1585R, 1841R, 1854, 1855, 1856
Simmonds, P., 2696
Simmons, A., 3325
Simon, J.R., 509R, 852, 1305R, 1778R
Simon-Vandenbergen, A.M., 1857, 1858
Simpson, D.W., 1610
Simpson, J.A., 3326
Singh, P., 1129
Siporin, R.L., 1859
Sisam, C., 274R, 334R, 450R, 562R, 1661R, 3327, 3328, 3329
Sisam, K., 2697, 3330, 3728
Sklar, E.S., 3807
Sklute, L.M., 2698
Skydsgaard, N.J., 3817R
Sledd, J., 153R, 1333R, 1715R, 2699
Slettengren, E., 853, 3331, 3332
Slover, C.H., 3580
Small, G.W., 1315, 1437R, 1611, 1612, 1613, 1614, 1817R
Smart, V., 3581, 3582, 3583
Smeaton, B.H., 3709R
Smetana, C., 467

Smith, A.B., 108
Smith, A.H., 96R, 415R, 1127R, 1167, 1450R, 1725R, 2666R, 3584
Smith, E.C., 37, 1316, 3677R, 3698R, 3699R
Smith, Colin, 3585
Smith, C.C., 3333
Smith, G.C.M., 1728R
Smith, G.G., 2700
Smith, H.L., Jr., 192R, 2701
Smith, J.J., 429, 3803
Smith, L.P., 215
Smith, Merete, 3334
Smith, M.E., 1011
Smith, P.H., Jr., 89, 90
Smith, Robin, 1031R
Smith, Roger, 2702
Smith, R.A., 3624R
Smith, R.M., 836R, 843R
Smithers, G.V., 112R, 416R, 430, 1007, 1367R, 2703, 3151R, 3335, 3336, 3337, 3620R
Smyser, H.M., 1860
Snortum, N.K., 1861
Snouffer, E.J., 1862
Snyder, L.L., 3729
Söderholm, T., 1031R
Sokolova, M.N., 2704
Soland, M., 2705
Soliño, J.S.G., 177R, 431, 432
Solo, H.J., 2706, 1615
Somerset, R.D.-N., 654
Sommerfelt, A., 161R
Sonnenschein, E.S., 234R
Sørensen, K., 78R, 1310R, 1317, 1318
Spamer, J.B., 1319, 3854
Spargo, J.W., 3338, 3339
Sparke, W., 216
Spearing, A.C., 511
Specht, F., 2707
Speedie, D.C., 854
Spencer, H., 3340
Spindler, R., 2666R
Spitsbardt, H., 2896R
Spitzer, L., 1863, 3341, 3342

Spolsky, E., 2708
Sprengel, K., 1926R, 1983
Sprockel, C., 454, 455
Spufford, P., 2895R
Squires, A., 295R, 560
St. Clair, R., 1031R
Stahl, L., 1864
Staines, D., 2910R
Standop, E., 240R, 241R, 251R, 1061R, 1220R, 1324R, 1325R, 1341R, 1342R, 1560R, 1616, 1684R, 1751R, 1798R, 1965R, 2327R, 2393R, 2896R
Standop, S., 162R
Stanley, E.G., xxvii, 7R, 9R, 46R, 85R, 89R, 90R, 97R, 104R, 106R, 107R, 108R, 109R, 120R, 125R, 141R, 158R, 162R, 208R, 236R, 241R, 268R, 288R, 290R, 450R, 481R, 495R, 512, 503R, 561, 855, 944R, 946R, 1141R, 1234R, 1464R, 1478R, 1550R, 1605R, 1644R, 1661R, 1686R, 1751R, 1784R, 1984, 1993R, 2081R, 2086R, 2230R, 2245R, 2283R, 2337R, 2393R, 2415R, 2482R, 2541R, 2587R, 2655R, 2709, 2710, 2711, 2712, 2713, 2714, 3246R, 3258R, 3343, 3344, 3418R, 3437R, 3586, 3680R, 3818R
Stanley, J.P., 1168, 2715
Stanzel, F.K., xxviii
Stapelkamp, C., 2716, 3345
Stark, D., 1130
Staun, J., 856, 857
Staedman, J.M., Jr., 949R, 3346
Štech, S., 2717
Steever, S.B., 1284
Stein, G., 38, 78R, 1932R, 3347
Steinberg, C.(B.), 1985, 3587, 3700
Steinki, J., 1865
Stemmler, T., 655
Stene, A., 656
Stenton, F.M., 3588, 3589, 3590, 3591, 3592, 3620R
Stephan, F., 450R
Stephens, J., 3818R

Stephenson, E.A., 539R
Steponavičius, A., 858, 859
Stern, G., 1008, 1914R, 2718, 2719
Stettner, L., 3121R
Steuernagel, K., 2720
Stevens, D., 86
Stevens, J., 117R
Stevens, M., 513, 514
Stevenson, J.A.C., 120
Stevick, R.D., 217, 294R, 314R,, 601, 1169, 1517R, 1853R, 1866
Stewart, A.H., 1131, 1320, 1617
Stewart, G.R., Jr., 3348, 3593
Stibbe, H., 2721
Stieve, E., 3349
Stiles, P.(V.), 680, 860, 3350
Stillwell, G., 418R
St-Jacques, R., 20R
Stobie, M.M.R., 1170
Stockwell, R.P., 657, 658, 861, 862, 863, 864, 865, 1009, 1010, 1011, 1012, 1013, 1321, 1618, 1841R
Stokes, M., 3904
Stone, R.K., 3905
Stones, M.A., 2895R
Storms, G., 232R, 249R, 263R, 454R, 866, 1014, 1313R, 1322, 1585R, 2655R, 3351, 3594
Strachan, L.R.M., 2722, 2723, 3595
Stracke, J.R., 2724, 2725, 2726
Strang, B.M.H., 78R, 158R, 218, 226R, 1052R, 1986, 2727
Straus, J., 2728, 2729
Strauss, O., 1619
Strickland, E.C., 3352
Strite, V.L., 2730, 2731
Strnadová, Z., 1274R
Stroh, F., 2746R
Strohm, P., 3353
Strøjer, L., 867
Ström, H., 3596
Stroud, T.A., 3872R
Stryker, W.G., 106R, 2732, 2733
Stuart, C.I.J.M., 2734
Stuart, H., 2735, 2736, 2737, 2738

INDEX OF NAMES

Stuip, R., 1631
Sturtevant, A.M., 1315R
Sturtevant, E.H., 1315R
Stürzl, E., 263R
Subbiondo, J.L., 156R
Suchan, E., 64
Suerbaum, U., 2657
Suggett, H., 433
Sullivan, S., 125R
Sundby, B., 160R, 509R, 917R, 1003R, 1015, 1744R, 1867, 1868, 2739, 3354, 3355, 3368R, 3701, 3808, 3809, 3810
Sundén, K.F., 3356, 3357, 3358, 3359, 3360
Süsskand, P., 1323
Suter, K., 1324
Sutherland, R.C., 2740
Suzuki, E., 1873R, 3361, 3362, 3363
Svartvik, J., 407R, 1869
Svoboda, A., 2393R
Swaen, A.E.H., 96R, 98R, 184R, 257R, 2666R, 2741, 2742, 2743, 2744, 2745
Swan, T., 1620
Swanton, M.J., 3702
Sweet, H., 284
Świeczkowski, W., 1870
Syrochvatova, V.P., 870
Szarmach, P.E., 1506
Szogs, A., 92R, 733R, 2508R, 2666R, 2746
Szwedek, A., 276R, 1401R, 2063
Taglicht, J., 515, 3364
Tajima, M., 1871, 1872, 1873, 1874
Takahashi, S., 871
Talentino, A.V., 2747, 2748
Tandy, K.A., 1621
Tatlock, J.S.P., 140, 3186R, 3906
Tatton-Brown, T., 3505R
Taylor, A.B., 1016
Taylor, A.R., 539R
Taylor, J., 434
Taylor, M.V., 1622
Taylor, P.B., 271R, 2749, 2750, 3818R
Tejada, P., 1381R

Tellier, A.R., 171R, 219, 251R, 263R, 613R, 651R, 1325, 1448R, 1616R, 1684R, 1800R
Temple, W.M., 2751
Templeton, J.M., 114R
Tengstrand, E., 1008R, 1623, 3365, 3597, 3598, 3703
Tengvik, G., 3599
Terasawa, J., 1326, 1624
Terasawa, Y., 21, 22, 39, 1875, 3907
Terrebonne, R.A., 872
Tester, S.K., 3366
Thacker, A.T., 2752
Thomas, C.K., 192R
Thomas, R., 1327, 1328
Thomason, S.G., 1017
Thompson, L.S., 78R
Thomson, R.L., 259, 1033R, 2641, 2753, 2754, 2755
Thomson, S.H., 602
Thornburg, L.L., 1329, 1330
Thornston, K.C., 360
Thun, N., 1987, 3367
Thuresson, B., 3368
Tilander, G., 3369
Tilgner, E., 3370
Tilling, R.M., xxvi
Tillman, N.P., 1018
Timmer, B.J., 105R, 250R, 282R, 452R, 1445R, 1553R, 1581R, 1616R, 1625, 1626, 1784R, 2756, 3840R, 3851R
Tinkler, J.D., 2757
Todd, R., 3889
Tolkien, J.R.R., 435, 436, 3371, 3372, 3373
Toll, J.M., 308R, 3374
Toon, T.E., 873, 874, 875, 876, 877, 2758, 2759
Toor, S.D., 3819
Topliff, D.E., 1171
Toppen, W.H., 25R
Torkar, R., 2760, 2797R
Toth, K., 29R, 85R, 2761
Touster, E.K., 878

Townsend, B., 3375
Trahern, J.B., Jr., 90R, 151R, 261R
Traugott, E.C., 1143R, 1331, 1332, 1388R, 1575R, 1639R, 1744R, 1824R, 1940
Tremaine, H.P., 2762
Tripp, R.P., Jr., 100, 101
Tristram, H.L.C., 493R
Trnka, B., xxxii, 196R, 270R, 288R, 879, 880, 944R, 1019, 1020, 1021, 1144R, 1560, 1800R, 1855R, 1876, 2763
Trudgill, P., 327
Trusler, M., 516
Tucker, S.I., 79R, 155R, 3376, 3377, 3817R
Turner, G.W., 1333R, 3817R
Turner, K., 1627
Turville-Petre, G., xxix, 3008
Turville-Petre, Joan, 556R, 3378
Turville-Petre, J.E., 603
Turville-Petre, T., 3379
Tuso, J.F., 2764, 2765
Twomey, M.W., 90
Tysdahl, B., 426
Ueda, M., 1877
Ufimzewa, A.A., 1988
Uhler, K., 2766
Ullmann, S., 2393R
Umpfenbach, H., 607
Unwin, P.T.H., 3601
Unwin, T., 3602
Urbanová, L., 263R
Urwin, K., 1878
Utley, F.L., 1879, 3704, 3705
Utz, H., 255, 292, 1220R
Vachek, J., 79R, 152R, 169R, 211R, 220, 221, 263R, 280R, 332R, 437, 610R, 659, 660, 661, 662, 663, 792R, 881, 941R, 1022, 1023
Valentine, G.E.W., 1172
Vallins, G.H., 222, 531, 532, 1333, 1989, 1990
Van Beeck, F.J., 1880
Van Beek, P., 1628, 2767

Van Dam, J., 1629
Van der Auwera, J., 1881, 1882
Van der Gaaf, W., 181R, 182R, 409R, 931R, 415R, 949R, 973R, 1024, 1127R, 1334, 1335, 1336, 1337, 1338, 1450R, 1630, 1725R, 1876R, 1883, 1884, 1885, 1886, 1887, 1888, 1889, 2768, 3380, 3381
Vanderheyden, J.F., 509R
Van der Leek, F.C., 1441, 1631
Van der Meer, H.J., 1890
Van der Merwe Scholtz, H., 2769
Van der Rhee, F., 882
Van de Velde, M., 1772
van Doren, M., 82
van Draat, P.F., 3670R
van Ek, J.A., 153R
Van Essen, A.J., 883
van Haeringen, C.B., 112R, 3374R
van Hamel, A.G., 1067R, 2446R
Van Kemenade, A., 664, 1632, 1633, 1634
Van Langenhove, G.C., 665, 666, 884
van Lessen Kloeke, W.U.S., 1632
van Loey, A., 257R
van Roey, J., 650R
Van Roosbroeck, G.L., 3382
van Spaendonck, C., 2746R, 3121R
van Wijngaarden, A., 3258R, 3594R
Varnas, L.A., 456
Vat, J. [pseudonym], 1635
Vaughan, M.F., 3603
Velten, H.V., 2770
Vendryes, J., 196R, 270R, 300R, 3624R
Venezky, R.L., 109, 110, 530, 2771, 2772, 2773
Verdonck, J., 101R, 693R, 2774, 2775
Verhoeff, P.J., 1800R
Vermeer, P.M., 46R, 218R, 580
Vest, E.B., 3505R
Vickers, B., 3873R
Vickrey, J.F., 2776, 2777, 2778
Viebrock, H., 2681
Viel, M., 1025
Viereck, W., 271R, 3809R

INDEX OF NAMES

Viethen, H.W., 1343R
Villa, F., 613R
Visser, F.T., 161R, 196R, 1339, 1340, 1341, 1342, 1343, 1344, 1636, 1684R, 1891, 1991, 3383, 3384, 3385, 3386
Visser, G.J., 1892
Vleeskruyer, R., 106R, 251R, 289R, 1445R, 2779
Vočadlo, O., 2780
Vogel, B., 3811, 3812
Vogt, A., 1637
Voitle, H., xxvii, 3482R, 3680R, 3697R, 3699R
Von Appel, M.F., 605
von Erhardt-Siebold, E., 931R, 2990R
von Feilitzen, O., 3422, 3433, 3434, 3604, 3605, 3606, 3607, 3608, 3609, 3706
von Lindheim, B., 438, 517, 1224R, 1992, 2781, 2782, 2783, 2784, 2785, 2786, 2799R, 3297R
von Rüden, M., 1993
Von Schaubert, E., 1638, 2787
von Schon, C.(V.), 145R, 1345
von Wartburg, W., 2252
Vorlat, E., 2899R
W., S.L.P., 2766R
Wadstein, E., 2788, 3610
Wagner, K.H., 1639
Wahlén, N., 1640
Wahrig, G., 1994, 1995
Waite, G.(G.), 448, 2789
Wakelin, M.F., 2790, 2791, 3707, 3789, 3813, 3814
Walcutt, C.C., 1893
Waldo, G.S., 1958R
Waldorf, N.O., 2792
Waldron, R.A., xxviii, 465R, 1996
Walker, J.A., 301, 1049R, 2793, 2794
Walker, W.S., 2795
Wall, C., 3855
Wallace, K.Y., 3387
Wallace-Hadrill, A., 121
Wallenberg, J.K., 3388, 3449R, 3529R, 3611, 3612

Wallner, B., 3389, 3390, 3391
Wallum, M.K., 1346
Wandeweghe, W., 1772
Wandl, E., 3392
Ward, A., 86R, 233, 306, 792R, 946R, 1031R, 1039R
Warner, A.R., 1894, 1895
Wärtli, H., 3856
Waterhouse, R., 1641, 1642, 1643, 1644, 1645, 1646, 1647, 2796, 3857
Watson, G., 23, 24, 25, 1132
Watson, J.W., Jr., 885, 886, 887, 888
Wattie, J.M., 1648
Watts, R.J., 1896, 2822
Watts, V.E., 3393, 3426R, 3435, 3505R, 3613, 3614
Way, A., 1897
Weber, C.A., 2666R
Weber, G., 223, 297R, 889, 913R, 939R, 1978R
Weber-Liel, B., 518
Webster, M., 3394
Wedel, A.R., 1649
Weekly, E., 207R, 224, 225, 1978R
Weese, W.E., 3908
Wegner, A., 198R, 1898, 1899, 1900
Wehrle, O., 3395
Weidmann, U., 2822
Weier, D., 414
Weimann, K., 285, 2797
Weinstock, H., xxx, 67, 187R, 218R, 294R, 307, 792R, 917R, 951R, 1026, 1806R, 2899R, 3769R, 3809R
Weiss, B.J., 164R
Weiss, C., 1517R
Weiss, H., 606
Weisweiler, J., 98R, 2798
Welch, M.G., 3615
Wells, C., 336R
Wełna, J., 218R, 242, 299R, 651R, 1218R, 1650, 1651, 3677R
Welte, W., 1839
Weman, B., 2799
Wenisch, F., 255R, 2800, 2801, 2802, 2803, 2804

Wenskus, R., 2662
Wentersdorf, K.P., 2805, 2806, 2807, 2808
Wermser, R., 3396
Wertheimer, E., 86
Wescott, R.W., 310R
West, F., 1347, 1348
Westergaard, E., 3397
Western, A., 666R, 1028
Wetzel, C.-D., 255R, 334R, 562, 2809
Weyhe, H., 1133
Whatley, E.G., 3616
Whitaker, H.A., 1349
Whitbread, L., 49R, 89R, 2810, 2811, 2812
White, B., 3398
Whitehall, H., 439, 607, 608, 3197, 3399, 3400, 3793, 4401
Whitelock, D., 3436, 3604R
Whitesell, J.E., 890
Whiting, B.J., 141, 3402, 3909
Whiting, H.W., 141
Whitman, F.H., 1652
Whitteridge, G., 3403
Whittier, P.G., 1653
Widdowson, J.D.A., 78R
Wiegand, N., 1350
Wiencke, H., 519
Wienold, G., 1778R, 2655R
Wiersma, S.M., 2813
Wietelmann, I., 2814
Wik, B., 1351
Wilcockson, C., 3404
Wild, F., xxix, 191R, 234R, 236, 243R, 296R, 308R, 415R, 931R, 944R, 973R, 3794R
Wild, H.-O., 1654
Wilkinson, G.T., 213
Willard, R., 192R, 229R, 563, 865, 931R, 2815, 2816, 3405
Williams, A., 3406
Williams, B.C., 149R, 246
Williams, E.G., 509R, 2817, 3407
Williams, J.M., 226
Williams, M.J., 129

Williams, N., 314R
Williamson, K., 3790
Wilson, B.D., 891
Wilson, E., 609, 1845R, 3408
Wilson, J., 3409
Wilson, R.H., 111R, 3708
Wilson, R.M., 11R, 168R, 211R, 218R, 294R, 301R, 306R, 319R, 391, 440, 454R, 471R, 520R, 1027, 1445R, 1684R, 1751R, 1800R, 1841R, 1965R, 3670R, 3730, 3818R, 3905R, 3910
Windeatt, B., 372R
Winkler, G., 1901
Winny, J., 511
Winter, W., 1997
Wirtjes, H., xxviii
Wisbey, R.A., 1906
Wise, C.M., 208R
Witting, K., 120R, 517R, 1029
Wokatsch, W., 98R, 533
Wölcken, F., 531R, 1980R
Wolff, D., 79, 89R, 1052
Wolff, E.J., 1998
Wolf, L., 917R
Wolfe, P.M., 1030, 1031, 1032
Wolf-Rottkay, W.H., 2818
Wood, F.A., 2819
Wood, F.T., 227
Woodbine, G.E., 441
Woodell, T.M., II, 1655, 1853R
Woodward, R.H., 2820
Woolf, H.B., xxix, 103R, 105R, 192R, 1217R, 1656, 3368R, 3599R, 3604R, 3617, 3618, 3619, 3620
Woolfson, A.P., 892
Workman, S.K., 3911
Woudhuysen, S.K., 2283R
Wrander, N., 3437
Wrenn, C.L., xxxii, 88R, 98R, 106R, 204R, 228, 230R, 257R, 274, 297R, 371, 415R, 454R, 534, 733R, 913R, 1368R, 1581R, 2013R, 2076R, 2799R
Wright, E.M., 243, 286, 308
Wright, H.G., 3410

Wright, J., 243, 286, 308
Wright, L.E., 3621
Wright, M.J., 509R
Wright, V.D., 1657
Wüst, W., 2821
Wyatt, A.J., 889R, 3411
Wyld, H.C., 81R, 229, 230, 442, 3412
Wyler, S., 1445R, 1585R, 1751R, 1784R, 1840R, 2822, 2836R, 3271R, 3413
Wynn, J.B., 503R
Wyss, S., 1658, 1659, 1660, 2823
Yamaguchi, H., 3414
Yamakawa, K., 1278R
Yeager, R.F., xxvii, 58
Yerkes, D., 1134, 1661, 2824, 2825, 2826, 3415, 3622
Yngve, V.H., 1352
Yoder, E.K., 893
Yonekura, H., 1902
Yorke, B.A.E., 2827
Young, G.A., 1662
Young, K., 3416
Zabulienė, L., 894, 895
Zachrisson, R.E., 229R, 443, 3612R, 3623, 3624, 3625, 3626, 3627, 3628, 3629, 3630, 3631, 3632, 3633, 3634
Zaic, F., xxviii
Zandvoort, R.W., 8R, 81R, 97R, 149R, 160R, 161R, 174R, 184R, 187R, 203R, 211R, 228R, 234R, 260R, 270R, 955R, 1322R, 1580R, 1708R, 1798R, 1817R, 1942R, 1943R, 2415R, 3244R, 3258R, 3417, 3482R
Zeeman, E., 3912
Zeitlin, J., 1315R
Zellmer, A., 184R
Zender, M., 3528
Zettersten, A., 520, 2828, 2980, 3418, 3419, 3420
Zettler, H.G., 1903
Zgusta, L., 2112
Ziegler, J., 1173
Zieglschmid, A.J.F., 1443R, 1663, 1999
Zimmermann, R., 271R, 1242R, 1353, 1671R, 1778R, 1791R, 1904, 3913
Zuck, L.V., 1664
Zupko, R.E., 83, 84
Zwanenburg, W., 1631

Wright, J., 243, 286, 308
Wright, L.E., 3621
Wright, M.J., 509R
Wright, V.D., 1657
Wüst, W., 2821
Wyatt, A.J., 889R, 3411
Wyld, H.C., 81R, 229, 230, 442, 3412
Wyler, S., 1445R, 1585R, 1751R, 1784R, 1840R, 2822, 2836R, 3271R, 3413
Wynn, J.B., 503R
Wyss, S., 1658, 1659, 1660, 2823
Yamaguchi, H., 3414
Yamakawa, K., 1278R
Yeager, R.F., xxvii, 58
Yerkes, D., 1134, 1661, 2824, 2825, 2826, 3415, 3622
Yngve, V.H., 1352
Yoder, E.K., 893
Yonekura, H., 1902
Yorke, B.A.E., 2827
Young, G.A., 1662
Young, K., 3416
Zabulienė, L., 894, 895
Zachrisson, R.E., 229R, 443, 3612R, 3623, 3624, 3625, 3626, 3627, 3628, 3629, 3630, 3631, 3632, 3633, 3634
Zaic, F., xxviii
Zandvoort, R.W., 8R, 81R, 97R, 149R, 160R, 161R, 174R, 184R, 187R, 203R, 211R, 228R, 234R, 260R, 270R, 955R, 1322R, 1580R, 1708R, 1798R, 1817R, 1942R, 1943R, 2415R, 3244R, 3258R, 3417, 3482R
Zeeman, E., 3912
Zeitlin, J., 1315R
Zellmer, A., 184R
Zender, M., 3528
Zettersten, A., 520, 2828, 2980, 3418, 3419, 3420
Zettler, H.G., 1903
Zgusta, L., 2112
Ziegler, J., 1173
Zieglschmid, A.J.F., 1443R, 1663, 1999
Zimmermann, R., 271R, 1242R, 1353, 1671R, 1778R, 1791R, 1904, 3913
Zuck, L.V., 1664
Zupko, R.E., 83, 84
Zwanenburg, W., 1631

In the LIBRARY AND INFORMATION SOURCES IN LINGUISTICS (LISL) series (Series Editor: E.F. Konrad Koerner) the following volumes have been published and will be published during 1988:

1. ANTTILA, Raimo & Warren A. BREWER: *Analogy: A basic bibliography.* Amsterdam, 1977.
2. SABOURIN, Conrad: *Adverbs and Comparatives: An analytical bibliography.* Amsterdam, 1977.
3. HUNTSMAN, Jeffrey F.: *Translation Theory: A comprehensive bibliography.* Amsterdam, 1988. n.y.p.
4. VERSCHUEREN, Jef: *Pragmatics: An annotated bibliography.* Amsterdam, 1978.
5. LAVER, John: *Voice Quality: A classified research bibliography.* Amsterdam, 1979.
6. McKAY, John C.: *A Guide to Romance Reference Grammars: The modern standard languages.* Amsterdam, 1979.
7. CANNON, Garland: *Sir William Jones. A bibliography of primary and secondary sources.* Amsterdam, 1979.
8. GUIMIER, Claude: *Prepositions: an analytical bibliography.* Amsterdam, 1981.
9. LEOPOLD, Joan: *The Letter Liveth: The Life, Work and Library of August Friedrich Pott (1802-87).* Amsterdam, 1983.
10. KOERNER, E.F. Konrad: *Bibliographie Saussurienne, 1876-1976.* Amsterdam, 1988. n.y.p.
11. KOERNER, E.F. Konrad & Matsuji TAJIMA: *Noam Chomsky: A personal bibliography.* Amsterdam, 1986.
12. SPILLNER, Bernd: *Error Analysis: A comprehensive bibliography.* Amsterdam, 1987. n.y.p.
13. TAJIMA, Matsuji: *Old and Middle English Language Studies: A Classified Bibliography 1923-1985.* Amsterdam, 1988.
14. DECHERT, Hans W., Monika BRÜGGEMEIER & Dietmar FÜTTERER (Comps.): *Transfer and Interference in Language. A Selected Bibliography.* Amsterdam, 1984.
15. McKAY, John C.: *A Guide to Germanic Reference Grammars.* Amsterdam, 1985.
16. ESCHBACH, Achim & Viktória ESCHBACH-SZABÓ (Comps.): *BIBLIOGRAPHY OF SEMIOTICS, 1975-1985.* Amsterdam, 1986. 2 vols.
17. NOPPEN, Jean-Pierre van et al. (comps.): *METAPHOR: A Bibliography of post-1970 publications.* Amsterdam, 1985.
18. BEARD, Robert & Bogdan SZYMANEK (comps): *BIBLIOGRAPHY OF MORPHOLOGY, 1960-1985.* Amsterdam, 1988.